March 11. 1971

Dear Lili:

Happy Birthday -

In the days ahead think of me while perusing these pages

Shirley Rapoport

Wisdom of the West

a historical survey of Western Philosophy in its social and political setting

Wisdom of the West

Bertrand Russell

editor Paul Foulkes

designer Edward Wright with ten Compositions by John Piper

Crescent Books, Inc.

Library of Congress Catalog Card No. 59-11326

Printed in Yugoslavia by Mladinska Knjiga, Ljubljana

Foreword

'A big book,' said Callimachus the Alexandrian poet, 'is a big evil!' On the whole I feel inclined to share this view. If, therefore, I venture to put the present volume before the reader, it is because, as evils go, this book is a minor one. Nevertheless, it calls for a special explanation; for I have some time ago written a book on the same subject. 'Wisdom of the West' is an entirely new work; though, of course, it would never have appeared had not my 'History of Western Philosophy' preceded it.

What is here attempted is a conspectus of Western Philosophy from Thales to Wittgenstein, together with some reminders of the historical circumstances in which this story unfolds itself. To support the account, there is a collection of pictures of men, places and documents, which have been chosen as nearly as possible from sources belonging to the period to which they refer. Above all, an attempt has been made, wherever this seemed feasible, to translate philosophic ideas, normally expressed only in words, into diagrams that convey the same information by way of geometrical metaphor. There is little to fall back on here, and the results are therefore not always entirely successful. However, it seems that such methods of presentation are worth exploring. Diagrammatic exposition, so far as it can be achieved, has the further advantage of not being tied to any particular tongue.

As to the appearance of yet another history of philosophy, two things may be said in extenuation. In the first place, there are few accounts that are compact and reasonably comprehensive at the same time. There are, indeed, many histories of greater compass that deal with each item at much greater length. With these works the present volume obviously does not set out to compete. Those who develop a deeper interest in the subject will no doubt consult them in due course, and will perhaps even go to the original texts. Secondly, the current trend towards more and fiercer specialisms is making men forget their intellectual debts to their forbears. This study aims to counter such forgetfulness. In some serious sense, all Western philosophy is Greek philosophy; and it is idle to indulge in philosophic thought while cutting the ties that link us with the great thinkers of the past. It used once to be held, perhaps wrongly, that it was meet for a philosopher to know something about everything. Philosophy claimed all knowledge for its province. However this may be, the prevailing view that philosophers need know nothing about anything is quite certainly wrong. Those who think that philosophy 'really' began in 1921, or at any rate not long before, fail to see that current philosophic problems have not arisen all of a sudden and out of nothing. No apology is therefore offered for the comparatively generous treatment of Greek philosophy.

An account of the history of philosophy may proceed in one of two ways. Either the story is purely expository, showing what this man said and how that man was influenced. Alternatively, the exposition may be combined with a certain measure of critical discourse, in order to show how philosophic discussion proceeds. This second course has been adopted here. It may be added that this should not mislead the reader into believing that a thinker may be dismissed out of hand merely because his views have been found wanting. Kant once said that he was not so much afraid of being refuted as of being misunderstood. We should try to understand what philosophers are attempting to say before we set them aside. It must be confessed, all the same, that the effort sometimes seems out of proportion to the insight achieved. In the end, this is a matter of judgment which everyone has to resolve for himself.

The scope and treatment of the subject in this volume differ from those in my earlier book. The new material owes much to my editor Dr. Paul Foulkes, who has helped me in the writing of the text and has also chosen many of the illustrations and devised most of the diagrams. The aim has been to provide a survey of some of the leading questions that philosophers have discussed. If, on perusing these pages, the reader is tempted to pursue the subject further than he might otherwise have done, the chief purpose of the book will have been attained.

Bertrand Russell

Prologue

What are philosophers doing when they are at work? This is indeed an odd question, and we might try to answer it by first setting out what they are not doing. There are, in the world around us, many things which are understood fairly well. Take, for instance, the working of a steam engine. This falls within the fields of mechanics and thermodynamics. Again, we know quite a lot about the way in which the human body is built and functions. These are matters that are studied in anatomy and physiology. Or, finally, consider the movement of the stars about which we know a great deal. This comes under the heading of astronomy. All such pieces of well defined knowledge belong to one or other of the sciences.

But all these provinces of knowledge border on a circumambient area of the unknown. As one comes into the border regions and beyond, one passes from science into the field of speculation. This speculative activity is a kind of exploration, and this, among other things, is what philosophy is. As we shall see later, the various fields of science all started as philosophic exploration in this sense. Once a science becomes solidly grounded, it proceeds more or less independently, except for borderline problems and questions of method. But in a way the exploratory process does not advance as such, it simply goes on and finds new employment.

At the same time we must distinguish philosophy from other kinds of speculation. In itself philosophy sets out neither to solve our troubles nor to save our souls. It is, as the Greeks put it, a kind of sightseeing adventure undertaken for its own sake. There is thus in principle no question of dogma, or rites, or sacred entities of any kind, even though individual philosophers may of course turn out to be stubbornly dogmatic. There are indeed two attitudes that might be adopted towards the unknown. One is to accept the pronouncements of people who say they know, on the basis of books, mysteries or other sources of inspiration. The other way is to go out and look for oneself, and this is the way of science and philosophy.

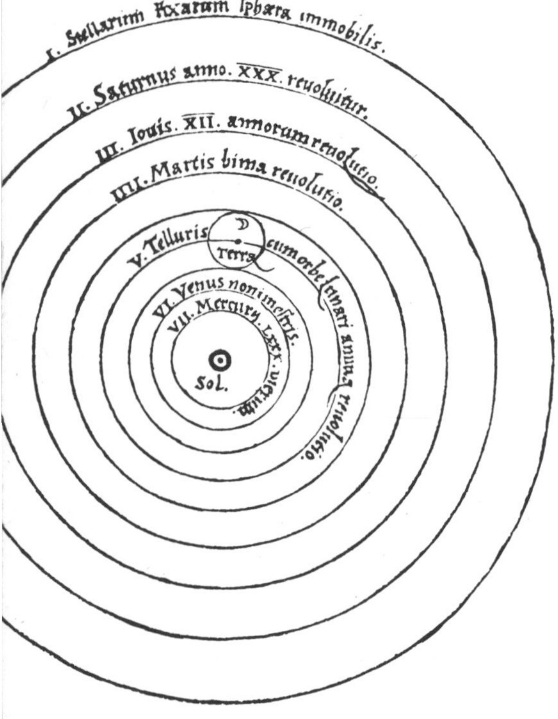

Science deals with known facts, philosophy with speculation

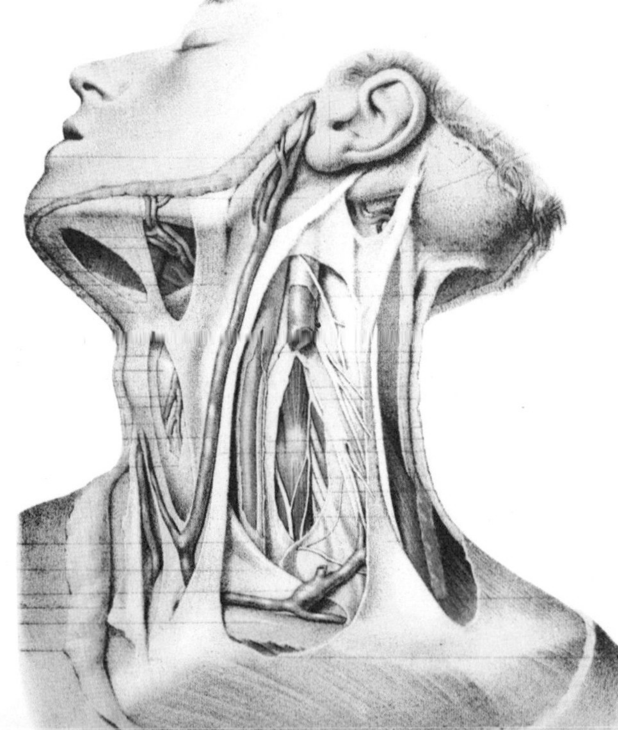

Lastly, we may note one peculiar feature of philosophy. If someone ask the question what is mathematics, we can give him a dictionary definition, let us say the science of number, for the sake of argument. As far as it goes this is an uncontroversial statement, and moreover one that can be easily understood by the questioner though he may be ignorant of mathematics. Definitions may be given in this way of any field where a body of definite knowledge exists. But philosophy cannot be so defined. Any definition is controversial and already embodies a philosophic attitude. The only way to find out what philosophy is, is to do philosophy. To show how men have done this in the past is the main aim of this book.

There are many questions that people who think do at some time or other ask themselves, where science cannot yield an answer. Neither will those who try to think for themselves be willing to take on trust the ready answers given by soothsayers. It is the task of philosophy to explore these questions, and sometimes to dispose of them.

Thus, we may be tempted to ask ourselves such questions as what is the meaning of life, if indeed it have any at all. Has the world a purpose, does the unfolding of history lead somewhere, or are these senseless questions?

Then there are problems such as whether nature really is ruled by laws, or whether we merely think this is so because we like to see things in some order. Again, there is the general query whether the world is divided into two disparate parts, mind and matter, and, if so, how they hang together.

And what are we to say of man? Is he a speck of dust crawling helplessly on a small and unimportant planet, as the astronomers see it? Or is he, as the chemists might hold, a heap of chemicals put together in some cunning way? Or, finally, is man what he appears to Hamlet, noble in reason, infinite in faculty? Is man, perhaps, all of these at once?

Along with this there are ethical questions about good and evil. Is there a way of life that is good, and another that is bad, or is it indifferent how we live? If there be a good way of life, what is it, and how can we learn to live it? Is there something we may call wisdom, or is what seems to be such mere empty madness?

All these are puzzling questions. One cannot settle them by carrying out experiments in a laboratory, and those of an independent frame of mind are unwilling to fall back on the pronouncements of dispensers of universal nostrums. To such as these the history of philosophy supplies what answer can be given. In studying this difficult subject we learn what others at other times have thought about these matters. And so we come to understand them better, for their way of tackling philosophy is an important facet of their way of life. In the end this may show us how to live though knowing little.

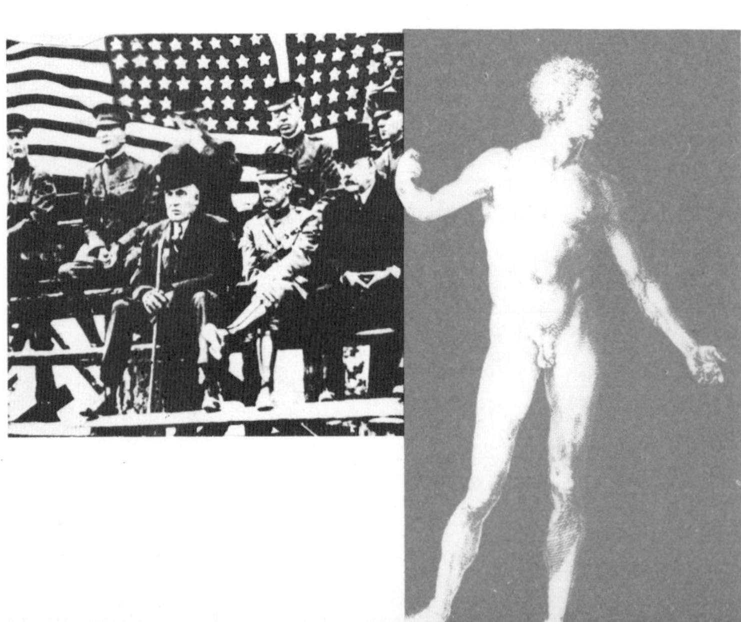

Is man a helpless dwarf?
Or is he a lump of earth?
Or is he as Hamlet sees him?

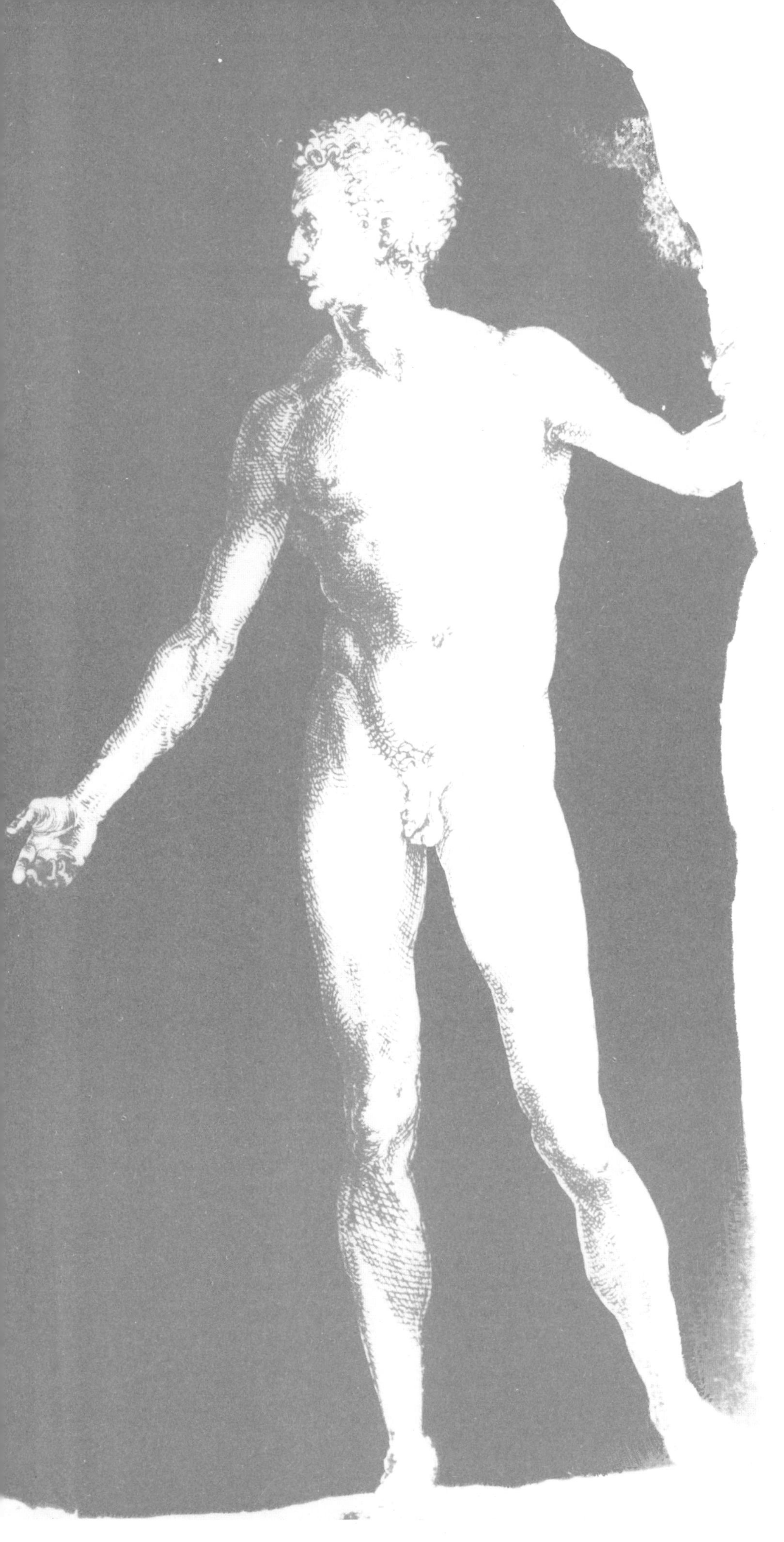

The palace at Cnossus; in Crete, the forbear of Greek civilization

Before Socrates

Philosophy begins when someone asks a general question, and so does science. The first people to evince this kind of curiosity were the Greeks. Philosophy and science, as we now know them, are Greek inventions. The rise of Greek civilisation which produced this outburst of intellectual activity is one of the most spectacular events in history. Nothing like it has ever occurred before or since. Within the short space of two centuries, the Greeks poured forth in art, literature, science and philosophy, an astonishing stream of masterpieces which have set the general standards for Western civilisation.

Philosophy and science begin with Thales of Miletus in the early sixth century B.C. What course of previous events had come to set off this sudden unfolding of the Greek genius? As best we may we must attempt to find an answer. With the help of archaeology, which has made great strides since the turn of the century, we can piece together quite a fair account of how the Greek world developed.

Among the civilisations of the world the Greek is a late comer. Those of Egypt and Mesopotamia are older by several millennia. These agricultural societies grew up along the great rivers and were ruled by divine kings, a military aristocracy and a powerful class of priests who presided over the elaborate polytheistic religious systems. The bulk of the population were serfs who worked the land.

Both Egypt and Babylonia furnished some knowledge which the Greeks later took over. But neither developed science or philosophy. Whether this is due to lack of native genius or to social conditions is not a fruitful question here, both no doubt play their part. What is significant is that the function of religion was not conducive to the exercise of intellectual adventure.

In Egypt religion was much concerned with life after death. The pyramids are funeral monuments. Some knowledge of astronomy was required to ensure effective prediction of the floods of the Nile, and as administrators, the priesthood had developed a form of picture writing. But no great resources were left over for development in other directions.

In Mesopotamia, the great semitic empires supplanted the earlier Sumerians from whom they adopted cuneiform writing. On the side of religion, the central interest lay more in welfare in this world. Recording the movement of the stars and the associated practices of magic and divination were directed to these ends.

Somewhat later we find the development of trading communities. Foremost among these were the inhabitants of Crete, whose civilisation has only recently come to light again. The Cretans probably came from the coast lands of Asia Minor and rapidly gained pre-eminence throughout the islands of the Aegean. A new wave of immigrants, towards the middle of the third millennium B.C., led to an extraordinary development of Cretan culture. Great palaces were built at Cnossos and Phaestos, and Cretan ships plied the Mediterranean from end to end.

From 1700 B.C. onwards, recurrent earthquakes and volcanic eruptions set off a Cretan migration to neighbouring Greece and Asia Minor. Cretan craftsmanship transformed the culture of the mainland peoples. In Greece, the best known site to show this is Mycenae in the Argolid, the traditional home of Agamemnon. It is the Mycenaean period whose memories are reported in Homer. About 1400 B.C., Crete suffered a violent earthquake which put a sudden end to Cretan supremacy.

The Greek mainland had hitherto absorbed two successive waves of invaders. The first of these were the Ionians, who came from the north, about 2000 B.C., and seem to have become gradually merged with the indigenous population. Three hundred years later followed the Achaean invasion, which this time formed a ruling class. The

The Liongate; at Mycenae, where Cretan influence took root

Earliest known Greek inscription, on an 8th century stone from Thera

masters of Mycenae and the Homeric Greeks in general belonged to this ruling caste.

The Creto-Achaeans had extensive trade relations throughout the Mediterranean. The Cretan catastrophe of 1400 did not interrupt this. Amongst the 'peoples of the sea' who threatened Egypt about 1200 B.C. we find the Cretans, called Peliset by the Egyptians. These were the original Philistines from whom Palestine, the land where they settled, took its name.

About 1100 B.C., a further invasion achieved what the blows of nature had failed to accomplish. Under the impact of the Dorian invasions, the whole of Greece and the Aegean fell to the vigorous uncivilised conquering hordes. The Achaeans had exhausted themselves in the Trojan War early in the 12th century B.C. and could not withstand the onslaught. Sea power falls to the Phoenicians, and Greece now enters a period of obscurity. It is about this time that the Greeks adopted the semitic alphabet from Phoenician traders, completing it by adding the vowels.

Greece proper is rugged in aspect as well as in climate. The country is divided by barren mountain ranges. Passage by land from valley to valley is difficult. Separate communities grew up in the fertile plains, and when the land no longer could carry their numbers, some would set out across the sea to found colonies. From the middle of the eighth to the middle of the sixth century B.C. the shores of Sicily, Southern Italy, and the Black Sea became dotted with Greek cities. With the rise of colonies trade developed, and the Greeks came into renewed contact with the East.

Politically, post-Dorian Greece underwent a regular sequence of changes beginning with kingship. Gradually power came into the hands of the aristocracy, which in turn was followed by a period of non-hereditary monarchs or tyrants. In the end, political power fell to the citizens, which is the literal meaning of 'democracy'. Tyranny and democracy henceforth alternate. Pure democracy may work so long as all the citizens can be gathered into the market place. In our time it survives only in a few of the smaller cantons of Switzerland.

The earliest and greatest literary monument of the Greek world is the work of Homer. About the man we know nothing definite. Some even think there was a line of poets later called by this name. At all events, the two great Homeric poems, the Iliad and the Odyssey, seem to have been completed by about 800 B.C. The Trojan War, around which the poems turn, took place shortly after 1200 B.C. We thus have a post-Dorian account of a pre-Dorian event, and hence a certain amount of inconsistency. In their present form, the poems go back to the recension of Peisistratus, the Athenian tyrant of the sixth century B.C. Much of the brutality of the earlier period has been softened in Homer, though traces of it survive. The poems indeed reflect the rational attitudes of an emancipated ruling class. Bodies are cremated, not buried as we know they were in Mycenaean times. The Olympic Pantheon are a noisy crew of hard living masters.

Dionysus, the Thracian god, symbol of the mystical and violent

Religion is as good as absent, whereas sophisticated customs, like hospitality to strangers, are strong. The more primitive elements, like human sacrifice in the form of ceremonial killing of prisoners, do occasionally break through, but very rarely. On the whole, the tone is one of restraint.

In a way, this symbolises the tension of the Greek soul. On the one side there is the orderly and rational, on the other side the unruly and instinctive. The former give rise to philosophy, art and science. The latter emerge in the more primitive religion connected with fertility rites. This element seems very much under control in Homer; in later times, especially with renewed contact with the East, it comes to the fore again. It is associated with the worship of Dionysus or Bacchus, originally a deity of Thrace. A reforming influence on this pristine savagery arises in the legendary figure of Orpheus, who is said to have been torn limb from limb by intoxicated Bacchantes. The Orphic doctrine tends towards asceticism and emphasises mental ecstasy. By this it is hoped to achieve a state of 'enthusiasm' or union with the god, and thus to gain mystical knowledge not to be had otherwise. In this refined form, Orphic religion had a profound effect on Greek philosophy. It first appears in Pythagoras who adapts it to his own mysticism. From there, elements of it found their way into Plato and into most other Greek philosophy, insofar as it was not purely scientific.

Apollo, the Olympian god, symbol of light and reason

But the more primitive elements survived even in the Orphic tradition. They are indeed the source of Greek tragedy. There, sympathy lies always on the side of those who are tossed by violent emotions and passions. Aristotle rightly speaks of tragedy as a catharsis, or purging of the emotions. In the end it is this twofold aspect of the Greek character which enabled it, once and for all, to transform the world. Nietzsche called these two elements the Apollonian and the Dionysiac. Neither alone could have brought forth the extraordinary explosion of Greek culture. In the East, the mystical element reigned supreme. What saved the Greeks from falling under its sole spell was the rise of the scientific schools of Ionia. But serenity on its own is just as incapable as mysticism, of causing an intellectual revolution. What is needed is a passionate search for truth and beauty. It seems that the Orphic influence provided just that conception. Philosophy, to Socrates, is a way of life. It is worth remembering that the Greek word theory first meant something like 'sight-seeing'. Herodotus uses it in this sense. A lively curiosity, bent on passionate yet disinterested inquiry, this is what gives the ancient Greeks their unique place in history.

The civilization of the West, which has sprung from Greek sources, is based on a philosophic and scientific tradition that began in Miletus two and a half thousand years ago. In this it differs from the other great civilizations of the world. The leading notion that runs through Greek philosophy is the logos. It is a term that connotes, amongst other things, 'word' and 'measure'. Thus, philosophic discourse and scientific inquiry are closely linked. The ethical doctrine that arises from this connection sees the good in knowledge, which is the issue of disinterested inquiry.

The philosopher asks general questions about order in things

The asking of general questions, we said, is the beginning of philosophy and science. What, then, is the form of such questions? In the widest sense they amount to seeking an order in what to the casual observer looks like a string of haphazard, fortuitous events. It is interesting to note whence the notion of order is first derived. Man, according to Aristotle, is a political animal. He lives, not on his own, but in a society. Even at the most primitive level this involves some kind of organisation, and from this source the notion of order is drawn. Order is first and foremost social order. Some regular changes in nature, such as the sequence of day and night, and the cycle of the seasons, were no doubt discovered a very long time ago. Still, it is in the light of some human interpretation that these changes were first understood. The heavenly bodies are gods, the forces of nature spirits, made by man in his own image.

The problem of survival means in the first place that man must try to bend the forces of nature to his own will. Before this was done in ways that we could now describe as scientific, man practised magic. The underlying general notion is the same in the two cases. For magic is an attempt to obtain specific results on the basis of certain rigidly defined rites. It is based on a recognition of the principle of causality, that given the same antecedent conditions, the same results will follow. Magic is thus proto-science. Religion, on the other hand, springs from a different source. There, the attempt is to obtain results against or in spite of regular sequence. It functions in the region of the miraculous, which involves the abrogation of causality. These two ways of thinking are thus quite different, even though in primitive thought we often find them mixed up together.

Out of the common activities in which groups participate, there develops the means of communication which we call language. The fundamental object is to enable men to apply themselves to a common purpose. Thus the basic notion here is agreement. Likewise, this might well be taken as the starting point of logic. It arises from the fact that in communicating, men eventually come to agree, even if they do no more than agree to differ. When such an impasse was reached our ancestors no doubt settled the matter by trial of strength. Once you despatch your interlocutor he no longer contradicts you. The alternative sometimes adopted is to pursue the matter by discussion, if it is pursued at all. This is the way of science and philosophy. The reader may judge for himself how far we have progressed in this since prehistoric times.

The philosophy of the Greeks reveals throughout its stages the influence of a number of dualisms. In one form or another these have continued to be topics about which philosophers write or argue. At the basis of them all lies the distinction between truth and falsehood. Closely connected with it in Greek thought are the dualisms of good and evil, and of harmony and strife. Then there is the dualism of appearance and reality which is very much alive today. Along with these we have the questions of mind and matter, and freedom and necessity. Further, there are cosmological questions concerning whether things are one or many, simple or complex, and finally the dualisms of chaos and order, and of the boundless and the limit.

The way in which these problems were tackled by the early philosophers is instructive. One school might come down on one side of a dualism, another subsequently would raise criticisms and adopt the opposite view. In the end a third would come along and effect some kind of compromise, superseding both the original views. It is by observing this see-saw battle between rival doctrines amongst the pre-socratic philosophers that Hegel first developed his notion of the dialectic.

Many of these dualisms are in some ways interrelated. In a rough and ready way we might however set them apart from each other to show what have been the different types of questions philosophy has been dealing with. Truth and falsehood are discussed in logic. Good and evil, harmony and strife, are questions belonging, on the face of it, to ethics. Appearance and reality, and the question of mind and matter, might be set down as the traditional problems of the theory of knowledge, or epistemology. The remaining dualisms belong more or less to ontology, or the theory of being. There is nothing hard and fast about these divisions, of course. In fact, some of the more characteristic features of Greek philosophy lie in the way in which these boundaries are broken down.

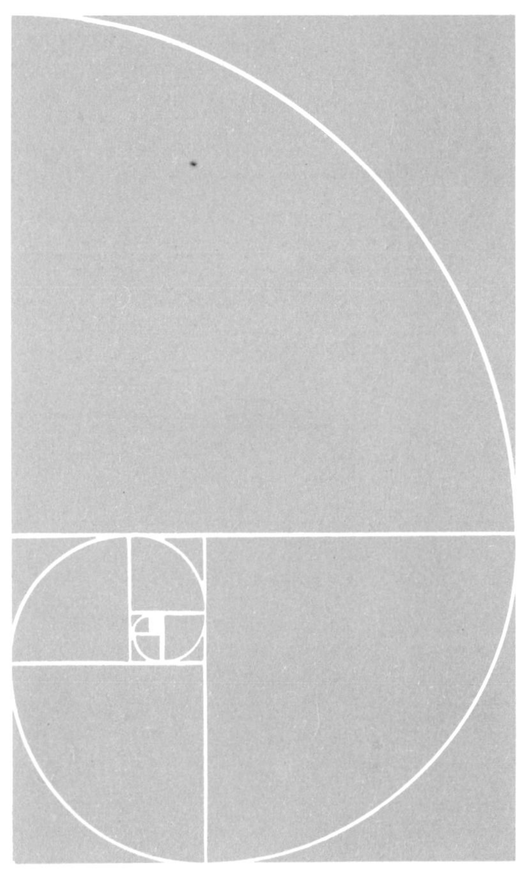

Is the universe simple or complex, ordered or chaotic?

The first school of scientific philosophers sprang up in Miletus. This town on the Ionian coast was a lively crossroads for trade and commerce. To the south-east lie Cyprus, Phoenicia and Egypt; to the north, the Aegean and the Black Sea, westward across the Aegean, the mainland of Greece and the island of Crete. In the east, Miletus is in close touch with Lydia, and through it with the empires of Mesopotamia. From Lydia the Milesians learnt the practice of striking gold coins for money. The port of Miletus was thronged with sails from many nations and her warehouses were stocked with goods from all over the world. With money a universal means of storing value and exchanging one kind of merchandise for another it is not surprising to find that the Milesian philosophers asked the question what all things are made of.

Thales of Miletus

'All things are made of water', Thales of Miletus is reported as having said. And so philosophy and science begin. Greek tradition counts Thales as one of the seven Wise Men. From Herodotus we gather that he predicted an eclipse of the sun. Astronomers have computed that this occurred in 585 B.C. which is therefore taken as his floruit. It is unlikely that Thales had a theory of eclipses, but he must have been familiar with Babylonian records on these phenomena, and would therefore know when to look out for them. As luck would have it, this one was visible in Miletus, which was a good thing for chronology, as no doubt for his own fame too. Likewise, it is very doubtful whether in geometry he had established the theorems concerning similarity of triangles. Certainly, however, he applied the Egyptian rule of thumb for the height of a pyramid to finding the distance of ships at sea, and of other inaccessible objects. He thus had some notion that geometric rules have general scope. This notion of generality is original and Greek.

Thales is also said to have stated that the magnet has a soul because it can move iron. The further statement that all things are full of gods is more questionable. This may well have been attributed to him on the basis of the former saying, but seems to make it superfluous. To say the magnet has a soul has sense only so long as other things have not.

Many stories have come to be linked with Thales, some of them possibly true. It is said that when challenged on one occasion, he showed his practical genius by cornering the market for olive oil. His grasp of meteorology told him beforehand that the harvest would be rich. He therefore hired all the presses he could lay hands on, and, when the time came, let them at his own price. He thus made quite a sum and showed the scoffers that philosophers can make money if they choose.

A logical development pervades Milesian materialism. Thales said all things are made of water, but did not explain how

The most important of Thales' views is his statement that the world is made of water. This is neither so far fetched as at first glance it might appear, nor yet a pure figment of imagination cut off from observation. Hydrogen, the stuff that generates water, has been held in our own time to be the chemical element from which all other elements can be synthetized. The view that all matter is one is quite a reputable scientific hypothesis. As for observation, the proximity of the sea makes it more than plausible that one should notice that the sun evaporates water, that mists rise from the surface to form clouds, which dissolve again in the form of rain. The earth, on this view, is a form of concentrated water. The details might thus be fanciful enough, but it is still a handsome feat to have discovered that a substance remains the same in different states of aggregation.

The next of the Milesian philosophers is Anaximander, who was born, it seems, about 610 B.C. Like Thales, he was an inventor and man of practical affairs. He is the first mapmaker and was the leader of one of the Milesian colonies on the coast of the Black Sea.

Anaximander criticised the cosmological theory of his predecessor. Why, indeed, choose water? The primary stuff that things are made of cannot be one of its own special forms. It must, therefore, be something different from all these, something more fundamental. For the various forms of matter are continually in strife with each other, hot against cold, and wet against dry. These continually encroach upon each other, or commit 'injustice' in the Greek sense in which this means lack of balance. If any one of these forms were the basic matter it would long since have overcome the others. The original matter is what Aristotle calls the material cause. Anaximander calls it the Boundless, an infinite fund of material extending in all directions. From it the world arises and into it will in the end return.

Harbour installations at Miletus

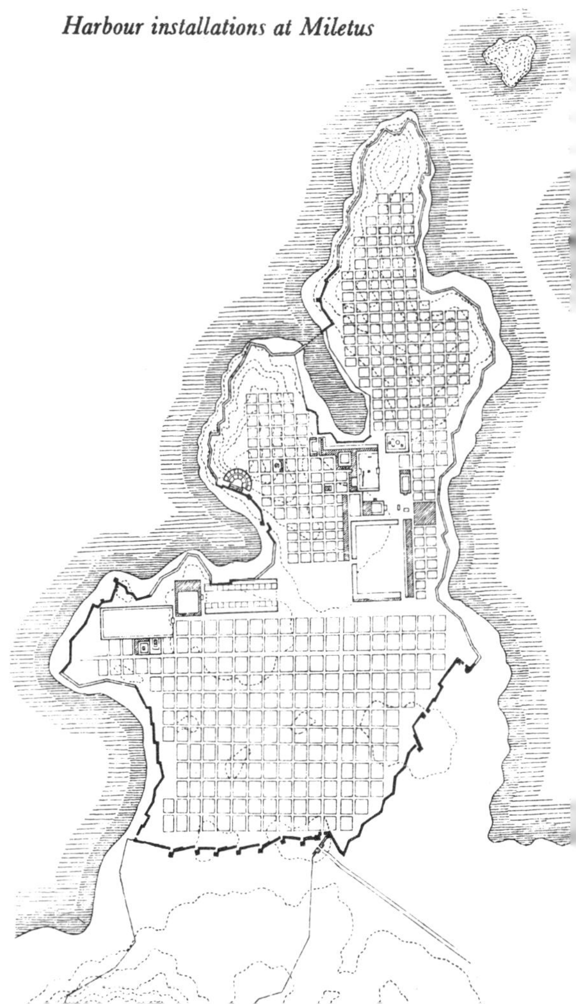

Anaximander tries to explain how all things are made: the 'Boundless' is the source; stresses somehow arise in it, causing wet and dry, hot and cold, to separate out. Their mixtures form all things, change being strife of opposites

Anaximander regarded the earth as a free floating cylinder with ourselves on one of the end faces. Moreover, our world is supposed to be surrounded by innumerable other worlds. A world here is what we should now call a galaxy. The internal function of each world is governed by a vortex motion which attracts the earth to the centre. The heavenly bodies are wheels of fires concealed by air except at one point. We might think of them as bicycle tubes, with the valve the unconcealed point. We must of course remember that air to the Greeks of that time is something that can make things invisible.

Concerning the origin of man, Anaximander held an extremely 'modern' view. Observing that the human young need a long period of care and protection, he concludes that, had man always been as he is now, he could not have survived. Therefore he must once have been different, that is, he must have evolved from an animal which can fend for itself more quickly. This kind of argument is called a reductio ad absurdum. From a given assumption you deduce something which is manifestly wrong, in this case that man did not survive. Hence the assumption must be rejected. If this argument is sound, that is if from the assumption that man always was as he is now it follows, as I feel inclined to think it does, that he could not have survived, then the argument establishes without further ado that some sort of evolutionary process does go on. But Anaximander did not content himself with this argument. He went on to state that man derives from the fish of the sea, and this he backed up by observations on fossil remains and on how sharks feed their young. It is no doubt on these grounds that Anaximander enjoins us not to eat fish. Whether our brethren of the deep cherish equally delicate sentiments towards us is not recorded.

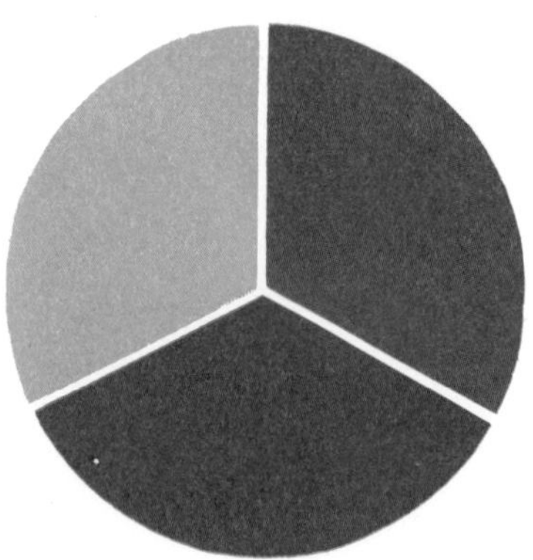

Anaximenes sees change as the working of the external forces of condensation and rarefaction on matter. Any form of matter may then serve as basic. He chose air

The third of the famous Milesian thinkers was Anaximenes. Beyond the fact that he was the youngest of the three, we know nothing definite about his date. His theories, in some ways, are a backward step from his precursor, but while his thinking was less adventurous, his views were on the whole more durable. Like Anaximander, he holds there is a basic matter, but sees this in the specific substance air. The different forms of matter we find around us arise from air through processes of condensation and rarefaction. Since this is a way of saying that all differences are differences of quantity, it is quite all right to take a specific substance as basic. Air is what the soul is made of, and just as it keeps us alive so it does the world. This is a view which was adopted later by the Pythagoreans. In his cosmology Anaximenes was on the wrong track. Fortunately the Pythagoreans in this respect followed Anaximander. For the rest, they rather tended to borrow from Anaximenes, and in a sense this is justified. He was the last representative of the school and had inherited its entire tradition. Besides, it was his theory of condensation and rarefaction which really completed the Milesian view of the world.

The philosophers of Miletus were men of different mettle from the specialists that pass under this head today. They were men engaged in the practical affairs of the city and able to meet all kinds of emergencies. It has been suggested that Anaximander's theories were expounded in a treatise on geography in a wide sense. The surviving titles of early treatises now lost mean 'accounts of the physical nature of things'. Thus the range of subjects was wide and the treatment probably not very deep. It was no doubt against this sort of 'knowledge of many things' that Heraclitus later protested.

In philosophy, what is important is not so much the answers that are given, but rather the questions that are asked. On this score the Milesian school deserves its fame. It is not surprising that Ionia, which had produced Homer, should also be the cradle of science and philosophy. As we saw, religion in Homer is olympian in character, and so it continued to be. Where no great weight of mysticism bears down on a society, scientific speculation is more likely to get under weigh. And while many of the later schools of Greek philosophy had their share of mysticism, it must always be remembered that all of them were indebted to the Milesians.

The Milesian school was in no way tied to any religious movement. Indeed, it is one of the remarkable features of the presocratics that they were all of them at variance with the prevailing religious traditions. This is true even of schools like the Pythagorean, which was not in itself opposed to religion. The religious practices of the Greeks were on the whole linked with the established customs of the various city states. When philosophers struck out along paths of their own it was not then surprising that they should come into conflict with the state religions of their cities, a fate apt to overtake the independent minded at all times and places.

Anaximander

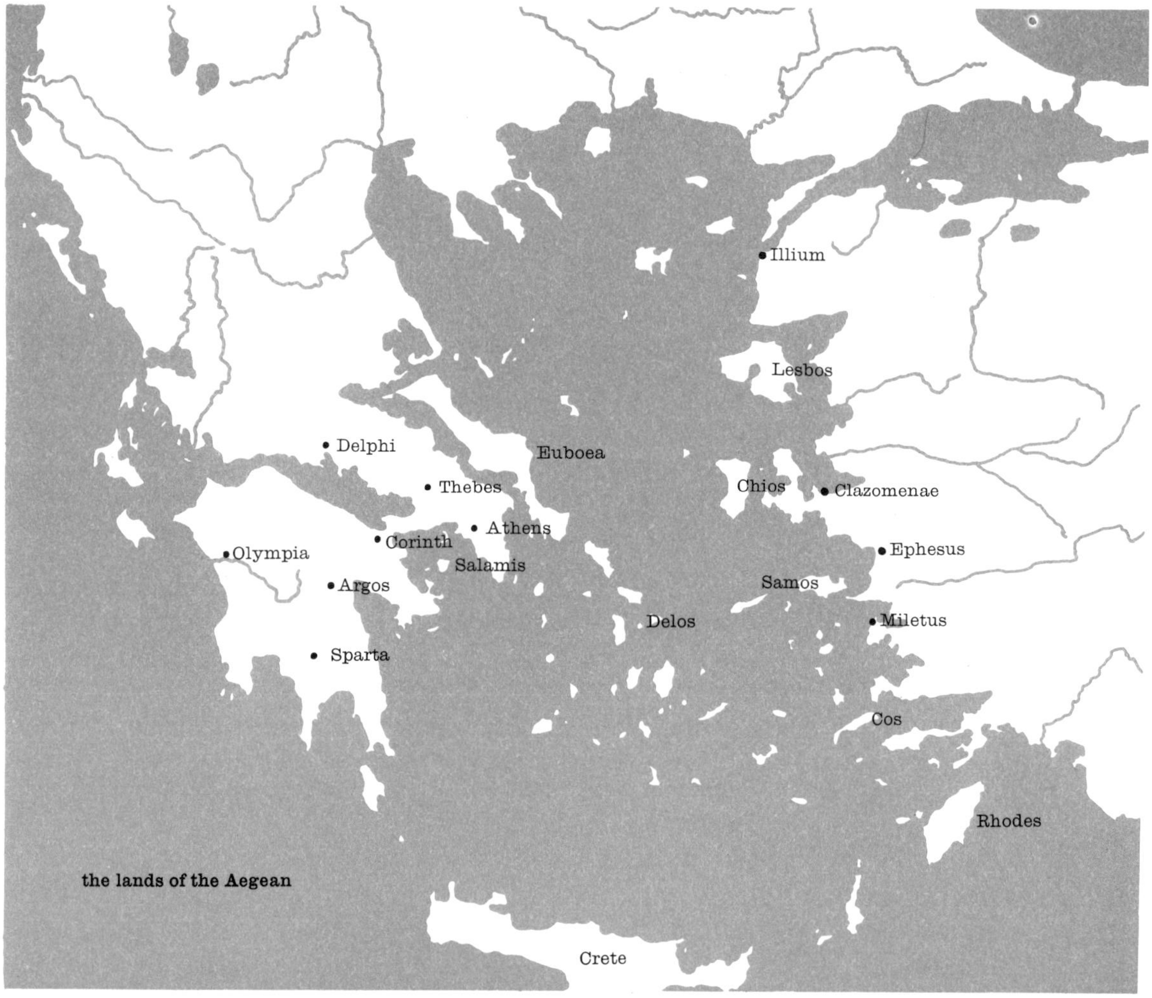

Illium
Lesbos
Delphi
Euboea
Thebes
Chios
Clazomenae
Athens
Corinth
Olympia
Ephesus
Salamis
Argos
Samos
Delos
Miletus
Sparta
Cos
Rhodes
Crete

the lands of the Aegean

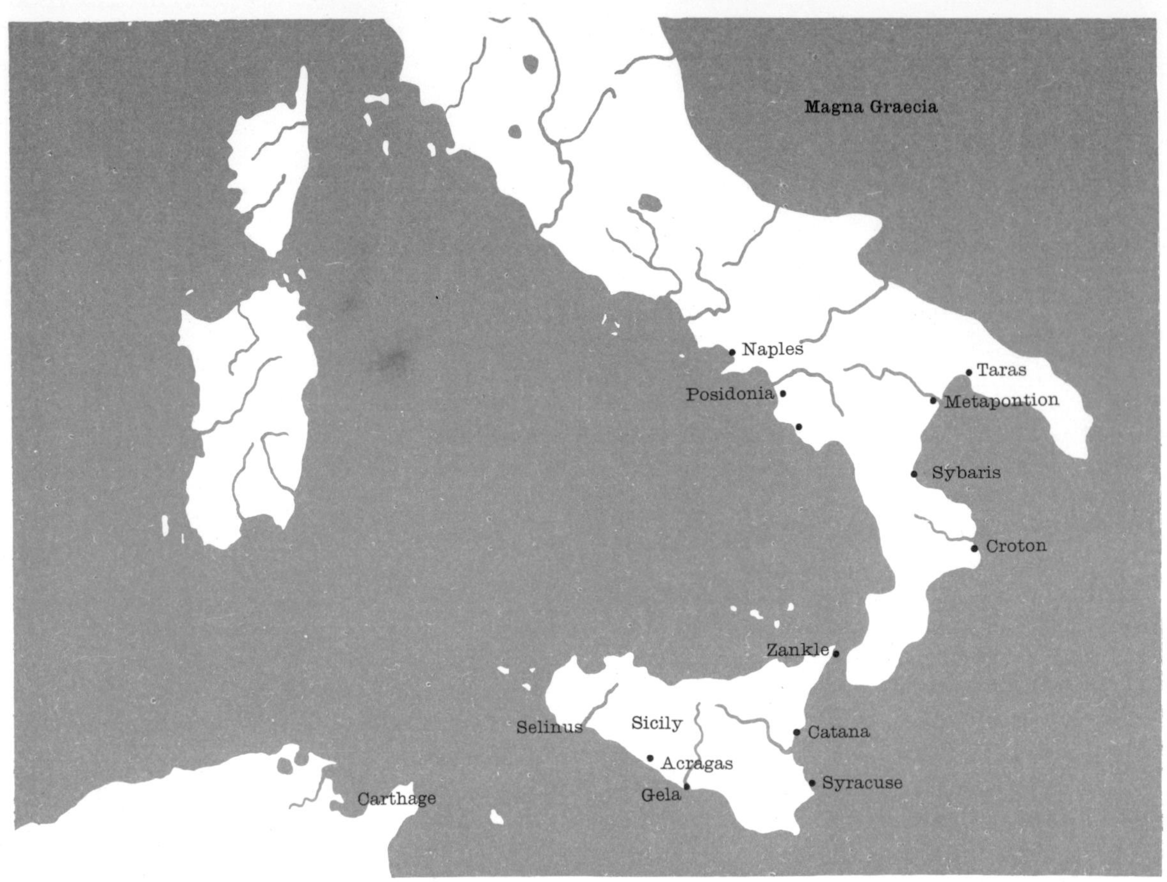

A stone's throw from the Ionian coast lies the island of Samos. In spite of physical nearness, however, the traditions of the islands were in some important respects more conservative than those of the mainland cities. Here, a greater continuity with the Aegean civilisation of the past seems to have survived, and in what follows it is well to keep in mind this difference. Whereas the Ionia of Homer and the early Milesian school was on the whole not inclined to take religion seriously, the island world was from the beginning more receptive to the orphic influence which came to graft itself on such beliefs as had remained from Creto-Achaean days.

The Olympian cult was very much a national affair without a strict religious dogma. Orphicism, on the other hand, possessed sacred texts and held its followers together by the bonds of shared belief. Philosophy in this context becomes a way of life, an outlook which was later adopted by Socrates.

Pythagoras, on a 4th century coin from Athens. On the back, the owl, symbol of wisdom and Athens

The pioneer of this new spirit in philosophy was Pythagoras, a native of Samos. Little is known about his date and the details of his life. He is said to have flourished in 532 B.C., during the tyrantship of Polycrates. The town of Samos was a rival of Miletus and other mainland towns which had fallen to the invading Persians after they had taken Sardis in 544 B.C. Samian vessels plied the length and breadth of the Mediterranean. Polycrates was for a time a close ally of Amasis, the King of Egypt. This no doubt gave rise to the story that Pythagoras travelled to Egypt and thence derived his mathematical knowledge. At all events he left Samos because he could not

bear Polycrates' oppressive rule. He settled down in Croton, a Greek city of Southern Italy, where he set up his society. He lived in Croton for twenty years, until 510 B.C. Following a revolt against the school, he retired to Metapontion where he remained until his death.

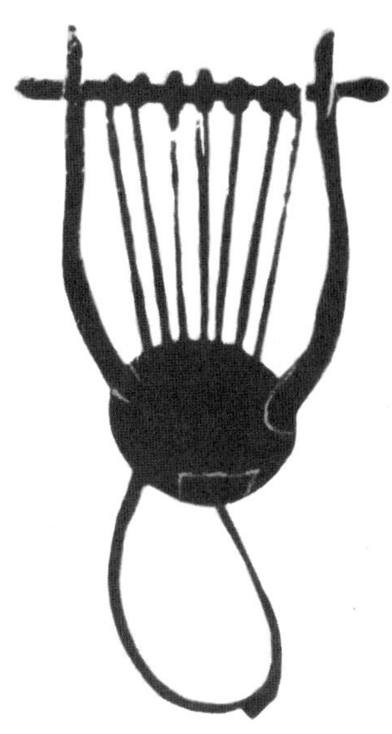

For the Milesians, as we have seen, philosophy was an intensely practical matter, and philosophers could be and were men of action. Within the Pythagorean tradition the opposite conception came to the fore. Here, philosophy becomes detached contemplation of the world. This is connected with the orphic influence embodied in the Pythagorean attitude to life. We have a division of men into three ways of life. Just as there are three kinds of men who come to attend the Olympic games, so there are three kinds of men in society. At the lowest level, there are those who come to buy and sell: next we have those who take part in the contest, and finally we have the spectators who come to see, the theoreticians in the literal sense. These last correspond to the philosophers. The philosophic way of life is the only one which holds out some hope for transcending the fortuities of existence, it provides an escape from the wheel of birth. For, according to the Pythagoreans, the soul is subject to a sequence of transmigrations.

This side of the tradition is connected with a number of primitive tabus and rules of abstinence. The tripartite division of ways of life will meet us again in Plato's Republic, as indeed much else in Pythagoreanism and in the other pre-socratic schools. Plato, it might be said, provides the synthesis of the doctrinal struggles of the early philosophers.

On the other hand, the Pythagorean school gave rise to a scientific and more especially a mathematical tradition. It is the mathematicians that are the true inheritors of Pythagoreanism. In spite of the mystical element arising from the orphic revival, this scientific side of the school is not really distorted by religious ideas. Science itself does not become religious, even if the pursuit of the scientific way of life is endowed with religious significance.

A powerful agent in the purifying aspect of this way of life is music. The Pythagorean interest in it may well arise from this influence. However this may be, Pythagoras discovered the simple numerical relations of what we call musical intervals. A tuned string will sound the octave if its length is halved. Similarly, if the length is reduced to three-quarters we obtain a fourth, if to two-thirds a fifth. A fourth and a fifth together makes one octave, that is $4/3 \times 3/2 = 2/1$. Thus these intervals correspond to the ratios in the harmonic progression $2 : 4/3 : 1$. It has been suggested that the three intervals of the tuned string were compared with the three ways of life. While this must remain speculation it is certainly true that the tuned string henceforth plays a central part in Greek philosophical thought. The notion of harmony, in the sense of balance, the adjustment and combination of opposites like high and low, through proper tuning, the conception of the mean or middle path in ethics, and the doctrine of the four temperaments, all of these go back in the end to Pythagoras' discovery. Much of this we shall find again in Plato.

The full string sounds the tonic. Clamped at $\frac{3}{4}$, it sounds a fourth higher. This shortened string is now clamped at $\frac{2}{3}$ of its length, sounding a fifth higher still. The final length is $\frac{1}{2}$ the original, and sounds an octave above it

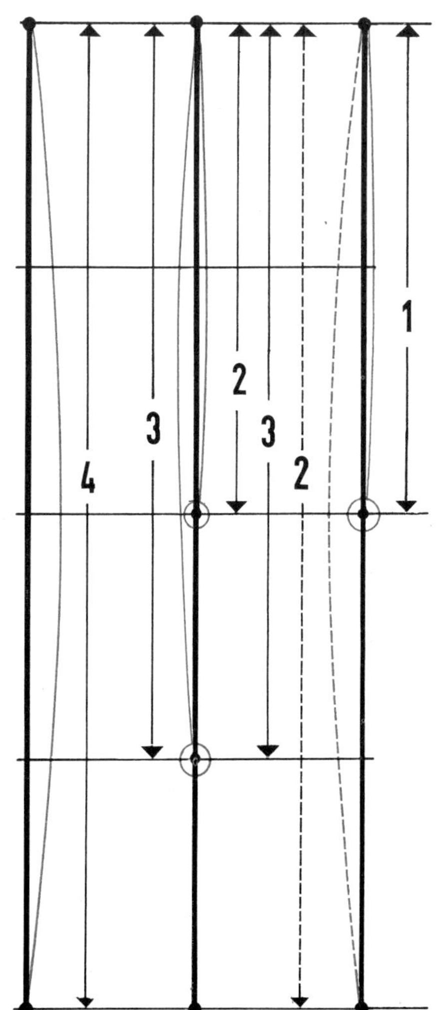

It is very likely that the discoveries in music led to the notion that all things are numbers. Thus, to understand the world around us, we must find the number in things. Once the numerical structure is grasped, we have control over the world. This is indeed a most important conception. While its significance suffered a temporary eclipse after Hellenistic times, it was once more recognised when the revival of learning brought forth a renewed interest in ancient sources. It is a dominant feature of the modern conception of science. With Pythagoras, too, we find for the first time an interest in mathematics not dictated primarily by practical needs. The Egyptians had some mathematical knowledge, but no more than was needed to build their pyramids or measure their fields. The Greeks began to study such matters 'for the sake of enquiry', to use a phrase of Herodotus, and Pythagoras was foremost amongst them.

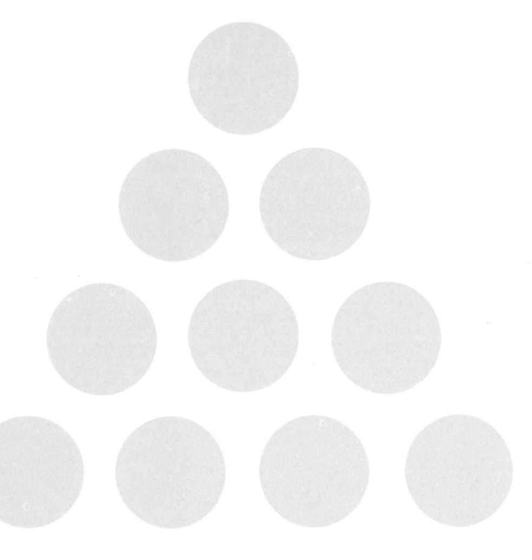

The tetraktys, 'Triangular' number of four rows, and symbol by which the Pythagoreans swore

He had developed a way of representing numbers as arrangements of dots or pebbles. This indeed is a method of reckoning which in some form or other survived for a long time. The Latin word 'calculation' means 'a handling of pebbles'.

'Square' numbers, the sums of successive odd numbers

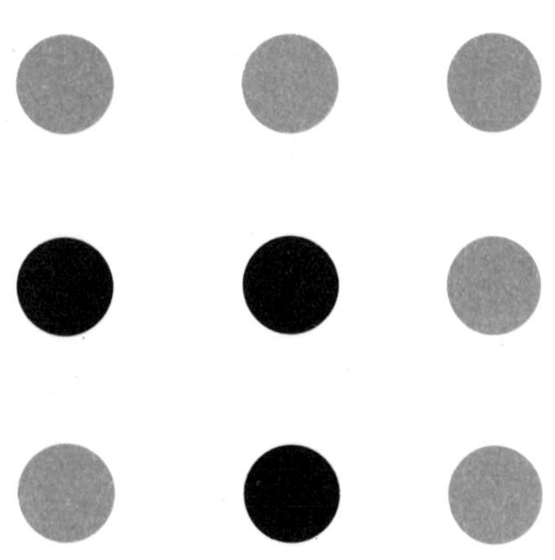

Connected with this is the study of certain arithmetical series. If we arrange lines of pebbles each containing one more than the first, starting with one, we obtain a 'triangular' number. Special significance was attached to the tetraktys, consisting of four lines and showing that $1+2+3+4=10$. Similarly, the sum of successive odd numbers gives rise to a 'square' number, and the sum of successive even numbers to an 'oblong' number.

In geometry, Pythagoras discovered the famous proposition that the square on the hypotenuse equals the sum of the squares on the other two sides, though we do not know what proof he gave of it. Here, again, we have an example of general method and demonstration as opposed to rule of thumb. The discovery of this proposition however led to a tremendous scandal in the school. For one consequence of it is that the square on the diagonal of a square equals twice the square on the side. But no 'square' number can be broken up into two equal square numbers. Hence the problem cannot be solved by means of what we now call rational numbers. The diagonal is incommensurable with the side. To solve the problem we need a theory of irrational numbers which was developed by later Pythagoreans. The name 'irrational' in this context evidently goes back to this early mathematical scandal. The story goes that one of the brotherhood was drowned at sea for divulging the secret.

'Oblong' numbers, the sums of successive even numbers

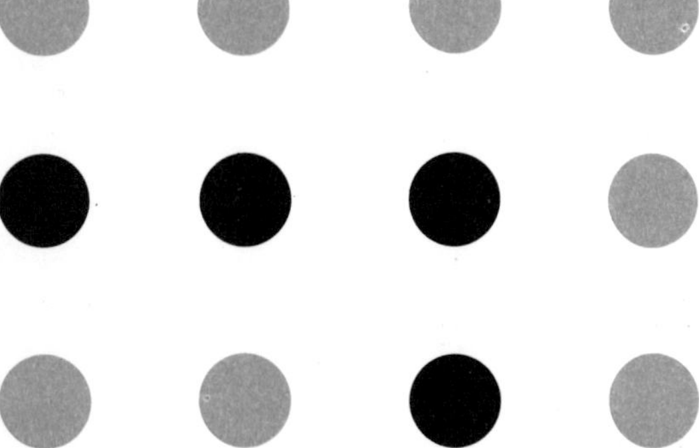

In his theory of the world, Pythagoras bases himself directly on the Milesians, and combines this with his own theories concerning number. The numbers in the arrangements mentioned earlier are called 'boundary stones', no doubt because this conception goes back to measuring fields, or 'geometry' in the literal sense. Our Latin word 'term' has the same literal meaning. According to Pythagoras, the boundless air is what keeps the units distinct, and the units are what gives measure to the boundless. Furthermore, the boundless is identified with the dark, and the limit with fire. This evidently is a conception arising from the sky and the stars. Like the Milesians,

Pythagoras thought there were many worlds, though on his view of number it is unlikely that he considered them to be innumerable. Developing the view of Anaximander, Pythagoras held that the earth was a sphere, and abandoned the vortex theory of the Milesians. It was, however, to be left to another, later native of Samos to put forward the heliocentric theory.

It is the Pythagorean preoccupation with mathematics that gave rise to what we shall later meet as the theory of ideas, or as the theory of universals. When a mathematician proves a proposition about triangles, it is not about any figure drawn somewhere that he is talking; rather, it is something he sees in the mind's eye. Thus arises the distinction between the intelligible and the sensible. Moreover, the proposition established is true without reservation and for all time. It is only a step from this to the view that the intelligible alone is the real, perfect and eternal, whereas the sensible is apparent, defective and transient. These are direct consequences of Pythagoreanism that have dominated philosophical thought as well as theology ever since.

We must remember, too, that the chief god of the Pythagoreans was Apollo, in spite of the orphic elements in their beliefs. It is the Apollonian strain which distinguishes the rationalistic theology of Europe from the mysticism of the East.

Pythagoras

$$c^2 = (a-b)^2 + 4 \times \tfrac{1}{2} a b$$
$$= a^2 + b^2$$

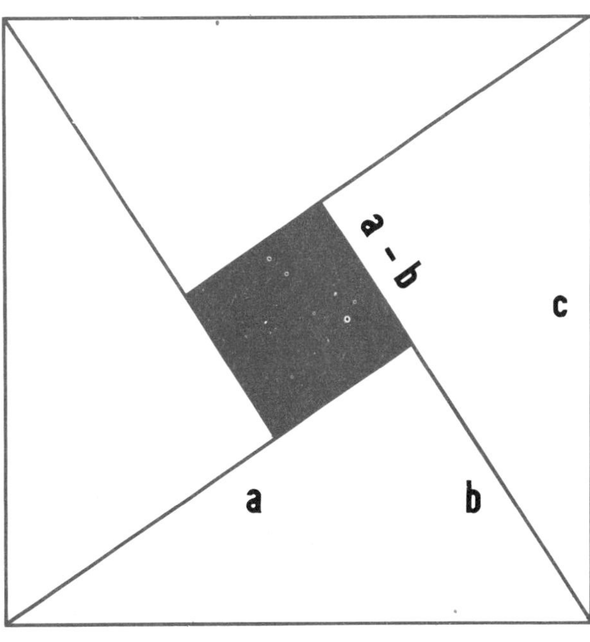

The famous theorem of Pythagoras. What proof he had is not known

An isosceles right-angled triangle of side 1 has a hypotenuse not expressible as a rational number

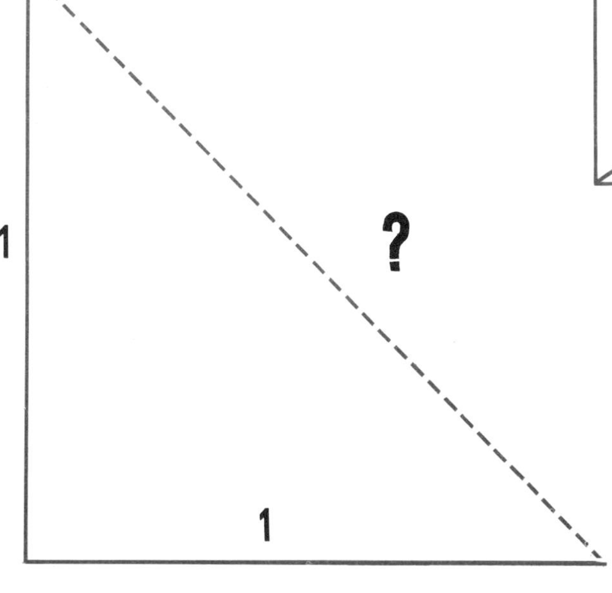

Under the influence of the early Pythagoreans the old Olympian religion was thus displaced, and a new religious conception developed in its stead. A much more virulent assault on the traditional gods was made by Xenophanes. Born probably in 565 B.C. in Ionia, he fled to Sicily when the Persians came, in 540. His principal object seems to have been to eradicate the Olympian pantheon with its gods made in the image of man. He was likewise opposed to the mysticism of the orphic revival and makes fun of Pythagoras. The next in line of the philosophic tradition was another Ionian, Heraclitus of Ephesus, who flourished about the turn of the sixth century. About his life we know almost nothing beyond the fact that he belonged to an aristocratic family. Some fragments of his writings have however survived. From these we can readily see why he was regarded as obscure. His sayings have the ring of prophetic utterances. The fragments are terse and elegant, and full of vivid metaphors. Speaking of the eternal round of life and death he says 'Time is a child playing draughts, the kingly power is a child's'. In his disdainful taunts of the undiscerning he gives rein to his contempt in biting phrases. 'Fools when they do hear are like the deaf: of them does the saying bear witness that they are absent when present', and again 'Eyes and ears are bad witnesses to men if they have souls that understand not their language'.

To remind us that worthwhile achievements cost much work and effort he says 'Those who seek for gold dig up much earth and find a little'. Those who find this too hard a task are dismissed with 'Asses would rather have straw than gold'. Even so, he foreshadows a thought later expressed in a famous saying by Socrates, that we should not be too proud of what we do learn. 'Man is called a baby by God, even as a child by man'.

A somewhat closer study of Heraclitus' theory will help to make some of these sayings a little clearer. Although Heraclitus did not have the scientific interests of his Ionian predecessors, his theorising nevertheless is grounded in the teachings both of the Ionians and of Pythagoras. Anaximander had said that the competing opposites return into the boundless to atone for their mutual encroachments. From Pythagoras comes the notion of harmony. Heraclitus develops a new theory from these ingredients, and this is his signal discovery and contribution to philosophy: the real world consists in a balanced adjustment of opposing tendencies. Behind the strife between opposites, according to measures, there lies a hidden harmony or attunement which is the world.

Anaximander's opposites and Pythagoras' tuned string lead to Heraclitus' view: harmony from opposing tensions, as in a bow

This universal notion is often not apparent, because 'nature loves to hide'. Indeed, he seems to have held that in a sense an attunement must be something which does not strike the eye at once. 'The hidden attunement is better than the open'. In fact, the existence of harmony is usually overlooked. 'Men do not know how what is at variance agrees with itself. It is an attunement of opposite tensions, like that of the bow and the lyre'.

Thus strife is the motive principle which keeps the world alive. 'Homer was wrong in saying, "Would that strife might perish from among gods and men!" He did not see that he was praying for the destruction of the universe, for, if his prayer were heard, all things would pass away'. It is in this logical sense, and not as a military maxim, that we must take his statement that 'War is the father of all'. This view requires a new fundamental matter which would emphasise the importance of activity. Following the Milesians in principle, though not in detail, he chose Fire. 'All things are an exchange for Fire, and Fire for all things, even as wares for gold and gold for wares'. This mercantile simile shows the point of the theory. The flame of an oil lamp looks like some fixed object. Yet all the while oil is being sucked up, fuel is transformed into flame, and soot settles down from the burning of it. Thus everything that goes on in the world is a process of exchanges of this kind, nothing ever stays the same. 'You cannot step twice into the same river, for fresh waters are ever flowing in upon you'. It is because of this kind of illustration that later writers attribute to Heraclitus the famous saying that 'All things are in flux'. Socrates speaks of the Heracliteans under the nickname of 'the flowing ones'.

It is important to contrast this with another fragment from Heraclitus which says that 'We step and do not step into the same river, we are and are not'. At first sight it seems this cannot be reconciled with the previous statement. However, this present saying belongs to a different aspect of the theory. The clue lies in the second half. We are and we are not is a somewhat cryptic way of saying that the unity of our existence consists in perpetual change, or to express it in the language later forged by Plato, our being is a perpetual becoming. Likewise with the example of the river. If I step into the Thames today, and again tomorrow, I step into the same river, yet the water I step into is not the same. The point is, I imagine, clear enough, as I would not recommend to the reader to try the exercise. Another statement of this is found in the saying that 'The upward and the downward path are one and the same'. We have already observed this in the case of the flames: the oil rises, the soot falls, both are part of the process of burning. It may well be that in the first place the statement must be taken literally. A sloping road goes both up and down, depending on which way you go. Heraclitus' theory of opposites here reminds us that what appear to be conflicting features are really essential parts of a situation. One of the most striking ways of putting it occurs in the statement that 'Good and ill are one'. This evidently does not mean that good and evil are one and the same thing. On the contrary, just as one could not conceive of an upward path without a downward path, so one could not understand the notion of good without at the same time understanding the notion of evil. In fact, if you destroy the way up, by removing the hillside, for example, you also abolish the way down; and likewise with good and evil.

Heraclitus, on a 4th century coin from Ephesus, his native town

Thus far the theory that all things are in flux is not really new. Anaximander held precisely similar views. But the explanation of why nevertheless things remain the same is an advance on the Milesians. The leading notion of measures comes from Pythagoras. It is by preserving proper measures that the perpetual change maintains things as they are. This is as true of man as of the world.

In nature things are transformed according to measures, and likewise within the human soul, where there are changes between the dry and the moist. A moist soul declines and stands in danger of disintegration if this goes unchecked by fire, a not altogether inaccurate piece of observation on a man in his cups. On the other hand, 'The dry soul is the wisest and best', though we must not err on the side of excellence either, for an excess of fire will kill the soul as surely as unbridled moistening. Annihilation by fire appears however to be reckoned as a more glorious end, since 'Greater deaths win greater portions'. The reason for this is presumably that fire is the eternal substance: 'This world, which is the same for all, no one of gods or men has made; but it was ever, is now and ever shall be an ever-living Fire with measures kindling, and measures going out'.

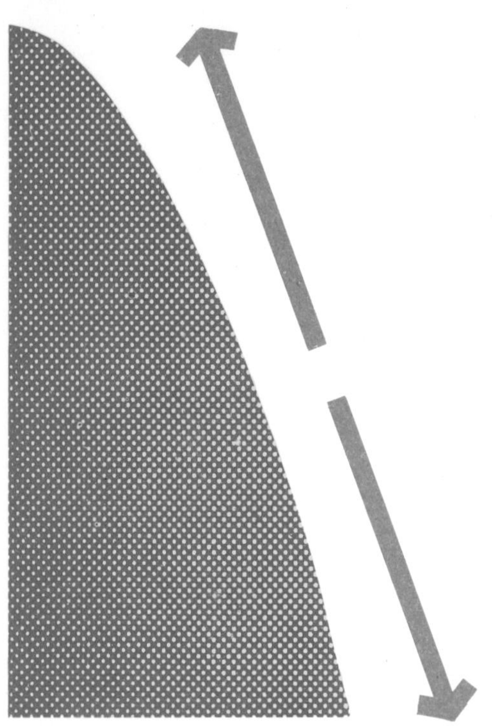

The way up, and down, are the same. Removing one, you remove both

As for the processes of nature, they all conform to their measures. Injustice is not, as Anaximander held, to be sought in the strife between opposites, but in the disregarding of the measures. 'The sun will not overstep his measures, if he does, the Erinyes, the handmaids of justice will find him out'. But the measures are not absolutely rigid, provided they do not exceed the bounds. They may in fact oscillate within certain ranges, and this accounts for such periodic phenomena as day and night in nature, waking and sleeping in man, and similar changes. It is tempting to connect the notion of oscillating measures with the Pythagorean construction of irrational numbers by continued fractions, where successive approximations alternately exceed and fall short of the exact value. However we do not know whether the early Pythagoreans did evolve this method, and though by Plato's time it was certainly well known, we cannot with certainty attribute such knowledge to Heraclitus.

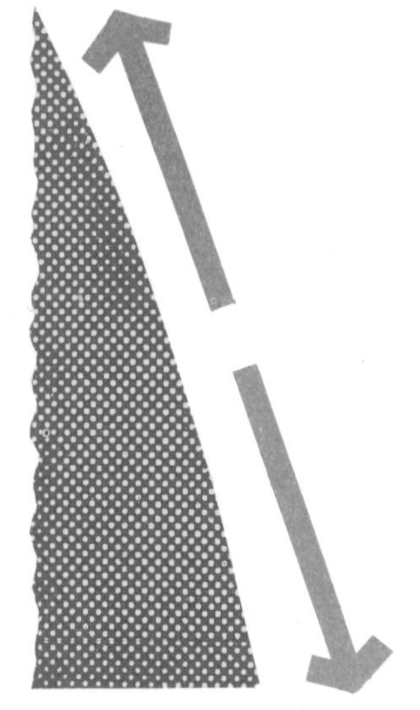

Like Xenophanes, Heraclitus was scornful of the religion of his day, both in its Olympian and Orphic form. It is not through rites and sacrifices that men will become good. He recognised clearly the superficial and primitive character of ritual practices. 'They vainly purify themselves by defiling themselves with blood, just as if one who had stepped into the mud were to wash his feet in mud. Any man who marked him doing this would deem him mad'. No good can come from this direction.

However, there is one way in which wisdom can be achieved, and that is by grasping the underlying principle of things. This formula is the harmony of opposites, but men do not recognise it, though it manifests itself everywhere. 'The formula, which is as I say, men always fail to grasp, before they hear it, and once they have heard it. For though all things happen according to this formula, men seem as though they had no experience of it, even when they experience such words and deeds as I explain, when I distinguish each thing after its kind and show how it is'. If we do not recognise the formula, then no amount of learning is going to be of any use. 'The learning of many things does not teach understanding'. This is a view which we shall find again in Hegel, and Heraclitus is the source of it.

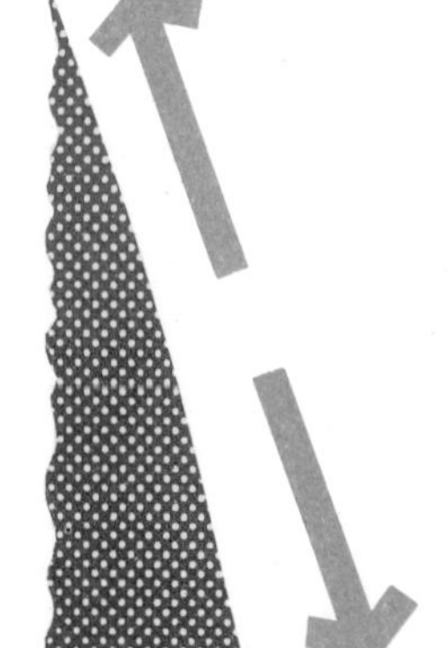

Wisdom, then, consists in grasping the underlying formula which is common to all things. This we must follow as a city follows its laws.

Indeed we must do it even more strictly, for the common formula is universal, even if the laws of different cities differ. Heraclitus thus insists on the absolute character of the common as against the notion of relativism which was developing at that time on the basis of comparisons between the various customs of different peoples. The Heraclitean doctrine is opposed to the pragmatic view of the Sophists, which Protagoras later expressed in the statement that 'Man is the measure of all things'.

But though the universal formula, or Logos, is found everywhere, the many are blind to this and behave as though each had a private wisdom of his own. Thus, the common formula is anything but public opinion. For this blindness Heraclitus despises the crowd. He is in the literal sense of the word an aristocrat, one who favours the power of the best. 'The Ephesians would do well to hang themselves, every grown man of them, and leave the city to beardless lads; for they have cast out Hermodorus, the best man among them, saying, "we will have none who is best among us; if there be any such, let him be so elsewhere and among others".'

Of himself Heraclitus no doubt had quite a good opinion, for which he may perhaps be forgiven. This personal kink set aside, he emerges as a powerul thinker, bringing together the leading conceptions of his predecessors, and exerting a vital influence on Plato.

The Heraclitean doctrine of flux draws attention to the fact that all things are involved in some kind of motion. The next turn in Greek philosophy takes us to the other extreme of the scale and denies motion altogether.

View of the site of Ephesus

A feature shared by all the theories so far reviewed is that in each an attempt is made to explain the world by means of some one principle alone. The individual solutions offered differ from school to school, but each of them propound one basic principle concerning what all things are made of. So far, however, no one had critically examined this general point of view. The critic who undertook this task was Parmenides.

About his life, as with so many others, we know little of interest. He was a native of Elea in Southern Italy, and founded a school which was named Eleatic, after the town. He flourished during the first half of the fifth century and, if we are to believe Plato, together with his follower Zeno, he visited Athens, where both of them met Socrates some time about 450 B.C. Of all the Greek philosophers, Parmenides and Empedocles were the only ones to set forth their theories in poetic form. The poem of Parmenides was entitled 'On Nature', as many other of the writings of the older philosophers were called. It is divided into two sections of which the first, 'The Way of Truth', contains his logical doctrine mainly of interest to us here. In the second part, 'The Way of Opinion', he sets out a cosmology which is essentially Pythagorean, but he is quite explicit in saying we must regard all this as illusory. He had himself been a follower of the Pythagorean doctrine, but abandoned it when he came to formulate his general criticisms. This part of the poem thus is intended as a catalogue of errors from which he had freed himself.

The Parmenidean 'what is, is' leads to a solid spherical world, rigid, uniform and motionless

Parmenides' criticism begins from a weakness common to the theories of all his predecessors. This he found in the inconsistency between the view that all things are made of some basic stuff and at the same time speaking of empty space. The material we can describe by saying, 'It is', and empty space by saying, 'It is not'. Now all previous philosophers had made the mistake of speaking of what is not as though it were. Heraclitus might even be described as saying that it is and is not both at once. As against all these, Parmenides asserts simply that 'It is'. The point is that what is not cannot even be thought of, for one cannot think of nothing. What cannot be thought cannot be, and therefore what can be can be thought. This is the general trend of the Parmenidean argument.

Some consequences emerge at once. 'It is' means that the world is full of matter everywhere. Empty space simply does not exist, either within it or outside it. Moreover there must be as much matter in one place as in any other, since, if this were not so, we should have to say of a place of smaller density that it somehow was not, and this is impossible. 'It' must be equally in all directions, and cannot reach out to infinity, since this would mean that it was incomplete. It is uncreated and eternal; neither can it arise from, or dissolve into, nothing, nor can it arise from something, since there is nothing else along with it. And so we arrive at a picture of the world as a solid, finite, uniform material sphere, without time, motion or change. This is indeed a monstrous blow to commonsense, but it is the logical conclusion of a thorough-going material monism. If this offend our senses, so much the worse for them; we must write off sense experience as illusory, and this is precisely what Parmenides does. By working through the monist theory to the bitter end he compels later thinkers to make a fresh start. The sphere of Parmenides illustrates what Heraclitus meant by saying that, if strife were ever to come to an end, so would the world.

It is worth noting that the Parmenidean criticism does not touch Heraclitus' theory taken correctly. For the view that things are made of fire is not really essential to his theory. Its function is metaphorical, in that the flame illustrates in a colourful way the important notion that nothing ever stays still, that all things are processes. How a statement like 'it is and is not' must be construed in Heraclitus was explained earlier. In fact, the Heraclitean doctrine already contains an implicit criticism of the linguistic metaphysics in Parmenides.

The Parmenidean theory in its linguistic form amounts simply to this: when you think or speak, you think or speak of something. It follows that there must be independent, external things to think and speak about. This you can do on many different occasions, and therefore the objects of thought or discourse must always exist. If they cannot fail to exist at any time, change must be impossible. What Parmenides overlooked is that on his view he could never deny anything, since this would involve him in saying what is not. But if this were so, then he could never assert anything either, and thus all discourse, all speech, all thought would be impossible. Nothing survives except 'It is', an empty formula of identity.

Ruins at Elea; 6th century Phocaean colony, birthplace of Parmenides

Nevertheless, the theory brings out the important point that if we can use a word intelligibly it must have some meaning, and what it means must exist in some sense or other. The paradox is removed if we remember Heraclitus. When the matter is made sufficiently explicit, we find that no one ever really says that it is not, but rather that it is not of a certain kind. Thus if I say 'grass is not red', I am not saying grass is not, but rather that it is not of a certain sort that other things are. I could indeed not say this if I had no examples to offer of other things that were red, for instance buses. The Heraclitean point is that what is red now may be green tomorrow, you might put a coat of green on a red bus.

This raises the general question of the conditions under which words are meaningful, which is too big an issue to be treated here. However, Parmenides' denial of change lies at the origin of all subsequent theories of materialism. The 'It' to which he attributes existence is what came later to be called substance, the invariable and indestructible stuff of which materialists say all things are made.

Parmenides and Heraclitus constitute the two extreme opposites amongst the thinkers of presocratic times. It is worth noting that, besides Plato, the atomists produced a synthesis of these two opposing points of view. From Parmenides they borrow their immutable elementary particles, while from Heraclitus comes the notion of ceaseless movement. This is one of the classical examples which first suggested the Hegelian dialectic. It is certainly true of intellectual progress that it arises from a synthesis of this kind, consequent upon an unrelenting exploration of extreme positions.

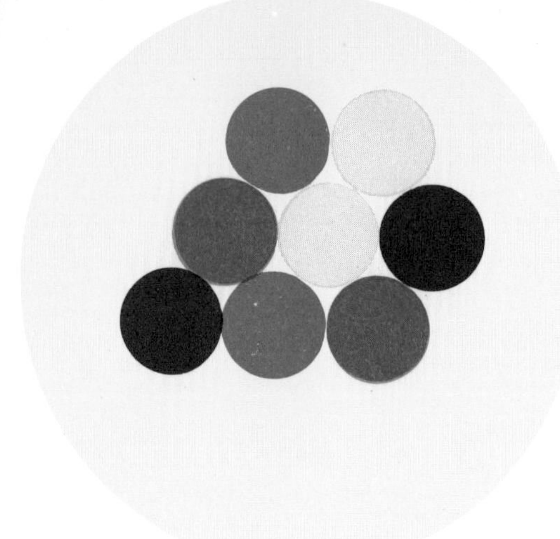

The criticism of Parmenides called for a new approach to the question of what the world was made of. This was supplied by Empedocles of Acragas. Once again, we know little about his date. He flourished in the first half of the fifth century. Politically, he was on the side of the many. Tradition tells of him as a democratic leader. At the same time there was a mystic streak in him which appears to be connected with the orphic influence of the Pythagoreans. Like Parmenides, he seems to have been under the spell of the Pythagorean teaching, and like him later broke away from it. Some miraculous tales survive about him. He could, so legend has it, influence the weather. Owing, no doubt, to his medical skill he succeeded in staying an epidemic of malaria in Selinus, an event which was later gratefully remembered on coins struck in that city. He is said to have considered himself a god, and when he died was supposed to have been wafted on high. Others say he jumped into the crater of Etna, though this seems quite incredible; no politician worth his salt ever jumps into a volcano.

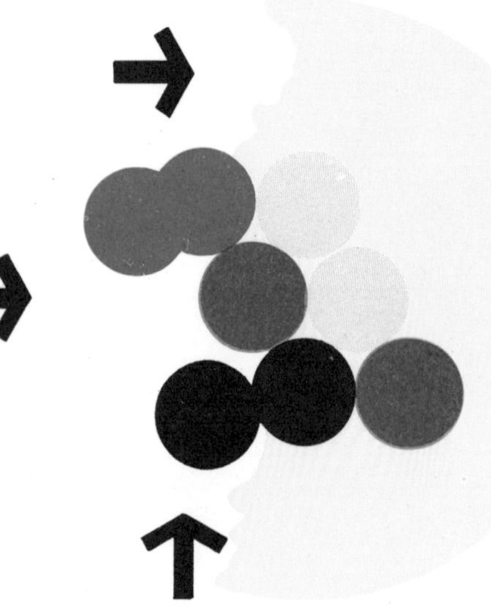

In order to strike a compromise between the Eleatic doctrine and the ordinary evidence of the senses, Empedocles adopted all of the items hitherto tried as basic, adding to them a fourth. These he called the 'roots' of things, and Aristotle later called them elements. This is the famous theory of the four elements, water, air, fire and earth, which dominated chemical science for nearly two thousand years. Vestiges of it survive in ordinary speech even now, as when we speak of the fury of the elements. This theory is really a hypostasis of the two sets of opposites, wet and dry, hot and cold.

We might note that to meet the criticism of Parmenides it is not enough merely to multiply the kinds of substance regarded as fundamental. There must be, in addition, something that causes the basic stuff to mix in various ways. This is supplied by Empedocles' two active principles of love and strife. Their only function is to unite and divide, though, as the notion of insubstantial agency had not then been developed, they had to be taken as substances. They were therefore themselves regarded as material or substantial and are counted along with the four others to make six. Thus, when the four substances were separated, strife takes up the space between them, whereas when they are united, love cements them together. We might note, incidentally, that there is some justification for the view that an agent must be material. For though this notion has been somewhat refined it is still the view of modern science that an agency must have a substantial source somewhere, even if not where it acts.

When Strife expels Love, the four elements are separated

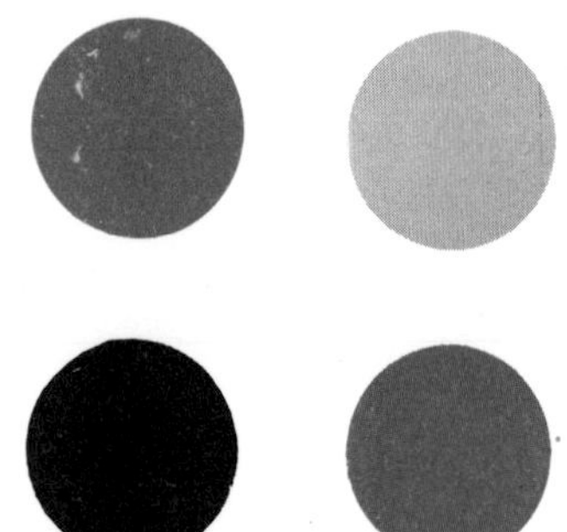

Already Anaximenes had taken air to be substantial, though we do not know on what grounds. Empedocles is on different ground, for he discovered the fact that air was material. This he found by experimenting with water-clocks. It is therefore worthy of note that where his predecessors speak of air he calls this substance aether, both of them Greek words. The latter gained new scientific status in the second half of the 19th century when electro-magnetic theory required some medium for the propagation of waves.

While making these innovations, Empedocles retained a good deal of the Eleatic theory. Thus, the elementary substances are eternal and unchanging and cannot themselves be further explained. This, too, remains an important, if often not explicitly stated, principle of scientific explanation. If, to take a familiar example, one explains the facts of chemistry in terms of atoms, these atoms themselves must be left unexplained. In order to explain them one has to take them as made up of still smaller bits which in their turn are not explained.

As before, then, what is is, nothing can arise from what is not, nor anything pass into it. All this is perfectly sound Eleatic materialism. We may note here a general point on which the Empedoclean revision of the materialist doctrine fails to meet the criticism of Parmenides. The point is that as soon as one admits change one has to admit the void as well. For if change is possible, then in principle it is equally possible that the amount of matter in a given space can be diminished until nothing is left. It is no good merely to increase the number of substances. Parmenides is thus quite right in denying the possibility of change once he has denied the possibility of empty space, and Empedocles does not really help to overcome this difficulty. We shall see later how the atomists solved the problem.

Empedocles knew that light takes time to travel and that the moon's light is indirect, though we cannot tell whence he derived this information. His cosmology is based on a series of cycles starting the world sphere with strife outside and love within, holding the other elements together. Then strife expels love until the various elements are quite separate and love without. Then the reverse happens until we come to the starting point again. His theory of life is tied to this cycle. In the last stage of the cycle, when love invades the sphere, different parts of animals are formed separately. Next, when strife is again quite without we have haphazard combinations subject to the survival of the fittest. When strife once more begins to enter, a process of differentiation develops. Our own world is in an advanced stage of this process, which is once more governed by the evolutionary principle of survival of the fittest.

Coin of Selinus, in honour of Empedocles' containing an epidemic

Finally we must note Empedocles, interest in medicine and physiology. From the physician Alcmaeon of Croton, a follower of the Pythagoreans, he took over the theory that health is a proper balance between the opposite components, and disease occurs if any one takes the upper hand. Likewise he adopted the theory of pores, or passages, through which the entire body breathes. It is these pores that enable us to have sense perceptions. In particular, his theory of vision, which held sway for a long time, provides for a meeting of effluences from the object seen and a ray of fire coming forth from the eye.

His religious views were in the orphic tradition, they are quite divorced from his philosophy and need not detain us. It is however of some interest that in his religious writings he seems to hold views which cannot be reconciled with his theory of the world. This kind of discrepancy is a very common occurrence, more especially amongst those who are not given to critical examination of their beliefs. It is indeed not possible to entertain such conflicting views together at one moment. But men cheerfully believe one thing now and the opposite to-morrow without even suspecting there might be inconsistency.

Our story has by now brought us well into the 5th century B.C. A good deal of what must be discussed under the heading of presocratic philosophy is in fact contemporary with Socrates. It is often not possible to avoid overlapping in some measure. To present a connected account one must from time to time overstep the bounds of mere chronology. This is a difficulty besetting all historical inquiry. History pays scant attention to the convenience of the chronicler.

Somewhat later, we shall be more specifically concerned with Athens. At present we must take a brief general glance at the social and political conditions of fifth century Greece.

Although the Persian Wars had given the Greeks a deeper understanding of their common bonds of language, culture and nationhood, the city state very much remained the centre of interest. Beyond the traditions belonging to all who spoke the tongue of Hellas, the local customs of each single city continued their own vigorous life and maintained their identity. Homer might indeed be a common heritage, but Sparta was as different from Athens as a prison from a playground, and either was different from Corinth or Thebes.

The development of Sparta had taken a peculiar turn of its own. Owing to the growth of their number, the Spartans had been forced into subduing the neighbouring tribe of the Messenians who were reduced to a race of servants. As a result the Spartan state became transformed into a military camp.

Warrior; from Sparta, which met economic with military pressure

The government consisted of a popular assembly which elected a council of elders and appointed two ephors or supervisors. There also were two kings, one each from a noble family, but the effective power lay in the hands of the ephors. The entire aim of education was to produce disciplined soldiers. The Spartan hoplites were famous throughout Greece,and did indeed represent a formidable force. The stand of Leonidas and his three hundred men against the Persian host of Xerxes at Thermopylae must count amongst the memorable feats of history. The Spartans were not a morbidly sentimental people. Discipline was harsh and private feelings subdued. Misshapen infants were exposed in order not to dilute the vigour of the race. The young were taken from their parents at an early age and brought up in institutions resembling military barracks. Girls were on the whole treated in the same way as boys, and the social position of women was largely one of equality. A good deal of Plato's ideal state is inspired by the example of Sparta.

The city of Corinth, on the isthmus, held a commanding position for trade and commerce. She was ruled by an oligarchy and had joined the Peloponnesian league under Spartan leadership. The Corinthians had their contingents in the Persian wars, but they exercised no leadership. Their interests were chiefly commercial, and Corinth was famous not as a home of statesmen and thinkers, but rather for her places of amusement. She also was the metropolis of one of the greatest of all Greek colonies, the city of Syracuse in Sicily. Between these two cities,and with Magna Graecia in general,there existed lively trade links along the sheltered sealane of the Gulf of Corinth.

In Sicily, the Greeks were next-door neighbours to the powerful Phoenician city of Carthage. In concert with Xerxes' invasion of Greece, the Carthaginians had tried to overrun the island in 480 B.C. The vast resources of Syracuse and the leadership of the tyrant of Gela foiled this attempt as permanently as the mainland Greeks had warded off the danger of conquest by the Great King.

The gradual displacement of Corinth by Athens in the course of the fifth century no doubt helped to spark off the Peloponnesian War, and it was the disastrous Syracusan campaign that in the end brought Athens down.

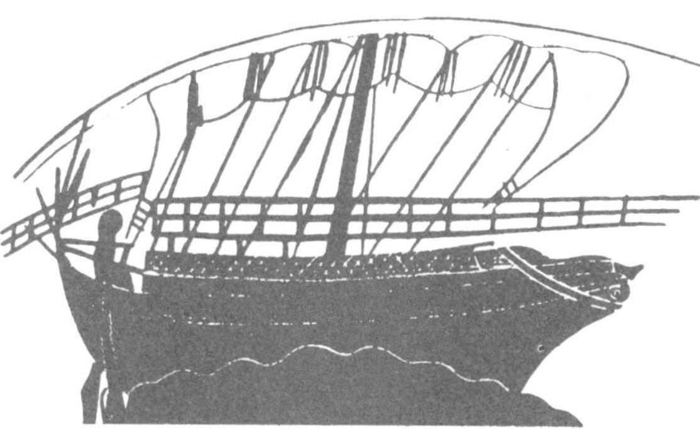

Merchant vessel; from Corinth, which saw its hope in trade

In the Boeotian plains, North West of Athens, stands the ancient city of Thebes, linked to the famous legends of Oedipus. During the fifth century Thebes, too, was ruled by an aristocratic oligarchy. Its role during the Persian Wars had not been altogether commendable. A Theban detachment had perished with Leonidas, but after Xerxes had overrun the country, the Thebans fought alongside the Persians at Plataea. For this defection Athens punished Thebes by depriving her of her leading position in Boeotia. The Thebans were thenceforth held in mild contempt by the Athenians. But as the power of Athens grew, Sparta sided with Thebes to counterbalance this growth. In the Peloponnesian War Thebes held out against Athens though the surrounding countryside was overrun. Yet when the Spartans had won, Thebes switched sides and lent her support to Athens.

Most of the city states controlled the territory of their immediate neighbourhood. Those who lived in the country might till the fields, but the power of government was concentrated in the city. Where there was scope for it, as in the democratic states, participation in the running of public affairs was universal amongst the citizens. A man who took no interest in politics was frowned upon, and was called an 'idiot', which is Greek for 'given over to private interests'.

Olive harvest, main Greek export

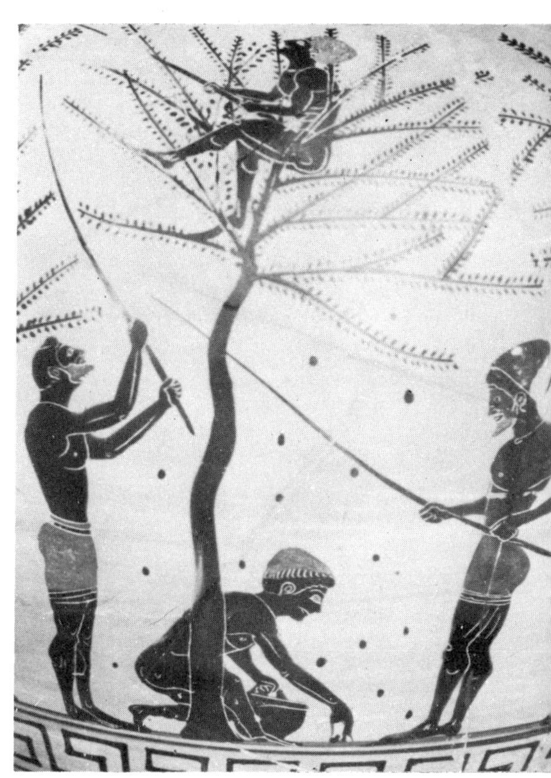

The soil of Greece is not suitable for cultivation on a large scale. As the population grew it thus became necessary to import grain from elsewhere. The main source of supply were the lands bordering the shores of the Euxine, where a large number of Greek colonies had been set up over the centuries. Greece in return exported olive oil and pottery.

The strong individualist streak of the Greeks shows itself in their attitude towards the law. In this they are quite on their own and utterly different from their contemporaries in Asia. There, the authority of a ruler is upheld by laws considered as godgiven, whereas the Greeks recognised that laws are made by and for men. If a law is no longer in conformity with the times it can be changed by common consent. But as long as it has the force of common backing it must be obeyed. The classical example of this respect for law is the refusal of Socrates to escape the death sentence of the Athenian court.

At the same time, this meant that different cities had different laws, so that there was no authority which could settle disputes between them in a peaceful manner.

Greece thus was too far divided by internal jealousies and disruptive individualism ever to achieve national stability. She fell to Alexander and later to Rome. Nevertheless there were common institutions and ideals which allowed for her survival as a cultural unit. The national epic has already been mentioned. But there were other bonds as well. All Greeks revered the shrine at Delphi, in the hills north of the Gulf of Corinth, and in some measure respected the Delphic Oracle.

Delphi was the centre of worship of the god Apollo, who stands for the forces of light and reason. Ancient legend had it that he had killed the Python, the mythical reptile symbolising darkness, and for this feat men built the shrine at Delphi. Here Apollo exercised his protection over the achievements of the Greek spirit. Along with this, the Apollonian cult contains an ethical strain linked with purifying rites. The god himself had had to expiate the miasma of his victory over the Python, and now he held out hope to others who had defiled themselves with blood. There is one exception however: a matricide could not be forgiven. It is an arresting symptom of the growth of Athenian self confidence to find, in Aeschylus' tragedy, Orestes finally acquitted of just this crime, by Athena and a somewhat anachronistic Aeropagus. The other main shrine of Apollo stood on the island of Delos which had been a religious rallying point for the Ionian tribes, and for a while was the home of the treasury of the Delian league.

Athena's temple; at Delphi, home of the oracle, pan hellenic shrine

Another great panhellenic institution were the games at Olympia, in the western Peloponnese. These recurred once every four years and took precedence over any other business, including war. No greater honour could be gained than an Olympic victory. A winner was crowned with a wreath of laurel, and his city would set up in its own shrine at Olympia a statue to commemorate the event. These competitions were first held in 776 B.C. and since then the Greeks reckoned time by Olympiads.

The Olympic Games were a living sign of the value the Greeks attached to the body. Once more this typifies the characteristic emphasis on harmony. Men have bodies as well as minds, and both must be disciplined. It is well to remember that the thinkers of Greece were not ivory tower intellectuals of the kind that our modern world has inherited from the scholastic traditions of the middle ages.

Finally, we must add a word about slavery. It has often been said that the Greeks failed as experimenters because this meant dirtying one's hands, a pastime strictly reserved for slaves. Nothing could be more misleading than such a summary conclusion. The evidence clearly points the other way, as is shown both by the records of their scientific achievements and the remains of their sculpture and architecture. In any case the importance of slaves must not be overrated, even though there was a strong snobbish feeling that gentlemen did not use their hands. It is true that those who worked the silver mines at Laurion bore an inhuman lot. But on the whole, the slave population of the cities was not treated with calculated cruelty. For one thing, a slave was too valuable, especially if he were skilled in some craft. Many slaves eventually became freed men. Slavery on a massive scale belongs to a later age than fifth century Greece.

What is perhaps most astonishing about the fifth century is the sudden outburst of intellectual experiment and invention. This is true in the arts as much as in philosophy. Where the sculpture of the previous century still retains the stiff formality of its Egyptian prototypes, now it comes suddenly to life. In literature, the formalistic rites of old change into the ever more flexible mould of Attic drama. Everything is expanding and no goal seems to be beyond the reach of man. This tremendous feeling of self confidence is nowhere better expressed than in the famous chorus of Sophocles' Antigone: 'many a mighty creature lives, but none mightier than man'. This kind of sentiment is lost in later ages, but revives again during the renaissance in modern times. In the writings of the Italian humanist Alberti one can find very similar views on the status of man. An age of such vitality does not take stock of itself. But self confidence is apt to lead to hybris. It was Socrates, in the later stages of the century, who began to remind men of the form of the good.

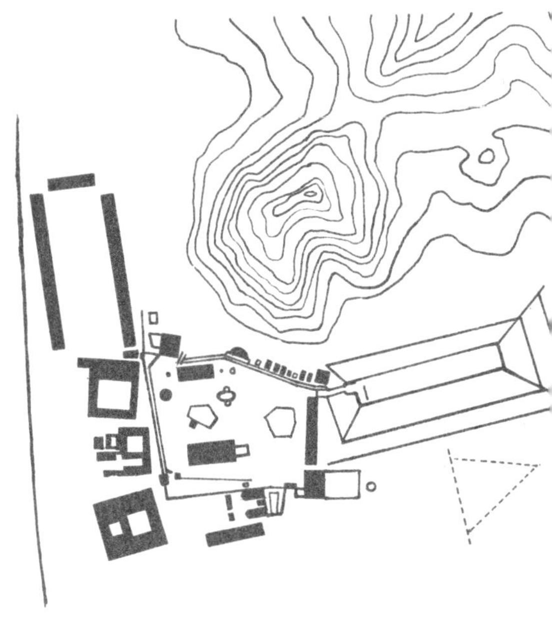

This, then, is the setting in which the civilization of Greece reached its unequalled heights. Based on an underlying principle of harmony, it was torn by internal strife, and this may in the end have enhanced its greatness. For though it never could evolve a viable panhellenic state, it conquered all those who conquered the land of Hellas, and to this day remains the framework of the civilization of the West.

View of Olympia, every four years the scene of pan-hellenic games

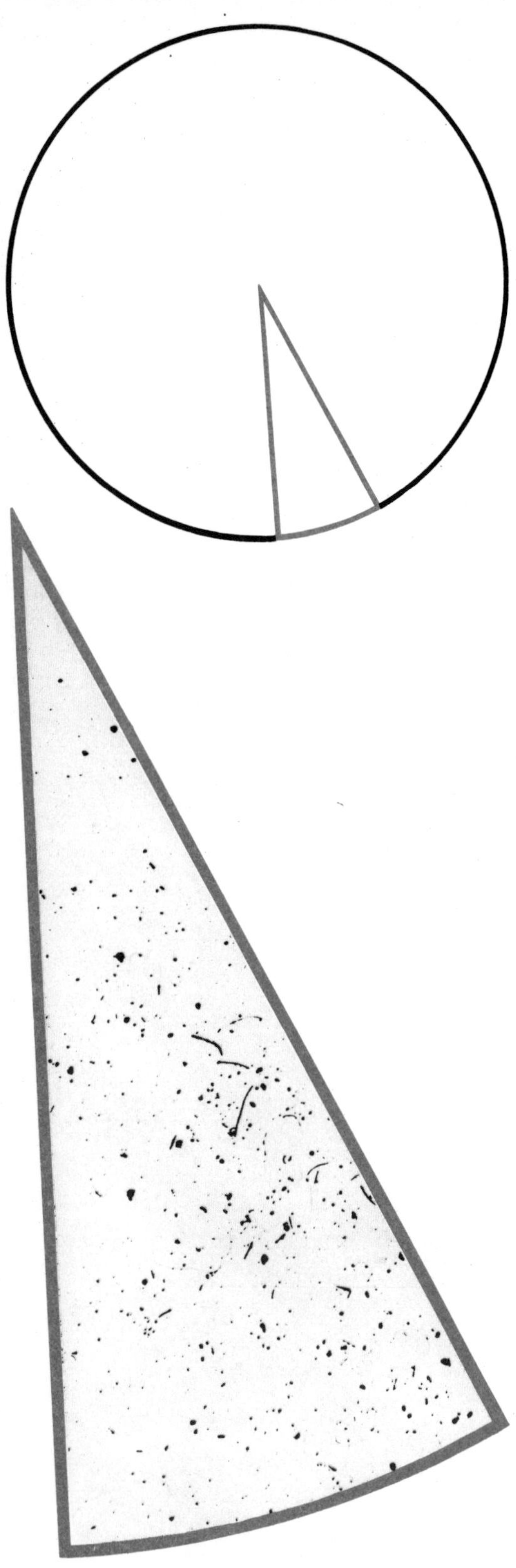

All things contain portions of everything. What seems white has, on looking close, some black in it

The first philosopher who came to live in Athens was Anaxagoras, who stayed there for a period of some thirty years, from the end of the Persian Wars to the middle of the century. By birth he was an Ionian, from Clazomenae, and in his interests he is the heir of the Ionian school at Miletus. His home town had been captured by the Persians at the time of the Ionian revolt, and it seems that he came to Athens with the Persian army. It is recorded that he became a teacher and friend of Pericles, and some even suggest that Euripides was once among his pupils.

Anaxagoras was mainly concerned with scientific and cosmological questions. We know of at least one piece of evidence that shows him as an astute observer. In 468–67 B.C. a sizeable hunk of meteoric rock fell into the river Aigospotamos, and it is no doubt partly on this account that Anaxagoras developed his view that the stars were made of glowing hot rock.

In spite of his influential friends at Athens, Anaxagoras aroused the ill will of the more narrow kind of Athenian conservatism. Independent and unpopular thinking is a precarious business at the best of times, and when it runs against the pious prejudices of those who imagine they know best it can become positively dangerous for the non-conformist. The case was moreover complicated by the fact that in his youth Anaxagoras had been a Persian sympathiser. It would seem indeed as though the pattern has not greatly changed these last 2500 years. At all events Anaxagoras was tried on charges of impiety and Medism. What the punishment might have been and how he escaped it is not quite certain. His friend Pericles probably snatched him from prison and whisked him away. Afterwards, he went to live in Lampsacus where he continued teaching until his death. Very commendably, the citizens of that town took a more enlightened view of his activities. Anaxagoras must be the only philosopher in history whose death was commemorated by an annual school holiday. The teaching of Anaxagoras was set down in a book and some fragments of this have survived in other sources. Socrates, who was later tried on similar charges of impiety, tells the judges that the unconventional views he is accused of holding really are those of Anaxagoras, whose book could be bought by anyone for one drachma.

The theory of Anaxagoras, like that of Empedocles before him, was a fresh attempt at digesting the Parmenidean criticism. Where Empedocles had thought of each of the parts of the pairs of opposites, hot and cold, dry and wet, as a basic stuff, Anaxagoras on the contrary thinks that each of these in varying proportions is contained in every tiny scrap of material, be it ever so small. To make his point he falls back on the infinite divisibility of matter. Merely cutting things into smaller bits, so he would say, does not eventually land us with something different, for Parmenides had shown that what is cannot in any way fail to be, or become what is not. The assumption that matter is infinitely divisible is interesting. This is the first time that it makes its appearance. That it is wrong is unimportant here. What it does bring to the fore is the notion of infinite divisibility which does apply to space. It seems that here we have a starting point from which the notion of empty space was later developed by the atomists.

Be that as it may, if we grant the assumption, Anaxagoras' criticism of Empedocles is so far sound.

The differences between things are due to the greater preponderance of one or the other of the opposites. Thus Anaxagoras would say that, in some measure, snow is black, but that white predominates. In a way there is a touch of Heraclitus in this. The opposites hang together and everything may change into anything else. Anaxagoras says that 'the things that are in the world are not divided nor cut off from one another with a hatchet' and that 'in everything there is a portion of everything except Nous, and there are some things in which there is Nous also'.

The Nous, or intelligence, which is here mentioned, is the active principle which takes the place of Empedocles' love and strife. But it is still considered as a substance, although a very rare and subtle one. Nous is different from other substances in that it is pure and unmixed. It is Nous that sets things into motion. Further, the possession of it sets apart the living from the inanimate.

For the origin of our world he put forward a view which in some way resembles much more recent speculation on this subject. Nous sets off an eddy motion somewhere, and as this gathers strength there is a separation of various things according to whether they are more or less massive. Heavy chunks of rock, hurled out by the earth's rotation, go farther than other objects. Because they move so fast they begin to glow, and this explains the nature of the stars. Like the Ionians, he thought there were many worlds.

Anaxagoras; coin from Clazomenae, the Ionian city of his birth

Concerning perception, he advanced the ingenious biological principle that sensation depends on contrasts. Thus, vision is a breaking in of light on the opposite dark. Very intense sensations cause pain and discomfort. These are views that are still current in physiology.

In some ways, then, Anaxagoras produced a more refined theory than his predecessor. There are at least hints that he tried to struggle through to a conception of empty space. But though at times it looks as though he wants to make Nous an insubstantial agent, he does not quite succeed. As in the case of Empedocles, therefore, the fundamental criticism of Parmenides is not met. In the meantime, however, the suggestion of infinite divisibility marks a new advance in the account of how the world is constituted. There remains the step of recognising that divisibility belongs to space, and the stage is set for atomism.

It would be wrong to imagine that Anaxagoras was an atheist. However, his conception of god was philosophical and not in line with the state religion of Athens. It is because of his unorthodox opinions that the charge of impiety was laid against him. For he equated god with Nous, the active principle which is the source of all motion. Such a view was bound to attract the unfavourable notice of the government, since it naturally raises doubts as to the value of established ritual performances, and to that extent touches upon the authority of the state.

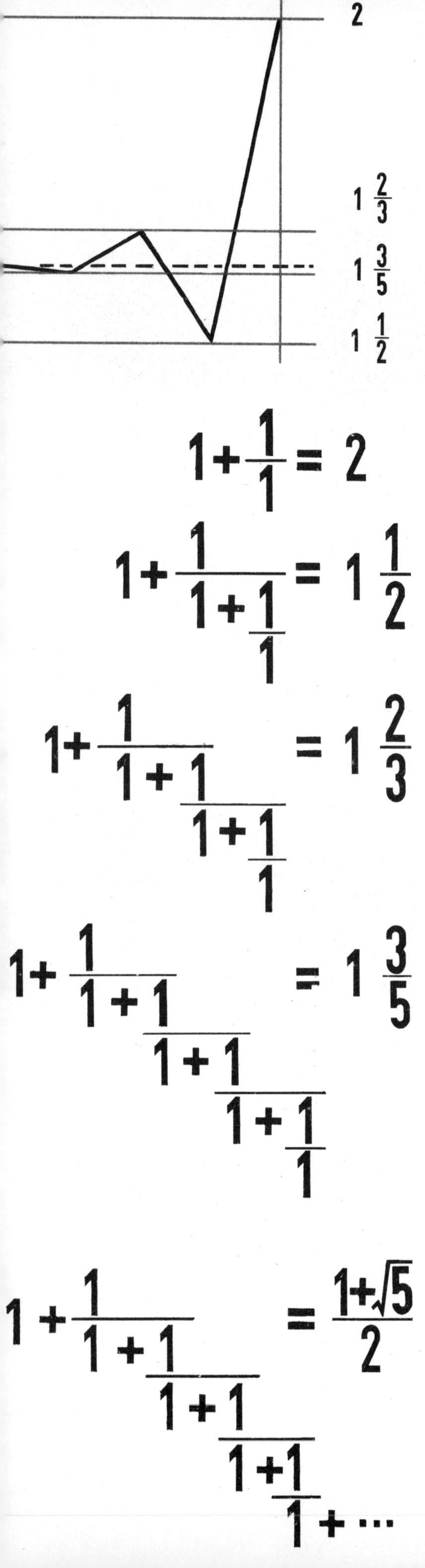

Why Pythagoras and his school had been expelled from Croton in 510 B.C. we shall probably never know. Still, it is not too difficult to see where the school might come into conflict with upright citizens. For we must remember, Pythagoras did meddle with politics, as was the wont with Greek philosophers. Although philosophers are on the whole viewed with forbearing indifference by the rest of mankind, it is remarkable, when they set forth a critical opinion, how they succeed in stirring up the murky waters of professional politics. Nothing annoys those who govern more than the suggestion that they might after all be not so wise as they themselves imagined. No doubt it was on grounds such as these that the Crotonians burnt the Pythagorean school. But burning schools, or men for that matter, has always proved singularly unhelpful in stamping out unorthodoxy. As a result of the disaster which had overtaken the original school, its views became more widely known than ever, through the activities of surviving members who returned eastward to Greece.

We have seen that the founder of the Eleatic school had been at first a follower of Pythagoras. From the Eleatic philosopher Zeno, the Pythagorean theory of number was to receive a devastating attack a little later. It is therefore essential to grasp what this theory involves.

Numbers were thought of as made up of units, and the units, represented by dots, were taken as having spatial dimensions. A point on this view is a unit having position, that is, it has dimensions of some sort, whatever they are. This theory of number is quite adequate for dealing with rational numbers. It is always possible to choose as unit a rational number in such a way that any number of rational numbers are integral multiples of the unit. But the account comes to grief when we meet irrational numbers. They cannot be measured in this way. It is worth noting that the Greek of which irrational is a translation meant measureless rather than bereft of reason, at any rate for Pythagoras. In order to overcome this difficulty, the Pythagoreans invented a method of finding these elusive numbers through a sequence of approximations. This is the construction of continued fractions mentioned earlier. In such a sequence, successive steps alternately exceed and fall short of the mark by ever diminishing amounts. But the process is essentially infinite. The irrational number aimed at is the limit of the process. The point of the exercise is that we can reach rational approximations as close as we like to the limit. This feature is indeed the same as that involved in the modern conception of a limit.

A theory of number can thus be worked out along these lines. Nevertheless the notion of the unit conceals a fundamental confusion between discrete number and continuous quantity, and this becomes patent as soon as the Pythagorean theory is applied in geometry. What the difficulties are we shall see in discussing Zeno's criticism.

The other main legacy of Pythagorean mathematics is the theory of ideas, which was adopted and further developed by Socrates. This, too, was effectively criticised by the Eleatics, if Plato is a reliable guide. We have already hinted at the mathematical origin of this theory. Take for instance the theorem of Pythagoras. It would be of no avail to draw an extremely accurate diagram of a right angled triangle and the squares on its sides, and then proceed to measure their areas. However accurate the drawing, it is not perfectly accurate, indeed it could never be. It is not such diagrams as these that give the proof of the theorem. For that we require a perfect diagram, of the kind that can be imagined but not drawn. Any actual drawing must needs be a more or less faithful copy of the mental image. This is the burden of the theory of ideas which was a well known part of the doctrine of the later Pythagoreans.

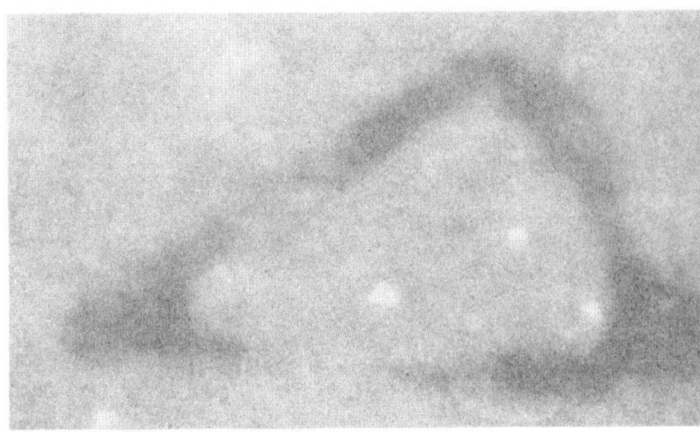

We saw how Pythagoras had developed a principle of harmony from his discovery on tuned strings. From it stem the medical theories which consider health as some sort of balance between opposites. The later Pythagoreans took this one stage further and applied the notion of harmony to the soul. According to this view the soul is an attunement of the body, so that the soul becomes a function of the well ordered condition of the body. When the organization of the body breaks down the body disintegrates and so does the soul. We might think of the soul as the stretched string of a musical instrument, and of the body as the framework on which it is strung. If the frame is destroyed the string becomes slack and loses its attunement. This view is quite at variance with the earlier Pythagorean notions on this subject. Pythagoras, it seems, believed in the transmigration of souls, whereas on this more recent view souls die as surely as bodies.

In astronomy, the later Pythagoreans developed a very bold hypothesis. According to this, the centre of the world is not the earth, but a central fire. The earth is a planet revolving round this fire, but it is invisible for us because our side of the earth always points away from the centre. The sun, too, was considered as a planet, receiving its light by reflection from the central fire. This was a long step forward to the heliocentric hypothesis later put forward by Aristarchus. But in the form in which the Pythagoreans had developed their theory so many difficulties remained that Aristotle reinstated a flat earth view. Because of his greater authority in other matters this, instead of the true view, came to prevail in later times when the sources were forgotten.

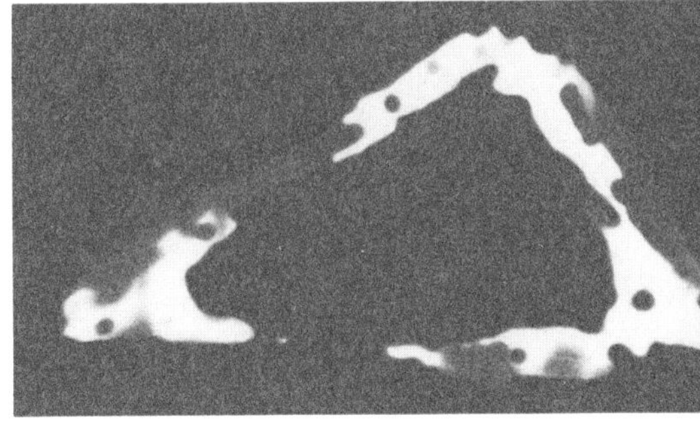

As for the growth of theories on the constitution of things, Pythagoreanism recognises one feature which is overlooked or misunderstood by many of the earlier thinkers. This is the notion of the void. Without it a satisfactory account of motion is impossible. Here, too, the Aristotelian doctrine was later to return to the backward view that nature abhors the vacuum. It is to the atomists that we must look for the true line of development of physical theory.

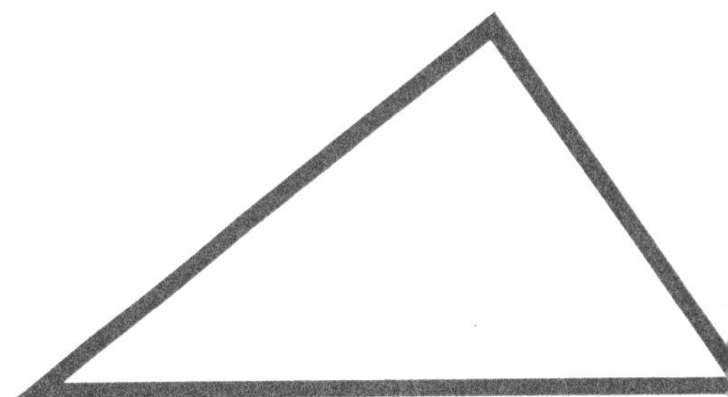

A perfect triangle cannot be drawn, it is seen with the mind's eye

Meanwhile the Pythagorean school sought to accommodate the advances made by Empedocles. Their mathematical outlook did not, of course, allow them to adopt these elements as ultimate. Instead, they produced a compromise which laid the foundations of a mathematical theory of the constitution of matter. The elements were now considered as consisting of particles of the shape of regular solids. This theory is further developed in Plato's 'Timaeus'. The word 'element' itself seems to have been coined by these later Pythagorean thinkers.

None of the materialist attempts to meet the criticism of Parmenides up to this point can be considered as altogether satisfactory. Whatever the weaknesses of the Eleatic theory itself, the fact remains that mere multiplication of fundamental substances cannot provide a solution. This point was brought home very forcefully by a series of arguments put forward by the followers of Parmenides. Foremost amongst these is Zeno of Elea, a countryman and disciple of Parmenides. Zeno was born about 490 B.C. Beyond the fact that he took an interest in political affairs, the one important thing we know about him is that he and Parmenides met Socrates in Athens. This is reported by Plato, and there is no reason for disbelieving him.

A figure is infinitely divisible; there can be no ultimate units, either finite or sizeless

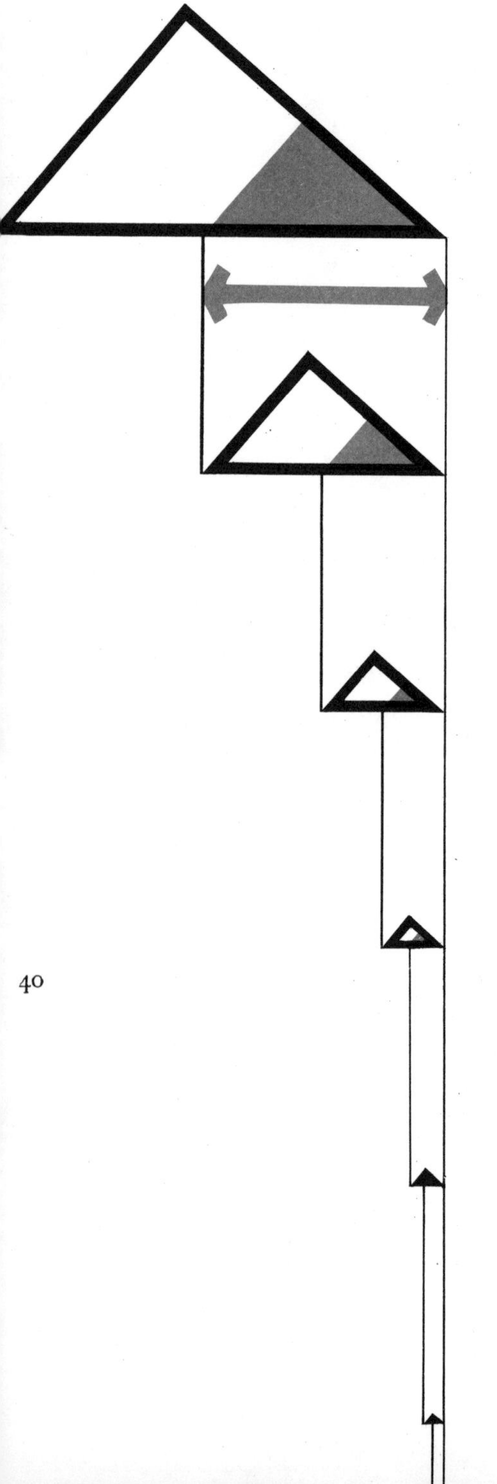

The Eleatic doctrine, as was shown earlier, leads to very startling conclusions. For this reason many attempts were made to patch up the materialist doctrine. What Zeno was trying to show was that if Eleaticism did not commend itself to common sense, rival theories purporting to overcome this impasse led to even stranger difficulties. Thus, instead of giving a direct defence of Parmenides, he tackled the opposition on its own ground. Starting from the assumption of an opponent, he would show by deductive argument that this involved impossible consequences. Therefore the original assumption could not be entertained and was in fact destroyed.

This kind of argument is similar to the reductio ad absurdum argument mentioned in the discussion of Anaximander's theory of evolution. But there is an important difference. In the ordinary reductio ad absurdum, one argues that since the conclusion is in fact false, therefore one of the premisses is in fact false.

Zeno, on the other hand, tries to show that from a certain assumption one can derive two contradictory conclusions. This means that the set of conclusions is not just in fact untrue, but impossible. Hence, so he argues, the assumption from which the conclusions follow is itself impossible. This kind of argument proceeds without any comparison between the conclusions and the facts. It is in this sense purely dialectic, that is, in the realm of question and answer. Dialectic argument was first systematically used by Zeno. It has a very important function in philosophy. Socrates and Plato adopted it from the Eleatics and developed it in their own way, and it has loomed large in philosophy ever since.

The arguments of Zeno are in the main an attack on the Pythagorean conception of the unit. Connected with this there are certain arguments against the void and against the possibility of motion.

Let us first consider an argument showing the unsoundness of the notion of unit. Whatever is, so Zeno would argue, must have some magnitude. If it had no magnitude at all it would not exist. So much being granted, the same may be said of each part, it too will have some magnitude. It is all the same to say this once and to say it always, he goes on to state. This is a terse way of introducing infinite divisibility; no part could be said to be the smallest. If, then, things are many, they will have to be small and large at the same time. Indeed, they must be so small as to be without size, for infinite divisibility shows that the number of parts is infinite, which requires units without magnitude, and therefore any sum of these has no magnitude either. But at the same time, the unit must have some magnitude, and therefore things are infinitely great.

Zeno denied infinite space, for if the earth were contained in space, what contained it in turn?

This argument is important in showing that the Pythagorean theory of number fails in geometry. If we consider a line, then, according to Pythagoras, we ought to be able to say how many units there are in it. Clearly, if we assume infinite divisibility, then the theory of units breaks down at once. At the same time it is important to grasp that this does not prove Pythagoras wrong. What it does prove is that the theory of units and infinite divisibility cannot be entertained together, or, in other words, that they are incompatible. One or the other must be given up. Mathematics required infinite divisibility, therefore the Pythagorean unit must be abandoned. A further point worth noting concerns reductio ad absurdum itself. A single proposition which makes sense cannot have immediate consequences that are incompatible. It is only when other propositions are combined with it that contradictions can be generated, to wit, when in two different arguments the additional proposition in one argument is incompatible with the additional proposition of the second argument. Thus, in the present case we have two arguments; first, things are many and units have no size, therefore things have no size; second, things are many and units have size, therefore things are infinite in size. The two incompatible additional premisses are that units have no size, and that they have some size. On either count, the conclusion is manifestly absurd. It follows that something is wrong with the premisses in each argument. What is wrong is the Pythagorean conception of the unit.

To vindicate Parmenides' position against the void, Zeno put forward a new argument. If space exists it must be contained in something, and this can only be more space, and so on indefinitely. Unwilling to accept this regress, Zeno concludes there is no space. What this really amounts to is a denial of the view that space is an empty container. Thus, on Zeno's view we must not distinguish between a body and the space in which it is. It is easy to see that the container theory could be turned against the sphere of Parmenides. For to say that the world is a finite sphere would in this case mean that it was in empty space. Zeno here tries to preserve his master's theory, but it is doubtful whether it makes sense even so to speak of a finite sphere if beyond there is nothing.

An argument of this kind which can be repeated over and over again is called an infinite regress. This does not always lead to a contradiction. Indeed, no one would nowadays object to the view that any space is part of a bigger space. For Zeno a contradiction arises just because he takes it for granted that 'what is' is finite. He therefore is confronted with what is called a vicious infinite regress.

Regressive arguments of the vicious type are really a form of reductio ad absurdum. What they show is that the basis of the argument is incompatible with some other proposition which is assumed to be true.

The most famous of Zeno's arguments are the four paradoxes of motion, and foremost amongst these, the story of Achilles and the tortoise. Once again, the defence of Parmenides' theory is indirect. The onus is thrown on the Pythagoreans to produce something better since their own theory cannot account for motion either. The argument is that if Achilles and the tortoise run a handicap race, Achilles can never overtake his competitor. Suppose the tortoise starts a certain distance down the track, then while Achilles runs up to the starting point of the tortoise, the latter will have moved somewhat further ahead. While Achilles runs to this new position, the tortoise again will have gained a point slightly further on. Every time Achilles closes in on the tortoise's previous position, the wretched creature will have moved away. Achilles does of course come closer and closer to the tortoise, but he will never catch up with it.

Achilles and the tortoise

We must remember that the argument is directed against the Pythagoreans. Their assumption is therefore adopted and a line is taken as made up of units, or points. The conclusion is therefore a way of saying that however slowly the tortoise moves, it will have to cover an infinite distance before the race is run. Here, then, is another form of the argument that things are infinite in size.

Although it is not difficult to show what is wrong with the conclusion, it must be quite clear that, as a counter to Pythagorean doctrines of the unit, the argument is impeccable. It is only when we abandon this view of the unit that we can develop a theory of infinite series which shows where the conclusion errs. If, for instance, a series consists of terms diminishing in a constant ratio, as do the lengths of successive stages in the race, then we can work out where Achilles will overtake the tortoise. The sum of such a series is defined as a number such that the sum of any number of terms, however large, will never exceed it, but the sum of a sufficiently large number of terms comes as close to it as we like. That there is one such number, and one only, for a given series, must here be stated without demonstration. The kind of series involved in the race is called geometrical. Anyone familiar with elementary mathematics can cope with it nowadays. But let us not forget that it was precisely the critical work of Zeno that has made it possible to develop an adequate theory of continuous quantity on which to base these sums that now seem child's play to us.

Another paradox, sometimes called the racecourse, brings out the other half of the dialectic attack. The argument is that one could never cross from one side of the racecourse to the other, for this would mean that we must traverse an infinite number of points in a finite time. More precisely, before reaching any point, one must reach the halfway mark, and so on indefinitely. Therefore, one could never start moving at all. This, together with Achilles and the tortoise, which shows that having started one could never stop, disposes of the hypothesis that a line consists of infinitely many units.

Two more paradoxes are given by Zeno to show that we cannot mend matters by supposing there is only a finite number of units in a line. First, let us take three equal parallel segments of lines, made up of the same finite number of units. Let one of them be at rest, and the other two moving in opposite directions with equal speed, in such a way that they all come to lie alongside each other when the moving lines pass the stationary one. The relative velocity of the two moving lines is twice as great as the relative velocity of each of these and the stationary line. The argument now depends on the further assumption that there are units of time as well as of space. Speed, then, is measured by the number of points to move past a given point in a given number of moments. While one of the moving lines passes half the length of the stationary line it passes the entire length of the other moving line. Hence the latter time is twice the former. But to reach their position alongside each other the two moving lines take the same time. Thus it would seem that the moving lines move twice as fast as they move. The argument is a little complicated because we do not normally think in moments so much as in distances, but it is a perfectly sound criticism of the theory of units.

Finally, there is the paradox of the arrow. At any moment the arrow in flight occupies a space equal to itself and is therefore at rest. Hence it is always at rest. This shows that motion cannot even start, whereas the previous paradox showed that motion is always faster than it is. By having thus demolished the Pythagorean theory of discrete quantity, Zeno has laid the foundations for a theory of continuity. And this is just what is needed to defend the theory of Parmenides' continuous sphere.

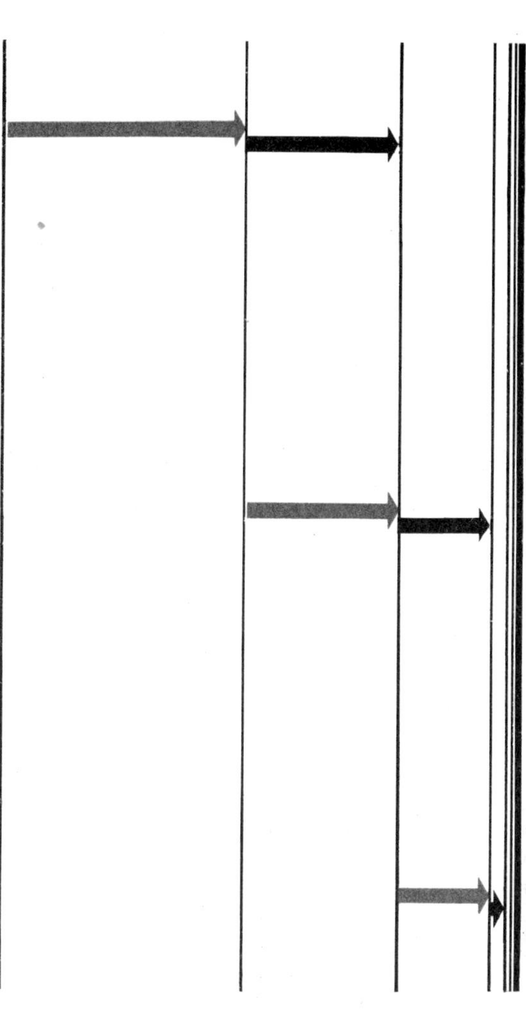

While Achilles runs the handicap, the tortoise has gone ahead some distance, and so on, indefinitely

The other Eleatic philosopher of note was Melissus of Samos, a contemporary of Zeno. Of his life we know only that he was a general during the Samian revolt and defeated an Athenian fleet in 441 B.C. Melissus amended the theory of Parmenides in one important respect. We saw already that Zeno had to reassert the denial of the void. But it is not then possible to speak of what is as a finite sphere, because this suggests that there is something outside it, to wit, empty space. The void being ruled out, we are compelled to regard the material universe as infinite in all directions, which is Melissus' conclusion.

In his defence of the Eleatic One, Melissus went so far as to foreshadow the atomic theory. If things are many, so he argues, then each of these must itself be like the One of Parmenides. For nothing can come to be or pass away. Thus the only tenable theory that there are many is obtained by breaking up the sphere of Parmenides into little spheres. This is just what the atomists went on to do.

If distance and time consist of units, the middle row moves at two different speeds at once

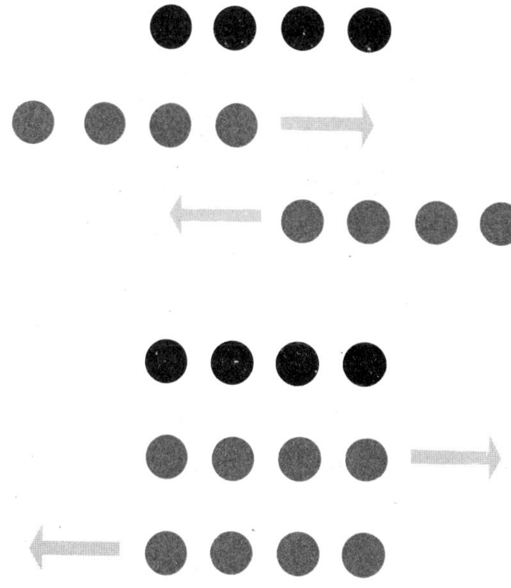

The dialectic of Zeno was in the main a destructive attack on Pythagorean positions. At the same time it provides the foundations of the dialectic of Socrates, in particular for the method of hypothesis which we shall meet later. Moreover, here for the first time one finds a systematic use of close argument on a specific issue. The Eleatics were presumably well versed in Pythagorean mathematics, and it is in that field one expects to see applications of this procedure. About the actual ways in which Greek mathematicians carried out analysis unfortunately very little is known. It seems clear, however, that the rapid development in mathematics during the latter half of the fifth century was in some measure linked with the emergence of settled canons of argument.

How can we account for the changing world around us at all? Evidently it is of the very nature of explanation that its grounds should not themselves be shifting. The first to ask the question were the early Milesians, and we have seen how subsequent schools gradually transformed and refined the problem. In the end it was another Milesian thinker who gave the final answer to this question. Leucippus, of whom nothing else of note is known, was the father of atomism. The atomic theory is a direct outcome of Eleaticism. Melissus had all but stumbled on it.

The theory is a compromise between the one and the many. Leucippus introduced the notion of innumerable constituent particles, each of which shared with the sphere of Parmenides the feature of being rigid, solid and indivisible. These were the 'atoms', the things that cannot be cut. They are always moving in empty space. The atoms were all supposed to be the same in composition, but could differ in shape. What was indivisible or 'atomic' about these particles was that they could not be physically broken asunder. The space they occupy is of course mathematically divisible without limit. The reason why atoms are not seen in the ordinary way is that they are so extremely small. An account can now be given of becoming or change. The ever-changing aspect of the world arises from re-arrangements of atoms.

Change as rearrangement of atoms that remain themselves unchanged

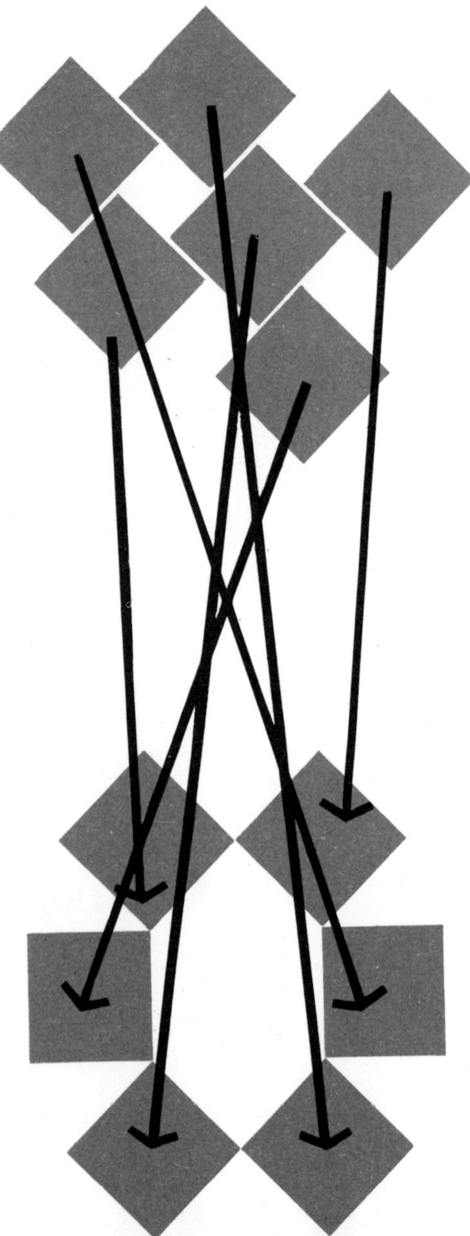

In the language of Parmenides, the atomists would have to say that what is not is just as real as what is. In other words, there is such a thing as space. What this is it would be difficult to say. On this score I do not think we are any further ahead today than were the Greeks. Empty space is that of which in some sense geometry is true. That is really all one can say with confidence. The earlier difficulties of materialism arose from the insistence that everything must be corporeal. The only one who had a clear notion of what the void might be was Parmenides, and he, of course, had denied its existence. All the same, it is worthwhile to remember that to say what is not is does not, in Greek, amount to a contradiction in terms. The clue lies in the fact that there are two Greek words for 'not'. One of them is categorical, as in the statement 'I do not like X'. The other is hypothetical and is used in commands, wishes and the like. It is this hypothetical 'not' which figures in the phrase 'what is not', or 'not being', as used by the Eleatics. If the categorical 'not' were used in 'what is not is' it would of course be plain gibberish. In English the distinction is lacking, and this digression therefore unavoidable.

It has often been asked whether the atomic theory of the Greeks was based on observation, or whether it was merely a lucky shot in the dark, having no other groundwork than philosophic speculation. The answer to this question is not at all so simple as might be thought. On the one hand, it is clear from what was said above that atomism is the only viable compromise between common sense and Eleaticism. The Eleatic theory is a logical criticism of the earlier materialist doctrine. On the other hand, Leucippus was a Milesian and well versed in the theories of his great countrymen and predecessors. His own cosmology bears witness to this, for he returned to the earlier views of Anaximander instead of following the Pythagoreans.

Anaximenes' theory of condensation and rarefaction is evidently in some measure based on observation of such phenomena as the condensing of mists on smooth surfaces. The problem thus was one of incorporating the Eleatic criticism into a theory of particles. That the atoms should be subject to perpetual motion may well be suggested by the same observation, or from the dancing of dust in a beam of sunlight. In any case the theory of Anaximenes does not really work unless we think of more or less densely packed batches of particles. It is thus certainly not true that Greek atomism was just a lucky guess. When Dalton revived the atomic theory in modern times, he was well aware of the Greek views on the subject and found that this provided an account of his observation on the constant proportions in which chemical substances combine.

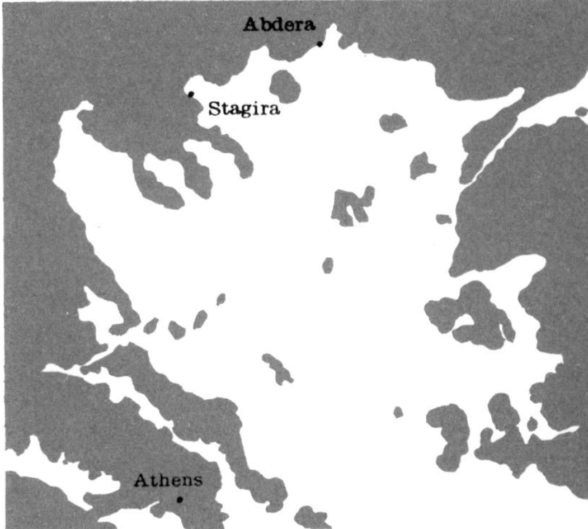

There is however a deeper reason why the atomic theory was not a fortuitous discovery. This is connected with the logical structure of explanation itself. For what is it to give an account of something? It is to show how what occurs is a consequence of the changing configuration of things. Thus if we wish to explain a change in a material object, we must do this by reference to changing arrangements of hypothetical constituents that remain themselves unexplained. The explicative force of the atom remains intact as long as the atom is not itself under investigation. As soon as this happens the atom becomes the object of an empirical enquiry, and the explicative entities become sub-atomic particles, which in their turn remain unexplained. This aspect of the atomic theory has been discussed at great length by the French philosopher E. Meyerson. Thus, atomism as such conforms to the structure of causal explanation.

The atomic theory was further developed by Democritus, a native of Abdera, who flourished about 420 B.C. In particular, he went on to distinguish between things as they really were and as they seemed to us. Thus, on the atomic view, the world around us really consists just of atoms in motion, whereas we experience it in a variety of ways. This gives rise to a distinction between what were much later called primary and secondary qualities. On the one side there are shape, size and matter, and on the other, colours, sounds, tastes and the like. The latter are then explained in terms of the former, which belong to the atoms themselves.

Democritus of Abdera

The theory of atoms we shall meet several times more in the course of our enquiry. What might be its limitations will be discussed in the appropriate places. Here, let us merely note that atomism is the outcome not of fanciful speculation, but a serious answer, one hundred and fifty years in the making, to the Milesian question.

Beyond its importance for natural science, atomism also gave rise to a new theory of the soul. Like everything else the soul is made up of atoms. These constituents of the soul are more refined than other atoms, and are distributed throughout the body. On such a view death means disintegration and personal immortality does not exist, a consequence later drawn by Epicurus and his followers. Well being, which is the end of life, consists in a balanced state of the soul.

The sophists taught at a price, training for practical success

Along with the development of the philosophic schools during the fifth century, there arose a class of people who were in a sense on the fringe of philosophy. There were the men who were generally referred to as the sophists. It is to them that Socrates refers contemptuously as those who make the weaker seem the stronger reason. It is important to understand how this movement came into being, and what was its function in Greek society.

The shifting scene of philosophic combat had made it difficult to see on what side the truth might be. If there is one thing that practical men have no time for it is an issue which remains open. To those who want to get things done merely to be active, an undecided question is anathema. This, on the whole, was the predicament in which the sophists found themselves. The conflicting theories of the philosophers held out no hope that knowledge was possible at all. Besides, the broadening experience of contact with other nations had shown that there were unbridgeable gaps between the customs of different nations. Herodotus tells an anecdote on this. At the Great King's court, delegations from tribes of different lands in the Persian Empire were present. Each gasped with horror when they learned of the funeral customs of the others. One lot used to incinerate the dead, the other gobble them up. Herodotus quotes Pindar in conclusion: custom is King of all.

Since the sophists felt that knowledge could not be had, they declared that it was unimportant. What mattered was useful opinion. There is of course some truth in this. In the conduct of practical affairs success is indeed the one overriding consideration. Here again, the Socratic view is the very opposite. Where the Sophists were interested in sound practice, Socrates held that this was not enough, that in fact the unexamined life was not worth living.

At a time when there was little if any systematic education in Greece, the Sophists fulfilled just this task. They were itinerant teachers who would give lectures or tuition on a professional basis. One of the things Socrates dislikes about them is their taking of fees. One may well feel that Socrates was here a little unfair, for even talkers have to eat sometimes. Still, it is worth noting that the academic tradition holds salaries to be a kind of retainer which should enable the professor to forget about material problems.

In their teaching, the Sophists severally emphasised different subject matters. The most respectable of their activities was simply the provision of a literary education. But there were others who taught subjects of more immediate practical bearing. With the spread of democratic constitutions during the fifth century, it became important to be able to make speeches. This need was catered for by the teachers of rhetoric. Likewise, there were teachers of politics who would instruct their disciples on how to handle affairs in the assembly. Finally, there were the teachers of disputation, or eristic, men who could make the worse appear the better case. This art has obvious uses in the law courts, where the accused had to conduct his own defence, and its teachers taught how to twist arguments and produce paradoxes.

It is important to distinguish eristic from dialectic. Those who practise the former are out to win, whereas the dialecticians are trying to discover the truth. It is really the distinction between debate and discussion.

While in the field of education the sophists thus performed a valuable task, their philosophical outlook was inimical to enquiry. For theirs was a scepticism of despair, a negative attitude to the problem of knowledge. The sum of this position is the famous saying of Protagoras, that 'Man is the measure of all things, of things that are that they are, and of things that are not that they are not'. Thus, each man's opinion is true for him, and disagreements between men cannot be decided on the score of truth. Small wonder, then, that the sophist Thrasymachus defines justice as the advantage of the stronger.

While, therefore, Protagoras abandons the quest for truth, he still seems to allow that one opinion can be better than another, in the pragmatic sense, though this position is open to the general logical criticism against pragmatism. For if we ask which of two opinions is in fact the better, we are at once driven back to the notion of absolute truth. At all events, Protagoras is the originator of pragmatism.

An amusing tale shows how the sophists came to be viewed. Protagoras, convinced his teaching was foolproof, told an indigent pupil to pay from the proceeds of his first court case. Once trained, the youngster would not begin to practise. Protagoras prosecuted to recover his fee, arguing before court that the student must pay: by the bargain if he won, and by the verdict if he lost. The accused gave as good as he got and better. The payment was forfeit, he declared: by the verdict if he won, and by the bargain if he lost.

Socrates taught informally, bringing men to know themselves

The word sophist itself means something like man of wisdom. Since Socrates, too, was a teacher, it is not surprising that the undiscerning in his own time called him a sophist. That this classification is wrong we have already shown. Not until Plato's time, however, was the distinction properly recognised. In one sense, of course, philosophers and sophists provoke similar responses from the crowd.

Towards philosophy in general, those who are not philosophically minded have from time immemorial evinced a rather curious and inconsistent attitude. On the one hand, they tend to treat philosophers with mild and benevolent condescension as harmless fools, as cranks who walk with their heads in the clouds and ask silly questions, out of touch with the real concerns of men, and unmindful of those things to which sensible citizens ought to attend. On the other hand, philosophic speculation can have a profoundly unsettling influence on established practice and custom. The philosopher is now regarded with suspicion as a non-conformist who upsets traditions and conventions and does not give unconditional assent to the habits and views that seem to be good enough for everyone else. To have their cherished beliefs called into question makes those who are not used to such treatment feel insecure, and they react with hatred and hostility. Thus Socrates was accused of subversive teaching just as much as the sophists in general, and the teachers of eristic in particular.

Athens

The three greatest figures in Greek philosophy were all of them linked with Athens. Socrates and Plato were born Athenians, and Aristotle studied and later taught there. It is thus helpful to look at the city in which they lived, before we discuss their work. The barbarian hordes of Darius had been beaten by the Athenians alone, on the plains of Marathon in 490 B.C. Ten years later, the combined efforts of the Greeks broke the land and sea forces of Xerxes. At Thermopylae, a Spartan rearguard had taken fearful toll of the Persians, and later, at Salamis, the Greek ships under Athenian leadership dealt a death blow to the enemy navy. The following year, at Plataea, the Persians suffered final defeat.

But Athens lay waste; her people had been evacuated, and the Persians had burnt the city and the temples. A great reconstruction now began. Athens had borne the brunt of the fighting. She had been a leader during the War. Now that the danger was past, she became a leader in peace time as well. The mainland Greeks had now been saved, the next step was to free the islands of the Aegean. In this the army of the Spartans was of little use, so it fell to the lot of naval Athens to keep the Great King at bay. Thus, Athens came to hold sway in the Aegean. What began as the Delian League, with its centre on the island of Delos, ended as the Athenian Empire, with the treasury taken from Delos to Athens.

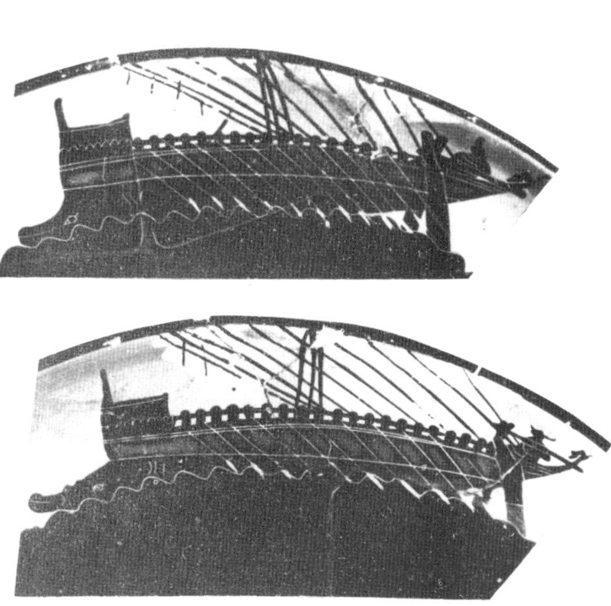

Athens had suffered in the common cause; now it was only right, so she felt, that her temples should be built again from the common funds; and so rose the new Acropolis, the 'city on the peak', with the Parthenon and other buildings, whose ruins still remain today. Athens became the most magnificent city in Greece, and the meeting place of artists and thinkers, as well as a centre of shipping and trade. Pheidias the sculptor made statues for the new temples, especially the colossal image of the goddess Athena which, dominating the Acropolis, overlooked the entrance hall and steps. Herodotus the historian, from Halicarnassus in Ionia, came to live in Athens and wrote his history of the Persian wars. Greek tragedy came into its own with Aeschylus who had fought at Salamis. The 'Persae', in which he tells of Xerxes' defeat, for once deals with a theme not derived from Homer. The tragedians Sophocles and Euripides lived to see the decline of Athens, and so did the comic poet Aristophanes, whose biting satire spared no one. Thucydides, who was to become thc recorder of the great war of Sparta and Athens, was the first scientific historian. Both politically and culturally Athens reached her peak in these decades between the Persian and the Peloponnesian wars. The man whose name this period bears is Pericles.

Pericles, leader of Athens in deed, though not in title

Pericles was an aristocrat by birth. His mother was a niece of Cleisthenes the reformer, who had begun the work of making the Athenian constitution more democratic. Anaxogaras had been one of Pericles' teachers, and from the philosopher the young nobleman had learnt a mechanical theory of the universe. Pericles grew into a man free from the popular superstitions of the time, reserved and moderate in character, and on the whole somewhat disdainful of the people. Yet it was under him that Athenian democracy attained full maturity. Already the council of the Areopagus, a kind of upper house, had lost much of its power. Except for the trial of homicide, all its functions were taken over by the council of five hundred, the Assembly and the law courts. All members of these became paid state officials elected by simple lot. A new system of social services somewhat changed the old and traditional virtues.

But Pericles was of the stuff that makes a leader. After the ostracism of Thucydides in 443 B.C., Pericles was chosen as one of the generals year after year. As he was well liked by the people, a powerful speaker and able statesman who far outshone his colleagues, he ruled almost like an autocrat. Thucydides was later to write of Periclean Athens that she had been in word a democracy, but in deed the rule of the first citizen. Only during the years just before the Peloponnesian war did the democratic party begin to ask for more power. By then, the bad effects of the restriction of citizenship to Athenians born of Athenian parents, dating back to 441 B.C., and the strain on finance due to lavish building programmes, began to be felt. The war, brought about by Spartan jealousy of Athenian imperialism, lasted from 431 to 404 B.C. and ended in total defeat for Athens. Pericles himself died in the early part of it in 429, as the result of the plague that had hit the city the year before. But as a cultural centre Athens outlived her political downfall. To our own day she has remained a symbol of all that is great and beautiful in the endeavours of man.

The Erechtheion, seen from the Parthenon; built on the Acropolis in the time of Pericles

Aeschylus

Sophocles

Euripides

We come now to Socrates the Athenian. He is perhaps the one philosopher whose name at least is known to all. About his life we do not know a great deal. He was born about 470 B.C. He was a citizen of Athens, had little money, nor tried very hard to get more. Indeed, his favourite pastime was discussion with friends and others, and teaching philosophy to young Athenians. But, unlike the Sophists, he took no money for it. In 'The Clouds' the comedian Aristophanes makes fun of him, so he must have been a well known sight around town. In 399 B.C. he was condemned for un-Athenian activities and executed by poisoning.

Socrates

For the rest, we have to rely on the writings of two of his pupils, Xenophon the general, and Plato the philosopher. Of these Plato is the more important. In several of his dialogues he shows us Socrates as he lived and talked. We learn from the 'Symposium' that Socrates was apt to go into fits of absent-mindedness. He would suddenly stop somewhere and remain lost in thought, sometimes for hours on end. At the same time he was physically tough. From his days of military service it was known that he stood up to heat and cold better, and could do without food or drink longer, than anyone else. We also know that he was courageous in battle. At great risk to himself he once saved the life of his friend Alcibiades, who, wounded, had stumbled to the ground. In war and peace alike, Socrates was a man unafraid, and so he remained in the hour of death. He was an ugly man to look at and took little care in dress. His tunic was shabby and crushed, and he was always barefoot. In all he did he was moderate and had amazing control over his body. Though he rarely took wine, when the occasion arose he could drink all his companions under the table without getting tipsy.

In Socrates we find a forerunner of both the Stoic and the Cynic schools of later Greek philosophy. With the Cynics he shares his lack of concern about worldly goods, with the Stoics his interest in virtue as the greatest good. Except in his younger days, Socrates was not much given to scientific speculation. His foremost interest was with the Good. In the early dialogues of Plato, where Socrates stands out most clearly, we find him looking for the definition of ethical terms. In the 'Charmides', the question is what is moderation; in the 'Lysis', what is friendship; in the 'Laches', what is courage. We are not given final answers to those questions, but we are shown that it is important to ask them.

This brings out the main line of thought in Socrates himself. Though he always says he knows nothing, he does not think knowledge lies beyond our reach. What matters is precisely that we should try to seek knowledge. For he holds that what makes a man sin is lack of knowledge. If only he knew, he would not sin. The one overriding cause of evil is therefore ignorance. Hence, to reach the Good we must have knowledge, and so the Good is knowledge. The link between Good and knowledge is a mark of Greek thought throughout. Christian ethics is quite opposed to this. There, the important thing is a pure heart, and that is likely to be found more readily among the ignorant.

Socrates, then, tried to clarify these ethical problems by discussion. This way of finding out things by question and answer is called dialectic, and Socrates was a master of it, though he was not the first to use it. It is stated in Plato's dialogue 'Pamenides' that Socrates as a young man met Zeno and Parmenides and was given a dialectic thrashing of the kind he later dealt out to others. The dialogues of Plato show Socrates as a man with a very lively sense of humour and a biting wit. He was famous and feared for his irony. The literal meaning of 'irony', which is a Greek word, is something like that of the English word 'understatement'. Thus when Socrates says he knows only that he knows nothing he is being ironical, though, as always, there is a serious point lurking beneath the top layer of fun. Socrates was no doubt familiar with the achievements of all the thinkers, writers and artists of Greece. But what we know is little, and as nothing when set against the infinite vastness of the unknown. Once we see this, we can truly say we know nothing.

Drinking cup; 'symposium' is Greek for 'drinking party'

The best picture of Socrates in action is the 'Apology', which shows us his trial. It is his speech in defence of himself, or rather what Plato later remembered him as saying, not a word for word report, but something of the kind that Socrates could and would have said. Such 'reporting' was not unusual, Thucydides the historian does it quite openly. The Apology is thus a piece of historical writing.

Socrates was accused of non-conformism with state religion, and of corrupting the young by his teaching. This was only a sham indictment. What the government had against him was his link with the aristocratic party, to which most of his friends and pupils belonged. But since there had been an amnesty the court could not press this charge. The formal accusers were Anytus, a democratic politician, Meletus, a tragic poet, and Lycon, a teacher of rhetoric.

From the outset Socrates gives free rein to his irony. His prosecutors, so he says, are guilty of eloquence and make nicely ornamented speeches. He himself had reached seventy years of age, had never appeared in court before, and asks the judges to bear with his unlegal way of talking. Socrates now mentions a class of accusers older and more dangerous, because more elusive. They are those

Delphic Apollo; his oracle told Socrates none was wiser than he

Homer, Hesiod, Orpheus, Musaeus; once dead, Socrates may meet them

who have been going round speaking of Socrates as 'a wise man, who speculated about the heavens above and searched into the earth beneath, and made the worse appear the better cause'. He replies that he is not a scientist, nor does he teach for money like the Sophists, nor does he know what they know.

Why, then, do people call him wise? The reason is that the Delphic Oracle once said that none was wiser than Socrates. He had tried to show the oracle wrong. Thus, he sought out men held to be wise and questioned them. He asked politicians, poets, craftsmen, and found that none could give an account of what they were doing, none were wise. In showing up their ignorance he made many enemies. In the end he understood what the oracle meant: God alone is wise, man's wisdom is paltry, he is wisest among men who sees, like Socrates, that his wisdom is worth nothing. So he spent his time debunking pretence to wisdom. This has left him a poor man, but he must live up to the oracle.

Socrates

Questioning his prosecutor Meletus, he forces him to admit that everyone in the state improves the young except Socrates himself. But it is better to live among good men rather than bad. He thus would not corrupt the Athenians wittingly, and if he did it unwittingly, Meletus should put him right, not prosecute him. The charge says that Socrates had set up new gods of his own, but Meletus slates him as an atheist, a clear contradiction.

Socrates now tells the court that his duty is to fulfil the God's order to search into himself and other men, even at the risk of falling foul of the state. This attitude of Socrates reminds us that the problem of divided loyalties is one of the main themes of Greek tragedy. He goes on to speak of himself as a gadfly to the state and mentions an inner voice which always guides him. It forbids, but never commands him to do something. It is this voice which stopped him from going into politics, where no one can stay honest for long. The prosecution have produced none of his former pupils present in the court. He would not plead for mercy by bringing his weeping children, he must convince the judges, not beg favours.

When the verdict was guilty, Socrates made a biting and sarcastic speech, and offered to pay a fine of 30 minae. This was bound to be rejected, and the death penalty was confirmed. In a final speech, Socrates warns those who had condemned him that they in turn will be heavily punished for this misdeed. Then, turning to his friends, he tells them what has happened was not evil. Death should not be feared. Either it is a dreamless sleep, or it is life in another world where he can talk undisturbed with Orpheus, Musaeus, Hesiod and Homer, and there they certainly do not kill a man for asking questions.

Socrates spent one month in prison before drinking the hemlock. Until the return of the stateship, delayed by storms on its yearly religious trip to Delos, no one could be executed. He refused to escape, and the 'Phaedo' shows him spending his last hours with friends and disciples discussing immortality.

Plato

If you look through the pages of this volume you will find that no single philosopher has been given as much space as Plato, or Aristotle. That this should be so results from their unique position in the history of philosophy. First, they come as the heirs and systematisers of the presocratic schools, developing what had been handed down to them, and making explicit much that had not fully broken through in the earlier thinkers. Next, they have exercised throughout the ages a tremendous influence on the imagination of men. Wherever speculative reasoning has flourished in the West, the shadows of Plato and Aristotle were hovering in the background. Finally, their contribution to philosophy is more substantial than that of probably any thinkers before or since. There is hardly a philosophic problem on which they did not say something of value, and anyone who nowadays sets out to be original, while ignoring Athenian philosophy, does so at his own peril.

The life of Plato spans the period from the decline of Athens to the rise of Macedonia. He was born in 428 B.C., one year after the death of Pericles, and thus grew up during the Peloponnesian war. He lived to over eighty and died in 348 B.C. His family background was aristocratic, and so was his upbringing. Ariston, his father, traced his own ancestry back to the Athenian royalty of old, whereas Perictione, the mother of Plato, came from a family which had long been active in politics. Ariston died when Plato was still a boy, and Perictione subsequently married her uncle Pyrilampes, a friend and partisan of Pericles. Plato seems to have spent his formative years in the home of his stepfather. With such a background it is small wonder that he held strong views on the political duties of a citize These he not only put forward, notably in the Republic, but practised himself. In his early years it seems that he showed promise as a poet, and it was more or less understood that he should take up a political career. This ambition came to a sudden end when Socrates was condemned to death. This fearful piece of political intrigue and spitefulness left an indelible impression upon the young man's mind. No one could long maintain his independence and integrity within the framework of party politics. It is from this time forward that Plato finally turned to a life devoted to philosophy.

Socrates had been an old friend of the family, and Plato had known him since childhood. After the execution, Plato together with some other followers of Socrates took refuge in Megara, where they remained until the scandal had died down. After this, Plato appears to have travelled for some years. Sicily, Southern Italy and possibly even Egypt were on his itinerary, but we know very little about this period. At all events we find him again in Athens in 387 B.C., when he laid the foundations of a school. This place of learning was established in a grove a little distance north west of the town. The piece of land was linked with the name of the legendary hero Academus, and the institution was therefore called Academy. Its organisation was modelled on the Pythagorean schools of Southern Italy with whom Plato had been in contact during his travels. The Academy is the ancestor of the universities as they developed from the Middle Ages onward. As a school, it survived for over 900 years, which is longer than any such institution before or since. In A.D. 529

it was finally closed down by the Emperor Justinian, whose Christian principles were offended by this survival of classical traditions.

The Academic studies ran roughly parallel to the traditional subjects of the Pythagorean schools. Arithmetic, geometry both two and three dimensional, astronomy, and sound, or harmonics, constituted the basic substance of the curriculum. As might be expected with the strong Pythagorean links, great emphasis was placed on mathematics. It is said that the entrance to the school carried an inscription bidding any who might dislike such studies refrain from entering. Ten years were spent on training in these disciplines.

The aim of this course of instruction was to turn the thoughts of men from the shifting changes of the experienced world to the immutable framework lying behind it, from becoming to being, to use the words of Plato.

None of these disciplines are, however, autonomous. In the end they are all responsible to the canons of dialectic, and it is a study of these which is the real distinguishing feature of education.

In a very real sense this remains the object of genuine education even today. It is not the function of a university to cram the heads of students with as many facts as can be squeezed in. Its proper task is to lead them into habits of critical examination and an understanding of canons and criteria which bear on all subject matters.

The grove of Academus, site of Plato's school, a mile from town

How the Academy was organised in detail we are unlikely ever to know. But from literary hints we can infer that it must have resembled modern institutes of higher learning in many ways. It was provided with scientific equipment and a library, and conducted lectures and seminars.

With the provision of education in such a school, the Sophist movement declined rapidly. No doubt those who attended its courses must have contributed something to its upkeep. But then the question of money is not really the vital point, quite apart from the fact that Plato, being well-to-do, could afford to ignore such matters. The important thing is the Academic aim, which was to train men's minds to think for themselves in the light of reason. No immediate practical goal was envisaged, in contrast with the Sophists who sought nothing beyond proficiency in practical affairs.

Aristotle, student at the Academy

One of the earliest students at the Academy was also the most famous. As a young man, Aristotle went to Athens to attend the school and remained there almost twenty years, until Plato's death. Aristotle tells us that his master lectured without prepared notes. From other sources we learn that in seminars or discussion groups, problems would be put forward for the students to solve. The dialogues were literary philosophic essays aimed not at his students so much as at a wider educated public. Plato never wrote a text book and always refused to set down his philosophy as a system. He seems to have felt that the world at large is too complex to be strained into a preconceived literary mould.

The Academy had been running for twenty years when Plato once more went abroad. In 367 B.C. Dionysius I, the ruler of Syracuse, died. His son and heir, Dionysius II, succeeded him, a somewhat raw and callow youth of thirty who was ill equipped for the task of directing the fortunes of so important a polity as Syracuse. The real power lay in the hands of Dion, brother-in-law of the young Dionysius, and an ardent friend and admirer of Plato. It was he who invited Plato to come to Syracuse in order to put Dionysius through his paces and make a well informed man of him. The odds against success in such an enterprise are slender at the best of times, but Plato agreed to try, partly no doubt because of friendship for Dion, but also because this was a challenge to the reputation of the Academy. Here indeed was Plato's chance of putting his theory of the education of rulers to the test. Whether a scientific education as such makes a statesman a clearer thinker in political affairs is of course questionable, but Plato evidently thought it did. A strong ruler in Sicily was essential if the Western Greeks were to hold their own against the growing power of Carthage, and if some training in mathematics might turn Dionysius into such a man much would be gained, while, if the treatment failed, nothing, at any rate, would be lost. Some headway was made at first, but not for long. Dionysius had not the mental vigour to withstand prolonged educational treatment, besides which he was a thoroughly unpleasant schemer in his own right. Envious of his brother-in-law's influence in Syracuse and friendship with Plato, he forced him into exile. Plato could now do nothing further by staying on, and therefore returned to Athens and the Academy. He tried, as best he could, to mend matters from a distance, but without avail. In 361 B.C., he went once more to Syracuse in a final attempt to put things right. Nearly a year was spent on trying to work out some practical measures to unite the Sicilian Greeks in the face of the Carthaginian peril. In the end the ill will of the conservative faction proved to be an insuperable obstacle. Not without first incurring some danger to his own life, Plato finally managed to leave for Athens, in 360 B.C. Dion, in the sequel, recovered his position by force, but, in spite of Plato's warnings, showed himself to be an impolitic ruler, and got himself murdered in due course. Still Plato urged the followers of Dion to pursue the old policy, but his advice went unheeded. The final fate of Sicily was conquest from abroad, as Plato had foreseen.

Stadium entrance; at Syracuse, scene of Plato's political work

On his return in 360, he went back to his teaching and writing at the Academy, remaining active as an author to the last. Of all the philosophers of antiquity Plato is the only one whose works have come down to us nearly complete. The dialogues, as has been mentioned, are not to be taken as formal and technical treatises on philosophical topics. Plato was much too aware of the difficulties besetting this kind of enquiry ever to aspire at laying down a system to end all systems, as so many philosophers have done since. Furthermore, he is unique amongst philosophers in being not only a great thinker but a great writer as well. The works of Plato mark him as one of the outstanding figures in world literature. This distinction has unfortunately remained exceptional in philosophy. There are great masses of philosophic writing which are turgid, dull and bombastic. Indeed, there is, in some places, what almost amounts to a tradition that philosphic works must be obscure and clumsy in style in order to be profound. This is a pity, because it frightens off the interested layman. It must not be imagined, of course, that the educated Athenian of Plato's day could read the dialogues and appreciate their philosophic importance at first blush. It would be just as reasonable to expect a layman innocent of mathematics to pick up a book on differential geometry and be a better man for it. At all events, however, you can read Plato, which is more than can be said of most philosophers.

Apart from the dialogues, there survive some letters of Plato, mainly to his friends in Syracuse. These are valuable as historical documents but are otherwise of no special philosophic interest.

Something must here be said of the role of Socrates in the dialogues. Socrates himself never wrote anything, so that his philosophy has survived mainly through what we learn from Plato. At the same time, Plato in his later work developed theories of his own. One must therefore distinguish in the dialogues what is Plato and what is Socrates. This is a task of some delicacy but nevertheless not impossible. For one thing, in what we can judge on independent grounds to be later dialogues, Plato criticises some of the earlier theories which are set forth by Socrates. It used to be thought that the Socrates of the dialogues was merely a mouthpiece of Plato, who by means of this literary device put forward whatever views happened to exercise his mind at the time. This appraisal, however, does violence to the facts and no longer prevails.

Plato

The influence of Plato on philosophy is probably greater than that of any other man. The heir of Socrates and the presocratics, the founder of the Academy and Aristotle's teacher, Plato stands at the centre of philosophic thought. It is this, no doubt, that leads the French logician E. Goblot to write that Plato's is not a metaphysic, but the one and only metaphysics. If we keep in mind the distinction between Socrates and Plato, then it might be more accurate to say that it is the Platonic Socrates whose doctrines have mainly influenced philosophy. The revival of Plato in his own right is a much more recent thing. In the scientific field it dates back to the early seventeenth century, whereas in philosophy proper it belongs to our own times.

In studying Plato, it is important to keep in mind the central role of mathematics. This is one of the features which distinguishes Plato from Socrates, whose interests had early grown away from science and mathematics. Subsequent ages, that were not subtle enough to grasp the theories of Plato, turned his serious studies into numerical mystery-mongering, an aberration which is unfortunately not as uncommon as one might wish. Mathematics, of course, remains a field of special interest to the logician. We must now proceed to examine some of the problems which are treated in the dialogues. The literary merit of the works cannot so easily be conveyed and is in any case not our main concern. But even in translation sufficient colour survives to show that philosophy need not be unreadable to be significant.

When Plato is mentioned one thinks at once of the theory of ideas. It is set out by Socrates in several dialogues. Whether it is due to Socrates rather than Plato has long been controversial. In the 'Parmenides', which, though a later dialogue, describes a scene when Socrates was young and Plato not yet born, we see Socrates trying to uphold the theory of ideas against Zeno and Parmenides. In other places we find Socrates talking to people who, it is taken for granted, are familiar with the theory. Its origins are Pythagorean. Let us look at the account of it in the 'Republic'.

Without philosophy, we are like shadows; the form of the Good shows the world in full colour

Let us begin with the question: what is a philosopher? Literally, the word means a lover of wisdom. But not everyone who is curious to know is a philosopher. The definition must be narrowed down: a philosopher is one who loves the vision of truth. An art collector loves beautiful things, but that does not make him a philosopher. The philosopher loves beauty in itself. The lover of beautiful things is dreaming, the lover of beauty itself is awake. Where the art lover has only opinion, the lover of beauty itself has knowledge. Now knowledge must have an object, it must be of something that is, or else it is nothing, as Parmenides would have said. Knowledge is fixed and certain, it is truth free from error. Opinion, on the other hand, can be mistaken. But since opinion is neither knowledge of what is, nor yet nothing, it must be of what both is and is not, as Heraclitus would put it.

Thus, Socrates thinks that all particular things, which we grasp through our senses, have opposite features. A particular beautiful statue also has some ugly aspects. A particular thing which is large from some point of view is also small from another. All these are objects of opinion. But beauty as such and largeness as such do not come to us through our senses, they are unchanging and eternal, they are objects of knowledge. By taking Parmenides and Heraclitus together, Socrates works out his theory of 'ideas' or 'forms', something new which is not in either of the two earlier thinkers. The Greek word 'idea' means 'picture' or 'pattern'.

This theory has a logical side and a metaphysical side. On the logical side we have the distinction between particular objects of some kind and the general words we call them by. Thus the general word 'horse' refers not to this horse or that horse, but to any horse. Its meaning is independent of particular horses and what happens to them, it is not in space and time, but eternal. On the metaphysical side, it means there is somewhere or other an 'ideal' horse, the horse as such, unique and unchanging, and this is what the general word 'horse' refers to. Particular horses are what they are in so far as they fall under, or have a part in, the 'ideal' horse. The idea is perfect and real, the particular is deficient and only apparent.

To help us understand the theory of ideas, Socrates outlines the famous simile of the cave. Those who are without philosophy are like prisoners in a cave. They are in chains and cannot turn round. Behind them is a fire, and before them the empty cave shut off at the back by a blank wall. On this, as on a screen, they see their own shadows, and that of things between them and the fire. Because they can see nothing else, they think the shadows are the real things. In the end, one man throws off his fetters and gropes his way towards the mouth of the cave. There, for the first time, he sees the light of the sun, shining on the full-blooded things of the real world. He goes back into the cave to tell his fellow creatures about his findings, and tries to show them that theirs is no more than a dim reflection of reality, a world of mere shadows. But, having seen the light of the sun, his sight has become dazzled by its brilliance, and he finds it harder now to make out the shadows. He tries to show them the way to the light, but to them he seems more stupid than before, and therefore it is no easy task to convince them. If we are strangers to philosophy, then we are like the prisoners. We see only shadows, appearances of things. But when we are philosophers, we see things outside, in the sunlight of reason and truth, and this is reality. This light, which gives us truth, and the power of knowing, stands for the idea of the Good.

The theory as here set forth is, in the main, inspired by Pythagorean notions, as has been stated earlier. That it was not Plato's own view, at any rate in his later and maturer period, seems to be fairly well attested by the fact that in the later dialogues the theory of ideas is first demolished, and then disappears altogether. The task of refuting it is one of the central themes of the 'Parmenides'. The meeting of Parmenides and Zeno with Socrates is not in the least implausible and may be taken as historical, though, of course, what was said on the occasion is less likely to be reported in the dialogue. Still, the speakers all of them run true to character, and they express views that are in line with what we know about them from independent sources. Parmenides, it will be remembered, had in his younger days been influenced by the Pythagoreans, and later broke his connections with their teaching. The theory of ideas is therefore not new to him, and he finds ready criticisms for the formulations given it by the young Socrates.

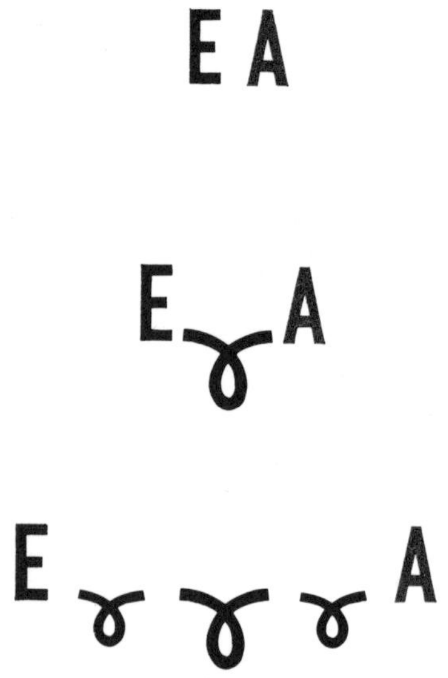

E A

E A

E A

The form (E) cannot be linked to the particular (A); each attempt produces two more gaps

To begin with, Parmenides points out that there is no good reason why Socrates should allow forms for mathematical objects and for notions like the good and the beautiful, but deny them to the elements and meaner things. This leads on to a very much more serious matter. The central difficulty in the Socratic theory of forms is the connection between the forms and the particulars. For the form is one and the particulars are many. Socrates' account of the link between them uses the notion of participation, but it is some puzzle to see how the particulars could participate in the forms. Clearly the whole form cannot be present in each particular, since then it would not be one form. The alternative is that each particular contains a part of the form, but then the form explains nothing.

But there is worse to come. In order to explain the connection between the form and the particulars that come under it, Socrates has to introduce participation, and this itself, being exemplified in many cases, is a form. But then we must ask at once how this form is connected on the one side to the original form and on the other to the particular. Two more forms are, it seems, required, and we are led into a vicious infinite regress. Every time we try to close a gap by introducing a form, two further gaps appear. Bridging the gap is thus a Herculean task without Hercules' escape. This is the famous Third Man argument, so called after the special case of it where the form in question is that of man. Socrates tries to evade the difficulty by suggesting that the forms are patterns and that particulars resemble them. But this falls victim to the Third Man argument too. Thus, Socrates can give no account of how the forms are linked with their particulars. But this can be shown directly too. For it has been assumed that forms are not sensible, but intelligible. Within their own realm they can only be linked amongst themselves, and likewise with particulars. The forms thus seem to be unknowable. If the forms are unknowable, then, of course, they are superfluous and once again incapable of explaining anything. We may put the matter differently thus: if the forms are by themselves, unrelated to our world, they are vacuous; if on the other hand they are so related, then they cannot belong to a world of their own, and the metaphysical doctrine of forms is untenable.

How Plato himself tackles the problem of universals we shall see later. Here we need merely note that the Socratic doctrine does not stand close examination. In the 'Parmenides' this matter is not pursued any further. Parmenides turns to the different problem of showing that all is not well even within the realm of Socrates' forms. The elaborate dialectic in the style of Zeno shows the unsoundness of Socrates' original contention that the forms are all separate from each other, and this prepares the ground for Plato's solution.

There is, however, another difficulty which harks back to the Pythagorean origin of the theory of ideas. We saw earlier how that side of the theory springs from an account of the objects of argument in mathematics. When the mathematician establishes a theorem about triangles he is apparently not concerned with any figure that one might actually draw on paper. For any such figure has imperfections which fall outside mathematical considerations. However hard one might try to draw an accurately straight line, it will never be perfectly accurate. From this it is concluded that the perfectly straight line belongs to a different world, and hence we have the view that forms belong to an order of existence different from that of sensible objects.

Inequality is a form, yet here it is seen in the world of sense

At first glance this view is not without a certain plausibility. It seems not unreasonable, for instance, to hold that two sensible objects are nearly but not quite equal, that they might tend towards equality but never quite achieve it. At any rate it may be difficult, if not impossible, ever to decide that they were perfectly equal. On the other hand, let us take two unequal things. Here, we often see at once that they are unequal, so that the form of inequality seems to reveal itself quite plainly in the sensible world. Instead of formulating this in the terminology of forms, let us turn to how we ordinarily put these matters. We say altogether naturally of two things that they are almost equal but not quite. But no good sense attaches to saying of two things that they are nearly, but not quite, unequal. This criticism directly shows up the theory of forms.

Why, it might be asked, if the theory of ideas had suffered such damaging criticism at the hands of the Eleatics, did Socrates continue to hold it unchanged? For the force of the attack must surely have been clear to him. It seems, however, more to the point to turn this question round. It is precisely because of the difficulties that Socrates, in his intellectual interests, retreated to questions of ethics and aesthetics. The goodness of man is in any case not seen quite in the same sense as, for example, the colour of his hair. But even in this field Socrates eventually became somewhat dissatisfied with the theory of participation, though he never put forward anything else. There is nevertheless a hint that the solution must be sought not in things, but in what we can say about them, in arguments. It is in this direction that Plato's own efforts on the problem of universals continue.

The matter is mentioned in passing by Socrates in the 'Phaedo', though he does not go on to develop this aspect of the problem. Plato takes it up again in the 'Theaetetus' and the 'Sophist'.

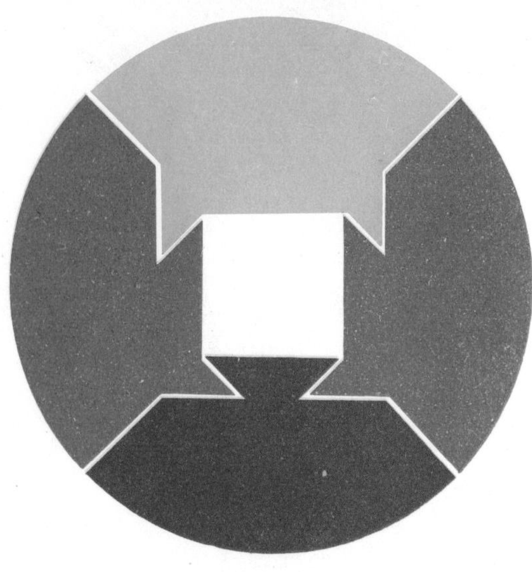

The ideal state: each part plays its proper role

The 'Republic' is probably the most famous of Plato's dialogues. It contains the forerunners of many a line of enquiry taken up by later thinkers down to our own times. The building up of an ideal state discussed in it has given the dialogue its name. It is this polity which we shall now describe. As we saw, the Greeks thought of the state as a city. This is shown by the Greek word 'polity' which means roughly 'township', in the sense in which this includes the whole social fabric that goes with a well run town. This word is the Greek title of the dialogue. Our word 'political' comes from it.

For Plato, the citizens in the ideal state are divided into three classes: the guardians, the soldiers and the common people. The guardians are a small élite which alone wields political power. When the state is first set up, the lawmaker appoints the guardians, and thereafter they will be succeeded by their own kin. Outstanding children from the lower classes may, however, be raised into the ruling class, while worthless offspring of their own may be sent down into the soldiery or the common herd. The guardians' task is to see that the lawgiver's will is done. To make sure they will do this, Plato has a whole set of plans on how they must be brought up and live. They will be educated both in mind and body. For the mind, there is 'music', that is, any art watched over by the muses; for the body, 'gymnastics', sports for which no teams are needed. Training in 'music', or culture, is to produce gentlemen. It is from Plato that the notion of a gentleman, as understood in England, is derived. The young must be taught to behave with dignity, grace and courage. To attain this there is strict censorship of books. The poets must be banned: Homer and Hesiod show the gods carrying on like quarrelsome intemperate men, which is bad for respect. God should be shown as the creator not of the whole world, but only of what is not evil in it. Again, there are passages likely to inspire fear of death, or admiration for riotous behaviour, or suspicion that the wicked may thrive while the good suffer. All this must be banned. Music, in the narrow sense of today, is also censored: only those modes and rhythms are allowed that further courage and temperance. They must live on plain fare, they will then need no doctors. When they are young they must be sheltered from what is nasty, but at a certain age they are to meet both terrors and temptations. Only if they resist them both are they fit to be guardians.

The social and economic life of the guardians shall be a rigid communism. They have small houses and own barely what they need for their personal existence. They eat together in groups, feeding on simple fare. There is complete equality of the sexes; all women are the common wives of all men. To maintain their numbers, the rulers will bring together, at certain festivals, a suitable group of men and women, chosen allegedly by lot, but actually with a view to producing sound offspring. Children are taken away at birth and brought up together in such a way that no one knows who his physical parents or children are. Those born from unsanctioned unions are illegitimate, those that are deformed or of inferior stock are done away with. Thus will private sentiments grow weak and public spirit strong. The best are chosen for training in philosophy. Those who master it are at last fit to rule.

The government has the right to lie if the public interest demands it. In particular, it will inculcate the 'royal lie' which presents this brave new world as god-given. In two generations this would come to be believed without protest, at any rate by the herd.

We finally come to the definition of justice which was the pretext for the whole discussion, since Plato introduced his ideal city because he felt it might be easier to discuss justice on a large scale first. Justice reigns when everyone minds his own business. Each is to do the work of his station without meddling in other men's affairs. In this way the body politic functions quietly and efficiently. Justice, in this Greek sense, is linked with the notion of harmony, the smooth working of the whole through the proper function of each part.

The ideal state's three classes: Guardians, soldiers, workers

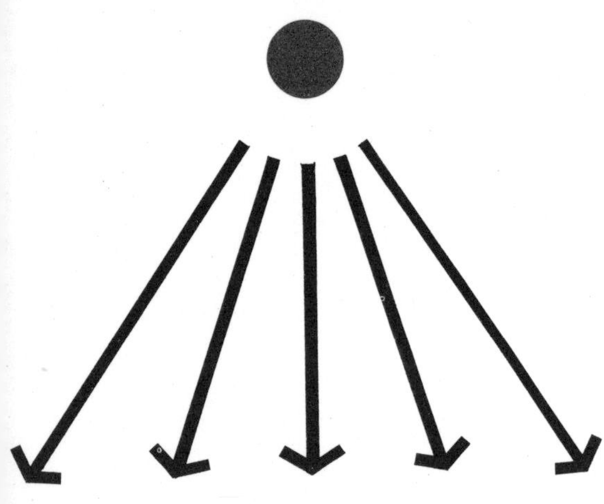

Monarchy, the rule of one; under rule of law, to be preferred

Here, indeed, we have a fearful picture of a state machine in which men as individuals almost disappear. The utopia described in the 'Republic' is the first of a long line of similar phantasies right down to Aldous Huxley's Brave New World. No doubt, too, it has given inspiration to potentates who were in a position to effect major social changes with complete disregard for the suffering inflicted. This is bound to happen wherever the view prevails that men are made to fit into preconceived systems. That the state might be the servant of its citizens, rather than they its slaves, would even now be regarded as heretical in some quarters. Just where the balance lies is a complicated issue which is not here at stake. In sum, however, the ideal state of the 'Republic' has led many who oppose its principles to bestow all kinds of lurid labels on Plato. We must therefore examine what precisely is the import of the political theory it propounds.

At the outset, it must be remembered that Plato's own later development in political matters took quite a different turn. This we shall examine a little later. The ideal state of the 'Republic' is Socratic more than Platonic and seems to be directly inspired by Pythagorean ideals. This brings us to the crux of the matter. The ideal state is really a scientist's view of the proper way to run the country. As a scientist's model, it may well tempt a social engineer to wreak vast changes in the fond belief that he was being scientific. If technologists had their way this is the sort of thing they would do. At the same time, this recognition takes a good deal of the sting from the conception of the ideal state. For, after all, it is simply a model, for discussion and clarification of certain issues. It is clearly with this intention that it is put forward by Socrates. This is obvious from what may appear some of the more extreme provisions in this paradise on earth. Besides, we must take into account a certain measure of irony. No one, for instance, really wants to ban the poets. Nor does anyone really contemplate introducing a thoroughgoing sexual communism. Some of the features of the ideal state are, of course, derived from observing Sparta as she actually was. Nevertheless, the model remains a model. It is not suggested as a practical plan for setting up an actual city. When Plato later became involved in the politics of Syracuse he was not trying to establish an ideal state on this pattern. As we saw, his aim was the more modest and practical one of making a spoilt prince into a man fit to conduct the affairs of an important city which was already a going concern. That Plato was unsuccessful is another matter and merely shows that education is not so universal a remedy as is often thought.

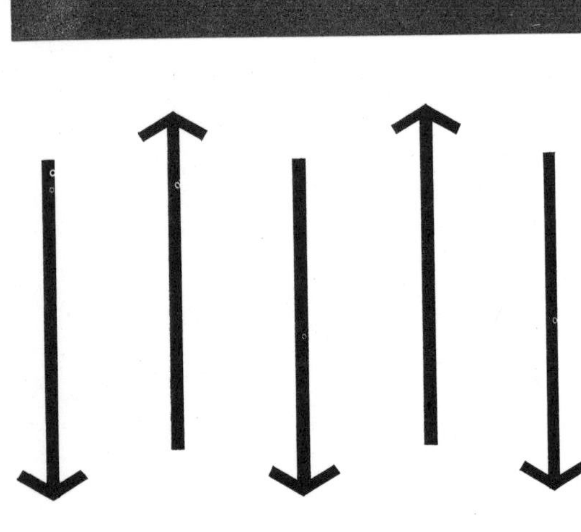

Democracy, the rule of many; in the absence of law, the least evil

In the later dialogues Plato twice returns to a discussion of political questions. In the 'Statesman' we find an account of the various political organisations that might exist in a city. The different possibilities depend on the number of rulers and on the manner of their rule. We may have a monarchy, or an oligarchy, or a democracy, and each of these may function either according to legal principles, or else without them, giving in all six different combinations. If there is no rule of law, power in the hands of the many is considered to be productive of the least evil, since there will be no unity of purpose. On the other hand, if there is rule of law, democracy is the worst constitution, because now a common purpose is required if anything is to be achieved. Here, then, a monarch is to be preferred.

There remains the possibility of a mixed constitution, taking some of the elements of the six simple ones. In his last work, the 'Laws', Plato finally decides that in this world of ours, in which, it seems, philosopher kings are not to be found, the best we can do is to combine, under the rule of law, the rule of One with the rule of Many. The 'Laws' give very detailed instructions on how this kind of system is to be organised, and how office bearers are to be elected. On matters of education, too, a great deal of detail is given to the timing and content of what we now call secondary education. In hellenistic times, grammar schools were a firmly established stage in the education of the young. The basis for this kind of institution is laid down in the 'Laws'.

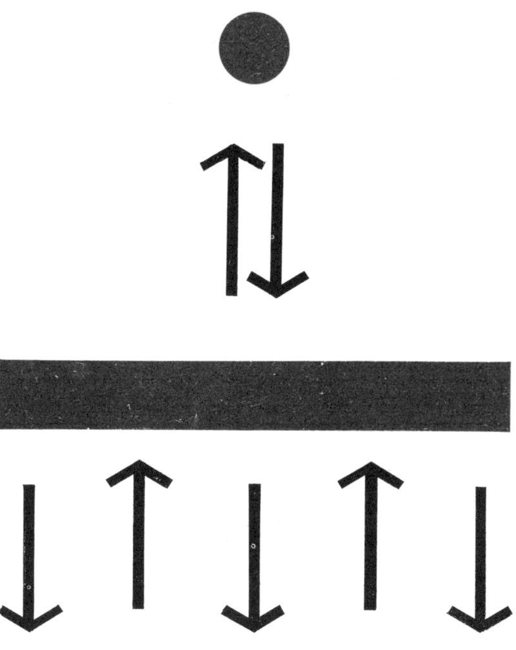

The best state combines monarchy with democracy

The political ideals of the 'Republic', as we have said, are not recommendations to be translated into fact. In this respect, the later thought of Plato is quite different. His political and educational suggestions are extremely practical and down to earth. Many of them were quietly adopted in later times, whereas their origins were soon forgotten. It is otherwise with the system of the 'Republic'. As a system it has generally been misunderstood, but its spectacular provisions have more than once found ardent supporters, much to the detriment of the human guineapigs that suffered the consequences. It is from this circumstance that Plato is occasionally described as a precursor of those who first failed to understand him and then rushed into misguided action on the strength of it.

For all that, it must be allowed that even Plato displays a certain narrowness in his political thinking. In this he simply shares the common Greek feeling of distance to the barbarian. Whether this was a selfconscious feeling of superiority, or merely a natural way of thinking that arose from the unquestioned supremacy of Greek culture, it would be difficult to decide. At any rate, the Plato of the 'Laws' still thinks that in founding a new city, which is the artificial pretext for the dialogue, one should select a site remote from the sea, to avoid the corrupting influence of trade and contact with foreigners. This, of course, leads to difficulties, since some measure of trading activity must go on. It is necessary for those who are not endowed with independent means to make a living somehow. Characteristically, when talking of the teachers in his proposed grammar schools, Plato says these will have to be paid and must therefore be foreigners.

This attitude of isolation in political matters is in the end responsible for the Greek world's inability to achieve a viable organisation of wider scope. The kind of political life that they envisaged was static, whereas the world around them was changing rapidly. This was the main weakness in the political thinking of the Greeks. In the end imperial Rome was to establish a world state. If the Romans lacked Greek originality, they were also free from the excessive individualism of the city state.

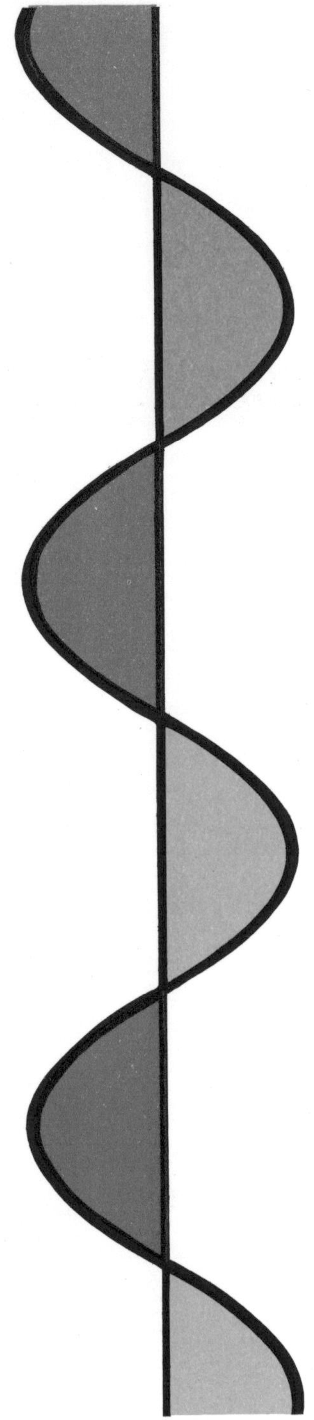

If the soul alternates between life within and without a body, learning is remembering. Hence the importance of dialectic

While, then, in matters of political theory, we can distinguish a Socratic theory from the later, Platonic, developments, there remain certain features of social theory in general which are common to both men. These are their views on the nature of education. Indeed, their approach merely makes explicit the outlook of Greek traditions of enquiry. We recall that science and philosophy were pursued in schools or societies where there was close collaboration between teachers and students. The important truth which seems to have been understood, implicitly at least, from the very beginning is that learning is not a process of dishing out information. Some of this, of course, there must be. But it is neither the sole function of the teacher, nor yet the most important one. This is indeed more evident today than it was at that time, for written records were rarer and harder to find than they are now. With us, it stands to reason that anyone who can read can collect information from a library. Less than ever before should a teacher need to pass on mere information. All the more is it to the credit of the philosophers of Greece that they should have grasped how genuine education must be pursued. The role of the teacher is one of guidance, of bringing the pupil to see for himself.

But learning to think independently is not an ability that comes all of a piece. It must be acquired by dint of personal effort and with the help of a mentor who can direct these efforts. This is the method of research under supervision as we know it today in our universities. It may be said that an academic institution fulfils its proper function to the extent that it fosters independent habits of mind and a spirit of enquiry free from the bias and prejudices of the moment. In so far as a university fails in this task it sinks to the level of indoctrination. At the same time such a failure has more serious consequences still. For where independent thinking dies out, whether from lack of courage or absence of discipline, there the evil weeds of propaganda and authoritarianism proliferate unchecked. The stifling of criticism is thus a much more serious thing than many people realise. Far from creating a living unity of purpose in a society, it imposes a kind of insipid, brittle uniformity upon the body politic. It is a pity that men in places of power and responsibility are not more often aware of this.

Education, then, is learning to think for oneself under the guidance of a teacher. This was, in fact, the practice from the beginning of the Ionian school, and it was recognised explicitly by the Pythagoreans. Indeed, it has been suggested by the French philosopher, G. Sorel, that philosophy originally meant not love of wisdom, but rather, 'the Friends' wisdom', the Friends in question being, of course, the Pythagorean brotherhood. Whether this be so or not, it does at least emphasise that science and philosophy grow as traditions and not as isolated, individual efforts. At the same time we see why it was that Socrates and Plato were so violently opposed to the Sophists. For these were simply purveyors of useful knowledge; their teaching, if such it may be called, was superficial. They may be able to instruct a man in some measure to make adequate responses in a variety of situations, but such piling up of information is ungrounded, unexamined. This is, of course, not to say that a genuine teacher may not run up against hopeless cases. Indeed, it is a distinctive feature of the educative process that there must be effort on both sides.

In Socrates, this educational theory is linked with another notion that goes back to the early Pythagoreans. In the 'Meno', the process of learning is called a remembering of things learnt in a previous existence and since forgotten. It is this that requires the joint effort described above. As for the notion of remembering, or anamnesis, it is based on the view that the soul goes through a series of alternate embodied and disembodied states, a view that has obvious links with the theory of transmigration as held by Pythagoras. The disembodied soul is as if asleep, and that is why, when it is in a waking and embodied state, what it has learned in a previous existence must be awakened too. Socrates here tries to show this by questioning one of Meno's slave boys. Beyond a knowledge of ordinary Greek, the boy is quite uneducated, as we might put it. Yet Socrates, merely by asking simple questions succeeds in eliciting from the youngster the construction of a square of twice the area of a given square. It must be admitted that the account is not altogether convincing as a proof of the theory of anamnesis. For it is Socrates who draws the figures in the sand and puts the boy on the track of his errors whenever he does go astray. On the other hand, here is a pretty accurate description of an educational situation. It is the interplay of student and teacher in the way set out in this example that produces genuine learning. It is in this sense that learning may be described as a dialectic process, where the word has its original Greek meaning.

It is not without interest to note that the educational theory here described has left its mark on ordinary language as spoken quite apart from learning or philosophy. For we commonly speak of someone's interest in a subject being awakened or aroused. This is an instance of a general phenomenon in the growth of idiom. Ordinary language is the resting-ground of bits and pieces of philosophic speculation from the past. It would be a good thing if this were occasionally remembered by those who tend to deify ordinary speech as though it were somehow beyond the canons of enquiry.

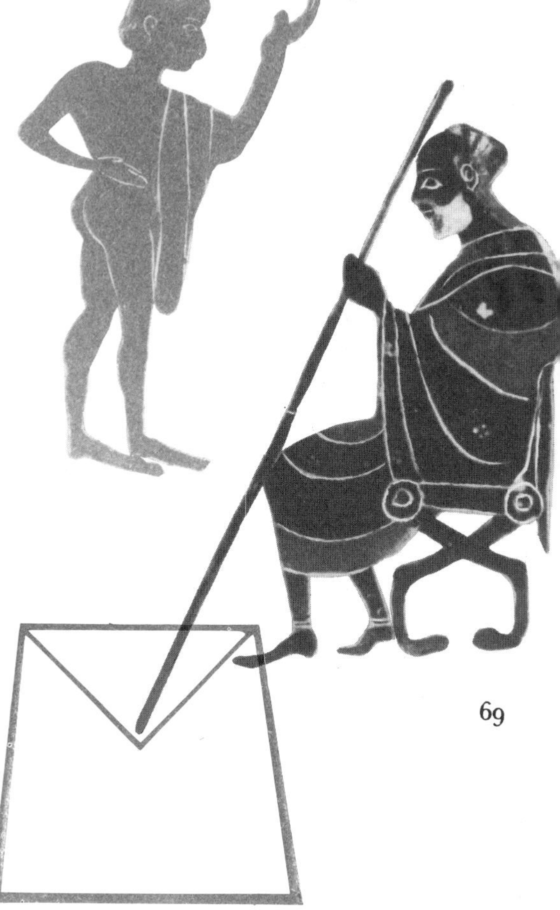

As for the theory of anamnesis, it was used by Socrates in an attempt to prove that the soul is immortal. This is described in the 'Phaedo', though it may be remarked that the case is not successful. At all events, it is worth remembering that the theory of transmigration was dropped by the later Pythagoreans. As we saw earlier, they adopted a view based on the notion of harmony, which in fact leads to the opposite result that the soul is mortal. On the educational aspect of the remembering process we may note that the practice of psychoanalytic therapy is based precisely on this notion of reawakening memories from the past. For all its more mysterious elements, psychoanalysis has a sounder grasp of the connection between education and therapy than did the associationist psychology based on Hume. In a wide sense, education, for Socrates, is therapy of the soul.

It is a process leading to knowledge and therefore to the Good. Ignorance might thus be regarded as something in the way of freedom, a free way of life being achieved by knowledge and insight. A similar view is found in Hegel's philosophy, where freedom is described as meaning that one understands the working of necessity.

There is another and perhaps more important problem which is treated in the 'Meno', though its discussion in the 'Euthyphro' is more interesting. This is the logical problem of definition. The question asked in the 'Euthyphro' is what is the holy, and the dialogue shows Euthyphro attempting to give a definition of it. That all his efforts turn out to be fruitless in the end is not important. In the course of the discussion Socrates makes him see what is required in the framing of a definition and thus clarifies the formal logical character of what is called definition by genus and difference.

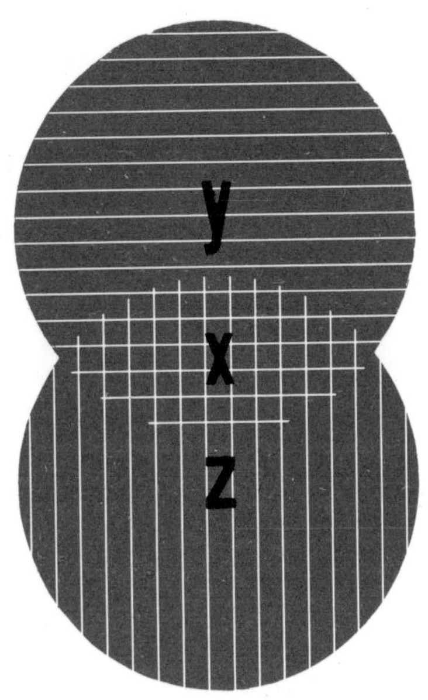

Definition by genus and difference: X is defined as YZ

To the modern reader this manner of treatment of matters of logic seems somewhat odd. One is used today to dry and stolid text book accounts, in the manner of Aristotle. The writing of philosophical dialogues, which was invented by Plato, found many imitators but has now gone out of fashion. This is perhaps a pity, for it cannot be said that the style of philosophic writing in our day is what it could be. Dialogue imposes on the author a greater measure of literary discipline than any other form of writing. In this respect the early dialogues of Plato are without equal. We must remember that we are dealing with pieces written shortly after the death of Socrates at a time when Plato's own thought was still in the making, and his powers as a dramatic artist at their best. As a result of it these dialogues are easier to read as literature than the later ones, but their philosophic content is harder to glean.

In several of the earlier dialogues we meet speakers who commit an elementary if common blunder when asked to give a definition of a term. What they do instead is to give instances of it. It is no good to reply to the question what is the Holy as Euthyphro does. The Holy, says Euthyphro, is to prosecute the offender against religion. But in effect this is not a definition at all. The statement merely says that prosecuting the offender is a holy act. There may be others. As to what holiness is, we are as much as ever in the dark. It is as though someone, when asked what is a philosopher, were to reply Socrates is a philosopher. The situation is delightfully ironic if we recall the setting of the conversation. Socrates, on his way to court in order to discover the nature of the charge laid against him, meets Euthyphro who also has legal business on hand. He is arraigning his own father for manslaughter of a slave who had died of neglect. Euthyphro is acting according to the proper rites and religious practices of the community, and evinces the usual cocksureness and self-certainty of those who give uncritical if virtuous assent to the formal customs of their tribe. Socrates therefore flatters him as an expert and feigns to be asking ethical advice from Euthyphro, who must surely be an authority in such matters.

Leaving the ethical question aside for the moment, we find that Socrates succeeds in explaining what is required logically. We are asking for the 'form' of the Holy, a statement of that which makes holy things what they are. Using more familiar language, we should now state the case in terms of necessary and sufficient conditions. Thus, if and only if, an animal is rational is it human, leaving out perhaps toddlers, who start on all fours with other quadrupeds. Schematically, we can show this by means of two intersecting circles. Man, the term to be defined, is the common part of the two circles which cover respectively what is rational and what is animal. The way in which we arrive at such a definition is by taking one of the terms, in this case animal, and limiting it by the second term, rational. The first is called the genus, the second the difference, that which singles out from amongst animals the species man. Man, if you like, is an animal with a difference, the difference of being rational. So at least the text books seem to think. Looking round, one wonders if, though formally correct, this definition might not in substance be a pious error.

On the ethical side, the dialogue throws some light on the Athenian state religion, and on how the ethic of Socrates differed from this. It is the difference between authoritarian and fundamentalist ethics. Socrates brings the question into focus when he asks for some clarification of Euthyphro's suggested definition of the Holy as that which the gods approve of unanimously. Socrates wants to know whether a thing is holy because the gods approve of it, or whether the gods approve of it because it is holy. The question is really a veiled criticism of what evidently is Euthyphro's attitude to the problem. For him all that matters is that the gods should have issued a command that something be done. In the Athenian context where there was a state religion, this meant in effect that the ordinances of the ecclesia were to be obeyed as such. Curiously enough, Socrates himself agreed with this as a matter of political practice. But at the same time he felt himself compelled to ask the ethical question about the activity of the state itself, a move which to the Euthyphros of this world would and could not occur. And this at once leads us to the age-old dilemma of divided loyalties which, as we noted earlier, is one of the great themes of Greek drama. That this is by no means a dead and buried issue is clear from the fact that the problem of law and justice is always with us. What is the relation between the two? What are we to do when called upon to obey a law which we find unjust? The question is more alive than ever when blind obedience to our political masters threatens to plunge the world into total and irreparable destruction.

The difference between Euthyphro and Socrates is in the end that the former thinks of the law as something static, whereas the Socratic view implies that the law is not unalterable. Although he does not say this in so many words, Socrates here appears as an empiricist in social theory. As such it behoves him to enquire into whether certain practices are good or evil, no matter who commanded them. That this will make him liable to ill-will from, and persecution by, the state, he must surely have known. It seems, indeed, that this is not an uncommon fate of heretical thinkers who strike at the roots of orthodoxy. No matter that they might act from the purely disinterested motive of righting wrongs done to others, the hostility evinced towards them will be the same.

Socrates' attitude to the laws of Athens is set out in the 'Crito', which shows him unwilling to flee and so escape sentence. Though the laws be unjust they must be obeyed lest the rule of law fall into disrepute. He fails to see that this might happen precisely because of injustice.

His inconsistent attitude in matters concerning authority led Socrates to spurn the easy solution of escape. In refusing to compromise he forced the hands of the prosecution and became a martyr of free thought. His last hours are described in the 'Phaedo', a work which ranks amongst the masterpieces of Western literature. The discussion in the dialogue centres on an attempt to prove that the soul is immortal. We need not here consider the arguments in detail. They are not very sound as arguments, though they raise interesting issues about the mind-body problem. Towards the end of the dialogue, the discussion reaches a point where no one is prepared to raise further objections. It cannot well have escaped the notice of the Pythagoreans present that fresh difficulties could have been produced. But it seems that the ominous character of the event, together with a feeling of piety, made Socrates' friends refrain from casting ultimate doubts on his conclusions. What is philosophically perhaps the most important part in the dialogue is the description of the method of hypothesis and deduction, which is the framework for all scientific argument.

Socrates explains the matter when a certain feeling of dismay seems to settle on the company because of insuperable difficulties in the argument. He warns his friends against misology, the mistrust and rejection of argument in general, and a little later proceeds with a formal outline of his method.

We must start with some supposition, or hypothesis. The two words mean the same, a putting underneath of something. The point is that we must lay the groundwork on which the argument is to be built. From the hypothesis we deduce the consequences that follow from it and see whether they square with the facts. This is what was originally meant by the phrase 'saving appearances'. A hypothesis whose consequences do justice to the facts saves the appearances, the things around us as they appear. This notion is in the first instance no doubt connected with the astronomy of the later Pythagoreans, more particularly with the notion of the trampstars, or planets. Their apparent motion is irregular, a feature which does not fit in with certain metaphysical demands for simplicity. Hence the need for a simple hypothesis which will save the appearances.

If the facts do not agree with the consequences of the hypothesis, the latter is destroyed, and we must try some other hypothesis. The important thing to notice is that hypotheses themselves remain unproved. This is not to say that one chooses starting points quite arbitrarily, but it does mean that in argument one must begin with something which is admitted by all participants, if not from conviction then at least for the sake of argument. The proving of hypotheses is quite another matter. Here we must begin from a higher starting point of which the hypothesis in question may be shown to be a consequence. This is precisely the task of dialectic as Socrates conceives it. We must destroy the special hypotheses of the various sciences, in the sense of removing them as special. In the end, the aim of dialectic is to reach the one supreme starting point, the form of the Good. This, of course, may strike us as a somewhat vain hope. Still, it remains the case that theoretical science is always moving

A B C

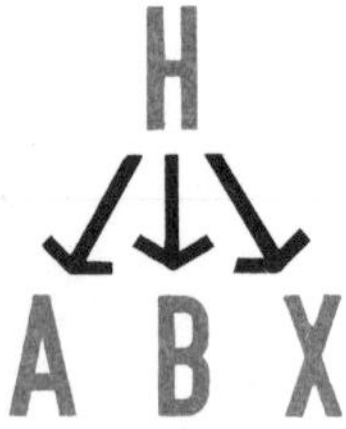

X

The method of hypothesis: A, B, C are appearances to be saved. H fails to save C; X destroys H. H_2 *does save the appearances*

in the direction of greater generality, and unification of fields that might at first seem quite disparate. What was more especially in the minds of the mathematical philosophers was a unification of arithmetic and geometry, a problem which was finally solved with great brilliancy by Descartes some two thousand years later.

That Socrates was not the first to use argument from hypothesis we have already seen. The Eleatics had already used this procedure for their polemics against those who held that things were many. But theirs was on the whole a destructive purpose. What is new here is the notion of saving the appearances. In other words, the problem is one of giving a positive account, or logos, of facts as we observe them. By giving an account, we explain the facts in terms of the hypothesis. It is worth noting that in this approach there is a concealed ethical notion that an explained fact is somehow better than an unexplained one. We may recall that Socrates held that the unexamined way of life was not worth living. Ultimately, all this is connected with the Pythagorean ethic that enquiry as such is good. Moreover, the tendency towards greater and greater unification until everything is ultimately subsumed under the form of the Good points in some measure to the positive content of Eleaticism. The form of the Good and the Eleatic One have this in common, that theoretical science works in the way these notions hint at.

The method of hypothesis and deduction has never been stated better than in the 'Phaedo'. Oddly enough, Socrates never seems to have spotted a curious inconsistency between this and his theory of knowledge and opinion. For, clearly, the theory of deduction from hypotheses requires that the appearances to be saved can as such be unmistakable. Otherwise there could be no comparison between them and the consequences of the hypothesis. On the other hand, appearances are apprehended by the senses, and these are held to be productive of opinion which is fallible. If, therefore, we are to take the theory of hypothesis and deduction seriously, we must abandon the theory of knowledge and opinion, and indirectly this undermines the theory of ideas in so far as it is built on the distinction between knowledge and opinion. This is what empiricism has done.

One question which has not been touched at all is how a hypothesis is set up in the first place. To this we can give no general answer. There is no formal prescription which will ensure success in enquiry. It is perhaps a measure of Socrates' insight that he does not even raise the question. There is no such thing as a logic of invention.

The 'Phaedo' is evidently a historical document in the same sense as the 'Apology'. As such it shows Socrates maintaining his attitude to life right to the end. He is considerate to others, proud in an unselfconscious way, courageous and composed. Excessive display of emotions he finds undignified, and he rebukes his friends who threaten to break down under the strain of the final moments before the hemlock is brought to him. With great indifference and detachment he drinks the poison and lies down to await death. His last request is to his friend Crito, to sacrifice a cock to Asclepius, as though death, the release of soul from body, were like a healing.

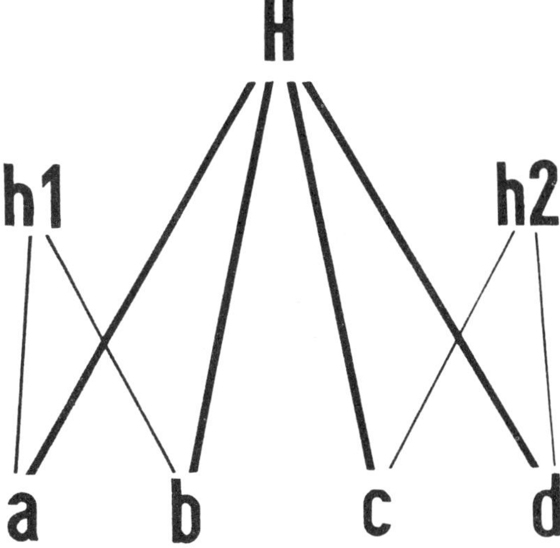

Destroying special hypotheses: H destroys h_1 and h_2, unifying what was hitherto disparate

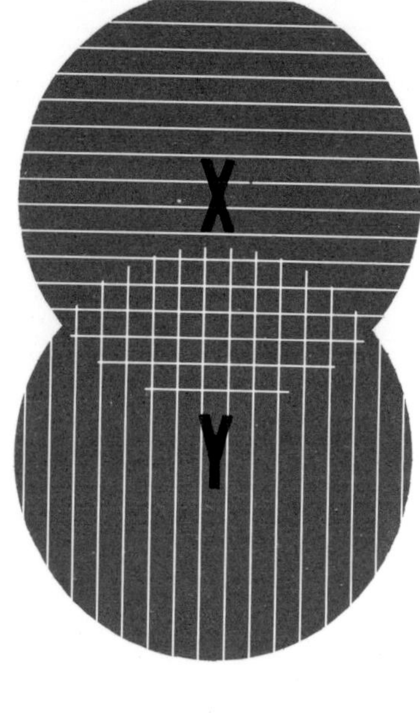

We have already discussed the criticism of the Socratic theory of ideas by Parmenides, in the dialogue of that name. In the 'Theaetetus', which was written, it seems, at the same time as the 'Parmenides', we are definitely moving away from the theories of Socrates, and Plato's own views are beginning to take shape. We may recall that, for Socrates, knowledge is of the forms, whereas the senses give rise merely to opinion. This view correctly underlines a certain difference between mathematical knowledge and sense experience, but as a general theory of knowledge it is never made good. Indeed, the 'Parmenides' shows that it could not be. In the 'Theaetetus' a new attempt is made to dispose of the problem.

Socrates still appears as the central figure in the dialogue. Since here we are given a criticism of the theory of knowledge implicit in the 'Republic' it seems not inappropriate that it should be discussed by Socrates himself. Already, however, the Socratic point of view no longer dominates. In subsequent dialogues, where Plato at last has reached mature views of his own, he uses the device of introducing a stranger to propound his theories, and Socrates subsides.

Theaetetus, after whom this dialogue was named, was a famous mathematician who had distinguished himself both in arithmetic and geometry. He invented a general method for working out quadratic surds and completed the theory of the regular solids. In the dialogue we meet him as a promising lad, shortly before the trial of Socrates. The piece is dedicated to the memory of Theaetetus, victim to wounds and sickness after the battle of Corinth in 369.

Truth and falsehood belong to judgements. If X and Y overlap, some X is Y is true. If they do not overlap, some X is Y is false

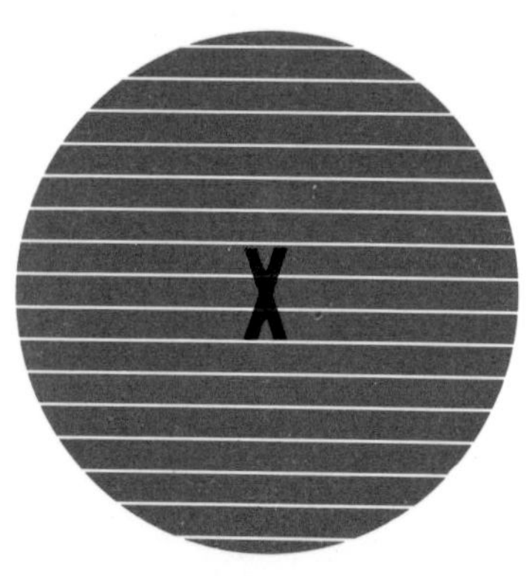

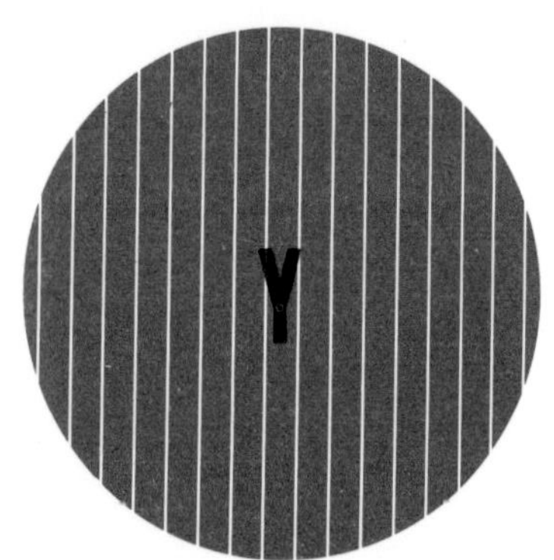

The question to which the introductory banter leads up is what is knowledge. Theaetetus first makes the usual mistake of giving instances instead of a definition, but quickly sees the error and proceeds to give a first definition. Knowledge, he says, is aesthesis. This is the general Greek term for perception of any kind. Our own word anaesthetic simply means a blotting out of perception. More particularly, we are here concerned with sense perception. The view that knowledge is sense perception is really the same as the formula of Protagoras, that man is the measure of all things. In sense perception things appear as they appear, so that we cannot go wrong. In the ensuing discussion it becomes clear that the proposed definition of knowledge is not adequate. To begin with, it will not do to say that something is as it appears, since nothing really is; things are always in a state of becoming, as Heraclitus had said. Sense perception is, in fact, an interaction between perceiver and perceived. Moreover, Protagoras himself would have admitted that in matters where a decision must be made, one man's view is not as good as another's, the expert is a better judge than the layman. Besides, a man untainted by philosophic thought will hardly give assent to the formula, so on his own showing Protagoras must admit that for such a person the theory is not true. The upshot of the discussion is this: if we try to describe knowledge in terms of a Heraclitean theory of flux we find that nothing can be said. Before anything can be pinned down by a word it has melted away into something else. We must therefore try some other way of answering the question what is knowledge.

Let us then consider the fact that while the senses each have their proper objects, anything which involves connection between perceptions by different senses requires the function of some overall sense. This is the soul or mind, the two are not distinct in Plato. The soul apprehends such general predicates as identity, difference, existence, number, as well as the general predicates of ethics and art. Hence it is not possible to define knowledge simply as sense perception. Let us therefore try to see whether we can find a definition on the side of the soul. The function of the soul is to conduct dialogues with itself. On reaching a settlement of a question we say that it has made a judgement. We must now examine whether we may define knowledge as true judgement. On investigation we find that it is impossible on this theory to give a satisfactory account of false judgement, or error. That errors are made is obviously granted by all. The distinction between truth and error is not worked out at this stage. Plato merely clears the ground, his own account of the problem may well not have been fully developed at that time.

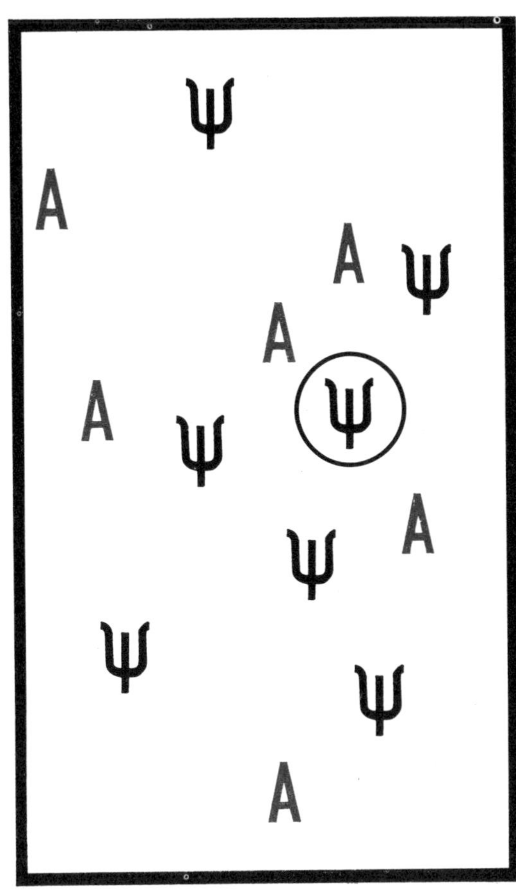

If knowledge were purely mental, how explain error? The birdcage simile fails: if, catching, we know, error would be unmasked at once

But false judgement is impossible if judgement is an activity of the soul alone. We might suppose that the mind was like a tablet with memory marks impressed on it. Error might then consist in connecting a present sensation to the wrong imprint. But this fails for mistakes in arithmetic when there is nothing to have sensations of. If we suppose the mind to be some sort of birdcage, the birds in which are pieces of knowledge, then we might occasionally net the wrong bird, and that would be error. But then, to commit an error is not the same as to utter an irrelevant truth. We must therefore suppose that some of the birds are pieces of error. But if we catch one of these we know that it is an error as soon as it is caught, so that we could never be in error. Besides, we may note the point which the argument overlooks, that if one introduces pieces of error, then the entire story becomes circular as an account of error.

Again, a man may well utter a true judgement by accident, or from other causes, such as wanting to hold a view which happens to be in fact true. The final definition tries to meet this: knowledge is true judgement supported by argument. In the absence of argument there is no knowledge. We may think of letters which can be named but have no meaning, and their combination into syllables which can in turn be analysed and therefore are objects of knowledge. But if the syllable is the sum of its letters it is as unknowable as they are, if more, then it is this additional feature which makes it knowable, and the statement becomes empty. Besides, what is meant by argument here? Clearly, an account of how the thing differs from all others. This is either a further judgement, or amounts to a knowledge of the difference. The first implies a regress, the second a circle in definition. No solution to our problem is given, but the air is cleared of certain misconceptions. Neither sense perception nor ratiocination can, on its own, account for knowledge.

The problem of knowledge and the problem of error are evidently two sides of the same question. As neither of them is settled in the present discussion, a fresh start must be made. To this we shall now turn our attention.

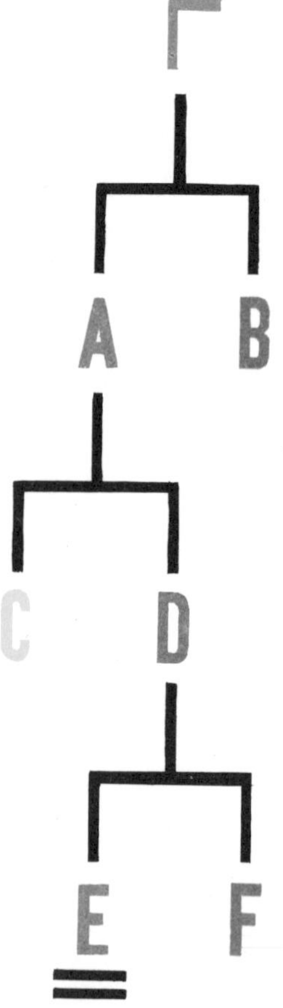

X=ΓADE

Definition by division, the basis of classification. At each stage the genus is divided in two

We come now to a piece which purports to continue the conversation of the 'Theaetetus' on the following day. This is the 'Sophist', a dialogue which on stylistic grounds can be dated as a good deal later than the 'Theaetetus'. The company assembled are the same, but in addition an Eleatic stranger appears on the scene. It is the stranger who stands at the centre of the dialogue, whereas Socrates plays a very minor part in the discussion. Outwardly, the 'Sophist' is concerned with a problem of definition. The question is to define what is a sophist, and to distinguish him from the philosopher. The veiled antagonism implied in this seems to be directed mainly against the Socratic school of Megara, which had developed a one-sided and destructive mode of Eleatic logic chopping. The Eleatic stranger, in whom we may see the voice of Plato himself, shows a truer grasp of the issues and produces a brilliant solution of the problem of error. By using the stranger as a mouthpiece, Plato gives us to understand that he himself stands in the true tradition of philosophic development, whereas the sophistical paradoxmongers of Megara have strayed from the path.

The real problem which is tackled in the 'Sophist' is the Parmenidean puzzle about Not-being. In Parmenides this was of course mainly a matter concerning the physical world. In his followers, it spread into logic as well, and it is this problem that we find here examined. Before turning to this, the central question of the dialogue, we may add a few comments on the method of division, especially since it is the classificatory procedure which was used in the Academy. The work of Aristotle on the classification of animals belongs to his Academic period. The method provides us with detailed definitions of terms, starting with the genus and dividing it into two at each step, by giving sets of alternative differences. A preliminary example is given in the 'Sophist' to explain the procedure. The term to be defined is angling. To begin with, angling is an art, so that the arts constitute the first genus. We may divide them into arts of production and arts of acquisition, and angling evidently belongs to the latter. Acquisition is now divided into cases where its objects give consent, and where they are simply captured. Again, angling belongs to the second of these. Capture can be divided into open and concealed, angling being of the latter kind. The things taken may be inanimate or living; angling is concerned with living things. The animals in question may live on land or in a fluid, and again the term to be defined belongs to the second class. Inhabitants of fluids may be birds or fish, fish may be caught by net or by striking, and you may strike by night or day. Angling is done in daylight. We may strike from above or below, and angling is of the latter kind. Retracing our steps and collecting all the differences, we define angling as the art of acquiring by concealed capture animals that live in water, catching by day and striking from below. The example is not to be taken too seriously, it is chosen because the sophist may also be taken as an angler, his quarry being the souls of men. Various definitions of the sophist follow, but we need not pursue this matter.

Instead, we shall now turn to the discussion of the Eleatic problem. The difficulty about Not-being arises because the philosophers have not properly understood what is meant by Being, as the stranger shows with great acumen. Referring back to the 'Theaetetus', we may recall that knowledge, whatever else it may also require, at least requires interaction and therefore Motion. But it also requires Rest, since otherwise there would be nothing to be talked about. Things must in some sense stay put if they are to be objects of enquiry. This gives us a hint for attacking the problem. For Motion and Rest undoubtedly both exist, but as they are opposites, they cannot be combined. Three possibilities for combination seem to suggest themselves. Either all things remain completely separate, in which case Motion and Rest cannot have a part in Being. Or all things can merge, in which case Motion and Rest could come together, which they clearly cannot. It therefore remains that some things can, and others cannot, combine. The solution of our difficulties lies in recognising that Being and Not-being are meaningless expressions on their own. It is only in a judgement that they make sense. The 'forms' or kinds, like Motion, Rest, Being, are the general predicates already mentioned in the 'Theaetetus'. They are clearly quite different from the forms of Socrates. This Platonic theory of forms is the starting point of what later developed into the theory of categories.

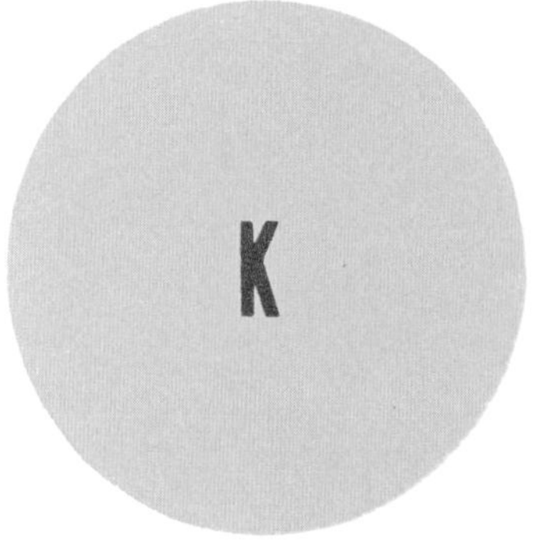

The function of dialectic is to study which of these forms or 'highest kinds' combine, and which do not. Motion and Rest, as we have seen already, do not combine with each other, but each of them combines with Being, each is. Again, Motion is the same as itself but other than Rest. Sameness, or identity, and otherness, or difference, like Being, are all-pervasive. For each is identical with itself and different from all the others.

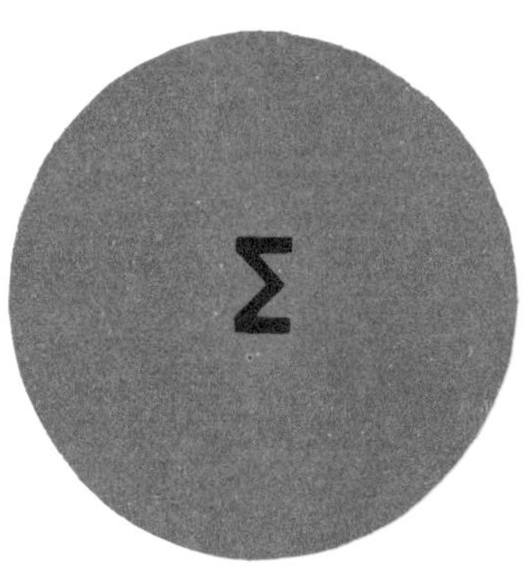

'Platonic' forms answer Parmenides who said it is or is not, but Motion (K) both is and is not: it is, Rest (Σ) is, but Motion is not Rest

We can see now what is meant by Not-being. Motion, we might say, both is and is not. For it is Motion, but it is not Rest. In this sense, then, Not-being is on the same level as Being. But it is plain that the Not-being here evolved must not be taken in complete abstraction. It is a Not-being such and such, or better, a Being other than such and such. Plato has thus brought out the source of the difficulty. In modern jargon, we must distinguish the existential use of 'is' from the use of it as a copula in a proposition. It is the second of these which is logically important.

On this basis we can now give a simple account of error. To judge truly is to judge something to be as it is. If we judge something to be as it is not, we judge falsely, and so we commit error. It may surprise the reader that the outcome is no more formidable or mysterious than that. But then as much holds of any problem once we know the solution.

We may note, in conclusion, that the problem of the 'Theaetetus' has been incidentally disposed of as well. In a sense it is not a proper question. We must stick to judgements, and these, as we can now see, may be true or false. But how do we know whether a given judgement is one or the other? The answer is just that it is true if things are so, and if not, not. There is no formal criterion which ensures us against error.

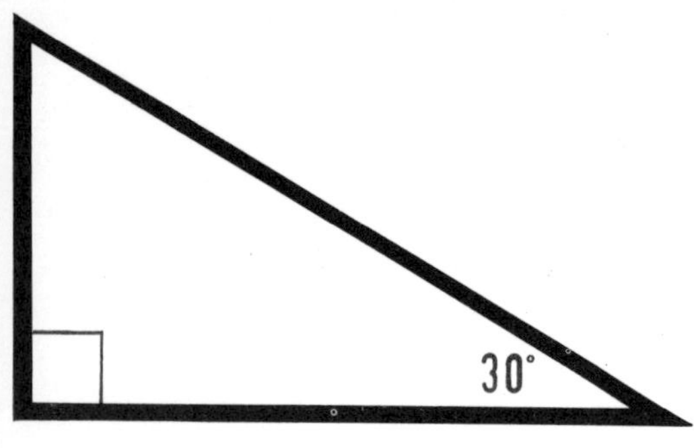

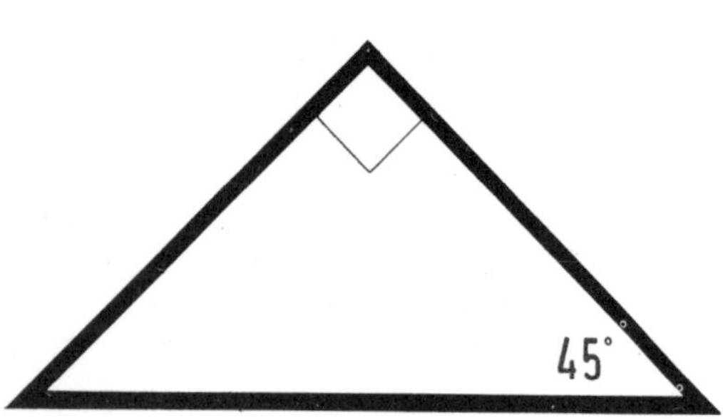

The two basic triangles, Plato holds the elements are made of these, a geometric nuclear theory

The account of Not-being we have just outlined enables us henceforth to dispose of the problem of change. It makes the Heraclitean theory explicit and removes from it the apparent aura of paradox. Yet there is in Plato another theory of change which links up directly with both atomism and mathematical physics as we know it today. The theory is given in the 'Timaeus', another dialogue belonging to the last and mature period of Plato's thought. An account of the cosmogony set out in that dialogue would lead us too far afield, we merely note that there is a great deal of advanced Pythagoreanism in it, together with hints on the proper explanation of planetary motion. Indeed, it is likely that the heliocentric hypothesis was an Academic discovery. A good many other scientific matters are touched on in the dialogue, but we must leave these aside. Let us turn at once to what might well be called Plato's geometrical or mathematical atomism. According to this view we have to make a threefold distinction between forms, basic matter and the corporeal reality of the sensible world. The basic matter here is simply empty space. Sensible reality is the outcome of a mixture between forms and the space on which they are somehow imprinted. On this basis we are now presented with an account of the material world, both physical and biological, in terms of the four elements. But these in turn are now considered as geometrical bodies made up of two kinds of elementary triangles, that which consists of half an equilateral triangle, and the right-angled isosceles triangle, which is half a square. Out of these triangles we can construct four of the five regular solids. The tetrahedron is the basic particle of fire, the cube of earth, the octohedron of air and the icosahedron of water. By breaking up these bodies into their constituent triangles and rearranging them we can effect transformations between the elements. Again, the fiery particles, having sharp points, penetrate the other bodies. Water consists of much smoother particles, hence the gliding of fluids.

The theory of transformation here suggested is in fact a remarkable precursor of modern physical theories. Indeed, Plato goes much further than the materialist atomism of Democritus. The basic triangles are evidently counterparts of what in modern physics are called nuclear or elementary particles. They are the constituents of the basic particles. We may note, too, that these particles are not called atoms. This, to a Greek, would be a flagrant solecism, and so indeed it really remains. The word atom means literally an indivisible thing. A thing which is made up of other things should in all strictness not be called an atom.

Plato here appears as the precursor of the main tradition of modern science. The view that everything can be reduced to geometry is explicitly held by Descartes, and in a different way by Einstein. That Plato should confine himself to four elements is of course in one sense a limitation. The reason for this choice is that such was the prevailing view of the times. What Plato tried to do is to give a 'logos' or account of this view in order to save the appearances, and the hypothesis he employs is mathematical. That the world is ultimately intelligible in terms of number was, as we saw, a part of the Pythagorean doctrine which Plato accepted. We thus have a mathematical model for physical explanation. In method this is just the aim of mathematical physics today.

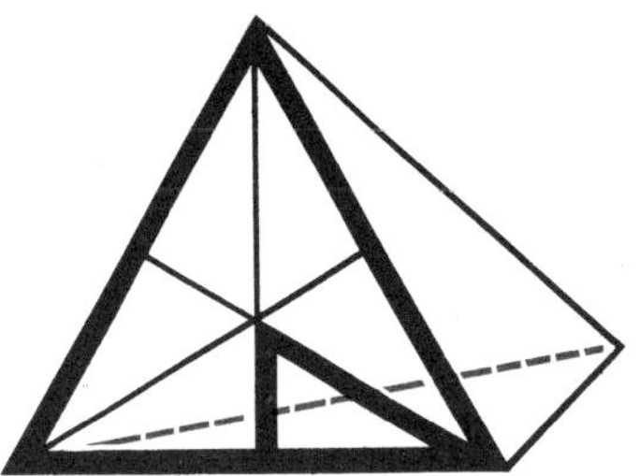

That this theory should be linked more particularly to the theory of the regular solids is perhaps a streak of Pythagorean mysticism. Indeed, there remains, on this scheme, no place for the dodecahedron. This alone, of the five solids, has faces not made up from the two elementary triangles, but from regular pentagons. The pentagon, it may be recalled, was one of the mystical symbols of the Pythagoreans, and its construction involves the irrational number shown when we discussed the later Pythagoreans. Furthermore, the dodecahedron looks rounder than any of the other four solids. Plato therefore makes it stand for the world. This speculation does not affect the soundness or otherwise of the mathematical model.

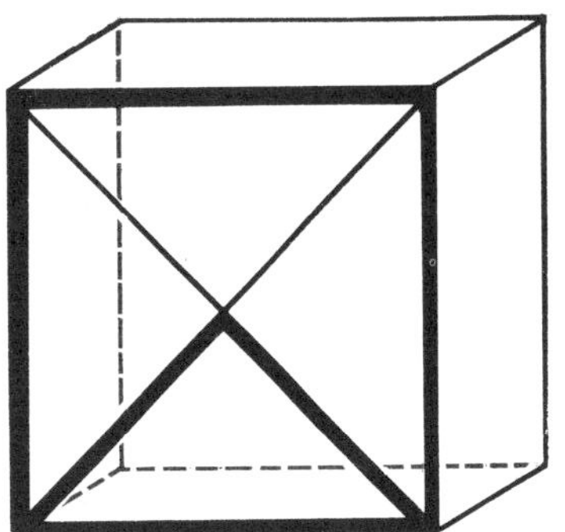

Plato's theory of mathematics we have not the time to treat fully here. It must in any case be pieced together from a few hints in the dialogues and statements in Aristotle. It is nevertheless important to note two items. The first is that Plato, or at any rate the Academy, revised the Pythagorean doctrine of number in order to escape the Eleatic criticisms of it. In this, again, an extremely modern view is foreshadowed. The beginning of the number series is recognised to be zero instead of the unit. This makes it possible to develop a general theory of irrationals, which, if one were pedantic, should now no longer be called irrational. Likewise, in geometry, lines are now thought of as generated by the motion of a point, a view which plays a central part in Newton's theory of fluxions, which was one of the early forms of what came to be called differential calculus. We see clearly the way in which these developments make for a unification of arithmetic and geometry in the spirit of the dialectic.

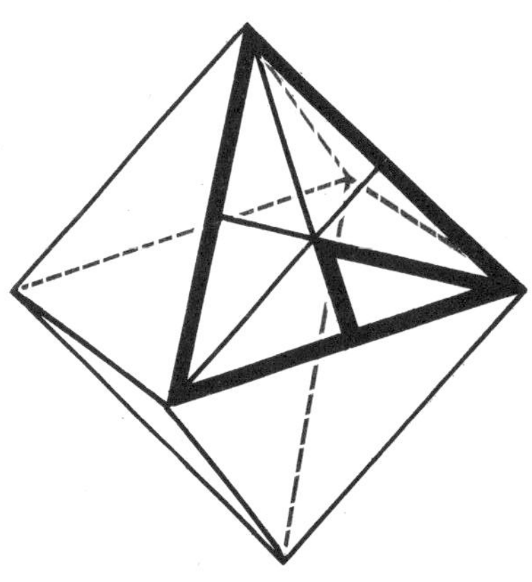

The elements, the tetrahedron fire, the cube earth, the octohedron air, the icosahedron water

The second important matter is a statement of Aristotle's that Plato said numbers could not be added. This somewhat lapidary pronouncement contains in fact the germs of an extremely modern view of number. Following the Pythagoreans, Plato regarded numbers as forms. These evidently cannot be added together. What happens when we make additions is that we put together things of a certain kind, let us say pebbles. The sort of thing that mathematicians talk about is, however, different from the pebbles as well as from the forms. It is somehow intermediate between the two. What mathematicians add together is things of an unspecified kind, any kind, provided that in the relevant respect the kind is the same for all the things added. All this stands out very clearly in terms of the definition of number that was given by Frege, and later by Whitehead and myself. The number three, for example, is the class of all triplets. A triplet is a class of objects of a given kind. Likewise for any other cardinal number. The number two is the class of couples, a couple being a class of things. You can add a triplet and a couple of one kind, but not the number three and the number two.

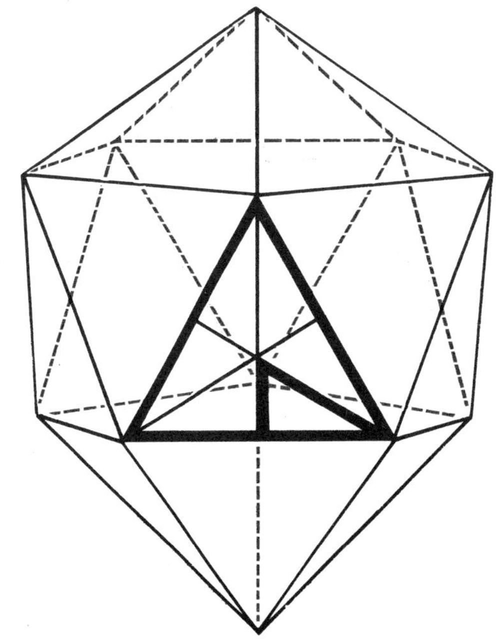

This concludes a bare outline of some of the more important theories of Plato. Few, if any, philosophers have ever reached his range and depth, and none has surpassed him. Anyone who would engage in philosophic enquiry is unwise to ignore him.

Aristotle, the last of the three great thinkers who lived and taught in Athens, was probably the first professional philosopher. With him the climax of the classical period is already passing. Politically Greece was becoming less important; Alexander of Macedon, who as a lad had been Aristotle's pupil, laid the imperial foundations on which the hellenistic world began to flourish. But of this later.

Aristotle

Unlike Socrates and Plato, Aristotle was a foreigner in Athens. He was born in about 384 B.C. at Stagira in Thrace. His father was court physician to the Kings of Macedon. At the age of eighteen Aristotle was sent to Athens to study under Plato at the Academy. He remained a member of the Academy until the death of Plato in 348-7 B.C., some twenty years in all. The new head of the Academy, Speusippus, was strongly in sympathy with the mathematical strain in Platonic philosophy, the feature which Aristotle understood least and disliked most. He therefore left Athens and during the next twelve years we find him working in a number of places. Following an invitation from his former schoolfriend, Hermeias, a ruler in Mysia on the coast of Asia Minor, Aristotle joined a group of Academicians there and married the niece of his host. Three years later he went to Mitylene on the island of Lesbos.

His work on the classification of animals belongs, as we have said, to his Academic period. During his stay in the Aegean he must have conducted his researches in marine biology, a field in which he made contributions that were not improved on until the 19th century. In 343 he was called to the Macedonian court of Philip II, who was looking for a tutor to his son Alexander. For three years Aristotle filled this office, but on this period we have no trustworthy sources. This is perhaps unfortunate; one cannot help wondering what hold the wise philosopher had on the unruly prince. Still, it seems safe to say that there was not a lot on which the two might see eye to eye. Aristotle's political views were based on the Greek city state which was all but on the way out. Centralised empires like that of the Great King would seem to him, as indeed to all Greeks, a barbarian invention. In this, as in cultural matters generally, they had a healthy respect for their own superiority. But the times were changing, the city state in decline and hellenistic empire in the offing. That Alexander admired Athens for her culture is true enough, but then so did everyone else, and Aristotle was not the cause of it.

From 340 until the death of Philip in 335, Aristotle lived in his home town once more, and from then until Alexander's death in 323, he worked in Athens. It is at this time that he founded a school of his own, the Lyceum, named after the nearby temple of Apollo Lykeius, that is the wolf-slayer. Here Aristotle would lecture his classes, walking through the halls and gardens and talking as he went. From this habit the teaching of the Lyceum came to be known as the peripatetic, or walk-about, philosophy. It is interesting to note that our own word discourse literally means a running about. Its Latin forbear did not come to be used with its present meaning of reasoned argument until the Middle Ages. It may have acquired this sense from being used in connection with the peripatetic philosophy, though this is entirely problematic.

Following the death of Alexander, the Athenians rose in revolt against Macedonian rule. Aristotle was naturally suspected of pro-Macedonian sympathies and was charged with impiety. As the case of Socrates had shown, such legal exercises could on occasion lead to somewhat unpleasant consequences. Aristotle was no Socrates and decided to shun the fangs of the patriots, lest the Athenians score another crime against philosophy. He left the running of the Lyceum to Theophrastus, withdrew to Chalcis, and died there in 322.

The grove of Apollo Lukeios, site of the Lyceum, Aristotle's school

It is to the second Athenian period that most of what has come down to us as the writings of Aristotle belongs. Not all of these are actually books. There seems little doubt that some of the Aristotelian corpus is based on lecture notes. Thus Aristotle appears to be the first writer of text books. Some of the works even seem to be records taken down by students. As a result of this, Aristotle's style is rather dull and uninspired, though it is known that he also wrote dialogues in the manner of Plato. None of these survives, but it is evident from the rest that Aristotle was not a literary figure of the stature of Plato. Where Plato wrote dramatic masterpieces, Aristotle turned out dry schoolbooks. Where Plato poured forth rambling dialogues, Aristotle produced systematic treatises.

To understand Aristotle we must remember that he is the first critic of Plato. Still, it cannot be said that Aristotelian criticism is always well informed. It is usually safe to trust Aristotle when he states the doctrine of Plato, but when he proceeds to explain its significance he is no longer reliable. It may of course be assumed that Aristotle was acquainted with the mathematics of his day. His membership of the Academy would seem to vouch for that. But it is equally clear that he was out of sympathy with the mathematical philosophy of Plato. Indeed, he never really understood it. The same reservations must be made where Aristotle comments on the presocratics. Where we have straight reports we can rely on them, the interpretations must all be taken with a grain of salt.

While Aristotle was a biologist of note, even if we allow for some rather peculiar lapses, his views on physics and astronomy were hopelessly muddled. Plato, combining the Milesian and Pythagorean traditions, had been much nearer the mark, and so were later Hellenistic scientists like Aristarchus and Eratosthenes. Aristotle's most famous contribution to systematic thought is probably his work in logic. Much of it is derivative from Plato, but where in Plato logical doctrines are scattered amidst much other material, in Aristotle they are gathered together and set out in a form in which they have continued to be taught almost unchanged until the present. Historically, Aristotle's influence has been rather obstructive, mainly because of the blind and slavish dogmatism of many of his followers. For this, of course, we cannot lay the blame on Aristotle himself. It still remains that the scientific revival of the renaissance was a breakaway from Aristotle and a return to Plato. In his outlook, Aristotle remained a child of the classical age, though Athens was declining before he was born. He never understood the significance of the political changes that took place during his lifetime. The classical period had long since reached its term.

Alexander the Great

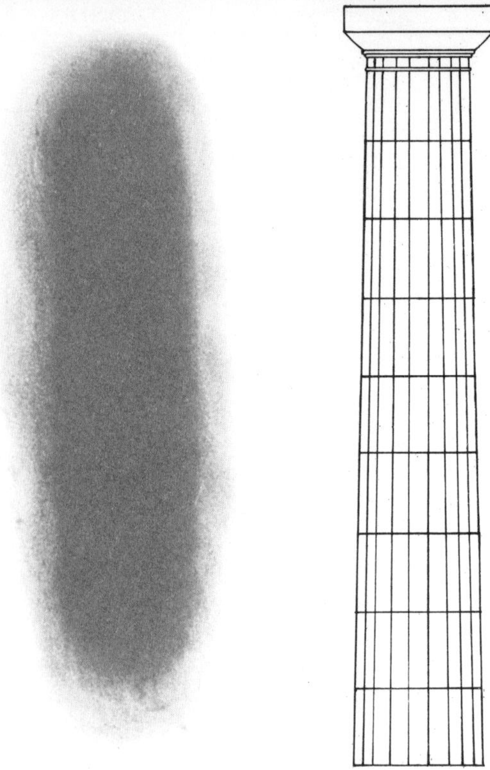

Matter and form are abstractions, a concrete thing has both

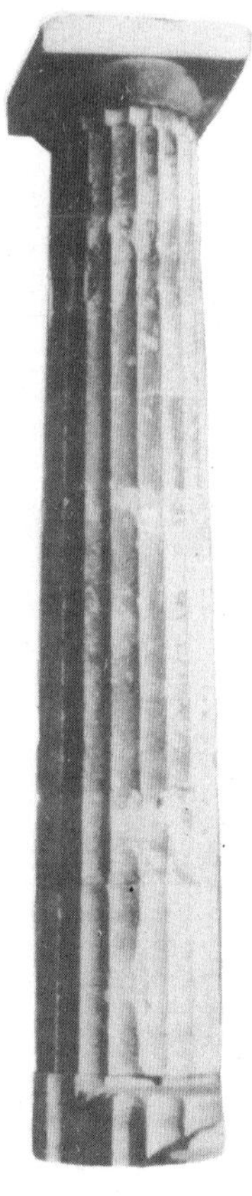

The metaphysics of Aristotle is not easy to discuss, partly because it is widely scattered throughout his work, and partly because there is a certain want of clearcut commitment. It is worth noting from the outset that what we now call metaphysics did not go by that name in Aristotle's time. 'Metaphysics' literally means simply 'after physics'. The book received this title because an early editor placed it after the Physics in his arrangement of the works. It would have been more to the point to have placed it before physics, because that is where it naturally belongs. Aristotle would have called it 'first philosophy', a discussion of the general preconditions of enquiry. The name metaphysics has however gained currency.

Aristotle's work in this field may be considered as an attempt to replace the Socratic theory of ideas by a new theory of his own. The chief criticism of Aristotle is the third man argument applied to the doctrine of participation. This merely re-echoes the criticism Plato had already put forward in the 'Parmenides'. The alternative suggested by Aristotle is the theory of matter and form. Take for instance the stuff that goes into the making of a column. This would be the matter. The form is something like the architect's drawings of the column. Both these are in a sense abstractions, in that the real object is a combination of the two. Aristotle would say that it is the form, when imposed on the matter, which makes the latter what it is. The form confers characteristics upon the matter, turns it, in fact, into a substance. It is important not to confuse matter with substance if we are to understand Aristotle aright. Substance is a literal translation from Aristotle's Greek and simply means the underlying thing. It is some immutable thing which is the carrier of qualities. It is because we naturally tend to think in terms of some kind of atomic theory that we are prone to identify substance with matter. For atoms are, in the sense here required, substantial entities whose function it is to carry qualities and account for change. This we have already hinted at in connection with the atomists.

In the Aristotelian theory, forms turn out after all to be more important than matter. For it is form that is creative, matter being of course required too, but merely as raw material. The form turns out to be substantial in the literal sense. From what has just been explained it will be clear that this means forms are immutable and eternal entities underlying the process of the real world. They are thus after all not so very different from the ideas or forms of Socrates. To say that forms are substantial implies that they exist independently of particular things. How these substances exist is never clearly explained. At any rate, there seems to be no attempt at assigning to them a distinct world of their own. It is worth noting that Aristotle thinks his forms to be quite different from universals. The criticism of the theory of ideas is really linked to a simple point of language. There are in ordinary talk words for things and words for what these things are like. The former are nouns, the latter adjectives. In technical jargon nouns are sometimes called substantives. This is a term that goes back to hellenistic times and shows how strongly Aristotelian theories influenced the grammarians. Nouns, then, are substance words, whereas adjectives are quality words. But it is wrong to infer from this that there must be separately existing universals of which adjectives are the names. Aristotle's view of universals is a more organic one, as might well be expected from a biologist. Universals somehow intervene in the production of things, but they do not exist in a shadowy world of their own. For all that Aristotle does not intend his theory of matter and form to take the place of universals, it nevertheless bears on this problem; and, as we saw, does not really succeed in breaking away from the theory of ideas. It is important to remember, too, that on Aristotle's theory one may quite properly speak of immaterial substances. One example of this is the soul, which, as that which gives form to the body, is a substance but not material.

Along with the problem of universals goes the perennial question of accounting for change. Some find this so difficult that, like Parmenides, they simply deny it. Others adopt a refined Eleaticism and resort to atomic explanations, while others still make use of some theory of universals. All this we have already mentioned. In Aristotle we find a theory of actuality and potentiality more akin to universals than to atomism.

In discussing the problem of potentiality we must be careful to set aside one rather trivial form of it. There is a way of talking in which the word potential merely functions as idle wisdom after the event. If a flask of oil begins to burn we may say that this is because it was potentially so even beforehand. But this is clearly no explanation at all. Indeed, for reasons of this kind some philosophic schools denied that anything useful could be said on the subject. Antisthenes of Megara was one of these, as we shall see later. According to this view, either a thing is of a certain sort or it is not, anything beyond this is nonsense. But clearly, we do make statements like 'oil is inflammable' and they make perfectly good sense. Aristotle's analysis provides the correct answer. In saying that a thing is potentially A, we mean that under certain conditions it will in fact be actually so. To say that oil is inflammable is to recognise that, given a set of circumstances that can be specified, it will burn. Thus, if the temperature is right and you strike a match holding it to the surface of the oil you will set fire to it. The conditions in question must of course be such that they can in fact occur, or be actual. In this sense the actual is logically prior to the potential. An account of change can now be given in terms of a substance which is the potential bearer of a series of qualities that become successively actual in it. Whatever shortcomings such an account might have in practice, it is at least not trivial in principle, if we remember the Aristotelian analysis of potentiality. Such an approach is clearly more reminiscent of Socrates and Plato than of the atomists. The Aristotelian view is partly influenced by scientific interests in biology, where the notion of potentiality is particularly useful. The account here given is incomplete in one important respect. It does not mention how and why changes occur. On this Aristotle has a very detailed answer which we shall consider when we come to his theory of causality. As to cosmogony and the view of God as the first cause or unmoved mover, this too will be left till later. We should however remember that Aristotle's theology is considered by him as part of what we now call metaphysics.

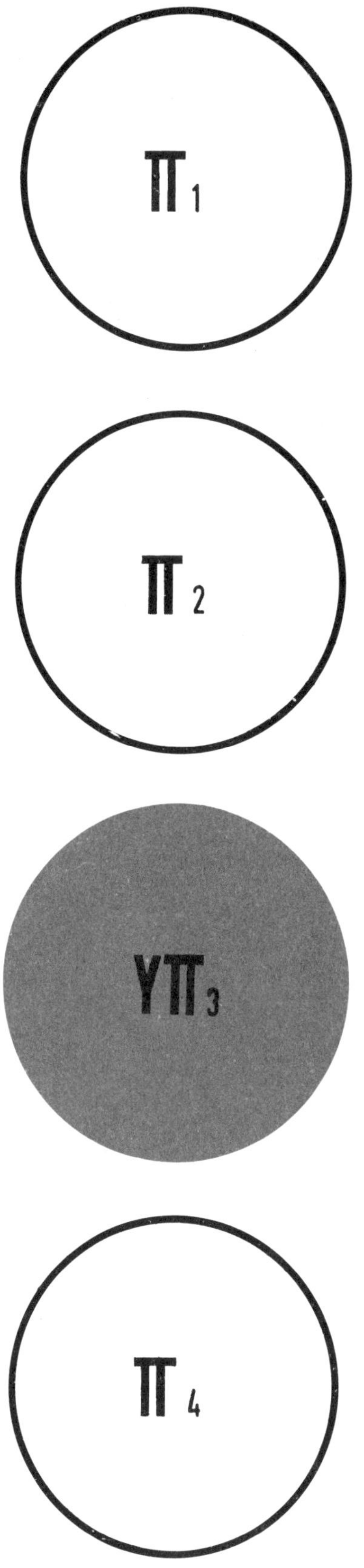

Change; potential qualities become actual, by turns, in a substance

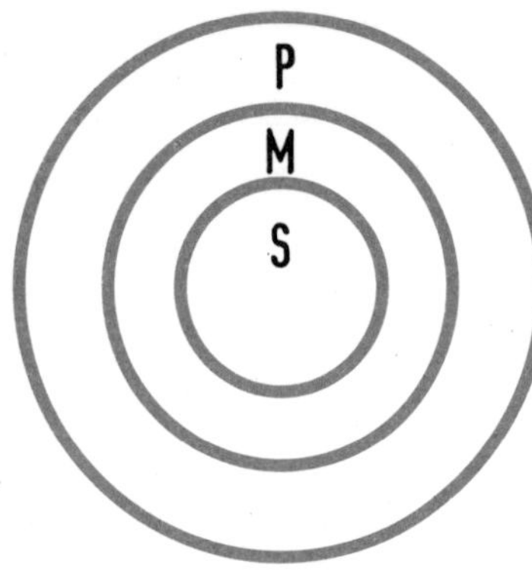

All M are P, all S are M ∴ all S are P
A first figure syllogism called Barbara, using Euler's circles

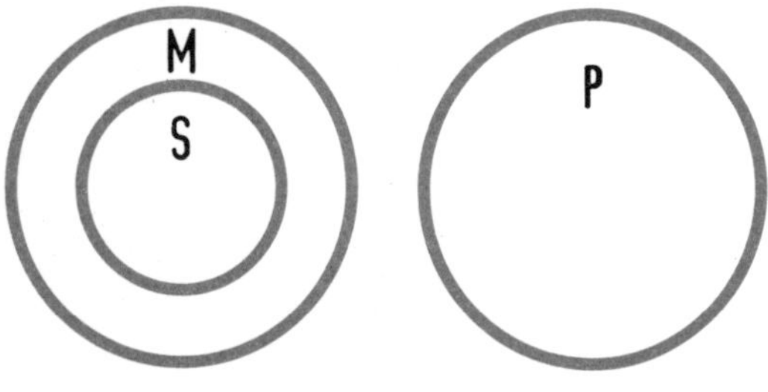

No M are P, all S are M ∴ no S are P
A first figure syllogism called Celarent

Let us now turn to Aristotle's work in logic. We have said earlier that one distinctive feature of Greek science and philosophy is the notion of proof. Where the astronomers of the East had been content to record appearances, the thinkers of Greece sought to save them. The process of proving a proposition involves the construction of arguments. This, of course, had been going on for a long time before Aristotle; but no one, to our knowledge, had ever given a detailed general account of the form which arguments take. Here Aristotle's work supplies a survey which he, and Kant, at any rate, imagined to be complete. That in this he was sadly mistaken is not really important; the vital step was to have seen the possibility of giving a general account of formal logic. It is perhaps best to emphasize straight away that there is no such thing as informal logic. What is meant is the general form of arguments, a study which belongs to the field of logic. The Aristotelian logic depends on a number of assumptions which are connected with his metaphysics. First of all it is taken for granted that all propositions are of the subject-predicate type. Many propositions in ordinary speech are of this type and this is one of the sources of the metaphysics of substance and quality. The subject-predicate form is of course suggested already by Plato in the 'Theaetetus' whence presumably Aristotle derived it in the first place. It is in this context that the problem of universals arises. Propositions are divided according to whether they are about universals or individuals. In the former case they may encompass the whole scope of the universal, as in 'all men are mortal', which is called a universal proposition. Alternatively, the statement may cover only part of the universal, as in 'some men are wise', and this is called a particular proposition. The case of the individual proposition is exemplified by a proposition like 'Socrates is a man'. When we come to combining propositions in an argument the individual must be treated as a universal proposition. Propositions are affirmative or negative according to whether something is asserted or denied of a subject.

On the basis of this classification we may now consider what happens in argument. Starting from one or more propositions called premisses, we deduce other propositions which follow from, or are consequences of, these premisses. The fundamental type of all argument, according to Aristotle, is what he called syllogism. A syllogism is an argument with two subject-predicate premisses that have one term in common. This middle term disappears in the conclusion. Thus, all humans are rational, babies are human, therefore babies are rational, is an example of a syllogism. In this case the conclusion does follow from the premisses, so that the argument is valid. As to the truth or otherwise of the premisses, that is of course quite a different question. Indeed, it is possible to derive true conclusions from false premisses. The important thing however is that if the premisses are true, then any conclusion validly derived is also true. It is therefore important to discover which syllogistic arguments are valid and which are not. Aristotle gives a systematic account of valid syllogisms. Arguments are first classified as to their figure, which depends on the arrangement of the terms. Three different configurations were recognised by Aristotle, and the Stoics later discovered a fourth. In each figure some arguments are valid and some not. An ingenious method of testing syllogistic arguments was invented by the 18th century Swiss mathematician Euler. By representing the scope of a term by means of a circle it becomes easy to see whether an argument is sound or not. Thus, the example we gave previously is easily seen to be correct. It is a first figure syllogism to which the scholastics gave the technical name Barbara. Similarly, no mammal can fly, all pigs are mammals, therefore no pig can fly, is a valid first figure argument. This form is called Celarent. Notice that in this particular example the conclusion is true though one of the premisses is false. For bats are mammals and yet can fly.

As a result of the authority which Aristotle commanded in later times, syllogism remained for some two thousand years the only type of argument recognised by logicians. Some of the criticisms that were levelled against it in the end were forestalled by Aristotle himself. Thus, in the case of an argument like all men are mortal, Socrates is a man, therefore Socrates is mortal, it has been supposed that to know the first premiss one would already have to know the conclusion so that the argument begs the question. This is based on a misunderstanding of how we come to know a statement like all A are B. It is not necessary nor even usual to look at each A in turn and see that it is B. On the contrary, it is often enough to look at a single exemplar to see the connection. This is obviously so in geometry. All triangles have the sum of their angles equal to two right angles, but no geometer worth his salt is going to charge about peering at triangles to satisfy his mind before risking a universal statement.

The three Aristotelian figures of syllogism

M - P
S - M
―――――
S - P

P - M
S - M
―――――
S - P

M - P
M - S
―――――
S - P

This, in brief, is the gist of the theory of syllogism. Aristotle also dealt with syllogisms made up of modal propositions, that is statements that contain 'maybe' or 'must' instead of 'is'. Modal logic is coming to the fore again in the field of contemporary symbolic logic. The doctrine of syllogism, in the light of more recent developments, appears now as rather less important than it used to be thought. As far as science is concerned, the operation of syllogism leaves the premisses unproved. This raises the question of starting points. According to Aristotle science must begin with statements that stand in no need of demonstration. These he called axioms. They need not be especially common in experience, provided only that they are clearly understood as soon as they are explained. It is perhaps not superfluous to point out that this concerns the setting out of a body of scientific fact rather than the process of scientific enquiry. The expository order always conceals the order of discovery. In the actual pursuit of enquiry, there is a great deal of haze and imprecision which is cleared as soon as the problem is solved.

What Aristotle seems to have had in mind when talking about axioms is geometry, which was by his time beginning to appear in systematic form. Only a few decades separate Aristotle from Euclid. No other science at that time had reached a stage where it could be presented in the manner of geometry. That sciences can be ordered in some sort of hierarchy seems to follow from this. Mathematics is here supreme. Astronomy, for instance, would come below it, for it must call on mathematics to give the reasons for the motions it observes. In this field Aristotle foreshadows later work, especially the classification of sciences of the French positivist Comte.

Substance	**Socrates**
Quality	**philosopher**
Quantity	**five foot eight**
Relation	**friend of Plato**
Place	**in the Agora**
Time	**at noon**
Position	**standing**
State	**ill-clad**
Action	**talking**
Affection	**being taunted**

The ten Aristotelian categories

The study of language, for Aristotle, is an important philosophic pursuit. A beginning here too was made by Plato, in the 'Theaetetus' and the 'Sophist'. Indeed, one of the leading notions in Greek philosophy is the conception of logos, a term which we first meet in this context with Pythagoras and Heraclitus. It variously means word, measure, formula, argument, account. This range of significance must be kept in mind if one is to grasp the spirit of Greek philosophy. The term 'logic' is evidently derived from it. Logic is the science of the logos.

But logic somehow has a peculiar status. It is not quite of the same kind as what are normally called sciences. Aristotle distinguished three types of science according to the main purpose achieved by each. Theoretical science provides knowledge, in the sense in which this is opposed to opinion. Mathematics is the most obvious example here, though Aristotle also includes physics and metaphysics. Physics in his sense is not quite what we understand by it today. It is rather a general study of space, time and causality some of which we should probably consider under the heading of metaphysics, or perhaps even logic, if given a sufficiently wide sense.

There are, next, practical sciences like ethics which are designed to govern man's conduct in society, and finally productive sciences whose function it is to guide us in the creation of objects for use or artistic contemplation. Logic, it seems, fits into none of these. It is therefore not a science in the ordinary sense, but rather a general way of dealing with things which is in fact indispensable for science. It affords criteria for discrimination and demonstration and should be considered as a tool or instrument which is brought to bear on scientific enquiry. This is the meaning of the Greek 'organon' which Aristotle used when speaking of logic. The term logic itself was invented later by the Stoics. As to the study of the form of argument, this Aristotle called analytics, which literally means a setting free. What is thus set free for inspection is the structure of argument.

Though logic, then, has to do with words, it is not, for Aristotle, concerned with mere words. For most words are more or less fortuitous marks that stand for non-verbal things. Thus, logic is not the same as grammar, though logic may influence grammatical science. Neither is logic the same as metaphysics, for it is not so much about what is as about our way of knowing this. It is here that Aristotle's rejection of the theory of ideas is important. For someone who holds such a theory, logic in the restricted sense we are considering might be identified with metaphysics. Aristotle, on the contrary, held them to be distinct. His attempt at solving the problem of universals proceeds with the help of what we may call 'concepts' which at any rate do not live in a world other than ours. Finally, logic is not the same as psychology. This stands out especially well in the case of mathematics. The deductive order of Euclid's Elements is one thing, the tortuous mental writhings involved in the mathematical enquiry that brought this knowledge to light is quite another. The logical structure of science and the psychology of scientific enquiry are two distinct and separate things. So in aesthetics, the merits of a work of art have nothing to do with the psychology of production.

By way of introduction, a survey of logic must somewhere assess the structure of language and what can be said in it. In the Aristotelian organon this is dealt with in a work called the 'Categories'. Here, too, there is a beginning in Plato, as we saw in discussing the 'Sophist'. The Aristotelian discussion is however much more down to earth and more closely concerned with the facts of language. It distinguishes ten different general items that can be discerned in discourse. These are substance, quality, quantity, relation, place, time, position, state, action and affection. The first is substance, which is what any statement is about. The other categories cover the various sorts of statement that may be made of a substance. Thus, if we speak about Socrates, we may say that he has a certain quality, to wit that he is a philosopher. There is a certain amount of him, whatever the size may be. This answers to quantity. He stands in certain relations to other things and is located in space and time, and interacts with his surroundings by doing and suffering certain things. The theory of categories has had many distinguished successors as we shall see later, though in most cases these have been more metaphysically tainted than the linguistic study of Aristotle. This is particularly so with Kant and Hegel.

Categories are of course abstractions. They answer the most general questions that may be asked about anything. Aristotle considers that the categories are what words mean on their own. The meanings of words are objects of knowledge in a different sense from the import of judgements. In the former case, Aristotle would say, one has a direct apprehension. In modern linguistics this is sometimes expressed as 'having the concept of' whatever it might be. The sort of knowledge one has in the case of a true judgement is quite a different matter. Here concepts combine to signify a state of affairs.

$$\frac{A > B \quad B > C}{A > C}$$

One kind of relational argument. Aristotle did not recognise them

The logic of Aristotle is a first attempt to set out in systematic fashion the general form of language and argument. Much of it is inspired from sources in Plato, but this does not diminish its merit. In Plato, logical points arise here and there throughout the dialogues, and some particular issue might be taken up and dropped again as the mood of the moment dictates. Aristotle in a way did for logic what Euclid was shortly going to do for geometry. Aristotelian logic has reigned supreme until the 19th century. Like much else in Aristotle, the logic came to be taught in a fossilized condition by men who were so overawed by Aristotle's authority as not to dare question him. It is characteristic of most modern philosophers of the period of the revival that they were thoroughly dissatisfied with the Aristotelians of the schools. This has produced a reaction against everything connected with the name of Aristotle, which is unfortunate since much that is valuable can be learnt from him. In one important respect, however, the logic of Aristotle was seriously incomplete. It did not concern itself with relational argument which is especially important in mathematics. Take a simple example like A is greater than B, B is greater than C, therefore A is greater than C. The vital thing here is the transitive character of the relation 'greater than'. With some ingenuity this argument can be forced into the mould of syllogism, but in more complicated cases it seems hopeless. Even so, the relational character of the argument is lost from sight.

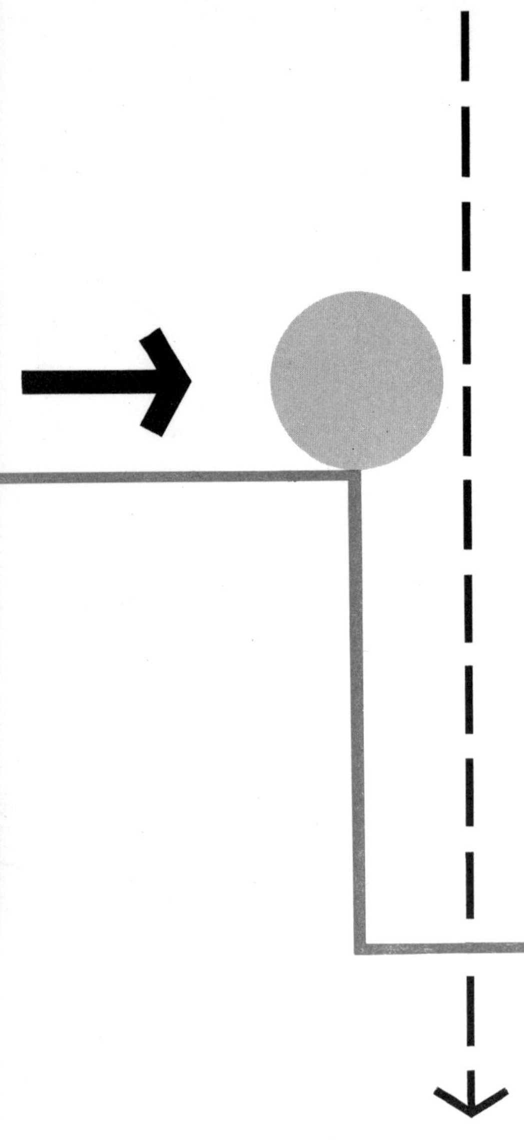

A material sphere, placed in a certain way, pushed off the step seeks a lower level: an example of Aristotle's four causes

We must now turn to a number of general problems which might be discussed under the heading of philosophy of nature. This is the title of the book in which they are principally discussed. The Greek word physics, it should be recalled, means nature. When Aristotle wrote he could look back on a long line of predecessors who had published works entitled 'On Nature'. From the time of Thales everyone who thought he had at last discovered the true workings of the world had written in this vein. Physics nowadays connotes something rather more specific, though these more general questions do intervene. Until not so long ago, it used to be called natural philosophy, a term which survives in the universities of Scotland. This is not to be confused with the philosophy of nature of the German idealists, which is a kind of metaphysical aberration in physics. Of this we shall learn more later.

One of the most important items here is Aristotle's theory of causality. This is connected with the theory of matter and form. In a causal situation there is a material aspect and a formal aspect. The latter is itself divided into three parts. There is first the formal aspect in the restricted sense, what might be called the configuration. Secondly we have the agent which actually sets off the change, as the pulling of a trigger sets off a rifle. Thirdly, there is the purpose or end which the change is striving to achieve. These four aspects are called the material, formal, efficient and final causes, respectively. A simple example will make this clear. Consider a stone tottering on the brink of a step, being pushed over the edge and about to fall. The material cause in this situation is the matter of the stone itself. The formal cause is the general lie of the land, to wit the step and the position of the stone on it. The efficient cause is whatever does the pushing. The final cause is the stone's desire to seek the lowest possible level, that is the attractive force of gravitation.

About material and formal causes little need be said. We do no longer speak of these as causes. They are necessary conditions in a causal situation in the sense that something has to be somewhere for anything to happen at all. As for efficient and final causes, both of these merit some comment. The efficient cause is what in modern terminology is called simply the cause. Thus, a stone falls from a step, because someone or something gives it a push. In physical science, this is the only kind of causality recognised. On the whole, the tendency in science is to try to establish explanations in terms of efficient causes. The notion of final cause is not admitted into physics nowadays, though vestiges of teleology survive in its vocabulary. Words like attraction and repulsion, seeking the centre and the like, are remnants of teleological notions and remind us of the fact that Aristotle's theory of causality was undisputed until some three hundred and fifty years ago. The trouble with final causality is very similar to the danger incurred in using the notion of potentiality which we discussed earlier. To say a stone falls because it has a tendency to fall is really to give no account at all. But here again there are occasions on which the terminology of ends does fulfil a reasonable purpose. In the field of ethics, for instance, it is not trivial to point to a goal as a cause for conduct or action of a certain kind. The same is true in the field of human activity in general. Present expectations of future events are motives for our actions. This is true of animals too, and there are cases when one might feel inclined to use this sort of talk even of plants. Clearly, then, finality is not merely trivial when we consider biological and social problems. It is from his biological interests that Aristotle derived the notion of final causes. In this context it becomes clear that potentiality and finality go together. The biologist is confronted with the question how a seed gives rise to the full-grown plant or animal. In Aristotelian terms, he would say that the acorn potentially contains the oak, and what turns it into a tree is the tendency to realise itself. This way of talking is of course an example of the trivial use of these notions. Quite generally, as a science develops, final explanations are replaced by accounts using efficient causes. Even psychology follows this trend. Psycho-analysis, whatever its merits or failings might be, tries to explain behaviour by means of what happened before rather than by what might yet befall.

The teleological view ultimately derives its force from the fact that our natural surroundings appear to display some sort of order. Causal necessity, which is connected with efficient causality, seems to be a blind force whose operation does not account for this order. Teleology, on the other hand is as though informed with foresight. Here, again, the biological order might well incline one in favour of a teleological view. But in any case, Aristotle recognises the operation of both necessity and finality. It is clear that on such a basis natural science was not going to prosper. The science of physics in particular suffered a serious setback which was not made good until with Galileo there came, in the field of method, a return to Plato. To a mathematician, the notion of finality is not so likely to occur as to a biologist, and we need not be surprised to find that Plato is free from it. Teleology is ultimately at fault in being anthropomorphic or theological. It is men who have purposes and pursue ends. Accordingly it is in this sphere that finality does make sense. But sticks and stones harbour no goals, and no good can come from trying to talk as though they did. With proper safeguards we may of course use the notion of tendency just as we saw was possible with potentiality.

Necessity is blind; in contrast Finality seems to have foresight

To say a stone has a tendency to fall means that given certain conditions it will fall. This, however, is not what Aristotle has in mind. For him finality is linked with purpose, and this he infers from the existence of order which to him indicates design. That on such principles the study of physical science cannot flourish is clear enough. For if the enquirer's curiosity is soothed with sham explanations, then real accounts of natural phenomena will not be forthcoming. In the field of astronomy, in particular, Aristotle did grave disservice to science. The theory of finality which assigned to everything its proper place led him to make a distinction between the sublunary regions and what lies beyond the moon. The two parts are held to be governed by different principles. This entirely fanciful speculation is rank lunacy when compared with the advanced astronomy of the Academy. The real damage was however done by those who would not treat Aristotle in a critical manner, accepting him wholly instead of rejecting what was bad, thus bringing him generally into disrepute.

Another general topic which is discussed in natural philosophy is space, time, and motion. The last of these we have already mentioned in connection with change. Aristotle's procedure here is worth noting. Where the Eleatics found insuperable difficulties in trying to construct an account of motion, Aristotle approaches the question from the other end. Movement does occur, and this must be our starting point. Taking this for granted, the problem is to give an account of it. To apply a modern distinction here, Aristotle stands out as an empiricist as against the Eleatic rationalists. The point is not without importance, especially since it is often wrongly believed that there is something unreliable and untidy about the empirical procedure. In the case of motion, for instance, Aristotle maintains the view that there is continuity, and this is a perfectly sensible thing to do. It is then possible to go on to find out what this continuity involves, but it is not possible to manufacture continuity out of the discontinuous. This latter point is often overlooked by mathematicians who from the time of Pythagoras have hoped to build a mathematical world out of nothing. While an analytic theory of continuity can be constructed in a purely logical manner, its application to geometry depends on a postulate of continuity.

Place and time are treated in a similar way by Aristotle: all places are within other places, all times within other times

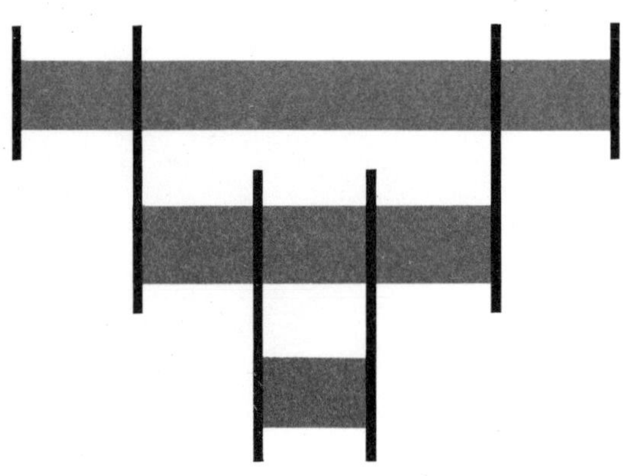

The case of movement we considered earlier was change of quality. There are two other kinds of movement, change of quantity and change of place. These are the only three categories under which movement may fall. On Aristotle's theory, it is not possible to reduce all change to movement of particles as the atomists do. For it is not possible to reduce one category to another. Here again, the Aristotelian view is on the side of empiricism, while the atomists, who, as we saw, are heirs of the Eleatic tradition, think in terms of the rationalist principle of reduction.

On space and time, the theory of Aristotle has much in common with modern views. That there is such a thing as position Aristotle infers from the fact that different objects may at different times occupy the same space. One must therefore distinguish space from what is in it. In order to determine the location of an object we may begin by specifying a region in which it is, and this is then progressively narrowed down until we come to its proper place. Proceeding in this manner, Aristotle defines the place of a body as its boundary. This, on the face of it, is a rather meagre conclusion to have reached in what might seem so formidable a problem. However, in analysing this kind of question the outcome is often surprisingly simple and down to earth. Moreover, anodyne as such solutions appear, they always carry some interesting consequences. In the present case we conclude that it makes sense to ask of any object where it is, but it is nonsense to ask where the world is. All things, that is, are in space; but the universe is not. For it is not contained in anything, it is in fact not a thing in the sense in which chairs and tables are. We can thus quite confidently tell anyone who wishes to travel to the ends of the world that he is setting out on a wild goose chase. It should perhaps be mentioned that in his analysis of place or location Aristotle is not providing a theory of space in the sense in which mathematicians or physicists might. What he is doing is more akin to linguistic analysis. The two are however not unrelated. If we can analyse the meaning of location, this will evidently help us to improve our understanding of statements about space.

In opposition to the atomists, Aristotle holds that there is no void. For this view he advances a number of arguments all of which are unsound. The most interesting of these is a reductio ad absurdum starting from the fact that in a medium the speed of bodies varies according to the density of the medium and the weight of the body. From this he concludes first that in a void bodies should move with infinite speed,which is absurd: all movement takes some time. Next, a heavier body should move faster than a lighter one, but in a void there is no reason why this should be. On these two counts he declares a vacuum to be impossible. The conclusions however do not follow from the premisses. It does not follow from the fact that in a rarer medium a body moves faster that in the void it will move infinitely fast. As to the other point, observation shows that in an evacuated space a light body does fall at the same speed as a heavy one. The Aristotelian misconceptions concerning the void were not clarified until some two thousand years later. All the same it is only fair to say that even in modern times scientists have felt uneasy about the void. They have filled it with peculiar matter like the aether, or more recently with distributions of energy.

Aristotle's discussion of time is very similar to his analysis of place. Events are within a sequence of times just as objects are within a sequence of places. Just as an object has a proper place, so an event has a proper time. With regard to continuity, Aristotle distinguishes three ways in which things may be ordered. First of all, they may be consecutive, one thing coming after another without any intervening term of the series being considered. Next, we may have things in contact, as when consecutive terms are adjacent, and finally the order may be continuous, when successive terms actually share their boundaries. If two things are continuous with each other they are also in contact, but the reverse does not follow. Likewise,two things in contact are also consecutive,but not the other way round.

Things are 1) consecutive, or 2) contiguous, or 3) continuous: if 2) then 1) but not vice versa, if 3) then 2) but not vice versa

With these preliminaries settled, we see that a continuous quantity cannot be made up of indivisible elements. Evidently an indivisible can have no boundaries, otherwise it can be further divided. If on the other hand the indivisibles have no size, it makes nonsense to speak of them as consecutive, adjacent or continuous. Between any two points of a line, for example, there are other points, and likewise between any two moments in a stretch of time there are other moments. Space and time are thus continuous and infinitely divisible. In this context, Aristotle proceeds to give an account of Zeno's paradoxes. The solution he provides is in fact correct, but misses the point of Zeno's arguments. As we have seen, Zeno did not put forward a positive theory of his own but rather set out to show that all was not well with the Pythagorean theory of units. His Eleatic preconceptions set aside, he might well have agreed with Aristotle.

The detailed scientific theories of Aristotle need not concern us here. Though he did some good work, especially in biology, his record is marred by extravagancies no pre-Socratic would have countenanced.

The soul's rational, sensitive, nutritive faculties; man has three, animals two, plants one

We have seen earlier that final causes may with some plausibility be sought in ethics. It is from this field that teleology is derived in the first place. The good, for Aristotle, is that towards which all things strive. Since he rejects the theory of ideas we shall of course not find a form of the good. He notes the fact that the word good has various different uses which cannot all be brought under one head. Nevertheless, the good in any of its manifestations is ultimately derived from the goodness of God. It is thus neither so very different nor so far removed from the theory of ideas as might at first appear. This sort of vacillation is found throughout Aristotle's philosophy. On one side he breaks away from the Academy and on the other he seems to come back to it. In some cases, as in the present, it is possible to separate the two sides and consider the first on its own merits. The analysis of the uses of the word good provides some valuable distinctions that may sometimes be overlooked. This is interesting but does not take us very far, though some modern linguistic analysts would say that nothing remains to be done beyond this point. In this they are perhaps a little rash. For they fail to do justice to the wide and popular spread of some kinds of nonsense. Truth is after all not a matter of majority decisions. As to the metaphysical status of God, this for Aristotle is quite an impersonal matter. God is the unmoved prime mover who gives the world its original impulse. This task performed, he ceases to take an active interest in the world, and certainly does not watch the doings of mankind. It is a colourless philosopher's God, an adjunct to the theory of causality.

In order to grasp the drift of Aristotle's ethics we must say something about his theory of the soul. From Plato he borrows the tripartite division. He speaks of the nutritive, sensitive and rational soul. The first of these belongs to all living things, they all have a metabolism, as we might put it. Sensitivity belongs to animals and men but not to plants, whereas reason is peculiar to the human race. It is only at the rational level that ethics intervenes. Plants merely vegetate and animals merely live like animals. The soul, giving unity to the body, is form to its matter. It does not survive death in a personal sense, though reason as such is immortal.

The ethical question arises when we ask what is the end of human life. Aristotle sees it in the wellbeing of the rational soul, and this in turn connotes for him a life of active rational activity, informed with virtue and pursued with continuity. Virtue, on the Aristotelian theory, is thus a means to an end. This end is of course not achieved by everyone to the same extent, but it is nevertheless the highest goal a man may reach. As with Socrates, the theoretical life is the best.

It is important to understand that this does not, to a Greek of Aristotle's time, imply seclusion from the world and a turning away from its affairs. In the first place, the ethical life involves activity, though this should be disinterested. Thus, the theoretical life is not the reason why the experimental method fell into abeyance, though in Aristotle the emphasis is on a contemplative review of truth already gathered rather than on new discovery. This raises a difficulty which he overlooks, for in order to have something to assess, one must make an initial intellectual effort, and who is to say when an adequate measure of it has been spent? The truth of the matter is that enquiry cannot be limited in this way. In the second place, the good citizen must fulfil his civic duties and perform various services, both in peace and war. The ivory tower conception of philosophy is due to the Stoics. It was their turning away from the world of sense that caused the drying up of the scientific movement.

In connection with the moral virtues, or virtues of character, Aristotle puts forward the theory of virtue as a mean. In each case there may be a deficiency or a surfeit neither of which constitute proper conduct. Virtue is somewhere between these extremes. Thus, steadfast courage is neither rash aggressiveness nor timid withdrawal. The theory of the mean is inspired by the doctrine of attunement which goes back to Pythagoras and Heraclitus. Aristotle proceeds to give a picture of the man who has all the virtues, the man with the great soul. This gives us a fair picture of the kind of thing that was generally held to be admirable in the comportment of citizens at that time. The result, in sum, is somewhat overpowering, though the absence of false modesty is rather refreshing. A man should not overestimate his worth, but likewise he should not belittle himself. But in the end the magnanimous man must be a very rare specimen if only for the fact that most men never have the opportunities of exercising all these virtues. As with Socrates and Plato, the emphasis tends to be on an ethical élite. The doctrine of the mean is not altogether successful. How, for instance, is one to define truthfulness? This is recognised as a virtue; but we can hardly say that it is halfway between telling big lies and little lies, though one suspects that in some quarters this view is not unpopular. In any case such definitions do not apply to the intellectual virtues.

Virtue a mean between extremes: Composure, the mean between aggressiveness and subservience

Of the good and evil that men do Aristotle holds that action is voluntary, except where there is compulsion or ignorance. As against the Socratic view he allows that one may act deliberately in an evil manner. Along with this he develops an analysis of the meaning of choice, a problem that could of course not arise in the theory which holds that no one ever sins wilfully.

In his theory of justice, Aristotle adopts the distributive principle, which operates in Socrates' definition in the 'Republic'. Justice is done if everyone receives his fair portion. The inherent difficulty in such a view is that it does not provide a basis for deciding what is fair. What are to be the criteria? Socrates at least insists on one criterion which seems reasonably objective, to wit the measure of education. This is a view which is largely in force with us today, though during the Middle Ages it was not. The question of deciding what is fair must evidently be resolved somehow if the theory of justice is to be applied.

Finally, we must mention Aristotle's views on friendship. To live the good life one must have friends to consult and lean on as circumstances might require. Friendship, for Aristotle, is an extension of self-esteem to others. It is in your own interest that you must love your brother as you love yourself. Here, as in general, Aristotle's ethics suffer from being somewhat smug and self centred.

Two things strike us from the outset when we come to consider Aristotle's political theory. First, we note that in politics argument is of necessity teleological, and Aristotle is quite aware of it. Secondly, there is an almost exclusive concentration on the city state. As to the latter, Aristotle simply did not grasp that the days of the Greek city state were fast running out in his own lifetime. Macedonia was taking over the leadership in Greece and, under Alexander, went on to conquer an empire, but the political problems of such an organisation do not interest Aristotle. There are, it is true, a few pale references to the Great King, Egypt and Babylon, but such minor barbarian excursions only sharpen the contrast. The Greek city state, for Aristotle, exhibits political life in its highest form; what goes on abroad is barbarism of one kind or another.

The teleological approach, which we have seen elsewhere, is used from the beginning. Associations are formed in order to pursue some end. The state, being the greatest and most comprehensive of these, must pursue the greatest end. This is of course the good life of the Ethics and is achieved in a community of a certain size, namely the city state, formed by the banding together of smaller groups which in turn are based on the household or family. It is natural for man to live as a political animal because he strives after the good life. No ordinary mortal is so self-sufficient that he can live alone. Aristotle goes on to discuss the problem of slavery and says that throughout nature we find a dualism of the superior and the inferior. The cases of body and soul, man and animals, spring to mind. In such circumstances it is best for both sides that there should be ruler and ruled. Greeks are naturally superior to barbarians and it is therefore in order for foreigners to be slaves, though not for Greeks. In a way this is already a recognition that slavery cannot in the end be justified. Every barbarian tribe will no doubt consider itself superior and treat the question from its own point of view. Indeed, this the semi-barbarians from Macedonia were then doing.

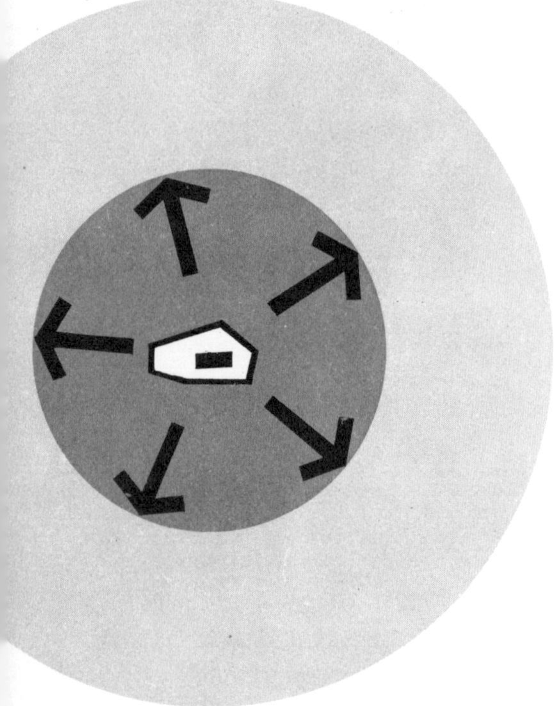

Aristotle's ideal state: it must be within sight from a hill top

In his discussion of wealth and the means of acquiring it, Aristotle brings out a distinction which came to exercise great influence during Medieval times. A thing is said to have two values. The first of these is its proper value, or value in use, as when a man wears a pair of shoes. The second is value in exchange; and this gives rise to a kind of unnatural value, as when a pair of shoes is exchanged not for some other commodity for immediate proper use, but for money. Money has certain advantages in that it constitutes a compact form of value which can be carried more easily, but it has disadvantages in that it acquires a kind of independent value of its own. The worst example of this is when money is lent at a rate of interest. Much of Aristotle's objection is probably due to economic and social prejudice. It will not do for a gentleman to indulge in money-making at the expense of cultivating the good life. What he overlooks is that without some financial resources it is impossible to pursue such aims. As for money-lending, the objection here is based on a rather narrow view of the function of capital. No doubt an impoverished freeman may fall into slavery through enlisting the help of a lender at a time when his own fortunes are on the decline, and to this one may quite properly object. But there are also constructive uses of capital to finance commercial ventures. This kind of money-lending may not have commended itself to Aristotle since large scale trade, especially with foreigners, was regarded as an unfortunate necessity.

Turning now to the discussion of the ideal state we find that its provisions are more mellow than those of the blue-print in the 'Republic'. In particular, Aristotle emphasises the importance of the family unit. In order to develop real affection there must be some restriction of the area in which it operates. To receive proper attention a child must be in the care of its own parents; purely communal responsibility in this sphere tends to produce neglect. The ideal state of the 'Republic' is altogether too monolithic. It overlooks the fact that within certain limits the state is a community of many different interests. We may note incidentally that if one recognises the plurality of interests there would be no need for royal lies. With regard to the ownership of land, Aristotle recommends that it should be private but its products should be enjoyed by the community. This amounts to a form of enlightened private ownership where the owner uses his wealth to the advantage of the community. What produces this spirit of responsibility is education.

In his conception of citizenship Aristotle adopts a rather narrow point of view. Only those men who are equipped not only to cast a vote but to take a direct and active part in the process of governing the state are to be called citizens. This excludes the vast mass of farmers and labourers who are deemed unfit to exercise political functions. The possibility of government by representation could not well occur to anyone at that time.

On the question of the various different types of constitution, Aristotle largely follows Plato's scheme in the 'Politicus'. He does however bring out the importance of wealth as against numbers. It does not matter whether the few or the many govern, but whether they do or do not command economic power. As to just claims to power, Aristotle recognises that all and sundry will demand power for themselves invoking the same principle of justice in each case. This is that equals should have equal shares and unequals not. The trouble is how to assess equality and inequality. Those who excel in one sphere often think themselves superior in everything. In the end the only way out of this impasse lies in the recognition of the ethical principle. Equality must be judged on the criterion of goodness. It is the good that should have power.

Northern and Eastern barbarian, a Greek in the middle: only Greeks combine Northern brawn with Eastern wit

After a long survey of the various types of constitution Aristotle reaches the conclusion that on the whole the best constitution is one in which there is neither too much nor too little wealth. Thus, the state with a preponderant middle class is the best and most stable. The causes of revolution and their prevention are next discussed. The basic cause is perversion of the principle of justice: because men are equal or unequal in some respects it does not follow they are so in all. Finally, there is an account of the ideal state. Its population must have the right size with the right skills, it should be taken in at a glance from a hilltop, and its citizens should be Greeks who alone combine the vitality of the North with the intelligence of the East.

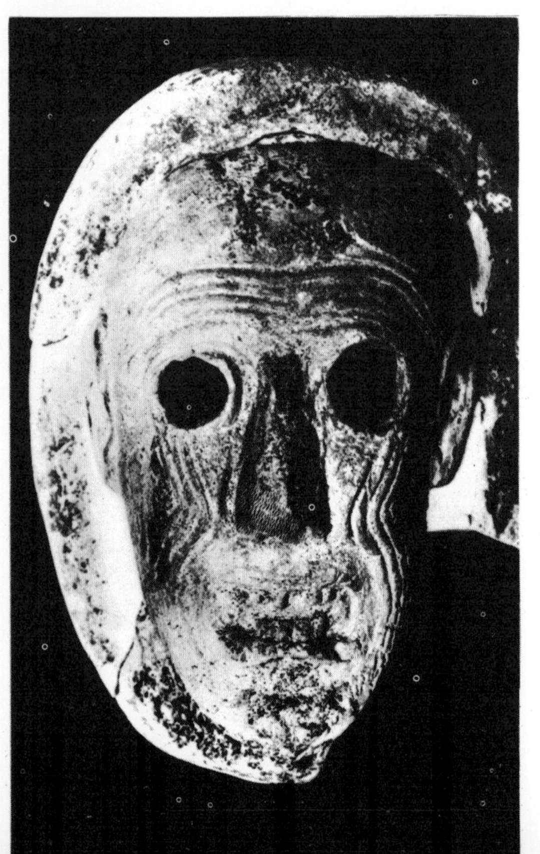

In conclusion, we must touch on a work which, though slender in size, has had great influence on the history of art criticism, particularly in the field of dramatic literature. This is Aristotle's 'Poetics', a book devoted chiefly to the discussion of tragedy and epic poetry. The word poetics itself, it should be noted, means literally a process of making things. In general it could therefore be used of any productive activity, but in the present context it is restricted to artistic production. A poet, in the sense this carries today, is a versewright.

All art, according to Aristotle, is imitative. His classification first separates painting and sculpture from the rest, leaving music, dancing and poetry in the modern sense as one group. The various ways in which imitation intervenes distinguish the different types of poetry from each other. What is meant by imitation is never actually explained. The notion is of course familiar from the theory of ideas, where particulars may be said to imitate universals. In Aristotle, imitation seems to imply an evoking by artificial means of sentiments that are like the real thing. The entire discussion seems to have been worked out with an eye on dramatic art, since it is in that field that the imitative principle is most naturally applied. This becomes even clearer when Aristotle goes on to speak of imitation of human action. The behaviour of men can be portrayed in three ways. We can show them precisely as they are, or we may aim at imitating either something above normal standards of conduct or something below it. By this means we can differentiate between tragedy and comedy. In tragedy, men are shown greater than life size, though not so far removed from us as to preclude our taking a sympathetic interest in their affairs. Comedy, on the other hand, shows men worse than they are, for it emphasises the ridiculous side of life. The farcical element in human character is held to be a defect, though not a particularly harmful one. We note here a certain running together of artistic values with ethical ones. This is a bias which comes from the 'Republic', where artistic assessment is closely linked to social and ethical criteria. Sheer villainy could never be aesthetically valuable, a limitation modern literary standards do not admit.

Aristotle next distinguishes between poetry that tells a story and poetry which presents an action. This sets aside epic from drama. The origin of dramatic art is to be found in the recitations connected with religious rites. It is clear that Greek tragedy began from certain incantations taking place at Orphic ceremonies. One possible explanation of the term itself is that it refers to a goat song, the animal being one of the symbols of Orpheus. Tragos is Greek for goat, and ode means song. In its earliest form tragic ceremony had a leader who spoke verses, and a responding crowd, much as in a religious function today. From this developed the first actor and the chorus, as Aristotle points out. Comedy, on the other hand arose from Dionysian revelry, as is indicated by the name which means a song of revels.

Epic poetry makes use of the same metre throughout, whereas tragedy has a variety, for different portions. But, what is more important, tragedy is more circumscribed in the setting of its scene. Aristotle does not put forward a clear-cut theory of unity of place, time and action. It is more a matter of practical limitations inherent in the two kinds of composition. A play must be performed at one sitting within a confined space, whereas an epic can be as long as you like and uses the imagination for a stage. Aristotle defines tragedy as the imitation of human action. It should be good, complete and of reasonable dimensions, and should produce in the beholder sympathetic feelings of fear and pity which thereby become purged from the soul.

As to completeness, Aristotle insists that a tragedy should have a beginning, a middle and an end. At first sight this does not seem to be a very informative pronouncement. What is meant is however quite sensible: a tragedy must have a plausible point of departure, develop in a rational manner and come to a conclusive issue. It must be complete in the sense of being self-contained. Size matters, for the mind falters if a piece is too long; if too short, it does not register.

The final cause of tragedy is the cleansing of the soul by a purging of the emotions. This is the meaning of the Greek word catharsis. It is through the experience of vicarious emotions of fear and pity that the soul can unload itself from this burden. Thus tragedy has a therapeutic purpose. The terminology here is borrowed from medicine. Where Aristotle's views are original is in suggesting a cure by a mild form of the complaint itself, a kind of psychiatric inoculation. In this account of the end of tragedy it must of course be taken for granted that fear and pity haunt us all, which is probably true.

Aristotle goes on to examine various aspects of a work of tragedy. The most important of these is the plot. Without it there can be no drama. In so far as it is through the plot that characters realise themselves, they are secondary to it. Potential character becomes actual in the plot. With regard to the action, two types of incidents are especially important. These are first a sudden reversal of fortune, and secondly the discovery of some unexpected circumstance bearing on the plot. These events should overtake a person not too outstanding in any of the virtues, and his downfall should be caused not by vice but by lack of judgement, which drags him from high position and influence and makes him an outcast. There are many examples of this kind of situation in Greek drama.

Of the treatment of character, Aristotle requires primarily that it should be true to type. As in the case of the plot, the characters must commend themselves as being lifelike. It is in this sense that one must take Aristotle's statement elsewhere that poetry deals with universal situations, whereas history describes the particular. In tragedy, we recognise general features of human life which give a theme to the work. It is of importance to note that what we might call the aspect of stage production, although mentioned by Aristotle, is regarded by him as of minor weight. This places the emphasis almost entirely on the literary quality of a work. He may well have considered tragedy fit for reading as much as for stage performance. The 'Poetics' does not provide a full-blown theory of art and of beauty. But it sets out with clarity a number of criteria which have greatly influenced literary criticism ever since. Above all, there is a refreshing absence of talk about authors' feelings and intentions, and a concentration on the works themselves.

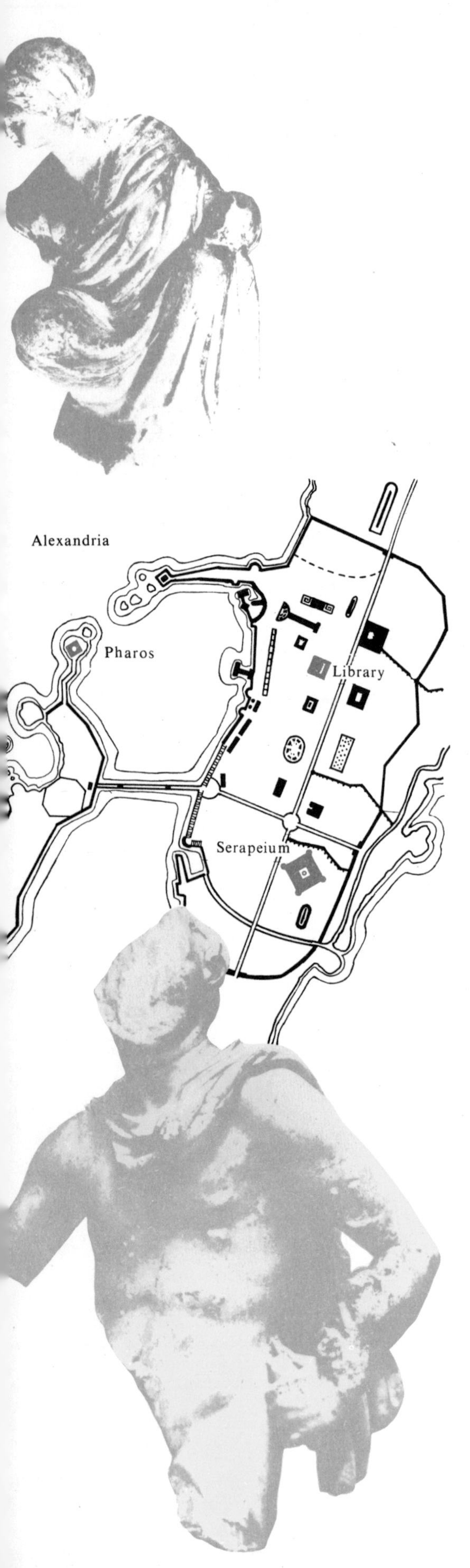

We have seen that Greek philosophy is coeval with rational science. It lies in the nature of the case that philosophic questions arise at the border lines of scientific enquiry. In particular this is true of mathematics. Since the time of Pythagoras, arithmetic and geometry have played a vital part in Greek philosophy. There are several reasons why mathematics is especially important here. First of all, a mathematical problem is clear cut and simple. This does not mean it is always easy to solve, it need not be simple in this sense. But ordinary problems in mathematics are simple when one compares them with questions in physiology, for example. Secondly, there is an established mode of procedure in demonstration. We must of course remember that someone had to find this out to begin with. Generality of proof and demonstration are precisely Greek inventions. In mathematics the function of proof stands out more clearly than in most other sciences, even though what really goes on in a mathematical demonstration has often been argued about and frequently misunderstood. Thirdly, the conclusions of a mathematical argument, once properly understood, do not admit of doubt. This much is of course true of the conclusion of any valid argument whose premisses are accepted. The point of mathematics is that it is part of the procedure that you do accept the premisses, whereas in other fields one always compares conclusions with facts, for fear that one of the premisses might have been wrong. In mathematics there are no facts outside itself which call for comparison. Because of this certainty, philosophers of all times have usually allowed that mathematics affords knowledge of a kind superior and more reliable than is to be gathered in any other field. Many have said that mathematics is knowledge and have denied this description to any other information. To use the language of the 'Republic', we might say mathematics belongs to the realm of forms and therefore yields knowledge, where other fields deal in particulars of which at best opinion is to be had. The theory of ideas owes its origin to Pythagorean mathematics. In Socrates it was expanded into a general theory of universals, while with Plato it is confined once more to the field of mathematical science.

Towards the end of the fourth century, the centre of mathematical activity moves to Alexandria. The city had been founded by Alexander in 332, and rapidly became one of the foremost trading communities in the Mediterranean. Standing as it does at the gateway to Eastern lands, it provided a point of contact between the West and cultural influences from Babylonia and Persia. A large Jewish community grew up in a short period and became rapidly hellenized. Scholars from Greece built up a school and a library which became famous throughout antiquity. There was no other collection of books to rival the holdings of Alexandria. Unfortunately, this unique source of ancient science and philosophy fell to the flames when Julius Caesar's legions took the town in 47 B.C. It is at this time that much material on the great writers of the classical period was irretrievably lost. No doubt much of lesser value also burnt. This reflection affords some minor consolation when libraries are gutted.

The best known of Alexandrian mathematicians is Euclid, who taught round about 300 B.C. His Elements remain one of the greatest monuments to Greek science. Here is set out, in deductive fashion, the collected geometrical knowledge of the time. Much in Euclid is not of his own invention. But to him is due the systematic presentation of the subject. The Elements have been throughout the ages an example which many have striven to attain. When Spinoza set out his ethics 'more geometrico', it was Euclid that served as the model, and the same is true of Newton's Principia.

One of the problems that, as we saw, was tackled by the later Pythagoreans was the construction of irrationals as limiting values of sequences of continued fractions. Nevertheless, a full arithmetical theory of this problem was never formulated. As a result of this, an account of proportions could not be worked out in arithmetical terms. For it remained impossible to give an irrational, or unmeasurable, number a numerical name. With lengths, the matter is different. Indeed, the difficulty was first discovered in the attempt to give a number to the hypotenuse of an isosceles right-angled triangle of side one unit long. It was, therefore, in geometry that a fully fledged theory of proportions emerged. Its inventor, it seems, was Eudoxus, a contemporary of Plato. The form in which the theory has come down to us is found in Euclid, where the whole matter is set out with admirable clarity and rigour. A final return to arithmetic occurs with the invention, some two thousand years later, of analytic geometry. When Descartes assumed that geometry can be handled by means of algebra he was, in fact, pursuing the scientific ideal of Socratic dialectic. In destroying the special hypotheses of geometry he found more general principles on which to base it. This is precisely the aim that was pursued, with what measure of success we shall never know, by the mathematicians of the Academy.

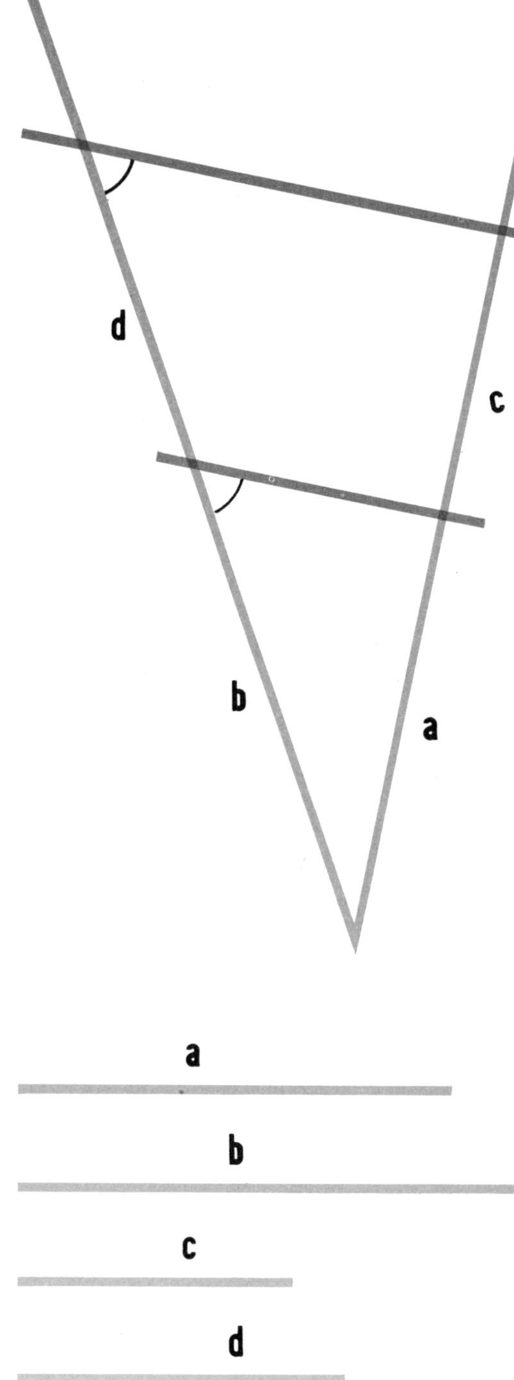

The theory of proportions, as expounded by Euclid of Alexandria

The Elements of Euclid are pure mathematics in the modern sense. Conforming in this to the traditions of the Academy, the mathematicians of Alexandria pursued their researches because they were interested in the problems. Nowhere is this more clearly apparent than in Euclid. There is not the slightest trace of a suggestion that geometry might be useful. Moreover, to master such a subject required long application. When Euclid was asked by the King of Egypt to teach him geometry in a few easy lessons, he made the famous retort that there is no royal road to mathematics. Yet it would be wrong to imagine that no use was made of mathematics. It would be equally wrong to think that mathematical problems do not often spring from practical problems. But it is one thing to delve into the origins of some particular theory and quite another to treat it on its own merits. These two concerns are often not sufficiently distinguished. It is pointless to cavil at Euclid because he pays little heed to the sociology of mathematical discovery. This is something he is simply not interested in. Given a certain body of mathematical knowledge, however this may have grown, he proceeds to deal with it and puts it into a rigorous deductive order. This is a scientific exercise that does not depend for its validity on the state of the nation or indeed on anything else. These same remarks indeed apply to philosophy itself. It is no doubt the case that the conditions of the times draw men's attention to certain problems now rather than earlier or later, but this in no way alters the merit or otherwise of the theories put forward to meet them.

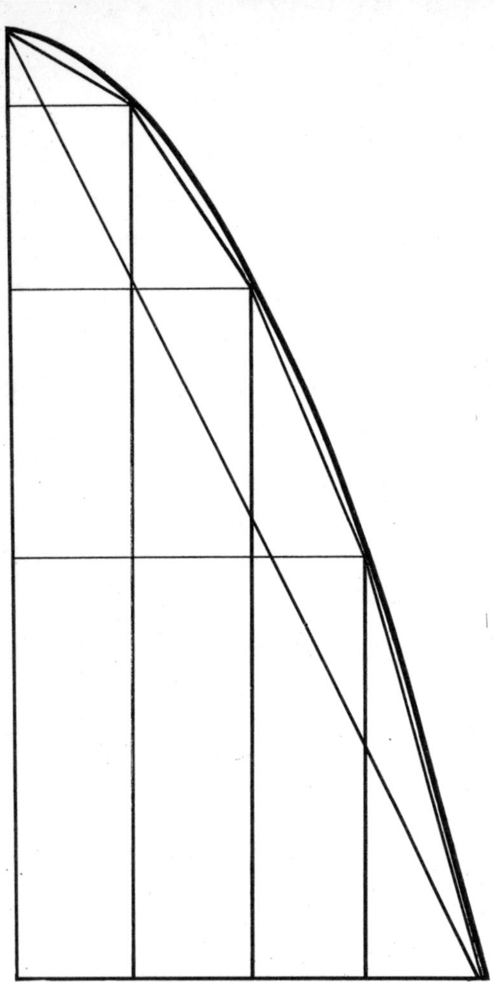

Archimedes used the method of exhaustion to square parabolas, a forbear of integral calculus

Another invention attributed to Eudoxus is the so-called method of exhaustion. This is a procedure used to calculate areas bounded by curves. The aim is to exhaust the space available by filling it with simpler figures whose areas can be readily found. In principle this is precisely what happens in integral calculus, of which the method of exhaustion is really a precursor. The most famous mathematician to use this method of calculation was Archimedes, who was not only great in the field of mathematics but was also an outstanding physicist and engineer. He lived in Syracuse, and, according to Plutarch, more than once his technical skills helped to preserve the city from being overcome by hostile armies. In the end, the Romans conquered the whole of Sicily and with it Syracuse. The city fell in 212 and during the sack Archimedes was killed. Legend has it that a Roman soldier stabbed him to death as he was busy working out some geometric problem on a patch of sand in his garden.

Archimedes used the method of exhaustion to square the parabola and the circle. For the parabola, the inscribing of an infinite sequence of smaller and smaller triangles leads to an exact numerical formula. In the case of the circle, the answer depends on the number π, the ratio of circumference to diameter. As this is not a rational number, the method of exhaustion can be used to work out approximations of it. By inscribing and circumscribing regular polygons of increasing number of sides, we approximate the circumference more and more closely. The inscribed polygons are always less in perimeter than the circle, the circumscribed ones always more, but the difference becomes smaller and smaller as the sides grow in number.

The other great mathematician of the third century was Apollonius of Alexandria, who invented the theory of conic sections. Here, too, we have another clear example of the destruction of special hypotheses. For a pair of straight lines, a parabola, ellipse, hyperbola and circle now all appeared as special cases of one and the same thing: the section of a cone.

In other fields of science, the most spectacular Greek successes probably belong to astronomy. Some of these we have mentioned already when discussing various philosophers. The most amazing achievement of this period is the discovery of the heliocentric theory. Aristarchus of Samos, a contemporary of Euclid and Apollonius, appears to be the first to have given a full and detailed account of this view, though it is possible that it was held in the Academy towards the end of the fourth century. At any rate, we have the reliable testimony of Archimedes that Aristarchus did hold this theory. We also find references to it in Plutarch. The gist of the theory was that the earth and the planets move round the sun which, together with the stars, remains fixed, the earth revolving on its own axis while it runs through its orbit. That the earth turns on its axis once a day was known already to Heraclides, a fourth century Academic, while the obliquity of the ecliptic was a fifth century discovery. The theory of Aristarchus was thus by no means an utter novelty. Nevertheless, there was some opposition and even hostility to this daring departure from the commonsense view of the time. It must be confessed that even some philosophers were against it, probably mainly on ethical grounds. For to remove the earth from the centre of things must surely break down moral standards. Cleanthes, the stoic philosopher, went so far as to demand the Greeks should indict Aristarchus for impiety. Eccentric opinions on sun, moon and stars are quite as dangerous at times as unorthodox views in politics. It appears that after this outburst Aristarchus voiced his opinions with somewhat greater diffidence. The view that the earth moves has since upset religious feelings on one other famous occasion, when Galileo upheld the Copernican theory. Copernicus, it may be noted, in effect merely revived or rediscovered the theory of the astronomer from Samos. A marginal entry of the name of Aristarchus in one of Copernicus' manuscripts puts this beyond doubt. As to the relative sizes and distances within the solar system, the results are not all equally successful. The best estimate of the sun's distance from the earth is roughly half the actual size. The moon's distance was worked out fairly accurately. The diameter of the earth was obtained to within fifty miles of the correct figure. This feat was due to Eratosthenes, who was librarian at Alexandria and an ingenious scientific observer. To determine the earth's circumference, he selected two points of observation that lay fairly nearly on the same meridian. One of these was Syene, on the tropic of cancer, where at midday the sun is in zenith. This was observed by the reflection of the sun in a deep well. Four hundred miles north, in Alexandria, it was merely necessary to determine the angle of the sun, which is easily done by measuring the shortest shadow of an obelisk. From this information, the circumference of the earth and the diameter are easily derived.

Much of this knowledge was soon forgotten, mainly because it clashed with the religious prejudices of the period. That even philosophers were guilty in this is really quite understandable. For the new astronomy threatened to subvert the ethic doctrine of the stoic movement. The impartial observer is inclined to remark that this shows stoicism is a bad doctrine and therefore should be upturned. But this is counsel of perfection, and those whose views are thus impugned will not give up their position without a fight. It is one of the rarest gifts to be able to hold a view with conviction and detachment at the same time. Philosophers and scientists more than other men strive to train themselves to achieve it, though in the end they are usually no more successful than the layman. Mathematics is admirably suited to foster this kind of attitude. It is by no means accidental that many great philosophers were also mathematicians.

In conclusion, it is perhaps worth emphasising that mathematics, besides the simplicity of its problems and the clarity of its structure, affords some scope for the creation of the beautiful. The Greeks, indeed, possessed a very acute sense of aesthetics, if the linguistic anachronism be allowed. The term aesthetics as used today was first coined by the 18th century German philosopher Baumgarten. At all events, the sentiment expressed by Keats in saying that truth is beauty is a thoroughly Greek conception. It is precisely the kind of thing a platonist may well feel in contemplating the geometrical proportions of a Grecian urn. The same holds of the structure of mathematical proof itself. Notions like elegance and economy in this field are aesthetic in character.

Eratosthenes found the earth's girth: with the sun in zenith, its angle to the normal elsewhere on the same meridian gives the answer

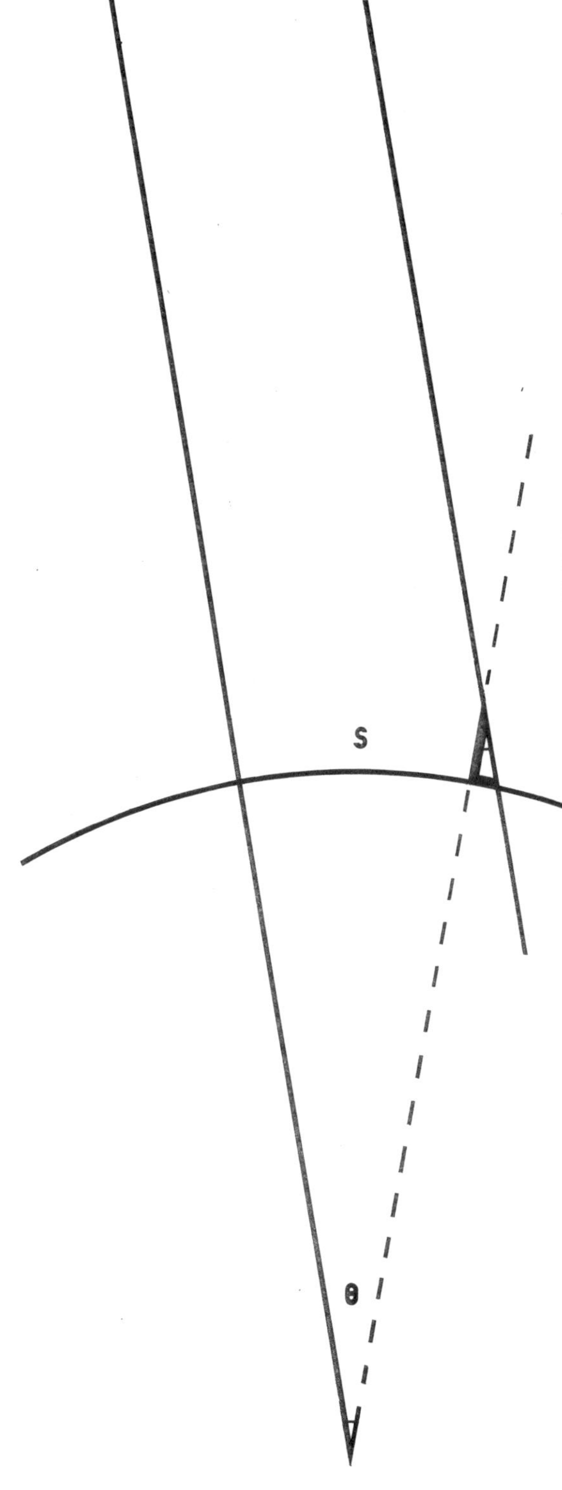

Hellenism

If the early fifth century B.C. had seen the Greeks fighting against the invading Persians, the early fourth showed that the Great King's empire was a giant on clay feet. For had not Xenophon proved that a small band of well-led and disciplined Greek soldiers could hold its own against the might of Persia, even within her own territories?

With Alexander the Great, the Greek world went over to the attack. In ten short years, from 334 to 324 B.C., the Persian empire fell to the young Macedonian conqueror. From Greece to Bactria, from the Nile to the Indus, the world for one brief spell came under the single rule of Alexander, who, though to the Greeks he was a Macedonian overlord, looked upon himself as the carrier of Greek civilisation. And so indeed he proved to be. He was not just a conqueror, but a coloniser as well. Wherever his armies had carried him he founded Greek cities run on Greek lines. In these centres of Greek life the original Greek or Macedonian settlers would fuse with local people.

Alexander at Issus, beating Darius. As his lands grew, Greek culture spread, from Nile to Indus: allegory of the Nile, Indo-Greek Buddha

Alexander encouraged his Macedonians to marry Asian women and was not shy himself to practice what he preached. For good measure he took two Persian princesses for wives.

As a state, the empire of Alexander was an ephemeral thing. After his death, his generals in the end divided the territory into three parts. The European, or Antigonid empire, fell to the Romans within little more than a hundred years. The Asiatic, or Seleucid kingdom, broke up and was taken over by the Romans in the West and the Parthians and others in the East. Egypt under the Ptolemies became Roman under Augustus. But as a carrier of Greek influence, the Macedonian conquest was more successful. Greek civilisation fairly poured into Asia. Greek became the language of the educated everywhere, and quickly developed into the common tongue for trade and commerce, much as English has done in recent decades. Around 200 B.C. a man could speak Greek from the Gates of Hercules to the Ganges.

The science, philosophy and, above all, the art of the Greeks was thus coming to bear on the old civilisations of the East. Coins, vases, architectural and sculptural remains and, to a lesser extent, literary influences, bear witness to this cultural invasion. Likewise, the East exerted a new influence on the West. This was, however, something of a step backward. For what seems to have caught the fancy of the

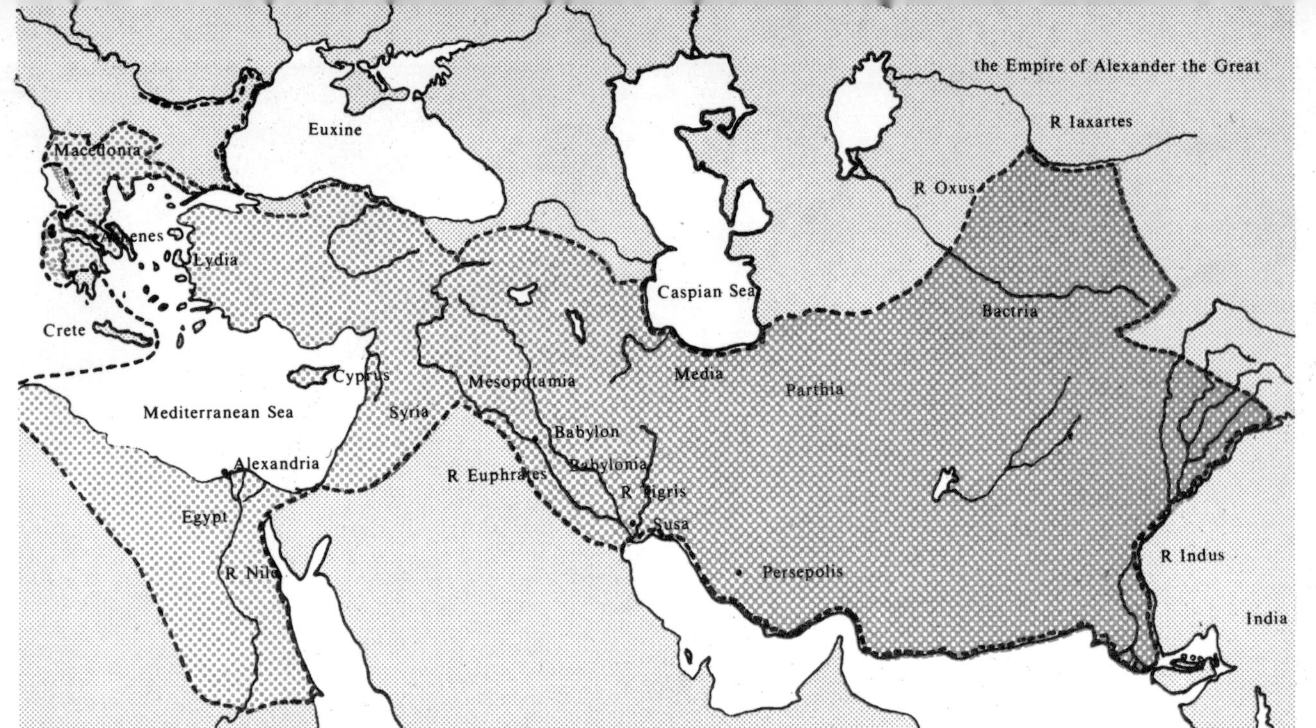

Three hellenistic Kings: Ptolemy I of Egypt, Demetrius Poliorcetus of Macedon, Seleucus I of Syria

Greeks more than anything else at that time was Babylonian astrology. Thus, for all its scientific and technical expansion, the hellenistic age was far more superstitious than the classical times had been. The same thing is recurring under our own eyes. When I was a young man, astrology was the preserve of some few unhinged cranks. Today, this disease is powerful enough to persuade those who control the popular press to carry columns on what is in the stars. Perhaps this is not to be wondered at. For until the Romans came, the whole hellenistic period was unchecked, unsettled and unsafe. The mercenary armies of warring factions infested the countryside from time to time. Politically, the new cities of Alexander lacked the stability of the older colonies which had traditional links with their metropolis. The general climate of the times lacked a feeling of security. Mighty empires had fallen, their successors were fighting for supremacy on a shifting scene. The transience of things was brought home to men in no uncertain fashion.

Roman coin of Janus, cruder than hellenistic coins of that time

Culturally, we find an increasing spread of specialisation. The great men of the classical period, as members of a city state, could turn their hands to many things, as occasion and circumstances might demand. The enquirers of the hellenistic world confined themselves to one specific field. The centre of scientific research shifted from Athens to Alexandria, the most successful of Alexander's new cities, the meeting place of scholars and writers from all over the world. Eratosthenes the geographer was for some time the chief librarian of the great library. Euclid taught mathematics, and so did Apollonius, while Archimedes had studied there. Socially, the basis of stable existence was being undermined by the growth of the slave population. A free man could not easily compete in fields where slaves were used to do the work. The only thing to do was to become a soldier of fortune and hope to be in on some lucrative plundering exploit. While the wider sphere of Greek influence had taught men ideals wider than that of the city state, there was neither a man nor a cause strong enough to rally the scattered remnants of Alexander's world.

The everlasting sense of insecurity brought with it a lack of interest in public affairs and a general decay of intellectual and moral fibre. The Greeks of old had failed to rise to the political problems of their time, the men of the hellenistic period failed likewise. In the end it fell to the organising genius of Rome to produce order from chaos and to transmit to later ages the civilisation of the Greeks.

A section of the Peutinger map; good roads helped Roman control

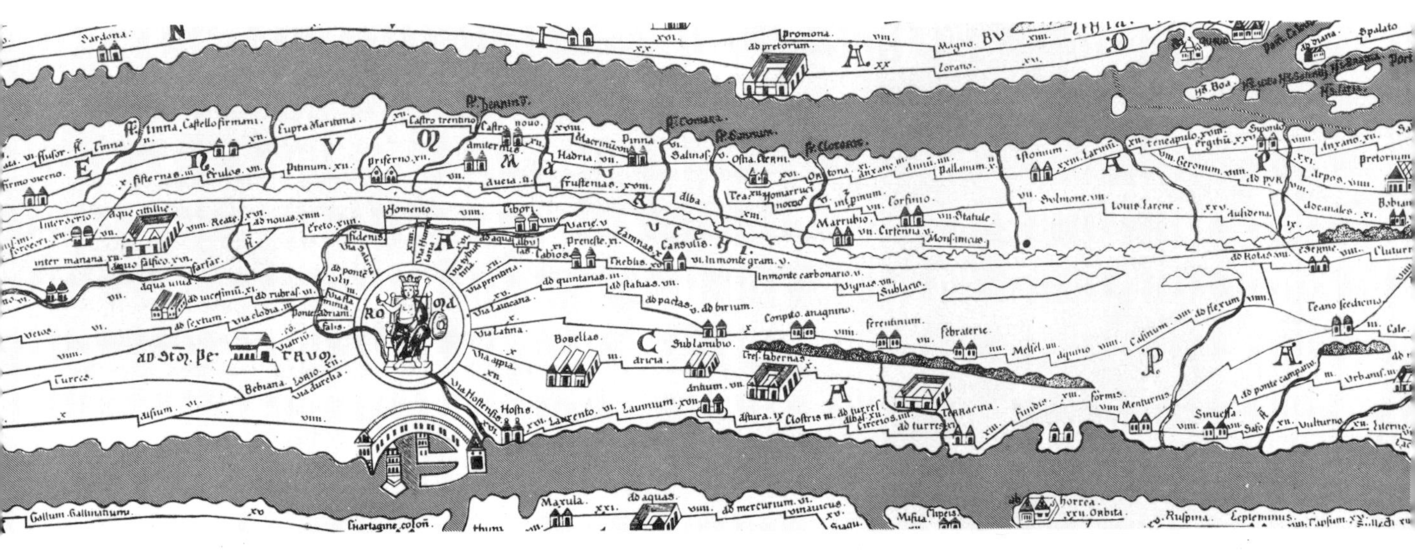

Antisthenes, logician from Megara

Diogenes, the cynic

Along with the passing of the golden age of city states, a general decline in freshness and vitality overtakes the Greek world. If there is one outstanding feature that all the great Athenian philosophers had in common, it is a boldly cheerful attitude to life. The world was not a bad place to live in, the state could be taken in at one glance. Aristotle, as we saw, had made this a feature of his ideal city.

As a result of Macedonian expansion this complacent outlook was shattered once and for all. In the philosophic trends of those days this reflects itself in an overall pessimism and sense of insecurity. No longer do we meet the self-assurance of citizen aristocrats like Plato.

In a sense it is the death of Socrates which marks the watershed of Greek culture. Though Plato's work was still to come, we are in fact descending into the plains of hellenistic culture. In philosophy a number of new movements are beginning to emerge. The first of these is linked directly with Antisthenes, one of Socrates' disciples. His name is associated with a paradox in the Eleatic tradition. According to this, it is impossible to make significant statements. A is A, which is true but not worth saying, or A is B, where B is not A, and this must needs be false. No wonder Antisthenes came to lose faith in philosophy. In his later years he renounced his upper class life and background and took to leading the simple life of the common people. He rebelled against the customs of his time and wished to turn back to a primitive life untrammelled by the conventions and restrictions of the organised state.

One of his disciples was Diogenes, a native of Sinope, a Greek colony on the Euxine. From him the new movement derived its label. Diogenes lived a life as primitive as a dog, which earned him the nickname of 'cynic', meaning dog-like. Legend has it that he lived in a tub and that Alexander once came to visit the famous man. The young Macedonian asked him to utter a wish and it would be granted. 'Stand out of my light' was the reply, and so impressed was Alexander that he retorted, 'Were I not Alexander, I would be Diogenes'.

The burden of cynic teaching was a turning away from worldly goods and a concentration on virtue as the only good worth having. This is clearly one of the strains of socratic doctrine. As a reaction to world events it is a somewhat negative approach. It is true that the weaker one's ties the smaller becomes the likelihood of being hurt or disappointed. But from such sources no further inspiration can be expected. The cynic doctrine in due course grew into a widespread and powerful tradition. During the third century B.C. it had great popular support throughout the hellenistic world. This, of course, merely means that a form of debased cynic teaching happened to reflect truly the ethical conditions of the times. It was a kind of opportunistic attitude to life, taking with both hands when there were things to take, yet not complaining when times were lean, enjoying life when it could be enjoyed, but accepting the whims of fortune with a shrug of the shoulder. It is from this development of the doctrine that the word 'cynical' acquired its uncomplimentary tinge of meaning. But cynicism as a movement was not a sufficiently deliberate affair to last as such. Its ethical content came to be absorbed by the stoic school, of which we shall speak a little later.

Another, rather different product of the period of philosophic decline was the sceptic movement. Literally, a sceptic is just a doubter, but as a philosophy, scepticism raises doubt to the rank of a dogma. It denies that anyone could ever know anything with certainty. The trouble, of course, is that one would like to know whence the philosophic sceptic gathers this piece of information. How does he know that this is the case if his position explicitly denies the possibility of knowledge? This is a criticism applicable as soon as the dubiety of our opinions is made into a principle. As a healthy reminder that it pays to be cautious, there is of course nothing wrong with it.

The first philosophic sceptic was Pyrrho, a citizen of Elis, who had seen the world with Alexander's armies. Sceptic doctrines were not a new thing, for, as we saw earlier, doubt had been thrown upon the reliability of the senses by the Pythagorean and Eleatic schools, whereas the sophists had introduced similar notions as a basis for their social and ethical relativism. But none of these thinkers had made a central issue of doubt as such. When 17th and 18th century writers speak of Pyrrhonian philosophers, it is to sceptics of this kind that they refer. Of Pyrrho himself next to nothing is known, but his disciple Timon appears to have denied that first principles of deduction could ever be attained. Since the Aristotelian account of scientific argument relies on first principles, this was a serious attack on the followers of Aristotle. It explains why the scholastic Middle Ages were so hostile to Pyrrhonian philosophy. The Socratic account of the method of hypothesis and deduction is not affected by the sceptic onslaught. Philosophically, the revival of learning in the 17th century was a turning away from Aristotle and a return to Plato.

Forms of design relax along with decaying intellectual standards

After Timon, who died in 235 B.C., scepticism, too, ceased to be an independent school. Instead, it was absorbed by the Academy, which preserved a sceptic bias for nearly two hundred years. This was, of course, a distortion of the Platonic tradition. True enough, we find passages in Plato which out of context look like a giving up of all attempt at constructive thinking. The dialectic puzzles in the 'Parmenides' spring to mind. But dialectic, in Plato, is never an end in itself. Only if it is misunderstood in this way can it be twisted in a sceptical sense. Still, in an age which was becoming submerged in superstition, the sceptics did perform a valuable service as debunkers. By the same token, however, they might well decide to go through the motions of some superstitious rites without feeling inwardly committed. It is because of this completely negative outlook that, as a system, scepticism tended to bring forth amongst its devotees a generation of half-baked scoffers who were clever rather than sound.

During the first century B.C., scepticism once more became an independent tradition. Lucian, the satirist of the second century A.D., and Sextus Empiricus, whose works are extant, belonged to later scepticism. But the temper of the times ultimately demanded a more definite and comforting system of beliefs. The growth of a dogmatic outlook gradually overshadowed the sceptic philosophy

When one compares the philosophic speculations of the hellenistic age with that of the great Athenian tradition and its precursors, one is forcibly struck by the wan and tired look of the age of decadence. Philosophy to the thinkers of old had been an adventure, requiring the alertness and courage of the pioneer. Later philosophy too may be said to have drawn on the courage of its practitioners, but it is now the courage of resignation and patient endurance rather than the boisterous valour of the explorer. In an age where the framework of the old society had crumbled, men sought peace, and if they could not easily secure this commodity, they made a virtue out of putting up with hardships that could not be eschewed. This is nowhere more clearly evident than in the philosophic school of Epicurus.

Born in 342 B.C., of Athenian parents, Epicurus at the age of eighteen came from Samos to Athens and shortly afterwards went to Asia Minor, where he came under the spell of the philosophy of Democritus. When just over thirty, he founded a school, which from 307 B.C. until his death in 270 B.C. functioned in Athens. The school lived as a community in his house and grounds, seeking as far as possible to isolate itself from the rush and strife of the outside world. All his life, Epicurus was dogged by minor ailments which he trained himself to bear without flinching. The central aim of his doctrine is the attainment of an undisturbed condition of peacefulness.

The prime good for Epicurus is pleasure. Without it the good life is impossible. The pleasures in question include those of the body as much as those of the mind. The latter consist in the contemplation of bodily pleasures, and are not in any vital sense superior. Still, since we have greater control over the direction of our mental activities, we can in some measure select the objects of our contemplation, whereas the affections of the body are largely imposed on us. Here lies the only advantage of pleasures of the mind. On this view the virtuous man is circumspect in the pursuit of his pleasures.

This general theory gives rise to a conception of the good life quite different from that of Socrates and Plato. The whole tendency is away from activity and responsibility. Socrates did, of course, consider the theoretic life as the best of all. But this did not mean complete detachment and aloofness. On the contrary, one of the duties of the elite is precisely to take an active part in the conduct of public business. Plato, too, was strongly imbued with this sense of duty. The philosopher who has emerged from the cave must go back and help free those less gifted with insight than he. It was this conviction that led him into his Sicilian ventures. In Epicurus, none of the vitality of living remains. He does indeed distinguish between active and passive pleasures, but gives the latter pride of place. An active pleasure is experienced in the striving for some pleasurable end under the motive power of desire for the thing that is wanting. The goal once attained, a passive pleasure is achieved in the absence of any further desire. It is an anaesthetic revelling in a state of satiety.

One can understand that this kind of prudential ethic commended itself to a period weary of the uncertainties of life. As an account of the Good it is, however, very onesided. It overlooks, amongst other things, the fact that the absence of desire or feeling is a feature precisely of the active pursuit of enquiry. Socrates was fundamentally right in holding that knowledge was a Good. It is in disinterestedly striving for understanding that we achieve the kind of unselfconscious alertness that Epicurus is seeking.

His temperament as a man did, however, lead Epicurus into being less consistent than his somewhat austere opinions might suggest. For he valued friendship above all else, even though this can evidently not be counted amongst passive pleasures. That epicurean came to be a byword for luxurious living is due to the fact that Epicurus was much maligned by his stoic contemporaries and their successors, who despised what seemed to them the grossly materialistic outlook of the Epicurean doctrine. This is all the more misleading for the circumstance that the Epicurean circle really led a frugal existence.

Epicurus; his atomic theory of the soul supersedes immortality

Following Democritus' atomism, Epicurus was in this sense a materialist. He does not, however, adopt the view that the motion of atoms is rigidly governed by laws. As we have pointed out before, the notion of law is in the first place derived from the social sphere and only later came to be applied to the happenings of the physical world. Religion, likewise, is a social phenomenon, and in the notion of necessity these two lines of thought seem to cross. It is the gods who are the ultimate lawgivers. In his rejection of religion, Epicurus was thus bound to dismiss the rigid rule of necessity as well. The atoms of Epicurus are therefore allowed a certain measure of capricious independence, though once a certain process was under weigh, its further course was in accordance to laws, as in Democritus.

As for the soul, that simply was a special kind of material, whose particles were intermingled with the constituent atoms of the body. Sensation is explained as the impinging of emanations from objects upon the atoms of the soul. When death supervenes, the soul atoms lose their connection with the body and are scattered, surviving as atoms but no longer capable of sensation. In this way Epicurus shows that fear of death is irrational, because death itself is not something that we can experience. Though he is violently opposed to religion, Epicurus allows that the gods exist. However, we are neither better nor worse off for their existence. Themselves superb practitioners of Epicureanism, they take no interest in the concerns of men.

They mete out neither reward nor punishment. In sum, it behoves us to steer a course of prudence and moderation with the aim of achieving a state of unruffled equilibrium, the supreme of pleasures and therefore the highest Good.

Unlike other schools, Epicureanism did not develop a scientific tradition. Its freethinking attitude and its opposition to superstitious practices continued to be respected by a select few amongst the upper classes of the early Roman Empire, though even on the ethical side it was gradually displaced by Stoicism. Only one other outstanding name figures in the Epicurean tradition, that of the Roman poet Lucretius who lived from 99 to 55 B.C. In a famous poem entitled 'De rerum natura' he sets forth the Epicurean doctrine.

Zeno the Stoic

The most influential philosophic movement which flourished in hellenistic times is Stoicism. Less rigidly bound to the soil of metropolitan Greece than the great schools of Athens, it drew some of its most famous representatives from the East and later from the Roman West. The founder of the movement was a Phoenician Cypriot by the name of Zeno. The date of his birth is uncertain but falls within the second half of the fourth century B.C. The commercial activities of his family first took the young man to Athens, and there he developed an interest in philosophy. He abandoned trade and eventually set up a school of his own. He used to lecture in the Stoa Poikile, which means a covered hallway painted in many colours. It is after this building that the doctrine was called Stoicism.

The stoic philosophy spans a period of some five centuries. During that time, its doctrines underwent considerable changes. What holds the movement together, however, is its ethical teaching which remained much the same throughout. This aspect of stoicism has its origin in the socratic way of life. Courage in the face of danger and suffering, indifference to material circumstances, these are virtues that the stoics valued. It is this emphasis on endurance and detachment that has given the word stoic its modern meaning.

Stoicism, as an ethical theory, is a somewhat colourless and austere discipline when set over against the theories of the classical age. As a doctrine, however, it succeeded in gaining wider adherence than the doctrines of Plato and Aristotle. It may be that Plato's emphasis on knowledge as the supreme good did not easily commend itself to men who stood in the midst of a life of action. At all events, it was the stoic doctrine which seemed to capture the imagination of the hellenistic kings and rulers. Whether this was enough to achieve the results that Socrates had hoped for in saying that philosophers must become kings and kings philosophers is, of course, more doubtful.

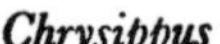

Chrysippus

Little survives of the work of the earlier stoics except in fragments, though it is possible to piece together a reasonable account of their doctrines. Zeno's own preoccupations seem to have been mainly ethical. One of the principal issues which remained a central interest throughout stoic philosophy is the great problem of determinism and free will, a philosophic question which has remained sufficiently alive to attract the attention of philosophers down the ages to our own day. According to Zeno, nature is strictly ruled by law. His cosmological theory appears to be inspired in the main by presocratic views. The original substance, according to Zeno, is fire, as with Heraclitus. From this, the other elements are in course of time separated, somewhat after the manner of Anaxagoras' theories. In the end there supervenes a large-scale bonfire, everything returns into the pristine fire and the whole thing starts all over again, as in Empedocles' theory of cycles. The laws in conformity with which the world runs its course emanate from some supreme authority which governs history in all its details. Everything happens for some purpose in a preordained manner. The supreme or divine agency is thought of not as something outside the world, but running through it, like moisture seeping through sand. God is thus an immanent power, part of which lives within each human being. This kind of view has become famous in modern times through the philosophical writings of Spinoza who was influenced by the stoic tradition.

The foremost good is virtue, which consists in living at one with the world. This is, however, not to be construed as a mere tautology, on the grounds that everything that is, is thus far forth at one with the world. It is rather a matter of a person's will being directed in such a way that it blends with nature instead of opposing it. Worldly goods are held to be of small account. A tyrant may deprive a man of all the external things he owns, even of life, but he cannot take from him his virtue, that is an internal inalienable possession. And so we reach the conclusion that on rejecting the false claims of external goods, a man becomes perfectly free, since his virtue, which alone matters, cannot be touched by outside pressure.

Admirable though some of these suggestions might be as precepts for dignified living, there are serious flaws in the doctrine as an ethical theory. For if the world is ruled by law it is of small avail to preach the supremacy of virtue. Those who are virtuous will be so because that is the way it had to be, and likewise for the wicked. And what are we to make of the Godhead which preordains evil? The suggestion made at one point in Plato's 'Republic', that God is the author only of what is good in the world evidently would be of little use here. Very similar objections face both Spinoza and Leibnitz, who try to turn the difficulty by holding that the human mind cannot grasp the necessity of things as a whole, but that in reality everything is arranged for the best in this best of possible worlds. But quite apart from the logical difficulties in the theory, there are, it would seem, plain factual mistakes. It is much to be feared that misery on the whole is not conducive to enhancing virtue or ennobling the soul. Besides, it is one of the melancholy discoveries of this progressive age of ours that with sufficient skill it is possible to break probably anyone, however strong his fibre. What is, however, very much to the point in stoicism is the recognition that in some sense the internal good of virtue is more vital than other things. Losses of material possession can always in some measure be repaired, but if one lose his self respect, he becomes less than human.

A stoa; Zeno taught in Athens in such a hall, whence Stoicism

The first systematic account of stoicism is said to go back to Chrysippus (280–207 B.C.), though his works have not survived. It is at this stage that the stoics took a more lively interest in logic and language. They formulated the theory of hypothetical and disjunctive syllogism, and discovered an important logical relation which in modern jargon is called material implication. This is the relation between two propositions when it is not the case that the first is true and the second false. Take the statement 'if the barometer falls, it will rain'. The relation between 'the barometer falls' and 'it will rain' is one of material implication. The stoics likewise invented the terminology of grammar which in their hands first became a systematic field of enquiry. The names of the grammatical cases is of stoic invention. The Latin translations of these, including the mistranslation of a Greek term into 'accusative', have come down from the Roman grammarians and are still used today.

The stoic doctrines gained ground in Rome through the literary activities of Cicero, who had studied under the stoic philosopher Posidonius. This Greek from Syria had travelled widely and contributed to many fields. His astronomical researches we have mentioned earlier. As a historian he carried on the work of Polybius. His philosophic position contained a fair measure of the older Academic tradition, at a time when the Academy itself had come under sceptic influence as we have already seen.

Although philosophically the later exponents of stoicism are less important, the writings of three of them have been very fully preserved and quite a lot is known about their lives. Though their social stations differed enormously, their philosophies are very much the same. Seneca, the Roman senator of Spanish origin, Epictetus, the Greek slave who had gained his freedom under Nero, and Marcus Aurelius, the emperor of the second century A.D., all of them alike wrote ethical essays in the stoic strain.

 Seneca, Roman Senator and Stoic

Seneca was born in 3 B.C. or thereabouts, and belonged to a well-to-do Spanish family that had come to live in Rome. He entered politics and in due course rose to ministerial office. His fortunes suffered a temporary setback under Claudius, a somewhat anodyne individual who at the request of Messalina, his wife, sent Seneca into exile in 41 A.D. The senator, it seems, had been a trifle too free in criticising the even freer mode of life of his empress, who some years later was indeed overtaken by a rather sudden end. Claudius' second wife was Agrippina, the mother of Nero. In 48 A.D. Seneca was recalled from his Corsican refuge to undertake the education of the imperial heir. The Roman prince was not a hopeful target for the pedagogic exertions of the stoic philosopher. But Seneca himself was far from leading the kind of life that might have been expected from one who preached the stoic ethic. He gathered a massive fortune, largely through lending money at exorbitant rates to the inhabitants of Britain. This may have been one of the grievances which led to the rebellion in the British province. Luckily it now takes more than high interest rates to goad Britons into a revolutionary frame of mind. As Nero became more autocratic and insane, Seneca once more fell into disgrace. In the end he was invited to commit suicide on pain of execution. This he did in the manner of the time by slashing his veins. Though his life had not on the whole been stoic in character, his manner of death was true to his philosophy.

Epictetus was a Greek, born probably in 60 A.D. His very name reminds us that he had been a slave, for it means the acquired one. From ill-treatment suffered during his early days of servitude he retained a lame leg and a general debility of health. On gaining his freedom, Epictetus began teaching in Rome until 90 A.D., when Domitian expelled him along with other stoics because they were critical of the Emperor's tyrannical rule and constituted a moral force set against the imperial throne. His last years were spent in Nicopolis, in the north west of Greece, where he died in about 100 A.D. Through his pupil Arrian some discourses of Epictetus have been preserved. In them we find the stoic ethic set out much along the lines explained above.

If Epictetus was born a slave, the last of the great stoic writers was on the contrary an emperor. Marcus Aurelius, who lived from 121 to 180 A.D., had been adopted by his uncle, Antoninus Pius, one of the more civilised among Roman emperors, as the epithet indeed suggests. Marcus Aurelius succeeded to the throne in 161 A.D. and spent the rest of his life in service to the Empire. The times were troubled by natural and military disturbances, and the Emperor was incessantly engaged in curbing barbarian tribes whose inroads upon the imperial borders were beginning to threaten Roman supremacy. The burden of office lay heavy on him, but he considered it his duty to sustain it. The state being endangered from within as well as without, he took such measures as seemed to help maintain order. He persecuted the Christians, not from malice, but because their rejection of the state religion was a troublesome source of dissidence. In this he was probably correct, though at the same time persecution is always a sign of weakness on the part of the persecutor. A society firmly established and confident of itself has no need to persecute heretics. The 'Meditations' of Marcus Aurelius, written in Greek like the discourses of Epictetus, have come down to us in their entirety. They are a diary of philosophic reflections, recorded, as time might permit, during moments of rest snatched from military duty or public business. It is worth noting that in spite of subscribing to the general stoic theory of the Good, Marcus Aurelius held a view of public duty which is more in line with that of Plato. Man being a social creature, it behoves us to play our part in the body politic. This underlines on the ethical plane the difficulty about free will and determinism we have hinted at earlier. For we have seen that on the general stoic view a man's virtue or vice is a private matter which does not affect others. But on the social view of man, the ethical qualities of each can have a very definite effect on everyone else. Had the Emperor taken a laxer view of his duties, there would undoubtedly have been far more strife than existed already. No very convincing solution of this difficulty was ever produced by stoicism.

On the question of first principles, which was a problem left over from the time of Plato and Aristotle, the stoics developed a theory of innate ideas, clear and self evident starting points from which the deductive process could begin. This view dominated the philosophy of the Middle Ages and was adopted by some modern rationalists as well. It is a metaphysical cornerstone of the Cartesian method. In its conception of man, the stoic doctrine was more generous than the theories of the classical age. Aristotle, we may recall, had gone so far as to admit that a Greek should not be a slave to his fellow countryman. Stoicism, taking its lead from Alexander's practice, held that in a sense all men were equal, even though during imperial times slavery existed on a more massive scale than ever before. Following this line of thought, stoicism put forward the distinction between natural law and the law of nations. By natural right here is meant the kind of thing a man is entitled to precisely because of his human nature. The doctrine of natural rights had some beneficial influence on Roman legislation in mitigating the lot of those who were deprived of full social status. It was revived for similar reasons in the post-Renaissance period in the struggle against the conception of the divine right of kings.

Marcus Aurelius, Emperor and Stoic

A consul of the Republican era

Forum Romanum, the state's centre

While Greece herself had been the intellectual workshop of the world, she was unable to survive as a free and independent nation. Greek cultural traditions, on the other hand, spread far and wide and have left a permanent mark, at any rate on Western civilisation. The Middle East was hellenized through the influence of Alexander; in the West, Rome became the carrier of the Greek heritage.

Contact between Greece and Rome first occurred though the Greek colonies of Southern Italy. Politically, the campaigns of Alexander had not disturbed the countries west of Greece. At the beginning of the hellenistic period, the two important powers in this area were Syracuse and Carthage. Both fell to Rome in the course of the third century, as a result of the first two Punic wars. Spain was annexed during these operations. The second century saw the conquest of Greece and Macedonia. A third Punic war ended with the complete levelling of the city of Carthage in 146. In the same year Corinth received similar treatment at the hands of the Roman legions. Such wantonly ruthless acts of destruction were rather exceptional and found their critics at the time as in later ages. In this regard our own period is fast relapsing into barbarism.

During the first century B.C., Asia Minor, Syria, Egypt and Gaul were added to the territories of Rome, while Britain fell during the first century A.D. These successive conquests were not the result of a mere thirst for adventure. They were dictated by the search for a natural frontier which could be held without too much hardship against encroachments by hostile tribes beyond. In the early days of the Empire this goal had been reached: in the north, the lands of Rome were bounded by two great rivers, Rhine and Danube. Eastwards lay the Euphrates and the Arabian desert, in the south the Sahara and in the west the Ocean. In this setting, the Roman Empire lived in comparative peace and stability for the first two centuries of our era.

Politically, Rome had begun as a city state similar in many ways to those of Greece. A legendary period under Etruscan Kings was followed by a republic dominated by an aristocratic ruling class which controlled the Senate. As the state grew in size and importance, constitutional changes in the direction of democracy imposed themselves. While the Senate retained a good deal of power, the popular assembly came to be represented by tribunes who had a voice in affairs of state. The consulship, too, became in the end accessible to men of origin other than aristocratic. As a result of conquest and expansion, however, the ruling families gained immense fortunes, while the small freeholder was driven off the land by the use of slave labour on large-scale holdings owned by absent landlords. The Senate thus ruled supreme. A popular democratic movement, led by the Gracchi, towards the end of the second century B.C., did not succeed, and a series of civil wars eventually led to the establishment of Imperial rule. Octavian, the adopted son of Julius Caesar, finally restored order, was granted the title of Augustus, and ruled as Emperor, though democratic institutions were formally retained.

Cameo of Augustus Caesar

For some two hundred years after the death of Augustus in 41 A.D., the Roman Empire lived on the whole in peace. There were, it is true, internal troubles and persecutions, but they were not of such proportions as to upturn the foundations of Imperial rule. Warfare went on along the borders while Rome lived a placid, ordered life.

A Roman Legion's standard bearer

In the end, the army itself began to take advantage of its power, which it used to extract gold in return for the favour of its support. In this way emperors came to the throne with military backing, and likewise fell as soon as such support was withdrawn. For a time disaster was staved off by the energetic efforts of Diocletian (286–305) and Constantine (312–337), but some of the emergency measures adopted only helped to accelerate the decline. Large numbers of Germanic mercenaries fought on the side of the Empire. This, in the end, proved to be one of the reasons for its fall. Barbarian princes, trained in the arts of war by serving with the Legions of Rome, at length came to suspect that these their new won skills might be employed with greater gain if used in their own interests rather than for the benefit of their Roman masters. A short hundred years later, the city of Rome fell to the Goths. Something of the cultural heritage of the past did, however, survive through the influence of Christianity which under Constantine had been promoted to official state religion. In so far as the invaders became converts, the Church was able to preserve in some measure the knowledge of Greek civilisation. The Eastern Empire suffered a different fate. There, the Moslem invaders imposed their own religion and through their own culture transmitted the traditions of Greece to the West.

Culturally, Rome is almost entirely derivative. In its art, architecture, literature and philosophy, the Roman world imitates more or less successfully the great examples from Greece. Nevertheless, there is one sphere in which the Romans succeeded where Greece and even Alexander had failed. This is the sphere of large-scale government, law and administration. Here, Rome had some influence on Greek thought. We saw earlier that in matters of politics the Greeks of

Roman cavalry riding down Gauls

classical times had been unable to transcend the ideals of the city state. Rome, on the other hand, had wider visions, and this impressed itself on the historian Polybius, a Greek born about 200 B.C. who had fallen into Roman captivity. Like Panaetius the stoic, he belonged to a circle of men of letters which had gathered round the younger Scipio. Beyond this political influence, Rome could yield nothing that might inspire Greek thinkers with new ideas. Greece, for her part, though destroyed as a nation, was in the sphere of culture victorious over her Roman conquerors. Educated Romans spoke Greek, as until recently educated Europeans spoke French. The Academy at Athens attracted the sons of Roman nobility. Cicero was a student there. In every field the standards of Greece were being adopted, and in many respects the products of Rome are pale copies of Greek originals. Roman philosophy, in particular, is peculiarly barren of original thought.

The irreverent and inquisitive character of the Greek tradition, coupled with the decay of hellenistic times, did something to soften the old Roman virtues, especially when with the advent of overseas expansion great riches poured into the country. The genuinely Greek influence diminished in strength and became centred on some few individuals, especially amongst the aristocracy of the city of Rome. The non-Greek elements of hellenistic culture, on the other hand, grew stronger with time. The East, as we have noted earlier, supplied an element of mysticism which was on the whole less dominant in the civilization of Greece. In this way religious influences from Mesopotamia and further afield seeped through to the West, producing a vast syncretic ferment from which Christianity ultimately emerged supreme. At the same time, the mystic strain encouraged the spread of all kinds of superstitious beliefs and practices. As men became less satisfied with their earthly lot and less confident in their own powers, the forces of unreason gained ground. The Empire did, it is true, enjoy two centuries of peace, but the Pax Romana was not an era of constructive intellectual effort. Philosophy, as far as there was any, was in the stoic strain. On the political side this was an advance over the parochialism of the great classical thinkers. For stoicism preached the brotherhood of man. With Rome the ruler of the known world for several centuries, this stoic notion did acquire tangible significance. In its own way, of course, the Empire regarded the world beyond its borders with just as much condescension as might the Greek city states. There were some contacts with the Far East, but not enough to impress the Roman citizen with the fact that there were other great civilizations that could not simply be dismissed as barbarian. For all its greater breadth of outlook, Rome thus was subject to the same arrogance as her cultural forebears the Greeks. This astigmatism was inherited even by the Church, which called itself Catholic, or universal, though in the East there were other great religions whose ethic was at least as advanced as the Christian. Men still dreamt of universal government and civilisation.

The supreme role of Rome, then, has been one of transmitting a culture older than, and superior to, its own. This was achieved because of the organising genius of Roman administrators and the social cohesion of the Empire. The remnants of the vast network of

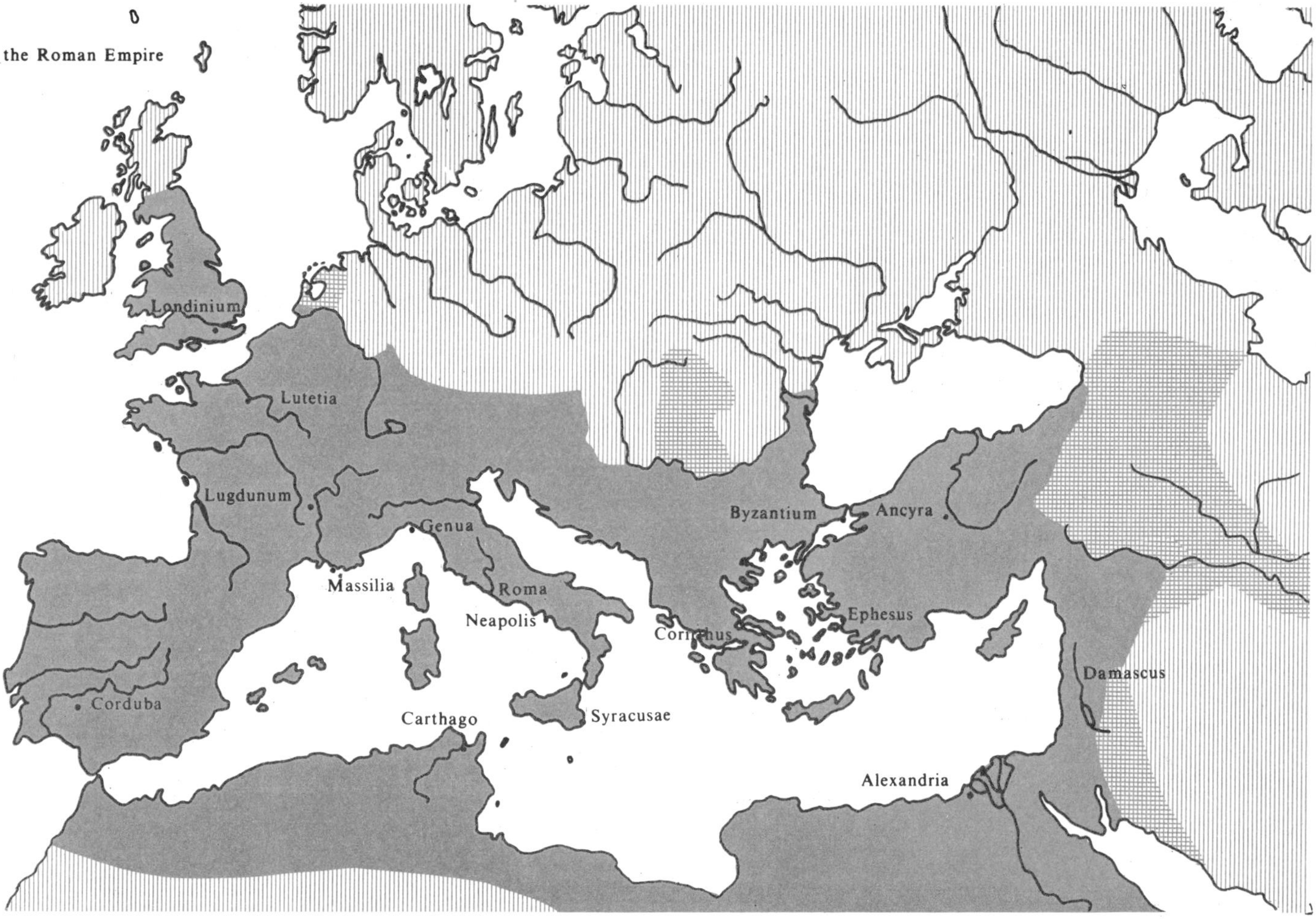

the Roman Empire

Londinium
Lutetia
Lugdunum
Genua
Massilia
Roma
Neapolis
Corinthus
Byzantium
Ancyra
Ephesus
Damascus
Corduba
Carthago
Syracusae
Alexandria

roads throughout Roman territories remind us of this great organising task. Roman expansion ensured that much of Europe should continue to function largely as one cultural unit, in spite of national differences and feuds that arose in later times. Not even the barbarian invasions were able to destroy this cultural basis beyond repair. In the East, the influence of Rome has been less lasting. The reason for this lies in the great vitality of the conquering Moslem Arabs. Where in the West invaders became absorbed within a tradition that owed much to Rome, the Middle East became almost completely converted to the religion of the conqueror. But the West owes to the Arabs much of its knowledge of the Greeks, which was transmitted to Europe by Moslem thinkers, especially through Spain.

In Britain, which was Roman for three centuries, the Anglo-Saxon invasions seem to have produced a complete break with Roman traditions. As a result of this, the great Roman legal tradition, which has survived everywhere else in Western Europe where Rome ruled, did not gain a hold in Britain. English common law to this day remains Anglo-Saxon. In philosophy, this has one interesting consequence worth noting. The scholastic philosophy of the Middle Ages is linked closely with the law, and philosophic casuistry was paralleled by a rigid and formal exercise of the old Roman tradition. In England, where Anglo-Saxon legal traditions were in force, philosophy, even at the height of the scholastic period, has mostly been of a more empirical temper.

Jupiter's Temple; Baalbek, in Syria

Plotinus, the Neo-Platonist

The syncretic tendencies which, under the Empire, worked in the field of religion were accompanied by a similar development in philosophy. Broadly speaking, the mainstream of philosophy during the early Empire was stoic, while the more cheerful doctrines of Plato and Aristotle had been somewhat supplanted. By the third century, however, a new interpretation of the old ethic in the light of stoic doctrine came to the fore, a move which was well in tune with the general conditions of the time. This amalgam of different theories came to be called Neo-Platonism and was to exercise great influence on Christian theology. It is, in a sense, a bridge from antiquity to the Middle Ages. With it, the philosophy of the ancients comes to an end, while medieval thought starts from this point.

Neo-Platonism arose in Alexandria, the meeting place of East and West. Here were to be found religious influences from Persia and Babylon, remnants of Egyptian rites, a strong Jewish community practising its own religion, Christian sects, and with it all a general background of hellenistic culture. The Neo-Platonic school is said to have been founded by Ammonius Saccas, of whom little is known. The most important of his pupils was Plotinus (204–270), the greatest of the Neo-Platonic philosophers. He was born in Egypt and studied in Alexandria where he lived until 243.

Being interested in the religions and mysticism of the East, he followed the Emperor Gordian III in a campaign against Persia. This enterprise did not, however, prosper. The Emperor was young and inexperienced, and somehow incurred the displeasure of his lieutenants. Such conflicts were at that time resolved in summary fashion, and the young Caesar met an untimely end at the hands of those he was supposed to command. Accordingly in 244 Plotinus fled from Mesopotamia, the scene of the murder, and settled in Rome, where he remained and taught until the end of his life. His writings are based on lecture notes from his later years, edited by his pupil Porphyry, who was somewhat of a Pythagorean. As a result of this, the works of Plotinus as they have come down to us are overlaid with a certain amount of mysticism, due perhaps to the editor.

Consisting of nine books, the extant works go under the title of the 'Enneads'. Their general tenor is platonic, though they lack both the scope and the colour of Plato's works, being almost wholly confined to the theory of ideas and some of the Pythagorean myths. There is in his work a certain detachment from the real world. This is not surprising when one considers the state of the Empire. It would take a man of utter blindness or else supreme fortitude to maintain an even temper of straightforward cheerfulness in face of the disorders of the time. A theory of ideas which treats the world of sense and its miseries as unreal is well suited to reconcile men to their fate.

The central doctrine of Plotinus' metaphysics is his theory of the trinity. This consists of the One, Nous, and Soul, in that order of priority and dependence. Before we go into this, let it be noted that for all the influence exerted on theology by this theory, it is not itself Christian, but Neo-Platonic. Origen, a contemporary of Plotinus who had studied under the same teacher, was a Christian and also put forward a theory of the trinity. This, too, put the three parts on different levels for which it was later condemned as heretical. Plotinus, as an outsider, was not thus marked for censure, and probably for that reason his influence until Constantine was greater.

The One of Plotinus' trinity is very much like the sphere of Parmenides, of which at best we may say 'It is'. To describe it in any other way would imply that there might be other things greater than it. Plotinus sometimes speaks of it as God, and sometimes in the manner of the 'Republic' as the Good. But it is greater than Being, omnipresent and nowhere, indefinable and pervasive. Of it one had better be silent than say anything, and in this we clearly see the influence of mysticism. For the mystic, too, takes refuge behind a barrier of silence and inability to communicate. It is in the last analysis the greatness of Greek philosophy to have recognised the central role of the logos. In spite of some mystical elements, Greek thinking is therefore essentially opposed to mysticism.

The next element in the trinity Plotinus calls Nous. It seems impossible to find an adequate translation for this. What is meant is something like spirit, not in a mystical but in an intellectual sense. The relation between Nous and the One is best explained by an analogy. The One is like the sun which provides its own light. Nous is then this light by which the One sees itself. It may, in a sense, be compared with selfconsciousness. By exercising our own minds in the direction away from sense we can come to know both Nous, and through it the One, of which Nous is the image. We see here a parallel to the notion of dialectic in the 'Republic', where a similar process is said to lead to vision of the form of the Good.

The third and final member of the trinity is called the Soul which is twofold in nature. In its inner aspect it is directed upwards to Nous; its outer manifestation leads down to the world of sense of which it is the creator. Unlike the stoic identification of God with the world, Plotinus' theory denies pantheism and goes back to the view of Socrates. But though Nature is considered as the downward emanation of Soul, it is not held to be evil as the Gnostics taught. On the contrary, the mysticism of Plotinus allows quite freely that Nature is beautiful, and as good as it is in the scheme of things that it should be. This generous outlook was not shared by later mystics and religious teachers, nor even philosophers. In their otherworldliness they came to curse beauty and pleasure as base and evil. How far such dire doctrines are ever practised by any but unbalanced fanatics is of course dubious in the extreme. Nevertheless, the inverted cult of ugliness did hold sway for many centuries. Christianity officially retains the quaint notion that pleasure is sinful.

Plotinus' Trinity: The One (E), Nous or 'Spirit', and lastly the Soul (Ψ). Christian theology owes it much

On the question of immortality, Plotinus adopts the view set out in the 'Phaedo'. A man's soul is said to be an essence, and as these are eternal so is the soul. This is parallel to Socrates' account, where the soul is said to be on the side of the forms. Nevertheless, Plotinus' theory has a certain Aristotelian element in it. Though the soul is eternal, it tends to merge in Nous, and therefore loses its personality even if not its identity.

We have now reached the end of our survey of Ancient philosophy. In the course of it we have spanned some nine centuries, from the time of Thales to that of Plotinus. If the line of division is set here, this is not to say that there have not been later thinkers that might properly be considered as belonging to the traditions of the Ancients. In one sense this is indeed true of all philosophy. Nevertheless, it is possible to discern certain major breaks in the development of cultural traditions. Such a point is reached with Plotinus. From now on, in the West at any rate, philosophy comes under the wing of the Church. This remains true even if there are exceptions, like Boethius. At the same time, it is well to keep in mind that when Rome fell there continued in Eastern parts, first under Byzantium and then Moslem rule, a philosophic tradition free from religious ties.

In looking back over the philosophic endeavours of the Ancient world, one is struck by the extraordinary power of the Greek mind in discerning general problems. Plato has said that the beginning of philosophy lies in puzzlement, and this capacity to be struck with wonder and amazement the Greeks of early times possessed to an unusual degree. The general notion of enquiry and research is one of the great Greek inventions that has shaped the Western world. It is of course always invidious to make comparisons between different cultures, but if one were to characterise Western civilisation in a single short phrase, one may well say that it is built on an ethic of mental enterprise which is essentially Greek. The other vital feature of Greek philosophy is that it basically aims at publicity. Its truths, such as they are, do not claim an aura of ineffability. From the beginning, great emphasis attaches to language and communication. There are, it is true, some mystical elements as well, and from quite early on. The Pythagorean mystical strain runs through the entire course of Ancient philosophy. But in a way this mysticism is really external to the enquiry itself. It tends much rather to govern the ethic of the enquirer. Only when decay sets in does mysticism assume a more important role. As we suggested in discussing Plotinus, mysticism is opposed to the spirit of Greek philosophy.

120 *Pre-Socratic Greek thinker*

One of the foremost problems which faced Ancient thinkers in a much more serious way than it does the moderns arose from the fact that, while we nowadays can fall back on the traditions of the past, no such support existed for the early philosophers of Greece. We largely take our philosophic, scientific and technological vocabulary from classical sources, often without fully appreciating their import. To the Greek enquirer everything remained to be done from the beginning. New ways of talking had to be forged and technical vocabularies invented, built up from the material provided by everyday speech. If therefore at times it seems to us that their ways of putting things are clumsy, we must remember that they were often groping for expression where the necessary tools were still in the making. Some effort of the mind is required to think oneself back into such a position. It is as though we had to do philosophy and science in Anglo-Saxon, cut off from Greek and Latin.

From the time we have reached, to the revival of learning and the emergence of modern science on the basis of a return to early sources, some twelve centuries had to elapse. It is perhaps an idle question to ask why this period of arrested development had to occur. Any attempt at answering it is bound to be oversimplified, Still, it is no doubt true that the thinkers of Greece and Rome did not succeed in evolving an adequate political theory.

If the failure of the Greeks had been due to a certain arrogance born of superior intellectual powers, the Romans failed from sheer lack of imagination. This heaviness of mind reveals itself in various ways, not least in the monumental architecture of Imperial times. The difference between the Greek and Roman spirit might well be symbolised by contrasting a Greek temple with a late Roman basilica. In Roman hands, the intellectual heritage of Greece becomes something rather less subtle and elegant.

The philosophic tradition of Greece is essentially a movement of enlightenment and liberation. For it aims at freeing the mind from the bonds of ignorance. It removes the fear of the unknown by presenting the world as something accessible to reason. Its vehicle is the logos and its aspiration the pursuit of knowledge under the form of the Good. Disinterested enquiry is itself regarded as ethically good; through it, rather than through religious mysteries, do men achieve the good life. Along with the tradition of enquiry we find a certain cheerful outlook devoid of false sentiment. For Socrates, the unexamined life is not worth living. Aristotle holds that what is important is not to live long but to live well. Some of this freshness, it is true, is lost in hellenistic and Roman times, when a somewhat more selfconscious stoicism gains ground. It remains none the less that all that is best in the intellectual framework of Western civilisation goes back to the traditions of the thinkers of Greece.

Constantine, who made Christianity the state religion.

Maxentius' Basilica, heavy in style

Early Christianity

In Graeco-Roman times, as today, philosophy was in the main independent from religion. Philosophers might, of course, ask questions which would also be of interest to those who were concerned with religious matters. But priestiy organisations had no influence on, or power over, the thinkers of those times. The intervening period from the fall of Rome to the end of the Middle Ages differs in this respect from both the preceding and subsequent eras. Philosophy in the West became an activity which flourished under the patronage and direction of the Church. For this there are a number of reasons.

Miniature of Boethius

Wisdom sitting in the Temple, from a Prudentius ms.

When the Western Roman Empire broke up, the function of the God-Emperors of Rome had already been split into two powers.

Since Christianity had become the state religion under Constantine, the Church had taken over all matters touching God and religion, leaving the Emperor to look after temporal affairs. The authority of the Church remained in principle undisputed, though it gradually declined, until the Reformation undermined its hold by insisting on the personal nature of man's dealings with God. Thereafter the churches became instruments of the rising national states.

While in the central parts of the old Empire secular traditions of learning lingered on for some time, the barbarian north had nothing to fall back on. Literacy thus came to be almost exclusively a mark of members of the Church, or clerics, an historical development whose memory survives in our modern word 'clerk'. What survived of the traditions of the past was preserved by the Church, and philosophy became a branch of learning designed to justify the dominion of Christianity and its guardians. So long as its tenets were on the whole accepted, the Church achieved and maintained a position of power and wealth. But there were other traditions which were striving for supremacy, the old Roman traditions through whose decline the Church had first risen into prominence, and the new Germanic tradition from which sprang the feudal aristocracies

St. Luke in his study

Aurelian walls of Rome, with the pyramid of Sestius

Pope Zacharias; a square halo is used to show him as still alive

Barbarian invaders

that took the place of the political organisation of the old Empire. However, neither of these was represented by a properly worked out social philosophy, and not least on this account they were unable successfully to challenge the power of the Church. The Roman tradition reasserted itself gradually from the Italian renaissance of the 14th century onwards, and the Germanic tradition broke through with the Reformation in the 16th century. But during the Middle Ages philosophy remains closely bound up with the Church.

Along with the replacement of the God-Emperor by the two powers of the Pope as God's representative on the one hand, and of the Emperor on the other, several other latent dualisms came to the fore. There is first of all the tangible reality of the dualism of Latin and Teuton. The power of the Church remained Latin, whereas the Empire fell to the teutonic descendants of the barbarian invaders. Until it fell under the attacks of Napoleon it was known as the Holy Roman Empire of the German nation. Next, we have the division of men into clergy and laity. The former were the guardians of the orthodox creed, and since the Church successfully withstood the impact of various heresies, at any rate in the West, the position of the clergy became greatly strengthened. Some of the Christian Emperors of the early period had been sympathetic to Arianism, but in the end orthodoxy won. Then there is the contrast between the Kingdom of Heaven and the various earthly kingdoms. The source of this is to be found in the Gospels, but it gains more direct importance after the fall of Rome. Though the barbarians might destroy the city, the City of God cannot be sacked. Finally, there is the opposition between the spirit and the flesh. This is of much older origin, going back to the socratic theories of body and soul. In their Neo-Platonic form these notions became central in the Pauline version of the new religion. It is from this source that the asceticism of early Christianity was inspired.

This, in bare outline, is the world in which what might for short be called Catholic Philosophy developed. It came to a first maturity in St. Augustine who was influenced mainly by Plato, and reached its peak in St. Thomas Aquinas who set the Church on an Aristotelian foundation which its chief apologists have defended ever since. Because this philosophy is so closely linked with the Church, an account of its development and its influence on later ages will involve what might at first appear to be more than a fair proportion of history. But some account of these events is necessary if we are to understand the spirit of the period, and its philosophy.

A Byzantine Emperor

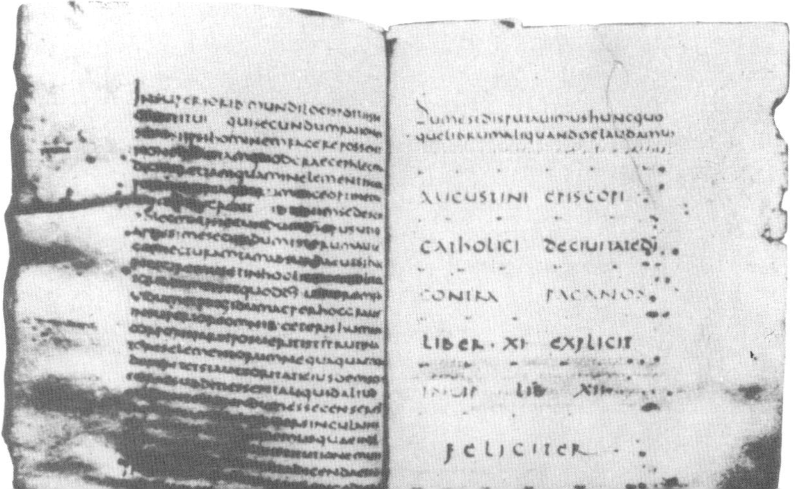

Page from Augustine's 'City of God'

Semitic deities, Babylonian idols

Christianity, which came to dominate the West, is an offshoot from the religion of the Jews, with certain Greek and Eastern admixtures.

With Judaism, Christianity shares the view that God has His favourites, though of course the chosen ones are different in the two cases. Both religions have the same view of history, starting with divine creation and moving towards some divine end. There were, it is true, some differences of opinion as to who was the Messiah, and what He was going to accomplish. For the Jews, the Saviour was still to come and would bring them victory on earth, whereas the Christians saw him in Jesus of Nazareth, whose Kingdom, however, was not of this world. Likewise, Christianity took over the Jewish conception of righteousness as a guiding principle of helping one's fellow man, and also the insistence on a dogma. Both later Judaism and Christianity subscribe to the essentially Neo-Platonic notion of another world. But while the Greek theory is philosophical and not readily grasped by everyone, the Jewish and Christian view was more one of settling accounts in the hereafter, when the righteous would go to heaven and the wicked burn in hell. The element of retribution in this theory made it universally intelligible.

To understand how these beliefs developed, we must remember that Yahweh, the God of the Jews, was in the beginning first and foremost the Deity of a semitic tribe Who protected His own people. Along with Him there were gods presiding over other tribes. There is not at this time any hint of another world. The Lord God of Israel directed the earthly fortunes of His tribe. He is a jealous God and will not suffer His people to have other gods besides Him. The prophets of old were political leaders who spent quite a lot of time on stamping out the worship of other gods, for fear of incurring Yahweh's dis-

Mt. Sinai, home of Yahweh, the invisible God of the Jews

pleasure and jeopardising the social cohesion of the Jews. This nationalistic and tribal character of the Jewish religion was enhanced by a series of national disasters. In 722 B.C. Israel, the northern kingdom, fell to the Assyrians, who deported most of its inhabitants. In 606 the Babylonians captured Nineveh and destroyed the Assyrian Empire. The southern kingdom of Judah was conquered by the Babylonian King Nebuchadrezzar who took Jerusalem in 586, burnt the Temple and led large numbers of Jews into captivity in Babylon.

Not until the year after Cyrus, the Persian king, had taken Babylon in 538 were the Jews allowed to go back to Palestine. It was during the Babylonian captivity that the dogma and national character of the religion hardened. Since the Temple was destroyed, the Jews had to dispense with sacrificial rites. Much of the traditional lore of their religion as it survives today goes back to this period.

Jewish captives in Babylon

Coin struck under the Maccabees

From this period, too, stems the dispersion of the Jews. For not all of them returned to their homeland. Those that did survived as a relatively unimportant theocratic state. After Alexander they managed somehow to hold their own in the long drawn out disputes between Seleucid Asia and Ptolemaic Egypt. An important Jewish population grew in Alexandria and in all but religion soon became completely hellenized. The Hebrew scriptures therefore had to be translated into Greek, giving rise to the Septuagint, so called because legend has it that seventy translators independently produced identical versions. But when the Seleucid King Antiochus IV tried to hellenize the Jews by force in the first half of the second century B.C., they rose in revolt under the leadership of the Maccabean brothers. With great courage and fortitude the Jews fought for the right to worship God in their own way. In the end they won and the family of the Maccabeans ruled as High Priests. This line of rulers is called the Hasmonean dynasty and governed until the time of Herod.

It was largely the successful resistance of the Maccabeans which, at a time when the Jews of the dispersion were becoming rapidly hellenized, ensured the survival of the Jewish religion, and thereby provided the conditions without which Christianity, and later Islam, could not have arisen. It is also at this time that the notion of another world hereafter creeps into the Jewish religion, since the events of the rebellion had shown that here below disaster often overtakes those first who are the most virtuous. During the first century B.C., beside the powers of orthodoxy, there developed, under hellenistic influence, a rather more mellow movement foreshadowing in its teachings the ethical reappraisal of the Jesus of the Gospels. Primitive Christianity is in fact a reformed Judaism, just as Protestantism was at first a movement of reform within the Church.

'No Gentiles in the precincts, on pain of death'; near the Temple gate

The triumph of Titus at Rome, Jewish captives and Temple spoils

Under Marc Antony, the rule of the High Priests was abolished and Herod, who was a thoroughly hellenized Jew, was appointed as King. After his death in 4 B.C. Judaea was directly governed by a Roman procurator. But the Jews did not take kindly to the Roman God-Emperors. Neither, of course, did the Christians. But unlike the Christians, who, in principle at least, subscribed to the practice of humility, the Jews on the whole were proud and disdainful, resembling in this the Greeks of classical times. Stubbornly they refused to recognise any but their own God. The advice of Jesus to give unto Caesar what is Caesar's and unto God what is God's, is a typical example of this Jewish recalcitrance. Though on the face of it a compromise, it is nevertheless a refusal to recognise the identity of God and Emperor. In 66 A.D. the Jews rose in revolt against the Romans, and after a bitter war Jerusalem was taken in 70 A.D. and the Temple destroyed a second time. The record of this campaign survives in the Greek of the hellenistic Jewish historian Josephus.

From this event derives the second and final dispersion of the Jews. As at the time of the Babylonian captivity, orthodoxy became more severe. After the first century A.D. Christianity and Judaism face each other as two distinct and antagonistic religions. In the West, Christianity aroused a fearful sentiment of anti-semitism so that the Jews from now on live at the fringe of society, persecuted and exploited, until their enfranchisement in the 19th century. It was only in Mohammedan countries, especially in Spain, that they flourished. When the Moors were finally expelled, it was largely through the polyglot Jewish thinkers of Moorish Spain that the classical tradition, along with the learning of the Arabs, was handed on to the clerics. In 1948 the Jews once more took possession of the Promised Land. Whether they will develop a new cultural influence of their own it is yet too early to say.

Arabesque, in synagogue at Toledo

Paul of Tarsus, sinner and saint, inventor of Christianity

The dissident Jewish sects which constituted primitive Christianity did not at first intend that the new creed should come to hold sway over gentiles. In their exclusiveness these early Christians maintained the old traditions. Judaism had never sought to convert outsiders, nor could it now, in its reformed condition, attract recruits so long as circumcision and ritual food restrictions were enforced. Christianity might have remained a sect of unorthodox Jews, had not one of its adherents set himself to broaden the basis for membership. Paul of Tarsus, a hellenised Jew and Christian, removing these external obstacles, made Christianity universally acceptable.

Still, to the hellenised citizens of the Empire it would not do that Christ should be the son of the God of the Jews. This blemish was avoided by gnosticism, a syncretic movement that arose at the same time as Christianity. According to gnosticism the sensible, material world was created by Yahweh, who was really a minor deity, having fallen out with the supreme godhead and thereafter practised evil. At last the son of the supreme god came to live among men in the guise of a mortal, in order to upturn the false teaching of the Old Testament. These, along with a dose of Plato, were the ingredients of gnosticism. It combines elements of Greek legend and Orphic mysticism, with Christian teaching and other eastern influences, rounding if off with an eclectic admixture of philosophy, usually Plato and Stoicism. The Manichaean variety of later gnosticism went so far as to equate the distinction between spirit and matter with the antithesis of good and evil. In their contempt for things material they went further than the Stoics had ever ventured. They forbade the eating of meat and declared sex in any shape or form to be altogether a sinful business. From their survival for some centuries it seems proper to infer that these austere doctrines were not practised with complete success.

The gnostic sects became less important after Constantine but still exercised a certain influence. The sect of the Docetics taught that it was not Jesus who was crucified, but some ghost-like substitute. One is reminded here of the sacrifice of Iphigenia in Greek legend. Mohammed, who allowed that Jesus was a prophet, though not as important a one as himself, later adopted the Docetic view.

As Christianity became more firmly established, its hostility to the religion of the Old Testament grew fiercer. The Jews, it held, had failed to recognise the Messiah announced by the prophets of old, and therefore must be evil. From Constantine onwards anti-semitism became a respectable form of Christian fervour, though in fact the religious motive was not the only one. It is odd that Christianity, which had itself been suffering appalling persecution, should, once in power, turn with equal ferocity on a minority which was just as steadfast in its beliefs.

In one respect, the new religion took a new and notable turn. The religion of the Jews is, on the whole, a very simple and untheological affair. This candidness survives even in the synoptic Gospels. But with John we find a beginning of that theological speculation which steadily grew in importance as Christian thinkers sought to accommodate the metaphysics of the Greeks within the framework of their own new creed. We are no longer concerned simply with the figure of the god-man Christ, 'the anointed one', but with his theological aspect as The Word, a conception which goes back through the Stoics and Plato to Heraclitus. This theological tradition found a first systematic expression in the work of Origen who lived from 185-254, in Alexandria. He had studied under Ammonius Saccas, the teacher of Plotinus, with whom he has much in common. According to Origen, God alone is incorporeal, in all his three aspects. He holds the old Socratic theory that the soul exists in an independent state before the body, entering it at birth. For this, as for the view that in the end all shall be saved, he was later to be regarded as guilty of heresy. But he fell foul of the Church during his lifetime too. When young he had unwisely taken extreme precautions against the weakness of the flesh by emasculation, a remedy of which the Church did not approve. Being thus diminished he was no longer eligible for the priesthood, though on this question there appears to have been some divergence of opinions.

Dionysian revelry: ancient rituals in contrast with the new religion

In his book 'Against Celsus', Origen gives a detailed reply to Celsus, whose book against the Christians has not survived. Here for the first time we find the apologetic strain of argument which insists on the divinely inspired nature of The Book. Amongst other things, the fact that belief has a socially valuable influence on its adherents is taken as proof of the validity of the belief. This last is a pragmatic view which was put forward by as recent a thinker as William James. It is easy to see, however, that such an argument is a double edged weapon. For it all depends on what it is that you hold to be valuable. The Marxists, who do not hold with institutional Christianity, call religion the opium of the people, and would, on pragmatic grounds, be perfectly entitled to do what they can to oppose it. The centralisation of the Church was a gradual process. In the beginning, bishops were elected locally by the members of the Church. Only after Constantine did the bishops of Rome grow more and more powerful. Through its support of the poor, the Church acquired a crowd of clients much as the senatorial families in Rome had done in the past. The time of Constantine was one of doctrinal struggles which caused much disturbance in the Empire. To settle some of these questions the Emperor exerted his influence to have the council of Nicaea convened in 325. This determined the standards of orthodoxy as against Arianism. By such methods did the Church henceforth resolve differences in doctrinal development. The doctrine of Arius, an Alexandrian priest, held that God the Father had priority over the Son, the two being distinct. The opposite heresy was defended by Sabellius, who maintained that they were merely two aspects of one and the same person. The orthodox view which ultimately won the field puts them on the same level, holding that they are alike in substance but different as persons. Arianism, however, continued to flourish, and so did a variety of other heresies. The chief protagonist of the orthodox camp was Athanasius, bishop in Alexandria from 328 to 373. Arianism was favoured by Constantine's successors, with the exception of Julian the Apostate who was a pagan. But with the advent of Theodosius in 379, orthodoxy received imperial support as well.

Saints, from the Arian chapel in Ravenna, Gothic Arian stronghold

To the last and Christian period of the Western Roman Empire belong three important clerics who in various ways helped strengthen the power of the Church. All three were later canonized. Ambrose Jerome and Augustine all were born within a few years of each other during the middle of the fourth century. Together with Pope Gregory the Great, who belongs to the sixth century, they came to be called the Doctors of the Church.

Ambrose, Milan's bishop

Of the three only the last one was a philosopher. Ambrose, a fearless protagonist of Church power, laid the foundations for the relation between State and Church which prevailed throughout the Middle ages. Jerome was the first to produce a Latin translation of the Bible. Augustine speculated on theology and metaphysics. The theological framework of catholicism up till the Reformation is mainly due to him, so are the leading principles of the reformed religions. Luther himself was an Augustinian monk.

Ambrose was born in 340, at Treves. He was educated in Rome and took up a legal career. At thirty he was appointed governor of Liguria and Aemilia in the North of Italy, a position which he held for four years. At that stage, for some reason unknown, he abandoned the secular life, though not his political activities. He was elected bishop of Milan, which was then the capital city of the Western Empire. From his episcopal position, Ambrose exercised far reaching political influence through his fearless and often uncompromising insistence on the spiritual supremacy of the Church.

At first, the religious position was clearcut and no threats to orthodoxy seemed likely while Gratian, himself a catholic, was Emperor. Neglectful of his imperial duties, he was however finally murdered, and with the succession trouble began. Power was usurped by Maximus throughout the West except for Italy, where the rule passed rightfully to Gratian's younger brother Valentinian II. As the young emperor was still a minor, his mother Justina did in effect hold sway. Justina being Arian, a clash was bound to occur. The focal point where paganism and Christianity collided most spectacularly was of course the city of Rome itself. Under Constantine's son Constantius, the statue of victory had been removed from the Senate House. Julian the Apostate had it restored, Gratian once more whisked it away, whereupon some senators asked for it to be put back. But the Christian faction in the Senate, with the help of Ambrose and Pope Damasus, prevailed. With Gratian out of the way, the pagan party came to the fore again in 384 with a petition to Valentinian II. To prevent this new move from inclining the Emperor to favour the pagans, Ambrose took up his quill to remind him that the Emperor was liable to serve God just as much as the citizens were to serve the Emperor as soldiers. By implication this goes much further than Jesus' request to give to God and Caesar what each of them severally was entitled to receive. Here we have a demand which asserts that the Church, being God's vehicle for commanding obedience on earth, was higher than the State. In a sense, this gives a true reflection of the way in which the power of the state was at that time receding. The Church, as a universal and international institution, was to survive the political dissolution of the Empire. That a bishop could hint at such things with impunity is a sign of the decay of the Roman Empire. The affair of the statue of victory was however not finished. Under Eugenius, a later usurper, it was restored, though after his defeat by Theodosius in 394, the Christian party won once and for all.

David doing penance. This example Ambrose bade Theodosius follow after the Thessalonica massacre

With Justina, Ambrose quarelled because of her Arianism. She had asked that a place of worship should be reserved in Milan for the Gothic legionaries who were Arian. This the bishop would not allow and in his stand the people sided with him. The Gothic soldiery which were sent to take over the basilica made common cause with the people and refused to resort to force. It was a signal act of courage for Ambrose, faced with barbarian mercenaries in arms, not to yield. The Emperor gave in, giving Ambrose a great moral victory in his fight for ecclesiastic independence.

But not all the actions of the bishop were equally commendable. During the reign of Theodosius, he opposed the Emperor who had ordered a local bishop to pay for the rebuilding of a burnt synagogue. The fire had been caused deliberately at the instigation of that cleric, and the Emperor was intent on not encouraging this kind of intimidation. But Ambrose argued that no Christian should on any count be held responsible for making good such damage, a dangerous doctrine that led to much persecution during the Middle Ages.

A raised platform, habitation of hermits, precursors of monasticism

While the chief merits of Ambrose lay in the field of administration and statesmanship, Jerome on the other hand was one of the outstanding scholars of his day. He was born in 345 at Stridon, near the Dalmatian border. At eighteen he went to Rome to study. After some years of travel in Gaul he settled in Aquileia, near his native town. Following some quarrel, he left for the East and spent five years as a hermit in the Syrian desert. Subsequently he went to Constantinople and back to Rome where he remained from 382 to 385. Pope Damasus had died the year before, and his successor seems to have disliked the quarrelsome cleric. Once more Jerome set out eastward, accompanied this time by a flock of virtuous Roman ladies who subscribed to his precepts on celibacy and abstinence. They finally settled down to a monastic life at Bethlehem, in 386, where he died in 420. His masterpiece is the Vulgate, the Latin Bible which became the recognised orthodox version. The Gospels were translated from the original Greek during his last stay at Rome, for the Old Testament he went back to the Hebrew sources, a task undertaken, with help from Jewish scholars, in the final period.

Through his way of life, Jerome became a powerful influence in furthering the monastic movement which was gaining strength at that time. His own retinue of Roman disciples who went with him to Bethlehem established four monasteries there. Like Ambrose, he was a great writer of letters, many of them to young ladies, exhorting them to remain in the paths of virtue and chastity. When Rome was sacked by Gothic invaders in 410, his attitude seems to have been one of resignation, and he continued to be more preoccupied with praising the worth of virginity than with the possibilities of taking steps to save the Empire.

Augustine, bishop of Hippo; writer on theology and philosophy

Augustine was born in 354 in the province of Numidia. He received a thoroughly Roman education and at twenty went to Rome together with his mistress and their young son. A little later we find him in Milan where he made a living as a teacher. On the religious side, he was a Manichaean during this period. But in the end, the continued pressure of remorse and a scheming mother brought him within the orthodox fold. In 387 he was baptised by Ambrose. He returned to Africa, became Bishop of Hippo in 396 and so remained until his death in 430.

In his Confessions, we find a colourful account of his struggles with sin. One early incident continued to obsess him throughout life. The episode is trivial enough, as a boy, he once ransacked a pear tree in a neighbour's garden, out of pure wanton high spirits. His morbid preoccupation with sin so magnified this misdeed that he could never quite forgive himself. Tampering with fruit trees, it would seem, is at all times a risky enterprise.

Sinfulness which in the early times of the Old Testament was considered as a national shortcoming had gradually come to be regarded as a blemish of the individual. For Christian theology, this shift in emphasis was vital, since the Church as an institution could not err. It was individual Christians that might commit sins. By emphasising the individual aspect, Augustine is a precursor of protestant theology. In catholicism, the function of the Church came to be regarded as the vital thing. For Augustine both sides are important. Man, being essentially damned and sinful, is saved through the mediation of the Church. But observance of religious practices and even the leading of a virtuous life cannot ensure salvation. God being good, and man evil, the granting of salvation is a favour, but the withholding of it is in no way blameworthy. This doctrine of predestination was later adopted by the more inflexible brands of reformed theology. On the other hand, his view that evil was not a material principle, as the Manichaeans had held, but the outcome of a bad will, was a valuable doctrine taken over by the reformed religions. It is the basis for the protestant conception of responsibility.

The theological work of Augustine was chiefly aimed at controverting the more moderate views of Pelagius. This Welsh cleric was a man of more humane temper than most of the churchmen of his time. He denied the doctrine of original sin and taught that man can through his own efforts achieve salvation, by choosing to lead a virtuous life. Moderate and civilized, this theory was bound to find many supporters, especially amongst those who still retained something of the spirit of the Greek philosophers. Augustine, for his part, fought the Pelagian doctrine with great fervour, and was not a little responsible for its being finally declared heretical. He construes the doctrine of predestination from the epistles of Paul, who might well have been astonished to see such fearful propositions deduced from his teaching. The theory was later taken up by Calvin, at which time the Church wisely dropped it.

Augustine's preoccupations are in the main theological. Even where he is concerned with philosophic questions, his aim is primarily to reconcile the teaching of the Bible with the philosophic heritage of the Platonic school. In this he is the precursor of the apologetic tradition. None the less, his philosophic speculations are interesting in their own right and reveal him as a thinker of some subtlety. This material is found in the eleventh book of the Confessions. It has no gossip value and is, therefore, usually omitted from popular editions.

The problem which Augustine sets himself is to show how the omnipotence of God can be reconciled with the fact that creation took place as outlined in Genesis, assuming this to be a fact. To begin with it is necessary to distinguish the Jewish and Christian notion of creation from that to be found in Greek philosophy. To a Greek, at any time, it would have seemed quite absurd that the world could be conjured up out of nothing. If God created the world, he is to be thought of as the master builder who constructs from raw materials that are already there. That something could come from nothing was alien to the scientific temper of the Greek mind. Not so with the God of the Scriptures, he is to be thought of as creating the building materials as well as putting up the structure. The Greek view naturally leads to pantheism, for which God is the world, a line of thought which has at all times attracted those with a strong leaning towards mysticism. The best known philosophic exponent of this view is Spinoza. Augustine adopts the Creator of the Old Testament, a God outside this world. This deity is a timeless spirit, not subject to causality or historical development. When he created the world he created Time along with it. We cannot ask what came before, because there was no Time of which this can be asked.

A bishop's mantle and cross on imperial throne: Church v. State

Bishop's cathedra; ivory, 6th cent.

Time, for Augustine, is a threefold present. The present properly so called is the only thing that really is. The past lives as a present memory, and the future as a present expectation. The theory is not without its defects, but the point of it is to emphasise the subjective character of time as being part of the mental experience of man, who is a created being. It makes therefore no sense, on this view, to ask what came before creation. The same subjective interpretation of time is found in Kant, who makes it a form of the understanding. This subjective approach led Augustine to foreshadow the Cartesian doctrine that the only thing that one cannot doubt is that he thinks. Subjectivism is, in the end, not a logically tenable theory. Still, Augustine is one of its able expositors.

The time of Augustine was marked by the fall of the Western Empire. Alaric's Goths took Rome in 410. The Christians may have seen in this a deserved chastisement for their sins. To the pagan mind the case stood otherwise: the old gods had been abandoned, and Jupiter had justly withdrawn his protection. To meet this argument from a Christian point of view Augustine wrote his 'City of God', which in the course of writing became a fully fledged Christian theory of history. Much in it is now of no more than antiquarian interest, but the central thesis of the independence of Church from State was of great importance during the Middle Ages, and continues to linger in some places even now. The view that the State, in order to partake of salvation, must obey the Church, is in fact based on the example of the Jewish State of the Old Testament.

Boethius, Platonist philosopher and Roman aristocrat

Under Theodoric's reign there lived in Rome a remarkable thinker whose life and work stand in sharp contrast with the general decay of civilization at the time. Boethius was born in Rome about 480, the son of a nobleman, and well connected with the senatorial class. He was a friend of Theodoric, and when the Gothic king became ruler of Rome in 500, Boethius was eventually appointed consul in 510. His fortunes suffered a reversal in later years. In 524 he was imprisoned and executed on a charge of treachery. It was in gaol, while waiting for death, that he composed the book which made him famous, the Consolations of Philosophy.

Even in his own time, Boethius enjoyed the reputation of being a wise and learned man. His are the earliest Latin translations of the logical writings of Aristotle. Along with these he produced commentaries and works of his own on Aristotelian logic. His treatises on music, arithmetic and geometry were long regarded as standard works in the liberal art schools of the middle ages. His plan to produce a complete translation of Plato and Aristotle unfortunately was never completed. The Middle Ages, oddly enough, revered him not only as a great student of classical philosophy, but also as a Christian. He had, it is true, published some tractates on theological matters, which were believed to be by his own hand, though it seems unlikely that they should be authentic. His own position, as set forth in the Consolations, is Platonic. It is of course more than likely that he was a Christian, as most people then were, but if so, his Christianity could have been no more than nominal, so far as his thinking was concerned. For the philosophy of Plato had much more influence on him than did the theological speculations of the Fathers. Yet perhaps it was well that he should have been thought reliably orthodox, since to this circumstance we owe that much of his Platonism could safely be absorbed by clerics of later centuries, when the taint of heresy might easily have condemned his works to oblivion.

At all events, the Consolations is free from Christian theology. The book consists of alternating prose and verse sections. Boethius himself speaks in prose, and philosophy in the shape of a woman replies in verse. In doctrine and outlook the work is quite removed from the interests that agitated the Churchmen of the time. It opens with a passage reaffirming the primacy of the three great Athenian philosophers. In pursuing the good way of life Boethius is following the tradition of the Pythagoreans. His ethical doctrines are largely stoic, and his metaphysics goes straight back to Plato. Some of the passages are pantheistic in tone, and accordingly he develops a theory in which evil is regarded as unreal. God, being equated with goodness, can do no evil, and since he is omnipotent evil must be illusory. Much of this is utterly at variance with Christian theology and ethics, but somehow it did not seem to upset anyone in the orthodox camp. The spirit of the entire book is reminiscent of Plato. It shuns the mysticism of the Neo-Platonic writers like Plotinus and is free from the superstitions prevailing at the time. The feverish sense of sin which overshadows Christian thinkers of that era is quite absent. What is perhaps the most remarkable feature of the work is that it was written by a man imprisoned and condemned to death.

It would be wrong to think of Boethius as an ivory tower thinker, remote from the practical concerns of his time. On the contrary, much in the manner of philosophers of old, he stood in the midst of practical affairs, an able and cool-headed administrator who did faithful and valuable service to his Gothic master. In later times he came to be regarded as a martyr to Arian persecution, an error which may have helped his popularity as a writer. Still, as a disinterested thinker not given to fanaticism, he was never canonized, whereas Cyril (of whom more presently) became a saint.

The work of Boethius in its historical setting raises the perennial problem of how far a man is bound to be the product of his age. Boethius lived in a world hostile to detached and reasonable enquiry, an era infested with superstition and rank with deadly zeal. Yet in his work none of these outside pressures seem to show, nor are his problems in any way peculiarly those of his time. It is of course true that aristocratic circles in Rome were less prone to yield to the passing fashions and enthusiasms of the day. If anywhere it was in these surroundings that some of the old virtues survived long after the empire ceased to exist, and this may to some extent account for the stoic strain in the ethical thinking of Boethius. But then this fact itself, the continued existence of such a group in spite of the inroads of barbarians from without and fanaticism from within, in turn must be explained. The answer, I think, is twofold. It is true enough that men are the products of traditions. In the first instance they are moulded by the surroundings in which they grow up, and later their way of life gains support from those traditions to which either in full conscience or else in more or less blind obedience they give their allegiance. On the other hand, traditions are not time bound in this way, they assume a life of their own and can survive for long periods, smouldering below the surface as it were, to be fanned once more into open fire when gaining renewed support. In some measure the traditions of classical times survived in the precarious circumstances of the barbarian invasions,and in this way a man like Boethius could emerge. Nevertheless he must have been aware of the gulf that separated him from his contemporaries. Depending upon the vigour of a tradition, it takes correspondingly more or less fortitude to support it, and Boethius surely needed all the courage he could muster.

Boethius writing the Consolations while awaiting death in prison

We can now answer another, related question. Is it necessary to study the history of philosophy in order to understand a philosophic question? And do we need to know something of the history of a period to understand its philosophy? Evidently on the view outlined above there is some interplay between social traditions and philosophical traditions. A superstitious tradition will not produce thinkers free from superstition. A tradition which values abstinence more highly than enterprise will not produce constructive political measures to meet the challenge of the moment. On the other hand, a philosophic question may well be understood without the entire apparatus of historical scholarship behind it. The point of looking at the history of philosophy lies in the recognition that most questions have been asked before, and that some intelligent answers to them have been given in the past.

The sack of Rome ushers in a period of invasion and strife, leading to the fall of Western Rome and the establishment of Germanic tribes throughout its territories. In the north, Britain was overrun by Angles, Saxons and Jutes, Frankish tribes spread into Gaul, and the Vandals went south into Spain and North Africa. The names of countries and regions have survived as reminders of these events, the Angles gave their name to England, the Franks to France, and the Vandals to Andalusia.

The south of France was occupied by Visigoths and Italy was conquered by Ostrogothic invaders, who had earlier been defeated in an unsuccessful attempt at smashing the Eastern Empire. Since the end of the third century, Gothic mercenaries had fought in Roman service, and had thus come to learn Roman skills and practices in warfare. The Empire lingered on for some few years after Rome fell, to be ultimately destroyed in 476 by Ostrogoths under their king Odovaker; he ruled until 493 when he was murdered at the behest of Theodoric, who became king of the Ostrogoths and reigned in Italy until his death in 526. Behind the Goths, from the East, the Mongolian tribe of the Huns under their king Attila were pressing westward. Though at times in league with their Gothic neighbours, they were on bad terms with them when Attila invaded Gaul in 451. A joint Gothic and Roman force stopped the invaders at Chalons. A subsequent attempt at taking Rome was foiled by moral pressure courageously exerted by Pope Leo. The Mongol prince died shortly afterwards and left his tribes without the leadership to which they were accustomed. The power of the marauding Asian horsemen vanished.

It might be thought that these upheavals would have called forth some bold reaction from the Church. But their attention was absorbed in niceties of doctrine pertaining to the rarer regions of Christ's degrees of multiplicity. There were those who held that he was one person with two aspects, the view which won in the end. Its chief protagonist was Cyril, the Alexandrian patriarch from 412 to 444. A staunch and narrow minded supporter of orthodoxy, he showed his zeal in practical ways by encouraging persecution of the Jewish community in Alexandria, and contriving the brutal murder of Hypatia, one of the few women who grace the annals of mathematics. He was in due course canonized.

Justinian tried to reconquer West. Orthodox, he closed the Academy

On the other side, the followers of Nestorius, the Patriarch of Constantinople, favoured the opinion that there were two persons, Christ the man and Christ the Son of God, a view which as we saw had Gnostic antecedents. The Nestorian doctrine had its supporters mainly in Asia Minor and Syria. An attempt was made to resolve this theological impasse, and a council was therefore summoned to assemble at Ephesus in 431. The faction siding with Cyril managed to reach the place of assembly first and quickly decided in favour of themselves, before the opposition had time to gain entry. Nestorianism was declared to be henceforth heretical. The view that there was only one person prevailed. After the death of Cyril, a synod at Ephesus, in 449, went even further and declared that Christ not only was one person but had only one nature. This doctrine came to be known as the Monophysite heresy. It was condemned at the Council of Chalcedon in 451. Had Cyril not died when he did, it is more than likely that instead of achieving sainthood he would have become a monophysite heretic. But though oecumenical councils might lay down standards of orthodoxy, heresy lingered on, especially in the East. It is not a little due to the intransigence of the orthodox power towards the heretic churches that the forces of Islam later met with such signal success.

In Italy, the Gothic invaders did not blindly destroy the social fabric. Theodoric, who reigned until his death in 526, preserved the old civil administration. In religious matters, he was apparently moderate. He was himself an Arian and seems to have countenanced the non-Christian elements that continued to survive especially amongst the patrician families in Rome. Boethius, the Neoplatonist, was Theodoric's minister. The emperor Justin was however a man of narrower views. In 523 he outlawed the Arian heretics. Theodoric was embarrassed by this move, for his Italian territories were solidly Catholic, while his own power was insufficient to withstand the emperor. Fearing a plot amongst his own supporters he had Boethius imprisoned and executed in 524. Theodoric died in 526, Justin the year after, to be succeeded by Justinian. It was on his commission that the great compendia of Roman law, the Codex and the Digests, were compiled. Justinian was a staunch champion of orthodoxy. Early in his reign, in 529, he ordered the closure of the Academy at Athens, which survived as a last stronghold of the old traditions, though by this time its teachings had become considerably diluted by Neoplatonic mysticism. In 532, the building of St. Sophia in Constantinople was begun. It remained the centre of the Byzantine Church until Constantinople fell to the Turks in 1453.

The emperor's interest in religion was shared by his spouse, the famous Theodora, a lady of indifferent past and a monophysite to boot. It was for her that Justinian embarked on the controversy of the Three Chapters. At Chalcedon three Fathers with Nestorian leanings had been declared orthodox, a clause offensive to monophysite opinion. Justinian decreed the three men were heretics, which led to long drawn out discussions in the Church. In the end he fell into heresy himself, adopting the Aphthartodocetic view that Christ's physical body was incorruptible, a monophysite corollary.

Under Justinian a last attempt was made to wrest the Western Provinces from their barbarian overlords. Italy was invaded in 535 and the country was torn by war for some eighteen years. Africa, too, was reconquered after a fashion, but Byzantine rule proved on the whole a doubtful blessing. In any case, the powers of Byzantium were not equal to the task of recovering the whole empire, even though the Church was on the Emperor's side. Justinian died in 565, and three years later Italy suffered a new barbarian onslaught. The Lombard invaders took permanent possession of the northern parts which came to be called Lombardy. For two centuries they struggled with the Byzantines who, being pressed by Saracens from the south, eventually withdrew. Ravenna, the last Byzantine stronghold in Italy, fell to the Lombards in 751.

Theodora, the monophysite spouse of Justinian

Theodoric's tomb at Ravenna

Coffin, thought to be of Benedict

Benedict, founder of Monte Cassino

During the period we are discussing a figure like Boethius was quite exceptional. The temper of the age was not philosophical. However, we must mention two developments which came to have important consequences for the philosophy of the Middle Ages. The first of these is the growth of monasticism in the West, the second the increase in power and authority of the papacy. They are linked respectively with the names of Benedict and Gregory. Monasticism began in the Eastern empire in the fourth century. In the early stages, it was not linked with the Church. It was Athanasius who took the first steps that finally brought the monastic movement under Church domination. Jerome, as we have seen, was a great champion of the monastic way of life. During the sixth century monasteries came to be established in Gaul and in Ireland. But the decisive figure in Western monasticism was Benedict, after whom the Benedictine order is named. Born in 480 of noble parentage, he grew up amidst the ease and luxuries of the Roman nobility. As a young man of twenty he suffered a violent reaction to the traditions of his early upbringing, and for three years went to live as a hermit in a cave. In 520 he founded a monastery on Monte Cassino. This became the centre of the Benedictine Order. Its rule, drawn up by the founder, enjoins upon its members vows of poverty, obedience and chastity. The excessive austerities practised by Eastern monks were not to Benedict's liking. Their traditions had taken very literal notice of the Christian view that the flesh was sinful. Accordingly they vied with each other who could achieve the rankest state of bodily neglect. To these unwholesome eccentricities the Benedictine rule put a determined stop. Authority and power was placed in the hands of the abbot who was appointed for life. In later times, the Benedictine Orders developed traditions of their own which were somewhat at variance with the intentions of their founder. A large library came to be collected at Monte Cassino, and Benedictine scholars did much to preserve the lingering traditions of classical learning.

Benedict remained at Monte Cassino until his death in 543. Some forty years later the Lombards sacked the monastery and the order fled to Rome. Twice more in its long history Monte Cassino suffered destruction, first at the hands of the Saracens in the ninth century, and once again during the second world war. Its library, fortunately was saved, and the monastery has now been completely rebuilt.

Some details on the life of Benedict are recorded in the second book of dialogues of Gregory. Much of this consists of tales of miraculous events and deeds, which throw some light on the general state of mind of the educated at that time. Reading, it must be remembered, had sunk by then to the level of a skill possessed by a very small minority. These writings were not at all produced for a gullible mass of illiterates, as are the superman and science fiction trash of today. For the rest, these dialogues constitute our main source of information on Benedict. Gregory the Great, their author, is counted as the fourth Doctor of the Western Church. He was born in 540, a scion of Roman nobility, and he grew up amidst wealth and luxury. He received the sort of education befitting his state, though he did not learn Greek, an oversight which he could never make good in spite of six years residence at the Imperial court in later years. In 573 we find him as the prefect of the city. But shortly afterwards he seems to have felt the call. He resigned his office and gave away his fortunes to become a Benedictine monk. The harsh and frugal life which followed hard upon this remarkable conversion did permanent damage to his health. His was however not to be the life of meditation he had yearned for. His political skills had not been forgotten, and Pope Pelagius II chose him as his ambassador at the Imperial court in Constantinople, to which the West still allowed a token allegiance. From 597 to 585 Gregory stayed at the court, but failed in his main task which was to entice the Emperor into war against the Lombards. But the period for military intervention was past. The last such attempts under Justinian had led to momentary success, only to come to nothing in the end. On returning to Rome, Gregory spent five years in the monastery which had been established in his former palace. The Pope died in 590 and Gregory, who would have much preferred to remain a monk, was chosen to succeed him. It required all the statesmanship of Gregory to deal with the precarious situation in which the crumbling of Western Roman authority had left the country. Italy was being ravaged by Lombards, Africa was the scene of struggles between a weak Byzantine exarchy beset by Moorish tribes, Visigoths and Franks were at war in Gaul, and Britain, dechristianized by the Anglo-Saxon invaders, had become pagan England. Heresies continued to plague the Church, and the general decay of standards tended to undermine those Christian principles that ought to have governed the way of life of the clerics. The practice of simony was widespread and could indeed not be checked effectively for some five-hundred years. Gregory fell heir to all these troublesome difficulties and did what he could to contain them. Yet the very confusion which reigned throughout the west enabled him to establish papal power on a firmer basis than it had ever hitherto possessed. Never until that time had the bishop of Rome been able to impose his authority so widely and with so great a measure of success as did Gregory. This he did mainly by writing numerous letters to clerics and secular rulers who might be failing in what seemed to him their proper duties, or guilty of exceeding the rightful scope of their authority. By issuing a Book of Pastoral Rules he laid the foundations for Roman supremacy in regulating Church affairs in general. This compendium was highly respected throughout medieval times and even found its way into the Eastern Church, where it was used in a Greek version. His theological teaching influenced biblical studies in the direction of symbolic interpretation, ignoring the purely historical content, which did not come to the fore until the revival of learning.

Gregory the Great, promoter of papal authority

For all his resolute endeavours in strengthening the position of Roman Catholicism, Gregory was a man of somewhat hidebound outlook. In politics, he would condone Imperial excesses if they might suit his own interests, or when he felt that opposition might be dangerous. Compared with a man like Ambrose he was a crafty opportunist. He did much to spread the influence of the Benedictine order, which became a prototype for later monastic foundations. But in his time the Church showed scant respect for secular learning and Gregory was no exception to the rule.

Scholasticism

As the central authority of Rome decayed, the lands of the Western Empire began to sink into an era of barbarism during which Europe suffered a general cultural decline. The Dark Ages, as they are called, are reckoned from A.D. 600 to 1000 approximately. Any attempt at carving up history like this into neat compartments is of course highly artificial. Not too much ought to be made of such divisions, at best they may hint at some overall features prevailing during the period. It must therefore not be imagined that with the turn of the 7th century Europe was suddenly plunged into gloom from which she emerged four centuries later. For one thing, the classical traditions of the past survived in some measure, though their continued influence was somewhat precarious and restricted. Some learning was fostered in monasteries, especially in far off corners like Ireland. Still, it is not inappropriate to call these centuries dark, especially if they are set over against what went before and what came after. At the same time it is well to remember that the Eastern Empire did not share this general decay in equal measure. Imperial control in Byzantium survived and thus caused learning to remain more secular than it was to become for many centuries in the West. Likewise, while Western culture languished, the young and vigorous civilisation of Islam, encompassing much of India, the Middle East, North Africa and Spain, rose to its greatest heights. Further afield, the civilisation of China under the Tang dynasty saw one of its most important literary epochs.

Charles Martel, victor at Tours over the Arab invaders

In order to understand why philosophy came to be so closely linked with the Church we must sketch in outline the main trends of development of the papacy and the secular powers through the period we are considering here. It was largely due to the political vacuum left by the disappearance of Imperial Rome that the Popes were able to secure their commanding position in the West. The Eastern patriarchs, besides being more restricted by the existence of Imperial authority, had never taken kindly to the pretensions of the bishops of Rome, and ultimately the Eastern Churches went their own several ways. Moreover, the barbarising influence of the invading tribes in the West had set back the general standards of literacy that had in Roman times prevailed throughout the Empire. The clerics, who did preserve what vestiges of learning had survived, thus came to be a privileged group that could read and write. When after some centuries of strife Europe emerged into a stabler period, it was the clerics who founded and ran the schools. The scholastic philosophy remained unrivalled until the renaissance.

In Western Europe, the papacy during the 7th and 8th centuries was steering a hazardous course between the rival political forces of Byzantine Emperors and barbarian kings. The Greek connection was in some ways preferable to dependence on the invaders. At least the Emperor's authority was based on proper legal foundations, whereas the rulers of conquering tribes had gained power by force. Besides, the Eastern Empire maintained the standards of civilization that had ruled when Rome was great, and in this way kept alive some kind of universal outlook which stood in sharp contrast with

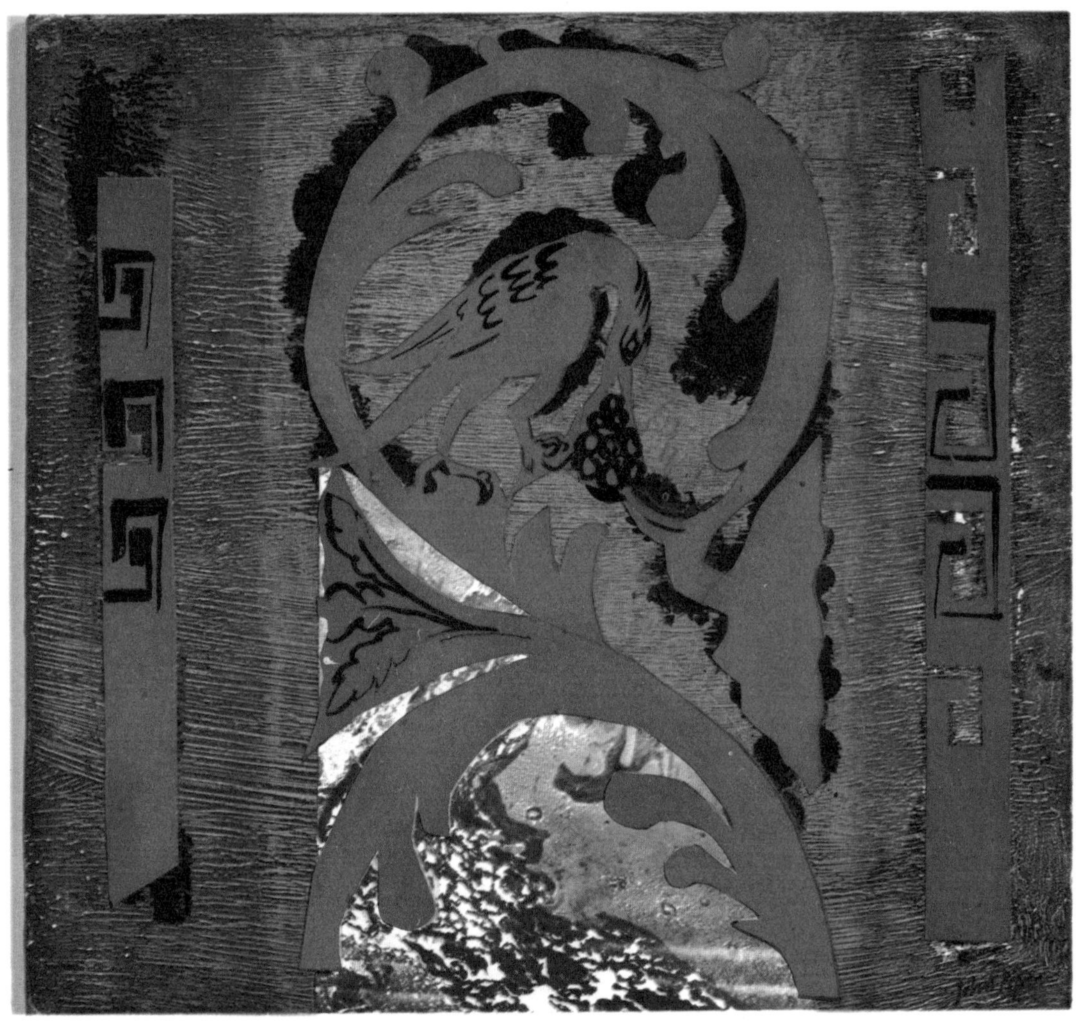

the narrow nationalism of the barbarian. Furthermore, both Goths and Lombards had within recent memory adhered to Arianism, while Byzantium was at least more or less orthodox, even if she refused to bow to the ecclesiastic authority of Rome.

However, the Eastern Empire was no longer strong enough to maintain its authority in the West. In 739 the Lombards made an unsuccessful attempt at conquering Rome. To counterbalance the Lombard threat, Pope Gregory III tried to enlist the help of the Franks. The Merovingian kings who succeeded Clovis had by then lost all real power in the Frankish Kingdom. The effective ruler was the major domus. During the early 8th century this office was held by Charles Martel, who stopped the rising tide of Islam at the battle of Tours in 732. Both Charles and Gregory died in 741. Their successors, Pepin and Pope Stephen III, came to an understanding. The major domus required from the Pope official recognition of kingship, thus supplanting the Merovingian dynasty. Pepin, in turn, gave the Pope the town of Ravenna, which the Lombards had captured in 751, together with other territories of the exarchate. This brought about the final break with Byzantium.

In the absence of a central political power, the papacy became much more powerful than the Eastern Church ever could in its own domain. The disposal of Ravenna was not, of course, in any sense a legal transaction. To give this business some semblance of proper title, certain clergy forged a document which came to be known as the Donation of Constantine. This instrument purported to be a decree of Constantine whereby he made over to the Holy See all territories that had belonged to Western Rome. In this way the temporal power of the Popes was established and maintained throughout the Middle Ages. The forgery was not exposed until the 15th century.

The Lombards tried to resist Frankish interference, but in the end Pepin's son Charlemagne crossed the Alps in 774 and inflicted a decisive defeat on the Lombard armies. He assumed the title of king of the Lombards and marched on Rome, where he confirmed his father's donation of 754. The papacy was favourably disposed to him, and he on his side did much to spread Christianity into Saxon territory, though his methods of converting pagans relied on the power of the sword more than on persuasion. On the Eastern border he conquered most of Germany, but in the South his efforts to push back the Arabs in Spain were less successful. The defeat of his rear-guard in 778 gave rise to the famous Roland legends.

But Charlemagne aimed at more than mere consolidation of his frontiers. He saw himself as the true heir of the Western Empire. On Christmas Day in the year 800, he was crowned Emperor by the Pope in Rome. This marks the beginning of the Holy Roman Empire of the German Nation. The break with Byzantium which had been caused in fact by Pepin's donation was thus completed by the creation of a new Western Emperor. Charlemagne's pretext for this move was somewhat flimsy. The throne at Byzantium was at that time occupied by the Empress Irene. This, he argued, was not allowed by Imperial practice, and therefore the office was vacant. By having himself crowned by the Pope, Charlemagne was able to function as the legal successor of the Caesars. At the same time, the papacy through this event became interlinked with the Imperial power, and though in the sequel headstrong Emperors might remove or install popes to suit their purposes, the Pope must still confirm an Emperor in his position by placing the crown on his head. The temporal and spiritual powers thus were locked together in fateful interdependence. Dissension was naturally inevitable, and Pope and Emperor, with varying fortunes, were engaged in a constant tug o' war. One of the chief causes of conflict arose over the question of episcopal appointments, of which more will be said later. By the 13th century, the opposing factions found compromise no longer possible. In the ensuing struggle, the papacy emerged victorious, only to lose its hard won advantage through the declining moral standards of the early renaissance popes. At the same time the rise of national monarchies in England, France and Spain released new forces which undermined the unity that had survived under the spiritual leadership of the Church. The Empire lingered on until Napoleon's conquest of Europe, while the papacy remains to the present day, though its supremacy was broken by the Reformation.

144 *Charlemagne, crowned Emperor at Rome in 800, heir to the Caesars*

While Charlemagne lived he gave welcome protection to the Popes, who in their turn were careful not to cross his purposes. He was himself illiterate and free from piety, but not inimical to learning or pious living in others. He encouraged a literary revival and patronised scholars, though his own recreations were of a less bookish nature. As for straight Christian conduct, this was deemed beneficial for his subjects, but must not unduly hamper the life of the court.

Under the successors of Charlemagne, the power of the Emperor declined, especially when the three sons of Louis the Pious divided its domains amongst themselves. From these events developed the rift which came to set the Germans against the French in later times. Meanwhile the Papacy gained in strength where from secular strife the Empire lost it. At the same time, Rome had to enforce its authority with bishops who, as we saw, had been more or less independent within their own areas, especially if they were at some distance from the seat of central power. In the matter of appointments, Pope Nicholas I (858–67) was by and large successful in maintaining Roman authority. Still, this whole question was somewhat contested not only by the secular powers but within the Church itself. A clever and determined bishop might well hold out against a Pope who lacked these qualities. In the event, the papal power lapsed again when Nicholas died.

The tenth century saw the papacy managed by the local aristocracy of Rome. The City had sunk into a state of barbarism and chaos as a result of the recurrent devastations occasioned by the struggles between Byzantine, Lombard and Frankish armies. Throughout the West, the land was made unsafe by independent minded vassals whom their feudal lords were unable to keep in check. Neither the Emperor nor the French king could enforce any kind of effective control over their unruly barons. Hungarian raiders encroached upon Italian territory in the North, while Viking adventurers spread fear and havoc throughout the coast and river lands of Europe. The Normans were eventually given a strip of land in France and in return accepted Christianity. The threat of Saracen domination from the South, which had been mounting during the 9th century, was averted when Eastern Rome defeated the invaders on the river Garigliano near Naples in 915, but the Imperial forces were too weak once more to govern in the West as had been tried in the time of Justinian. In this general confusion, the papacy, forced to obey the whims of wilful Roman noblemen, not only lost such remains of influence that hitherto it might have had in the affairs of the Eastern Church, but also found its control of Western clergy melting away while local bishops once again asserted their independence. In this, however, they were not successful, for though the ties with Rome might be loosened, the links with local secular powers grew stronger. The character of many of the incumbents of the throne of St. Peter during this period was not such as might have stemmed the tide of social as well as moral dissolution.

With the eleventh century, the great movements of peoples was coming to an end. The external threat of Islam had been contained. From now on, the West goes over to the offensive.

Coronation chair of Charlemagne, in the cathedral, Aix la Chapelle

Charles the Bald, King of France, patron of John the Scot

In far off Ireland the knowledge of Greek survived at a time when it had been forgotten in most other Western parts. The culture of Ireland flourished while the West was on the whole experiencing a decline. In the end it was the coming of the Danes which destroyed this pocket of civilization.

It is thus not surprising that the greatest figure among learned men of that age should be an Irishman. Johannes Scotus Erigena, the ninth century philosopher, was a Neoplatonist and Greek scholar, pelagian in outlook and pantheist in his theology. In spite of his unorthodox opinions he somehow seems to have escaped persecution. The vitality of Irish culture at that time was due to an interesting set of circumstances. When Gaul began to suffer successive waves of barbarian invasion, there was a great drift of learned men towards what protection the extreme West might afford. Those that went to England could find no foothold among the Angles, Saxons and Jutes who were pagan. But Ireland offered safety, and in this way many scholars found refuge there. In England, too, we must reckon the Dark Ages somewhat differently. There is a break at the time of the Anglo-Saxon invasions, but a revival under Alfred the Great. The dark period thus begins and ends two hundred years earlier. The Danish invasions of the ninth and tenth centuries produced a hiatus in the development of England and a permanent setback in Ireland. This time there was an exodus of scholars in the opposite direction. Meanwhile Rome was too far away to exercise control in Irish Church affairs. The authority of bishops was not overbearing, and the monastic scholars lost no time in quarrels of dogma. The liberal outlook of John the Scot was possible when elsewhere it would have met with swift correction.

Of John's life we know little, except for the period when he was at the court of Charles the Bald of France. He lived, it seems, from 800 to 877, the dates are uncertain. In 843 he was invited to the French Court to take charge of the court school. Here he became involved in a controversy on the question of predestination as against free will. John supported the free will side, holding that one's own efforts towards virtue do count. What gave offence was not so much his Pelagianism, though this was bad enough, but the fact that his treatment of the question was simply philosophical. Reason and revelation, he says, are independent sources of truth that neither overlap nor conflict. But if it looks as though there were conflict in a given case, reason must be trusted above revelation. In fact true religion is precisely true philosophy, and conversely. This point of view did not commend itself to the less vigorous minded clerics of the King's Court, and John's treatise on these subjects was condemned. Only the King's personal friendship helped to protect him from punishment. Charles died in 877, and so did his Irish scholar.

In his philosophy, John was a realist, in the scholastic sense of the term. It is important to be clear on this point of technical usage. Taking its origin from the theory of ideas as expounded by the Platonic Socrates, realism holds that universals are things, and that they come before particulars. The opposite camp based itself on the conceptualism of Aristotle. This theory is called nominalism, holding that universals are merely names and that particulars come before universals. The battle between realists and nominalists on the question of universals was hotly fought throughout the Middle Ages. It survives to the present day in science and mathematics. Because scholastic realism is connected with the theory of ideas it has in modern times also been called idealism. One must distinguish all this from later non-scholastic uses of these terms, which will be explained in the appropriate places.

John's realism stands out clearly in his main philosophic work, entitled 'On the division of Nature'. He recognises a fourfold division of Nature according to whether a thing creates or not, or is created or not. First, we have what creates and is not created, which evidently is God. Secondly, we come to what creates and is created, under which heading we find the ideas, in the sense of Plato and Socrates, which create particulars and are created by God, in whom they subsist. Thirdly, there are things in space and time which are created but do not create. This, finally, leaves what does not create and is not created, and here we turn full circle and come back to God as the ultimate goal towards which all things must strive. In this sense, God, being indistinguishable from his own purpose, does not create.

So far for things that are; but he also includes in Nature the things that are not. First amongst these are ordinary physical objects, which in true Neo-platonic style, are excluded from the intelligible world. Likewise, sin is regarded as a defect or privation, a falling short of the divine pattern, and so belongs to the realm of what is not. All this goes back ultimately to the Platonic theory in which, as we saw, the Good is equated with knowledge.

The view that, as explained, God is identical with his purposes leads directly into a pantheistic theology which is anything but orthodox. God's own essence is unknowable not only for men but for God himself, since he is not an object that could be known. The logical reason for this, though not stated by John, is that God is everything; and therefore the knowing situation, in which there is a knower and an object of knowledge, cannot arise. His theory of the Trinity is not unlike that of Plotinus. The being of God reveals itself in the being of things, His wisdom in their order, and His life in their movement; and these respectively correspond to Father, Son, and Holy Ghost. As for the realm of ideas, they constitute the Logos, which through the agency of the Holy Ghost cause, or give rise to, the particulars, which have no independent material being. God creates things out of nothing in the sense in which this nothing is God himself who transcends all knowledge and therefore is no thing. John thus opposes the Aristotelian view which allows material being to the particulars. On the other hand, the first three divisions on the criterion of creating and being created come from Aristotle's similar criterion of moving and being moved. The fourth division derives from the Neo-Platonic doctrine of Dionysius. Dionysius, an Athenian disciple of St. Paul, was the supposed author of a treatise reconciling Neo-Platonism with Christianity. John had translated this work from the Greek, and may well thus have gained protection, since the pseudo-Dionysius, through his connection with St. Paul, was wrongly held to be orthodox.

(1) God creates. (2) 'Ideas', in God, are created and create. (3) The spatio-temporal is created. (4) God, as total aim, is not created, nor creates

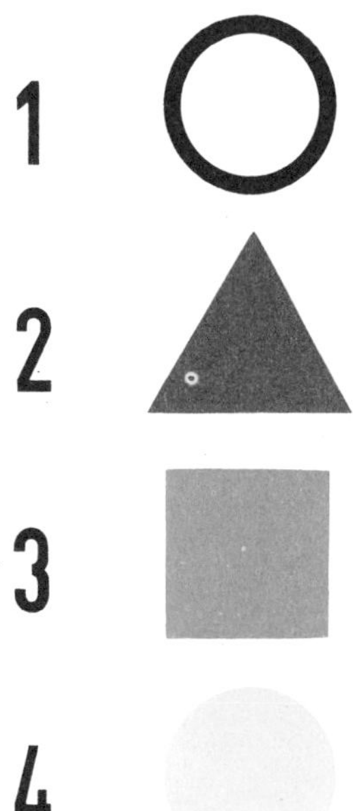

Abbey of Cluny, centre of reform

hic excomunicat Heinrici regis teutonicorum
B[eate] Petre apostolorum princeps. Inclina quesumus pias aures tuas
nobis. et audi me servum tuum quem ab infantia nutristi. et

Henry IV, excommunicated, begs the abbess Mathilda to intercede

During the 11th century, Europe at last begins to enter a period of regeneration. External threats from North and South were checked by the Normans. Their conquest of England put an end to Scandinavian encroachments, while their campaigns in Sicily freed that island once and for all from Saracen rule. Reforms of monastic institutions gained ground and the principles of papal elections and Church organization came under review. Standards of literacy began to rise as education improved, not only among clerics but to some extent with the aristocracy too.

The two chief difficulties that beset the Church at the time were the practice of simony and the question of celibacy. Both are in a sense linked with the status of the priesthood as it had developed over the years. Because priests were the ministers of religious miracles and powers. they came gradually to exercise considerable influence in secular affairs. This kind of influence remains effective only so long as people are on the whole given to believing that these powers are genuine. Throughout the Middle Ages this belief remained sincere and widespread. But the taste of authority generally whets the appetite. Unless there are strong and effective moral traditions to guide those in positions of vantage, they will tend to feather their own nests. In this way the granting of church office in return for a money payment became a source of wealth and power for those who could dispense such favours. These practices in the end corrupted the institution, and efforts were made, from time to time, to combat this evil. On the other hand in the matter of clerical celibacy the issues are not so clear cut. The moral aspect of this question has never been finally settled. Neither in the Eastern Church, nor later in the reformed churches of the West, was celibacy ever considered as morally valuable. Islam, it may be added, goes so far as to condemn it. Meanwhile, from a political point of view, there were not unreasonable grounds for the changes that were brought about at the time. If priests were married they would tend to develop into a hereditary caste, especially if the economic motive of preserving wealth was also involved. Besides, a priest must not be like other men; celibacy advertised this distance between them.

The centre from which monastic reform took its rise was the abbey of Cluny, founded in 910. A new principle of organisation was here put into practice for the first time. The abbey was solely and directly responsible to the Pope. The abbot in turn exercised authority over foundations that owed their origin to Cluny. The new regime strove to avoid the extremes both of luxury and asceticism. Other reformers followed suit and founded new orders. The Camaldolese go back to 1012, the Carthusians to 1084, and the Cistercians, who followed the Benedictine rule, to 1098. As for the papacy itself, reform was principally the outcome of struggles for supremacy between the Emperor and the Holy See. Gregory VI bought the papacy from his predecessor Benedict IX in order to reform it. But the Emperor Henry III (1039–56) who was himself a young and energetic reformer could not countenance such a transaction, however praiseworthy the motives might have been. In 1046, at the age of twenty-two, Henry descended upon Rome and deposed Gregory. Henry continued thenceforth to appoint Popes, which he did with discretion, and to remove them from office, if they should not come up to expectation. During the minority of Henry IV, who ruled from 1056 until 1106, the papacy once more recovered some of its independence. Under Pope Nicholas II a decree was passed which placed papal elections virtually into the hands of cardinal bishops, the Emperor being quite excluded. Nicholas also strengthened his hold over archbishops. In 1059, he sent Peter Damian, a Camaldolese scholar, to Milan in order to assert papal authority and support the local movements for reform. Damian is interesting as the author of the doctrine that God is not bound by the law of contradiction, and can undo that which is done, a view which was later rejected by Aquinas. Philosophy, for Damian, was the handmaiden of theology, and he opposed dialectic. The demand that God should be able to override the principle of contradiction brings out, by implication, the difficulty in the notion of omnipotence. If God is omnipotent, might He not be able, for instance, to make a stone so heavy that He cannot lift it? And yet He must be able to, if He is really omnipotent. Therefore, it seems, He both can and cannot lift it. Omnipotence turns out to be an impossible notion, unless one abandon the principle of contradiction. This last move would make discourse impossible. It is for this reason that Damian's theory was bound to be rejected.

Death of Pope Gregory VII

The election of the successor of Nicholas II sharpened the conflict between papacy and Emperor, with the scale turning in favour of the cardinals. The new incumbent after this, elected in 1073, was Hildebrand, who took the name of Gregory VII. Under his tenure came the great clash with the Emperor on the question of investitures, which was to last for several centuries. The ring and staff, with which a newly consecrated bishop was invested as symbols of office, had hitherto been given by the secular ruler. Gregory, in order to strengthen papal authority, arrogated this right to himself. Matters came to a head over the Emperor's appointment of a new archbishop of Milan, in 1075. The Pope threatened to depose and excommunicate the Emperor. The Emperor declared himself supreme and the Pope was pronounced deposed. Gregory retaliated and excommunicated Emperor and bishops, declaring them deposed in turn. The Pope gained the upper hand at first, and in 1077 Henry IV came to do penance at Canossa. But Henry's repentance was a political move. Though his enemies had elected a rival in his stead, Henry in time prevailed over his opponents, and when in 1080 Gregory at last pronounced in favour of the rival Emperor Rudolf it was too late. Henry had an antipope elected and with him entered Rome in 1084 to be crowned. Gregory, with Norman help from Sicily, forced Henry and his antipope to retreat in haste, but remained prisoner to his protectors and died the following year. Though Gregory was not successful, his policies later were.

A manuscript of Anselm, Archbishop of Canterbury

Men like Anselm, Archbishop of Canterbury (1093–1109) soon followed Gregory's example and quarrelled with secular authority. Anselm is important in philosophy as the inventor of the ontological argument for God's existence. God, being the greatest possible object of thought, cannot lack existence, else he would not be greatest. What is really wrong here is the view that existence is a quality. But many philosophers have since grappled with this argument.

The Prophet, from a Persian ms.

Expansion of the Moslem world

Whereas the West was overrun by barbarians who came to adopt Christianity, the Eastern Empire gradually fell to the onslaught of Mohammedans who, though not bent on converting the conquered peoples, granted exemption from tribute to such as would join their religion, a privilege of which the vast majority did avail themselves. The Mohammedan era is reckoned from the Hegira, Mohammed's flight from Mecca to Medina in 622. After his death in 632, the Arab conquests transformed the world in the short space of a century. Syria fell in 634–36, Egypt in 642, India in 664, Carthage in 697 and Spain in 711–12. The battle of Tours in 732 turned the tide, and the Arabs retreated to Spain. Constantinople was besieged in 669 and again in 716–17. The Byzantine Empire held out with diminishing territories until the Ottoman Turks took the city in 1453. This remarkable explosion of Moslem vitality was helped by the general state of exhaustion of the empires overrun. Besides, in many places the invaders were helped by conflicts in those areas. Syria and Egypt more especially had suffered for not being orthodox.

The new religion proclaimed by the Prophet was in some ways a return to the austere monotheism of the Old Testament, divested of the mystic accretions of the New. Like the Jews, he forbade graven images, but unlike them he banned the use of wine. How far this latter prohibition remained effective is doubtful; the former coincided with iconoclastic tendencies amongst Nestorians. Conquest was almost a religious duty, though the people of the Book were to be left unharmed. This affected Christians, Jews and Zoroastrians, who severally adhered to the canons of their own sacred scriptures.

The Arabs did not at first set out for systematic conquest. Their land being arid and poor, they were wont to make border raids for loot. But as resistance was feeble, the raiders became conquerers. In many cases the administration of these new lands remained untouched under its new masters. The Arab Empire was ruled by caliphs, successors of the Prophet and heirs to his authority. Though at first elective, the caliphate soon became dynastic under the Umayyads, who ruled till 750. This ruling family followed the teachings of the Prophet for political rather than religious reasons and was opposed to fanaticism. The Arabs were on the whole not too religiously inclined, their motives for expansion remaining, as at first, material gain. This very lack of fervour enabled them, though weak in numbers, to rule over vast regions inhabited by men more civilised and alien in creed. In Persia, however, the teaching of the Prophet fell on ground well prepared by the religious and speculative traditions of the past. After the death of Mohammed's son-in-law Ali in 661, the faithful split up into the Sunni and Shiah sects. The latter were somewhat of a minority whose loyalties lay with Ali, and who would have none of the Umayyads. The Persians belonged to this minority, and it is largely through their influence that the dynasty was supplanted and replaced by the Abbasids, who removed the capital from Damascus to Baghdad. The policies of this new dynasty gave freer rein to fanatical sections of Islam. However, they lost Spain where, at Cordova, an independent caliphate was set up by the one Umayyad who had survived the fall of his clan. Under Abbasid rule the Empire rose to great splendour with Harun-al-

Rashid, a contemporary of Charlemagne, and well known from the legends of the 'Arabian Nights'. After his death in 809, the Empire began to suffer from large scale use of Turkish mercenaries, just as Rome had from using barbarian soldiers. The Abbasid Caliphate declined and fell with the sack of Baghdad by the Mongols in 1256.

Moslem culture arose in Syria but soon became centred on Persia and Spain. In Syria, the Arabs inherited the Aristotelian traditions favoured by the Nestorians, at a time when orthodox Catholicism adhered to Neo-Platonic doctrines. Much confusion was however caused by the fact that Aristotelian theories became mingled with a certain Neo-Platonic influence. In Persia, Moslems became acquainted with Indian mathematics and introduced Arabic numerals which ought really to be called Indian. The civilization of Persia produced poets like Firdousi and maintained its high artistic standards in spite of Mongol invasion during the 13th century.

Nestorian traditions, through which the Arabs first came in contact with Greek learning, had also spread into Persia at an earlier stage, after the Byzantine Emperor Zeno had closed down the school at Edessa in 481. From both these sources, the Moslem thinkers learnt their Aristotelian logic and philosophy, along with the scientific heritage of the Ancients. The greatest of the Mohammedan philosophers in Persia was Avicenna (980–1037). Born in the province of Bokhara, he eventually taught philosophy and medicine at Ispahan, and finally settled at Teheran. He was fond of good living and incurred the enmity of theologians for his unorthodox opinions. His works therefore had greater influence in the West, through Latin translation. One of his main philosophic concerns is the perennial problem of universals which later became a central question in scholasticism. Avicenna's solution is an attempt at squaring Plato with Aristotle. He begins by saying that generality in forms is engendered by thought, an Aristotelian view repeated by Averroes and later Albertus Magnus, the teacher of Aquinas. But Avicenna goes on to qualify this view. Universals are before, in, and after things all at once: before in God's mind, when he creates things on a pattern; in things as far as they belong to the external world; and after them in human thought, which discerns patterns through experience.

Spain, too, produced one outstanding Mohammedan philosopher, Averroes (1126–98), born in Cordova of a line of cadis. He himself studied law amongst other things, and was a cadi in Seville and later in Cordova. In 1184 he became court physician, though he was finally exiled to Morocco for holding philosophic views instead of contenting himself with the faith. His main contribution was to free Aristotelian studies from the distorting influence of Neo-Platonism. He believed, as did Aquinas later, that God's existence can be proved on rational grounds alone. As for the soul, he holds with Aristotle that it is not immortal, though 'nous' is. Since this abstract intelligence is unitary, its survival does not mean personal immortality. Christian philosophers naturally rejected these views. Averroes in Latin translation not only influenced the scholastics, but also found favour with free thinkers at large who rejected immortality and came to be called Averroists.

Title page of Avicenna ms., 17th cent.

Averroes

The policies of Gregory VII seemed, at the time of his death in 1085, to have wrenched from the Holy See its power and influence in the affairs of the Empire. But in the sequel it turned out that the tug of war between temporal and spiritual powers was by no means at an end. Indeed, the papacy had not yet reached the summit of its political career. In the meantime, the vicar of God found his authority in matters spiritual enhanced by the support of the rising cities of Lombardy, while the Crusades at first strengthened his prestige.

The struggle over investitures was resumed by Pope Urban II (1088–99) who once more arrogated these rights to himself. When in 1093 Conrad, the son of Henry IV, rose in rebellion against his imperial father, he sought and found support from Urban. The Northern cities were favourably disposed towards the Pope, so that the whole of Lombardy was easily conquered. Philip, the King of France was also conciliated, and in 1094, Urban could set out on a journey of triumph through Lombardy and France. There, at the council of Clermont in the following year, he preached the first Crusade.

Emperor Frederick Barbarossa

Urban's successor, Paschal II, successfully continued the papal policy on investitures until the death of Henry IV in 1106. Thereafter, in German lands at least, the new Emperor, Henry V, prevailed. The Pope suggested that Emperors should not meddle with investitures in return for which clerics would forego the right to temporal property. The men of God, however, were more firmly anchored in this world than such a pious proposal seemed to suppose. When its provisions became known, the German clerics cried havoc. Henry, who was in Rome at the time, threatened the Pope into submission and had himself crowned Emperor. But his triumph was short-lived. Eleven years later, in 1122, Pope Calixtus II, by the Concordat of Worms, regained control over investitures.

During the reign of Emperor Frederick Barbarossa (1152–90), the struggle entered a new phase. In 1154, Hadrian IV, an Englishman, was elected to the Holy See. In the beginning, Pope and Emperor joined forces against the city of Rome which defied them both. In their movement of independence the Romans were led by Arnold of Brescia, a forceful and courageous heretic who inveighed against the temporal splendours of clerics. Church men who held worldly possessions could not enter the Kingdom of Heaven, he maintained. This view did not commend itself to princes of the Church, and Arnold was savagely attacked for this heresy. These troubles had begun under the previous pope but came to a head when Hadrian was elected. He punished the Romans for a civil disturbance by placing them under an interdict. In the end their spirit of independence was broken and they agreed to banish their heretic leader. Arnold went into hiding but fell into the hands of Barbarossa's troops. He was duly burnt and in 1155 the Emperor was crowned, not without a ferocious crushing of attendant popular demonstrations. But two years later the Pope broke with the Emperor. Two decades of war between the two powers followed. The Lombard League fought for the Pope, or perhaps rather against the Emperor. The fortunes of war were varied. Milan was razed in 1162, but later in that year Barbarossa and his antipope were overtaken by disaster when in their march on Rome the army was ravaged by pestilence. A final attempt at breaking papal power ended in Barbarossa's defeat at Legnano in 1176. An uneasy peace was concluded. The Emperor joined the third Crusade and died in Anatolia in 1190.

In the end the struggle between Church and Empire was to benefit neither party. It was the city states of Northern Italy that began to emerge as a new power. They supported the Pope as long as the Emperor threatened their independence. When, later, this threat disappeared, they followed their own interests and developed a secular culture distinct from that of the Church. Though nominally adhering to Christianity, they developed a largely free thinking outlook, much in the way in which Protestant society has tended to do after the 17th century. The maritime cities of Northern Italy gained greatly in importance as providers of ships and supplies during the Crusades. Religious fervour may have been one of the original forces contributing to the crusading movement, but powerful economic motives also were at work. The East held out fair promise of loot, to be acquired, what is more, in a virtuous and saintly cause, while close at hand the Jews of Europe were a profitable target for religious indignation. That in the Moslem world the knights of Christendom were set against a culture immeasurably superior to their own was not at first apparent to them.

Hadrian IV, the only English Pope

Scholasticism, as a movement, differs from classical philosophy in that its conclusions are circumscribed before the event. It must function within the orbit of orthodoxy. Its patron saint amongst the Ancients is Aristotle, whose influence gradually displaces that of Plato. In method it tends to follow the classificatory approach of Aristotle, using dialectic argument with scant reference to facts. One of the greatest theoretical issues was the problem of universals which split the philosophic world into opposing camps. The realists held that universals were things, basing themselves on Plato and the theory of ideas. The nominalists on the contrary maintained that universals were mere names, invoking the authority of Aristotle. Scholasticism is usually reckoned from Roscelin, a French cleric who was the teacher of Abelard. Little is known about him, and his philosophic views are recorded mainly in the writings of Anselm and Abelard. He was a nominalist and, according to Anselm, held that universals were a mere breath of the voice. From denying the reality of universals he went on to deny that a whole was real over and above its parts, a view which must have led to a rigid logical atomism. In connection with the Trinity this naturally produces heretical views which he was made to recant in Rheims in 1092. Abelard, born in 1079, was a more important thinker. He studied and taught in Paris, and after a theological interlude, returned to teaching in 1113. To this period belongs his affair with Heloise, whose irate uncle, Canon Fulbert, had the rash lover castrated and sent both of them severally into clerical retreat. Abelard lived on until 1142 and retained great popularity as a teacher. He, too, was a nominalist. More precise than Roscelin, he points out that we predicate a word not as an occurrence, but as having significance. Universals arise from the resemblances between things, but a resemblance is not itself a thing, as realism wrongly supposes.

During the 13th century, the scholastic movement reached its highest peak. Likewise, the struggle between Pope and Emperor entered its fiercest phase. In many ways this period marks the climax of the Medieval world in Europe. In subsequent centuries, new forces emerge, from the Italian renaissance of the 15th to the revival of science and philosophy in the 17th century.

The greatest of the political Popes was Innocent III (1198–1216), under whom papal authority attained a level never afterwards achieved. Sicily had been conquered by Barbarossa's son Henry VI who had married Constance, a princess in line of succession to the Norman Kings of the island. Henry died in 1197 and his son Frederick became King at two years old. His mother placed him under the guardianship of Innocent III upon the latter's accession. In return for respecting Frederick's rights, the Pope gained recognition of his own supremacy. Similar acknowledgements were obtained from most of the rulers of Europe. While in the fourth Crusade his plans were thwarted by the Venetians who forced him to take Constantinople for their own purposes, his venture against the Albigenses was entirely successful. Southern France was cleared of heresy, being totally destroyed in the process. In Germany, the Emperor Otto was deposed and Frederick II, now fully grown up, elected in his stead. Thus did Innocent III hold sway over Emperor and Kings. Within the Church itself, a greater measure of power was secured for the Curia. But in a way the very extent of its temporal success already foreshadowed the decline of the papacy. For as its hold on this world grew firmer, its authority in matters touching the next decayed; one circumstance that later led to the Reformation.

154 *Pope Innocent III, protagonist of papal supremacy*

Frederick II had been elected with papal support at the expense of promises concerning the Pope's supremacy. None of these the young Emperor intended to keep longer than necessary. This young Sicilian of German and Norman parentage grew up in a society where a new culture was in the making. Here Moslem and Byzantine, German and Italian influences combined to produce a modern civilization which gave the Italian renaissance its first impulse. Being steeped in all these traditions, Frederick was able to command respect with East and West alike. In outlook far beyond his time and modern in his political reforms, he was a man of independent thought and action. His forceful and construetive policies earned him the sobriquet of 'stupor mundi,' wonder of the world.

Within two years of each other both Innocent III and Frederick's defeated German opponent, Otto, died. The papacy passed to Honorius III, with whom the young Emperor soon fell out. Being familiar with the refined civilization of the Arabs, Frederick was not to be prevailed upon to go crusading. Next, there were difficulties in Lombardy, where German influence was on the whole disliked. This created further friction with the Pope who was generally supported by the Lombard cities. In 1227 Honorius III died and his successor, Gregory IX, forthwith excommunicated Frederick for failing to go on Crusade. The Emperor was not too much perturbed by this move. He had married the daughter of the Norman King of Jerusalem and in 1228, while still an outcast from the fold, went to Palestine and settled matters there by negotiation with the Moslems. Jerusalem was of scant military value, but Christians had religious attachments to it. The Holy City was thus surrendered by treaty, and Frederick was crowned King of Jerusalem.

To the Pope's way of thinking, this was altogether too reasonable a manner of composing differences, but in the face of success he had to make his peace with the Emperor in 1230. There followed a period of reform during which the Kingdom of Sicily was given a modern administration and a new legal code. Trade and commerce were encouraged by abolition of all internal customs barriers, and education promoted by the founding of a university at Naples. In 1237, hostilities in Lombardy revived, and Frederick, until his death, in 1250, was engaged in constant war with successive Popes. The mounting ferocity of the struggle tarnished the earlier and more enlightened years of his reign.

The rooting out of heresy was pursued with great thoroughness, though not on the whole with complete success. The Albigenses, a manichaean sect in Southern France, were, it is true, completely wiped out in the Crusade against them in 1209. Other heretical movements, however, survived. The Inquisition which was instituted in 1233, never entirely stamped out the Jews in Spain and Portugal. The Waldenses, a late 12th century movement foreshadowing the reformation, followed their leader, Peter Waldo, into exile from Lyons to the alpine valleys of Piedmont, west of Turin, where to this day they survive as Protestant and French speaking communities. In the light of such events one might suspect that later generations had learnt one cannot easily kill ideas by witch-hunt methods. History seems to show that this lesson has not been learnt.

In spite of the immensely powerful position of the Church, the thirteenth century was thus not a period of undisputed supremacy even within the purely ecclesiastical sphere. But if the established Church did not on the whole conform to the tenets of its founder, there arose within it two orders which at first somewhat restored the balance. Both the early Dominicans and Francisans followed the precepts of their founders, St. Dominic (1170–1221) and St. Francis of Assisi (1181–1226). But though these orders were originally mendicant, the vows of poverty were not to burden them for long. Both Dominicans and Franciscans became prominent in handling the business of the Inquisition. This institution fortunately never spread to England or Scandinavia. It is likely that at one time the tortures it inflicted were intended in the interest of the victims, on the view that temporary pain here below might save a soul from being eternally damned. Nevertheless, practical considerations no doubt helped at times to strengthen the pious intentions of the judges. The English had no objection in seeing Joan of Arc thus disposed of. However, the orders of Dominic and Francis, against what their founders would have wished, became devoted to the pursuit of learning. Albertus Magnus and his pupil Aquinas were Dominicans, while Roger Bacon, Duns Scotus and William of Occam belonged to the Franciscan order. It is in philosophy that they made their really valuable contribution to the culture of their period.

Emperor Frederick II, founder of a modern state in Sicily

Albertus Magnus, foremost Aristotelian of his time, taught Aquinas

If hitherto churchmen had found their philosophic inspiration mainly from Neo-platonic sources, the thirteenth century saw the triumph of Aristotle. Thomas Aquinas (1225-1274) sought to establish Catholic doctrine on Aristotle's philosophy. How far such an undertaking might meet with success in a purely philosophic way is of course doubtful. The theology of Aristotle, for one thing, is quite out of tune with the notion of God favoured by Christianity. But there can be no doubt that, as a philosophic influence within the Church, the Aristotelianism of Aquinas gained a hold which was complete and permanent. Thomism has become the official doctrine of the Roman Church, and is taught as such in all its colleges and schools. No other philosophy today enjoys so prominent a status and such powerful backing, except the Dialectical Materialism which is the official doctrine of Communism. In Aquinas' own time, his philosophy did not, of course at once achieve this privileged position. But in the sequel, as his authority became more rigidly established, so the mainstream of philosophy gradually moved once more into secular channels, reverting to the spirit of independence that pervades the philosophy of the Ancients.

Thomas belonged to the family of the Counts of Aquino, whose residence was in a village of that name, not far from Monte Cassino, where he began his studies. After six years at the University of Naples, he joined the Dominican order in 1244 and continued his work at Cologne, under Albertus Magnus, the foremost Dominican teacher and Aristotelian scholar of his time. Having spent some time in Cologne and Paris, Thomas returned to Italy in 1259, and devoted the following five years to the writing of the 'Summa contra Gentiles', which is his most important work. In 1266 he began writing his other main work, the 'Summa Theologica'. During these years, too, he wrote commentaries on many of the works of Aristotle, of which his friend William of Moerbeke provided him with translations straight from the Greek. In 1269, he left once more for Paris, where he stayed for three years. The university of Paris at that time was hostile to the Aristotelian doctrine of the Dominicans because this suggested some link with the Averroists there. On immortality, the Averroist view was, as we have seen, closer to Aristotle than the Christian doctrine. This augured ill for Aristotle, and Thomas took great pains to dislodge Averroist opinion from its stronghold. His efforts in this direction were entirely successful, a victory that saved the Stagyrite for Christian theology even if this meant giving up some of the original texts. In 1272, Thomas returned to Italy, where he died two years later, while on his way to the council of Lyons.

His system of philosophy soon gained recognition. In 1309, it was pronounced the official doctrine of the Dominican order, and canonization followed close afterwards, in 1323. Philosophically, the Thomist system is perhaps not quite so important as its historical influence might suggest. It suffers from the fact that its conclusions are inexorably imposed beforehand by Christian dogma. We do not find the disinterested detachment of Socrates and Plato, where the argument is allowed to take us whither it will. On the other hand, the great systems of the 'Sums' are monuments of intellectual labour. Opposing points of view are always stated clearly and fairly. In the commentaries on Aristotle, Thomas reveals himself as a thorough and intelligent student of the Stagyrite, which is more than could be said of any of his predecessors, his teacher included. His contemporaries called him the 'angelic doctor'. To the Church of Rome, Thomas Aquinas was indeed a messenger and a teacher.

In the earlier, neo-platonic theologians, the dualism of reason and revelation was external to the system. Thomism produced a reversal of doctrine against neo-platonic theory. Neo-platonism has a dualism in the sphere of being, as between universals and particulars. More precisely, perhaps, there is a hierarchy of degrees of being starting with the One and descending through ideas to the particulars which are lowest in respect of being. The gap from universals to particulars is somehow bridged by the Logos, which stated in more down to earth language is quite a sensible view. For words have general meaning but may be used to refer to particular things. Along with this dualist theory of being, we have a unitary theory of knowing. There is an intellect or reason which has one way of knowing that is essentially dialectical. With Aquinas the position is exactly the opposite. Here, in Aristotelian fashion, being is seen exclusively in the particulars, and from this the existence of God is somehow inferred. To the extent that particulars are accepted as raw material this view is empirical in contrast with the rationalist attempt at deducing particulars. On the other hand, the Thomist approach, while holding a unitary view of being, creates a dualism in the sphere of knowing. Two sources of knowledge are now postulated. First, as before, we have reason, which obtains its food for thought from the experience of the senses. There is a well known scholastic formula which says that there is nothing in the intellect which was not first in sense experience. But in addition, there is revelation as an independent source of knowledge. Where reason produces rational knowledge, revelation gives men faith. Some things, it would appear, lie altogether beyond the reach of reason, and these must be grasped, if grasped they can be, by the ministrations of revelation. To this group belong specific points of religious dogma, such as articles of faith that are past understanding. The triune nature of God, the resurrection and the Christian eschatology are examples of this. The existence of God, however, though it may in the first instance commend itself through revelation, may also be established dialectically on rational grounds, and to this end we find the various attempts at proving this proposition. Thus, insofar as principles of religion are amenable to rational treatment, it is possible to argue with non-believers; for the rest, revelation is the only way towards seeing the light. In the last analysis, Thomism does not really treat the two sources of knowledge as quite on the same footing. Somehow, it seems, faith is required before rational knowledge may be pursued. Men must believe before they can reason. For though the truths of reason are autonomous, it is a matter of revelation that they should be pursued at all. But this way of talking is not without some danger. The truths of revelation are arbitrary, and though for Aquinas there is no conflict between reason and revelation, nor therefore any opposition between philosophy and theology, one does in fact undermine the other. Where reason can cope with the facts, revelation is redundant, and conversely.

Ms page of a letter of Aquinas

Thomas Aquinas, founder of the official philosophy of the Church

As for theology, we must remember that this really falls into two parts. There is first what is called natural theology, which deals with God in the context of topics like first causes, prime movers and the like. This is what Aristotle calls theology; it may be set on the side of metaphysics. But Aquinas, as a Christian, also developed what may be called a dogmatic theology. This treats of matters accessible only through revelation. Here he falls back on earlier Christian writers, mainly Augustine whose views on grace and salvation he seems on the whole to endorse. These are indeed matters that lie beyond reason. Dogmatic theology is of course quite alien to the spirit of Ancient philosophy; nothing like it is found in Aristotle.

It is because of the theological element that Aquinas in his metaphysics goes beyond Aristotle in one important respect. We recall that Aristotle's God is a kind of disinterested architect. Existence is not considered as having to be conferred on particular things. They are simply there, and so was the raw material from which they were fashioned. For Aquinas, on the other hand, God is the fount of all existence. A finite thing is said to exist only contingently. It depends for its existence either directly or indirectly on something which exists of necessity, and this something is God. In scholastic language this is expressed in terms of essence and existence. The essence of a thing is roughly a quality, or what the thing is. Existence is a term pointing to the fact that a thing is. It is that whereby the thing is. Both these terms are of course abstractions in the sense that neither an essence nor an existence can be on its own. A concrete thing invariably has both. But there are facts of language which suggest a distinction here. Frege hints at precisely this point when he distinguishes between sense and reference. The meaning of a word raises one question, whether or not there is in fact an object to which the word applies is quite another matter. Finite things then are said to have existence and essence as distinguishable, though of course not separable, features. In God alone there is no objective difference between essence and existence. Now the metaphysical theory of the existential dependence of finite being gives rise to the third of the five proofs of the existence of God in the 'Summa theologica'. We begin from the ordinary fact of experience that things arise and pass away, which means that their existence is not necessary, in the technical sense. Things of this kind, so the argument runs, do at some time or other in fact not exist. But if so, there was a time when nothing existed, and hence there would be nothing now, since no finite thing can confer its own existence on itself. There must therefore be something which has necessary existence. This is what is called God.

Several comments on this argument may be useful. First, of course, it takes for granted that the being there at all of anything needs to be justified or accounted for. This is a central point of Thomist metaphysics. If this view is not held, as in fact it was not held by Aristotle, for instance, then nothing further can be said. But allowing the premiss for the sake of discussion, there is an internal weakness in the argument which makes it invalid. From the fact that any finite thing does at some time not exist it does not follow that there is any time at which none whatever exists.

The terminology of essence and existence is underpinned in Aquinas by the Aristotelian theory of potentiality and actuality. An essence is purely potential and an existence purely actual. In finite things there is thus always a mixture of these two. To exist is somehow to be engaged in an activity; and this must, for any finite object, derive from something else.

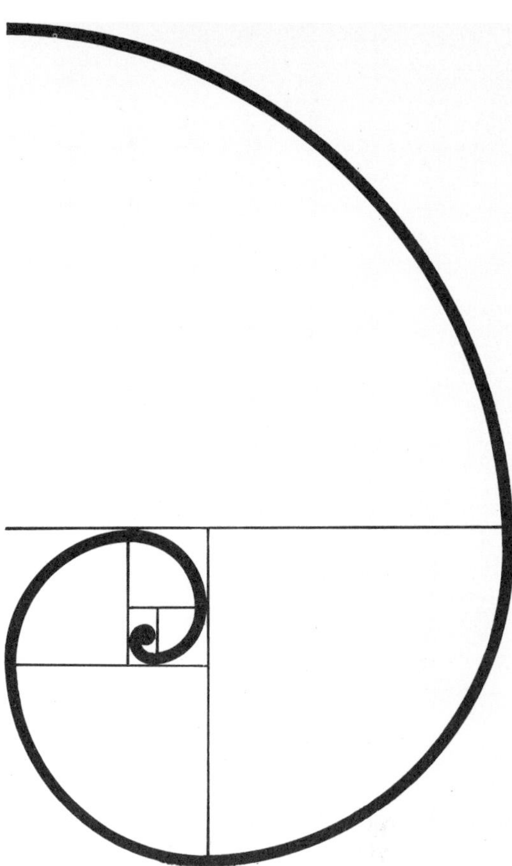

The argument from design: order implies a designer, hence God exists

The first and second proof for the existence of God are in effect Aristotelian in character. Aquinas argues to an unmoved mover and an uncaused cause, in each case stipulating that an infinite regress of movers and causes is inadmissible. But this simply destroys the premiss of the argument. To take the second argument, if every cause has itself a further cause, one cannot in the same breath go on to say that there is one cause which has no further cause. This is simply a contradiction. It should be mentioned, however, that Aquinas is not concerned with causal chains in time. It is a matter of sequence of causes, one depending on the other here and now, rather like the links in a chain suspended from a hook in the ceiling. The ceiling would be the first or uncaused cause, since it is not a link suspended from anything else. But there is no good reason why a regress should be rejected, provided only it leads to no contradictions. The series of rationals greater than zero up to and including one is infinite, and yet has no first member. In the case of motion, the question of a regress need not even arise. Two gravitating particles circling round each other like sun and planet will continue to do so indefinitely.

The fourth proof for God's existence proceeds from the recognition of various degrees of perfection in finite things. This, it is said, presupposes the existence of something completely perfect. The fifth and last argument notes that inanimate objects in nature appear to minister to some end, in that the world is pervaded by some kind of order. This is taken to point to an outside intelligence whose ends are thus served, since inanimate things cannot have ends of their own. In this argument, which is called the teleological, or argument from design, it is assumed that order must be accounted for. There is certainly no logical reason for such an assumption; we might equally well say that disorder needs explanation, and the argument runs the other way. The ontological argument of St. Anselm which we mentioned earlier was rejected by Aquinas, though curiously enough on practical rather than logical grounds. Since no created and therefore finite mind can ever grasp the essence of God, his existence, which is implied by his essence, can never in fact be deduced like this.

Whereas the God of Neo-Platonism is somehow coextensive with the World, the God of Aquinas is a kind of incorporeal highpriest set over and above the created world. As such he possesses to an infinite degree all positive qualities, which is taken to follow somehow from the bare fact of his existence, though what can be said on this subject is negative. A finite mind cannot reach a positive definition.

It is in the version of Aquinas that Aristotle dominated the philosophic field until the renaissance. What was rejected at that time was however not so much the teaching of Aristotle or even Aquinas, but rather certain ill-informed habits of using metaphysical speculation.

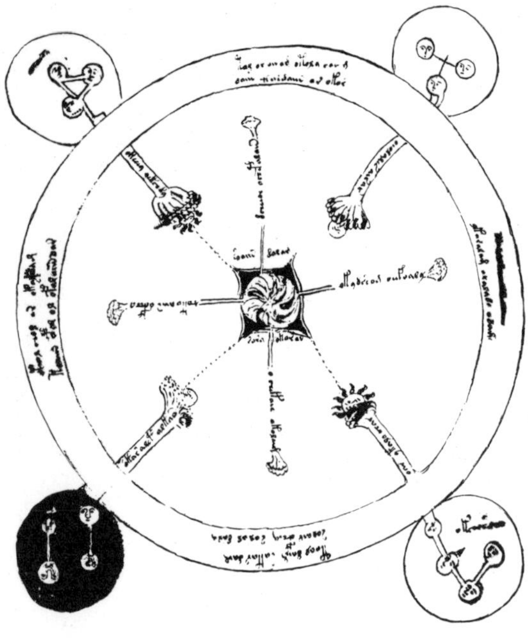

The importance of empirical study as against metaphysical speculation was emphasised by Roger Bacon, one of a line of Franciscan scholars under whose impact medieval ways of thinking began to disintegrate. Bacon was a contemporary of Aquinas and by no means opposed to theology. In laying the foundations on which more modern lines of enquiry later developed he had no wish to undermine the authority of the Church in spiritual matters. This is true in general of the Franciscan thinkers of the late 13th and early 14th centuries. Nevertheless, by their approach to the problem of faith and reason they hastened the breakdown of the Middle Ages.

For Thomism, reason and revelation, as we just saw, may overlap. The Franciscan scholars viewed this matter afresh and sought sharper definition between the two. By clearly separating the sphere of intellect from that of faith, they intended to liberate theology proper from its dependence on classical philosophy. At the same time, however, philosophy was thus severed from its subservience to theological ends. Along with a free pursuit of philosophic speculation goes scientific research. More especially, the Franciscans mark a renewed emphasis of Neo-Platonic influence which encouraged the study of mathematics. The strict exclusion of rational enquiry from the domain of faith henceforth demanded that science and philosophy refrain from cavilling at articles of faith. But, likewise, faith must not pretend to pronounce dogmata where rational science and philosophy can hold their own. This circumstance brings with it occasion for sharper conflicts than had till then occurred. For if the ministers of faith decree on matters which are found in fact to be not so, then it follows that they must retreat or else give battle on ground to which they hold no title. Only by not entering the lists of dialectics can revelation maintain its independence. In this way men may devote their lives to scientific research and at the same time hold a variety of beliefs about God. The Thomists weaken their theological position in attempting to prove God's existence, quite apart from the fact that the arguments are not successful. On the side of religious belief this means that the criteria of reason simply do not apply, and in a sense the soul is free to give allegiance to what it fancies.

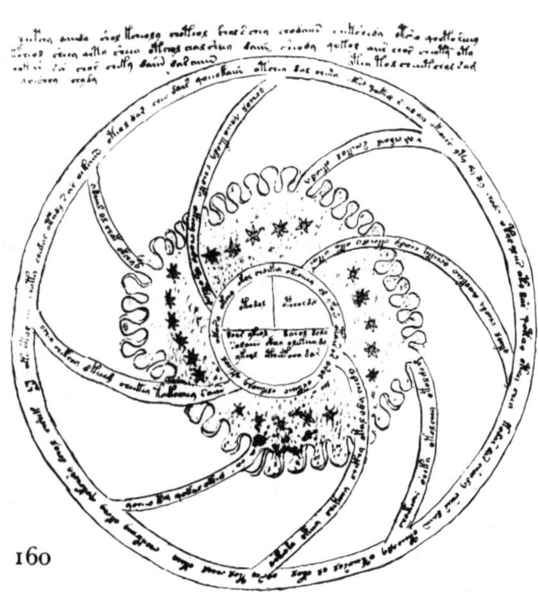

From an early ms. of Roger Bacon, an account of eclipses and comets

Roger Bacon lived, it seems, from 1214 to 1294, both dates are somewhat uncertain. Studying in Oxford and Paris, he acquired an encyclopaedic grasp of all branches of learning, somewhat in the manner of the Arab philosophers of the past. In his opposition to Thomism he did not mince words. It seemed odd to him that Aquinas should write authoritatively on Aristotle without being able to read him. Translations were unreliable and not to be trusted. Furthermore, while Aristotle does count as important, there are other things that are equally so. In particular, the Thomists were ignorant of mathematics. As for the gaining of new knowledge, we must resort to experiment rather than fall back on authorities. Bacon does not condemn the deductive method of scholastic dialectic as such, but he insists that it is not enough to derive conclusions. To carry conviction they must weather the test of experiment.

Such novel views could not fail to attract the unfavourable attention of orthodoxy. In 1257, Bacon was banished from Oxford and went into exile in Paris. The former papal legate in England, Guy de Foulques, became Pope Clement IV in 1265. Being interested in the English scholar, he requested from Bacon a summary of his philosophy. This was supplied in 1268, a Franciscan prohibition notwithstanding. Bacon's doctrines were favourably received and he was allowed to return to Oxford. But the Pope died that year, and Bacon continued to be less tactful than he might have been. In 1277 came the great condemnation. Bacon, with many others, was called to give account of his views. On what precise head he was found guilty is not known, but he spent fifteen years in prison. He was freed in 1292 and died two years later.

Of greater philosophic interest is Duns Scotus (about 1270–1308), a Scot as the name suggests, and a member of the Franciscan Order. He studied in Oxford where he became a teacher at twenty-three years old. Later he taught in Paris and Cologne, where he died. With Duns Scotus the breach between faith and reason becomes more definite. While this involves on the one side a narrowing down of the scope of reason, on the other it restores to God complete freedom and independence. Theology, which is concerned with what may be said about God, is no longer a rational discipline, but rather a set of useful beliefs inspired by revelation. In this spirit, Duns rejected the Thomist arguments for God's existence, on the grounds that they rest on sense experience. Likewise he rejected the arguments of Augustine, because these draw to some extent on divine illumination. Since argument and proof belong to philosophy, and theology and philosophy are mutually exclusive, he cannot accept the Augustinian proofs. On the other hand, he is not averse to a conceptual proof based on the notion of a first uncaused being, somewhat in the vein of Avicenna. This is really a variation on Anselm's ontological argument. But knowledge of God is not possible through created things whose existence is merely contingent and dependent on His will. In fact, the existence of things is identified with their essence. For Aquinas, it will be remembered, this identification serves to define God. Knowledge is of essences, and these are therefore different from the Ideas in God's mind, since we cannot know Him. Since essence and existence coincide, that which makes each individual what it is cannot be matter but must be form, in opposition to Aquinas' view. Although forms, for Duns, are substantial, he does not subscribe to a full blown Platonic realism. Thus there may be a variety of forms in an individual, but these are distinct in a formal manner only, so that there is no question of their existing independently.

For Duns, Will (red) rules Reason; Plato held the opposite view

Just as the supreme power lies with God's will, so within the human soul Duns holds that it is the will which rules the intellect. The power of the will gives men freedom, where intellect is constrained by the object to which it attends. From this it follows that the will can grasp only what is finite, since the existence of infinite being is necessary and therefore annuls freedom. The doctrine of freedom as opposed to necessity is in line with the Augustinian tradition. In the hands of the Franciscan scholars it became a powerful influence for scepticism. If God is exempt from the eternal laws of the world, then what may be believed of him may also be doubted.

An even more radical empiricism is found in the works of William of Occam, the greatest of the Franciscan scholars. He was born in Ockham in Surrey some time between 1290 and 1300. He studied and taught at Oxford and later at Paris. His doctrines being somewhat unorthodox, he was ordered in 1324 to attend the Pope in Avignon. Four years later he had another disagreement with the Pope, John XXII. The Spirituals, an extreme section of the Franciscan order who took their vow of poverty in earnest, had been the target of papal displeasure. A compromise arrangement, by which the Pope retained formal ownership of the property of the order, had been in force for some time. This was now revoked, and many members defied papal authority. Occam, Marsiglio of Padua, and Michael of Cesena, the order's general, were on the side of the rebels and were excommunicated in 1328. Fortunately they were able to flee from Avignon, and found protection at the court of the Emperor Louis, in Munich.

St. Francis of Assisi, founder of the Franciscan Order

In the struggle between the two powers, the Pope was backing a rival Emperor and excommunicated Louis, who in his turn laid charges of heresy against the Pope through a General Council. In Occam, the Emperor, in return for his protection, found a ready and forceful pamphleteer. The scholar penned some strong attacks against the Pope and his concerns in worldly affairs. Louis died in 1338, but Occam remained in Munich until his death in 1349.

Marsiglio of Padua (1270–1342), a friend and fellow exile of Occam, was equally opposed to the Pope and put forward quite modern views on the organisation and competence of both secular and spiritual powers. The ultimate sovereignty resides in the majority of the people in both cases. General Councils are to be formed by popular election. Only such a Council should have the right to excommunicate, and even then not without secular sanction. Councils alone should lay down standards of orthodoxy, but the Church is not to meddle in affairs of state. Occam's political thought, while not quite so extreme as this, is strongly influenced by Marsiglio.

In his philosophy, Occam goes much further towards empiricism than any of the other Franciscans. Duns Scotus, while removing God from the sphere of rational thought, nevertheless still retained a more or less traditional metaphysic. Occam, on the other hand, was roundly antimetaphysical. A general ontology as is found in Plato, Aristotle and their followers, is, according to Occam, quite impossible. Reality attaches to the individual, singular thing, and this alone could be an object of experience yielding direct and certain knowledge. This meant that for an account of being, the elaborate apparatus of Aristotelian metaphysics was quite superfluous. It is in this sense we must interpret Occam's statement that 'it is vain to do with more what can be done with less'. This is the basis of the different, better known saying, that 'entities should not be multiplied beyond necessity'. Though not in his writings, this maxim has come to be known as 'Occam's razor'. The entities in question are of course the forms, substances and the like, with which traditional metaphysics was concerned. However, a rather different twist has been given to this formula by thinkers of later ages who were primarily interested in questions of scientific method. Occam's razor there becomes a general principle of economy in the process of saving the appearances. If a simple explanation will do, it is idle to seek a complex one. While thus holding that being belongs to the individual, Occam allowed that in the sphere of logic, which deals with words, there is a kind of general knowledge of meaning. This is not, as with individuals, a matter of direct apprehension, but of abstraction. Besides, there is no guarantee that what has thus been arrived at has existence as a thing. Occam is thus a thorough going nominalist. Logic, in the strict Aristotelian sense, must be regarded as a verbal instrument. It is concerned with the meaning of terms. In this, Occam amplifies the views of the early nominalists of the 11th century. Indeed, already Boethius had maintained that the categories of Aristotle were about words.

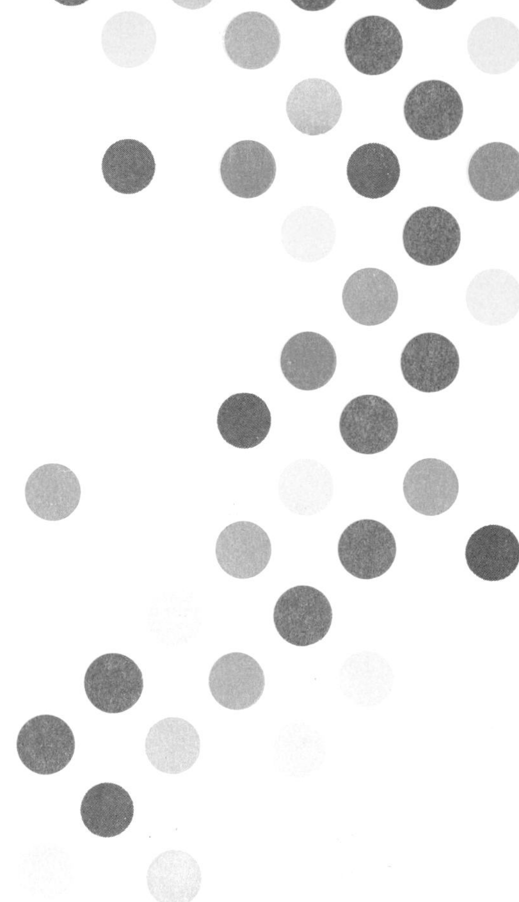

Occam's razor, principle of economy: use the simplest hypothesis

The concepts or terms used in discourse are entirely the product of the mind. Insofar as they are not verbalised they are called natural universals or signs, in contrast with words as such, which are conventional signs. To avoid absurdities, we must be careful not to confuse statements about things with statements about words. When, as in science, we talk about things, the terms used are said to be of first intention. If, on the other hand, we talk about words, as in logic, the terms are of second intention. It is important, in argument, to ensure that all the terms used have the same intention. Using these definitions, we may express the nominalist position by saying that the term 'universal' is of second intention. The realists think that it has first intention, but this is wrong. Here Thomism agrees with Occam in rejecting the notion of universals as things. They further agree in allowing the existence of universals before things, as ideas in the mind of God, a formula due originally to Avicenna, as we saw earlier. But whereas Aquinas held this to be a metaphysical truth which could be supported by reason, for Occam it was a proposition of theology in his sense, and thus divorced from the rational sphere. As for theology, this, to Occam, was altogether a matter of faith. God's existence could not be established by logical proof. In this he goes further than Duns Scotus and rejects Anselm as well as Aquinas. God cannot be known through sense experience and nothing can be established about him by our rational apparatus. Belief in God and in his various attributes depends on faith, and so does the entire system of dogmata about the Trinity, the immortality of the soul, creation and the like.

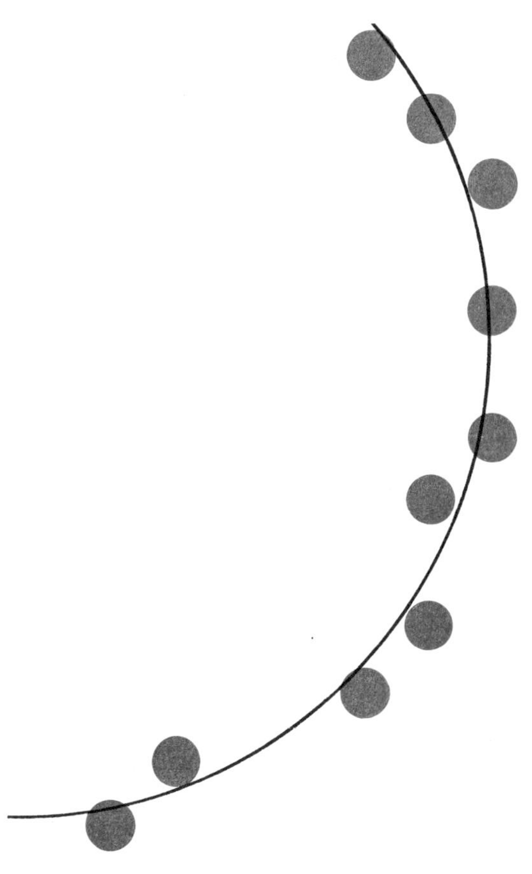

In this sense, then, Occam may be described as a sceptic. But it would be wrong to think of him as an unbeliever. By limiting the scope of reason, and freeing logic from metaphysical and theological encumbrances, he did much to promote renewed efforts of scientific enquiry. At the same time, the field of faith was left wide open to every kind of extravagance. It is therefore not surprising that there should have developed a mystical movement going back, in many ways, to Neo-Platonic traditions. Its best known representative is Master Eckhart (1260-1327), a Dominican whose theories completely ignored the demands of orthodoxy. To the established Church, a mystic is as much if not more of a menace than a freethinker. In 1329, Eckhart's doctrines were declared heretical.

Perhaps the greatest synthesis of medieval thought is to be found in the work of Dante (1265-1321). At the time when he wrote the Divine Comedy, the Middle Ages were indeed beginning to dissolve. Here, then, we have a conspectus of a world that was past its prime, looking back to the great Aristotelian revival of Aquinas, and the faction fights between Guelfs and Ghibellines that lingered in the city states of Italy. Dante, it is evident, had read the works of the Angelic Doctor. Likewise, he was conversant with the general cultural activities of his time, and with the classical culture of Greece and Rome, insofar as this was then known. The Divine Comedy is manifestly a journey through hell, purgatory and into heaven, but in the course of this trip we are actually presented with a compendium of medieval thought, in the form of digressions and allusions. Dante was banished from his native Florence in 1302, when in the eternal seesaw of civic disturbances between the rival parties, the Black Guelfs came to power. Dante's family supported the White party, and he himself had strong views on the function of the Empire. Much of these political struggles, together with recent past history that had led up to these events, receive mention in the Divine Comedy. At heart a Ghibelline, Dante admired Emperor Frederick II, who in his broad outlook and background was an ideal example of what the poet wished an Emperor to be. Dante belongs to the handful of greatest names of Western literature. But this was not his only title to fame. Above all, he forged the vulgar tongue into a universal literary instrument which for the first time was able to set a standard transcending the variations of local dialect. Whereas until that time Latin alone had fulfilled this office, Italian now became a medium for literary work. As a language, it has changed very little from that day to this. The first beginnings of poetry in Italian go back to Pietro della Vigna, the minister of Frederick II. Adopting what seemed best to him from a number of dialects, Dante built around his native Tuscan the literary language of modern Italy. At roughly the same time, the vulgar tongue developed in France, Germany and England. Chaucer lived shortly after Dante. The language of learning, however, remained Latin for some considerable time. The first philosopher to write in his native tongue was Descartes, and then only on occasions. Latin gradually declined until, in the early 19th century, it disappeared as a medium of expression by the learned. From the 17th to the 20th century, this function of universal communication was taken over by French, and in our time English is replacing it.

Dante Alighieri, whose great poem sums up the medieval outlook

In Dante's conception, we find that Hell is a stageless amphitheatre

In his political thinking, Dante was a champion of strong Imperial power at a time when the Empire had lost much of its pristine influence. The national states of France and England were in the ascendant, and the idea of universal Empire somewhat at a discount. It is in line with Dante's generally medieval outlook that this change of political emphasis did not strike him as significant. Had he been able to see this, the development of Italy into a modern state might well have occurred much earlier. This is not to say that the old tradition of an all embracing Imperial state did not have much to commend it. But the times were not ripe for it. As a result of this, Dante's political theories remained quite unimportant in the sphere of practical politics.

There are, in the Divine Comedy, some quaint problems touching the status of the Ancients, which to us would seem quite unimportant. The great philosophers of the classical past are of course not to be rated as mere heathens that deserve eternal damnation. Aristotle in particular, the 'master of those who know', surely deserves our praise. Still, not having gone through baptism, these thinkers certainly were no Christians. A compromise is therefore contrived. As heathens, the Ancient philosophers belong into hell, which is where we do indeed find them. But a special corner is set aside for them, a kind of Elysian enclave in an otherwise somewhat forbidding locality. So strong were the bonds of dogma in those days that it was felt to be a problem to fit in the great non-Christian thinkers of the past.

Medieval life, in spite of its fears and superstitions, was essentially an ordered affair. A man was born to his station and owed loyalty to his feudal lord. The whole body politic was nicely divided and ranged into grades, and nothing could alter this. In the field of political theory this tradition was exploded by Marsiglio and Occam. As to the spiritual power, which was the main wielder of those fears which kept men in check, its influence began to wane so soon as it was felt that dogma might be dispensed with. This cannot have been Occam's intention, but it was certainly the effect his doctrines came to have on the reformers. Among scholastics, Luther valued Occam above all the rest. None of these upheavals is yet foreshadowed in Dante. His opposition to the Pope is based not on any departure from orthodoxy, but on the meddling of the Church in matters that belonged to the Emperor's competence. But although papal power in Dante's own time had greatly diminished, it was no longer possible for a German Emperor to maintain his authority in Italy. After 1309, when the papacy was transferred to Avignon, the Pope became virtually an instrument of the King of France, and the conflict between Pope and Emperor became a struggle of France against Germany, England siding with the Empire. When Henry VII of Luxemburg became Emperor in 1308, it looked as though the Empire might once again recover, and Dante hailed him as a saviour. But Henry's successes were incomplete and ephemeral. Though he descended into Italy and was crowned in Rome in 1312, he was unable to assert himself against Naples and Florence, and died the following year. Dante died an exile in Ravenna in 1321.

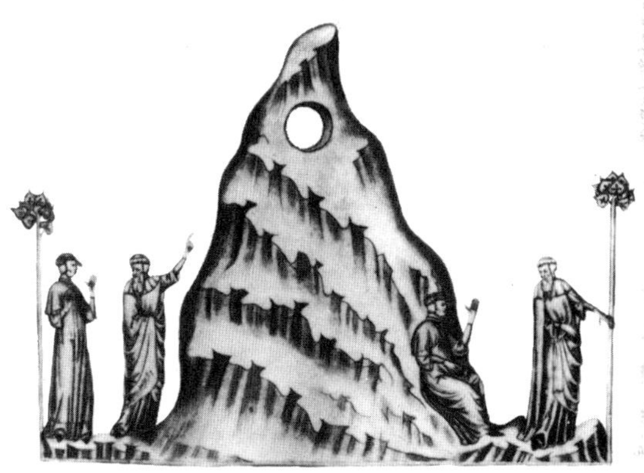

Similarly for the other place: Paradise is like a step-pyramid

With the rise of the vulgar tongues, the Church lost some of its hold on the intellectual activities in philosophy and science. At the same time, there occurs a great outburst of secular literature, beginning in Italy and gradually moving north. The wider scope of enquiry together with a measure of scepticism, born of the gulf between faith and reason, turned men's minds away from things not of this world and taught them to try to improve their lot, or at least alter it. All these tendencies were beginning to show themselves in the first half of the 14th century. Dante does not foresee them, he is essentially looking back to the times of Frederick II. Whereas the medieval world was in principle centralised, the new forces of the renaissance tended to disrupt the monolithic structure of medieval society. Nevertheless, it seems that in our own time, for different reasons, the idea of universal dominion may once again emerge.

The great schism ends when Council of Constance elects Martin V

During the 14th century the papal power suffered a rapid decline. Though in the struggle with the Empire, the Holy See had proved itself the stronger, it was no longer an easy matter for the Church to control Christians through holding the threat of excommunication constantly over their heads. Men were beginning to dare think about God for themselves. The papacy had lost its moral and spiritual hold on thinkers and scholars, while Kings and the masses of the people were alike uneasy about the enormous moneys that were levied by the Pope's envoys. All these trends were beginning to take shape, though at the turn of the century this might not yet have broken through into open conflict. Indeed, Pope Boniface VIII, in the Bull 'Unam Sanctam', stressed papal supremacy beyond even the claims of Innocent III. In 1300, he declared a Jubilee year, during which plenary indulgence would be accorded any of the flock who might come in pilgrimage to Rome. While this tended to underline the spiritual power of the Pope, it also helped to pour vast sums into his treasury besides enriching the people of Rome whose livelihood was bound up with looking after the temporal needs of pilgrims. The success of the Jubilee was such that its renewal was set down for fifty years hence, and then for twenty-five, instead of a hundred.

In spite of this outward show of supremacy, the power of Boniface VIII was flimsily grounded. As a man, he loved gold more than becomes a prince of the Church, and in matters of faith he was no paradigm of orthodoxy. During his entire tenure, he was in conflict either with French prelates or with their King, Philip IV. From this quarrel it was the King of France who emerged the victor. The next Pope, elected in 1305, was Clement V, a Frenchman who, in 1309, established his seat in Avignon. It was during his office and with his connivance that Philip IV suppressed the Templars. This purely predatory measure was undertaken on quite unfounded pretexts of heresy. In general, the quarrels of the papacy from now on tend to undermine its authority. The dissension between John XXII and the Franciscans produced the polemics of Occam. In Rome, the absence of the Popes in Avignon led to a temporary break away under the leadership of Cola di Rienzi. This Roman citizen began by fighting the corrupt nobility in Rome, and in the end defied both Pope and Emperor, declaring Rome to be ruler as of old. In 1352, Pope Clement VI succeeded in capturing Rienzi, who was not released until the Pope's death two years later. Rienzi returned to power in Rome but was killed by the populace some months later.

Through its exile in France, the papacy lost much of its prestige. Gregory XI tried to remedy this drift by returning to Rome in 1377. But he died the following year and his Italian successor, Urban VI, quarrelled with the French cardinals, who elected Robert of Geneva as their Pope. As Clement VII, this Frenchman returned to Avignon, and the Great Schism which was thus begun lasted until the Council of Constance. The French supported their Pope at Avignon, while the Empire recognised his Roman counterpart. As each Pope appointed his own Cardinals who in their turn elected his successor, the breach could not be healed. An attempt was made to break the deadlock by means of a Council called at Pisa in 1409. The two existing Popes were declared deposed and a new conciliar Pope was elected. But the deposed would not resign, so that instead of two Popes now there were three. The Council of Constance, which was called in 1414, at last restored some order. The conciliar Pope was deposed, the Roman incumbent was prevailed upon to resign, and the Avignon line dissolved for lack of support because of English ascendancy in France. In 1417, the Council appointed Martin V, thereby bringing the Great Schism to an end. But the Church failed to reform itself from within, and through his opposition to the conciliar movement, the Pope further diminished such respect as the papacy might still command.

John Wycliffe, heretic and critic of the Church. The peasants' revolt in 1381 was partly inspired by him

In England, opposition to Rome was carried further by John Wycliffe (about 1320-1384), a native of Yorkshire and a scholar and teacher at Oxford. It is worth remarking that England had long been less subservient to Rome than continental Europe. Already William the Conqueror had stipulated that no bishop could be appointed in his realm without the sanction of the King.

Wycliffe was a secular priest. His purely philosophic work is less important than that of the Franciscans. Abandoning the nominalism of Occam, he tended rather towards some form of Platonic realism. Where Occam had endowed God with absolute freedom and power, Wycliffe inclined to view God's ordinance as necessary and binding on Him. The world could not be other than it is, a view clearly inspired by Neo-Platonic doctrine and found again in the 17th century in Spinoza's philosophy. Late in life Wycliffe came to oppose the Church, at first because of the worldy style of life the popes and bishops indulged in, while the masses of the faithful lived in stark poverty. In 1376 he expressed a novel view on civil dominion in a course of lectures at Oxford. Only the righteous can lay claim to property and authority. The clergy, insofar as they might fail this test, were really forfeit of their property, a matter which should be decided by the State. In any case property was evil: if Christ and his disciples had had none, neither should the clergy have any now. These doctrines were not to the liking of propertied clerics, but found favour with the English government intent on stopping papal tribute. Pope Gregory XI, noting that Wycliffe's heretical opinions were in line with those of Marsiglio of Padua, ordered a trial, but the proceedings were broken up by the citizens of London. Besides, the University asserted its academic freedom to obey the King, and denied the Pope's competence to bring its teachers to court.

After the Great Schism, Wycliffe went so far as to declare the Pope to be Antichrist. Together with some friends he produced an English version of the Vulgate. He established a secular order of poor priests, who worked as itinerant preachers dedicated to the service of the poor. In the end he denounced the doctrine of transubstantiation much as the leaders of the reformation later did. During the Peasants' Revolt of 1381, Wycliffe remained neutral, though his past marked him as a rebel sympathiser. He died in Lutterworth in 1384. Alive, he had escaped persecution, The Council of Constance took revenge on his bones. His English followers, the Lollards, were ruthlessly stamped out. In Bohemia his doctrines inspired the Hussite movement which survived until the reformation.

If we ask ourselves what is the main difference between the Greek and the medieval outlook we might well say that the former lacked a sense of sin. To the Greeks, man did not appear afflicted with an inherited personal load of sinfulness. They might indeed observe that life on earth was a precarious thing that could be crushed at the whim of the gods. But this was in no way to be construed as a just and equitable portion for evils committed in the past. It follows that to the Greek mind there was no problem of redemption or salvation. Accordingly the ethical thinking of the Greeks is, on the whole, a fairly unmetaphysical affair. In hellenistic times, especially with stoicism, a note of resigned acceptance creeps into ethics, and is later transmitted to the early Christian Sects. In sum, however, Greek philosophy was not confronted with theological problems and therefore remained thoroughly secular.

When the Christian religion took hold of the West, the situation in ethical matters suffered a radical change. The Christian regarded earthly life as a preparation for a greater life to come, and the miseries of human existence as trials imposed on him to cleanse him from the congenital burden of sin to which he was heir. But this was literally a superhuman task. In order to survive the test successfully, man needed divine help, and this might or might not be forthcoming. Where to a Greek virtue was its own reward, the Christian must be virtuous because God tells him so. Though following the narrow path of virtue might not of itself ensure salvation, it was at any rate a prerequisite. Some of these tenets must, of course, be taken on trust, and here is where divine assistance first intervenes. For it requires the grace of God for man to acquire faith and thenceforth respect its articles. Those who could not take even this first step were irremediably damned.

Aristotle, through medieval eyes: from Chartres cathedral, 13th cent.

In this context philosophy came to have a religious function. For although faith transcends reason, it behoves the believer as best he may to fortify himself against doubt by letting reason shed on faith such light as it could. Philosophy, therefore, in medieval times, becomes the handmaiden of theology. So long as this attitude prevailed, the Christian philosophers were necessarily churchmen. Secular learning, insofar as it survived at all, was preserved by clerics, and schools, and later universities, were run by men who belonged to one or other of the great religious orders. The philosophic apparatus which was called into play by these thinkers goes back to Plato and Aristotle. More particularly, the Aristotelian strain gains the upper hand in the thirteenth century. It is easy to see why Aristotle is more adaptable to Christian theology than Plato. Using scholastic language, we may put the matter thus: a realist theory does not leave much room for a divine power with any vital function in the running of things. Nominalism provides much wider scope in this respect. Though, of course, the God of the Jews and Christians is a very different thing from the Aristotelian divinity, it is nevertheless true that Aristotelianism fits much better into the Christian scheme than Platonism. The Platonic theory is calculated to inspire pantheistic doctrines, as, for instance, with Spinoza, though his brand of pantheism is purely logical, as we shall see later. This union between philosophy and theology can last so long as it is allowed that reason can underpin faith to some extent. When the Franciscan scholars of the fourteenth century denied this possibility, and held reason and faith to be mutually irrelevant, the stage is set for a gradual withering away of the medieval outlook. No further employment remains for philosophy in the theological field. In freeing faith from all possible links with rational enquiry, Occam set philosophy on the road back to secularism. From the sixteenth century onwards, the Church no longer dominates in this field.

At the same time, this schism enables men to keep their rational and their religious activities strictly separate from each other. It would be quite wrong to think of this as hypocrisy. There have been, and remain, vast numbers of men who will not let their practical beliefs interfere with their religious ones. It is, on the contrary, quite certain that only in this way can a religion maintain itself free from the assault of doubt. For as long as theology comes out into the arena of dialectic, it must conform to the canons of rational discussion.

On the other hand, an impossible impasse is reached whenever one must take on faith a proposition which is incompatible with the findings of empirical enquiry. Take, for example, the age of our planet: the Old Testament computes it at some five and three-quarter millennia or so, and this the orthodox must believe. Geologists, on the other hand, give reasons for believing the earth to be over 4000 million years old. One or other of these two beliefs must thus be modified, unless the religious-minded enquirer is prepared to hold one view on Sunday and the other for the rest of the week. The important point here is that where religious principles conflict with the findings of enquiry, religion is always in a defensive situation and has to modify its position. For it is in the nature of the case that faith must not conflict with reason. Since conflict here lies within the field of rational dialectic, it is always religion that has to retreat. With this proviso, however, the religious position after retreat remains distinct and separate.

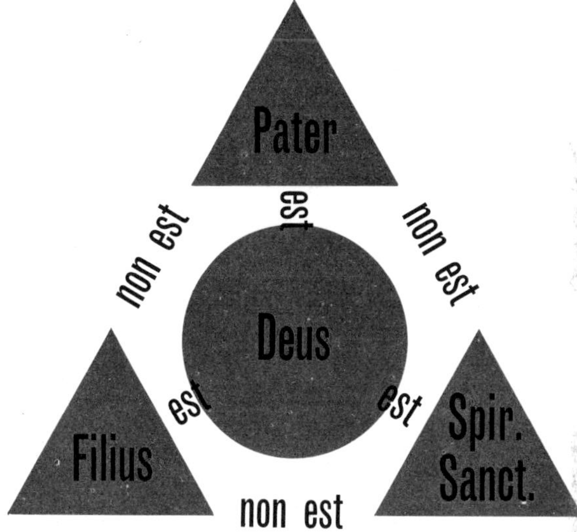

The nature of the holy trinity: a perennial scholastic problem

In their efforts to give a rational account of religious dogma so far as this is possible, the scholastic philosophers often showed great ingenuity and subtlety of mind. The long-range effect of these exercises was to sharpen the linguistic tools which were inherited by the renaissance thinkers that followed. This is probably the most valuable task scholasticism has performed. Where it was at fault was in not giving sufficient weight to empirical enquiry. It was left to the Franciscan scholars to draw attention to this defect. That the findings of experience should be thus underrated is natural enough in an age which was more concerned with God and the hereafter than with the problems of this world. The renaissance thinkers once more draw man into a central position. It is in such a climate that human activity will be valued for its own sake, and, therefore, scientific enquiry, too, takes new and formidable strides.

An ethic of activity is in the end what has set the West apart from the rest of the world during the last three or four hundred years. As Western technology has conquered the world, so the ethic that goes along with it has gained some measure of new influence.

Rise of modern philosophy

While during the 14th century the medieval outlook began to decline, there gradually emerged new forces which have forged the modern world of today. Socially, the feudal structure of medieval society became unstable through the rise of a powerful class of merchants who made common cause with sovereigns against unruly barons. Politically, the nobles lost some of their immunity when better weapons of offence made their customary strongholds untenable. If the crude sticks and pikes of peasants cannot breach castle walls, gunpowder will. Four great movements mark the period of transition which leads from the decline of the Middle Ages to the great forward surge of the 17th century.

Venus rising from the waves, symbol of cultural revival, in popular art, too

There is first the Italian renaissance of the 15th and 16th centuries. Whereas Dante was still steeped in medieval ways of thinking, he had provided in the vulgar tongue the instrument which made the written word accessible to the layman who had no Latin. With writers like Boccaccio and Petrarch there is a return to secular ideals. A rebirth of interest in the secular culture of the ancients is found throughout the arts and sciences, and marks a break with the clerical traditions of the Middle Ages. Whereas the medieval scene was dominated by preoccupations concerning God, the renaissance thinkers were more interested in man. From this circumstance the new cultural movement derives the name of Humanism, the second of the great new influences. Whereas the renaissance as a whole directly affected the general outlook on life, the humanist movement remained the province of thinkers and scholars. The Italian renaissance was not accompanied by a durable rebirth of national unity. The country was broken up into small territories ruled by city states and anarchy was rife. Italy fell to the Habsburg dynasties of Austria and Spain, and did not emerge as a sovereign nation until the middle of the 19th century. The renaissance movement, however, exerted a strong influence and gradually moved north into Germany, France and the Low Countries. The great humanists of these regions emerged roughly a century after their Italian precursors.

Here, the humanist movement is contemporary with the Lutheran reformation, the third of the major forces which changed the medieval world. That some kind of reform was due had indeed been recognised within the Church for some time. Humanist thinkers had criticised the malpractices which infested Church government, but the hold of ambitious and goldhungry Popes was too strong. When the reformation did break out it was severely opposed and condemned by Rome. What might otherwise have been accommodated as a new movement within the sphere of the Universal Church was thus forced into isolation, and developed into a number of National Protestant Churches. When at last the Catholic Church began to reform itself it was too late to heal the religious schism. Henceforth Western Christianity remains divided. The reformed religions owe to the humanist influence the conception of universal priesthood. Every man is in direct contact with God; Christ needs no vicars. The fourth important development arises directly from the revival of empirical studies initiated by the criticism of Occam. During the

next two centuries great advances are made in the scientific field. Of central importance was the rediscovery of the heliocentric system by Copernicus. The account of it appeared in print in 1543. From the 17th century onwards, the physical and mathematical sciences make rapid progress and by promoting great technical development secure the dominant position of the West. The scientific tradition, besides conferring material benefits, is in itself a great promoter of independent thought. Wherever Western civilization spreads, its political ideals eventually follow in the wake of its material expansion.

The outlook which is generated by the growth of scientific enquiry is essentially once more the outlook of the Greeks. Doing science is to save appearances. The authority which these traditions acquire is utterly different from the dogmatism with which the Church in medieval times had sought to impose its dominion on men. It is true, of course, that a hierarchy which lives by a dogmatic system of beliefs may to a large extent speak with one voice on all manner of things when enquirers hold various opinions. By some it is assumed that monolithic unanimity is a sign of superiority, though why this should be so has never been explained. That it may give those who support it a feeling of strength is no doubt the case, but this does not make their position any the more plausible, just as a proposition does not become any truer for being pronounced with a louder voice. The only things enquiry has to respect are the universal canons of rational discourse, or, in Socratic language, the dialectic.

The spectacular successes of science in its technological applications have, however, conjured up a danger of a different kind. For it has come to be thought by many that there is literally nothing man might not achieve if only his efforts are suitably directed and applied. The great advances of modern technology depend on the collaboration of many minds and hands, and to those whose task it is to initiate new schemes it must, indeed, appear that their own powers are without limit. That all these projects involve human effort and should serve human ends is apt to be forgotten. In this sphere our own world is fairly threatening to overstep the measures.

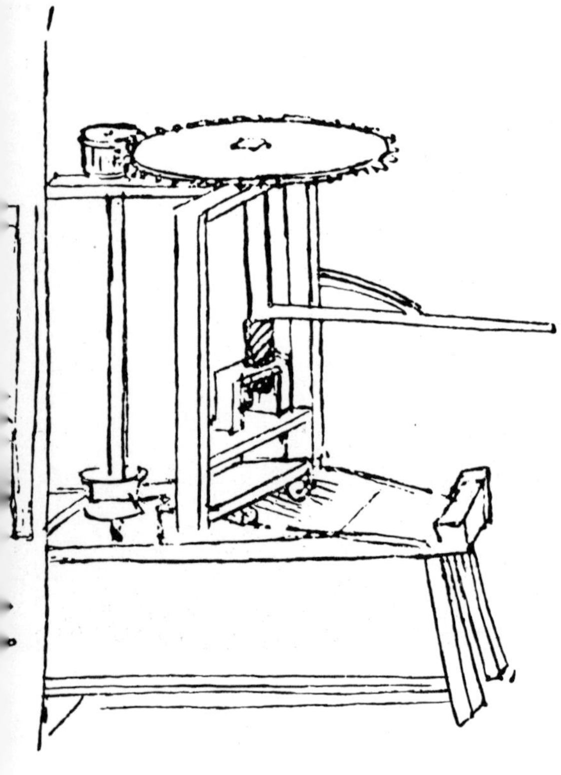

In the philosophic field, the emphasis on man gives an inward slant to speculation, and this leads to a point of view diametrically opposed to that which inspires the philosophies of power. Man now becomes a critic of his own faculties, nothing is allowed to stand unchallenged except certain immediate experiences. This subjective attitude leads to an extreme form of scepticism which in its own way is just as overwrought as the tendency to ignore the individual altogether. Some intermediate solution, evidently, must be found.

A printing press, instrument for spreading literature

Meanwhile, the transition period we are discussing is marked by two especially important developments. First there is the invention of the printing press using movable types. This goes back to the 15th century, so far, at any rate, as the West is concerned. The Chinese had used this process already five hundred years earlier, but this was not known in Europe. With the advent of printing, the scope for circulating new ideas grew enormously. It was this that in the end helped undermine the old authorities. For as the Bible, rendered into vulgar tongues, became freely available in print, the Church could no longer plausibly maintain its guardianship over matters of faith. As for learning in general, the same causes hastened a return to secularism. Not only did printing provide a means for spreading new political doctrines which were critical of the old order, but also it enabled the humanist scholars to publish editions of the works of the ancients. This in turn promoted a wider study of the classical sources and tended to improve standards of education generally.

It is perhaps not superfluous to point out that the invention of printing is a doubtful blessing if it is not accompanied by the safeguarding of freedom of discussion. For falsehood is printed just as easily as truth, and just as easily spread. It avails a man precious little to be able to read if the material put in front of him must be accepted without question. Only where there is freedom of speech and criticism does the wide circulation of the printed word enhance enquiry. Without this freedom it would be better if we were illiterate. In our own time this problem has become more acute because printing is no longer the only powerful medium for mass-communication. Since the invention of wireless telegraphy and television it has become even more important to exercise that eternal vigilance without which freedom in general begins to languish.

Along with the wider spread of information, men began to form a juster view of the earth they live on. This was accomplished through a series of voyages of discovery which gave new outlets to the drive and enterprise of the West. These adventurous exploits were made possible by technical improvements in shipbuilding and navigation, and also by a return to ancient astronomy. Until the 15th century ships did not venture far from the coast lines of the Atlantic, partly because there was no point in doing so, but above all because it was unsafe to venture into regions where there were no landmarks to guide the seafarer. The use of the compass opened up the high seas, and henceforth explorers might cross the oceans in search of new lands and sealanes.

Type of vessel used by Columbus. His discovery of America in 1492 opened up new horizons

For medieval man, the world was a static, finite and well-ordered place. Everything within it had its appointed function, the stars to run in their courses and man to live in the station to which he was born. This complacent picture was rudely shattered by the renaissance. Two opposing tendencies produce a new outlook. On the one hand, there is great confidence in the power and ingenuity of man, who now takes up the centre of the stage. But at the same time, man's position in the universe becomes less commanding, for the infinity of space begins to exercise the imagination of philosophers. These views are adumbrated in the writings of the German Cardinal Nicolas Cusanus (1401–1464), and in the following century become incorporated in the Copernican system. Similarly, there is a return to the old view of Pythagoras and Plato that the world is built on a mathematical pattern. All these speculations upset the existing order of things and undermined the old established authorities both in the clerical and secular sphere. The Church tried to contain the spread of heresy, but with little success. All the same it is well to remember that as recently as 1600 the Inquisition condemned Giordano Bruno to be burnt at the stake. As so often before, the ministers of the existing order, from fear of subversion, dealt out savage sentence on one who dared to be different. But this very verdict showed how weak was the position it was supposed to uphold. In the political field new conceptions of authority gradually developed and the powers of hereditary rulers came to be more and more restricted.

The break occasioned by the reformation was not in all respects a fruitful development. It might be thought that with a plurality of religions men should at last have come to see that one and the same God may be worshipped in many different ways. This was a view which Cusanus had advocated already before the reformation. But this rather obvious conclusion did not commend itself to the faithful.

The renaissance did not, of course, begin as a sudden awakening from a past during which the knowledge of the ancients lay dormant. Indeed, we have seen that throughout the Middle Ages there remained some vestiges of the older traditions. History is simply not broken up by such sharp lines of division. Nevertheless, distinctions of this kind are useful if handled with care. If, therefore, it is legitimate to speak of an Italian renaissance, this means that there are certain obvious differences between the medieval past and the modern period. A clear contrast, for example, exists between the ecclesiastic literature of the scholastics and the secular literature in the vulgar tongue which begins to appear with the 14th century. This literary revival precedes the humanist rebirth of learning based on classical sources. The new literature used as its vehicle the language of the people, and thus came to have a wider appeal than the works of scholars who retained Latin as their medium.

Plato and Aristotle, as seen by the Italian renaissance painter Raphael

In all fields of endeavour the limitations of the medieval outlook were now being thrown off. The sources of inspiration lie, to begin with, in the emerging secular interests of the period, and later in an idealized vision of the ancient past. The conception of antiquity which developed at that time was, of course, more or less distorted by the enthusiasm of a generation which had rediscovered a continuity with its own history. This somewhat romantic view of the ancients survived until the 19th century. We are certainly much better informed on these matters now than were the artists and writers of the renaissance.

In Italy, where the remnants of ancient civilisation provided tangible symbols of past ages, the renaissance movement gained a wider foothold than did its later forms north of the Alps. Politically, the country was divided much in the manner of ancient Greece. In the north, there were numerous city-states, in the centre the papal dominions and in the south the kingdom of Naples and Sicily. Of the northern cities, Milan, Venice and Florence were the most powerful. There was constant strife between states, as well as faction fights within each city. While individual intrigues and vendettas were conducted with supreme skill and cruelty, the country as a whole did not suffer grave damage. Nobles and cities would fight each other with the help of hirelings whose professional interest was to stay alive. This relaxed state of affairs was radically altered when Italy became the battleground of the French king and the Emperor. Italy was, however, too far divided to rally against invasion from abroad. The country thus remained disunited and largely under foreign dominion. In the repeated struggles between France and the Empire, it was the Habsburgs who emerged as victors. Naples and Sicily remained Spanish while the papal dominions enjoyed a tolerated independence. Milan, a Guelf stronghold, became a dependency of the Spanish Habsburgs in 1535. The Venetians occupy a somewhat special position, partly because they had never suffered defeat at the hands of the barbarians, and partly because of the Byzantine connection. They had acquired strength and wealth through the crusades, and after defeating their rivals the Genoese, controlled trade throughout the Mediterranean. When Constantinople fell to the Ottoman Turks in 1453, Venice began to decline, a process which was hastened by the discovery of the Cape route to India and the opening up of the New World.

The foremost bearer of the renaissance movement was the city of Florence. No town except Athens has brought forth such a company of artists and thinkers. Dante, Michelangelo and Leonardo, to mention only a few, were all of them Florentines, and so, later was Galileo. The internal troubles of Florence which had caused Dante's exile, eventually led to the rule of the Medicis. From 1400 onwards, except for short interruptions, this family of merchant nobles ruled the city for over three centuries.

As for the papacy, the renaissance had a twofold effect. On the one hand, the popes took an enlightened interest in the scholarly pursuits of the humanists and became great patrons of the arts. Papal claims to temporal power derived from the spurious Donation of Constantine, but Pope Nicholas V (1447–55) greatly admired Lorenzo Valla, who exposed the forgery and held other questionable opinions. The literary detective was made apostolic secretary in spite of his unorthodox views. On the other hand, this relaxation of standards of belief led to such secular preoccupations as to lose the papacy much of its spiritual influence. The private lives of men like Alexander VI (1492–1503) fell somewhat short of the piety which might be expected from God's representative on earth. Moreover, the temporal pursuits of 16th century popes drained off large sums of money from abroad. All this gave rise to grievances that culminated in the reformation.

Jerome, from a majolica dish of the renaissance period

In philosophy, the Italian renaissance did not, on the whole, produce great works. It was a period of rediscovery of sources rather than of great philosophic speculation. In particular, the study of Plato once more begins to challenge the Aristotelianism of the schools. Florence, under Cosimo dei Medici, saw the rise of the Florentine Academy in the early 15th century. This institution favoured Plato as against the established universities. In general, the labours of humanist scholars paved the way for the great philosophic developments of the 17th century.

For all that the renaissance emancipated men from the dogmatism of the Church, it did not save them from all kinds of ancient superstition. Astrology, which had constantly been discouraged by the Church, now gained widespread popularity, infecting not just the ignorant but the learned as well. As for witchcraft, this too was widely believed in, and hundreds of harmless eccentrics were burnt at the stake as witches. Witch-hunting is, of course, not unknown even in our own time, though it is no longer the custom to burn the quarry. Along with the rejection of medieval dogmatism went a loss of respect for established codes of conduct and behaviour. It is this, amongst other things, that prevented Italy from acquiring some form of national integrity in the face of foreign dangers from the North. The times were rife with treacherous intrigue and double dealing. The gentle art of disposing of rivals or enemies was developed to an unsurpassed level of craftsmanship. In such a climate of deceit and distrust no viable form of political collaboration could be born.

In the field of political philosophy, the Italian renaissance produced one outstanding figure. Niccolo Machiavelli (1469–1527) was the son of a Florentine lawyer. His political career began in 1494, when the Medici were expelled from Florence. It is at this time that the city came under the influence of Savonarola, the Dominican reformer who stood out against the vice and corruption of his time. In his zealous efforts he ultimately fell foul of Alexander VI, the Borgia pope, and was burnt at the stake in 1498. These events were calculated to provoke reflections on the nature of power and political success. Machiavelli later wrote that unarmed prophets always failed, giving Savonarola as an example. During the exile of the Medici, Florence was a republic and Machiavelli remained in public office until their return to power in 1512. Throughout this time he was opposed to them and therefore now fell into disgrace. He was forced to retire from public life, and thenceforth devoted himself to writing on political philosophy and related matters. An attempt to regain the favour of the Medici by dedicating his famous book 'The Prince' to Lorenzo II in 1513 was not successful. He died in 1527, the year the mercenaries of the Emperor Charles V sacked Rome.

Machiavelli, Florentine diplomat, political philosopher

Machiavelli's two great works on politics are 'The Prince' and the 'Discourses'. Of these, the first sets out to study the ways and means in which autocratic power is won and maintained, while the latter provides a general study of power and its exercise under various types of rule. The doctrine of 'The Prince' makes no attempt at giving pious advice on how to be a virtuous ruler. On the contrary, it recognises that there are evil practices which are conducive to the acquisition of political power. It is from this circumstance that the term Machiavellian has taken on its somewhat sinister and derogatory meaning. In fairness to Machiavelli it must be stated that he does not advocate villainy as a principle. His field of enquiry lies beyond good and evil, just as the researches of a nuclear physicist do. If you wish to gain power, so the argument runs, you must be ruthless. Whether this is good or bad is quite another question, but not of interest to Machiavelli. It is possible to find fault with him for not giving attention to this matter, but it is pointless to condemn him for his study of power politics as it actually existed. For what is set down in 'The Prince' is more or less a summary of practices that were common in renaissance Italy.

During his public life in the service of the Florentine republic, Machiavelli had been sent on a variety of diplomatic missions which had given him ample opportunity of studying at first hand the intricacies of political intrigue. In the course of his diplomatic work he became well acquainted with Caesar Borgia, the son of Alexander VI, and as vigorous a scoundrel as his father. With great skill and daring, Caesar Borgia planned to ensure his own position against the day when his father should die. His brother, standing in the way of these ambitions, was eliminated. On the military side, Caesar helped his father enlarge the papal dominions, fully intending later to keep these territories for himself. As for the papal succession, everything must be done that one of his own friends should come to occupy the Holy See. Caesar Borgia displayed admirable ingenuity, and diplomatic cunning in pursuing these ends, now feigning friendship, and now dealing death. The victims of these exercises in statesmanship cannot, of course, be consulted about their feelings, but the chances are that from a detached point of view they might well have admired Caesar Borgia's undoubted skill; such was the temper of the times. In the end, his plans failed because he was himself ill at the time his father died in 1503. The successor to the papal throne was Julius II, an inveterate enemy of the Borgias. Given the aims of Caesar Borgia, one may well recognise that he pursued them ably. For this, Machiavelli allows him generous praise. In 'The Prince', he commends him as an example to others who might be aspiring to power. That practices of this kind seemed to him defensible is in keeping with the general standards of the period. From the 17th to the 19th century such ruthless methods were, on the whole, not condoned, at least not praised in public. The 20th century has once again produced a number of political leaders in the tradition that Machiavelli knew.

Caesar Borgia, son of Alexander VI, ruthless renaissance potentate

From 1513 to 1521, the papal throne was occupied by Leo X, a member of the Medici family. Since Machiavelli was trying to ingratiate himself with the Medicis, we find that in 'The Prince' the question of papal authority is avoided with a few pious platitudes. In the 'Discourses' a rather more critical view is taken of the papacy. The entire approach here is more informed with ethical notions. Machiavelli considers, in order of merit, the various types of men in power, ranging from the founders of religions to those of tyrannies. The function of religion in the state he conceives along pragmatic lines. The truth or falsehood of religious belief matters not at all, provided only that the state should gain some measure of social cohesion. On such a view it is, of course, quite proper to persecute heretics. As for the Church, it is condemned on two counts: first, because the evil way of life of many of its ministers has shaken popular confidence in religion; and secondly, because the secular and political interests of the papacy were an obstacle to national unity in Italy. It may be noted, incidentally, that this is quite consistent with a recognition that, in pursuit of their own ends, some of the political popes had acted with great dexterity. 'The Prince', is not concerned with ends, whereas the 'Discourses' sometimes are.

As to conventional moral standards, 'The Prince' makes it quite clear that rulers are not bound by them: unless expediency demands that moral laws should be obeyed, a ruler may break them all. Indeed, he often must if he wishes to remain in power. At the same time, he should appear to others to be virtuous. It is only by means of this duplicity that a ruler can hold his position.

In the general discussion of the 'Discourses', Machiavelli expounds the theory of checks and balances. All orders in society should have some constitutional power so that they can exercise some measure of mutual control. This theory goes back to Plato's 'Politicus', and becomes prominent in the 17th century with Locke, and with Montesquieu in the 18th century. Machiavelli has thus influenced the theories of the liberal political philosophers of modern times as well as the practice of contemporary autocrats. The doctrine of duplicity is practised by many as far as it will carry them, though it has limitations which Machiavelli does not consider.

From Erasmus' book, 'In praise of folly'

The renaissance movement which swept Italy during the fifteenth century took some time to make itself felt north of the Alps. In that northward spread the forces of revival suffered some significant changes. For one thing, in the north the new outlook remained much more a concern of the learned. In a sense, it is not even strictly correct to speak of a renaissance, for there is nothing here that once existed and could now be reborn. Where in the south the traditions of the past had some vague meaning for people in general, in northern lands the influence of Rome had been temporary or non-existent. The new movement was thus led primarily by scholars, and its appeal therefore somewhat restricted. Not finding the same outlet in the artistic sphere, this northern humanism was in some ways a more serious affair. In the end, its break with medieval authority was more abrupt and spectacular than in Italy. Although many of the humanist scholars did not favour the religious split occasioned by the reformation, it was in a way to be expected that this should occur, if at all, in the wake of the northern renaissance.

Since the renaissance, the function of religion in the lives of the people was quite a different one on the two sides of the Alps. In Italy, the papacy in some sense represented the direct connection with the imperial past. As for the practice of religion itself, this was more a matter of routine, a part of ordinary life which was negotiated with the same unruffled attitude as eating or drinking. Even today religion in Italy retains this somewhat unfervid flavour when compared with the same creed as practised elsewhere. There was therefore a twofold reason why a complete severance with the existing religious traditions was impossible. First, the Church was in some sense a part of the establishment, even if, as Machiavelli had pointed out, the papacy was somewhat of a hindrance to Italian national unity ; and secondly, beliefs were not held with that kind of deep conviction that might have led to radical changes when called for. The humanist thinkers of the north were men who had a serious interest in religion and the abuses from which it suffered. In their polemical writings they were bitterly hostile to the debased practices of the curia. Added to this was a feeling of national pride for which Italian prelates had not always made due allowance. It was not merely a matter of general concern about the monetary contributions towards the upkeep and embellishment of Rome, but also of direct resentment of the condescension with which the quick-witted Italians regarded the more serious-minded Teutons from the north.

Erasmus of Rotterdam (1466-1536), scholar and editor

The greatest of the northern humanists was Erasmus of Rotterdam (1466–1536). Both his parents died before he was twenty, and this, it seems, prevented him from going straight on to a university. His guardians sent him to a monastic school instead, and in due course he joined an Augustinian monastery at Steyn. The result of these early experiences engendered in him a lasting hatred for the severe and unimaginative scholasticism which had been inflicted on him. In 1494, the bishop of Cambrai appointed Erasmus as his secretary and thus helped him to break away from the monkish seclusion of Steyn. Several visits to Paris followed, but the philosophic atmosphere at the Sorbonne was no longer conducive to furthering the new learning. For, in the face of the revival, the Thomist and Occamist factions had buried their hatchets and were now making common cause against the humanists.

At the end of 1499, he went for a short visit to England where he met Colet and above all More. Upon his return to the continent he took up Greek to good effect. When he visited Italy in 1506 he took his doctorate at Turin but found no one to excel him in Greek. In 1516 he published the first edition of the New Testament in Greek to appear in print. Of his books, the best remembered is 'The Praise of Folly', a satire composed at More's house in London in 1509. The Greek title is a pun on More's name. In this book, besides much ridicule on the failings of mankind, there are bitter attacks on the degradation of religious institutions and their ministers. In spite of his outspoken criticisms he did not, when the time came, declare openly for the reformation. He held the essentially protestant view that man stands in direct relation with God and that theology was superfluous. But at the same time he would not be drawn into religious controversies arising in the wake of the reformation movement. He was more interested in his scholarly pursuits and his publishing, and felt in any case that the schism was unfortunate. While in some measure it is true enough that controversies of this kind are a nuisance, these issues could not be ignored. In the end, Erasmus declared for Catholicism, but at the same time became less important. The stage was held by men of stronger mettle.

It is in education that the influence of Erasmus came to leave its most lasting impression. The humanist learning which, until recently, was the core of secondary education wherever Western European views prevailed, owes much to his literary and teaching activities. In his work as a publisher he was not always concerned with exhaustive critical examination of texts. He aimed at a wider reading public rather than at academic specialists. At the same time he did not write in the vulgar tongue. He was on the contrary intent on strengthening the position of Latin.

In England, the most prominent of the humanists was Sir Thomas More (1478–1535). At the age of fourteen he was sent to Oxford and there began to study Greek. This was at that time apt to be regarded as a trifle eccentric, and was certainly viewed with suspicion by the young scholar's father. More was destined to follow his father's footsteps and take up law. In 1497 he met Erasmus on his first visit to England. This renewed contact with the new learning strengthened More's interest in his Greek studies. Shortly after this he went through a phase of asceticism and practised the rigours of the Carthusian order. In the end, however, he abandoned monastic ideas, partly perhaps owing to contrary advice from his friend Erasmus. In 1504 we find him in Parliament, where he distinguished himself by his forthright barring of Henry VII's financial requests. The king died in 1509 and More once more devoted himself to his profession. But Henry VIII soon called him back to public affairs. In due course he rose to the highest office, becoming Chancellor in Wolsey's stead, after the latter's fall in 1529. But More did not remain in power long. He was opposed to the King's divorce from Catherine of Aragon, and resigned his office in 1532. He provoked the King's active displeasure by refusing to accept an invitation to the coronation of Anne Boleyn. When, in 1534, the act of supremacy established the King as the head of the new church, More would not take the oath. He was sent to the Tower, and at his trial, in 1535, was found guilty of treason for having said that Parliament could not make the King head of the Church. On the strength of this view he was executed. Toleration in matters of politics was not the custom of the times.

Thomas More (1478-1535), the English humanist

More was a voluminous writer, but most of his works are hardly read today. His fame rests entirely on a political phantasy best known under the title of 'Utopia'. This is a piece of speculative social and political theory, evidently inspired by Plato's 'Republic'. It is in the form of a report by a shipwrecked sailor who lived five years in this island community. As in Plato, there is great emphasis on communal property, and for similar reasons. Where things are privately owned, it is held, a thorough respect for the common weal cannot emerge. Besides, if men possess goods for themselves, they are divided from each other in the measure that their riches differ. That all men should be equal is, in Utopia, a basic fact taken for granted. From this it is inferred that private property is a corrupting influence and therefore not to be admitted. When their visitor tells the Utopians about Christianity, it appeals to them mainly for the communist streak in its teaching concerning property.

The organisation of this ideal state is described in great detail. There is a capital city and fifty-three other towns, all built on the same pattern, with identical dwellings to which all and sundry have free access. Where private property does not exist there is no point in stealing. The countryside is dotted with farms all run on similar lines. As for dress, everyone wears the same kind of clothes, except for a useful, though minor sartorial distinction between married women and spinsters. Clothes are inconspicuous and always remain the same, the vagaries of fashion are unknown. The working lives of citizens all run to the same pattern. They all work a six hour day and invariably turn in at eight in the evening and rise again at four in the morning.

Those who have the making of scholars concentrate on their intellectual labours and do not do any other kind of work. It is from this group that the governing body is selected. The system of rule is a form of representative democracy by indirect election. The head of state is elected for life, provided he behaves himself; if not, he may be deposed. The social life of the community is also subject to strict rules. As to relations with foreign countries, these are confined to the essential minimum. Iron does not exist in Utopia and must therefore be imported. Military training is given both to men and women, though war is never waged except in self-defence, or in assistance of allies or oppressed nations. So far as possible, the fighting is done by mercenaries. A fund of precious metal is built up by trade in order to pay for mercenary troops in time of war. For their own purposes they need no money. Their way of life is free from bigotry and asceticism. There is, however, one minor restriction: atheists, though allowed to hold their views without interference, do not enjoy the status of citizens and cannot belong to the government. For some of the more menial tasks there are bondsmen, recruited from the ranks of those convicted of serious crimes, or from foreigners who have escaped to avoid punishment in their own countries.

No doubt life in so well contrived a state as this would be desperately uninteresting. This is a common feature of ideal states. What is, however, much more relevant in More's discussion is the new liberal approach to the question of religious toleration. The reformation had shaken the Christian community of Europe out of its complacent attitude to authority. That there were precursors to these events, preaching toleration in religious matters, we have already mentioned. When the reformation led to a permanent religious split in Europe, the notion of toleration had eventually to prevail. The alternative of wholesale extermination and suppression was tried and found wanting in the end. In the sixteenth century, however, the notion that all and sundry might have their religious beliefs respected was still sufficiently eccentric to attract attention.

More's phantasy, inspired by Plato, tale of a sailor stranded on the island of 'Utopia'

One of the results of the reformation was that religion became more overtly a political matter, often on a national basis as in England. This, evidently, could never happen so long as one universal religion prevailed. It was this new political character of religious allegiance that men like More deplored in withholding their support for the reformation. That they substantially agreed on the necessity for some kind of reform we saw already in connection with Erasmus. But they deplored the violence and strife that attended the emergence of a completely separate creed. In this they were of course quite right. In England, the national character of the religious split stands out very clearly. Here the newly established Church fits closely into the political framework of the machinery of government. At the same time, the break was in some ways not so violent as elsewhere, for there had been a long standing tradition of comparative independence from Rome. Already the Conqueror had insisted on having his voice in episcopal appointments. The anti-Roman bent of the new Church survives in the maintenance of the Protestant succession which goes back to William and Mary, and in the unwritten law that no Roman Catholic succeeds to the Presidency of the United States.

We have seen that for some centuries before the storm of the reformation broke, a gradual change in intellectual climate had undermined the old views of Church supremacy. The causes which brought about this revolutionary change are varied and mixed. On the face of it we are merely confronted with a rebellion against vicarious authority between God and Man. But this commendable principle may well not have broken through unaided if the Church had not by its own abuses attracted men's attention to the disparity between what it preached and what it practised. The clergy often were substantially provided with landed property. This might not in itself be reckoned objectionable if it were not for the fact that the teaching of Jesus cannot be easily reconciled with the worldly deportment of his ministers. As for questions of religious doctrine, already Occam had maintained that Christianity could function without the unbridled supremacy of the Bishop of Rome. All the elements for a thorough reform of the religious life of Christendom were thus extant within the Church. In the end it was owing to political forces that the search for reform developed into a schism.

Martin Luther (1483-1546), Augustinian friar, reformer, bible translator

The reformers themselves were intellectually inferior to the humanist scholars that had prepared the ground. But they supplied the revolutionary fervour which critical thinkers often find it difficult to summon up. Martin Luther (1483—1546) was an Augustinian friar and a teacher of theology. The debased practice of selling indulgences caused him acute moral distress, as it did to many others. In 1517 he came out into the open and proclaimed the famous ninety-five theses, a document which he nailed to the door of the Castle Church of Wittenberg. In challenging the curia on this point, he had no intention of setting up a new religion. However, this vexed question involved the whole political problem of large scale financial contributions to a foreign power. By the time Luther publicly burned the papal bull of excommunication in 1520, the matter was no longer simply one of religious reform. The German princes and rulers were beginning to take sides, and the reformation became a political revolt of the Germans against the subtler power of the Pope.

John Calvin (1509-1564), the French reformer of Geneva

After the Diet of Worms in 1521, Luther was in hiding for ten months and produced a New Testament in the Vulgar Tongue. As a literary document this, in some measure, did for the Germans what the Divine Comedy had done for the Italians. At all events, it greatly helped to spread the words of the Gospels among the people. That there were grave discrepancies between the teaching of Jesus and the existing social order could now be seen by everyone who could read. It was largely on this and the new Protestant conception of the bible as the sole authority that the Peasants' revolt of 1524 based its own virtue. But Luther was not a democratic reformer and declared openly against those who had defied their political masters. In his political thinking he remained medieval in outlook. The revolt was attended by much violence and cruelty on all sides, and in the end was brutally crushed. This abortive attempt at a social revolution did something towards weakening the initial impulse of the reformed religion. The term Protestant itself stems from an appeal issued by supporters of the reformed religion in protest against the emperor's attempt, in 1529, to reintroduce the provisions of the Diet of Worms.

On that occasion, the reformer and his party had been declared outlaws, but this measure was being held in abeyance since 1526. Now once more Luther was under the ban of empire, and therefore did not attend the Diet of Augsburg in 1530. But the Protestant movement was by now too strong to be crushed, and in 1532 the emperor was forced, by the religious peace of Nuremberg, to give reluctant guarantees to those who sought free exercise of their new religion.

Emblem of Jesuit Order, founded by Ignatius of Loyola (1491-1556)

The reform movement spread rapidly into the low countries, France and Switzerland. After Luther, the most influential reformer was John Calvin (1509–1564), a Frenchman who established himself at Geneva. He became converted to the reform movement in his early twenties, and thereafter was spiritual leader of protestantism in France and the Netherlands. Calvinism as a doctrine, in its Augustinianism, is fiercer and more uncompromising than Lutheran evangelism. It is strongly imbued with puritan ideals and maintains that salvation is a matter of predestination. This is one of the less engaging features of Christian theology, and the Roman church did well to dissociate itself from the doctrine. In practice, of course, it does less harm than might at first appear, since everyone is free to consider himself as one of the elect.

The latter half of the sixteenth century saw France torn by the wars of religion between the reformed Huguenots and the Catholics. As in Germany, the causes of these upheavals were not merely religious, but partly economic. More precisely, we might say that both the religious and the economic causes were symptoms of general changes that marked the transition from medieval to modern times. For the reformed religion and its puritan features go hand in hand with the rise of modern trade. In France, the religious dissensions were for a time composed by the edict of toleration, proclaimed at Nantes in 1598. When it was revoked in 1685, large numbers of Huguenots left their homeland and settled in England and Germany.

As Protestantism was not a universal religion, it required protection from political heads of state, who tended to become the heads of their national churches as well. This was a blessing in disguise, for lacking the power of the Roman clergy, Protestant churchmen, though they were often as bigoted and intolerant as anyone, had not the unchecked power to do much harm. In the end, men saw that religious strife was wasteful and inconclusive, as neither side was strong enough to eliminate the other. It was from this negative realisation that effective religious toleration eventually developed.

Within the Roman Church itself, a new movement of reform developed towards the middle of the sixteenth century. This was centred on the Jesuit Order, which was founded by Ignatius of Loyola (1491–1556) and gained official recognition in 1540. The society of Jesus was organised on military principles inspired by Loyola's earlier career as a soldier. In doctrine, the Jesuits opposed the Augustinian teaching that the Protestants had adopted, and emphasised free will above all. Their practical activities were concerned with missionary work, education and the rooting out of heresy. They became the main organisers of the Spanish inquisition.

Alberti (1404-1472), architect, humanist thinker

Whereas the humanism of the north led to a new conception of Christianity, the Italian humanist thinkers were not much concerned with religion. Then, as now, catholicism in Italy was a part of daily life that did not deeply engage men's consciousness. In a sense, religion played a smaller part in their lives and was certainly less calculated to arouse their feelings. Besides, since Rome was the central point of the hierarchy, Roman catholicism could not disturb the national pride of Italians. In a very real form this was some kind of survival of the principles of state cult as it existed in ancient imperial days. The preponderance of Italian influence in the government of the Church of Rome remains to the present day.

Of much greater importance in the thinking of the Italian humanists was the renewed emphasis on the mathematical tradition of Pythagoras and Plato. The numerical structure of the world was once again emphasized, thus displacing the Aristotelian tradition that had overshadowed it. This was one of the principal developments which led to the spectacular revival of scientific enquiry in the sixteenth and seventeenth centuries. Nowhere is this more apparent than in the theory and practice of Italian renaissance architecture. Here, there was a direct link with the old classical traditions, especially as laid down in the works of Vitruvius, the Roman architect of the first century A.D. Great importance was attached to the proportions between the various parts of a building, and along with this went a mathematical theory of the beautiful. As Vitruvius had said, basing himself on Greek sources, beauty consists in the harmony of proper proportions. This view goes straight back to Pythagorean sources. It shows, incidentally, another way in which the theory of ideas may gain a foothold. For it is clear that, to the naked eye, it is not possible to judge precisely the numerical relationships between different parts of a structure. And yet, when certain precise proportions are achieved, some kind of aesthetic satisfaction seems to result. Therefore the existence of such proportions, as an ideal, guarantees perfection.

Pythagorean module: Giorgio used these proportions for design

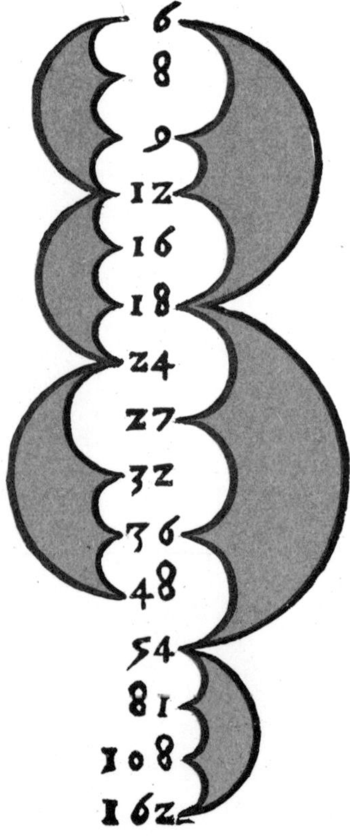

Amongst the Italian humanist thinkers one of the most important was Alberti (1404–1472). In the manner of the time, this Venetian was a versatile craftsman in many fields. His most lasting influence was probably in the field of architecture, but he also was a philosopher, poet, painter and musician. Indeed, just as some elementary knowledge of harmony is essential to understand the Pythagorean influence in Greek philosophy, so in the case of renaissance architecture the same knowledge is required to grasp the proportions involved in design. Briefly, the rationale of this theory was that the audible consonance of the Pythagorean intervals was the criterion for visual consonance in architectural design. When Goethe later speaks of architecture as frozen music, this, to a renaissance architect, would convey something which was literally true of his own practice. The theory of harmony based on the tuned string thus provided a general standard of excellence in art and was so interpreted by men like Giorgio and Leonardo. The principle of proportions was found also in the structure of the human body and in the adjusted function of men's moral existence. All this is straight and deliberate Pythagoreanism. But mathematics here assumes a further role which had great influence on the scientific revival of the following centuries.

For in so far as an art might partake of number it was at once raised onto a more exalted level. This is most obvious in the case of music, but also applies to the other arts. It also explains in some measure the versatility of the humanist thinkers of this period, and in particular the fact that so many of them were artists and architects. For the mathematics of proportions provided a universal key to the design of the universe. Whether such a theory can be made a sound basis for a general aesthetics remains, of course, controversial. But it has in any case the great merit of setting up unquestionably objective criteria for excellence not tied to feelings or intentions.

A grasp of the numerical structure in things thus conferred on man new powers over his surroundings. In a way it made man more like God. The Pythagoreans had viewed him as the supreme mathematician. If man was able in some measure to exercise and improve his mathematical skills he came closer to divine status. This is not to say that humanism was impious or even opposed to the received religion. But it does show that the current religious practices tended to be accepted as a matter of routine, and what really fired the imagination of thinkers was the old presocratic doctrine. Thus, in the field of philosophy, a neoplatonic strain comes to the fore again. The emphasis on man's power is reminiscent of the optimism of Athens at the peak of her power.

This was the intellectual climate in which modern science began to grow. It is sometimes thought that at the turn of the seventeenth century, science sprang into life fully armed, as Athena from the head of Zeus. Nothing could be further from the truth. The revival of science is based directly and consciously on the Pythagorean tradition of the renaissance. Likewise, it is worth emphasising that in this tradition there was no opposition between the work of the artist and the scientific enquirer. Both in their several ways sought after truth, whose essence was grasped through numbers. These numerical patterns were discernible to any who would take the trouble to look. This new approach to the world and its problems was radically different from the Aristotelianism of the schools. It was anti-dogmatic in that it did not rely on texts, but on the sole authority of the science of numbers. In this it may at times have gone too far. As in all other fields, the danger of overstepping the measures must always be remembered. In the present case, the excess would be mathematical mysticism, which relies on numbers as on symbols of magic. This, amongst other things, brought the theory of proportions into disrepute in later centuries. Besides, it was felt that the Pythagorean intervals imposed unnatural and stifling restrictions on the inventive genius of the designer. This romantic reaction against rules and criteria may well have run its course in our own time, and a return to some of the principles that animated the renaissance is a distinct possibility for the near future.

In philosophy proper, the fifteenth and sixteenth centuries are on the whole not very spectacular. On the other hand, the spread of the new learning, the dissemination of books, and, above all, the renewed vigour of the ancient traditions of Pythagoras and Plato, paved the way for the great philosophic systems of the 17th century.

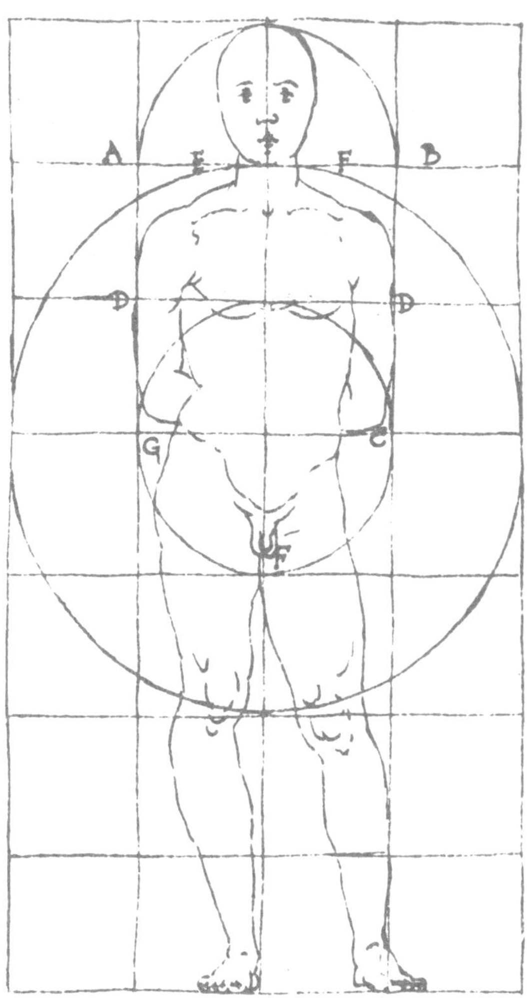

Man drawn over plan of basilica, sketch by Giorgio to show that proportions rule everything

Leonardo sketch of a skull

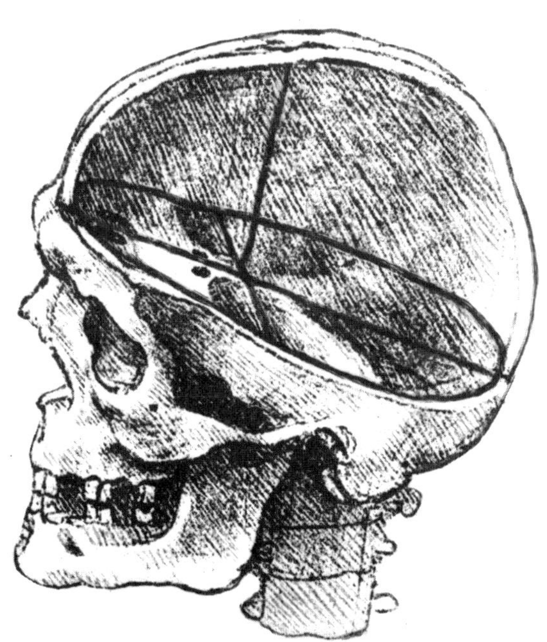

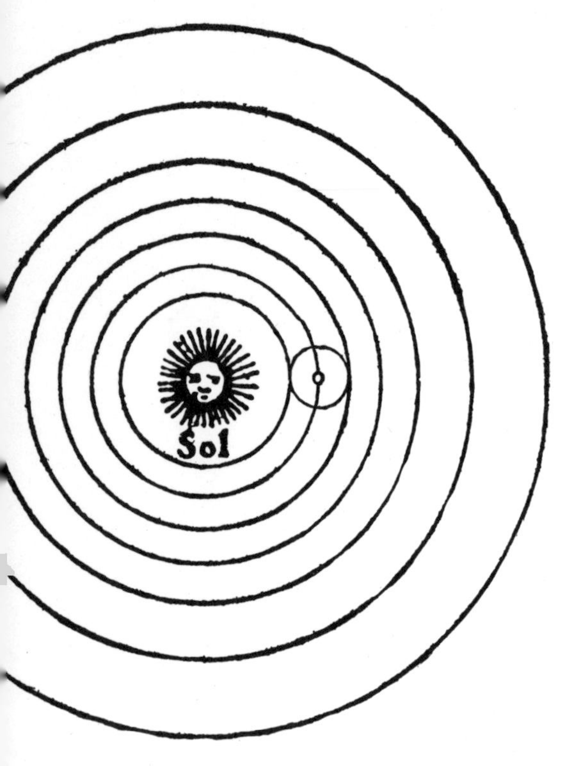

The heliocentric system of Copernicus

Copernicus (1473-1543), cleric and astronomer

It was in the wake of this revival of ancient modes of thought that the great scientific revolution began. Starting from a more or less orthodox Pythagoreanism, it gradually overthrew the established notions of Aristotelian physics and astronomy, to finish by going right behind the appearances and discovering an immensely general and powerful hypothesis. In all this, the men who furthered such enquiries knew that they stood directly in the Platonic tradition.

The first to revive the heliocentric theory of Aristarchus was Copernicus (1473–1543). This Polish cleric had in his earlier years gone south to Italy where we find him teaching mathematics in Rome in 1500. It was there that he came in contact with the Pythagoreanism of the Italian humanists. After some years of study at several Italian universities he returned to Poland in 1505, and after 1512 resumed his work as a canon of Frauenburg. His work was mainly administrative, though he had occasionally to practice medicine, which he had studied in Italy. In his spare time he pursued astronomical researches. The heliocentric hypothesis had come to his notice during his stay in Italy. Now he was trying to test his views with what instruments could be mustered at that time.

The work in which all this is fully set out is entitled 'De revolutionibus orbium coelestium', which was not published until the year of his death. The theory as he propounded it was not free from difficulties, and in some ways was dictated by preconceived notions going back to Pythagoras. That the planets must move steadily in circles seemed to Copernicus a foregone conclusion, because the circle is a symbol of perfection, and uniform motion the only kind becoming a heavenly body. Within the scope of the observations available, the heliocentric view with circular orbits was, however, much superior to the epicycles of Ptolemy. For, here, at last was a simple hypothesis which by itself alone saved all the appearances.

The Copernican Theory was received with violent hostility by Lutherans as well as Catholics. For it was sensed, quite rightly, that here was the beginning of a new anti-dogmatic movement which was going to undermine, if not religion itself, at least the authoritarian principles on which religious organisations rely. That in the end the great development of the scientific movement occurred mainly in protestant countries is due to the relative impotence of the national churches in the control over the opinions of its members.

Astronomical research was continued by Tycho Brahe (1546–1601), whose main contribution lay in the provision of extensive and accurate records of planetary motions. He also cast doubt on Aristotelian doctrines in astronomy by showing that the region beyond the moon was not exempt from change. For a new star that appeared in 1572 was found to have no daily parallax and must therefore be at a vastly greater distance than the moon. Comets, too, could be shown to be moving beyond the moon's orbit.

A great step forward was taken by Kepler (1571–1630), who as a young man had worked under Tycho Brahe. By careful study of the records of observation, Kepler found that the circular orbits of

Copernicus did not properly save the appearances. He recognised that the orbits were ellipses with the sun in one focus. Furthermore, the area swept out in a given time by a radius connecting the sun to a planet was found to be constant for that planet. Finally, the ratio of the square of the period of revolution to the cube of the mean distance from the sun turned out to be the same for all planets. These are the three laws of Kepler, which constituted a radical break with the somewhat literal Pythagoreanism that had guided the researches of Copernicus. It became clear that such extraneous elements as the insistence on circular motion had to be abandoned. Previously, where a simple circular orbit was inadequate, it had been the custom since Ptolemy to compound more complicated orbits by means of epicyclic motions. This device approximately accounts for the motions of the moon with regard to the sun. But more careful observations showed that no amount of epicyclic complication could adequately describe the observed orbits. Kepler's first law cut this Gordian Knot at one blow. At the same time, his second law showed that the motion of planets in their orbit was not uniform. When they are closer to the sun they move faster than in the more remote portions of the orbits. All this forced men to recognise that it was dangerous to argue without reference to the facts, from preconceived aesthetic or mystical principles. On the other hand, the central mathematical principles of Pythagoreanism were brilliantly vindicated by Kepler's three laws. It seemed, indeed, that it was the numerical structure in appearances that gave the key to understanding them. Likewise, it became clear that in order to find a proper account for appearances it was necessary to look for relationships that were usually not obvious. The measures according to which the universe runs are hidden, as Heraclitus had put it, and it is precisely the task of the enquirer to discover them. At the same time it is of utmost importance not to do violence to the appearances merely to safeguard some extraneous principle.

But if on the one hand it is dangerous to ignore appearances, on the other a blind recording of them can be just as frustrating to science as the wildest of speculations might be. Aristotle is a case in point. For he was right in saying that if you do not keep on pushing a body it will come to a halt. This is certainly what we observe with such bodies as we can push about. It was wrongly inferred that the same must be true of the stars which, indeed, we ourselves cannot push round the heavens, and which therefore must, it was thought, be moved in some other way. All this unsound theorising in dynamics rested on a set of appearances that had been taken too much at face value. Here, too, the proper analysis lay hidden. What causes bodies to slow down when not continuously impelled is the operation of obstructions. Remove these, and the body will continue moving of its own accord. In practice, of course, we cannot completely remove obstructions, but we can diminish them and observe that motions persist longer to the extent that the path has been cleared. In the limiting case, when there is nothing to impede a body, it will go on moving freely. This new hypothesis in dynamics was formulated by Galileo (1564–1642), one of the great founders of modern science. This new approach to dynamics was a radical departure from Aristotelianism in two ways. First, it postulated that rest was not a

Tycho Brahe's system, a step back from the theory of Copernicus

Quadrant used by Tycho Brahe

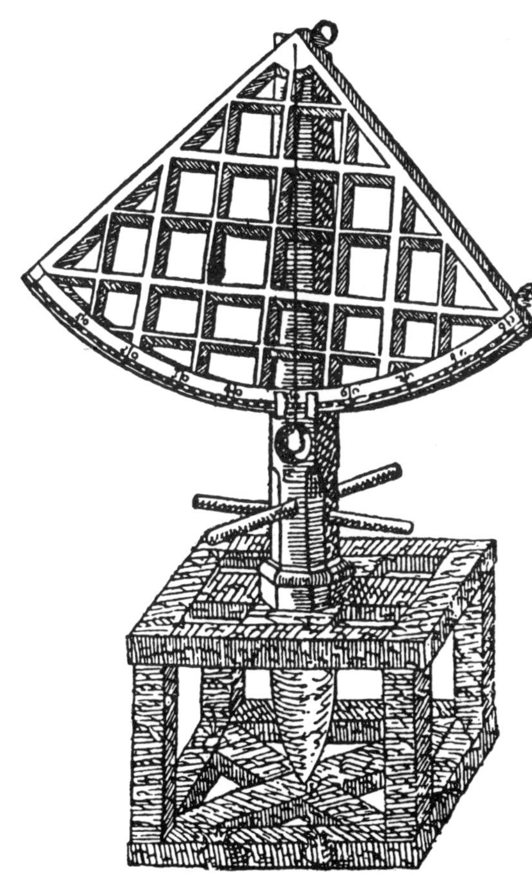

Galileo Galilei (1564-1642), scientist and inventor

Part of Pascal's logic machine

privileged condition of bodies, but that motion was just as natural. Secondly, it showed that not circular motion, as had been thought, but rectilinear motion was 'natural', in the special sense in which this word was used. If a body is not interfered with in any way it goes on moving at uniform speed in a straight line. The same insufficiently critical approach to observations had hitherto prevented a sound understanding of the laws governing falling bodies. It is as a matter of fact true that in the atmosphere a dense body falls faster than a light one of equal mass. Here again, it is the obstruction of the medium in which the bodies fall that must be taken into account. If the medium becomes rarer all bodies fall more nearly at the same rate, and in empty space this becomes strict equality. Observations on falling bodies showed that the speed of fall increases by thirty-two feet each second. Thus, as the speed was not uniform, but accelerated, there must be something interfering with the natural motion of bodies. This is the force of gravity exerted by the earth.

These findings were of importance in Galileo's researches on the path of projectiles, a matter of some practical military importance to the Duke of Tuscany who was Galileo's patron. An important principle of dynamics was here first brought to bear on a striking example. If we consider the path of a projectile we may take the motion to be compounded of two separate and independent partial motions. One of these is horizontal and uniform, the other vertical and therefore governed by the laws of falling bodies. The combined motion turns out to follow the course of a parabola. This is a simple case of the composition of directed quantities that obey the parallelogram law of addition. Velocities, accelerations and forces are quantities that can be dealt with in this way.

In astronomy, Galileo adopted the heliocentric theory and went on to make a number of important discoveries. Perfecting a telescope that had lately been invented in Holland, he observed a number of facts that once and for all destroyed the Aristotelian misconception about the heavenly regions. The Milky Way turned out to consist of vast numbers of stars. Copernicus had said that in his theory the planet Venus must show phases, and this was now confirmed by Galileo's telescope. Likewise, the telescope revealed the satellites of Jupiter, and it was shown that these moved round their parent planet in accordance with Kepler's laws. All these discoveries upset long cherished prejudices and led orthodox scholastics to condemn the telescope which had thus undermined their dogmatic slumbers. It is worth noting in advance that a very similar thing occurred three centuries later. Comte condemned the microscope for upsetting the simple form of the laws of gases. In this sense positivists have a good deal in common with Aristotle and his uncompromising superficiality of observation in physics.

Sooner or later Galileo was bound to fall foul of orthodoxy. In 1616 he was condemned in a closed session of the Inquisition. But his behaviour seemed to remain too unsubmissive, so that in 1633 he was once more dragged before court, this time in public. For the sake of peace he recanted and promised henceforth to abandon all thoughts of the earth moving. Legend has it that he did as he was bidden but mumbled to himself 'and yet it moves'. His recantation was of course only for show, but the Inquisition had succeeded in stamping out scientific enquiry in Italy for several centuries.

The final step in putting forward a general theory of dynamics was taken by Isaac Newton (1642–1727). Most of the notions involved had been hinted at or used in an isolated manner. But Newton was the first to understand the full significance of the gropings of his predecessors. In his 'Principia Mathematica philosophiae naturalis', published in 1687, he sets out the three laws of motion and then develops, in the manner of the Greeks, a deductive account of dynamics. The first law is a generalised statement of Galileo's principle. All bodies, if unimpeded, move at constant speed in a straight line, in technical terms, with uniform velocity. The second law defines force as the cause of non-uniform motion, stating that force is proportional to the product of mass and acceleration. The third law is the principle that to every action there is an equal and opposite reaction. In astronomy he gave the final and complete account for which Copernicus and Kepler had taken the initial steps. The universal law of gravitation states that between any two particles of matter there is a force of attraction proportional to the product of their masses and in inverse ratio of the square of the distance. In this way the motion of the planets, their satellites, and comets could all be accounted for to the smallest known detail. Indeed, since every particle affects every other particle, this theory made it possible to calculate exactly the perturbations of orbits caused by other bodies. This no other theory had ever been able to do. As for Kepler's laws, these were now merely consequences of Newtonian theory. Here, at last, the mathematical key to the universe seemed to have been discovered. The ultimate form in which we now state these facts are the differential equations of motion, which are stripped of all extraneous and incidental details of the concrete reality to which they apply. The same holds of Einstein's even more general account. Still, relativity theory to this day remains controversial and suffers from internal difficulties. But to return to Newton, the mathematical vehicle for expressing dynamics is the theory of fluxions, one of the forms of differential calculus, which was also discovered independently by Leibniz. From this time onwards mathematics and physics advance in leaps and bounds.

Other great discoveries were made in the seventeenth century. Gilbert's work on magnetism was published in 1600. Towards mid-century, Huygens put forward the wave theory of light. Harvey's discoveries on the circulation of blood appeared in print in 1628. Robert Boyle in 'The Sceptical Chymist' (1661) put an end to the mystery-mongering of the alchemists and returned to the atomic theory of Democritus. Great advances were made in the construction of instruments which in their turn provided more accurate observations leading to further developments of theory. This tremendous outburst of scientific activity was followed by a corresponding technological development that made Western Europe supreme for some three centuries. With the scientific revolution the spirit of Greece had once more come into its own. All this is reflected in philosophy too.

[1]

PHILOSOPHIÆ
NATURALIS
Principia
MATHEMATICA

Definitiones.

Def. I.

Quantitas Materiæ eſt menſura ejuſdem orta ex illius Denſitate & Magnitudine conjunctim.

AEr duplo denſior in duplo ſpatio quadruplus eſt. Idem intellige de Nive et Pulveribus per compreſſionem vel liquefactionem condenſatis. Et par eſt ratio corporum omnium, quæ per cauſas quaſcunq; diverſimode condenſantur. Medii interea, ſi quod fuerit, interſtitia partium libere pervadentis, hic nullam rationem habeo. Hanc autem quantitatem ſub nomine corporis vel Maſſæ in ſequentibus paſſim intelligo. Innoteſcit ea per corporis cujuſq; pondus. Nam ponderi proportionalem eſſe reperi per experimenta pendulorum accuratiſſime inſtituta, uti poſthac docebitur.

B Def.

First page of the Principia, by Isaac Newton (1642-1727)

In the process of saving appearances, philosophers had hitherto discussed mainly the aspect of saving. As to the appearances themselves, little if anything had been said. For this there are, of course, excellent reasons. But by way of reaction to the excessive concentration on the purely logical side of deduction, the time was ripe for something to be said about the material of observation without which empirical enquiry remains barren. The old Aristotelian instrument, or organon, of the syllogism could not serve the advancement of science. A new organon seemed to be required.

Francis Bacon (1561-1626)

The first to state these problems explicitly was Francis Bacon (1561–1626). Being the son of the lord keeper of the Great Seal, and trained in the legal profession, Bacon grew up in a climate which naturally led him into a government career. At twenty-three he entered parliament and later became the adviser of the Earl of Essex. When Essex fell into disgrace for treason, Bacon sided with the crown, though he was never able to command the full confidence of Elizabeth. But when James I succeeded to the throne in 1603, the outlook became more hopeful. By 1617, Bacon had advanced to his father's office and in the following year he became Lord Chancellor, being created Baron Verulam. In 1620 his enemies contrived to wreck his political career by accusing him of accepting bribes in chancery suits. Bacon did not contest the issue, admitting the charge but pleading that his judgement had never been swayed by gifts. The lords condemned him to a fine of £40,000, and decreed he should be detained in the Tower at the King's pleasure. As to political office or a seat in parliament, from these he must henceforth be excluded. Of this dire sentence, the first part was remitted and the second confined to four days detention. His exclusion from politics was, however, enforced, and from now on he lived in literary retirement.

Bacon was a man of wide interests in the tradition of the renaissance. He wrote on law and history, and is famous for his essays, a literary form which had of late been invented by Montaigne (1533–1592) in France. In philosophy Bacon's best known book is 'The Advancement of Learning', published in 1605 and written in English. Here Bacon sets the stage for his later enquiries. As the title of the book suggests, he is concerned with enlarging the scope of knowledge, and man's power of control over his surroundings. In matters of religion he adopts what amounts to an Occamist position. Let faith and reason each treat of their several concerns and not encroach upon each other. The only function assigned to reason in the religious sphere is to deduce consequences from principles accepted on faith.

As for the proper pursuit of science, what Bacon emphasized is the need for a new method or instrument of discovery, to replace the evidently bankrupt theory of the syllogism. This he found in his own new version of induction. In itself, the notion of induction was not new, Aristotle had already used it. But hitherto, the form in which induction had been practised was by simple enumeration of instances. Bacon thought he had found something of a more powerful procedure. This consisted in the drawing up of lists of things that shared a given quality under investigation, as well as lists of things that lacked it, and lists of things that possessed it in varying degrees.

In this way it was hoped one would discover the peculiar character of a quality. If this process of tabulation could ever be complete and exhaustive, we must of necessity reach the end of our enquiry. In practice we must content ourselves with a partial list and then venture some guess on the basis of it.

This, very briefly, is the gist of Bacon's account of scientific method, which he considered to be a new instrument for discovery. The title of the treatise in which the theory is set forth conveys this view. The 'Novum Organum', published in 1620, was to take the place of the organon of Aristotle. As a practical procedure it has not commended itself to scientists, and as a theory of method it is wrong, though in its insistence on observation it was a valuable antidote to the excesses of traditional rationalism. Basically, the new instrument really never goes beyond Aristotle. It relies solely and simply on classification, and on the notion that by sufficient refinement the proper pigeonhole will be found for everything. Once we have found the proper place, and with it the appropriate name, for any particular quality, we are held somehow to be in control of it. This account is adequate enough for statistical enquiry. But as to the formulation of hypotheses, Bacon is wrong in thinking that this is based on induction, which is concerned rather with the testing of hypotheses. Indeed, in order to conduct a series of observations one already has to have a preliminary hypothesis. But for the discovery of hypotheses one cannot lay down a set of general prescriptions. Bacon is quite wrong in thinking that there could be an instrument of discovery, the mechanical application of which would enable one to unearth startling new secrets of nature. The setting up of hypotheses does not proceed in this manner at all. Again, Bacon's rejection of the syllogism led him to underestimate the function of deduction in scientific enquiry. In particular, he had little appreciation of the mathematical methods which were developing in his time. The role of induction in the testing of hypotheses is one small facet of method. Without the mathematical deduction which leads from the hypotheses to a concrete, testable, situation, there would be no knowing what to test.

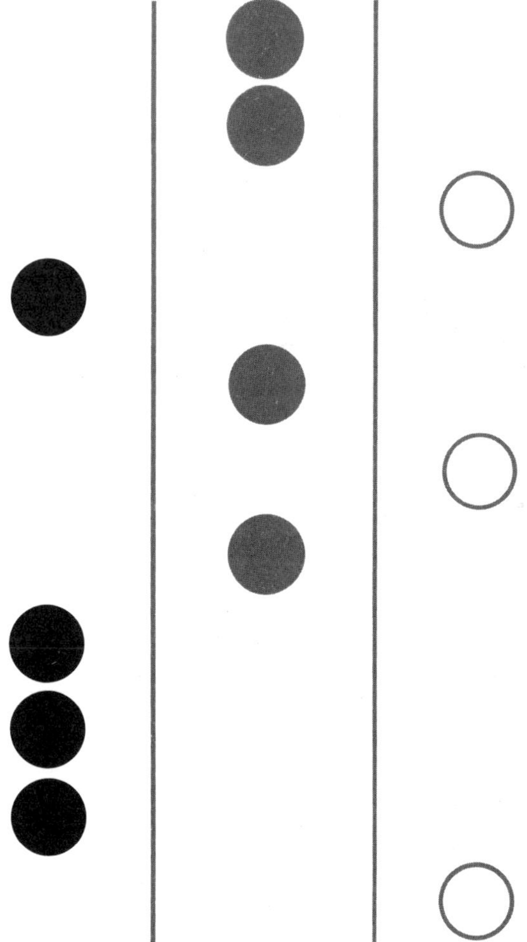

Bacon's method of science: listing items having a given quality

Bacon's account of the various kinds of error to which man is subject is one of the most colourful parts of his philosophy. We are prone, so he says, to yield to four types of mental weaknesses, which he calls 'idols'. First, there are the idols of the tribe', which belong to us because we are human. Wishful thinking would be an example, especially the expectation of greater order in natural phenomena than does in fact exist. Next, there are 'idols of the cave', which are the individual kinks of each man, and these are numberless. The 'idols of the market-place' are errors caused by the tendency of the mind to be dazzled by words, an error particularly rampant in philosophy. Lastly, the 'idols of the theatre' are those errors which arise from systems and schools of thought. Aristotelianism is Bacon's stock example of this.

For all his interest in scientific enquiry, Bacon missed practically all the most important developments of his own time He was unaware of the work of Kepler; and, though he was a patient of Harvey, did not know of the doctor's researches on the circulation of the blood.

Thomas Hobbes (1588-1679)

In France, Hobbes knew Charles II, later King, when Cromwell died

Of greater importance to British Empiricism, as for philosophy in general, was Thomas Hobbes (1588–1679). While in some respects he belongs to the empiricist tradition, he also has an appreciation of the mathematical method which links him with Galileo and Descartes. Being thus aware of the function of deduction in scientific enquiry he had a much sounder grasp of scientific method than Bacon could ever reach.

Hobbes' early family life was unpromising. His father was a wild and woolly-minded vicar who disappeared in London when Hobbes was yet a child. Fortunately, the vicar's brother was a responsible man who, being himself childless, took on the upbringing of his young nephew. At fourteen years Hobbes went to Oxford and studied classics. Scholastic logic and Aristotle's metaphysics were part of the curriculum, and for these Hobbes developed a thorough dislike which remained with him all his life. In 1608, he became tutor to William Cavendish, son of the Earl of Devonshire, and two years later accompanied his pupil on the traditional grand tour of the continent. Succeeding to the title, the young nobleman became Hobbes' patron. Through him Hobbes became acquainted with many of the leading men of his time. When his master died in 1628, Hobbes went to Paris for a time and then returned to become tutor to the son of his former pupil. With the young earl he went abroad in 1634 to visit France and Italy. In Paris he met Mersenne and his circle, and in 1636 visited Galileo in Florence. He returned home in 1637 and began working on an early version of his political theory. His views on sovereignty pleased neither side in the impending struggle between royalists and republicans, and Hobbes, being by nature inclined to caution, left for France where he remained from 1640 to 1651.

During these years in Paris he associated once more with Mersenne's circle and met Descartes. Being at first on friendly terms with the royalist refugees from England, including the future Charles II, he fell out with everybody when he published the 'Leviathan' in 1651. His royalist friends disliked the scientific and impersonal treatment of the problem of loyalty, while the French clergy took exception to his anti-catholicism. He therefore decided to flee once more, this time in the reverse direction back to England. He submitted to Cromwell and withdrew from political life. It was at this time in his life that Hobbes became involved in a bout of circle squaring, with Wallis from Oxford as his critic. Hobbes' admiration for mathematics was greater than his skill in that science, and the professor easily won in the controversy. Hobbes continued his polemics against mathematicians until the end of his life.

After the Restoration, Hobbes once more gained the favour of the King and even obtained a pension of £100 a year, an endowment as generous as the payment of it remained unreliable. But when, after the Plague and the Great Fire, popular superstition prompted a parliamentary enquiry into atheism, Hobbes' 'Leviathan' became a particular target of unfavourable criticism. Henceforth the author could publish nothing controversial on social or political matters except abroad, where during the last years of his long life he was held in higher repute than at home.

In philosophy, Hobbes laid the groundwork of much that was later characteristic of the British Empiricist school. His most important work is the 'Leviathan', in which he applies his general philosophic views to the working out of a theory of sovereignty. But before turning to social theory, the book contains, by way of introduction, a fairly complete summary of his general philosophic position. In the first part there is an account of man and human psychology in strictly mechanical terms, together with some general philosophic reflection on language and epistemology. Like Galileo and Descartes, he holds that whatever we experience is caused by mechanical motion in external bodies, whereas sights, sounds, smells and so on are not in the objects but are private to us. On this subject he mentions in passing that the universities still teach a crude theory of emanations based on Aristotle. Slyly he adds that he does not disapprove of universities in general, but seeing that he will later speak of their place in a commonwealth, he must tell us of their chief defects to be amended, 'amongst which the frequency of insignificant speech is one'. He has an associationist view of psychology and adopts a thorough-going nominalism with regard to language. Geometry, he considers, is so far the only science. The function of reason is of the character of argument as in geometry. We must start from definitions, being careful not to use self-contradictory notions in framing them. Reason, in this sense, is something that is acquired through practice, it is not inborn, as Descartes holds. There follows an account of the passions in terms of motions. In their natural state, Hobbes thinks, all men are equal and severally seek to preserve themselves at the expense of others, so that there is a state of war of all against all.

Title page of the 'Leviathan'

In it the sovereign figures as the sum of individuals

To escape this uneasy nightmare, men band together and delegate their own powers to a central authority. This is the subject of the second part of the book. Men, being rational and competitive, have to come to an artificial agreement or convenant, by which they agree to submit to some authority of their choice. Once such a system gets under weigh, there is therefore no right of rebellion, since it is the ruled that are bound by the agreement but not the ruler. Only if a ruler fails to provide the protection for which he was chosen in the first place can men rightly declare the agreement null and void. A society based on this kind of contract is a commonwealth. It is like a giant man made up of ordinary men, a 'Leviathan'. It is bigger and more powerful than a man, and therefore is like a god, though it shares with ordinary men their mortality. The central authority is called the sovereign and has absolute power in all spheres of life. The third part outlines why there should be no universal church. Hobbes was thoroughly Erastian, and therefore held that a church must be a national institution subject to the civil authorities. In the fourth part, the church of Rome is taken to task for failing to see this.

Hobbes' theory was influenced by the political upheavals of his time. What he abhorred above all was civil strife. His views therefore incline towards peace at any price. The notion of checks and balances, as worked out later by Locke, is alien to his way of thinking. His approach to political questions, though free from mysticism and superstition, tends to oversimplify the problems. His conception of the state is inadequate to the political situation in which he lived.

The renaissance period, as we have seen, gradually brought to the fore a preoccupation with mathematics. A second main question which interested post-renaissance thinkers was the importance of method. This we have noted already with Bacon and Hobbes. For René Descartes (1596–1650) these two influences became fused into a new philosophic system in the grand manner of the ancients. He is thus rightly regarded as the founder of modern philosophy.

Descartes' family belonged to the lower nobility, his father being a Councillor of the Parliament of Brittany. From 1604 to 1612 he attended the Jesuit College of La Flèche where, besides a sound classical education, he received as good a grounding in mathematics as was to be had at the time. After leaving college he went to Paris, and in the following year began studying law in Poitiers, where he graduated in 1616. His interests, however, lay elsewhere. In 1618 he went to Holland to enlist in the army, which left him a good deal of time for mathematical study. In 1619, the Thirty Years war began in earnest, and Descartes, intent on seeing the world, enrolled in the Bavarian army. In the winter of that year he found the leading notions that inspire his philosophy. The experience is described in the 'Discourse on Method'. One day when it was colder than usual, Descartes took refuge in a cottage and sat by the tiled oven. Thus properly warmed he began to meditate, and at the end of the day the outline of his entire philosophy had clearly presented itself to him. Descartes stayed with the army until 1622 and then returned to Paris. The following year he visited Italy, where he remained for two years. Returning to France he found that life at home offered too many distractions. Being by nature somewhat retiring, and intent on working in an undisturbed atmosphere, he left for Holland in 1628. Having sold his small estate, he was able to live independently in reasonable comfort. Except for three brief visits to France, he stayed in Holland for the next twenty-one years. Gradually he worked out his philosophy, along the lines that he had conceived on the occasion of the discovery of his method. An important work on physics, in which he adopted the Copernican theory, was held back from publication when Descartes heard of Galileo's trial in 1633. He was above all unwilling to be emmeshed in controversy, which to him seemed a waste of valuable time. He was, moreover, to all appearances a faithful Catholic, though with what doctrinal purity will remain forever unknown. Descartes therefore confined himself to publishing a collection of three volumes on Dioptrics, Meteors and Geometry. The 'Discourse', published in 1637, is intended as a preface to these three treatises. The most famous one is the Geometry, where the principles of analytic geometry are set out and applied. In 1641 there followed the 'Meditations', and in 1644 the 'Principles of Philosophy', dedicated to Princess Elizabeth, the daughter of the Elector Palatine. A treatise on the passions of the soul was written for the Princess in 1649. In that year, Queen Christina of Sweden became interested in Descartes' work, and at last prevailed upon him to come to Stockholm. This Scandinavian sovereign was a true renaissance character. Strong-willed and vigorous, she insisted that Descartes should teach her in philosophy at five in the morning. This unphilosophic hour of rising at dead of night in a Swedish winter was more than Descartes could endure. He took ill and died in February 1650.

René Descartes (1596–1650)

The method of Descartes is ultimately the outcome of his interest in mathematics. In the field of geometry, he had already shown how this could lead to far reaching consequences. For it was possible, with the analytic method, to describe the properties of whole families of curves by means of simple equations. Descartes believed that the method, which in the field of mathematics had been so successful, might be extended to other fields and thus enable the enquirer to reach the same kind of certainty as in mathematics. The 'Discourse' is aiming to show what precepts we must follow in order to make good use of our rational equipment. As to reason itself, it is held that all men are equal in this respect. We differ merely in that some use it better than others. But method is something acquired by practice, a point implicitly recognised by Descartes, for he does not wish to impose a method on us, but rather show how he himself has successfully employed his own reason. The account is autobiographical and tells of the writer's early dissatisfaction with all the inconclusive and uncertain talk that is to be found in all spheres. Of philosophy he says no view is so outrageous but has been held by someone. Mathematics impressed him for the certainty of its deductions, but he could not as yet see their proper use. He gave up book learning and began his travels, but he found that customs differed amongst themselves as much as the opinion of philosophers. In the end, he resolved he must look into himself to find the truth. There follows an account of the reflections by the stove mentioned earlier.

Noting that only a work completely finished by one single author gives any satisfaction, he decided to reject everything he had been taught and forced to take on trust. Logic, geometry and algebra alone survive this holocaust, and from these he finds four rules. The first is never to accept anything except clear and distinct ideas. Secondly, we must divide each problem into as many parts as are required to solve it. Thirdly, thoughts must follow an order from the simple to the complex, and where there is no order we must assume one. The fourth rule states that we should always check thoroughly in order to ensure that nothing has been overlooked. This is the method Descartes used in applying algebra to geometrical problems, thus creating what we now call analytical geometry. As for its application to philosophy, this, Descartes felt, must be postponed until he was a little older. In regard to ethics, we are in a dilemma. It is the last in the order of sciences, but in our lives we have to make immediate decisions. Descartes therefore adopts a provisional code of behaviour which, on a pragmatic criterion, will give him the best conditions of life. He therefore decides to abide by the laws and customs of his country and to remain faithful to his religion; to act with determination and perseverance once he had made up his mind to a course of action; and finally to attempt to rule himself rather than tempt fortune, and to adapt his wishes to the order of things rather than the reverse. From this time forward Descartes decided to devote himself to philosophy.

Going on to metaphysics, Descartes' method leads him to systematic doubt. The evidence of the senses is uncertain and must be called into question. Even mathematics, though less questionable, must be suspected, for God might be leading us systematically astray. Ulti-

DISCOURS
DE LA METHODE
Pour bien conduire sa raison & chercher
la verité dans les sciences.
PLUS
LA DIOPTRIQVE.
LES METEORES.
ET
LA GEOMETRIE.
Qui sont des essais de cete METHODE.

A LEYDE
De l'Imprimerie de IAN MAIRE.
CIↃ IↃ C XXXVII.
Auec Priuilege.

Discourse on Method, title page

Page listing the four precepts

20 DISCOURS.

Le premier estoit de ne receuoir iamais aucune chose pour vraye que ie ne la connusse euidemment estre telle: c'est à dire, d'euiter soigneusement la Precipitation, & la Preuention; & de ne comprendre rien de plus en mes iugemens, que ce qui se presenteroit si clairement & si distinctement a mon esprit, que ie n'eusse aucune occasion de le mettre en doute.

Le second, de diuiser chascune des difficultez que i'examinerois en autant de parcelles qu'il se pourroit, & qu'il seroit requis pour les mieux resoudre.

Le troisiesme de conduire par ordre mes pensées, en commenceant par les obiets les plus simples, & les plus aysez a connoistre, pour monter peu a peu comme par degrez iusques a la connoissance des plus composez: Et supposant mesme de l'ordre entre ceux qui ne se precedent point naturellement les vns les autres.

Et le dernier de faire partout des denombremens si entiers, & des reueuës si generales, que ie fusse assuré de ne rien omettre.

mately the one thing a doubter must admit is his own doubting. This is the basis of the fundamental Cartesian formula: 'I think therefore I am'. Here, Descartes thought, was the clear and distinct starting point for metaphysics. Thus, Descartes concludes that he is a thinking thing, quite independent of natural substances, and therefore likewise independent of the body. He now goes on to the existence of God for which he repeats essentially the ontological proof. Since God must be truthful he cannot deceive us as to our own clear and distinct ideas. Since we have such an idea of bodies, or extension, as he puts it, therefore they exist. Next comes an outline of the physical questions in the order in which these were to have been dealt with in the unpublished treatise. Everything is explained in terms of extension and motion. This is applied even in biology, and Descartes gives an account of the circulation of the blood as due to the heart's acting like a heater, causing blood that enters it to expand. This is, of course, at variance with Harvey's observations, and occasioned a lively controversy between the two men. But to return to the 'Discourse', this mechanical theory leads to the view that animals are automata, devoid of souls, which is moreover supposed to follow from the fact that they do not speak and therefore must lack reason. This reinforces the view that man's soul is independent of his body and leads us, since there are no other destructive forces, to conclude that it is immortal. Finally, the 'Discourse' hints at the trial of Galileo, and discusses the question whether to publish or not to publish. In the end the compromise is to release the 'Discourse' and the three essays to which it forms the preface. This, in bare outline is the message of the 'Discourse', giving a succinct picture of the principles of the Cartesian philosophy.

What is important in this doctrine is above all the method of critical doubt. As a procedure it leads into a universal scepticism, as it later did with Hume. But Descartes is saved from the sceptical conclusion by his clear and distinct ideas, which he finds in his own mental activity. Such general notions as extension and motion, being independent of the senses, are for Descartes innate ideas, and genuine knowledge is of these primary qualities. Sense perception is of secondary qualities like colour, taste, touch and the like, but these are not really in things. In the Meditations, Descartes gives the famous example of the piece of wax and its changing appearances to illustrate this point. What is constant throughout is extension; and this is an innate idea, known by the mind.

Christina of Sweden and Descartes

The Cartesian philosophy thus emphasizes thoughts as the indubitable starting points, and this has influenced European philosophy ever since, both in the rationalist and in the empiricist camp. This remains true even though the formula 'I think therefore I am', on which this development is based, is itself not very sound. For the statement is plausible only if we admit a concealed presupposition, that thinking is a self-conscious process. Otherwise we might as well say 'I walk therefore I am', for if I do walk it is indeed true that I must exist. This objection was raised by Hobbes and Gassendi. But, of course, I may think I walk when I am in fact not walking, whereas I could not think that I think when I am in fact not thinking. It is this self-reference, which is assumed to occur in the process of thinking, that confers on the formula its apparently indubitable character. Do away with self-consciousness, as Hume subsequently did, and the principle falls down. Still, it remains true that one's own mental experiences carry a peculiar certainty not shared by other events.

By sharpening the old dualism between mind and matter, the Cartesian philosophy brought to the fore the problem of the relation between mind and body that such a theory must face. For the material and the mental worlds now appear to run their several courses self-contained and ruled by their own principles. In particular, it is impossible on such a view to hold that mental operations such as willing could ever affect the physical world. Descartes himself made an exception here, by allowing that a human soul could alter the motion of the vital spirits as to direction, though not in quantity. This artificial escape was, however, out of keeping with the system. Besides, it did not agree with the laws of motion. Descartes' followers, therefore dropped it and held that mind cannot move body. To account for the relation we must suppose that the world is so preordained that whenever a certain bodily movement takes place, what passes for the appropriate mental concomitant does in fact supervene at the right moment in the mental sphere, without there being a direct connection. This view was developed by Descartes' followers, in particular Geulincx (1624–1669) and Malebranche (1638–1715). The theory is called occasionalism, because it holds that God so orders the Universe that the material and mental series of events run their parallel courses in such a way that an event in one always happens on the appropriate occasion of an event in the other. Geulincx invented the simile of the two clocks to illustrate this theory. If we have two clocks, each keeping perfect time, then we may look at one dial when the hand points to the hour and hear the other clock strike. This might incline us to saying that the first clock caused the second to strike. Mind and body are like these two clocks, wound up by God to run their independent but parallel courses. Occasionalism does, of course, raise some awkward difficulties. For just as in order to keep time we can dispense with one of our two clocks, so it seems that it is possible to infer mental events entirely by cross reference from physical events.

The Cartesian dualism: the mental and the physical are separate

The possibility of success of such an enterprise is guaranteed by the principle of occasionalism itself. We can thus work out a complete theory of mentality in terms of physical events only, an attempt which was in fact made by eighteenth century materialists, and amplified by the behaviourist psychology of the twentieth century. Thus, far from saving the soul's independence from the body, occasionalism ultimately makes the soul a redundant entity; or, if this be preferred, it makes the body superfluous at all times. Whichever view is taken, it ill agrees with Christian principles, and it is not surprising that Descartes' works found a secure place on the index. For one thing, Cartesianism cannot consistently accommodate free will. In the end, the rigid determinism of the Cartesian account of the material world, both physical and biological, did much to promote the materialism of the eighteenth and nineteenth centuries, especially when taken in conjunction with Newtonian physics.

Diagram from the Geometry

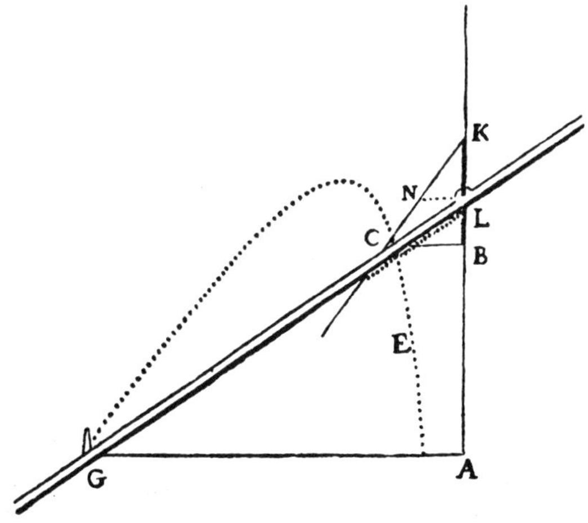

The Cartesian dualism is in the end the outcome of quite a conventional approach to the problem of substance, in the technical sense in which the scholastics had used the term. A substance is a carrier of qualities, but is itself independent and permanent. Descartes recognised matter and mind as two different substances which, being each sufficient unto itself, could not interact in any way. The occasionalist device is introduced to bridge the gap. It is clear, however, that if we admit such a principle there is no reason why we should not rely on it as heavily as we wish. One might, for instance, treat each mind as a substance of its own. Moving in this direction, Leibniz in his theory of monads developed a theory of infinitely many substances, all independent but co-ordinated. Alternatively, one could go back to a Parmenidean point of view, and maintain that there is only one substance. This latter course was taken by Spinoza, whose theory is perhaps the most consistent and uncompromising monism ever worked out.

Spinoza (1632–1677)

Spinoza (1632–1677), born in Amsterdam, was the son of a Jewish family whose forbears had, within living memory, abandoned their homes in Portugal to find a place where they might worship God after their own fashion. For, since the expulsion of the Moslems from Spain and Portugal, the Inquisition had instituted a reign of religious intolerance which made life for non-Christians, to say the least, uncomfortable. Reformed Holland, herself at war with the Spanish tyranny, offered refuge to these victims of persecution, and Amsterdam became the home of a large Jewish community. Within its bounds, Spinoza received his early upbringing and education.

But to his lively intellect these traditional studies were not enough. Through Latin he was able to acquaint himself with the writings of the thinkers who had brought about the great revival of learning and were developing the new science and philosophy. He soon found it impossible to remain within the bounds of orthodoxy, to the great embarrassment of the Jewish community. Reformed theologians were in their own way intransigent, and it was felt that any violently critical rejection of religion might upset the general atmosphere of tolerance then prevailing in Holland. Spinoza was finally expelled from his synagogue with all the curses in the Book.

Being naturally somewhat shy, he was thereafter completely isolated and thenceforth lived quietly amongst a small circle of friends, earning his living by polishing lenses and devoting himself to philosophic meditation. In spite of his retired way of life, his fame spread rapidly, and he was later to correspond with a number of influential admirers. Of these Leibniz was the most important, and it is known that the two met at the Hague. But Spinoza never consented to be drawn out of his retirement. In 1673, the Elector Palatine offered him the chair of philosophy at Heidelberg, but Spinoza politely refused to accept it. His reasons for declining the honour are revealing. In the first place, he says 'I think I should cease to promote philosophy were I to devote myself to teaching the young. Furthermore I do not know within what bounds I should have to contain the freedom of philosophising, so that I may not appear to wish to upset established religion ... you will therefore understand that I am not harbouring hopes for better fortune still, but will abstain from lecturing merely because I prize tranquillity, which I think I can best gain in this manner.'

Spinoza's writings are not bulky, but what there is reveals a concentration and logical rigour rarely ever attained. His views on God and religion were, however, so far ahead of his time, that for all his dignified ethical theorising he was reviled, both in his own time and for a hundred years to come, as a monster of iniquity. His greatest work, the 'Ethics', was felt to be so explosive that it could not be published until after his death. His political theory has much in common with Hobbes, but though indeed there is a fair measure of agreement between them on many of the features they thought desirable in a sound society, the grounding of Spinoza's theory is entirely different. Whereas Hobbes establishes his account in an empirical manner, Spinoza deduces his conclusions from his general metaphysical theory. In fact, to see the force of Spinoza's arguments one must treat his entire philosophical work as one great treatise. It is partly for this reason that Spinoza's writings made less of an immediate impression than the political works of the empirical philosophers. But it must be remembered that the problems discussed were then very live and real issues of the day. The vital part played by liberty in the function of the body politic was not then so generally admitted as it became in the nineteenth century.

Spinoza, unlike Hobbes, was a protagonist of freedom of thought. Indeed, it follows from his metaphysics and his ethical theory that only under such conditions can a state function properly. In the Tractatus Theologico-Politicus this is discussed with great emphasis. The book is somewhat unusual in that these topics are approached in an indirect way through biblical criticism. Spinoza here begins, mainly on the Old Testament, what two centuries later came to be called Higher Criticism. An examination of historical examples from this source leads on to a demonstration that freedom of thought is of the essence of social existence. On this matter, we find a quaint reflection by way of conclusion. 'And yet I must confess that from such freedom certain inconvenients may at times arise. But who has ever so wisely set up anything that no ills could arise from it? He who wishes to rule everything by laws will call forth imperfections rather than diminish them. What cannot be forbidden must needs be allowed, even if at times this leads to harm'.

Spinoza also differs from Hobbes in not regarding democracy as the most rational ordering of society. The most reasonable government issues sound decrees where they are competent, and remains aloof in matters of belief and instruction. It will arise where there is a politically responsible and privileged class on the basis of property. Under such a government men have the best chance to fulfil their intellectual potentialities, in Spinoza's sense; and that, in terms of his metaphysics, is what human beings naturally aim at. As to the question of the best government, it may well in fact be true that a trading community, where activity depends on some measure of freedom and safety, has the best chance of developing a liberal rule. His native Holland here illustrates Spinoza's point.

TRACTATUS
THEOLOGICO-
POLITICUS
Continens
Dissertationes aliquot,
Quibus ostenditur Libertatem Philosophandi non tantum salva Pietate, & Reipublicæ Pace posse concedi: sed eandem nisi cum Pace Reipublicæ, ipsaque Pietate tolli non posse.

Johann: Epist: I. Cap: IV. vers: XIII.
Per hoc cognoscimus quod in Deo manemus, & Deus manet in nobis, quod de Spiritu suo dedit nobis.

HAMBURGI,
Apud *Henricum Künrabt.* CIↃ IↃ CLXX.

Spinoza's house in The Hague

B. D. Spinoza

OPERA

POSTHUMA,

Quorum series post Præfationem exhibetur.

du Cabinet de M.r le C.te Wlgrin Taillefer

CIƆ IƆ C LXXVII.

Title-page of the book in which the Ethics appeared, posthumously

In turning to the 'Ethics' next, we are following the historical order in which Spinoza's system was published, even though the logical sequence would begin with it. The title of the book is somewhat misleading as to its contents. For here we have first of all Spinoza's metaphysics, which contains implicitly a statement of the rationalist blueprint for the scientific investigation of nature. This had become one of the foremost intellectual issues of the seventeenth century. There follows an account of the mind, the psychology of the will and of the passions, and an ethical theory based on the preceding.

The entire work is set out in the manner of Euclid. We start with definitions and a set of axioms, and from these we derive the entire corpus of propositions that follow, with all the attendant proofs, corollaries and explanations. This manner of philosophizing is not nowdays much in vogue; and to those who see no virtue in anything, save what comes hot off the press, the system of Spinoza will be a strange exercise indeed. But in its setting, it appears not so outrageous; and, in its own right, it remains a masterpiece of concise and lucid discourse.

The first part treats of God. Six definitions are set out, including one of substance and one of god in conformity with the traditional usage of scholastic philosophy. The axioms state seven basic assumptions which are not further justified. From here on we simply follow out the consequences, as in Euclid. From the way in which substance has been defined it appears that it must be something that completely explains itself. It is shown that it must be infinite, otherwise its limitations would have some bearing on it. Also, it is shown that there can be only one such substance, and it turns out to be the world as a whole; and likewise it coincides with god. Hence god and the universe, that is the totality of all things, are one and the same. This is the famous pantheistic doctrine of Spinoza. It must be emphasized that Spinoza's account has not a trace of mysticism in it. The whole affair is just an exercise in deductive logic, based on a set of definitions and axioms set up with prodigious ingenuity. It is perhaps the most outstanding example of systematic construction in the history of philosophy.

The identification of god with nature was utterly repugnant to the orthodox in all camps, and yet it was the outcome of a simple piece of deductive argument. As far as it goes it is sound enough, and if some were hurt in their precious beliefs this merely shows that logic is no respecter of feelings. If god and substance are defined in the traditional way there is nothing for it, Spinoza's conclusion imposes itself. One might well, as a result of this, come to recognize that there was something peculiar about these terms. In line with this theory, Spinoza regards our several human intelligences as parts of god's intelligence. He shares with Descartes the insistence on clarity and distinctness. For he says that 'falsehood consist in a lack of perception, which inadequate, that is mutilated and confused, ideas involve'. Once we have adequate ideas, we come to know indubitably the order and connection of things, which is the same as that of ideas. It is of the nature of mind to contemplate things not as contingent, but as necessary. The better we are able to do this the more closely we become one with god; or, what is the same, with the world. It is in this context that Spinoza coined the famous phrase that 'it is of the nature of mind to perceive things from a certain timeless point of view'. This is, indeed, a consequence of the fact that the mind sees things as necessary.

In the third section of the 'Ethics', it is shown how the mind is prevented from realising a full intellectual vision of the universe, because the operation of the passions militate against it. The motive power behind all our actions is self-preservation. It might be thought that this purely egotistic principle damns us all for self-seeking cynics. But this would be to miss the mark entirely. For in seeking his own advantage a man will sooner or later come to aspire to unity with god. This he achieves the more he can see things 'sub specie aeternitatis', that is from a timeless point of view, as mentioned above.

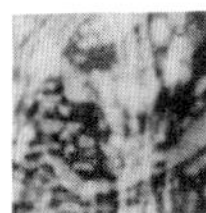

In the last two sections we find Spinoza's ethics properly so called. A man is in a state of slavery in so far as he is conditioned by outside influences and causes. This holds, indeed, for everything that is finite. But in so far as one may achieve community with god, one is no longer subject to such influences, because the universe as a whole is not conditioned. Thus, through becoming more and more attuned to the whole, one gains a corresponding measure of freedom. For freedom is precisely independence, or self-determination, and this holds true only of god. It is in this way that we can free ourselves from fear. Like Socrates and Plato, Spinoza holds ignorance to be the prime cause of all evil, and knowledge, in the sense of greater comprehension of the universe, the one condition conducive to wise and adequate action. But unlike Socrates, he does not think about death. 'A free man thinks of nothing less than of death; and his wisdom is meditation not of death, but of life'. Since evil is negative, god or nature, being a totality lacking nothing, cannot be evil. Everything is for the best in this one and only possible world. In practical affairs, it behoves man as a finite being to act in such a way as to preserve himself, in order to attain as great a measure of contact with the universe as he can.

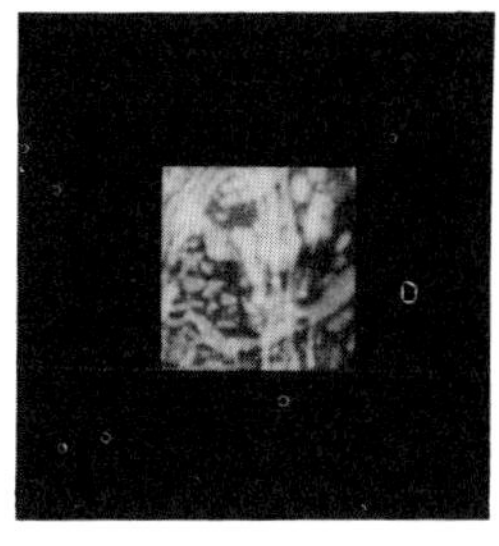

For Spinoza, mind and matter are two aspects of the one substance

This, very roughly, is the outline of Spinoza's system. Its importance for the scientific movement in the seventeenth century lies in the implicit suggestion of deterministic explanation on one and the same level for everything that goes on in the universe. In fact, this system is a blueprint for the future elaboration of a corpus of unified science. Such an attempt would not now be regarded as sound without certain serious qualifications. Likewise, on the ethical side, it cannot be admitted that evil is purely a negative thing. Every act of wanton cruelty, for instance, is a positive and permanent blemish on the world as a whole. It may be this that the Christian hints at in the theory of original sin. Spinoza's answer would have to be that no cruelty is ever wanton sub specie aeternitatis, but this would not be easy to establish. Nevertheless, the system of Spinoza remains one of the outstanding monuments of western philosophy. Though the severity of its tone has a certain Old Testament flavour, it is one of the great attempts, in the grand manner of the Greeks, to present the world as an intelligible whole.

Interior of synagogue whence Spinoza was expelled in 1656

The problem of substance led, as we have seen already, to very different solutions indeed. If Spinoza had maintained an extreme monism, the answer of Leibniz goes to the opposite extreme and postulates an infinity of substances. The two theories are in some ways related like that of Parmenides with atomism, though the parallel should not be pressed too far. Leibniz's theory is in the end based on the reflection that a substance, being one, cannot have extension; for this suggests plurality, and can only characterise a collection of substances. From this he infers that there are infinitely many substances, each of which is unextended and therefore immaterial. These substances are called monads, and have the essential property of being souls, in a somewhat general sense of the word.

Gottfried Wilhelm Leibniz (1646–1716)

Leibniz (1646–1716) was born in Leipzig where his father was a university professor. At an early age he showed signs of a lively and critical intellect; and at fifteen years old he entered the university, where he studied philosophy, graduating two years later and moving on to Jena to study law. At twenty he applied for his doctorate in law from the University of Leipzig, but this was withheld because of his age. At Altdorf, the university authorities were more tolerant and not only granted him his degree, but even offered him a chair. However, having very different things in mind, Leibniz did not avail himself of this offer. In 1667 he took up diplomatic service with the Archbishop of Mainz, one of the Electors and an active politician bent on raising the shattered remnants of the Empire from the holocaust of the thirty years war. Above all, it was necessary to keep Louis XIV of France from invading the country.

With this object Leibniz went to Paris in 1672 and stayed there for the best part of four years. His plan was to convince the Sun King to direct his military energies against the infidels and invade Egypt. This mission failed, but in the meantime Leibniz met many of the important philosophers and scientists of his time. Malebranche was then in vogue in Paris, and so were men like Arnauld, the chief representative of Jansenism since Pascal. The Dutch physicist Huygens, too, was amongst his acquaintances. In 1673 he came to London and met Boyle the chemist, and Oldenburg who was the secretary of the recently founded Royal Society, of which Leibniz became a member. Upon the death of his employer in the same year, Leibniz was offered a post by the Duke of Brunswick who needed a librarian at Hanover. Leibniz did not accept at once but remained abroad. In 1675, while in Paris, he began working on the infinitesimal calculus, which he discovered independently of Newton's slightly earlier work. Leibniz eventually published his version, which is closer to the modern form than Newton's theory of fluxions, in the Acta Eruditorum of 1684. Newton's Principia appeared three years later. A long and barren dispute ensued, and instead of dealing with the scientific issues involved, people took sides along nationalistic lines. As a result, English mathematics fell behind for a century, because the Leibnizian notation, adopted by the French, was a more flexible tool of analysis. In 1676, Leibniz visited Spinoza at The Hague, and then took up the librarianship at Hanover, a position in which he remained until his death. He spent much time on compiling a history of Brunswick, and for the rest pursued his scientific and philosophic studies. Besides, he continued to work out schemes to regenerate the European political scene. He tried to heal the great religious rift, but his schemes fell on deaf ears. When George of Hanover became King of England in 1714, Leibniz was not invited to follow the court to London, mainly no doubt because of the unfortunate repercussions of the controversy about the calculus. He stayed behind, embittered and neglected, and died two years later.

Leibniz's house at Hanover

The philosophy of Leibniz is not easy to discuss. For one thing, much of his work is fragmentary and often lacks the care of revision which would have brought to light inconsistencies before it was too late. The external circumstances of Leibniz's life are mainly responsible for this. Philosophical writing had to be done in rare moments of leisure and was subject to delay and interruptions. But there is a second and more interesting reason that renders Leibniz difficult at times. This arises from the twofold nature of his philosophy. On the one hand, there is his metaphysic of substance issuing in the theory of monads, on the other he put forward a logical theory which in many respects runs parallel to his metaphysical speculations. The logic is for us perhaps the more important of the two, but Leibniz himself evidently attached equal importance to both aspects of his work. Indeed, to him it seemed unquestionably the case that one could move from one sphere to the other without difficulty. This view is now on the whole discredited, at any rate by British philosophers; though the notion that language and logic are somehow self-contained is itself a metaphysical view with its own defects. As for the Leibnizian metaphysic, it is important to note that it receives some of its leading features from the scientific developments of the period. The metaphysical writings were published in his time and contain the theory of monads on which Leibniz's fame as a philosopher rested for some two centuries. The logical works remained unpublished and were not properly appreciated until the beginning of this century. In his metaphysical theories, Leibniz, as was stated above, produced an answer to the problem of substance by means of monads. With Spinoza he shares the view that substances cannot interact. This leads at once to the conclusion that no two monads can be causally connected. Indeed, there can be no real connections of any kind between them. This is expressed by saying that monads are windowless. How is this to be squared with the fact, admitted on all sides, that different parts of the universe appear to be in causal relations? The answer lay ready to hand in Geulincx' theory of the two clocks. We merely have to extend this to an infinite number and we reach the theory of pre-established harmony, according to which each monad mirrors the entire universe, in the sense that God has so ordained the entire business that all monads independently run their several courses in a gigantic system of craftily devised parallel courses.

1. La Monade, dont nous parlerons ici, n'est autre chose, qu'une substance simple, qui entre dans les composés; simple, c'est à dire sans parties. [1]).

2. Et il faut qu'il y ait des substances simples; puisqui'l y a des composés; car le composé n'est autre chose, qu'un amas, ou aggregatum des simples.

3. Or là, ou il n'y a point de parties, il n'y a ni étendue, ni figure, ni divisibilité possible. Et ces Monades sont les véritables Atomes de la Nature et en un mot les Elémens des choses.

4. Il n'y a aussi point de dissolution à craindre, et il n'y a aucune manière concevable par laquelle une substance simple puisse périr naturellement.[2])

5. Par la même raison il n'y en a aucune, par laquelle une substance simple puisse commencer naturellement, puisqu'elle ne sauroit être formée par composition.

From an early edition of the Monadology

Each monad being a substance, they are all qualitatively different as well as occupying different points of view. It will not do to say, strictly speaking, that they have different positions, since they are not spatio-temporal entities. Space and time are sensory appearances which are not real. The reality behind them is the arrangement of monads each with a different point of view. Each mirrors the universe in a slightly different way, no two of which are exactly alike. If

MENSIS OCTOBRIS A. M DC LXXXIV. 467

NOVA METHODUS PRO MAXIMIS ET MInimis, itemque tangentibus, quæ nec fractas, nec irrationales quantitates moratur, & ſingulare pro illis calculi genus, per G. G. L.

SIt axis AX, & curvæ plures, ut VV, WW, YY, ZZ, quarum ordinatæ, ad axem normales, VX, WX, YX, ZX, quæ vocentur reſpective, *v*, w, y, z; & ipſa AX abſciſſa ab axe, vocetur x. Tangentes ſint VB, WC, YD, ZE axi occurrentes reſpective in punctis B, C, D, E. Jam recta aliqua pro arbitrio aſſumta vocetur dx, & recta quæ ſit ad dx, ut *v* (vel w, vel y, vel z) eſt ad VB (vel WC, vel YD, vel ZE) vocetur d*v* (vel dw, vel dy vel dz) ſive differentia ipſarum *v* (vel ipſarum w, aut y, aut z) His poſitis calculi regulæ erunt tales: TAB.XII.

Sit a quantitas data conſtans, erit da æqualis o, & d $\overline{ax}$ erit æqu. a dx: ſi ſit y æqu *v* (ſeu ordinata quævis curvæ YY, æqualis cuivis ordinatæ reſpondenti curvæ VV) erit dy æqu. d*v*. Jam *Additio & Subtractio*: ſi ſit z − y + w + x æqu. *v*, erit d $\overline{z - y + w + x}$ ſeu d*v*, æqu dz − dy + dw + dx. *Multiplicatio*, d $\overline{xv}$ æqu. xd*v* + *v*dx, ſeu poſito y æqu. x*v*, fiet dy æqu xd*v* + *v*dx. In arbitrio enim eſt vel formulam, ut x*v*, vel compendio pro ea literam, ut y, adhibere. Notandum & x & dx eodem modo in hoc calculo tractari, ut y & dy, vel aliam literam indeterminatam cum ſua differentiali. Notandum etiam non dari ſemper regreſſum a differentiali Æquatione, niſi cum quadam cautione, de quo alibi. Porro *Diviſio*, d $\frac{v}{y}$ vel (poſito z æqu. $\frac{v}{y}$) dz æqu. $\frac{\pm v\,dy \mp y\,dv}{yy}$

Quoad *Signa* hoc probe notandum, cum in calculo pro litera ſubſtituitur ſimpliciter ejus differentialis, ſervari quidem eadem ſigna, & pro + z ſcribi + dz, pro − z ſcribi − dz, ut ex additione & ſubtractione paulo ante poſita apparet; ſed quando ad exegeſin valorum venitur, ſeu cum conſideratur ipſius z relatio ad x, tunc apparere, an valor ipſius dz ſit quantitas affirmativa, an nihilo minor ſeu negativa: quod poſterius cum fit, tunc tangens ZE ducitur a puncto Z non verſus A, ſed in partes contrarias ſeu infra X, id eſt tunc cum ipſæ ordinatæ

Nnn 3 z decre-

Leibniz's article on differential calculus, 1684; first page. diagrams

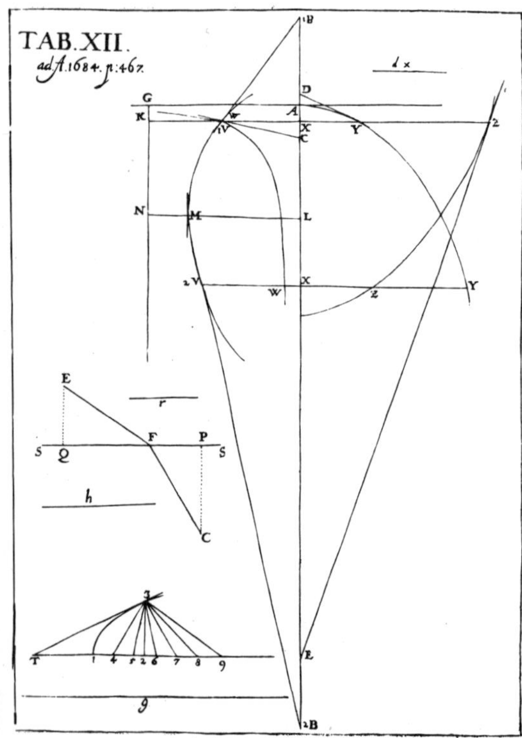

two monads are exactly alike then they are really just one and the same. This is the significance of Leibniz's principle of the identity of indiscernibles. It thus makes no sense to say, loosely speaking, that two monads could differ in position only.

Since all the monads are different we can arrange them in an order according to the clearness with which they mirror the world. Every object consists of a colony of monads. Human bodies, too, are organised in this way, but here there is a dominant monad which stands out for the clearness of its vision. This privileged monad is what is more specifically called the soul of a man, though in a wider sense all monads are souls, and all of them are immaterial, indestructible and therefore immortal. The dominant monad or soul stands out not only for the greater clearness of its perception but also in that it harbours the purposes for which its subordinates function in their pre-established harmonious manner. Everything in the universe happens for a sufficient reason, but free will is allowed for in that the reasons for which a human being acts have not the stringent compulsion of logical necessity. God, too, enjoys this kind of freedom, though he is not free to contravene the laws of logic. This theory of free will, which made Leibniz acceptable where Spinoza might offend, is really somewhat eternal to the systematic account in terms of monads, and is in fact at variance with it, as will be seen below.

As to the perennial question of the existence of God, Leibniz gives a complete exposition of the main metaphysical arguments which we have met already. Of the four arguments the first is St. Anselm's ontological argument, and the second a form of the argument from a first cause as found in Aristotle. Thirdly, we have an argument from necessary truth, which is said somehow to require a divine mind to exist in, and finally we have a proof from pre-established harmony, which is really a kind of argument from design. All of these we have dealt with elsewhere and shown what their weaknesses are. Kant was shortly to deny the possibility of metaphysical proofs of this kind in general. As for theology, it must be remembered that the god of metaphysics is a kind of finishing touch to a theory of the nature of things. He does not appeal to the emotions and has no connection with the god of the Book. Except for Neo-Thomists, theologians on the whole no longer rely on the theoretical divine entity of traditional philosophy.

The Leibnizian metaphysic was inspired in some measure by the new findings that were being accumulated with the help of the microscope. Leeuwenhoek (1632–1723) had discovered spermatozoa, and it had been shown that a drop of water was full of small organisms. It was, as it were, an entire world on a smaller scale than our own every day world. Considerations like these led to the notion of monads as ultimate unextended metaphysical soul-points. The new calculus with its infinitesimals seemed to be pointing in the same general direction. What is important for Leibniz here is the organic nature of these ultimate constituents. In this he departs from the mechanical outlook which had been promoted by Galileo and the Cartesians. Although this created difficulties, it led Leibniz to the discovery of the principle of conservation of energy in one of its early forms, and to the principle of least action. On the whole the development of physics followed the Galilean and Cartesian principles.

Whatever may be the relevance of this, it remains that in his logical doctrine Leibniz has provided a great number of hints that make his metaphysic, if not plausible, then at least somewhat easier to understand. Let us begin with the fact that Leibniz accepted the Aristotelian subject-predicate logic. Two general logical principles are taken as basic axioms. The first of these is the principle of contradiction, according to which of two contradictory propositions one must be true and the other false. The other is the previously mentioned principle of sufficient reason, in terms of which a given state of affairs follows from sufficient precedent reasons. Let us apply these two principles to the case of analytic propositions in Leibniz's sense; that is to say, propositions in which the subject contains the predicate, as in 'all metal coins are metallic'. Then it is seen from the principle of contradiction that all such propositions are true, whereas the principle of sufficient reason leads to the view that all true propositions, being sufficiently grounded, are of the analytic kind, though only God can see them in this way. To the human mind such truths appear to be contingent. Here, as in Spinoza, we find an attempt at grappling with the ideal programme of science. For what the scientist does in setting up theories is to try to grasp the contingent and exhibit it in such a way that it appears as a consequence of something else, and therefore in that sense necessary. God alone is in possession of a perfect science, and he therefore sees everything in the light of necessity.

Monads are non-spatio-temporal substances with a point of view

The non-interaction of substances is a consequence of the fact that the life-history of every logical subject is already contained in its own notion. This follows from the fact that its history is what is true of it, and the analyticity of all true propositions. Thus we are forced into admitting pre-established harmony. But in its own way this account is as strictly deterministic as Spinoza's theory, and free will in the sense previously explained has no place in it. As to God and his creation of the world, his goodness leads him to create the best possible world. There is, however, another Leibnizian theory on this subject, where God and creation do not figure at all. This is a view that seems to be inspired by the Aristotelian theory of entelechy, or striving from potentiality to actuality. That world will in the end exist which displays at any one time the greatest amount of actuality, keeping in mind that not all potentialities can simultaneously be realised.

But for his strict adherence to the subject-predicate logic, Leibniz might have published some of his attempts in mathematical logic, which would have got this subject under weigh more than a century earlier. He felt that it should be possible to invent a universal symbolic language which was perfect, and would reduce cerebration to calculation. In spite of electronic brains, this was perhaps somewhat rash, but nevertheless he foresaw much that has since become commonplace in the field of logic. As for the perfect language, this is only another expression of the hope that men could come to have the perfect science of God.

The preoccupation with clear and distinct ideas, and the consequent search for a perfect universal language, are the main rationalist pursuits of philosophy in the Cartesian tradition. That this, in some measure, corresponds to the aims of science we have already noted. At the same time we have here a road to follow rather than a final goal to reach. Leibniz already saw this at least implicitly, when he suggested that only God had perfect science. A very much more radical criticism of the rationalist line of thought is contained in the works of the great Italian philosopher Giambattista Vico (1668–1744). The Leibnizian statement, which every godfearing Christian, including Vico, would accept leads the Italian to set up a new principle of epistemology. God has perfect knowledge of the world because he has made it. Man, being himself created, knows the world imperfectly. For Vico, the condition for knowing something is to have made it. The basic formulation of the principle is that we can know only what we can do or make. We may put this by saying truth is the same as fact, provided the latter term is understood in its pristine meaning.

Giambattista Vico (1668–1744)

In his own time and for fifty years after his death Vico remained practically unknown. Born in Naples, the son of a small bookseller, he became, at the age of thirty-one, a professor of rhetoric at the university of his native city. This somewhat subordinate position he held until his retirement in 1741. Most of his life he was poor. To keep himself and his family he had to eke out his modest salary by giving private tuition and doing odd literary jobs for the nobility. Owing partly to the obscurity of his message he was not understood by his contemporaries, and never had the good fortune of meeting or corresponding with a thinker of his own stature.

The theory that truth is deed leads to a number of extremely important consequences. First of all, it provides a reason why mathematical truths are known with certainty. For man himself has made mathematical science by setting up rules in an abstract and arbitrary manner. Because we have literally made mathematics, we are able to understand them. At the same time, Vico thinks that mathematics does not enable us to promote a knowledge of nature nearly as much as the rationalists thought. For he thinks that mathematics are abstract; not in the sense of being distilled, as it were, from experience, but as being divorced from nature and in some ways an arbitrary construction of the human mind. Nature herself was made by God and therefore only he can fully understand her. As far as man goes, if he wishes to learn something about nature, he should adopt not so much a mathematical procedure, but an empirical approach through experiment and observation. Vico is much more in sympathy with Bacon than with Descartes. In warning against the use of mathematics Vico, it must be confessed, failed to see the role it plays in scientific research. At the same time one might allow that there was here a warning against unbridled mathematical speculation, which sometimes tries to pass for empirical research. That the proper approach lies somewhere between the two extremes we have already had occasion to suggest. The theory that mathematics gain their certainty from the doing of them has influenced many later writers, though they might disagree with Vico's notion that mathematics was in his sense arbitrary. The views of the marxist writer

Sorel may be mentioned here, as well as the accounts given by Goblot and Meyerson. The same holds of the utilitarian and pragmatist accounts of the nature of mathematics. On the other side, the notion of arbitrariness has commended itself to the formalists, who treat mathematics as an elaborate game. It would, of course, be difficult to state in all cases how direct the influence of Vico has been. Of Marx and Sorel we know that they studied Vico's work. But ideas often have subtle ways of making themselves felt without their influence becoming consciously seen. Though Vico's work was not very widely read, it nevertheless contains the germs of many developments in the philosophy of the nineteenth century.

Vico's house in Naples

The other main consequence of Vico's principle is his theory of history. Mathematics, he held, was perfectly knowable because man-made, but did not refer to reality. Nature was not perfectly knowable for it was made by God, but it did refer to the real. This paradox remains alive today wherever pure mathematics is held to be a mere construction. Vico tried to discover a 'new science' which was both perfectly knowable and about the real world. This he found in history, where man and god collaborate, a startling reversal of the traditional view; for the Cartesians had written off history as unscientific. The view that society is inherently more knowable than inert matter was revived in the last century by the German philosopher Dilthey, and the sociologists Max Weber and Sombart.

The new hypothesis is set forth most fully in a book called the 'New Science', of which Vico produced several versions. To the modern reader this book is somewhat of a problem, for it is a mixture of various ingredients that are not always properly distinguished. Apart from philosophical questions, the author deals with empirical problems and with straightforward questions of history, and these various strands of the enquiry are not always easy to disentangle. Indeed, at times Vico himself does not seem to be aware that he is sliding from one kind of question into the other. With all these faults and obscurities, there still remains a highly important theory developed in the book.

What, then, is meant by equating truth with the thing done, or fact? This somewhat unorthodox principle yields on closer inspection some quite sound corollaries on the epistemological question. For it is true that doing can help to improve our knowing. The intelligent performance of some action undoubtedly promotes one's understanding of it. It is evident that this occurs most naturally in the field of human action or endeavour. A good example is the understanding of music. To understand a piece of music thoroughly it is not enough to listen to it, but we must, as it were, reconstruct it by reading or playing the score, even if this is done with a relative lack of expert skill. The point is rather that expert skill is gained gradually in precisely this manner. But a similar comment holds true for scientific enquiry, too. An active knowledge of what can be done with the material under investigation gives one a firmer grasp on reality than mere external, abstract knowledge. This is at the basis of the pragmaticist philosophy of Peirce, as we shall see later. But in any case, there is nothing recondite here, ordinary common sense is aware of this in the saying that practice makes perfect. Thus it is not enough; in mathematics, to learn theorems, one should be able to bring to bear one's theoretical equipment on a variety of specific problems. This is not a demand for abandoning disinterested enquiry in favour of utility, on the contrary, it is through seeing concepts in action that a proper understanding of them is obtained. On the face of it this approach looks somewhat like the pragmatic doctrine of Protagoras. However, Vico does not make man the measure of all things in quite the Sophist sense. What is underlined is the active and literally reconstructive element in the knowing process, which is not at all the same as making what appears to each into the ultimate criterion. The emphasis on activity is quite opposed to the clear and distinct ideas of the rationalists.

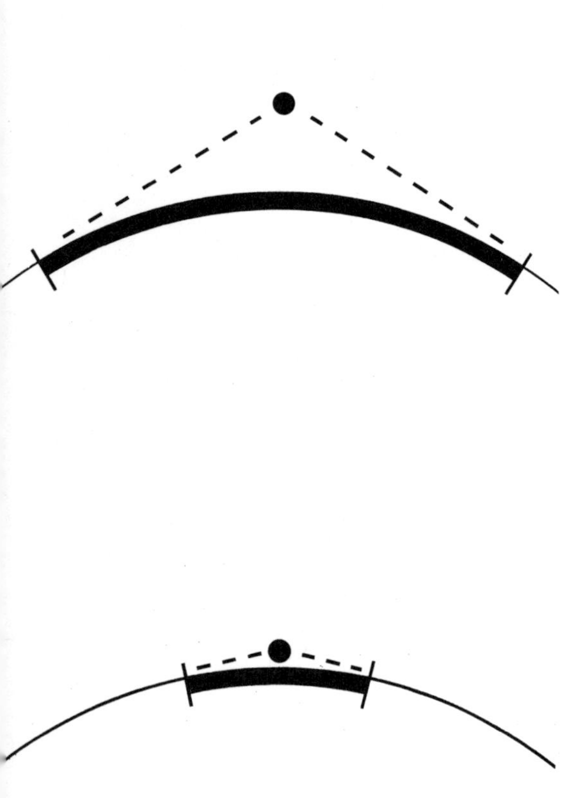

Truth is deed: the horizon of our knowledge extends as far as our field of action

Where rationalism shrinks away from the imagination as a source of confusion, Vico on the contrary emphasizes its role in the process of discovery. Before we reach concepts, he would hold, we think in terms of rather vague and ill-defined situations. This view is not entirely satisfactory, for however vague a thinking process might be it is difficult to see how it could be quite devoid of conceptual content. It might be better to say that primitive thought proceeds in terms of pictures and metaphors, whereas conceptual thinking is the last stage of sophistication. One valuable hint, that might arise from all this, is the fact that the rationalist account deals with science as a finished product, and presents it in an expository order. The account implicit in Vico shows science in the making and adopts the order of invention. But much of this is not at all clearly stated in Vico's work.

As to history, which is made by man, Vico holds that the greatest degree of certainty can be achieved. He felt that it was possible for the historian to discover the general laws of the historical process, and in terms of it explain why things have turned out as they have and will continue in a predictable manner. Vico is not saying that every detail is predicted in a mechanical way, but that the broad outlines are knowable in a general way. There is, for him, a tide in the affairs of men, and as the waters flow back and forth, so the fortunes of mankind run in cycles. The theory of cycles stems ultimately from presocratic sources, as we have seen. But Vico gives a new slant to these old notions by seeking the form of the recurrent phases of history in the mind of man, as the playwright and actor of the piece.

Thus Vico's theory, rather than looking back, points forward to Hegel's theory of history. At the same time, this approach to the historical problem fits in better with the empirical study of history than do the rationalist theories of order. Thus the theory of the social contract, as stated by Hobbes and later Rousseau, is a typical rationalist distortion. It is social theory seen in a mechanical, one might almost say mathematical way. Vico's theory allows him to see social organisation as a natural and gradual growth involving human beings who, through their accumulating traditions, slowly develop forms of communal living. The social contract, on the other hand, assumes men who suddenly find that they are perfectly reasonable and calculating beings who, through an act of rational decision, call into life a new society.

What is true of society in general is likewise true of language in particular. Language begins when in the course of their common activities men have to convey information to each other. In its primitive form, language consists of gestures and symbolic acts. When language becomes articulate its signs suffer a gradual change from direct, and in this sense, natural connection with simple objects, into conventional patterns. Indeed, language is to begin with poetic. Only gradually does it become scientific. The grammarians who codified the principles of linguistic structure were in error when they took the rationalist view here too and regarded language as a conscious and deliberate construction. That scientific and philosophic language is a late product of civilisation we have already seen when discussing ancient philosophy. There we saw how men struggled with the common language of their time in order to say new things. This remains an important principle that is occasionally forgotten. Starting from ordinary language it is precisely the business of science and philosophy to forge sharper linguistic tools for the purpose of handling new enquiries. This is the valuable message implied in the Cartesian demand for clear and distinct ideas. Vico himself does not seem to have seen the matter in this light, and therefore missed the significance of rationalist philosophy for science.

We may approach language in one of two opposite ways. Either we may take, with Leibniz, the extreme rationalist view of language as a calculus, with clear and distinct notions prevailing throughout, and rules for calculation set down explicitly. Alternatively, we may, in the spirit of Vico, regard the natural languages in the way in which they have grown as adequate media for communication, while rejecting any attempt at formalisation as a distortion. On such a view the function of logic really becomes superfluous, and the only criterion which can provide meaning is the active use of the language itself. Both these extreme points of view are wrong. The rationalist mistakes the direction in which development occurs for an ultimate goal that can be reached, whereas the refusal to formalise at all prevents any possiblity of breaking out of the narrow field of vision within which at any time we find ourselves. Besides, this latter approach is usually linked with the view that ordinary discourse is already as clear and distinct as it need or could be, an altogether rash and optimistic notion which fails to take into account past philosophic prejudices that survive in ordinary speech.

For all his unorthodox theorising in the sociological field, Vico nevertheless remained a devout Catholic. At any rate, he tried to accommodate the received religion within his system. Whether this is possible without inconsistency is of course another question. But then consistency is not one of Vico's merits. The importance of Vico lies much rather in his almost uncanny foreshadowing of the nineteenth century and its philosophic developments. In his sociology he moves away from the rationalist conception of the ideal commonwealth and applies himself to the empirical task of studying how societies grow and develop. In this he is highly original and for the first time provides a genuine theory of human civilization. All this is intimately connected with the leading notion central to all his thinking: that truth is deed, or 'verum factum', to use the Latin.

Allegorical Frontispiece of the 'Scienza Nuova'

British Empiricism

In the wake of the reformation there grew up in the north of Europe a new attitude to politics and philosophy. Its emergence as a reaction to the period of religious warfare and subservience to Rome was centred on England and Holland. England was largely spared the horrors consequent upon the religious schism of the continent. Protestants and Catholics, it is true, did for a while persecute each other in a half-hearted sort of way, and Puritanism under Cromwell was at loggerheads with the Church. But there were no large scale atrocities, and above all no foreign interference of a military kind. The Dutch, on the other hand, suffered the full impact of the religious wars. In a long and bitter struggle against Catholic Spain they finally achieved provisional recognition of independence in 1609, which was confirmed at the Treaty of Westphalia in 1648.

Horrors attending religious wars

This new attitude towards problems in the social and intellectual sphere is called liberalism. Under this somewhat vague heading one can discern a number of fairly distinct features. First of all, liberalism was essentially Protestant, but not in a narrow, Calvinistic manner. It was much rather a development of the protestant notion that each man must come to terms with God in his own way. Besides, bigotry is bad for business. Since liberalism was a product of the rising middle classes in whose hands commerce and industry was developing, it was opposed to the entrenched traditions of privilege of aristocracy and monarchy alike. The keynote is thus one of toleration. In the seventeenth century, at a time when most of the rest of Europe was torn with religious strife and tortured by instransigent fanaticism, the Dutch Republic was an asylum for non-comformists and free thinkers of all kinds. The Protestant Churches never acquired the political power that Catholicism had enjoyed during the Middle ages. State power was therefore becoming much more important.

The arbitrary power of monarchs came to be regarded with disfavour by the middle class merchants who had gained property and wealth through their own enterprise. The movement therefore was towards democracy based on the rights of property and the curtail-

Jacobean Parliament; England had reached some measure of stability

ment of the kingly powers. Along with the denial of the divine right of kings there arose a feeling that men can rise above their circumstances through their own efforts, and consequently a greater emphasis is beginning to be placed on the importance of education.

In general, government as such was viewed with suspicion, as interfering with the needs of expanding commerce and restricting its free development. At the same time the need for law and order was recognised as essential, and this somewhat tempered the attitude of opposition to government. From this period the English inherit their typical love for compromise. In social matters this implies a concern for improvement rather than revolution.

Guericke's experiments on vacua, upsetting Aristotle's views

Dutch navigators, then ranking amongst the foremost seafarers

Amsterdam stock exchange list

Cours van Negotie t'Amsterdam/ den 4 Juny.

Met Consent van de E. D. G. A. H.H. Burgermeesters.

ANNO 1674.

N° 1. Waren by 't ℔
Compagnise Peper — 17 a 17½
Nagelen in Soorten — 86 a 86
Fouten in Soorten — 47,8 a 48
Foely in Soorten — 18,10 a 20
Compagnie Canéel — 50 a 60 a 70
Francse Saffraen — 13 a 16 gl 10
Engels Saffraen — gl
[illegible] Gonfite Gemb. — 28 a 34
Natte Madery Sucaden — 13 a 14
Genees Greyn — 4
Nagel-hout — 18 a 20
Poever van Nagelen — 35 a 38

N° 2. Suyckeren by 't ℔
Candi Broot — 19 a 19
Poeyer Broot — 17,4 a 18
Nette Raf. 13,6 a 14 dito geplekt 13
Nette Mel. 12,8 a 13 dito geplekt 12 a 12
Lompen 12 dito gestot. 11
Wit Cand 20,4 a 25,4 a 26 Bruyn 15,6 a 14
Bresilse witte 12 a 13
Pan goet 9,5 a 10 Mascobad. 7,0 a 8
Panelen — 4 S. Tome
Christoffelse Suycker — 6 a 6
Barbadesse Suycker — 5,6 a 6
Suycker Syroop 't 100 ℔ 29
Marsilse Syroop 't vat

N° 3. Verwen by 't ℔ en 100 ℔. Contant.
Concenilje Mestique — ℔ 40 a 41
Indigo Guatimalo — ℔ 10 a 12
Dito Laure — ℔ 8,6 a 9
D. Karkees en Tripoli — ℔ 4 a 4
Spaens Groen — ℔ 20 a 23
Fernebouck — 100 ℔ 37 gl
Sint Martens Hout — gl
Sappon Hout — 13 a 15 gl
Campers Hout — 11 a 11 gl 10
Geel Hout 3 gl 5 Crappen 38 a 41 gl
Onberoofde — 29 a 33 gl
Gemeyn 21 a 25 gl Breslaute 12 a 13 gl
Wijnsteen van Duytslant — 22 a 26 gl
Italiaenten Wijnsteen — 15 a 18 gl
Dito Palem e Steen — 10 gl
Alepese Gal-noten — 35 a 36 gl 10
Dito Smerise — 29 a 30 gl
Gom de Semigal — 100 ℔ 18 gl
Pastel van St. Michiel. de bael 9 gl
Dito Thoulouse. de bael 20 gl
Smackde Port a Port 100 ℔ 16 a 18
Engels Coper-root — 6 a 6 gl
Dito Sweedts — gl
Roomsen Aluyn — 40
Dito Luycksen Aluyn — 37 a 38
Dito Engelse Aluyn 100 ℔ 35 a 36

N° 4. Drogeryen by 't ℔. Contant.
Quicksilver ℔ 36 Cinabrio 38
Borasa raf. ℔ a 20 Seduw. fijn 10
Rob fijn 50 a 8 gl Benju. fijn 24 a 60
Turbit — 80 Manna 24 a 32
Salarm. 10 a 11 8 Mastien 30
Selervat — 24 a 40 Lange Peper 4,8 a 8
Cassia Linge 15 a 15 Senebla 16 a 18 a 48
Salse Parille 43 Opoponare 44
Coloquinta ℔ 18 a 30 Cardemom 38 a 40
Wit Wierooch ℔ 8 a 16 Mechoacan 16 a 40
Coculus — ℔ 19 Gom Trag. ℔ 12 a 13
Corcu. 100 ℔ 28 a 40 Galanga 46
Bittere Amandelen 't 100 ℔ — 45 gl
Camfer rafinate 48 Cassia Fistula 40 gl
Sap van Soethout 't 100 ℔ — 30 a 34 gl
[illegible] 't 100 ℔ 30 gl Kubebe ℔ 15
Terbentina venet. 't 100 ℔ — 40 a 45 gl
Scamonium — ℔ 7 a 8 gl

By 't Ons.
Besar steen Orient. 14 a 18 Dito Occid. 66
Ambre Gris 66 Moschus 10 a 17 a 22 gl
Kramp. Peerlen — 36 a 42 a 6 a 10 gl
Amsterdams [illegible] Civet — 16 gl

Amsterdamse Goude Leeren / gemaeckt door Hans le Maire. D'Elle
Verheven Nieuw inventie — 54
Dito Geamaileerde — 56
Dito geschilderde bloemen — 88

N° 5. [illegible] Traen en Stockvis 't 100 ℔
Oosters Talck — 20 a 21 gl
Speten Talck — 22 gl 10
Moscovise Talck — 18 a 20 gl
Lever Traen — 18 a 19 gl
Groenlantse Traen — gl
Speck-traen — 37,10 a 38 gl
Robbe Traen — 37 a 38 gl
Inlantse Traen. de Ton 26 gl
Eylantse Walvis Baerden — 65 a 67 gl
Bontvis — 10,5 a 10 gl 10
Rootschaer — 8 a 9 gl
Lenge — 10 a 11 gl
Vlaemse Vis — 9,10 a 9 gl 15

N° 6. Honigh: Contant
Bordeuse Honigh 't vat — 40 a 41
Bajoensen Honigh 100 ℔ 10 a 10 gl 10
Honigh van Breta — 100 ℔ 12 a 13 gl
Bremer Honigh de Ton — 35 a 36 gl
Inlantse Honigh de Ton — 37 a 38 gl
Nantese Honigh — 12,10 a 13 gl

N° 7. Olyen by 't Vat en by de Aem Cont
Genuase Oly 60 a 62 Dito Poelse 47
Dito Civielse dito Portug. 48 a 52
Malegense — Majorca 52
Lijn Oly 34 gl Raep Oly 37 gl
Hennep Oly — 45 gl

N° 8. Waren by 't 100 ℔ Contant
Meleuse Rijs — 34
Root Korrel-Rijs
Bracke Rijs
Alsecantse Anijs — 27 gl
dito Roomse 13 gl 10 dito Poel. 18 gl
dito Maltese 14 gl dito Turcks 10 gl
Cumijn — 20 gl
Lange Amandelen — 53 gl
dito Val. n. N 43 gl Provense 40 gl
dito Barbar. 38 gl Lang. Rosijn N 33 gl 10
Cort Rosijn. de Cort N gl 10
Corenten San. Nao a 19 gl [illegible]
Lange Pruym. N 19 [illegible] Ronde
Vygen — gl
Alicantse Zeep — 23 a 25 gl
dito Marsilse — 22 gl
Toelonse Cappers fijne — 18 gl
Limoen — de Pijp 45 gl
Groote Olyven — gl
Dito in Barille gl Stijffel 10 a 11 gl
Droege Gember — 13 a 20 gl

N° 9. Huyden by de ℔. Contant.
Caraquese 50 a 55 ℔ — 20
Caraquese van 45 a 50 ℔ — 11 a 11
Idem van 25 a 27 ℔ — 10 a 10
Mexacam 31 a ℔ — 9,8 a 10
Cartageene 10 a 11 ℔ — 9
Havan. 38 a 40 ℔ 10 Idem 25 a 27 ℔ 9
Sando. 36 a 40 ℔ [illegible] 15 a 20 ℔ 8 9
Hondouras 38 a 40 ℔ — 8 a 8
Brasilianos 40 a 44 ℔ — 11 a 11
Dantz bank-Huyd. Somer-goet van 24 ℔ 9
Herfst Goet van 27 a 28 ℔ — 8
Poolse Zomer-goet van 24 ℔ 8
Idem 22 ℔ 7 4 Idem 13 a 14 6
Herfst-Goet van 25 ℔ — 6,8 a 6
Van 20 a 22 ℔ 5,12 a 6 4 van 14 a 15 ℔ 5,14 a 6
Deense van 15 a 17 ℔ — 5 a 5
Schev. van 18 a 19 ℔ 7 8 1,10 a 11 ℔ 6
Elants Huyden van Canid. van 13 a 14 ℔ 18 a 20 gl

Gesoute Huyden.
Inlantse Osse van 63 a 70 ℔ — 3,15 a 4
Vriesse Bulle van 60 a 65 ℔ — 3,14 a 3
Dito Koye van 60 a 64 ℔ — 3,18 a 2
Yrs. v. 70 ℔ 18 gl d'100 ℔ v 60 ℔ 17 gl
Van 50 ℔ 15 gl 10 v. 40 ℔ 14 a 14 gl 10
Juchten van 10 a 11 ℔ 't Paer 14 a 14 8
Van 12 a 13 ℔ [illegible] 15
Spaens-Leer van 24 ℔ 't Dozijn 38 a 33
Idem 17 a 18 ℔ — 32
Oosters 22 a 24 ℔ 24 a 26 Idem 15 a 18 ℔ [illegible]
Sool-Leer van 25 a 26 ℔ — 12 a 12
Idem 18 a 20 — 11,8 a 12

N° 10. Spaense Wynen. Contant.
Xerese Secken 't vat N 40 a 50
Pierre Semijn Wijn — N 40 a 46
Canary-Wijn —

Fransse Wynen. Contant
Petouwen Stom Wijn
Conjacken Schoon
Bordeuse — 5
Langonse Wijnen — 5
Libornse — 5
Hoogblanse wijn — 5
Nantese — 8
Nantse Frans. w. 30 vier
Conjackse —
Bord. Brandewijn. —
Bier Brandewijn. De Aem. 48 gl
Koorn Brandewijn. De Aem 44 gl

N° 11. Tin/ Loot en Was Contant.
Engels Loot — 26 a 27
Bronswijck Loot — 26
Engels block Tin — 52 gl
Fijn duytsch kulz Tin — 52 gl
Slachwalder kulz Tin — 52 gl
Oldenburger kulz Tin — 50 gl
Amsterdams proef Tin — 52 gl
Franckforder proef Tin 45 gl
Klaer Tin — 38 gl
Inlandts Was, met 100 ℔ 72 a 73 gl
Droog Oost. Was, 100 ℔ 71 a 73 gl
Gemeen Oosters 100 ℔ 68 gl
Oosters Ver-Was 100 ℔ 60 gl

N° 12. Wolle.
Segovia gesort. de prim. 31 a 33 a 36
Soorta 26 a 29 Soria Seg. 30 a 32
Petite Seg. gesort prim. 26 a 27
Mol. en Cast. gesort de pri 22 a 24
Alber Wol. e. pri. 27 Pet. Alb. Strijt
Sevilisse gesorteert de pri 19 a 20
Seg. Lam. Wolle. 100 ℔ 60 a 65 a 70 gl
Mol Cast. en Alb Lam W. 45 a 50 gl rise
Pomer ingeb. wol. 100 ℔ 31 a 32 gl m. r.
dito Fijne gryse 100 ℔ 39 gl cont
Rostocker — 100 ℔ 33 gl m. r.
Stettijnse — 100 ℔ 30 a 31 gl m. r.
Dantzicker — 100 ℔ 30 a 32 gl m. r.
Poolsse Lam. Wolle van 14 a 22 m. r.
Dito Somer Wolle — van 10 a 14 15 m. r.
Ennen Bre. scheor 100 ℔ 24 a 26 gl m. r.
Rijnse ingebond. 100 ℔ 26 a 28 gl cont.
Dito Uytgebond. 100 ℔ 35 a 37 gl cont.
Halb. en Duringer 100 ℔ 42 a 43 gl cont.
Rijnsse Pel-Wolle 100 ℔ 27 a 30 gl cont.
Bruwier Wolle — 100 ℔ 22 a 26 gl cont.

The liberalism of the seventeenth century thus was, as the name indeed suggests, a force for liberation. It freed those that practised it from all the tyrannies, political and religious, economic and intellectual, to which the dying traditions of medievalism were still clinging. Likewise, it was opposed to the blind fervour of extremist protestant sects. It rejected the authority of the Church to legislate in matters of philosophy and science. Until the Congress of Vienna plunged Europe into the neo-feudal morass of the Holy Alliance, early liberalism, fired by an optimistic outlook and driven by boundless energy, made tremendous strides without suffering major setbacks.

In England and Holland the growth of liberalism was so much bound up with the general conditions of the time that it created very little fuss. But in some other countries, notably France and North America, it had a revolutionary influence in shaping subsequent events. A dominant feature of the liberal attitude was its respect for individualism.

Protestant theology had emphasised the inadequacy of authority to lay down the law in matters of conscience. The same individualism penetrated into the economic and philosophic sphere. In economics it manifests itself in 'laisser faire' and its rationalisation in nineteenth century utilitarianism. In philosophy it brings to the fore an interest in the theory of knowledge, which has so largely occupied philosophers since then. Descartes' famous formula 'I think, therefore I am' is typical of this individualism, since it throws everyone back on his own personal existence as a basis for knowledge.

This doctrine of individualism was in the main a rationalist theory, and reason was held to be of paramount importance. To be ruled by the passions was generally considered to be uncivilised. During the nineteenth century, however, the individualist doctrine came to be extended to the passions themselves and, on the crest of the romantic movement, led to a number of philosophies of power which exalted the self-will of the stronger. This ends of course in something quite opposed to liberalism. Such theories are indeed self-defeating, since the man who succeeds must destroy the ladder to success, for fear of competition from others equally ambitious.

The liberal movement influenced the intellectual climate of opinion generally. It is therefore not surprising that thinkers who might otherwise hold radically different philosophic views were nevertheless liberal in their political theories. Spinoza was liberal as much as the British Empiricist philosophers.

With the rise of industrial society in the nineteenth century, liberalism was a powerful source for social improvement of the miserably exploited labouring classes. This function was later taken over by the more militant forces of the rising socialist movement. Liberalism remained on the whole a movement without dogma. As a political force it is now unfortunately quite spent. It is a sorry comment on our times, and perhaps the outcome of the international catastrophes of the present century, that most men no longer have the courage to live without a rigid political creed.

Ao. 1680. Einge- lauffene ORDI- NARI No. 28.

Post-Zeitung,

Von dem was wöchentlich in und ausserhalb des Heil. Römischen Reichs Merkwürdiges paßiret.

Praag/vom 8. Julii.

DAmit wir nicht so gar verlassen bleiben / und in eusserste Unordnung und vollen Ruin verfallen möchten / wollen Ihre Kayserl. Majest. dem Herrn Ober-Burggrafen und einen Herrn Stadthalter alhier zu residiren herein schikken. Der Herr General Montecuculi ist bey Hofe in eine solche Schwachheit gerahten / daß er in gar schlechter Disposition sich anderswohin bringen lassen müssen. Des Herrn Hof-Cammer Präsidenten Sache soll zu Lintz publiciret werden / deren Ausspruch aber übel lauten dörffte.

Ein anders / vom vorigen.

ZU möglichster Verwehrung des Schrekkens haben wir bißher unsere Todten nur in der Nacht wegführen und vergraben lassen / nun aber lehret uns die Noht den Tag damit nicht zu verschonen / denn es gehet fast über und über / also lauffen Gesunde und Kranke zusammen / und stekkt immer einer den andern an. Wo das Tribunal sich setzen wird / weiß man noch nicht. Gestern seynd beyde regierende Majest.

Early German news sheet

The philosophic work of Descartes gave rise to two main streams of development. One of these is the revived rationalist tradition whose main carriers in the seventeenth century were Spinoza and Leibniz. The other is what is generally called British Empiricism. It is important not to apply these labels too rigidly. One of the great obstacles to understanding in philosophy, as indeed in any other field, is a blind and over-rigid classification of thinkers by labels. Still, the conventional division is not arbitrary, but points to some leading features of the two traditions. This is true even though in political theory the British empiricists show a marked streak of rationalist thinking.

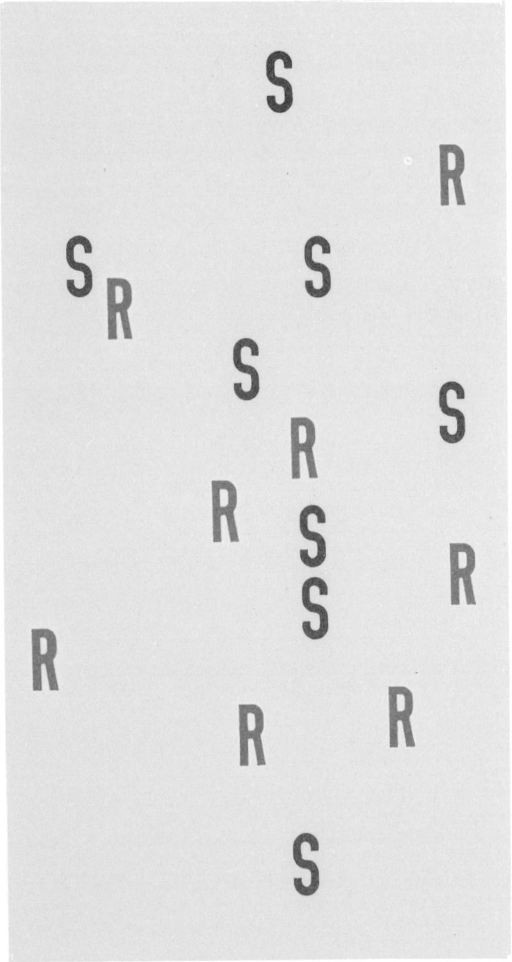

The three great representatives of this movement, Locke, Berkeley and Hume, roughly span the period from the Civil War in England to the French Revolution. John Locke (1632-1704) was given a strict puritan upbringing. His father fought with the forces of Parliament during the war. One of the basic tenets of Locke's outlook was tolerance. This eventually led him to break with both sides in the conflict. In 1646 he went to Westminster School where he acquired the traditional grounding in classics. Six years later he moved on to Oxford where he spent the next fifteen years, first as a student and then as a teacher of Greek and philosophy. The scholasticism then still prevailing at Oxford was not to his liking, and we find him taking an interest in scientific experiments and in the philosophy of Descartes. The established church held out no prospects for a man of his tolerant outlook, and so he finally took up the study of medicine. At this time he came to know Boyle, who was connected with the Royal Society that had been founded in 1668. Meanwhile he had accompanied a diplomatic mission to the Elector of Brandenburg in 1665, and in the following year had met Lord Ashley, later first Earl of Shaftesbury. He became Shaftesbury's friend and assistant until 1682. Locke's most famous philosophic work is his 'Essay concerning human understanding', begun in 1671 as a result of a series of discussion with friends, in which it became clear that a preliminary assessment of the scope and limitations of human knowledge might be helpful. When Shaftesbury fell in 1675, Locke went abroad and spent the next three years in France, where he met many of the leading thinkers of the time. In 1675 Shaftesbury re-emerged on the political scene and became Lord President of the Privy Council. Locke resumed his position as secretary with the earl the following year. Shaftesbury was trying to prevent the accession of James II and was implicated in the abortive Monmouth rebellion. In the end he died an exile in Amsterdam in 1683. Locke was suspect by association and escaped to Holland in the same year. For some time he lived under a pseudonym to avoid being extradited. It was at this time that he finished the Essay. To the same period belong his 'Letter on Tolerance' and the 'Two Treatises on Government'. In 1688 William of Orange took the English Crown and Locke returned home shortly afterwards. The Essay was published in 1690, and Locke spent most of his last years in preparing later editions and engaging in controversies arising from his work.

The mind starts like a blank sheet. Ideas of Sensation and Reflection are then inscribed on it

In the Essay, for the first time, we have a forthright attempt at setting forth the limitations of the mind and the sort of enquiries which it is possible for us to pursue. Whereas the rationalists had tacitly assumed that perfect knowledge was ultimately attainable, the new approach was less optimistic on this head. Rationalism is on the whole an optimistic doctrine and to that extent uncritical. The epistemological enquiry of Locke, on the other hand, is the foundation of a critical philosophy which is empirical in two senses. First, it does not, as the rationalists had done, prejudge the scope of human knowledge, and secondly it emphasises the element of sense-experience. This approach therefore marks not only the beginning of the empiricist tradition carried on by Berkeley, Hume and J. S. Mill, but also was the starting point of the critical philosophy of Kant. Locke's Essay thus sets out to sweep away old prejudices and preconceptions rather than to provide a new system. In this he had set himself a task which he considered more modest than the work of such master-builders as the 'incomparable Mr. Newton'. For his own part he feels 'it is ambition enough to be employed as an under-labourer in clearing the ground a little, and removing some of the rubbish that lies in the way of knowledge.'

The first step in this new programme was to base knowledge strictly on experience, which meant that the innate ideas of Descartes and Leibniz must be rejected. That we have from birth some kind of inborn equipment capable of development and enabling us to learn a number of things is admitted on all sides. But it will not do to assume that the untutored mind has dormant contents. If this were so we could never distinguish between this and other knowledge that genuinely comes from experience. We might then as well say that all knowledge is innate. This is of course precisely what is said in the theory of anamnesis that was mentioned in the 'Meno'.

The mind, then, is to begin with like a clean sheet of paper. What provides it with mental contents is experience. These contents Locke calls ideas, using the term in a very wide sense. In a general way, ideas are divided into two types, according to their objects. First there are ideas of sensation which come from the observation of the outside world through our senses. The other kind are ideas of reflection which arise when the mind observes itself. So far forth the doctrine does not introduce anything of startling novelty. That nothing is in the mind unless it had come through the senses was an old scholastic formula, and Leibniz had added a qualification excepting the mind itself from the general formula. What is new and characteristic of empiricism is the suggestion that these are the only sources of knowledge. Thus in the course of thinking and speculation we can never go beyond the confines of what we have gathered through sensation and reflection.

John Locke (1632–1704)

Locke proceeds to divide ideas into simple and complex. No satisfactory criterion for simplicity is provided, for he calls ideas simple when they cannot be broken up into parts. This is not very helpful as an explanation, and besides he is not consistent in his use of the phrase. But it is clear what he is trying to do. If there are only ideas of sensation and reflection, then it must be possible to show how mental contents are made up of these, or in other words, how complex ideas arise from a combination of simple ones. Complex ideas are subdivided into substances, modes and relations. Substances are complex ideas of things that can exist by themselves, whereas modes are dependent on substances. Relations, as Locke himself came to see, are not really complex ideas in his sense at all. They are a class of their own and arise from the mental operation of comparing. Take, for instance, the case of causality. This idea of relation supervenes upon the observation of change. The notion of necessary connection, Locke held, was based on a prior assumption and was not grounded in experience. Hume was later to emphasise the second of these points, and Kant the first.

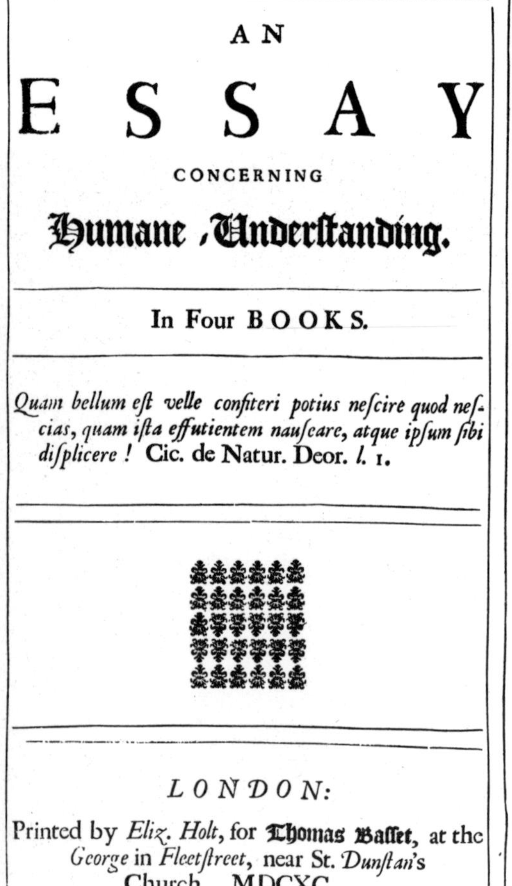

AN

ESSAY

CONCERNING

Humane Understanding.

In Four BOOKS.

Quam bellum eſt velle confiteri potius neſcire quod neſcias, quam iſta effutientem nauſeare, atque ipſum ſibi diſplicere! Cic. de Natur. Deor. *l.* 1.

LONDON:

Printed by *Eliz. Holt*, for **Thomas Baſſet**, at the *George* in *Fleetſtreet*, near St. *Dunſtan's* Church. MDCXC.

Title page of Locke's Essay

For Locke, to say that one knows something or other implies that one is certain. In this he merely follows the rationalist tradition. It is a use of the word 'know' which goes back to Plato and Socrates. Now what we know, according to Locke, are ideas, and these in turn are said to picture or represent the world. The representative theory of knowledge of course takes Locke beyond the empiricism which he so fiercely advocates. If all we know are ideas we can never know whether these correspond to the world of things. At all events, this view of knowledge leads Locke to the view that words stand for ideas much in the way that ideas stand for things. There is, however, this difference, that words are conventional signs in a sense in which ideas are not. Since experience provides us only with particular ideas, it is the operation of the mind itself that produces abstract, general ideas. As for his view on the origin of language, expressed incidentally in the Essay, it shares with Vico the recognition of the role of metaphor.

One of the chief difficulties of Locke's theory of knowledge is to account for error. The form of the problem is exactly the same as in the 'Theaetetus', if we substitute Locke's white sheet of paper for Plato's bird cage, and ideas for birds. It then appears that on such a theory we could never be in error, but Locke is not usually worried by this kind of problem. He is not systematic in his treatment and often leaves the argument when difficulties arise. His practical frame of mind led him to treat philosophic problems in piecemeal fashion without facing the task of achieving a consistent position. He was, as he had put it, an under-labourer.

In matters of theology, Locke accepted the traditional division of truth into rational and revealed, and always remained a devout, if independent, believer in Christianity. What he abhorred above all was 'enthusiasm', in the original Greek sense of the word. It means a state of being possessed by divine inspiration, and was characteristic of the religious leaders in the sixteenth and seventeenth centuries. Their fanaticism, Locke felt, was destructive of both reason and revelation, a view fearfully supported by the atrocities of the religious wars. In sum, Locke really puts reason first, following in this the general philosophic temper of his age.

The same mixture of reason and piecemeal empiricism is found in Locke's political theories. These are expressed in his two Treatises on Government, written in 1689-90. The first of these is a rebuttal of Sir Robert Filmer's pamphlet entitled Patriarcha, which contained an extreme formulation of the divine right of kings. This theory is based on the hereditary principle which Locke finds no difficulty in demolishing, though it may be remarked that the principle is not as such opposed to human reason. It is, in fact, widely accepted in the economic sphere.

In the second Treatise, Locke puts forward his own theory. Like Hobbes, he thinks that before there was civil government, men lived in a state of nature ruled by natural law. All this is traditional scholasticism. Locke's view on the rise of government is based, as in Hobbes, on the rationalist doctrine of the social contract. In its setting, this was an advance on those who held to the divine right of kings, though it was inferior to Vico's theory. The prime motive behind the social contract was, for Locke, the protection of property. In binding themselves to such agreements, men surrender the right to act as sole champions of their own causes. This right is now handed to the government. Since in a monarchy the king may well be himself involved in a dispute, the principle that no man should judge his own case requires that the judiciary must be independent of the executive. The division of powers was subsequently treated in great detail by Montesquieu. In Locke, we find the first full-blown account of these matters. What he has in mind more particularly is the executive power of the king as set over against the legislative function of parliament. It is the legislature which must be supreme, being responsible only to the community as a whole, of which it is the representative. What is to be done when the executive and the legislature are at loggerheads? Evidently the executive, in such cases, must be coerced into submission. This, indeed, is what had happened to Charles I, whose autocratic manner helped provoke the civil wars.

There remains the question of how one is to decide when force may rightfully be used against a fractious sovereign. In practice these matters are usually decided by the success or failure of the cause in question. Though Locke seems vaguely aware of this fact, his own view is in line with the generally rationalist trend of the political thinking of his time. It was assumed that any reasonable man knew what was right. Here, once more, the doctrine of natural law hovers in the background. For it is only on some intrinsic principle of this kind that the rightness of an action may be assessed. It is here that the third power of the judiciary has a peculiar role to play. Locke himself does not discuss the judiciary as a separate power. But where-ever the division of powers came to be accepted, the judiciary in time attained a fully independent status, enabling it to adjudicate between any other powers. In this way, the three powers constitute a system of mutual checks and balances that tend to prevent the rise of untrammelled authority. This is central to political liberalism.

In England today, the rigidity of party structure and the power yielded by Cabinet do somewhat diminish the division between executive and legislature. The most striking example of the division of powers as Locke conceived it exists in the government of the United States of America, where President and Congress function independently. As to the state in general, its powers since Locke's time have grown to vast dimensions, at the expense of the individual.

Of EDUCATION. 223

to be made, and what weight they out to have.

§. 177. *Rhetorick* and *Logick* being the Arts that in the ordinary method uſually follow immediately after Grammar, it may perhaps be wondered that I have ſaid ſo little of them: The reaſon is, becauſe of the little advantage young People receive by them: For I have ſeldom or never obſerved any one to get the Skill of reaſoning well, or ſpeaking handſomly by ſtudying thoſe Rules, which pretend to teach it: And therefore I would have a young Gentleman take a view of them in the ſhorteſt Syſtems could be found, without dwelling long on the contemplation and ſtudy of thoſe Formalities. Right Reaſoning is founded on ſomething elſe than the *Predicaments* and *Predicables*, and does not conſiſt in talking in *Mode* and *Figure* it ſelf. But 'tis beſides my preſent Buſineſs to enlarge upon this Speculation: To come therefore to what we have in hand; if you would have your Son *Reaſon well*, let him read *Chillingworth*; and if you would have him ſpeak well, let him be converſant in *Tully*, to give him the

Rhetorick. *Logick.*

Page from a pamphlet by Locke on education, published in 1695

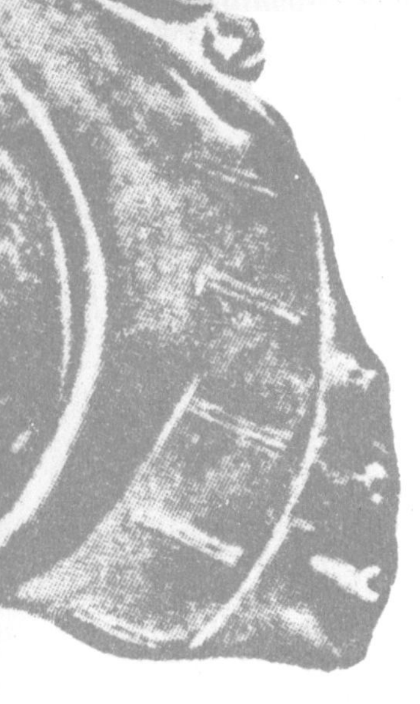

The Declaration of Independence shows Lockean influence, as in Franklin's use of 'self-evident'

Though amongst thinkers Locke is neither the profoundest nor the most original, his work came to exercise a strong and lasting influence both in philosophy and in politics. Philosophically he stands at the beginning of the new empiricism, a line of thought which was developed in the first instance by Berkeley and Hume and later by Bentham and John Stuart Mill. Likewise, the encyclopaedist movement of eighteenth century France was largely Lockean, with the exception of Rousseau and his followers. Marxism, too, owes its scientific flavour to Lockean influence.

Politically, Locke's theories were a summary of the kind of thing that was in fact being practised in England. No great upheaval is therefore to be expected. In America and France the case stood otherwise. As a result, Lockean liberalism led to some rather spectacular and revolutionary commotion. In America, liberalism became the national ideal, enshrined in the constitution. It is a way with ideals that they are not always faithfully observed, but as a principle early liberalism has continued to function in America almost unchanged.

Oddly enough, Locke's immense success is linked with the sweeping conquest of Newton. Once and for all, Newtonian physics had done away with the authority of Aristotle. Likewise, Locke's political theory, though hardly novel, repudiated the divine right of kings and sought to establish, on the basis of the law of nature of the scholastics, suitably altered to conform to modern conditions, a new doctrine of the state. The scientific temper of these efforts is reflected in its effects on subsequent events. The very wording of the

Declaration of Independence bears the stamp of it. When Franklin substituted 'self-evident' for Jefferson's 'sacred and undeniable' in the phrase 'we hold these truths to be self-evident', he echoes the philosophic language of Locke.

In France, the impact of Locke was, if anything, even stronger. The outdated political tyranny of the 'ancien regime' stood in painful and obvious contrast with the liberal principles of England. Besides, in the field of science Newtonian notions had ousted the older Cartesian view of the world. In economics, too, the English policy of free trade, though partly misunderstood, was much admired by the French. Throughout the eighteenth century there reigned in France an attitude of anglophilia built above all on the influence of Locke.

It is with the philosophy of Locke that the subsequent split in modern European philosophy first appears. Continental philosophy on the whole has been of the large scale system building kind. Its arguments are in the a priori strain and in its sweep it often takes no interest in matters of detail. British philosophy, on the other hand, follows more closely the method of empirical research in science. It deals with a host of smaller matters in piecemeal fashion, and when it does advance general principles it puts them to the test of direct evidence.

John Locke (1632–1704)

As a result of these differences in approach, the a priori system, while in itself consistent, will crumble to dust if its basic tenets are dislodged. The empiricist philosophy, being based on observed fact, will not collapse if in some places we find fault with it. The difference is as between two pyramids of which one is built upside down. The empirical pyramid stands on its base and does not fall if a slab is removed somewhere. The a priori stands on its head and topples over if you so much as squint at it.

In ethics, the practical results of this method are even more obvious. A theory of good worked out as a rigid system can wreak fearful havoc if some unenlightened despot fancies himself designed by fate to implement it. No doubt there may be some who despise utilitarian ethics because it starts from the base desire for happiness. It is quite certain, however, that the protagonist of such a theory will in the end do more to improve the lot of his fellow than will the austere and high minded reformer pursuing an ideal end no matter what the means. Together with these different points of view in ethics we find correspondingly different attitudes in politics developing. The liberals in the Lockean tradition had no great love for sweeping changes based on abstract principles. Every issue must be dealt with on its own merits in free discussion. It is this piecemeal, tentative and anti-systematic, rather than unsystematic, character of English government and social practice that continentals find so exasperating.

Rationalism, a pyramid standing on its head; Empiricism, on its feet

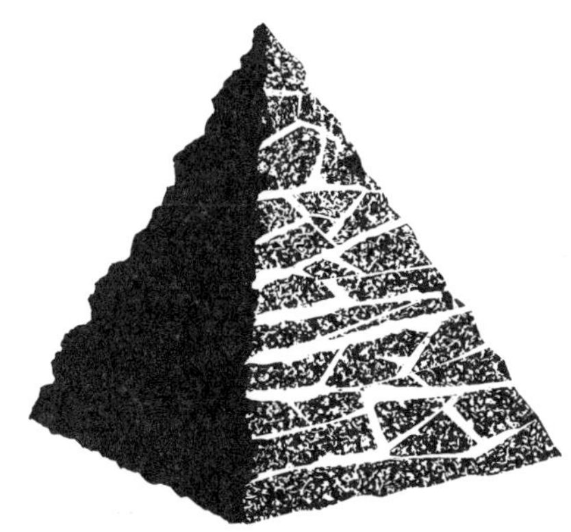

The utilitarian descendants of Lockean liberalism supported an ethic of enlightened self-interest. This conception may not have called forth the noblest sentiments in men; but by the same token, it avoided the truly heroic atrocities committed in the name of loftier systems that envisaged more dignified motives, while ignoring the fact that men are not abstractions.

One serious flaw that remains in Locke's theory is his account of abstract ideas. This, of course, is an attempt to cope with the problem of universals, left over on the Lockean theory of knowledge. The difficulty is that if we abstract from specific instances, what is left in the end is nothing at all. Locke gives as an example the abstract idea of a triangle, which must be 'neither oblique nor rectangle, neither equilateral, equicruval, nor scalenon, but all and none of these at once.' The criticism of the theory of abstract ideas is the starting point of Berkeley's philosophy.

George Berkeley (1685–1753)

George Berkeley (1685–1753), of Anglo-Irish descent, was born in Ireland in 1685. At fifteen years old he went to Trinity College, Dublin, where alongside the traditional subjects the new learning of Newton and the philosophy of Locke were beginning to flourish. In 1707 he was elected to a fellowship of his college. Within the next six years he published the works on which rests his fame as a philosopher.

Before he was thirty years old he had made his mark, thereafter his main energies were devoted to other causes. From 1713–1721 Berkeley lived and travelled in England and on the Continent. On returning to Trinity he took up a Senior Fellowship, and in 1724 became Dean of Derry. At this stage he began to work for the founding of a missionary college in Bermuda. With the assurance of backing from the government,he set out for America in 1728 to enlist support among the New Englanders. But the help promised from Westminster was not forthcoming,and Berkeley had to abandon his plans. In 1732 he returned to London. Two years later he secured preferment to the bishopric of Cloyne, a post he held until his death. In 1752 he left for a visit to Oxford where he died at the beginning of the following year.

The fundamental thesis of Berkeley's philosophy is that for something to exist is the same as its being perceived. This formula seemed to him so self-evident that he could never explain to his less convinced contemporaries what he was trying to do. For, on the face of it, the formula is of course outrageously at odds with common sense. No one normally thinks, as this view appears to demand, that objects which he perceives are in his mind. The point, however, is that Berkeley is implicitly suggesting that on the empirical view, that Locke had preached but not always practised consistently, there is something wrong with the idea of an object. To pretend to refute Berkeley by kicking stones as Dr. Johnson did is therefore completely beside the point. Whether Berkeley's own theory is in the end a cure for the difficulties of Locke is of course a different question. Meanwhile it must be remembered that Berkeley is not trying to mystify us with esoteric puzzles, but is attempting to rectify certain inconsistencies in Locke. In this at least, he is quite successful. The distinction between an inner and outer world cannot properly be maintained on Locke's epistemology. It is impossible, in one and the same breath, to hold a Lockean theory of ideas and a representative theory of knowledge. A very similar difficulty later faced the Kantian account of the same problem.

Title page of the New Theory of Vision, his first major work

AN
ESSAY
Towards a
New Theory
OF
VISION.

By GEORGE BERKELEY, M. A.
Fellow of *Trinity College, Dublin.*

DUBLIN:
Printed by AARON RHAMES, at the Back of *Dick's Coffee-Houſe,* for JEREMY PEPYAT, Bookſeller in *Skinner-Row,* MDCCIX.

The first work in which Berkeley criticises the theory of abstract ideas is the 'Essay towards a New Theory of Vision'. In this book he begins by discussing some confusions about perception which were at that time prevalent. In particular, he gives the proper solution to the apparent puzzle about our seeing things the right way up, though the image on the retina of the eye is inverted. This conundrum was much in vogue then, and Berkeley showed that it was due to quite a simple fallacy. The point is that we see with our eyes, and not by looking at them from behind as at a screen. Carelessness in sliding from geometrical optics into the language of visual perception is thus the cause of this misunderstanding. Berkeley goes on to develop a theory of perception which makes a radical distinction between the sorts of thing that different senses allow us to say about their objects.

Visual perceptions, he says, are not of external things but are simply ideas in the mind. Tactual perceptions, though in the mind as ideas of sensation, are nevertheless said to be of physical objects though in his later work this distinction is no longer allowed, and all perceptions yield ideas of sensation in the mind only. The reason why the senses are thus cut off from each other is that all sensations are specific. This, too, accounts for Berkeley's rejection of what he calls 'materialism'. For matter is simply some metaphysical carrier of qualities which latter alone gave rise to experiences that are mental contents. Bare matter as such cannot be experienced and is therefore an otiose abstraction. The same consideration applies to Locke's abstract ideas. If, for example, you take away from a triangle all the specific characters it has, in the end strictly nothing is left over, and of nothing no experience is to be had.

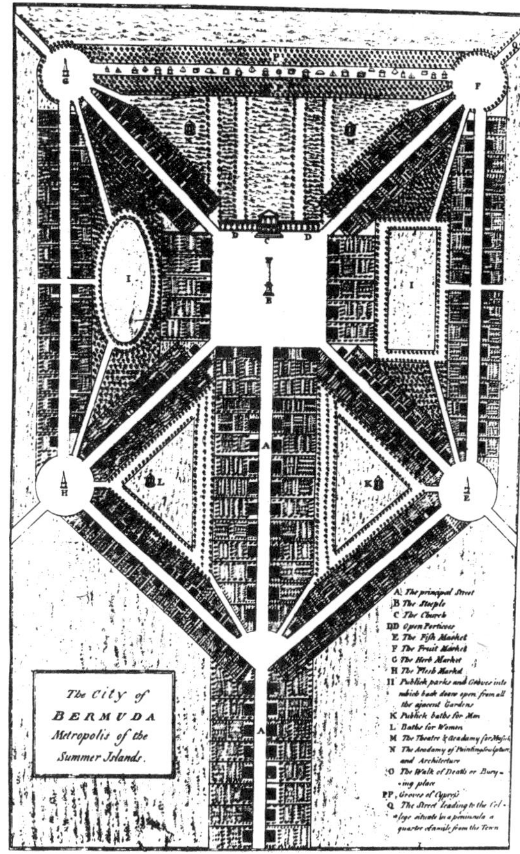

Plan for Berkeley's projects of a town in Bermuda

In the 'Principles of Human Knowledge', published in 1710, one year after the Essay, Berkeley states his basic formula without qualification or compromise: to be is to be perceived. This is the ultimate outcome of Locke's empiricism if one takes it seriously. For all we can then say is that we have experiences of certain sensations or reflections when we do in fact have them, and not at other times. Thus, not only are we confined to experiences which as such are registered in the mind, but we are reduced to admitting these only when we have them. In one sense this is not in the least odd: you have experiences when you have them and not at any other time. To speak of anything as existing only makes sense in and through experiences, and therefore to be and to be perceived are one and the same. It makes no sense, on this view, to speak of an unexperienced experience, or an unperceived idea, a position which continues to be held by contemporary philosophers who hold phenomenalist theories of knowledge. On such theories, there are no unsensed sense data. As for abstract ideas, if they were possible at all, they must be standing for some reality which cannot be experienced and this is a contradiction of Lockean empiricism. On the empirical view, reality is co-extensive with what can be experienced.

How, then, is the problem of universals to be tackled? Berkeley points out that what Locke thought of as abstract ideas were simply general names. But these do not refer to any one thing, rather they refer to any one of a group of things. Thus the word 'triangle' is used to speak about any triangle, but does not refer to an abstraction. The difficulty about the theory of abstract ideas is in fact not unrelated to that which we discussed in connection with the Socratic forms. They, too, are somehow totally unspecific and on this account live in another world than ours, yet it was thought possible to know them.

Berkeley, however, not merely rejects abstract ideas, but also the entire Lockean distinction between objects and ideas, together with the representative theory of knowledge that results from it. For how, as consistent empiricists, can we maintain on the one hand that all experience is of ideas of sensation and reflection, and on the other hand assert that ideas correspond to objects that are not themselves known, or even knowable? In Locke we already have a foretaste of a distinction, drawn later by Kant, between things in themselves and appearances. Berkeley will have none of the former, and is quite right in rejecting them as incompatible with Lockean empiricism. This is the point of Berkeleian idealism. All we may really know and talk of are mental contents. Along with the representative theory of knowledge, Locke held the view that words were signs for ideas. To each idea corresponds its word, and conversely. It is this erroneous view which is responsible for the theory of abstract ideas. Thus, Locke must hold that the utterance of a word in discourse summons up the idea, and in this way information is conveyed from one person to another.

Berkeley has no difficulty in showing that this account of language will not do. For what we understand in listening to someone is the drift of his speech rather than a series of verbal meanings cut off from each other and then strung together like beads. One might add that in any case the difficulty about representation occurs all over again. How is one to assign names to ideas? This would require that one could non-verbally convey that a certain definite idea was present in one's mind, and then go on to give it a name. But even then it would remain impossible to see how the correspondence could be stated since in the terms of the theory the idea itself is not verbal. The Lockean account of language is thus gravely deficient.

We have seen that one can give an account of Berkeley's idealism which makes it less startling than perhaps at first it seems. Some of the consequences that Berkeley is led to consider are less convincing. Thus, it seems to him inescapable that if there is perceiving activity going on, then there must be minds, or spirits, that engage in it. Now a mind, in having ideas, is not its own object of experience, therefore its existence consists not in being perceived, but in perceiving. This view of the mind, however, is not consistent with Berkeley's own position. For on examining the case we find that a mind conceived in this manner is precisely the sort of abstract idea that Berkeley has criticised in Locke. It is something that perceives, not something or other, but in the abstract. As for the question of what happens to the mind when it is inactive a special solution is required. Evidently, if existence means either perceiving, as in the case of active minds, or being perceived, as with ideas, then the inactive mind must be an idea in the constantly active mind of God. It is thus in order to meet a theoretical difficulty that this philosophical God is introduced. His function is merely to ensure the continued existence of minds, and incidentally, of what we call physical objects as well. This is a somewhat liberal way of bringing the whole account back to some-

A

TREATISE

Concerning the

PRINCIPLES

OF

Human Knowlege.

PART I.

Wherein the chief Caufes of Error and Difficulty in the *Sciences*, with the Grounds of *Scepticifm*, *Atheifm*, and *Irreligion*, are inquir'd into.

By *George Berkeley*, M. A. Fellow of *Trinity-College*, *Dublin*.

DUBLIN:

Printed by AARON RHAMES, for JEREMY PEPYAT, Bookfeller in *Skinner-Row*, 1712

Title page of the Principles of Human Knowledge

thing approaching common sense talk. This part of Berkeley's position is the least valuable and philosophically least interesting.

It is worth emphasising here that Berkeley's formula that to be is to be perceived does not state something that he thinks is a matter for experiment to decide He states, in fact, that we need only consider carefully how we use our vocabulary correctly to see that his formula must obviously be true. Thus what he is doing here has no metaphysical import, it is rather a question of laying down how certain words are to be used. In so far as we might decide to use 'existence' and 'being perceived' synonymously, there is of course no room for doubt. But Berkeley thinks not only that this is how we ought to use these words, but that in careful speech we do in fact already use them in this way. That this is not altogether an implausible view we have been at some pains to show. Nevertheless, one might well feel that this way of talking is not quite so appropriate as Berkeley thinks.

There is first of all the fact that he is led to a metaphysical theory of mind and God which is quite out of keeping with the rest of his philosophy. Without pressing this point, we may feel that the terminology of Berkeley is needlessly at variance with ordinary common sense ways of talking, though this might be arguable and is in any case not a reason why one must abandon it. But quite apart from this there is a philosophical weakness in Berkeley's account which lays much of it open to criticism. This is all the more remarkable for the fact that Berkeley himself had exposed just this kind of error in connection with vision. As we mentioned, he rightly insisted that a man sees with his eyes and does not look at them. Likewise, one might say in general that a man perceives with his mind, but in perceiving does not, as it were, hover over his mind, observing it. Just as we do not observe our eyes, neither do we observe our minds, and just as little as we should want to say that we see what is on the retina, should we say that we perceive what is in the mind. This shows at least that the phrase 'in the mind' needs a careful consideration which Berkeley does not give to it.

What this criticism shows is that there might be good reasons for rejecting Berkeley's way of talking in favour of a different terminology, and this on the basis of the analogy in the example. It seems clear that on this score, at any rate, the Berkeleian formulation is apt to be as misleading as anything. It might be felt that this is not a fair way of dealing with Berkeley. However, this is probably just what he himself would want a critic to do. For he held that it was the philosopher's business to disentangle misleading ways of talking. In the introduction to the Principles he puts the matter thus: 'upon the whole I am inclined to think that the far greater part, if not all, of those difficulties which have hitherto amused philosophers, and blocked up the way to knowledge, are entirely owing to ourselves. That we have first raised a dust, and then complain we cannot see.'

Berkeley's one other main philosophic work, 'The Dialogues of Hylas and Philonous', does not introduce new material for discussion, but reiterates, in the more readable form of dialogue, the views of the earlier works.

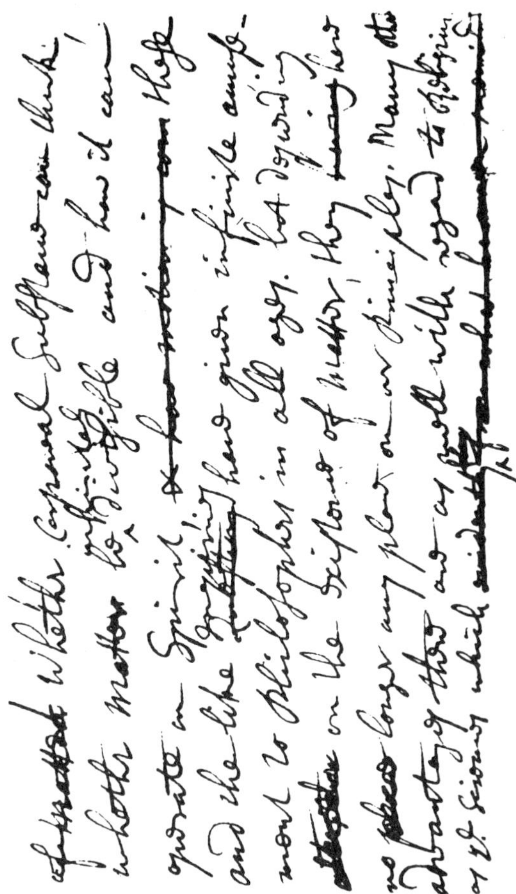

From the ms of the Principles

Library, Trinity College Dublin

A

TREATISE

OF

Human Nature:

BEING

An Attempt to introduce the experimental Method of Reaſoning

INTO

MORAL SUBJECTS.

Rara temporum felicitas, ubi ſentire, quæ velis; & quæ ſentias, dicere licet. Tacit.

Book I.

OF THE

UNDERSTANDING.

LONDON:
Printed for John Noon, at the *White-Hart*, near *Mercer's-Chapel* in *Cheapſide*.
MDCCXXXIX.

Title page of Hume's masterpiece: the Treatise of Human Nature

The doctrine of ideas as set forth by Locke is open to a number of serious criticisms. If the mind knows only sense impressions then Berkeley's criticism points out that no distinction can be made between primary and secondary qualities. A thorough-going critical account must, however, go further even than Berkeley, who still allowed the existence of minds. It was Hume who developed Lockean empiricism to its logical conclusion. In the end it is the extravagance of the sceptical position thus arrived at that shows up the flaws in the initial assumptions.

David Hume (1711–1776) was born in Edinburgh, where he entered the University at the age of twelve. After a conventional course of Art studies, he left the University before he was sixteen and tried for some time to apply himself to the law. But his true interests lay in philosophy which in the end he resolved to pursue. A short venture into business was speedily abandoned, and in 1734 Hume set out to France where he stayed for three years. Having no great means at his disposal, he had to adjust his mode of life to what little comforts his fortunes could afford. These restrictions he was quite willing to bear so that he might devote himself entirely to literary pursuits.

While in France, he wrote his most famous work, the 'Treatise of Human Nature'. By the time he was twenty-six, he had completed the book on which his philosophic fame has later come to rest. The Treatise was published in London shortly after Hume's return from abroad. It was, however, a resounding failure at first. The book bears traces of the youth of its author, not so much in its philosophic content, as in its somewhat brash and forthright tone. Nor did its unconcealed rejection of received religious principles help to increase its popularity. It was for similar reasons that Hume, in 1744, failed to secure the chair of philosophy at the University of Edinburgh. In 1746 he entered the service of General St. Clair with whom, in the following year, he went on a diplomatic mission to Austria and Italy. These duties enabled him to set aside sufficient money to retire from employment in 1748, and henceforth to devote himself to his own work. Within a period of fifteen years he published a number of works on epistemology, ethics and politics, and to crown it all, a History of England which brought him both fame and fortune. In 1763 he went once more to France, this time as personal secretary to the British Ambassador. Two years later he became secretary to the Embassy, and, upon recall of the ambassador, acted as chargé d'affaires until a new appointment was made later in the year. In 1766 he returned home and became an Under Secretary of State, a position he held for two years until his retirement in 1769. His last years were spent in Edinburgh.

Contemporary engraving of Hume and Rousseau

As he states in the introduction of the Treatise, Hume considers all enquiry in some measure governed by what he calls the science of man. Unlike Locke and Berkeley, Hume is concerned not only with clearing the ground, but keeps in mind the system which might subsequently be set up. And this is a science of man. The attempt at providing a new system suggests influence of continental rationalism, due to Hume's contact with French thinkers who continued to be dominated by Cartesian principles. At all events, a prospective science of man led Hume to enquire into human nature in general, and to begin with, into the scope and limitations of man's mental equipment.

Hume accepts the basic principle of Locke's theory of sensation, and on this view has no difficulty in criticising Berkeley's theory of the mind or self. For all we are aware of in sense experience are impressions, and none of these can give rise to the idea of personal identity. Berkeley had indeed suspected that his treatment of the soul as a substance was grafted on to his system in an artificial manner. He could not allow that we can have an idea of it, and therefore he suggests that we have a 'notion' of the soul. What these notions might be is never explained. But whatever he might say, this really undermines his own theory of ideas.

Hume's arguments are based on a number of general assumptions that run through his entire theory of knowledge. He agrees, in principle, with the Lockean theory of ideas, though his terminology is different. Hume speaks of impressions and ideas as the content of our perceptions. This distinction does not correspond to Locke's division of ideas of sensation and ideas of reflection, but cuts across this classification.

An impression, for Hume, may proceed both from sense experience and from such activities as memory. Impressions are said to produce ideas which differ from sense experience in that they have not the same vividness. Ideas are pale copies of impressions which at some time must have preceded them in sense experience. At all events, when the mind thinks, it attends to the ideas within it. The term 'idea' is here to be understood in the literal Greek sense of the word. Thinking, for Hume, is picture thinking, or imagining, to use a Latin word which originally meant the same. Collectively, all experience, whether in sensation or imagination, is called perception.

Several important points are to be noted. Hume follows Locke in holding that impressions are in some sense separate and distinct. Thus, Hume holds it possible to break down a complex experience into its simple constituent impressions. It follows from this that simple impressions are the building material for all experience, and can therefore be imagined separately. Moreover, since ideas are pale copies of impressions, it follows that whatever we can picture to ourselves in thinking can be the object of a possible experience. Furthermore, we conclude, on the same grounds, that what cannot be imagined can likewise not be experienced. Thus, the scope of possible imaginations is co-extensive with the range of possible experiences. It is essential to keep this in mind if we are to understand Hume's arguments. For he constantly invites us to try to imagine something or other, and on deeming us like himself unable to do this, he will assert that the supposed situation is not a possible object of experience. Experience thus consists of a succession of perceptions.

Beyond this succession, no other connection between perceptions is ever perceived. Here lies the fundamental difference between Cartesian rationalism and the empiricism of Locke and his followers.

Part of letter to his publisher from Hume, shortly before death

This, Dear Sir, is the last Correction I shall probably trouble you with: For Dr Black has promised me, that all shall be over with me in a very little time: This Promise he makes by his power of Prediction, not that of Prescription. And indeed I consider it as good News: For of late, within these few weeks, my Infirmities have so multiplyed, that Life has become rather a Burthen to me. Adieu then, my good and old Friend.

David Hume

The rationalists hold that there are close and intimate connections between things, and maintain that these can be known. Hume, on the other hand, denies that there are such connections, or rather suggests that, even if there were, we could certainly never know them. All we can know are successions of impressions or ideas, and it is therefore idle even to consider the question whether there are other, deeper connections, or not.

In the light of these general features of Humean epistemology we may now look more closely at the particular arguments put forward on some of the central issues in Hume's philosophy. Let us begin with the question of personal identity, discussed in the Treatise at the end of the first book, which is entitled 'Of the Understanding'. Hume begins by stating that 'there are some philosophers who imagine we are every moment intimately conscious of what we call our "self": that we feel its existence and its continuance in existence: and are certain, beyond the evidence of demonstration, both of its perfect identity and simplicity'. But an appeal to experience shows that none of the grounds on which the self is supposed to underlie experience will stand examination: 'Unluckily, all these positive assertions are contrary to that very experience which is pleaded for them: nor have we any idea of "self", after the manner here explained. For, from what impression could this idea be derived?' We are then shown that no such impression can be found, and thus there can be no idea of self.

226 *David Hume (1711–1776)*

There is the further difficulty that we cannot see how our particular perceptions are related to the self. And here Hume, arguing in his characteristic manner, says of perceptions that 'all these are different, and may be separately considered, and may exist separately, and have no need of anything to support their existence. After what manner therefore do they belong to self, and how are they connected with it? For my part, when I enter most intimately into what I call "myself", I always stumble on some particular perception or other, of heat or cold, light or shade, love or hatred, pain or pleasure. I can never catch "myself" at any time without a perception, and never can observe anything but the perception.' And a little later he adds 'if any one, upon serious and unprejudiced reflection, thinks he has a different notion of "himself", I must confess I can reason no longer with him. All I can allow is, that he may be in the right as well as I, and that we are essentially different in this particular'. But evidently he regards such people as cranks, and goes on to say 'I may venture to affirm of the rest of mankind that they are nothing but a bundle or collection of different perceptions, which succeed each other with an inconceivable rapidity, and are in a perpetual flux or movement'.

'The mind is a kind of theatre, where several perceptions successively make their appearance'. But this is qualified, 'the comparison of the theatre must not mislead us. They are the successive perceptions only, that constitute the mind: nor have we the most distant notion of the place where these scenes are represented, or of the materials of which it is composed'. The reason why men mistakenly believe in personal identity is that we tend to confuse a succession of ideas with the idea of identity we form of something remaining the same over a period of time. Thus, we are led to the notion of a 'soul', and 'self', and 'substance', to disguise the variation which does in fact exist in our successive experiences. 'Thus the controversy concerning identity is not merely a dispute of words. For when we attribute identity, in an improper sense, to variable or interrupted objects, our mistake is not confined to the expression, but is commonly attended with a fiction, either of something invariable and uninterrupted, or of something mysterious and inexplicable, or at least with a propensity to such fictions'. Hume then goes on to show how this propensity operates and gives an account, in terms of his associationist psychology, of how what passes for an idea of personal identity in fact supervenes.

To the principle of association we shall presently return. As for quoting Hume at length, his own elegance of style is excuse enough. Besides, there is really no better and clearer way of putting the matter than Hume's own. This circumstance has on the whole set a valuable precedent for philosophic writing in Britain, though Hume's perfection has perhaps never been equalled.

The other main question we must look at is Hume's theory of causality. The rationalists hold that the link between cause and effect is some intrinsic feature in the nature of things. As we saw, for instance with Spinoza, it was felt possible, by considering things in a sufficiently ample way, to show deductively that all appearances must be what they are, though it is usually allowed that only God can achieve such vision. On Hume's theory, such causal links cannot be known, for very much the kind of reason advanced in the criticism of the idea of personal identity. The source of our mistaken view as to the nature of this link lies in the propensity to attribute necessity of connection between the members of certain sequences of ideas. Now the linking together of ideas arises from association promoted by the three relations of resemblance, contiguity in space and time, and cause and effect. These he calls philosophical relations, in that they play a part in the comparison of ideas. In some ways they correspond to Locke's ideas of reflection, which, as we saw, arise when the mind compares its own contents. Resemblance in some measure intervenes in all cases of philosophic relation, since without it comparison cannot occur. Of such relations Hume distinguishes seven kinds: resemblance, identity, relations of space and time, numerical relations, degrees in quality, contrariety and causation. Of these he selects more particularly identity, relations of space and time, and causation, having shown that the other four depend only on the ideas being compared. Numerical relations in a given geometrical figure, for instance, depend only on the idea of that figure. These four relations alone are said to give rise to knowledge and certainty. But in the case of identity, spatio-temporal relations and causality, where we cannot conduct abstract reasonings, we must lean on sense experience. Causality is the only one of these that has a genuine function in reasoning since the other two depend on it. The identity of an object must be inferred on some causal principle, and likewise with spatio-temporal relations. It is worth noting here that Hume often inadvertently falls into ordinary ways of talking about objects, when in all strictness his theory should constrain him to mention only ideas.

For Hume, causality is association from habit; rationalists hold that cause and effect are linked

Hume then gives a psychological account of how the relation of causality is arrived at from experience. The frequent conjunction of two objects of a given kind in sense perception forms a habit of mind which leads us to associate the two ideas that are produced by the impressions. When this habit becomes strong enough, the mere appearance, in sensation, of one object, will call forth in the mind the association of the two ideas. There is nothing infallible or inevitable about this, causality is, so to speak, a habit of mind.

However, Hume's treatment is not altogether consistent, since earlier on we saw that association itself is said to arise from causality, whereas here causality is explained in terms of it. As an account of how mental habits are generated, the associationist principle is nevertheless a useful piece of psychological explanation which continues to exercise considerable influence. As for Hume, it is not really permissible for him to speak of mental habits or propensities, at least not of the formation of them. For, as we saw, in his stricter moments the mind just is the succession of perceptions. There is thus nothing that could develop habits, nor will it do to say that sequences of perceptions come as a matter of fact to develop certain patterns, since the bare statement spells mystery unless we can somehow make this appear as not just a fortunate accident.

Now it is certainly true that necessity of connection between cause and effect, as demanded by rationalism, cannot be spun out of Hume's epistemology. For however much we are confronted with constant and regular conjunctions, at no stage could we say that the impression of necessity had supervened over and above the sequences of impressions. It is thus not possible that there should be an idea of necessity. But since some men are rationalists and are prone to think otherwise there must be some psychological mechanism that misleads them. This is precisely where mental habits come in. We are so accustomed, from experience, to see effects following on their several causes that in the end we lapse into believing that it must be so. It is this last step which cannot be justified, if we accept Hume's empiricism.

Edinburgh, at the time of Hume

Hume concludes this discussion of causality by laying down certain 'rules by which to judge of causes and effects'. In this he anticipates by a hundred years the statement of J. S. Mill's canons of induction. Before setting out the rules, Hume recalls some of the main features of causality. 'Anything may produce anything', he says, reminding us that there is no such thing as necessary connection. The rules are eight in number. The first states that 'cause and effect must be contiguous in space and time,' the second that 'the cause must be prior to the effect,' the third that there must be constant conjunction between cause and effect. There then follow several rules that foreshadow Mill's canons. In four, we are told that the same cause always produces the same effect, a principle we are said to derive from experience. From this follows rule five, that where several causes might have the same effect, it must be by something they all have in common. Likewise we infer rule six, that a difference in effect shows a difference in cause. The remaining two rules we need not consider here.

The outcome of Hume's epistemology is a sceptical position. We saw earlier that the sceptics of ancient time were men opposed to the metaphysical system-builders. The term sceptic must not be understood in the popular sense that it has since acquired, which suggests some kind of chronic indecision. The original Greek simply means one who enquires with care. Where the system-builders felt they had found their answers, the sceptics were less sure and went on looking. In course of time it was their lack of confidence rather than their continued search which coloured the name by which they were known. Hume's philosophy is sceptical in this sense. For, like the sceptics, he comes to the conclusion that certain things that in everyday life we take for granted, cannot in any way be justified. One must not, of course, imagine that the sceptic is unable to make up his mind on the current problems that face him in the business of living. Having stated the sceptical position, Hume makes it quite clear that this does not disrupt one's ordinary pursuits. 'Should it here be asked me, whether I sincerely assent to this argument, which I seem to take such pains to inculcate, and whether I be really one of those sceptics who hold that all is uncertain, and that our judgment is not in any thing possessed of any measure of truth or falsehood: I should reply that this question is entirely superfluous, and that neither I, nor any other person, was ever sincerely and constantly of that opinion. Nature, by an absolute and uncontrollable necessity, has determined us to judge as well as to breathe and feel. . . . Whoever has taken the pains to refute the cavils of this total scepticism, has really disputed without an antagonist. . . .'

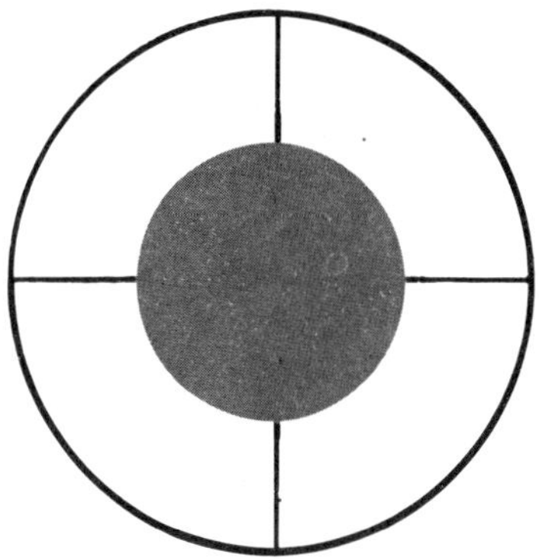

For rationalism things are intrinsically connected.

As to the doctrine of ideas which Locke put forward, Hume's development of it shows with relentless tenacity where this kind of theory leads us in the end. Further than this one cannot go along these lines. If one hold that when we ordinarily speak of causality we do not mean what Hume says we do or should mean, then a fresh start must be made. It is pretty clear that neither scientists nor the ordinary man thinks of causality in terms merely of constant conjunction. Hume's answer to this would be that they are all of them wrong if they mean something else. But perhaps here the rationalist doctrine is being somewhat too roundly dismissed. What the scientist does in fact do is much better described by rationalism, as we saw in connection with Spinoza. The aim of science is to exhibit causal relations in terms of a deductive system where effects follow from causes as the conclusion of a valid argument follows from its premisses, that is of necessity. But Hume's criticism remains valid for the premisses themselves. Towards these we should maintain an enquiring, or sceptical, attitude.

Scepticism denies all links

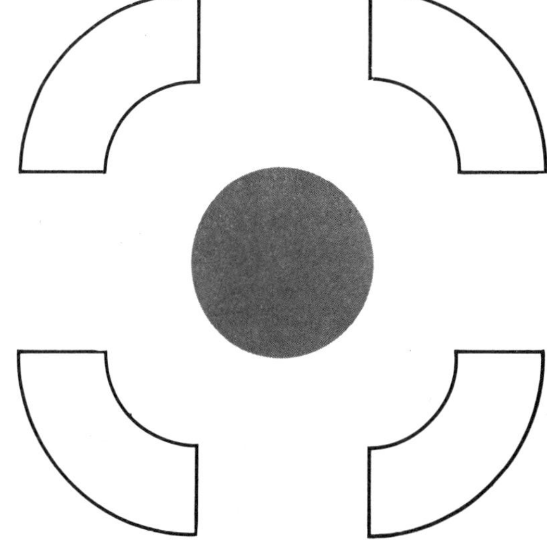

We recall that Hume's primary interest lay in the science of man. Here, the sceptical position produces a radical change in the fields of ethics and religion. For, once we have shown that we cannot know necessary connections, the force of moral demands is undermined as well, at any rate if it is desired to justify ethical principles by rational argument. The foundation of ethics now becomes no stronger than Humean causality itself. But of course, on Hume's own showing, this will leave us free in practice to adopt whatever view we wish, even if we cannot justify it.

Enlightenment and Romanticism

One of the outstanding features of the British Empiricist movement was its generally tolerant attitude to those that might be following different traditions. Thus Locke insisted that toleration must be extended without distinction, even to 'Papists', and though Hume makes fun of religion in general, and of Roman Catholicism in particular, he is opposed to that 'enthusiasm' which is a prerequisite for suppression. This generally enlightened attitude came to characterise the intellectual climate of the period. During the 18th century, it gained a foothold first in France, and later Germany. The movement of enlightenment, or 'Aufklärung' as it later was called by the Germans, was not tied invariably to a particular school of philosophic opinion. It was rather the outcome of the bloody and indecisive religious struggles of the sixteenth and seventeenth centuries. The principle of religious toleration, as we have seen already, commended itself to Locke as much as to Spinoza. At the same time, this new attitude in matters of belief had far-reaching political consequences. For it was bound to oppose unchecked authority in every sphere. The divine right of kings ill agrees with the free voicing of views on religion. In England, the political struggle had come to a head before the turn of the seventeenth century. The constitution that emerged from it was indeed not democratic, but it was free from some of the worst excesses that characterised the rule of privileged

Apotheosis of Rousseau, in 1794: part of the procession which took his remains to the Pantheon

nobles elsewhere. No violent upheavals were therefore to be expected. In France, the case stood otherwise. There, the forces of enlightenment did much to prepare the ground for the revolution of 1789. In Germany, 'Aufklärung' remained very much a matter of intellectual revival. Since the thirty years war, from which she was only gradually recovering, Germany was culturally dominated by France. It was not until the rise of Prussia under Frederick the Great, and the literary revival of the second half of the eighteenth century, that Germany began to cut loose from its subservience to French culture.

Byron (1788–1824)

Enlightenment, furthermore, was bound up with the spread of scientific knowledge. Where in the past much had been taken for granted on the authority of Aristotle and the Church, it now became the fashion to follow the work of the scientists. Just as in the sphere of religion, protestantism had thrown up the idea that everyone should use his own judgement, so in the scientific field men must now look at nature for themselves, rather than put blind trust in the pronouncements of those who stood for old-established doctrines. The findings of science were beginning to transform the life of Western Europe.

Whereas in France the old system was in the end shattered by the revolution, eighteenth century Germany was on the whole ruled by 'benevolent' despots. Freedom of opinion did exist in some measure, though it was not by any means untrammelled. Prussia, for all its military character, was perhaps the best example of a country where some form of liberalism, in the intellectual sphere at any rate, began to grow. Frederick the Great spoke of himself as the first servant of the state and allowed that within the confines of it everyone was free to gain salvation after his own fashion.

Enlightenment was essentially a revaluation of independent intellectual activity, aimed quite literally at spreading light where hitherto darkness had prevailed. It might be pursued with a certain sense of devotion and with intensity, but it was not on that account a way of life which favoured strong passions. Meanwhile,an opposite influence began to make itself felt: the more violent force of romanticism.

The romantic movement bears to enlightenment a relation which is in some ways reminiscent of the Dionysiac attitude as contrasted with the Apollonian. Its roots go back to the somewhat idealized conception of ancient Greece that had emerged with the renaissance. In eighteenth century France it grew into a cult of the emotions, by way of reaction against the somewhat cool and detached objectivity of rationalist thinkers. Where rationalist political thought, since Hobbes, had sought to establish and maintain social and political stability, the romantics were in favour of living dangerously. Instead of seeking safety they went out for adventure. Comfort and security were spurned as degrading, and a precarious way of life was held, in theory at any rate, to be a nobler thing. Hence springs the idealised notion of the poor peasant who ekes out a meagre living from his plot, but compensates for this by being free and uncorrupted by the urban civilization. Some special virtue was attached to being close to nature. The kind of poverty which was here approved of was essentially rural. Industrialism was anathema to the early romantics, and it is true enough that the industrial revolution produced much ugliness, both social and physical. In later decades, under Marxist influence, a romantic view came to be taken of the industrial proletariat. The just grievances of industrial labour have since then been righted, the romantic view of the 'worker' still lingers on in politics.

Linked with the romantic movement we find a revival of nationalism. The great intellectual efforts in science and philosophy had been essentially devoid of national feeling. Enlightenment was a force that knew of no political boundaries as such, even though in countries like Italy and Spain it could not flourish alongside Catholicism. Romanticism, on the other hand, sharpened national differences and favoured mystical conceptions of nationhood. This is one of the unexpected corollaries of Hobbes' Leviathan. A nation came to be viewed as a person on a large scale, endowed with some kind of will of its own. This new nationalism came to dominate over the forces that caused the revolution of 1789. England, being the fortunate possessor of natural boundaries, had acquired a sense of nationhood in very much more relaxed circumstances, and its own position in the scheme of things seemed to be unassailable. The young French Republic, beset on all sides by hostile rulers, could not develop so unself-conscious a conviction of its identity. Still less could the Germans, whose lands had been annexed by the imperial armies of Napoleon. A great outburst of national feeling had inspired the wars of liberation in 1813, and Prussia became the rallying point for German nationalism. It is interesting to note that some of the great German poets foresaw that this would lead to trouble.

Spurning utility, the romantics relied on æsthetic standards. This applies to their views on conduct and morals, as well as in economic matters, in so far as this ever touched their thinking. As to the beauties of nature, it was the violent and grandiose that won their approval. The life of the rising middle classes seemed to them dull and hedged in by crippling conventions. In this they were indeed not altogether unjustified. If today our outlook here is more tolerant, this is not least the outcome of romantic rebels who defied the approved customs of their age.

Philosophically, romanticism may be said to have exercised an influence in two opposite directions. First, there is the over-emphasis on reason, and along with it the pious hope that we need only apply our minds a little more intensely to the problems in hand and all our difficulties will be permanently solved. This kind of romantic rationalism, absent in the thinkers of the seventeenth century, figures in the work of the German idealists, and later in the philosophy of Marx. The Utilitarians also have a streak of it, in their assumption that man, in the abstract, is infinitely educable, which is clearly false. Utopian notions in general, whether purely intellectual or pertaining to social matters, are typical products of romantic rationalism. But on the other hand, the underrating of reason is equally an outcrop of romanticism. This irrationalist attitude, of which existentialism is perhaps the most notorious species, is in some ways a rebellion against the increasing encroachments of industrial society on the individual.

Romanticism found support above all amongst poets. The most famous romantic is probably Byron. Here we find all the ingredients that blend into a thorough romantic. There is rebellion, defiance, contempt for established conventions, recklessness and noble deeds. To die in the swamps of Missolonghi for the cause of Greek freedom was the greatest romantic gesture of all time. The later romantic poetry of Germany and France is influenced by him. The Russian poet Lermontov consciously styled himself a disciple. Italy, too, had a great romantic poet, Leopardi, whose work reflects the hopeless state of suppression of Italy at the beginning of the 19th century.

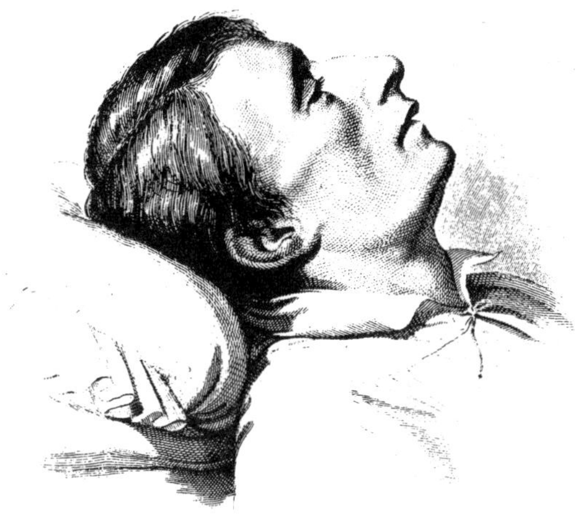

Leopardi (1798–1837), on his deathbed

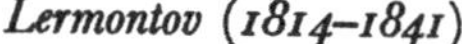

Lermontov (1814–1841)

The outstanding monument of the enlightenment period in the eighteenth century is the great Encyclopaedia compiled by a group of writers and scientists in France. Quite consciously, these men were turning their backs on religion and metaphysics, seeing in science the new intellectual driving force. By collecting together, in a vast work, the entire scientific knowledge of their time, not merely as an alphabetic record, but as an account of the scientific way of dealing with the world, these writers hoped to produce a powerful instrument in the struggle against the obscurantism of established authority. Most of the famous literary and scientific figures of eighteenth century France contributed to the enterprise. Two of these deserve special mention. D'Alembert (1717–1783) is probably best known as a mathematician. A vital principle in theoretical mechanics goes by his name. He was, however, a man of broad philosophic and literary interests. To him is due, amongst other things, the introduction to the Encyclopaedia. The man who bore the best part of editorial responsibility was Diderot (1713–1784), a writer on many subjects who had rejected all conventional forms of religion.

D'Alembert (1717–83), mathematician, co-editor of the Encyclopaedia

The encyclopaedists were not, however, irreligious in a wider sense. Diderot's view was akin to the pantheistic doctrine of Spinoza. Voltaire (1694–1778) who contributed extensively to the great work, had said that if God did not exist we should have to invent him. He was, of course, bitterly opposed to institutional Christianity, but did believe in some kind of supernatural power whose ends are served if men lived good lives. It is a form of Pelagianism devoid of all conventional attachments. At the same time, he ridiculed the Leibnizian view that ours is the best of all possible worlds, recognising evil as something positive that must be fought. Hence his fierce and bitter struggle against conventional religion.

Much more extreme in their rejection of religion were the French materialists. Their doctrine is a development of the theory of substance propounded by Descartes. We saw how the occasionalist principle really makes it superfluous to study mind as well as matter. Since the two realms function in a strictly parallel manner we can dispense with either one of the two. The best account of the materialist doctrine is found in Lamettrie's 'L'homme machine'. Rejecting the Cartesian dualism, he allows only one substance, to wit, matter. This matter is however not inert in the sense in which the earlier mechanistic theories had stipulated, on the contrary it is one of the features of matter as such that it should be in motion. There is no need of a prime mover, and God is merely what Laplace later called an 'unnecessary hypothesis'. On this view, mentality is a function of the material world. This theory has some connection with the Leibnizian conception of monads, even though it allows only one substance as contrasted with the infinity of monads. Nevertheless the view of monads as being 'souls' is somewhat akin to the notion of matter having, at times, a mind-like function. It is from this source, incidentally, that Marx derives the theory that the mind is a by-product of bodily organisation.

On the basis of such a theory, the materialists held a frankly atheist position. Religion in any shape or form is regarded as pernicious and deliberate falsehood, spread and encouraged by rulers and clerics in their own interests, since it is easier to exercise control over the ignorant. Here, too, Marx is indebted to the materialists when he speaks of religion as the opium of the people. By exposing religion and metaphysical speculation, the materialists wished to show mankind the path of science and reason which would usher in a kind of earthly paradise. This view they share with the encyclopaedists, and once again Marx's utopian socialism is inspired by these notions. In this respect however, they were all of them subject to a romantic illusion. While it is true that an enlightened attitude to life and its problems is of immense help in finding appropriate measures to meet our difficulties, it is plainly not to this world that ultimate and permanent solutions of the totality of all problems could belong.

What all these thinkers alike were emphasizing was the pre-eminence of reason. After the French revolution, which disestablished the reigning religion, a supreme being was invented and a special festival day set aside for it. Essentially, this was a deification of reason. At the same time, the revolution showed scant respect for reason in certain other matters. Lavoisier, the founder of modern chemistry, was arraigned before a revolutionary tribunal at the time of the terror. He had been a Farmer-general and had in fact suggested some valuable fiscal reforms. As an official of the ancien regime he was, however, held to be guilty of crimes against the people. When it was urged that he was one of the greatest scientists, the court replied that the republic had no need of scientists. And so he was guillotined.

ENCYCLOPEDIE,

OÙ

DICTIONNAIRE RAISONNÉ

DES SCIENCES,

DES ARTS ET DES MÉTIERS,

PAR UNE SOCIETE DE GENS DE LETTRES.

Mis en ordre & publié par M. *DIDEROT*, de l'Académie Royale des Sciences & des Belles-Lettres de Prusse; & quant à la PARTIE MATHÉMATIQUE, par M. *D'ALEMBERT*, de l'Académie Royale des Sciences de Paris, de celle de Prusse, & de la Société Royale de Londres.

Tantùm series juncturaque pollet,
Tantùm de medio sumptis accedit honoris! HORAT.

TOME PREMIER.

Gathering of the encyclopaedists, amongst them Voltaire (1), d'Alembert (4), Condorcet (5), and Diderot (6)

The Encyclopædia is in some ways the symbol of enlightenment during the eighteenth century. The emphasis lies on cool and rational discussion, and the aim is to work towards new and happier prospects for mankind. At the same time there grew up a romantic movement which was opposed to reason. One of the chief representatives of romanticism was Jean Jacques Rousseau (1712–1778). He was not, in the strict sense, a philosopher, except perhaps in his work on political theory and education. Through this and his vast literary activity he greatly influenced the later romantic movement.

Of Rousseau's life we have a record in his own 'Confessions', though the story is somewhat distorted through 'poetic' licence. Born in Geneva, of Calvinist descent, he lost his parents at an early age and was brought up by an aunt. Having left school at twelve years old he tried a number of different trades but liked none of them. At sixteen he ran away from home. At Turin he became converted to Catholicism, a faith he was to hold expediently for some time. He now entered the service of a lady, but was again stranded when she died three months later. On this occasion there was a famous incident which illustrates the ethical position of a man who relies merely on his own feelings. It was found that Rousseau had in his possession a ribbon he had stolen from his employer. Rosseau alleged that the object had been given him by a certain maid, who was duly punished for the theft. In the Confession he tells us that he was prompted to this deed by his affection for the girl, which caused her to be foremost in his mind when an explanation had been demanded of him. There is no hint of remorse. That he had borne false witness he would of course not deny. His excuse would probably be that he had done so without malice.

Jean Jacques Rousseau (1712–78)

We next find him under the wings of Madame de Warens, who also had been converted. This lady, considerably older than the young tramp, became his mother and mistress all in one. During the next decade, Rousseau spent much of his time in her house. In 1743, he became secretary to the French ambassador at Venice, but resigned when his salary was not forthcoming. In Paris, in about 1745, he met Thérèse le Vasseur, a servant girl with whom he thenceforth lived as his wife, concurrently running other affairs from time to time. The five children he had by her were all taken to the Foundling Hospital. Why he attached himself to this girl is not too clear. She was poor, ugly, ignorant and yet none too honest. It seems, however, that her defects ministered to Rousseau's feelings of superiority.

Not until 1750 did Rousseau become known as a writer. In that year, the Academy of Dijon held an essay competition on the question whether the arts and sciences had profited mankind. Rousseau carried the prize with a brilliantly argued denial. Culture, he maintained, taught men unnatural wants to which they became enslaved. He favoured Sparta as against Athens. Science he condemns because it had sprung from base motives. Civilized man is corrupted, it is the noble savage who is really in possession of virtue. These views were further developed in his 'Discourse on Inequality' (1754). Voltaire, who was sent a copy the following year, poured sarcastic scorn on the author, a slight which led to their eventual quarrel.

In 1754, Rousseau, now famous, followed an invitation to his native Geneva and reverted to Calvinism, in order to qualify for citizenship. In 1762 appeared 'Emile', a treatise on education; and 'The Social Contract', which contains his political theory. Both were condemned, the former for its account of natural religion, which displeased religious bodies all alike; and the latter for its democratic flavour. Rousseau fled first to Neuchâtel, then Prussian, and afterwards to England where he met Hume and even gained a pension from George III. But in the end he quarrelled with everyone and developed a persecution mania. He returned to Paris where he spent his last years in want and misery.

Rousseau's defence of the feelings as against reason has been one of the powerful influences in the shaping of the romantic movement. Amongst other things it has set Protestant theology on a new path that sharply differentiates it from the Thomist doctrine, which is in the philosophic tradition of the ancients. The new Protestant approach dispenses with proofs for the existence of God, and allows that such information wells up from the heart unaided by reason. Likewise, in ethics Rousseau contends that our natural feelings point in the right direction, whereas reason leads us astray. This romantic doctrine is of course diametrically opposed to Plato, Aristotle and Scholasticism. It is a most dangerous theory, since it is quite arbitrary and literally countenances any deed, provided only it has emotional backing on the part of the doer. This entire account of natural religion is an interlude in Emile and is presented as the 'Confessions of a Savoyard Vicar'. The new sentimentalist Theology that has sprung from Rousseau is in a sense unassailable. For, in the manner of Occam, it cuts itself loose from reason at the very start.

Contemporary picture of Rousseau in his study

The Social Contract is written in rather a different vein. Here Rousseau is at his theoretical best. On transferring their rights to the community as a whole, men as individuals lose all their liberties. It is true that Rousseau allows some safeguard, in that a man is said to retain certain natural rights. But this depends on the questionable assumption that the sovereign will in fact always respect such rights. The sovereign is not subject to any higher authority, and his will is the 'General Will', a kind of composite judgement which is enforceable on those whose individual wills might disagree.

Much hinges on the conception of the general will, but unfortunately it is not made very clear. The notion seems to be that taking away conflicting interests of individuals there is left over some self interest shared by all of them. But Rousseau never follows this to its last consequences. A state run on such lines would have to forbid all private organisations of whatever kind, and especially those with political and economic aims. Thus we have all the elements of a totalitarian system, and though Rousseau seems not altogether unaware of this, he fails to show how this consequence might be avoided. As for his references to democracy, it must be understood that he is thinking of the ancient City State and not of representative government. The book was, of course, misunderstood by those who first opposed its doctrine, and later by the leaders of the revolution who favoured it.

The post-Cartesian development of European philosophy took, as we saw, two different lines. On the one hand there are the various rationalist systems of continental philosophy, and on the other there is the general line of British Empiricism. Both are subjectivist in that they are concerned with private experience. Locke had set himself the task of conducting a preliminary enquiry to ascertain what was the scope of the human mind, and the great problem, which was brought out most clearly by Hume, is how to account for relation. Hume's answer was that we form certain habits which make us see things as connected. As we pointed out, even this is saying more than in all strictness Hume can be allowed. Still, it is a statement that contains a hint at one possible way out of the difficulty. It was his reading of Hume that woke Kant from his dogmatic slumber. By raising the habit Hume speaks of to the status of a rational principle, Kant simply disposes of the Humean problem; though, of course, he is saddled with some new difficulties of his own.

Immanuel Kant (1724–1804)

Immanuel Kant (1724–1804) was born in Königsberg in East Prussia, and never throughout his life moved far away from his native town. From his early upbringing he retained a streak of pietism which influenced his general mode of life and his ethical writing. Kant studied at the University of Königsberg, beginning with theology, but finally taking up philosophy, where he felt his real interests lay. For some years he earned a living as private tutor to the offspring of landed aristocrats, until, in 1755, he obtained a lectureship in philosophy at Königsberg. In 1770 he was promoted to the chair of logic and metaphysics which he retained until his death. Though not excessively ascetic, Kant led a very disciplined and industrious life. His habits were so regular that his fellow citizens used to set their watches by his passage. He was not a robust man but escaped illness because of his settled ways. At the same time, he was a brilliant conversationalist, and his attendance at social gatherings was always welcome. In political matters, he was a liberal in the best enlightenment tradition, and as to religion, he maintained a kind of unorthodox protestant position. He welcomed the French Revolution and favoured republican principles. Through his great philosophic works he achieved fame though never affluence. In his final years his mental powers declined; but the Königsbergers were proud of him, and when he died he was given a spectacular funeral, a distinction that overtakes very few philosophers indeed.

Kant's works cover an enormous range of subjects, on all of which he had at some time lectured. Little of this remains of interest today, except a cosmogonic theory based purely on Newtonian physics, a view that was later independently adopted by Laplace. What is of particular interest to us here is Kant's critical philosophy. The critical problem had first been mooted by Locke, who wished to clear the ground. But the way of ideas, after Locke, led inevitably to the scepticism of Hume. Kant staged what he himself called a Copernican revolution in this field. For instead of trying, as Hume had done, to explain concepts in terms of experience, Kant set out to explain experience in terms of concepts. In a sense we might say that Kant's philosophy holds a balance between the extreme position of British Empiricism on the one hand, and the innate principles of Cartesian rationalism on the other. The Kantian theory is difficult and involved and in many parts questionable. Nevertheless, we must attempt to grasp an outline of it if we are to understand its great influence on later philosophy.

With Hume and the empiricists, Kant held that all knowledge in fact arises through experience, but unlike them he added to this view an important remark. We must distinguish between what actually produces knowledge, and the form that such knowledge takes. Thus, though knowledge arises through experience, it does not solely derive from it. We might put this differently by saying that sense-experience is necessary but not sufficient for knowledge. The form that knowledge takes, the principles of organisation that transform the raw materials of experience into knowledge, these Kant would hold are not themselves derived from experience. Though Kant does not say so, it is obvious that these principles are innate in Descartes' sense.

The general concepts of reason which the mind thus supplies to shape experience into knowledge Kant, using the Aristotelian term, calls categories. Since knowledge is propositional in character, these categories must be linked with the form of propositions. Before showing how Kant derives the categories we must, however, pause to consider an important matter touching the classification of propositions. Kant, following Leibniz, adhered to the traditional Aristotelian subject-predicate logic. Indeed, he thought that logic was complete and unimprovable. Now propositions may be distinguished into such as already contain the predicate in the subject, and others in which this does not hold. Thus, 'all bodies are extended', is of the former type, because this is how 'body' is defined. Such propositions are called analytic, they only elucidate words. But 'all bodies have weight', is of the other type. The notion of being a body does not of itself include that of having weight. This proposition is synthetic, it may be denied without self-contradiction.

Alongside this way of distinguishing between propositions, Kant introduces another criterion of classification. Knowledge which is in principle independent of experience he calls 'a priori'. For the rest, whatever derives from experience is described as 'a posteriori'. The important thing is that these two classifications cut across each other. This is precisely how Kant escapes the difficulties of empiricists like Hume, who would have considered the two classifications as identical. The analytic would be coextensive with the a priori, and the synthetic with the a posteriori. Kant does allow the former, but insists that there may be a priori synthetic propositions. The aim of the 'Critique of pure Reason' is to establish how a priori synthetic judgements are possible. More particularly, what is here at stake for Kant is the possibility of pure mathematics, because in his view mathematical propositions are a priori synthetic. The example he discusses is the arithmetical one of adding five and seven, an illustration no doubt derived from Plato's 'Theaetetus' where the same numbers are used. The proposition that $5+7=12$ is a priori, since it does not derive from experience, while it is synthetic because the concept of twelve is not already contained in the concepts of five, seven and addition. On such grounds Kant holds mathematics to be a priori synthetic.

Critik
der
reinen Vernunft

von
Immanuel Kant
Professor in Königsberg.

Riga,
verlegts Johann Friedrich Hartknoch
1781.

Title page of the Critique of Pure Reason

Another important example is the principle of causality. The Humean account stumbled on the hurdle of necessary connection, which on the theory of impressions and ideas is impossible. For Kant, causality is an a priori synthetic principle. To call it a priori merely emphasises Hume's point that it cannot derive from experience, but instead of describing it as an externally conditioned habit, Kant treats it as a principle of cognition. It is synthetic because we can deny it without falling into verbal self-contradiction. Nevertheless, it is an a priori synthetic principle without which knowledge is held to be impossible, as we shall see a little later.

We can now turn to the Kantian theory of categories. These are the a priori concepts of the understanding other than those of mathematics. As we have suggested already, they must be sought in the form of propositions. Given Kant's view of logic, the list of categories seems to follow almost naturally. Indeed, Kant thought that he had found a method for deducing the complete list of categories. He first of all distinguished certain traditional formal features of propositions. These are quantity, quality, relation and modality. As to quantity, logicians since Aristotle recognise universal, particular and singular propositions. To these correspond the categories of unity, plurality and totality respectively. The quality of a proposition may be affirmative, negative or limitative, which points to the respective categories of reality, negation and limitation. Under relation we may divide propositions into categorical, hypothetical and disjunctive, whence we note the categories of substance and accident, cause and effect, and interaction. Lastly, a proposition may have one of three modal characters: it may be problematic, assertoric or apodeictic. The corresponding categories are those of possibility and impossibility, existence and non-existence, and finally necessity and contingency. With the details of Kant's deduction we need not here concern ourselves. Nor is it difficult to see that Kant's table of categories is not as complete as he thought, since it depends on a somewhat narrow view of logic. But the notion of general concepts, not derived from experience yet operating in the field of experience, is still of philosophic interest. It provides one answer to Hume's problem, though one might not accept the Kantian account of it.

Silhouette of Kant

Having deduced his list of categories from formal considerations, Kant goes on to show that without categories it is impossible to have any communicable experience at all. Thus, before the impressions which break in on the senses become knowledge, they must be organised or unified in some way by the activity of the understanding. We are here dealing with the epistemological problem. To explain Kant's position we must be clear on his use of terms. The knowing process is said to involve on the one hand the senses, which merely receive the impact of experience coming from without, and the understanding which ties these elements of sensation together. The understanding is to be distinguished from reason. Hegel later at one point expressed this by saying that reason is what unites men, understanding what sets them apart from each other. We might say that men are equal in so far as they are all rational, or endowed with reason; but unequal in regard to understanding: for this is active intelligence, in regard to which men are indeed notoriously unequal.

In order to have experience in a way that can be formulated in judgements, there must be what Kant calls a unity of apperception. Clearly, Hume's isolated impressions are not enough, however rapid their succession. Instead of the staccato of empiricist sense-experience Kant posits some kind of continuity. According to Kant it is impossible to have experience of anything eternal except through the framework of the categories. Their operation is thus a necessary condition for such experience. It is, of course, not sufficient, since the senses also must play their part. But the categories also intervene. What Kant thus seems to deny is the possibility of pure experience as a merely passive taking in of impressions, unless indeed we are concerned with ineffable streams of consciousness.

As for space and time, these are held to be two a priori particular notions that belong to pure intuition of outer and inner sense respectively. The discussion of these matters in Kant is rather complex and his arguments on the whole not very convincing. The gist of the whole theory seems to be that without a priori notions of space and time experience is impossible. In this respect space and time are somewhat akin to the categories. Experience is thus moulded by a priori concepts. But what gives rise to experience is also conditioned by things outside the mind. These sources of experience Kant calls 'things in themselves', or noumena, in contrast with appearances, or phenomena. On the Kantian theory it is impossible to experience a thing in itself, since all experience occurs with the concurrence of space, time and the categories. We may at best infer that there are such things from the postulated external source of impressions. Strictly speaking, even that is not permissible, since we have no independent way of finding out that there are such sources, and even if we had, we could still not say that they were causing our sense impressions. For if we speak of causality we are already inside the network of a priori concepts operating within the understanding. Here we have Locke's difficulty all over again. For just as Locke should not on his own theory speak of an external world giving rise to ideas of sensation, so Kant is not entitled to speak of noumena as giving rise to phenomena.

1 **Quantity**
unity
plurality
totality

2 **Quality**
reality
negation
limitation

3 **Relation**
substance and accident
causality and dependence
interaction

4 **Modality**
possibility—impossibility
existence—non-existence
necessity—contingency

The Kantian categories

The thing in itself, being outside space and time, is a piece of metaphysical furniture which ensured that in spite of a somewhat subjective epistemology, we should be able to avoid scepticism and recognise a field of experience which was at least inter-subjective. Kant is forced into this position because he does not allow the independent existence of space and time. Remove these two from the list of a priori concepts and the thing in itself becomes superfluous. This could certainly be done without affecting Kant's theory of the categories. There is however, another reason altogether for which Kant requires noumena. The clue lies in his ethical theory to which we shall come presently. Meanwhile let us note that the thing in itself falls completely outside the scope of a priori concepts and principles. One of the dangers in the speculative use of these concepts is precisely that we might overstep the bounds of their applicability. The limits of a priori concepts are those of the field of experience. If we go further we become involved in fruitless metaphysics and 'dialectic', which for Kant carries a derogatory meaning.

Kant's house in Königsberg

Zum

ewigen Frieden.

Ein philosophischer Entwurf

von

Immanuel Kant.

Königsberg,

bey Friedrich Nicolovius.

1795.

Title page of pamphlet on Perpetual Peace, 1795

But the 'Critique of Pure Reason' deals with only one of the three main questions that obtrude themselves on us. It sets the limits to cognition. This leaves volition and what Kant calls judgement. The former falls within the province of ethics, and is discussed in the 'Critique of Practical Reason.' As for judgement, this is meant in the sense of estimating purposes or ends. It is the subject of the 'Critique of Judgement', which we shall not examine here. However, we must briefly consider Kant's ethical theory, as discussed in the 'Critique of Practical Reason', and in the 'Metaphysics of Morals.'

Volition is called practical in the sense in which action is contrasted with the theoretical process of cognition. The two words, theoretical and practical, must here be understood in their original sense in Greek, being linked with 'seeing' and 'doing' respectively. The basic question of practical reason is this: how ought we to act? Here, too, Kant introduces somewhat of a revolution. For if hitherto ethics had always assumed that the will was ruled by external influences, Kant supposes that it gives its own law unto itself. In this sense the will may be described as autonomous. If we wish to arrive at some general principles of action, we cannot find them if we look for external goals or causes. We must, on the contrary, look within ourselves, if we wish to discover what Kant calls the moral law. But, evidently, this moral law cannot consist of specific injunctions. It cannot tell us how in any given case we should act. For this is precisely what, on the principle of autonomy, we must avoid. What remains is therefore a purely formal principle devoid of empirical content. This Kant calls the categorical imperative. Here we have another hybrid notion that, in the practical employment of reason, corresponds to the a priori synthetic in the theoretical employment of it. In traditional logic, the categorical and imperative moods are mutually exclusive. But Kant holds that certain statements involving 'ought' may be unconditional, and these he calls categorical imperatives. The supreme principle of ethics is thus found in the following categorical imperative: always act in such a way that the principles guiding the will could become the basis of a universal law. This somewhat austere pronouncement is really just a pompous way of saying that we should do unto others as we would that they do unto us. It is a principle which denies the justice of special pleading.

We note that the categorical imperative at the basis of Kantian ethics is a formal principle. As such it cannot belong to the sphere of theoretical reason, since this concerns itself with phenomena. Kant concludes from this that the good will, which is determined by this categorical imperative, must be noumenal. And here, at last, we see what function the noumenon has. Phenomena conform to the categories, in particular to the category of cause and effect. Noumena, on the other hand, are not subject to such restrictions, and in this manner Kant is able to escape the dilemma of free will as opposed to determinism. In so far as a man belongs to the phenomenal world, he is determined by its laws. But as a moral agent, man is noumenal, and therefore possesses free will. The solution is ingenious enough, though of course it falls along with the notion of the thing in itself. There is, in Kant's ethic, a somewhat forbidding streak of Calvinist rectitude. For, clearly, the only thing that counts is that our action should be inspired by the right principles. On this view, to like doing what you are ethically bound to do is a positive hindrance to moral action. Suppose I like my neighbour, and feel therefore inclined to help him when he is in difficulties. This, on Kant's principle, is not nearly so commendable as to extend the same charitable attitude to someone else who is perfectly loathsome. The whole thing becomes a rather unpleasant and dreary round of duties, performed not from desire but from principle. The performer is the good will, which alone counts as unconditionally good.

It is, of course, perfectly true that we cannot always give in to the whim of the moment. There are many occasions when we do act on principle, even if this runs against our immediate desires. But all the same it seems odd that all one's actions should be thus hemmed in. That Kant held such a view may be due to his having led on the whole an extremely theoretical life. Otherwise, it might have occurred to him that in the field of private affections there may be much that we might properly call good, without there being any question of turning anything into a general law. But the Kantian ethic is open to a much more serious objection still. If what counts is the frame of mind or intention, then you can cheerfully fall into a thorough mess, provided only you feel it is your duty. The miserable consequences that your action might call forth are of no account whatever. Well might Socrates warn the protagonist of such an ethic that ignorance was the overriding sin.

View of Königsberg Castle, house of Kant in foreground, left

As to the ethical function of the thing in itself, there are some further consequences. In the 'Critique of Pure Reason' Kant had shown that it is impossible, within the sphere of theoretical reason, to establish the existence of God by argument. The speculative activity of pure reason does indeed entertain the idea of the existence of God. But it is the practical reason which alone gives ground for such a belief. Indeed, in the practical field we are bound to accept this notion, since without it there can be no proper moral activity. For Kant the possibility of acting on the categorical imperative of the moral law carries the practical implication that God exists.

In a way, Kant's theory draws a dividing line reminiscent of Occam. For what the First Critique sets out to do is to delimit knowledge in order to make room for faith. That God exists cannot be known as a theoretical truth, but it imposes itself as a belief on practical grounds, always in the sense of theoretical and practical explained earlier. Nevertheless, Kant's ethic did not allow him to follow any religious dogma. For, as we see, it is the moral law which is really important. The specific dogmata of different religions are falsely asserted to be god-given. Though Kant held that Christianity was the only religion which did in fact conform to the moral law, his views on religion earned him official censure by the Prussian Government.

Equally radical for his time were the views on peace and international cooperation set forth in a pamphlet on 'Perpetual Peace', published in 1795. Representative government and world federation were two of the leading notions he proposed. We might do well to remember these in our own time.

The Kantian philosophy had, as we saw, provided some sort of answer to Hume's problem, but at the cost of introducing noumena. Kant's successors in the German Idealist movement were not slow to demonstrate the weakness of this conception, though their own developments in the theory of knowledge were questionable too.

One way of avoiding a dualism had been indicated by the materialists, for whom the mind is an accompaniment of certain forms of material organization. The other possibility is to turn this round and consider the outer world as in some sense the product of the mind. Kant, in positing noumena, had been unwilling to take this last step; Fichte took it deliberately.

Fichte (1762-1814)

Fichte (1762-1814), born in poor circumstances, was helped through his school and University days by a generous patron. Afterwards he made a precarious living as a tutor. When he came across Kant's writings he went at once to seek out the great philosopher, who helped him publish a critical essay on revelation. This gained immediate success, and Fichte became professor at Jena. His views on religion were, however, not to the liking of the authorities. He left for Berlin and entered government service. In 1808, he held his famous 'Addresses to the German Nation', in which he appealed to the Germans as a whole to resist Napoleon. In these speeches German nationalism takes a somewhat intense form. 'To have character and to be German undoubtedly mean one and the same', according to Fichte. It is not quite clear whether he thought this was an empirical fact or an appropriate verbal definition. The former is a discussible issue; as a definition it seems a trifle eccentric.

Part of Fichte letter to Schiller

When, in 1810, the University of Berlin was founded, he became professor, retaining this post until his death. When the wars of liberation broke out in 1813, he sent his students to fight against the French. Like so many others, he had been a supporter of the French revolution, but an opponent of the corruption of it by Napoleon.

In his political thinking, Fichte foreshadows Marxian notions of a socialist economy with state control over production and distribution. But philosophically of greater interest to us here is his doctrine of the Ego, which was designed to counter the Kantian dualism. The Ego, which in some ways corresponds to Kant's unity of apperception, is an active thing which is autonomous in Kant's sense. As for the world of experience, this is a kind of unconscious projection of the Ego, which he calls the non-Ego. It is because the projection is not a conscious one that we are said to be misled into thinking that we are constrained by an external world. As to things in themselves, this question can never arise, since what we know are appearances. To talk about noumena is self-contradictory; it is like knowing what can, by definition, not be known. The projection is however not only unconscious but unconditional as well. Since it is not experienced, it is not determined by the category of causality. As a free process it springs from the practical and moral nature of the Ego, where practical is to be understood in the etymological sense. For in this way the active principle which animates the Ego has some work to do in coming to terms with its own projection.

This somewhat fanciful theory does indeed avoid dualist difficulties. It is a precursor of Hegelianism as we shall see. One of the consequences of such a theory is that it must seem possible to spin the world out of the Ego. This was first attempted by Schelling, whose philosophy of nature later inspired Hegel.

Schelling (1775-1854) was, like Hegel and the romantic poet Holderlin, of Suabian origin. Both of them became his friends when he entered the University of Tübingen at the age of fifteen. Kant and Fichte were the main philosophic influence that he absorbed; and an early brilliance and literary elegance earned him a professorship at Jena before his twenty-third year. In this way he came to know the romantic poets Tieck and Novalis, and the two Schlegel brothers: Friedrich; and August, who with Tieck translated Shakespeare into German, and whose divorced wife Schelling married, though he was twelve years younger. He was interested in science and conversant with the latest developments. Before he was twenty-five he had published his 'Philosophy of Nature', in which he sets out to give an a priori account of nature. In this Schelling does not ignore the actual state of empirical science. He does, however, think that after the event it must be possible to deduce these findings from very general principles that are non-empirical. There is in this attempt a streak of spinozistic rationalism, combined with Fichte's notion of activity. For the a priori world that Schelling is trying to derive is conceived as active, whereas the world of empirical science seemed to him to be dead. This method was later taken up by Hegel. To the modern reader such rarified speculations about scientific matters are nearly incomprehensible. There is a lot of empty verbiage and a great deal of outright ludicrous detail in these discussions. It was this, amongst other things, that later brought idealist philosophy into disrepute.

Schelling (1775-1854)

What is, however, remarkable, is that Schelling himself in later years came to reject this kind of philosophising. Schelling's own interests had, after his early phase, moved towards religious mysticism. His first wife had died, and he had fallen out with Hegel. When in 1841 he was invited to write a preface to the German translation of the works of the French philosopher Victor Cousin, Schelling took the opportunity to launch a scathing attack on Hegel's philosophy of nature. No names are mentioned, and the culprit was in any case dead, but the intention was clear enough. Schelling here vigorously denies that it is possible to deduce empirical facts from a priori principles. Whether he was aware that this undermined his own philosophy of nature as well as Hegel's it is difficult to assess.

Both in Fichte and Schelling we find forms of what Hegel later used as the dialectic method. In Fichte we saw how the Ego is confronted with the task of overcoming the non-Ego. In Schelling's philosophy of nature there is a fundamental concept of polar opposites and their unity which foreshadows the dialectic even more clearly. However, the source of the dialectic goes to Kant's table of categories, where he explains that in the third in each group is a combination of the first and second, which are opposites. Thus, unity is in a sense the opposite of plurality, whereas a totality contains a manifold of units, and this unites the two first notions.

The German Idealist philosophy received its final and systematic form at the hands of Hegel. Taking up hints from Fichte and the early Schelling, he produced a philosophic edifice that for all its unsound features still remains interesting and instructive. Besides, Hegelianism exercised widespread influence on a whole generation of thinkers not only in Germany but later in England as well. France, on the whole, was not amenable to Hegelian philosophy, perhaps because of the great obscurity of the original which hinders a plausible rendering into clearcut French. The philosophy of Hegel survives especially in the dialectic materialism of Marx and Engels, which provides just as good an example of its untenability.

Ge. Wilh. Frid. Hegel,
Prof. p.o. an d. Kön. Universität

G. W. F. Hegel (1770-1831)

Hegel (1770–1831) was born in Stuttgart and studied at Tübingen at the same time as Schelling. For some years he worked as a private tutor and then joined Schelling in Jena in 1801. It was here that five years later he completed the 'Phenomenology of Mind', on the eve of the battle of Jena. He left before the victorious French and for some years worked as an editor and then as the head of a grammar school in Nuremberg, where his 'Science of Logic' was written. In 1816 he became professor at Heidelberg and produced the 'Encyclopaedia of the Philosophic Sciences.' Finally, in 1818, he was called to the chair of philosophy at Berlin, where he henceforth remained. He greatly admired Prussia, and his philosophy became official doctrine.

Hegel's writings are amongst the most difficult works in the entire literature of philosophy. This is due not only to the nature of the topics discussed, but also to the clumsy style of the author. The relief afforded by the occasional brilliant metaphors is not enough to offset the general obscurity. To try to understand what Hegel was aiming at we might recall the Kantian distinction between the theoretical and the practical. The Hegelian philosophy may then be described as insisting on the primacy of the practical, in the original sense of the word. For this reason, great emphasis is laid on history and the historical character of all human endeavours. As for the dialectic method, which has some roots in Kant, Fichte and Schelling, its plausibility for Hegel no doubt stems from a review of the see-saw development of historical movements. More particularly, the growth of pre-socratic philosophy seems to follow this pattern, as was mentioned earlier. Hegel raises this method to the status of a principle of historical explanation. Now as far as it goes dialectic progression from two opposing demands to some compromise solution is useful enough. However, Hegel proceeds to show how history had to go through its various stages on the basis of this principle. Needless to say this is only possible by distorting the facts. It is one thing to recognise a pattern of historical events, but quite another to deduce history from such a principle. Schelling's criticism can be applied to this as much as to the philosophy of nature.

The dialectic method is in some ways reminiscent of the socratic striving towards the form of the Good. To this latter corresponds what Hegel calls the Absolute Idea. Just as the socratic dialectic, through destroying special hypotheses, leads ultimately to the form of the Good, so the Hegelian dialectic ascends to the Absolute Idea. This process is explained for better or worse in the

Logic. It should be kept in mind that logic to Hegel is really synonymous with metaphysic. Thus, under this heading we find an account of the categories spun out of each other by a dialectic progression of thesis, antithesis and synthesis. This doctrine is evidently inspired by the Kantian discussion of the categories with which it shares the category of unity as a starting point. Thereafter Hegel goes his own way and constructs a long and somewhat arbitrary string of categories until he reaches the Absolute Idea, by which time we have turned full circle and are back again at unity. In a way Hegel regards this as a guarantee of completeness and sound argument. The Absolute Idea in fact turns out to be the supreme example of unity, in which all differences have been swallowed up.

As to the dialectic process that leads to the Absolute, it helps us to gain a fuller grasp of this difficult notion. To explain this in simple language is beyond Hegel's and no doubt anyone's power. But Hegel here falls back on one of those striking illustrations with which his works abound. The contrast is that between somebody whose notion of the Absolute is unsupported by a passage through the dialectic, and someone else who has gone through it. This is likened to the significance that a prayer has to a child and to an old man. Both recite the same words, but for the child they mean very little more than certain noises, whereas to the old man they evoke the experiences of a lifetime.

The dialectic principle thus proclaims that the Absolute, in which the progression comes to an end, is the only reality. In this particular, Hegel is influenced by Spinoza. It follows that no fragment of the whole has any viable reality or meaning by itself. Only if it is related to the entire universe can it be meaningful. It would seem as though the one and only proposition we should risk is that the Absolute Idea is real. Only the whole is true. Anything partial can only be partially true. As for a definition of the Absolute Idea, this is so obscure in Hegel as to be useless. The gist of it is however quite simple. The Absolute Idea, for Hegel, is the Idea which thinks itself.

This is a metaphysical showpiece that corresponds in some ways to Aristotle's God, an aloof and unknown entity wrapped up in its own thought. In some other respects it is reminiscent of Spinoza's God who is identical with the universe. Like Spinoza, Hegel rejects any form of dualism. Following Fichte, he starts from the mental, and therefore talks in terms of the Idea.

This general metaphysical theory is applied by Hegel to history. That it should fit certain general patterns in this field is not, of course, surprising, for it is precisely from history that Hegel derived the dialectic principle. But, as we said earlier, the detailed account of specific events should not be sought in this a priori manner. Again, the progression towards the Absolute in history provides an opportunity for some pretty crude nationalist propaganda. It would appear that history had reached its ultimate stage in the Prussian state of Hegel's day. Such is the conclusion that Hegel reaches in the 'Philosophy of History'. It now appears that the great dialectician was here somewhat hasty in his deduction.

Georg Wilhelm Friedrich Hegel's

Vorlesungen

über die

Philosophie der Geschichte.

Herausgegeben

von

Dr. Eduard Gans.

Dritte Auflage

besorgt

von

Dr. Karl Hegel.

Die Weltgeschichte ist nicht ohne eine Weltregierung verständlich.

Wilhelm von Humboldt.

Mit Königl. Würtembergischem, Großherzogl. Hessischem und der freien Stadt Frankfurt Privilegium gegen den Nachdruck und Nachdrucks-Verkauf.

Berlin, 1848.

Verlag von Duncker und Humblot.

Title page of Hegel's Philosophy of History

The same pattern of argument leads Hegel to favour a state which is organised in a totalitarian manner. The development of spirit in history is above all the task of the Germans, according to Hegel. For they alone have understood the universal scope of freedom. Now freedom is not a negative notion but must be linked to some code of law; on this we may agree with Hegel. From this it does not, however, follow that wherever there is law there is freedom, as Hegel seems in fact to think. If this were so, 'freedom' would be synonymous with 'obedience to law', which is somewhat at variance with the layman's view. At the same time there is a valuable hint in Hegel's notion of freedom. Someone who habitually runs his head into brick walls, from an unwillingness to allow that bricks are harder than skulls, might be described as persistent but not as free. In this sense freedom is to recognise the world as it is rather than harbour illusions, or to grasp the working of necessity, a thought foreshadowed, as we saw, already by Heraclitus. But when it comes to the specific laws of Prussia, there seems to be no reason why these should be logically necessary. To maintain that they are, as Hegel is inclined to do, merely enjoins upon the helpless citizen a blind obedience to the ordinances of his country. His freedom is to do as he is told.

Hegel in his study

The dialectic method is inspired by one other feature which comes from an observation of history. For it emphasises the aspect of struggle between opposing forces. Like Heraclitus, Hegel greatly values strife. He goes so far as to suggest that war is morally superior to peace. If nations have no enemy to fight against, they become morally weak and decadent. Evidently Hegel is here thinking of Heraclitus' dictum that war is the father of all. He rejects Kant's conception of world-wide confederation and is opposed to the Holy Alliance, which emerged from the Congress of Vienna. The entire discussion of politics and history is distorted by his one-sided interest in political history. In this he lacks the broad vision of Vico, who recognised the importance of the arts and sciences. Only from a political view in the narrow sense could Hegel come to the conclusion that external enemies were vital to the moral health of a nation. If one adopts a somewhat wider outlook it becomes clear that there is much within any given society that provides ample outlet for the healthy pugnacity of its citizens. The view that differences between nations must be resolved by war assumes that no social contract between them is possible, and that they must remain in their mutual dealings in a state of nature, where only power counts. On this matter Kant displayed greater insight than Hegel. For our own times have shown that war will in the end lead to universal destruction. That would indeed amount to a dialectic consummation which must satisfy even the most orthodox Hegelian.

The Hegelian doctrine of politics and history is oddly enough not really in harmony with his own logic. For the totality in which the dialectic process issues is not like the 'One' of Parmenides, which is undifferentiated; nor even like Spinoza's God or Nature, where the individual becomes more and more at one with the universe and ultimately becomes merged with it. Hegel, on the contrary, thinks in terms of organic wholes, a notion which was later to influence the philosophy of Dewey. On this view, it is precisely through being related to a whole, as are the parts of an organism, that the individual gains its full reality. One might have thought that this would lead Hegel to allow a variety of organisations within the state, but he will have none of it. The state is the one overriding power. As a good protestant, Hegel naturally proclaims the supremacy of state over church; for this ensures the national character of church organisation. To the Church of Rome, leaving aside all other considerations, Hegel would be opposed for what is in fact its main merit: that it is an international body. Likewise, no allowance is made for the independent pursuit of organised interests within society, even though on his organic view Hegel should welcome such activities. As for disinterested enquiry or the indulging of hobbies, this would not be entertained. But why, for instance, should stamp collectors not gather into a club merely to pursue their own common interest in philately? It is worth noting that the official Marxist doctrine retains a strong measure of Hegelianism here. All activities are somehow construed as having to minister directly to the welfare of the state. If a philatelic society under such a system does not view its work as helping to glorify the socialist revolution, its members will find themselves rudely cut off from collecting stamps or anything else.

Georg Wilhelm Friedrich Hegel's

Grundlinien

der

Philosophie des Rechts,

oder

Naturrecht und Staatswissenschaft

im Grundrisse.

Herausgegeben

von

Dr. Eduard Gans.

Dritte Auflage.

Mit Königl. Würtembergischem, Großherzogl. Hessischem und der freien Stadt Frankfurt Privilegium gegen den Nachdruck und Nachdrucks-Verkauf.

Berlin, 1854.

Verlag von Duncker und Humblot.

Title page of Hegel's Philosophy of Law

Hegel's political theory is inconsistent with his metaphysic in one other important respect. A thorough application of his own dialectic principle should have brought him to see that there is no ground for stopping short of an organisation between nations, perhaps somewhat along the lines suggested by Kant. As it is, the Absolute in politics seems to be the Kingdom of Prussia. The deduction of his conclusion is, of course, a sham. That there were men who honestly believed this proposition one would indeed not deny. But while it may give comfort to some to believe such things, it is somewhat disingenuous to proclaim them as dictates of reason. By this method one can find spurious excuses for every prejudice and atrocity under the sun. It is all a little too easy.

Let us now return to the dialectic, which is really the central notion of Hegel's system. We have previously noted how a dialectic step involves three stages. We first have a statement which is then opposed by a counter-statement, and finally the two are combined into a composite arrangement. A simple example will illustrate this. One might for instance put forward the thesis that gold is valuable. Against this may be pitted the antithesis that gold is not valuable. The synthesis may then perhaps be reached that the value of gold depends on circumstances. If you happen to be in Oxford Street, where you will find people willing to take your gold and give you sandwiches in exchange for it, gold is valuable. But if you should be lost in the Sahara desert with a bag of gold, and you are in need of water, then gold is not valuable. Thus, it seems, the attendant circumstances must be taken into account. Hegel might not approve of this example, but it serves our purpose here. Now the contention is that the synthesis becomes a new thesis and the same dialectic process begins again, and so on until we take in the whole universe. This amounts to saying that the full significance of anything emerges only when it is viewed in all its possible connections; that is, in its setting in the world as a whole.

Several comments suggest themselves. The first relates to the historical content of the dialectic. It is perfectly true that there are cases where irreconcilable demands are adjusted by some sort of compromise. I might say for instance that I am unwilling to pay income tax. Inland Revenue naturally take the opposite line and would carry away the lot. Finally we come to a kind of intermediate solution through which both parties attain some measure of satisfaction. In this there is nothing whatsoever mysterious. It is to be noted that the compromise arises not from two demands that are contradictory, but rather contrary to each other. This logical point needs some elucidation. Two statements are contradictory if the truth of one entails the falsity of the other, and vice versa. But two contrary statements might well both be false though they cannot both be true. Thus, in the above example, the compromise solution gives the lie to both of the opposing claims. What makes the dialectic work in the true historical case is the fact that from contrary demands some sort of agreement may often be arrived at. If, of course, the parties have insufficient patience to work out an acceptable scheme, the game is apt to become a little more drastic; and in the end, the stronger party wins and leaves the loser on the field. In such a case contrary demands may after the event be seen as contradictory. But only after the event: for it is not inevitable that this must happen. In holding contrary views on taxation, neither the citizen nor the authorities are compelled to exterminate the other.

Hegel lecturing

Secondly, it may be noted that intellectual development follows a similar pattern. In this aspect the dialectic goes back to the interplay of question and answer of Plato's dialogues. This is precisely how the mind works when confronted with a problem. A case is put forward, various objections may be raised, and, in the course of discussion, either an adjustment is reached, through taking a more refined view of the situation; or the original case is abandoned, if on reflection it seems that one of the objections must be accepted. Here, a compromise is possible, whether the statements pitted against each other are contradictory or contrary. Thus, Heraclitus' statement that everything moves, and Parmenides' statement that nothing moves, are contraries. But one might merely object to Heraclitus' view by saying that some things do not move, in which case the two statements are contradictory. In either case we may reach the compromise that some things move, and some not.

This brings out an important difference that Hegel is not prepared to recognise. Contradiction is something that occurs in discourse. One man can contradict another; or perhaps better, one statement can contradict another statement. But in the everyday world of facts there is no contradiction. One fact cannot be contradictory to another, whatever view may be taken of the relation between language and the world. Thus, poverty and wealth are not contradictory, but merely different. Because Hegel takes a spiritual view of the world, he is inclined to ride roughshod over this vital distinction. Again, it is easy to see, on this view, why the dialectic method is applied not only as an instrument of the theory of knowledge, but directly as a description of the world. To use technical terms, Hegel gives his method not only epistemological, but also ontological status. It is on this basis that Hegel proceeds to give a dialectic account of nature. Schelling's objection to it we have already mentioned. This kind of nonsense was taken over wholesale by the Marxists, except, of course, that they replaced Hegel's bias on the side of the mind by the materialist principles of Lamettrie.

Another peculiar prejudice which stems from the dialectic method is Hegel's predilection for the number three. Everything seems to come in threes, just because the dialectic consists of the three stages of thesis, antithesis and synthesis. Thus, wherever anything needs dividing up, Hegel divides it into three. In his account of history, for example, he recognizes the Oriental world, that of the Greeks and Romans, and finally that of the Germans. The rest does not seem to count at all. This is of course all right for symmetry, but seems not altogether convincing as a method of historical study. Likewise, we find a tripartite division in the Encyclopaedia, corresponding to the three stages of the spirit. There is first being-as-such, which gives rise to logic. Next, the spirit is said to pass through a phase of self-estrangement, in which it is in a state of being-other. This second stage is discussed in the philosophy of nature. Finally, the spirit completes the dialectric round-trip and returns to itself. Corresponding to this, there is the philosophy of spirit. The whole thing is conceived as a dialectic triad. This kind of theorising is so preposterous that even those who respect Hegel no longer try to defend it.

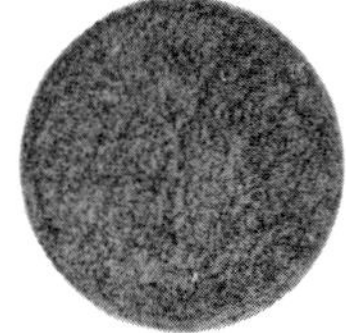

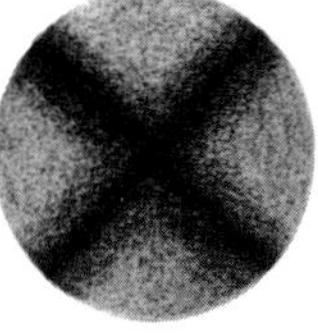

The dialectic process: a thesis opposed by an antithesis gives rise to a synthesis

But having made these critical comments, we must not overlook what is valuable in Hegel's philosophy. First of all, as far as the dialectic is concerned, it will be allowed that Hegel here shows considerable insight into the workings of the mind. For it is frequently on the dialectic pattern that the mind progresses. As a contribution to the psychology of intellectual growth, the dialectic is, up to a point, a piece of shrewd observation. Secondly, Hegelianism does emphasise the importance of history which had been suggested by Vico a century earlier. The way in which Hegel states his case sometimes suffers through want of precision in the use of words. This is perhaps linked with a certain poetic conception of language itself. Thus, when Hegel says that philosophy is the study of its own history, we must see this in the light of the dialectic principle. Hegel is saying that philosophy necessarily grows according to the dialectic pattern, and therefore a study of dialectic, which is the overriding philosophic principle, seems to coincide with a study of the history of philosophy. This is therefore a very oblique way of saying that for a proper understanding of philosophy one must know something of its history. One may disagree with this, but it is not nonsense. In his formulations, Hegel often plays on different meanings of words. Indeed, he held the view that language has a kind of inherent intelligence which is somehow superior to that of its users. Oddly enough, a very similar view is held by the ordinary language philosophers of present-day Oxford.

As to the historical situation, Hegel felt that the Absolute was at hand. It was therefore proper to set up philosophic systems, which in his view always supervene after the event. This he expressed most strikingly in the preface to the 'Philosophy of Law': 'the owl of Minerva begins her flight only when dusk breaks in.'

Berlin University in Hegel's time

Title page of 'The Logic', from Hegel's Encyclopaedia

Georg Wilhelm Friedrich Hegel's

Encyklopädie

der

philosophischen Wissenschaften

im Grundrisse.

Erster Theil.

Die Logik.

Herausgegeben und nach Anleitung der vom Verfasser gehaltenen Vorlesungen mit Erläuterungen und Zusätzen versehen

von

Dr. Leopold von Henning.

Zweite Auflage.

Mit Königl. Würtembergischem, Großherzogl. Hessischem, und der freien Stadt Frankfurt Privilegium gegen den Nachdruck und Nachdrucks-Verkauf.

Berlin, 1843.

Verlag von Duncker und Humblot

The Hegelian philosophy is inspired by a general principle which recurs throughout the history of philosophy. It is that no portion of the world can be understood unless it is seen in its setting in the universe as a whole. Consequently the whole is the only reality.

This view is found already amongst the presocratics. When Parmenides states that the universe is an immovable sphere, he is trying to express something of this kind. The mathematical philosophers of the Pythagorean school likewise hint at this notion when they say that all things are numbers. More recently, Spinoza was a representative of the view that the whole alone is ultimately real. Following the Pythagorean tradition, the mathematical physicists, in their search for the one supreme formula which will explain the whole universe, are moved by the same belief. The spectacular advances of Newtonian physics, culminating in cosmologies like that of Laplace, provide an example of this. It is not too difficult to show that the idealist notion of a universal system is untenable. At the same time, there is a danger of summarily dismissing it without trying to see what it is aiming at, even if only in an obscure and hazy manner.

The interesting point is that in one respect the system of the idealists correctly portrays the ambitions of scientific theory. The programme of science does indeed provide for an ever widening sweep of the systematic understanding of nature. Hitherto unsuspected interconnections are brought to light, more and more of the happenings in nature are brought within the compass of a system of theory, and in principle there is no end to this development. Moreover, a scientific theory allows of no exceptions, its hold must be universal, it is either all or nothing. We might then say that the system of the idealist is a kind of platonic idea of science as a whole, a divine science as Leibniz conceived of it. That everything is related to everything else in some manner is true enough, but it is not true that things change by being connected with other things. It is on the second score that this way of looking at science thus falls badly short of the mark. It is equally wrong in showing the whole thing as a finished product, whereas it is a peculiar feature of scientific inquiry that there can be no end to it. The Hegelian attitude is not a little connected with the scientific optimism of the latter 19th century, when everyone thought the answer to everything was just around the corner. In the event, this proved to be an illusion, as might have been foretold.

Rationalism is to Empiricism as a jigsaw puzzle with inseparable parts is to an isolated piece

Meanwhile, however, it is a trifle unprofitable to tinker with a divine science. Whatever might be said about it, this is not the world to which it belongs, and other worlds than ours can have no bearing on us. The idealist system is thus a spurious concept. But we can show this even more directly by an example. I entertain numerous true beliefs, such as for instance that Nelson's Column is taller than Buckingham Palace. A Hegelian will have none of this. 'You do not know what you are talking about', he would object. 'To grasp the fact you speak of, you have to know what kinds of material are used in the two structures, who built them and why, and so on indefinitely. In the end you will have to take in the entire universe before you are entitled to say you know what you mean in stating that Nelson's Column is taller than the Palace.' But, of course, the trouble is that on this showing I should have to know everything before I know anything, and thus could never even make a start. No one is going to be so modest as to proclaim himself literally and utterly empty-minded. Besides, it simply is not true. I do know that Nelson's Column is taller than the Palace, but otherwise lay no claim to divine omniscience. The fact is that you can know something without knowing everything about it; you can use a word intelligently without knowing the entire vocabulary. It is as though Hegel insisted that a piece from a jig-saw puzzle had no significance until the whole puzzle had been completed. The empiricist, on the contrary, recognizes that each piece has a significance of its own. Indeed, if it had not, you could not begin to put the pieces together.

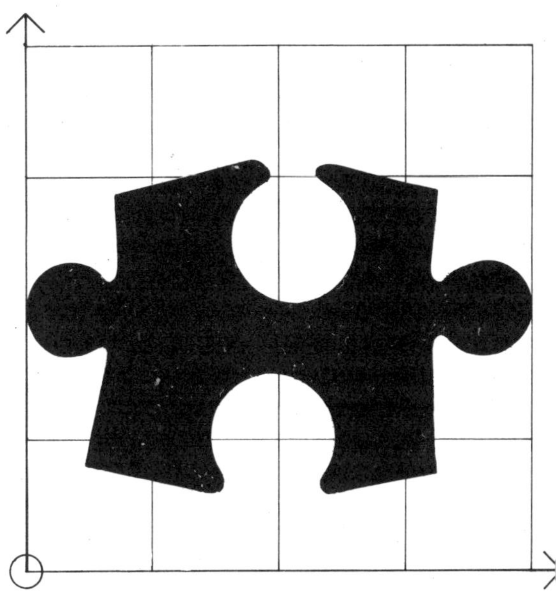

The criticism of the logical doctrine of system has important consequences in ethics. For if the logical theory were correct, the ethical theory built on it must be so too. As it is, the question is once more wide open.

Here Hegelianism and Lockean liberalism stand diametrically opposed to each other. For Hegel the state is in itself good, the citizens do not matter as such, but only insofar as they minister to the glory of the whole. Liberalism starts at the other end and regards the state as ministering to the individual advantages of its various members. The idealist view easily generates intolerance, ruthlessness and tyranny. The liberal principle fosters tolerance, consideration and compromise.

Sören Kierkegaard (1813-1855)

The idealism of Hegel is an attempt at viewing the world as a system. Although the emphasis is on spirit, Hegelianism is not in the least subjectivist in aim. We might call it an objective idealism. We have seen already how the dialectic system-building was later criticised by Schelling. Philosophically, this is the starting point of the violent anti-Hegelian outburst of Sören Kierkegaard, the Danish philosopher. His works had little influence at the time, but some fifty years later they became the source of the existentialist movement.

Kierkegaard (1813–1855) was born in Copenhagen, where at the age of seventeen he entered the University. His father had come to the capital as a young man and had exchanged farming for business, in which he was extremely successful. The son was thus not under pressure to make a living for himself. From his father, Kierkegaard inherited a lively wit and intelligence, as well as brooding temperament. By 1841, he had completed a master's degree in theology. In the meantime he had been inconclusively engaged to a girl who did not seem to him sufficiently appreciative of what he took to be his own theological mission. At all events, he broke off the engagement, and after finishing his studies went to Berlin, where Schelling was then lecturing. Henceforth he devoted himself to theological and philosophic speculation, while his one-time betrothed very sensibly married someone else.

Let us return to the criticism that Schelling directed against Hegel's system. Schelling distinguishes between negative and positive philosophy. The former is concerned with concepts, or universals, or essences, to use the scholastic term. It dealt with the 'what' of things. Positive philosophy, on the other hand relates to actual existence, or to the 'that' of things. Schelling holds that philosophy must start with a negative stage and then move on to the positive level. The formulation reminds one of Schelling's principle of polarity, and of the fact that in his own philosophical development he had traversed precisely this kind of path. The early Schelling is 'negative', the later works are 'positive' in this sense. The chief criticism against Hegel is then that, having become stuck in the negative region, he purports to deduce the positive world of fact. It is from this comment that existentialism takes its origin.

But this is only a logical objection to Hegel. What is at least equally important in Kierkegaard is an emotional objection. Hegelianism is a somewhat dry and theoretical affair, and leaves little if any scope for the passions of the soul. Indeed, this is true of the German Idealist philosophy in general, and even Schelling's later speculations do not escape from this. The enlightenment had tended to look upon the passions with some misgivings, Kierkegaard wants to make them philosophically respectable again. This is in line with the romanticism of the poets, and opposed to the kind of ethic that links good with knowledge and evil with ignorance. By cutting off the will from reason, in true Occamist fashion, existentialism is trying to attract our attention to the need for man to act and choose, not as a result of philosophic reflection, but from some spontaneous function of the will. This at once enables him to make room for faith in a very simple way. For it is now a free act of the will to accept religious beliefs.

The existentialist principle is sometimes expressed as stating that existence is prior to essence. Another way of putting it would be to say that we first know that a thing is, and afterwards what it is. Again, this amounts to putting the particular before the universal, or Aristotle before Plato. Kierkegaard puts will before reason and argues that, in regard to man, one should not be too scientific. Science, which deals with what is general, can only touch upon things from the outside. In contrast with this, Kierkegaard recognises 'existential' modes of thinking which grasp a situation from the inside. In the case of man, he feels we overlook what is really important if we approach him in the scientific way. The specific feelings of an individual can be understood existentially.

Kierkegaard's birthplace in Copenhagen; second from right

For Kierkegaard, ethical theories are too rationalistic to allow men to order their lives by them. The specific character of an individual's moral action are not duly appreciated by any of these theories. Besides, it is always easy to find counter-examples or exceptional cases where a rule is broken. It is on grounds such as these that Kierkegaard urges that we should base our lives on religious rather than on ethical principles. This is in the respected Augustinian tradition of protestantism. A man is responsible only to God and his command. No other human being can intervene to change this relation. For Kierkegaard, religion is a matter of existential thinking, since it comes from within the soul.

Kierkegaard was a fervent Christian; but, naturally enough, his views were bound to bring him into conflict with the somewhat rigid institutionalism of the Danish state church. He was opposed to rationalist theology in the grand manner of the scholastics. The existence of God has to be grasped existentially; no amount of demonstration, which moves in the realm of essence, can establish it. Thus, as we have said earlier, Kierkegaard severs faith from reason.

The criticism of Hegel, from which the reflections of Kierkegaard take their course, is in the main valid. The existentialist philosophy which has grown out of it is, however, not nearly so sound. In limiting the scope of reason, it lays itself open to all kinds of absurdities. At the level of faith this would indeed not only be expected, but almost welcome. 'Credo quia absurdum' is an old and respected motto of believers in revelation, and in a sense they may be right; if you are going to exercise your freedom to believe, you might as well fasten on to something unusual.

Caricature of Kierkegaard

Meanwhile, it is well to remember that underestimating reason is just as dangerous as overrating it. Hegel thought too highly of it and fell into the error that reason could generate the universe. Kierkegaard goes to the other extreme and in effect maintains that reason is unable to help us towards grasping the specific which alone is really worth knowing. Such a view denies all value to science, and is in accordance with the best principles of romanticism. Although Kierkegaard fiercely criticises the romantic way of life, as being purely determined by the vagaries of external influences, he is himself a thorough romantic. The very principle which postulates existential modes of thinking is a muddled romantic conception.

The existentialist rejection of Hegel was thus in the main a refusal to allow that the world itself constituted a system. Though Kierkegaard does not enter explicitly into the matter, his existentialism in fact presupposes a realist theory of knowledge, in the sense in which this is opposed to an idealist view. A very different objection to Hegel arises if one returns to a somewhat refined Kantian dualism, a move which occurs in Schopenhauer's philosophy.

Arthur Schopenhauer (1788–1860) was the son of a Danzig merchant who admired Voltaire and shared his respect for England. When, in 1793, Prussia annexed the free city of Danzig, the family moved to Hamburg. In 1797, Schopenhauer went to live in Paris, and during his two years stay he nearly forgot his mother-tongue. In 1803 he came to England and entered a boarding school for some six months. This sufficed to make him loathe our schools and learn the language. In later years he regularly took the London 'Times'. On returning to Hamburg he made a half-hearted attempt at a commercial career, but gave it up again as soon as his father died. His mother now moved to Weimar, where she soon became hostess of a literary salon frequented by many of the great poets and writers then residing there. In fact, she subsequently became a novelist herself. But meanwhile her son, whose morose temperament she did not share, began to resent her somewhat independent mode of life. At twenty-one, Schopenhauer acquired a small legacy, and thereafter mother and son gradually became estranged.

'The World as Will and Idea', title page

Die

Welt

als

Wille und Vorstellung:

vier Bücher,

nebst einem Anhange,

der die

Kritik der Kantischen Philosophie

enthält,

von

Arthur Schopenhauer.

Ob nicht Natur zuletzt sich doch ergründe?
Göthe.

Leipzig:
F. A. Brockhaus.
1819.

The legacy enabled him to take up university studies. He began in Göttingen in 1809, where he first came in contact with Kant's philosophy. In 1811 he moved to Berlin, where his studies were mainly in science. He attended some of Fichte's lectures, but held his philosophy in contempt. He completed his studies in 1813 when the wars of liberation broke out, but these events did not call forth in him any lasting enthusiasm. In the following years he came to know Goethe in Weimar, where he began his studies of Indian mysticism. In 1819 he began to lecture as a Privatdozent at the University of Berlin. He was fully convinced of his own genius, and felt that it would be less than honest to conceal this fact from the rest of mankind, who might as yet not be aware of it. Accordingly, he set his lectures for the same hour as Hegel. When he failed to attract the Hegelians in force, Schopenhauer decided to give up lecturing and to settle down in Frankfurt, where indeed he remained for the rest of his life. As a person he was conceited, sour and vain. The fame for which he yearned did not supervene until the end of his life.

Arthur Schopenhauer

Schopenhauer reached his philosophic views at an early age. His main work, 'The World as Will and Idea', appeared in 1818 when the author was just thirty years old. It was at first ignored completely. In this book is set forth a kind of modified Kantian theory which deliberately retains the thing in itself. Unlike Kant, however, Schopenhauer equates the thing in itself with the will. Thus, the experienced world is, as with Kant, regarded as consisting of phenomena, in the Kantian sense. What causes these phenomena is, however, not a range of unknowable noumena, but the noumenal will. This is pretty close to orthodox Kantian views. We saw that

Kant regards the will as on the side of noumena. If I exercise my will, there corresponds to it, in the world of experience, the movement of my body. It may be noted in passing that Kant here has really failed to go beyond occasionalism; for, as we saw, there can be no causal relation between noumena and phenomena. At any rate, Schopenhauer regards the body as an appearance whose reality resides in the will. As with Kant, the noumenal world lies beyond space, time and the categories. The will as noumenon is not subject to them either. Therefore it is timeless and non-spatial, which implies its oneness. As far as I am real, to wit in regard to my will, I am not distinct and separate, that would be a mere phenomenal illusion. On the contrary, my will is really the one universal will.

Arthur Schopenhauer (1788-1860), as a young man

Schopenhauer regards this will as thoroughly evil, and responsible for the suffering which inevitably accompanies life. Moreover, for him knowledge is not, as for Hegel, a fount of freedom, but rather a source of suffering. Thus, in place of the optimism of rationalist systems, Schopenhauer displays a gloomy outlook in which there is no room for happiness. As to sex, this was a wicked business too, because procreation merely provided new victims for suffering. Connected with this view is Schopenhauer's misogyny, for he felt that woman's part in this was more deliberate than man's.

There is no logical reason why Kantian epistemology should be thus linked with a pessimistic view of things. Schopenhauer himself was unable, by temperament, to be happy, and therefore declared that happiness could not be achieved. Towards the end of his brooding life, his work gained recognition and his financial circumstances became somewhat easier, both of which suddenly caused him to be more cheerful in spite of his theory. Still, it cannot be said that the rationalist over-confidence in the goodness of this world is sound either. Thus, where a thinker like Spinoza was, theoretically at least, not prepared to see evil, Schopenhauer went to the other extreme and could see no good in anything.

The solution to this painful state of affairs must, according to Schopenhauer, be sought in the myths of Buddhism. What causes our suffering is precisely our willing. By doping the will we may in the end achieve release in Nirvana, or nothingness. The mystic trance makes us see through the veil of Maya, which stands for illusion. Thus we may come to see the world as one and, having gained this knowledge, conquer the will. But knowledge of oneness here does not lead to communion with God, as in the western mystics like master Eckhart; or with the pantheistic world of Spinoza. On the contrary, insight into the whole, and sympathy with its suffering, afford us an escape into nothingness.

Schopenhauer in later years

As against the rationalist doctrines of the Hegelian school, Schopenhauer's philosophy emphasizes the importance of the will. This view was adopted by many later philosophers who have otherwise very little in common. We find it in Nietzsche as well as in the pragmatists. Existentialism, too, is greatly interested in the will as against reason. As to the mysticism of Schopenhauer's doctrine, this rather stands outside the mainstream of philosophy.

Jenseits

von Gut und Böse.

Vorspiel

einer

Philosophie der Zukunft.

Von

Friedrich Nietzsche.

Leipzig

Druck und Verlag von C. G. Naumann.

1886.

Beyond Good and Evil, title page

If the philosophy of Schopenhauer seeks, in the end, to provide an escape from the world and its strife, the opposite path is taken by Nietzsche (1844 – 1900). It is not easy to sum up the content of his thinking. He is not, in the ordinary sense, a philosopher, and has not left a systematic account of his views. One might perhaps describe him as an aristocratic humanist in the literal sense. What he tried above all to promote was the supremacy of the man who was best, that is healthiest and strongest in character. This brings with it a certain emphasis on toughness in the face of misery, which is somewhat at variance with received ethical standards, though not necessarily with actual practice. By concentrating on these features out of context, many have seen in Nietzsche the prophet of the political tyrannies of our own times. It may well be that tyrants have drawn some inspiration from Nietzsche, but it would be inappropriate to make him responsible for the misdeeds of men who have understood him at best superficially. For Nietzsche would have been bitterly opposed to the political developments in his own country, had he lived long enough to witness them.

Nietzsche's father was a protestant pastor. This made for a home background of piety and rectitude, a tinge of which remains in the high moral tone of Nietzsche's works even at their most rebellious. At an early age he showed himself a brilliant scholar, and at twenty-four he became professor of classical philology at the university of Basle. A year later the Franco-Prussian war broke out. As Nietzsche had become a Swiss citizen, he had to content himself with serving as a medical orderly. After being laid low with dysentry he was discharged and returned to Basle. He had never been in the best of health, and never quite recovered from his war service. By 1879 he had to resign his post, though a generous pension enabled him to live in reasonable comfort. The next ten years he spent in Switzerland and Italy, continuing his literary work, mostly in solitude and without recognition. In 1889, as a delayed result of a venereal infection contracted during his student days, he became insane and remained in this state until his death.

Nietzsche's work is in the first instance inspired by the ideals of presocratic Greece, and particularly Sparta. In his first major work, 'The Birth of Tragedy' (1872), he put forward the famous distinction between the Apollonian and the Dionysiac moods of the Greek soul. The dark and passionate Dionysiac strain is bound up with a recognition of the reality of tragedy in the existence of man. The olympian pantheon, on the other hand, is a kind of serene vision which counter-balances the stark unpleasantness of human life. This springs from the Apollonian streak of the soul. We might describe Greek tragedy as an Apollonian sublimation of Dionysiac cravings. Aristotle, as we saw, held similar views on these matters.

What Nietzsche eventually took from this account of the origins of tragedy is the conception of the tragic hero. Unlike Aristotle, he sees in tragedy not a vicarious cleansing of the emotions, but a positive acceptance of life as it is. Whereas Schopenhauer had reached a pessimistic conclusion, Nietzsche adopts an optimist position, which he thinks can be discerned in a proper interpretation of Greek tragedy. However, it must be noted that his is not an optimism in the popular sense. It is rather a kind of aggressive acceptance of the harsh and cruel realities of life. Like Schopenhauer, he recognizes the primacy of the will; but he goes further and regards a strong will as the pre-eminent feature of a good man, whereas Schopenhauer had seen the will as the source of all evil.

Nietzsche distinguishes between two types of person and their respective moralities. These are the masters and the slaves. The ethical theory based on this distinction is expounded in his book 'Beyond Good and Evil' (1886). On the one hand we have the master morality, in which good connotes independence, generosity, self-reliance and the like; in fact, all the virtues that belong to Aristotle's great-souled man. The opposed defects are subservience, meanness, timidity and so on, and these are bad. The contrast between good and bad is here roughly equivalent to that between noble and contemptible. The slave morality works on quite a different principle. For it the good lies in a kind of pervasive reticence, and in all those things that diminish suffering and striving; whereas it condemns the things that are good on the master morality, calling them evil rather than bad. The good of the master morality is apt to be terrifying, and all fear-provoking action is evil to the slave. The morality of the hero or superman lies beyond good and evil.

In 'Thus Spake Zarathustra' these doctrines had already been set out in the form of an ethical manifesto which imitates, in style, the writings of the Bible. Nietzsche was a great literary artist, and his works look more like poetic prose than philosophy.

What Nietzsche abhorred above all was the emergence of the new type of mass humanity that grew up along with the new technology. For him the proper function of society is to act as the seedbed for the few great who achieve the aristocratic ideal. The suffering that this might cause to the small fry does not seem to him to matter. The kind of state he envisages has much in common with the ideal state of Plato's 'Republic'. Traditional religions he considers to be props to the slave morality. The free man, according to him, must recognize that God is dead; what we must strive for is not God, but a higher type of man. The stock example of slave morality, Nietzsche finds in Christianity. For it is pessimistic in holding out hopes of a better life in another world, and values slavish virtues like meekness and sympathy. It was for Wagner's later leanings towards Christianity that Nietzsche came to attack the composer whom he had earlier counted as an admired friend. As for his hero-worship, this was accompanied by a fierce anti-feminism which advocated the oriental custom of treating women as chattel. In this we find a reflection of Nietzsche's own inability to cope with the fair sex.

There is in this ethical doctrine a good deal of useful observation of different types of human beings and their ways of tackling the business of living. There is much to be said for the exercise of a certain ruthlessness, provided this is administered to oneself. What is less convincing is the notion of total indifference to the suffering endured by the many in the interest of the few.

Oh Mensch! Gib Acht!
Was spricht die tiefe Mitternacht?
„Ich schlief, ich schlief —,
„Aus tiefem Traum bin ich erwacht: —
„Die Welt ist tief,
„Und tiefer als der Tag gedacht.
„Tief ist ihr Weh —,
„Lust — tiefer noch als Herzeleid:
„Weh spricht: Vergeh!
„Doch alle Lust will Ewigkeit —,
„— will tiefe, tiefe Ewigkeit!"

Ms of the famous song from Thus Spake Zarathustra

Nietzsche (1844–1900)

Utilitarianism and since

We must now turn back a century and take up another strand of our story. The idealist philosophy and its critics had developed in a world whose material circumstances were altering in a very radical manner. These changes were brought about by the industrial revolution which took its rise in eighteenth century England. At first, the introduction of machinery was a very gradual thing. Improvements were made in the construction of looms, and the output of textiles increased. The vital step was the perfection of the steam-engine, which provided a limitless source of power to drive the machines in the workshops that sprang up in great numbers. The most efficient way of producing steam was by means of coal-fired boilers. There was thus a great development of coal-mining, often under very harsh and ugly circumstances. Indeed, on the human side, the early days of industrialism were a thoroughly gruesome period.

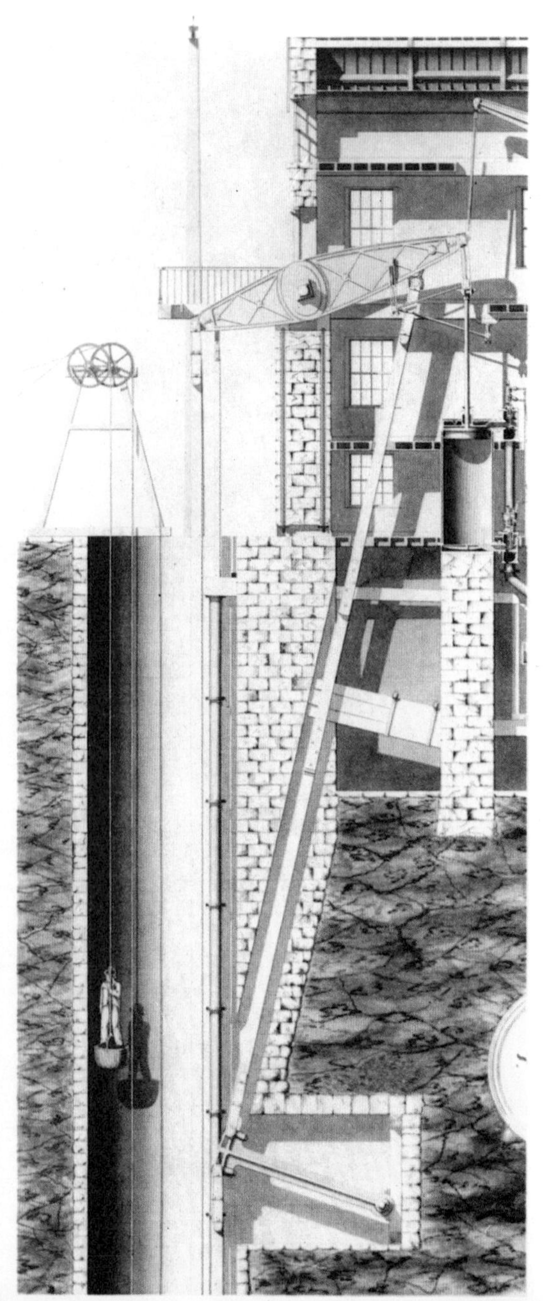

During the eighteenth century, the enclosure movement in England reached its peak. For several centuries past there had been cases of common land being enclosed by the nobility for their own use. This created some hardship to the rural population whose living was in some measure dependent on the benefits to be drawn from the common land. Not until the eighteenth century, however, did this encroachment of their privileges cause large numbers of country-folk to be uprooted and driven to the towns and cities in search for a new livelihood. It was these people who came to be absorbed in the new factories. Badly paid and exploited, they settled down in the poorest quarters of the towns as well as on the outskirts, laying the foundations for the huge industrial slums of the nineteenth century. The invention of machinery was at first viewed with considerable suspicion by those who felt that their skills in handicraft were being rendered superfluous. Likewise, with every improvement in the working of machines, the tendency of industrial labour was to resist for fear of having their livelihood cut off. This fear is not unknown even today; the introduction of electronically controlled machinery is viewed with suspicion by trade unions, as much as was the power loom in the nineteenth century. However, on this particular the pessimists have always been wrong. Instead of suffering a decline of living conditions, the industrial nations of the world have experienced a gradual rise in wealth and comfort at all levels. It must be confessed that the misery of the early industrial proletariate in England was pretty stark. Some of the worst evils were partly due to ignorance, for these were new problems that no one had ever had to face. The old liberalism, based on handicraft and peasant proprietorship, was not flexible enough to cope with the great new problems of industrial society. Reform was slow in coming, but did eventually correct these early mistakes. Where industrialism developed later, as in continental countries, some of the troubles that beset the development of industrial society were less severe because by then the problems were better understood.

During the early nineteenth century there begins a growing tendency of interplay between science and technology. In some measure this

has, of course, always existed. But from the days of industrialism onwards, the systematic application of scientific principles in the design and production of technical equipment has produced an accelerating growth of material expansion. The steam-engine was the source of the new power. The first half of the century saw a complete scientific investigation of the principles involved. The new science of thermodynamics in turn taught engineers how to build more efficient engines.

At the same time, the steam-engine began to replace all other forms of power in the field of transport. By the middle of the century a vast net of railways was growing up in Europe and North America, and at the same time, sailing ships began to be displaced by steamers. All these innovations produced vast changes in the lives and outlook of the people who were affected by them. On the whole, man seems to be a conservative animal. His technical prowess has therefore tended to outpace his political wisdom, thus creating a lack of balance from which we have not recovered yet.

The early development of industrial production gave rise to a renewed interest in questions of economics. As a study in its own right, political economy in modern times goes back to the work of Adam Smith (1723–90), a fellow countryman of David Hume and a professor of philosophy. His writings on ethics are in the Humean tradition but were on the whole less important than his work on economics. He owes his fame to the treatise on 'The Wealth of Nations' (1776). In this book for the first time an attempt is made to study the various forces at work in the economic life of a country. One particularly important problem which is brought to the fore is the question of division of labour. Smith shows at some length how the production of industrial goods is increased if the making of an article is broken up into a number of stages, each of which is carried out by a specialised worker. The particular example he chooses comes from the making of pins, and his conclusions are no doubt based on actual observations of production figures. At all events, the principle of division of labour was applied on a grand scale in industry ever since, and has been thoroughly vindicated. There are, of course, human problems which have to be considered too, for if the specialised operation becomes so fragmentary as to destroy a man's interest in his work, the worker suffers in the end. This difficulty, which was not too well understood in Smith's time, has become one of the major problems of modern industry and its dehumanizing effect on those who work its machines.

Adam Smith (1723–90), founder of modern political economy

Political economy remained for some considerable time a peculiarly British pursuit. The physiocrats of eighteenth century France had indeed been interested in economic problems, but their writings did not exert the same influence as Adam Smith's book, which became the bible of classical economics. The next important contribution in this field was Ricardo's labour theory of value which was taken over by Marx.

In the philosophic field, the rise of industrialism has brought with it a certain emphasis on utility which was hotly opposed by the romantics. At the same time this somewhat dull philosophy was in the end more productive of much needed reform in social matters than all the romantic indignation it provoked from poets and idealists. The changes it sought to bring about were piecemeal and orderly, and revolution was far from its aims. Not so with the somewhat more emotional doctrine of Marx, which in its own peculiar way retains much of the uncompromising idealism of its Hegelian source. Here the goal is a complete transformation of the existing order by violent means.

Early textile workshop

The great human problem of technological society did not at once reveal itself to those who did not suffer the indignities it inflicted on the industrial proletariat. Such unpleasant facts might be unfortunate but were at first regarded as inevitable. This somewhat smug and callous indifference was shattered during the later part of the century, when the problems involved came to be taken up by writers. The revolution of 1848 did something towards bringing these facts to the notice of society at large. As a political manoeuvre, the disturbances were somewhat of a failure. They did, however, leave behind some measure of uneasiness about social conditions. In the works of Dickens in England, and later Zola in France, these problems received an airing that helped to foster a greater awareness of the situation.

One of the great remedies to all social ills was seen in the provision of adequate education. In this the reformers were probably not quite right. Merely to teach everyone to read, write and reckon does not in itself dispose of social problems. Nor is it true that these no doubt admirable skills are essential for the proper working of an industrial society. A great deal of specialised routine work can in principle be done by illiterates. But education may indirectly help to solve certain problems, since it sometimes makes those who have to endure hardships seek ways to better their lot. At the same time, it is clear enough that a mere course of instruction need not lead to such results. On the contrary, it may lead people to believe that the existing order of things is as it must be. Indoctrination of this sort is at times quite effective. Nevertheless, the reformers are right in holding that certain problems cannot be properly tackled unless there is a fairly widespread understanding of what is at stake: and this does indeed require some measure of education.

Memorial coin for Adam Smith's Wealth of Nations

The division of labour which Adam Smith discussed in connection with the making of goods has overtaken intellectual pursuits to almost an equal extent. During the course of the nineteenth century, enquiry has, so to speak, become industrialized.

The utilitarian movement received its name from an ethical doctrine which goes back more particularly to Hutcheson, who had expounded it already in 1725. Briefly, the theory holds that the good is pleasure and the bad pain. Hence the best state to be achieved is one in which the balance of pleasure over pain is greatest. This view was adopted by Bentham, and came to be known as utilitarianism.

Jeremy Bentham (1748–1832) was above all interested in jurisprudence, where his main inspiration derived from Helvetius and Beccaria. Ethics, for Bentham, was mainly a basis for studies on legal ways of promoting the best possible state of affairs. Bentham was the leader of a group of men who were known as the 'Philosophical Radicals'. They were much concerned with social reform and education, and were generally opposed to the authority of the Church and the restrictive privileges of the ruling section of society. Bentham was a man of retiring disposition and had started from views that were not notably radical. In later life, however, he became, for all his shyness, an aggressive atheist.

Jeremy Bentham (1748–1832)

He was much concerned with education and shared with his fellow radicals a supreme confidence in its unlimited remedial powers. It is worth recalling that in his time England had only the two universities, and access to these was restricted to professing Anglicans. This anomaly was not corrected until the latter half of the nineteenth century. Bentham was intent on helping to provide opportunities for university education to those who failed to fulfil the narrow qualifications demanded by the existing institutions. He was one of the group who helped to establish University College, London, in 1825. No religious tests were imposed on students, and the college has never had a chapel. Bentham himself had by this time made a complete break with religion. When he died he stipulated that his skeleton, suitably accoutred and surmounted by a wax mask, should be kept at the college. The picture shown here was taken from this exhibit, which sits in a showcase as a permanent memorial to one of the founders.

Bentham's philosophy is based on two leading ideas that go back to the early eighteenth century. The first of these is the principle of association which had been given prominence by Hartley. It stems ultimately from Hume's theory of causality, where it is used to explain the notion of causal dependence in terms of the association of ideas. In Hartley and later Bentham, the principle of association becomes the central mechanism of psychology. Instead of the traditional apparatus of concepts pertaining to the mind and its operation, Bentham puts his one principle which works on the raw material provided by experience. This enables him to give a deterministic account of psychology, which does not involve mental concepts at all; these have, as it were, been shorn off by Occam's razor. The theory of the conditioned reflex later worked out by Pavlov is based on the same kind of outlook as the associationist psychology.

The second principle is the utilitarian maxim of the greatest happiness, which has already been mentioned. This is linked with psychology in that for Bentham what men try to do is to attain the greatest possible happiness for themselves. Happiness is here taken to mean the same as pleasure. The function of the law is to ensure that, in seeking his own maximum pleasure, nobody should impair this same pursuit for others. In this way is achieved the greatest happiness of the greatest number. This was, for all their differences, the common aim of the utilitarians. Thus baldly stated, the goal sounds somewhat uninspired and smug. But the intentions behind it are far from being so. As a movement devoted to reform, utilitarianism has certainly achieved more than all the idealist philosophies put together, and it has done this without much fuss. At the same time, the principle of greatest happiness for the greatest number was capable of bearing another interpretation. In the hands of liberal economists, it became a justification for 'laisser faire' and free trade. For it was assumed that the free and untrammelled pursuit by each man of his own greatest pleasure would, given jurisprudence, produce the greatest happiness of society. In this, however, the liberals were a little too optimistic. One might perhaps allow, in a Socratic vein, that if men took the trouble to inform themselves and gauge the repercussions of their actions, they would usually see that hurting society will in the end be hurtful to themselves. But men do not always consider such things with care, and often act on impulse and in ignorance. In our own time, the doctrine of 'laisser faire' has therefore come to be hedged about with certain restrictive safeguards.

The law, then, is considered as a mechanism to ensure that each may pursue his aims without detriment to his fellows. The function of punishment is thus not revenge, but prevention of crime. What matters is that certain encroachments should carry a penalty, not that the retribution should be savage, as in fact it tended to be in England at that time. Bentham was opposed to the indiscriminate infliction of the death penalty, which was then very freely dispensed for rather trifling offences.

Two great conclusions follow from the utilitarian ethic. First it seems clear that in some respects all men have equally strong urges towards happiness. Therefore they should all enjoy equal rights and opportunities. This view was somewhat of a novelty at the time, and constituted one of the central tenets of the reforming programme of the radicals. The other inference that suggests itself is that the greatest happiness can only be attained if conditions remain stable. Thus, equality and security are the overriding considerations. As for liberty, this Bentham thought less important. Like the Rights of Man, liberty seemed to him somewhat metaphysical and romantic. Politically, he favoured benevolent despotism rather than democracy. This, incidentally, brings out one of the difficulties in his utilitarianism. For evidently there is no mechanism which will ensure that the legislator will in fact take a benevolent course. On his own psychological theory this would require that legislators always act with extreme foresight on the basis of full knowledge. But, as we have suggested earlier, this assumption is not altogether sound. As a matter of practical politics, this difficulty cannot be removed once and for all. At best one may attempt to make sure that legislators are never allowed more than so much rope at a time.

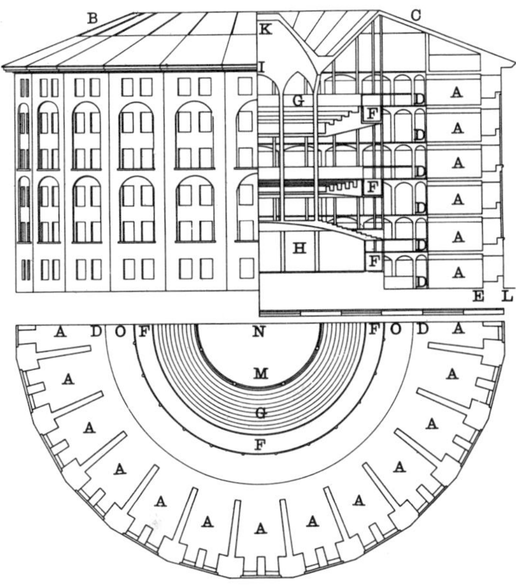

EXPLANATION

A *Cells*
B to C *Great Annular Sky Light*
D *Cell Galleries*
E *Entrance*
F *Inspection Galleries*
G *Chapel Galleries*
H *Inspectors Lodge*
I *Dome of the Chapel*
K *Sky Light to D°*
L *Store Rooms &c with their Galleries immediately within the outer wall all round place for an annular Cistern Q*
M *Floor of the Chapel*
N *Circular Opening in d° (open except at Church times to light the Inspectors Lodge*
O *Annular Wall from top to bottom for light air and seperation*

Plan of the Panopticon, Bentham's design for a prison

In his social criticism, Bentham is in line with eighteenth century materialism, and foreshadows much that Marx was later to maintain. He holds that the existing morality of sacrifice is a deliberate hoax imposed by the governing class in defending its vested interests. It expects sacrifices from others but does not make any itself. Against all this Bentham puts forward his utilitarian principle.

While Bentham remained the intellectual leader of the Radicals during his life-time, the driving force behind the movement was James Mill (1773–1836). He shared Bentham's utilitarian views on ethics, and despised the romantics. In political matters he thought that men could be persuaded by argument and were given to making rational assessments before taking action. Along with this goes an inordinate belief in the efficacy of education. The butt of these preconceptions was James Mill's son John Stuart Mill (1806–73), who had his father's educational doctrines ruthlessly inflicted on him. 'I never was a boy,' he complained later in life, 'never played at cricket. Instead he studied Greek from the age of three, with all the rest to follow at an equally premature age. This fearful experience led not unnaturally to a nervous breakdown just before he was twenty-one years old. Mill later took an active interest in the movement for parliamentary reform during the thirties, but did not bother to assume the leadership that had belonged to his father and to Bentham before him. From 1865 to 1868 he held the seat for Westminster in the House of Commons, continuing to press for universal suffrage, and pursuing a generally liberal, anti-imperialist course after the fashion of Bentham.

John Stuart Mill (1806–73)

In his philosophy, J. S. Mill is almost entirely derivative. The book which established his reputation perhaps more firmly than anything else is his Logic (1843). What was novel at the time was his discussion of induction. This is governed by a set of canons which are curiously reminiscent of some of Hume's rules for causal connections. One of the perennial problems of inductive logic has been to find a justification for arguing inductively. Mill takes the view that what gives ground for proceeding in this manner is the observed constancy of nature, which is itself a supreme induction. This, of course, makes the whole argument circular, a circumstance that did not seem to worry him. But there is a much more general problem involved here, which has continued to bedevil logicians to the present day. The difficulty is, roughly, that somehow people feel induction is not after all as respectable as it ought to be. Therefore it must be justified. But this would seem to lead to an insidious dilemma that is not always recognized. For justification is a matter of deductive logic. It cannot itself be inductive if induction is what must be justified. As for deduction itself, this no one feels compelled to justify, it has been respectable from time immemorial. Perhaps the only way out is to let induction be different without seeking to tie it to deductive apologies.

Mill's account of the utilitarian ethic is contained in an essay entitled Utilitarianism (1863). There is little here that goes beyond Bentham. Like Epicurus, who might be regarded as the first utilitarian, Mill is in the end prepared to regard certain pleasures as higher than others. But he is not really successful in explaining what might be meant by qualitatively better pleasures as contrasted with mere differences in quantity. This is not surprising, since the greatest happiness principle, and the calculus of pleasures that goes with it, implicitly eliminate quality in favour of quantity.

In trying to give an argument in favour of the utilitarian principle that pleasure is in fact what people pursue, Mill commits a serious blunder. 'The only proof capable of being given that an object is visible, is that people actually see it. The only proof that a sound is audible, is that people hear it: and so of the other sources of our experience. In like manner, I apprehend, the sole evidence it is possible to produce that anything is desirable, is that people actually desire it.' But this is a quibble based on a verbal similarity that conceals a logical difference. One says of something that it is visible if it can be seen. In the case of desirable there is an ambiguity. If I say of something that it is desirable, I may mean simply that I do in fact desire it. In speaking thus to someone else I assume, of course, that his likes and dislikes are roughly the same as mine. To say, in this sense, that the desirable is desired is trivial. But there is another sense in which we speak of something as desirable, as when we say that honesty is desirable. This really means that we should be honest, it is an ethical statement that is being made. Mill's argument is thus certainly unsound, for the analogy between 'visible' and 'desirable' is superficial. Already Hume had pointed out that one cannot deduce an 'ought' from an 'is'.

But in any case, it is easy to give direct counter-examples which invalidate the principle. Barring the trivial sense in which pleasure is defined as what is desired, it is not generally true that what I desire is pleasure, though the satisfaction of a desire will indeed give me pleasure. Besides, there are cases where I may desire something which has no direct bearing on my life beyond the fact that I have this desire. One might, for instance, desire that a certain horse should win a race without actually laying bets. The utilitarian principle is thus open to a number of serious objections. Nevertheless, the utilitarian ethic may still be the source of effective social action. For what the ethical doctrine proclaims is that the good is the greatest happiness of the greatest number. This may be held quite apart from whether men in fact always act in a way that will promote this universal happiness. The function of the law would then be to ensure that the greatest happiness is obtained. Likewise, the object of reform on such a basis is not so much an attainment of ideal institutions as of workable ones that do in fact bestow some measure of happiness upon the citizen. It is a democratic theory.

In opposition to Bentham, Mill was a passionate defender of freedom. The best exposition of his views on this matter is to be found in the famous Essay on Liberty (1859). He had written it together with Harriet Taylor, whom he had married in 1851, after her first husband's death. In this essay, Mill puts up a powerful defence for freedom of thought and discussion, and suggests a limitation of the state's power to interfere in the lives of its citizens. He is particularly opposed to Christianity's claims to be the fount of all goodness.

ON

LIBERTY

BY

JOHN STUART MILL.

LONDON:
JOHN W. PARKER AND SON, WEST STRAND.
M.DCCC.LIX.

Title page of J. S. Mill's pamphlet On Liberty

Malthus (1766–1834)

One of the problems that began to make itself felt by the turn of the eighteenth century was the rapid increase in population, which occurred once vaccination began to diminish the death-rate. A study of this problem was undertaken by Malthus (1766–1834), who was an economist, a friend of the radicals, and an Anglican clergyman to boot. In his famous Essay on Population (1797) he set out the theory that the rate of increase in population was fast outrunning the development of food supplies. While population increased in geometric progression, the provision of food grew only in arithmetic proportion. A point must come where numbers have to be limited, or else large-scale starvation will supervene. On the question of how such limitation is to be achieved, Malthus adopts a conventional Christian view. Men must be educated so that they might learn to practise 'restraint' and thus keep numbers down. Malthus, himself a married man, was outstandingly successful in implementing this theory in his own case; in four years he had a family of three children.

In spite of this triumph it now appears that the theory is not as effective as might be wished. It would seem that Condorcet had held sounder views on these matters. Where Malthus preached 'restraint', Condorcet had earlier suggested birth-control in the modern sense. This Malthus never forgave him, for in his own stern moral view such methods came under the heading of 'vice'. He regarded artificial birth-control as somewhat on a level with prostitution.

On this general question the radicals were at first divided. Bentham had once been in favour of Malthus, whereas the Mills tended to agree with the views of Condorcet. Young J. S. Mill, at the age of eighteen, was once arrested in the course of handing out birth-control pamphlets in a working-class slum, and sent to prison for this offence. It is not surprising, then, that the general subject of liberty was to remain one of his vital interests.

Ricardo (1772–1823)

The Essay on Population was nevertheless a very important contribution to political economy and provided certain basic notions that found their later developments in other fields. In particular, Darwin (1809–82) derived from it the principle of natural selection and the notion of the struggle for existence. In discussing the geometric rate of increase of organic beings and the struggle that ensues, Darwin says, in The Origin of Species (1859), that 'it is the doctrine of Malthus applied with manifold force to the whole animal and vegetable kingdoms; for in this case there can be no artificial increase of food, and no prudential restraint from marriage.' In this free for all fight for the limited means of subsistence, victory goes to the organism best adapted to its surroundings. This is Darwin's doctrine of the survival of the fittest. In a sense, it is merely an extension of the free competition of the Benthamites. However, in the social field this competition has to conform to certain rules, whereas Darwinian competition in nature knows no restrictions. Translated back into political terms, the doctrine of survival of the fittest was to inspire some of the political thinking of the dictatorships of the twentieth century. It is unlikely that Darwin himself would have countenanced these extensions of his theory, for he was himself a liberal, and supported the radicals and their programme of reform.

The other and much less original part of Darwin's work is the theory of evolution. This, as we saw, goes back to Anaximander. What Darwin did was to supply an immense amount of factual detail based on his own diligent observation of nature. His arguments for evolution are of unequal value, but certainly better backed than those of the great Milesian. Still, the Darwinian theory first brought the evolutionary hypothesis into the wider arena of public discussion. Since it explained the origin of species in terms of natural selection from a universal ancestral organism, it was opposed to the story of Genesis upheld by established religion. This led to a bitter struggle between Darwinists and orthodox Christians of all denominations.

Darwin (1809–82)

One of the chief protagonists in the Darwinist camp was T. H. Huxley, the great biologist. These issues have since then somewhat abated. But at the height of the controversy immense feeling could be aroused on the question whether or not man and the higher apes had a common ancestor. I rather suspect this suggestion must be offensive to apes, but in any case few people nowadays are upset by it.

Another line of development that began with the radicals led directly to Socialism and Marx. Ricardo (1772–1823), who was a friend of Bentham and James Mill, published his Principles of Political Economy and Taxation in 1817. In this treatise, Ricardo puts forward a sound theory of rent, which was neglected, and a labour theory of value, according to which the exchange value of a commodity depends simply on the amount of labour spent on it. This caused Thomas Hodgskin to suggest, in 1825, that labour was entitled to reap the benefit of the values that it produced. If rent was paid to the capitalist or the owner of land, this could only be robbery.

At the same time, working men found a champion for their cause in Robert Owen, who had introduced in his own textile factories in New Lanark some very novel principles of treating labour. He was a man informed with high ethical views, and declared that the inhuman exploitation of workers then prevailing was wrong. His practice showed that a business could be run with profit while men were paid a decent wage without working excessive hours. Owen was the driving force behind the first Factory Acts, though their provisions fell far short of what he had hoped to achieve. In 1827 we find Owen's followers referred to for the first time as Socialists.

Cartoon of Darwin and T. H. Huxley

The radicals were by no means pleased by Owen's doctrine, for this seemed to subvert the received notions of property. On this score the liberals were more inclined to subscribe to free competition and the prizes that this might fetch. The movement which grew up with Owen as its leader gave rise to the co-operative system and helped to promote early trade unionism. But, for want of a social philosophy, these early developments were not immediately successful. Owen was above all a practical man with a burning belief in his one leading idea. It remained for Marx to provide Socialism with a philosophic foundation. In this he based himself on the labour theory of value of Ricardo for his economics, and on the Hegelian dialectic as a tool for philosophic discussion. In this way, utilitarianism was a stepping stone to theories that proved in the end to be more influential.

The town of Treves, on the Moselle river, has in the course of its history been peculiarly productive of saints. For it is the birthplace not only of Ambrose, but also of Karl Marx (1818–83). As sainthood goes, Marx was undoubtedly the more successful of the two, and it is just that this should be so. For he is the founder of the movement that sanctified him, whereas his fellow townsman and saintly colleague was but a latter-day adherent of his own creed.

Karl Marx (1818–83), pupil of Hegel, social theorist, revolutionary

Marx came from a Jewish family which had turned protestant. During his university days he was strongly influenced by the Hegelianism then in vogue. His work as a journalist came to an abrupt end when the Prussian authorities banned the 'Rheinische Zeitung' in 1843. Marx then went to France and became acquainted with the leading French socialists. In Paris he met Friedrich Engels, whose father owned factories in Germany and at Manchester. Engels managed the latter, and was thus able to introduce Marx to the problems of labour and industry in England. On the eve of the revolution of 1848, Marx published the Communist Manifesto. He was actively involved in the revolution both in France and Germany. In 1849, the Prussian government sent him into exile, and he took refuge in London. There he remained, except for some brief trips to his homeland, until the end of his life. In the main it was through help from Engels that Marx and his family subsisted. But in spite of poverty, Marx studied and wrote with zeal, paving the way for the social revolution he felt imminent.

Marx's thinking was moulded by three major influences. There is first of all his connection with the Philosophic Radicals. Like them, he is opposed to romanticism and pursues a social theory which claims to be scientific. From Ricardo he adopted the labour theory of value,though he gave a different twist to it. Ricardo and Malthus had argued from a tacit assumption that the existing social order was immutable; free competition therefore keeps wages for labour at subsistence level, and so controls numbers. Marx, on the other hand, takes the point of view of the worker whose labour is used by the capitalist employer. A man produces value in excess of his remuneration, and this surplus value is drained off by the capitalist for his own benefit. In this way, labour is exploited. But this is not really a personal matter. For it requires the concurrence of large numbers of men and quantities of equipment to produce goods on an industrial scale. The exploitation is therefore to be understood in terms of a system of production, and the relations to it of the working class and the capitalist class as a whole.

Friedrich Engels (1820–95)

This brings us to the second strain in Marx's thinking, namely his Hegelianism. For what seems to count in Marx, as much as in Hegel, is the whole system rather than the individual. It is the economic system that must be tackled, rather than isolated grievances. In this particular Marx is utterly at variance with the liberalism of the Radicals and their reforms. The Marxist doctrine is tied very closely to philosophical theories that are in the main Hegelian. This may well be the reason why Marxism has never really been popular in England, for the English are not on the whole much impressed by philosophy.

From Hegel, too, stems Marx's historical view of social development. This evolutionary approach is connected with the dialectic, which Marx adopts unchanged from Hegel. The historical process advances in dialectic fashion. Here Marx's interpretation is thoroughly Hegelian in method, though the driving force is conceived differently in the two cases. In Hegel, the course of history is a gradual self-realization of the spirit which strives towards the Absolute. Marx substitutes modes of production for the spirit, and the classless society for the Absolute. A given system of production will, in the course of time, develop internal tensions between the various social classes that are linked with it. These contradictions, as Marx calls them, are resolved into a higher synthesis. The form that the dialectic struggle takes is the class war. The fight continues until, under Socialism, a classless society supervenes. Once this has been attained there is nothing left to fight, and the dialectic process may go to sleep. For Hegel the Kingdom on earth was the Prussian State, for Marx it is the classless society.

The development of history, for Marx, is just as inevitable as for Hegel, and both deduce it from a metaphysical theory. The criticism levelled against Hegel can be applied unchanged to Marx. In so far as Marx's observations reveal a shrewd assessment of certain historical events that did in fact occur, they do not require a logic from which they are allegedly deduced.

Manifest

der

Kommunistischen Partei.

Veröffentlicht im Februar 1848.

London.

Druck von R. Hirschfeld, English & Foreign Printer,

48, Clifton Street, Finsbury Square.

1848.

The Communist Manifesto of 1848

While the Marxist account is Hegelian in method, it repudiates Hegel's insistence on the spiritual nature of the world. Marx said that Hegel had to be put upside down, and this he proceeded to do by adopting the materialist doctrines of the eighteenth century. Materialism is the third main ingredient in Marxist philosophy. But here, too, Marx gives a new twist to the older theories. Leaving aside the materialist element in the economic interpretation of history, we find that Marx's philosophic materialism is not of the mechanical type. What Marx maintains is much rather a doctrine of activity which goes back to Vico. In his Eleven Theses on Feuerbach (1845) he put this point in the famous dictum that 'philosophers have only interpreted the world in various ways, the real task is to change it.' In this context, he puts forward a conception of truth which is very reminiscent of Vico's formula, and foreshadows certain forms of pragmatism. Truth, for him, is not a matter of contemplation, but something that has to be demonstrated in practice. The contemplative approach is linked with bourgeois individualism, which Marx, of course, despises. His own practical materialism belongs to the classless world of Socialism.

What Marx is trying to do is to capture, for materialism, the doctrine of activity which had been developed by the Idealist school in general, and Hegel in particular. The mechanistic doctrines had let this go by default and thus allowed Idealism to work out this aspect of theory; though, of course, it had to be put upside down before it was of any use. As to Vico's influence, this is perhaps not fully conscious, though Marx certainly knew the Scienza Nuova. He called his own new theory dialectic materialism, thus emphasizing the evolutionary and Hegelian element in it.

From all this it can be seen that the Marxist doctrine is a highly sophisticated affair. The theory of dialectic materialism is a philosophic system for which its supporters claim a universal scope. As might be expected, this has led to a great deal of philosophic speculation, in the Hegelian vein, about matters that had really better be left to the empirical enquiries of science. The earliest example of this is to be found in Engels' book 'Anti-Dühring', in which he criticizes the theories of the German philosopher Dühring. But detailed dialectic explanations on why water boils, in terms of quantitative changes accumulating into qualitative ones, contradictions, negations and counter-negations, are not a whit more satisfying than the philosophy of nature in Hegel. It really will not do to brand traditional science as pursuing bourgeois ideals.

Das Kapital.

Kritik der politischen Oekonomie.

Von

Karl Marx.

Erster Band.

Buch I: Der Produktionsprocess des Kapitals.

Hamburg
Verlag von Otto Meissner.
1867
New-York I. W. Schmidt, 24 Barclay-Street.

Title page of Capital. This book Marx wrote in the British Museum

Marx is very likely right in holding that the general scientific interests of a society reflect in some measure the social interests of its dominating group. Thus, one might hold that the revival of astronomy during the renaissance promoted the expansion of trade and enhanced the power of the rising middle class, though it may be remarked that one could not easily explain either in terms of the other. But in two vital respects this doctrine is inadequate. In the first place, it is evident that the solution of particular problems within a scientific field need have no connections whatsoever with social pressures of any kind. Of course, this is not to deny that there are occasions when a problem is tackled in response to some urgent need of the moment. But, in general, scientific problems are not resolved in this manner. This leads us to the second weakness in the dialectic materialist account, to wit the failure to recognize the scientific movement as an independent force. Again, no one would deny that there are important links between scientific enquiry and other things that go on in society. Nevertheless, the pursuit of science, in the course of time, has gathered a certain momentum of its own, which ensures for it some measure of autonomy. This is true of all forms of disinterested enquiry. While, therefore, dialectic materialism is valuable in pointing to the importance of economic influences as moulding the life of a society, it is at fault in oversimplifying in terms of this one leading notion.

In the social field itself this provokes some rather odd consequences. For if you do not agree with the Marxist doctrine, you are deemed not to be on the side of progress. The term of distinction reserved for those who have not been visited by the new revelation is the word 'reactionary'. Literally, the inference is that you are working against progress, in a backward direction. The dialectic process, however, ensures that you will be eliminated in due course, for progress must win in the end. This, then, becomes the rationale for violent removal of non-conformist elements. There is here a strong messianic streak in the political philosophy of Marxism. As the founder of an earlier creed had put it, he who is not with us is against us. This is clearly not the principle of a democratic doctrine.

All this points to the fact that Marx was not only a political theorist, but also an agitator and revolutionary pamphleteer. The tone of his writings is often one of indignation and ethical rectitude, which would seem to be quite illogical if the dialectic is going to run its inevitable course in any case. If, as Lenin later put it, the state is going to wither away, it is pointless to make a fuss about it before the event. But this distant historical goal, admirable though it might be in the contemplation, is of scant comfort to those who suffer here and now. And so, the pursuit of what relief can be obtained is after all respectable, even if it is not quite consistent with the theory of the dialectic evolution of history. For what this preaches is the overthrow of the existing order by violent means. In fact, of course, this aspect of the theory seems to be mainly a reflection of the desperate plight of the working-class in the nineteenth century. It is a good example of Marx's own economic interpretation of history, which explains the views and theories that are held at any time in terms of the prevailing economic order. This doctrine comes dangerously close to pragmatism in one respect at least. For it looks as though we are doing away with truth in favour of economically conditioned prejudices. If now we were to ask the same question about this theory itself, we should have to say that it, too, merely reflects certain social conditions at a particular time. But here Marxism implicitly makes an exception in its own favour. For it holds hat the economic interpretation of history on the dialectic materialist pattern is the true view.

Marx's grave, Highgate cemetery

In his forecasts on the dialectic evolution of history, Marx was not in all respects successful. He did predict, with some accuracy, that a system of free competition would eventually lead to the formation of monopolies. This much is indeed discernible from traditional economic theory. But where Marx went wrong was in assuming that the rich would become richer, and the poor poorer, until the dialectic tension of this 'contradiction' became so strong as to call forth the revolution. This is not at all what did happen. The industrial nations of the world, on the contrary, devised methods of regulation which softened the starkness of the economic struggle, by limiting freedom of action in the economic sphere and introducing social welfare schemes. When the revolution did come, it was not, as Marx had foretold, in the industrialized Western part of Europe, but in agrarian Russia.

The Marxist philosophy is the last great system that was produced by the nineteenth century. Its great appeal and widespread influence is due in the main to the religious character of its utopian prophecies, as well as to the revolutionary element in its programme for action. As for its philosophic background, this is, as we have tried to show, neither quite so simple nor quite so new as is often thought. The economic interpretation of history is one of a number of general theories of history that are ultimately derivative from Hegel. Another example, which belongs to the following generation, is Croce's theory of history as the story of liberty. In particular, the Marxist doctrine of contradiction is directly borrowed from Hegel, and subject to the same difficulties. Politically, this raises problems of some magnitude in our own time. Nearly half the world today is governed by states that put implicit trust in Marx's theories. The possibility of co-existence involves a certain relaxation of theoretical commitments.

Auguste Comte (1798–1857)

In France, the philosophic movement of the encyclopaedists found a successor in Auguste Comte (1798–1857). Sharing with the Philosophic Radicals their respect for science and opposition to established religions, he set out to provide a comprehensive classification of all the sciences, starting with mathematics and culminating in social science. Like his English contemporaries, he was opposed to metaphysics, though like them he knew little of German Idealism. Because he insisted that we must begin with what is given directly in experience, and refrain from trying to go behind phenomena, he calls his doctrine a positive philosophy. It is from this source that positivism derives its name.

Comte was born in the ancient university town of Montpellier, the son of a highly respectable and conventional family of government clerks. His father was a monarchist and a rigid catholic, but Comte soon outgrew the narrow purview of the parental home. When at the Polytechnique in Paris, he was expelled for taking part in a students' rebellion against one of their professors. This later prevented him from gaining university employment. At the age of twenty-six he published his first sketch of positivism, and from 1830 onwards the Course of Positive Philosophy appeared in six volumes. During the last ten years of his life, he devoted much time to the elaboration of a positivist religion, which was to take the place of the established creeds. Instead of God, this new gospel recognized humanity as supreme. Throughout his life, Comte was somewhat frail in health, and suffered from recurrent mental depression which drove him to the verge of suicide. He made a living by private tuition, eked out with gifts from friends and admirers, amongst whom we find J. S. Mill. But Comte appears to have been somewhat impatient of men who would not constantly acknowledge him as a genius, which in the end caused Mill's friendship for him to cool off.

Comte's philosophy shows certain affinities particularly with Vico, whose work Comte had studied. From Vico he derives the notion of the primacy of history in the affairs of man. Likewise, this source provides the concept of various stages in the historical development of human society. Vico himself had derived this observation from a study of Greek mythology. Comte adopts the view that society goes from an initial theological phase through a metaphysical phase, and finally moves on to what he calls a positive phase, which brings the historical process to its proper happy end. Vico, in this respect, was a more realistic thinker, and recognized that society can and does relapse from periods of refinement and civilized achievement into eras of new barbarism. The Dark Ages that followed the break-up of the Roman world are an example. So, perhaps, are our own times. To return to Comte, the positive stage is ruled by rational science. This is Comte's famous theory of the three stages of development. It has been suggested that there is some echo of Hegel here, but the similarity is superficial. For the development from one phase to the next is not conceived in dialectic terms, and the fact that there are three stages is entirely fortuitous. What Comte does share with Hegel is the optimistic notion of an ultimate state of perfection reached by the historical process. Marx, as we saw, held similar views. This is a general symptom of nineteenth century optimism.

Positive Philosophy, title page

COURS

DE

PHILOSOPHIE POSITIVE,

PAR M. AUGUSTE COMTE,

ANCIEN ÉLÈVE DE L'ÉCOLE POLYTECHNIQUE, RÉPÉTITEUR D'ANALYSE TRANSCENDANTE ET DE MÉCANIQUE RATIONNELLE A LADITE ÉCOLE.

TOME PREMIER,

CONTENANT

LES PRÉLIMINAIRES GÉNÉRAUX ET LA PHILOSOPHIE MATHÉMATIQUE.

PARIS,

BACHELIER, LIBRAIRE POUR LES MATHÉMATIQUES,

QUAI DES AUGUSTINS, N° 55.

1830

The positivist theory maintains that all scientific fields have undergone this evolution through three stages. The only one that has as yet completely cleared all hurdles is mathematics. In physical science, metaphysical concepts still abound, though it is to be hoped that the positive stage is not far off. We shall see later how within fifty years of Comte a positive account of mechanics came to be given by Mach. What Comte is trying to do above all is to arrange the entire field of scientific study in a comprehensive and logical order. In this endeavour he shows himself a true descendant of the encyclopaedists. The idea of such an order is, of course, extremely old, going back as far as Aristotle. Each science in the hierarchy contributes to an account of the entries that follow it, but not to those that precede. In this way we arrive at the Comtian list, headed by mathematics and followed by astronomy, physics, chemistry, biology and sociology.

The important entry is the last one. Comte himself coined the word sociology for what Hume would have called a science of man. According to Comte, this science has as yet to be established, and he considers himself as its founder. Logically, sociology is the last and most complex study in the hierarchy, but in point of fact we are all of us more familiar with the social surroundings in which we live than with the axioms of pure mathematics. This brings out another aspect of the primacy of the historical, which we have met in Vico. For man's social existence is the process of history.

	logical order	epistemological order
mathematics	1	6
astronomy	2	5
physics	3	4
chemistry	4	3
biology	5	2
sociology	6	1

The logical order is the reverse of the order of knowing

The positive stage of social existence, which fired the imagination of Comte, has the common drawbacks of all utopian systems. Here there is a marked streak of idealist influence in Comte's thinking, though how he came by it is not quite clear. Within each of the three phases of development there is a gradual unifying tendency that moves itself through three stages. Thus, in the theological stage we start with animism, which attributes divine status to all the objects discerned by primitive man. From this we move on to polytheism and monotheism. The tendency is always towards greater unification. In science, this means that we strive to subsume a variety of phenomena under some single head, and in society the goal is away from the individual towards humanity as a whole. This has, indeed, somewhat of a Hegelian ring about it. Positive humanity will be ruled by the moral authority of a scientific élite, while the executive power will be entrusted to technical experts. The arrangement is not dissimilar to the ideal state of Plato's 'Republic.'

On the ethical side, the system requires that the individual submerge his own desires in favour of a dedication to the progress of humanity. This emphasis on the 'cause' to the exclusion of private interests also characterizes the political theory of Marxism. As might be expected, positivism does not recognize the possibility of an introspective kind of psychology. This is specifically denied, because it is said to be impossible for the knowing process to know itself. So far as this suggestion is meant to imply that in a knowing situation it is not true in general that the knower knows his own knowing, we may accept it as sound. Nevertheless, in ruling out hypotheses in general as metaphysical, positivism misconstrues the nature of explanation.

A completely different outlook from positivism informs the philosophy of C. S. Peirce (1839–1914). Where Comte had discarded hypotheses as metaphysical, Peirce, on the contrary, was intent on showing that the framing of hypotheses is a vital activity with a logic of its own. The work of Peirce is voluminous and fragmentary. Besides, he was often struggling with difficult problems and novel suggestions. It is therefore not easy to obtain a clear view of his position. It is, however, beyond doubt that he was one of the most original minds of the later nineteenth century, and certainly the greatest American thinker ever.

II. What conception of a Law of Nature was entertained in England in Hume's day, not by those who wrote upon the subject, but by the silent mass of educated men?
In Hume's day, more than at other times, the great mass of educated Englishmen were grossly "practical". They did not waste thought upon anything not pretty directly concerning their own comfort, security, or amusement. They went to church, because doing so set a good example to the people, and so tended to maintain the supremacy of the upper classes. That was commonly regarded among university graduates as the chief function of the church; and consequently, anything that tended to weaken the church awoke in such men horror and dread.*
*For a picture of Oxford in 1721, see Amhurst's 'Terrae Filius'.

From ms of Peirce's article 'Hume on Miracles and Laws of Nature'

Peirce was born in Cambridge, Massachusetts. His father was professor of mathematics at Harvard, where Peirce himself became a student. Except for two spells of a few years of lecturing, Peirce never secured permanent academic employment. He held a government post in the Geodetic Survey, and produced, besides his scientific work, a steady flow of papers and articles on a wide range of philosophic topics. His failure to gain a professorship was somewhat linked with his disregard for the standards of conformity demanded by the society in which he lived. Moreover, few except some friends and scholars recognized his genius, and no one really understood him fully. It is a measure of his sense of purpose that he was not soured by such lack of recognition. During his last twenty-five years he was beset by poverty and ill health, but he worked until the end.

Peirce is commonly regarded as the founder of pragmatism. However, this view is subject to very serious qualifications. Contemporary pragmatism stems not from Peirce, but from what William James thought Peirce was saying. That this confusion arose is due to a number of causes. For one thing, Peirce's own views became clearer in his later writings, whereas James took his lead from earlier formulations, which were more open to misunderstanding. Peirce tried to disown the pragmatism James attributed to him. He therefore came to call his own philosophy pragmaticism, in the hope that this inelegant neologism would draw attention to the difference.

The doctrine of pragmatism is stated in some of Peirce's earlier work in a form which does permit, on the face of it, the inference that James drew from it. Peirce links his definition of truth to a general discussion of inquiry and the motives that animate its pursuit. Inquiry arises out of some kind of dissatisfaction or uneasiness, and its aim is said to be the attaining of a state of rest, in which the disturbing influences have been dispelled. The view one accepts at any of these intermediate stages of equilibrium is, to the best of one's knowledge, the truth. But one can never know that fresh evidence might not require one to change one's position. We can never rest assured that we have not committed an error. This general theory of inquiry Peirce calls fallibilism. In connection with it he says that truth is the opinion to which, in the end, the community settles down. Taken at face value, this is of course absurd. For if we all were to believe that twice two make five, and at that very instant the earth were destroyed, our erstwhile arithmetic eccentricity would still remain erroneous. It may be indeed the case that if all my neighbours did believe such things, it might be prudent of me at least to pretend that I shared their views, but that is altogether a different matter. Peirce's statement must thus be seen in the context of fallibilism.

As to the bearing of any particular truth, Peirce insists that any statement that claims to be true must have practical consequences. It must, that is, allow the possibility of some future action, and the formation of a disposition to act accordingly in all circumstances of the given kind. The meaning of a statement is said to consist in these practical consequences. It is in this form that James adopted pragmatism. But it must be made clear that Peirce's view is much rather in line with the 'verum factum' formula of Vico. Truth is what you can do with your statements. To take an example, if I make a statement about a chemical substance, then the import of it is enhanced by all the properties of the substance that can be subjected to experiment and tested. This, roughly, seems to be what Peirce is driving at. The pragmatism that James has culled from all this reminds one of the Protagorean formula of man as the measure of all things, in contrast with Peirce's intention, which is better expressed by Vico's theory.

Series of diagrams after Peirce: an elucidation of the syllogism

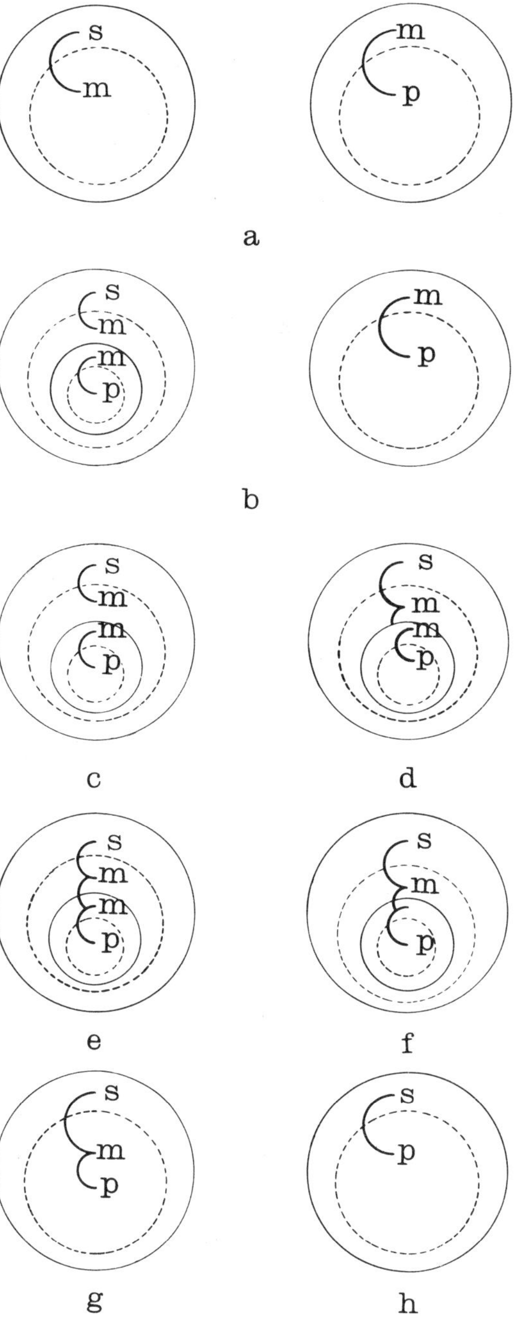

In the discussion of the logic of hypotheses, Peirce made a fundamental contribution. It had been variously supposed by philosophers that hypotheses are the result either of deduction, as rationalists might incline to hold, or of induction, as the empiricists think. Peirce saw that neither of these views was adequate. Hypotheses are the outcome of a third and radically different logical process, which Peirce in his customary colourful style calls 'abduction'. It amounts to tentatively adopting a hypothesis because it saves some particular appearance. That the appearance is saved is of course a matter of deduction, but not the acceptance of the hypothesis.

Like his father, Peirce was an accomplished mathematician, and in the field of symbolic logic he made a number of important discoveries. Amongst other things, he invented the method of truth-tables to determine the truth-values of a compound formula, a device much used by later logicians. To him is also due a new logic of relations.

Peirce laid much store by his system for diagrammatic argument, but the rules of the procedure are rather involved, and the idea does not seem to have gained much popularity. The pragmaticist outlook of Peirce led him to emphasize an interesting aspect of mathematical argument that is not often given its due weight. He insists on the importance of construction in the building up of a mathematical proof. These views are found again in Goblot and Meyerson.

Peirce had a thorough grasp not only of mathematics and of the scientific developments of his time, but also of the histories of science and of philosophy. From this broad outlook it seemed to him that science presupposes a metaphysical basis of a realist kind. He therefore elaborated a metaphysic of his own, leaning explicitly on the scholastic realism of Duns Scotus. Indeed, he holds that pragmaticism and scholastic realism go hand in hand. Whether this be so or not, it shows that his pragmaticism has little to do with James' pragmatism.

In his own time Peirce had very little influence; what made pragmatism into an influential philosophy was the interpretation given to it by William James (1842–1910). This by no means pleased Peirce, as we have mentioned already. For Peirce's doctrine is something rather more subtle than Jamesian pragmatism, and is only beginning to be properly appreciated.

James was a New Englander and a staunch protestant. This background survives in his thinking, though he was a free thinker and sceptically disposed towards all forms of orthodox theology. Unlike Peirce, he had a long and distinguished academic career at Harvard, where he was Professor of Psychology. His 'Principles of Psychology' appeared in 1890, and remains to this day one of the best general accounts of the subject. Philosophy was really a sideline for him, but he rightly came to be regarded as the leading American figure in that field. As a man, he was kind and generous, and strongly in favour of democracy, unlike his literary brother Henry. Compared with Peirce's philosophy, his thinking is rather less profound; but owing to his personality and position, he exercised a vastly greater influence on philosophic thought, particularly in America.

William James (1842–1910)

The philosophic importance of James is twofold. His influential role in spreading pragmatism we have just noted. The other main strand of his thinking is connected with a doctrine which he called radical empiricism. It was first stated in 1904, in an article entitled 'Does "Consciousness" exist?' James here set out to show that the traditional dualism of subject and object was a hindrance to a sound view of epistemology. According to James, we must abandon the notion of self-consciousness as an entity set over against the objects of the material world. The subject-object account of knowing seems to him a sophisticated rationalist distortion, which is in any case not truly empirical. For we really have nothing to go on beyond what James calls 'pure experience'. This is conceived as the concrete fulness of life, as contrasted with subsequent abstract reflection on it. The knowing process thus becomes a relation between different parts of pure experience. James did not go on to work out the full implications of this theory, but those who followed his suggestion came to replace the old dualistic theories by a 'neutral monism', which states that there is only one kind of basic stuff in the world. For James, then, pure experience is the stuff all things are made of. Here the radical empiricism of James is marred by his pragmatism, which does not recognize anything that has no practical bearing on human life. Only what forms part of experience, by which he means human experience, is of any relevance. James' English contemporary F.C.S. Schiller, who held rather similar views on this, called his own theory 'Humanism'. The trouble with this doctrine is that its scope is too narrow for what science, and for that matter common sense as well, have always regarded as one of their main tasks. The inquirer must see himself as part of a world which is always stretching beyond his ken. Otherwise there would be no sense in pursuing anything. If I am of necessity co-terminous with whatever the world might mean, I might as well sit back and drift. While James is right in criticizing the old dualistic theories of mind and matter, his own theory of pure experience cannot be entertained.

On the general question of rationalism versus empiricism, we must mention a famous distinction drawn by James. According to this view, rationalist doctrines tend to emphasize the mental at the expense of the material. They are optimistic in character and strive for unity, and favour reflection to the neglect of experiment. Those who incline towards accepting such theories James calls tender-minded. On the other side, there are the empiricist theories, which tend to occupy themselves more with the material world. They are pessimistic, recognize separateness in the world, and prefer experiment to excogitation. These views are supported by the tough-minded. The distinction must, of course, not be pressed too far. The pragmatic doctrine is definitely on the tough-minded side of this alternative. In a treatise entitled 'Pragmatism' (1907), James explains his theory and points out that there are two sides to it. On the one hand, pragmatism is a method, which James identifies with the empiricist attitude. He is careful to insist that as a method it does not prescribe any particular results, but merely a way of dealing with the world. What this method amounts to is roughly that distinctions carrying no practical differences are meaningless. Along with this goes a refusal to regard any issue as ever finally closed. This much comes straight from Peirce and would indeed commend itself to any empiricist enquirer. If nothing more were involved, James would be quite right in saying that pragmatism was merely a new name for some old ways of thinking.

From these admirable principles, however, James gradually slides into something very much more questionable. The pragmatic method leads him to the view that scientific theories are instruments for future action, rather than finally acceptable answers to questions about nature. A theory should not be treated as a magic spell of words, which enables the magician to maintain a hold on nature. The pragmatist insists on examining each word closely and asking for what James has called its 'cash-value'. From this it is only one further step to the pragmatist definition of truth as that which has fruitful consequences. Dewey's instrumental conception of truth comes to much the same thing.

At this point pragmatism becomes itself a metaphysical doctrine of the most dubious kind, and it is understandable that Peirce took great pains to dissociate himself from it. Leaving aside the difficulty of establishing here and now what are the consequences of a given view, and whether they will turn out to be fruitful, there remains in any case the fact that a certain set of consequences will either be fruitful, or they will not be so. This, at any rate, has to be decided in an ordinary, non-pragmatic way. It will not do to evade this issue by saying the consequences will be fruitful in some indeterminate measure; that would allow us simply to accept anything at all. Up to a point, James seems to sense this difficulty in that he recognizes a person's freedom to adopt certain beliefs if this is conducive to happiness. The case of religious belief provides a good example. But this is not at all the way in which a religious person holds his beliefs. He does not entertain them because of the contentment he estimates they will produce, but rather the reverse: it is because of his beliefs that he is happy.

PRAGMATISM

A NEW NAME FOR SOME
OLD WAYS OF THINKING

POPULAR LECTURES ON PHILOSOPHY BY
WILLIAM JAMES

LONGMANS, GREEN, AND CO.
39 PATERNOSTER ROW, LONDON
NEW YORK, BOMBAY, AND CALCUTTA
1907

Pragmatism, title page

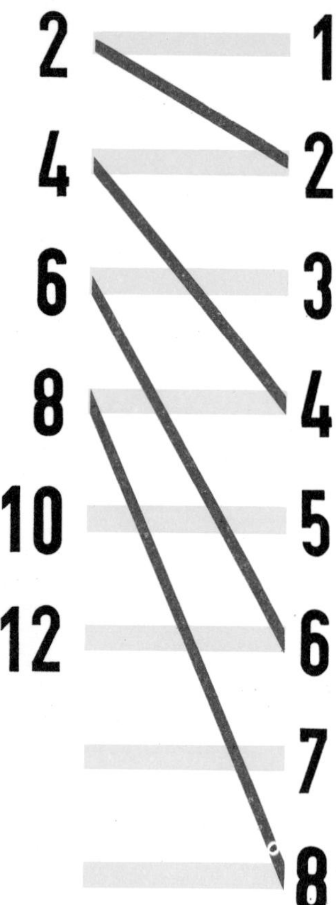

One of Cantor's paradoxes: there are as many even numbers as there are numbers

From the very beginning of philosophy in Greece, mathematics has always been a subject of special interest to philosophers. The advances of the last two hundred years bear this out in a striking manner. The infinitesimal calculus formulated by Leibniz and Newton led, in the eighteenth century, to a great outburst of mathematical invention. However, the logical foundations of mathematics were not properly understood, and considerable use was made of some rather ill-founded notions.

Mathematical analysis in those days laid much store by the concept of 'infinitesimals'. This, it was thought, played an essential part in the functioning of the newly invented calculus. An infinitesimal, so it was held, is a quantity neither sizeless nor finite, but 'vanishingly' small. It was supposed that it was such quantities that were at work in the forming of differential coefficients and integrals. At bottom, the infinitesimal is, of course, one of the mustiest of all skeletons in the mathematical cupboard. For it goes back to the unit of the Pythagoreans, which is a similar version of this entity. We have seen how Zeno exposed the Pythagorean doctrine. In modern times, critical comment on the theory of infinitesimals also came from philosophers. Berkeley was probably the first to point out the difficulties involved, and there are some telling points in Hegel's discussion of these matters. But mathematicians did not at first pay heed to these warnings. They went ahead and developed their science, and it is well that they should have done so. It is a peculiar fact about the genesis and growth of new disciplines that too much rigour too early imposed stifles the imagination and stultifies invention. A certain freedom from the strictures of sustained formality tends to promote the development of a subject in its early stages, even if this means the risk of a certain amount of error.

Nonetheless, there comes a time in the development of any field when standards of rigour have to be tightened. In mathematics, the period of rigour sets in with the beginning of the nineteenth century. The first onslaught was delivered by the French mathematician Cauchy, who worked out a systematic theory of limits. This, in conjunction with the later work of Weierstrass in Germany, made it possible to dispense with infinitesimals. The general problems of continuity and infinite number, which are lurking behind these developments, were for the first time investigated by Georg Cantor.

Numerical infinity had been causing trouble from the time of Zeno and his paradoxes. If we recall the race between Achilles and the tortoise, we might put one of the puzzling aspects of this contest as follows: for every place Achilles has been at, there is a place that the tortoise has occupied. The two runners have thus at any time assumed an equal number of stations. Yet obviously Achilles covers more ground. This seems to run counter the common sense notion that the whole is greater than the part. But when we deal with infinite collections this is no longer so. Thus, to take a simple example, the series of positive integers, which is an infinite collection, has in it odd and even numbers. Take away all the odd numbers, and you might think that what is left is half of what you began with. But there remain as many even numbers as there were numbers altogether at the start. This somewhat startling conclusion is quite easily demonstrated. First, we write down the series of natural numbers, and then, alongside it, a series resulting from it by doubling each member in turn. For every number in the first series there is a corresponding entry in the second. There is, as mathematicians put it, a one-one correspondence between them. The two series therefore have the same number of terms. In the case of infinite collections, therefore, a part contains as many terms as the whole. This is the property that Cantor uses to define an infinite collection.

On this basis Cantor developed a whole theory of infinite numbers. In particular, he showed that there are infinite numbers of different sizes, though one must not, of course, think of these quite in the way in which we talk about ordinary numbers. An example of a higher infinity than that of the series of natural numbers is the series of real numbers, or continuum, as it is sometimes called. Suppose all decimal fractions are listed in order of size. We now make up a new decimal by taking the first figure of the first entry, the second figure of the second entry, and so on, and raising each figure by one. The resulting decimal is different from all the decimals in the list, which we had supposed to be complete. This shows that a denumerable list cannot be made up in the first place. The number of decimal fractions is infinite to a higher degree than the number of natural numbers. This so-called diagonal process has later been of some importance in symbolic logic too.

Another question of basic interest to the logician came to be taken up towards the end of the nineteenth century. The ambition of mathematicians from the earliest times has been to show their entire science as a system of deductions from a single starting point, or at least from as few as possible. This is one of the aspects of Socrates' form of the Good. The Elements of Euclid provide an example of what was required, even if Euclid's own treatment was defective.

Peano's axioms: the successor of a number is a number, any number has one and only one such; 0 is a number but not a successor. Finally, the principle of mathematical induction

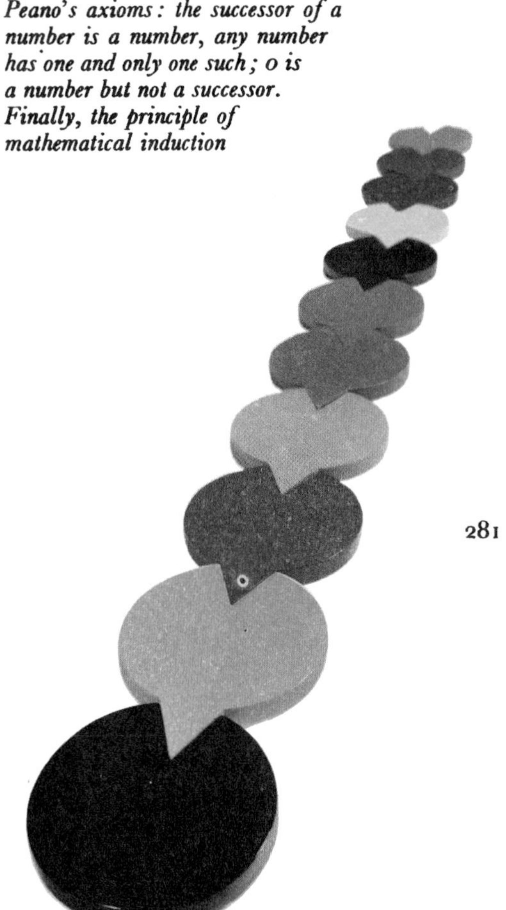

In the case of arithmetic, a small set of postulates, from which everything else could be deduced, was given by the Italian mathematician Peano. The basic statements are five in number. Together they define the class of progressions of which the natural number series constitutes one example. Briefly, the postulates state that the successor of every number is also a number, and that every number has one and only one successor. The series begins with zero, which is a number, but not itself the successor of a number. Finally, there is the principle of mathematical induction, by means of which the general properties belonging to all members of the series are established. This principle runs thus: if a given property of any number 'n' also belongs to its successor, and to the number zero, then it belongs to every number of the series.

From the time of Peano, a new interest was taken in questions about the foundations of mathematics. In this field there are two opposed schools of thought. On the one hand there are the formalists, whose main concern is consistency; and on the other the intuitionists, who take a somewhat positivist line, and demand that you should be able to point to what you happen to be talking about.

A common feature of these mathematical developments is their interest to the logician. Here, indeed, it seemed that logic and mathematics were beginning to merge at the fringes. Since the time of Kant, who had considered logic as complete, great changes had occurred in the study of logical theory. In particular, new forms of treating logical arguments by means of mathematical formulae had been developed. The first systematic account of this new way of dealing with logic is due to Frege (1848–1925), whose work was, however, completely ignored for twenty years, until I drew attention to it in 1903. In his own country he long remained an obscure professor of mathematics. It is only in recent years that his importance as a philosopher has come to be recognized.

G. Frege.

G. Frege (1848–1925)

Frege's mathematical logic goes back to 1879. In 1884, he published his Foundations of Arithmetic, in which the method is applied to a more radical treatment of Peano's problem. The axioms of Peano, for all their economy, were nevertheless unsatisfactory from a logical point of view. For it seemed somewhat arbitrary that it should be these rather than some other statements that were the basis of mathematical science. Peano himself never went so far as to consider these matters. To solve this question in the most general form was the task that Frege set himself.

What Frege set out to do is to exhibit the axioms of Peano as a logical consequence of his symbolic system. This would at once remove the blemish of arbitrariness, and show that pure mathematics was merely a prolongation of logic. In particular, it would be necessary to derive some logical definition of number itself. The notion of reducing mathematics to logic plainly suggests itself from Peano's axioms. For they limit the essential vocabulary of mathematics to the two terms of 'number' and 'successor'. The second of these is a general logical term; to turn our vocabulary entirely into logical terms we merely need give a logical account of the first. This Frege did, defining number by means of purely logical concepts. His definition comes to much the same as that given by Whitehead and myself in Principia Mathematica. It is there stated that a number is the class of all classes similar to a given class. Thus, every class of three objects is an instance of the number three, which itself is the class of all such classes. As for number in general, this is the class of all particular numbers, and thus turns out to be a class of the third order.

One perhaps unexpected feature resulting from this definition is that numbers cannot be added together. While you can add a triad of apples to a couple of pears and obtain five pieces of fruit, you cannot add the class of all triads, to the class of all couples. But, as we saw, this is not really so novel a discovery after all. Plato had already said that numbers cannot be added.

His treatment of mathematics led Frege to formulate the distinction between the sense and the reference of a sentence. This is required to account for the fact that equations are not merely empty repetitions. The two sides of an equation have common reference, but differ in sense.

As a system of symbolic logic, Frege's account did not gain much influence, partly no doubt because of its intricate notation. The symbolism used in Principia Mathematica owes something to that of Peano, and has been found more adaptable. Since then, quite a number of notations have come into use in the field of mathematical logic. One of the most elegant of these was developed by the famous Polish school of logicians, which was dispersed by the last war. Likewise, considerable improvements have been made in the way of economy both in notation and in the number of fundamental axioms of the system. The American logician Sheffer introduced a single logical constant, in terms of which those of the propositional calculus could be defined in turn. With the help of this new logical constant it was possible to base the system of symbolic logic on one single axiom. But all these are highly technical matters that cannot be explained in detail here.

Mathematical logic, on the purely formal side, is no longer the concern of philosophers as such. It is handled by mathematicians, though of course it is mathematics of a very special sort. What is of interest to the philosopher are the problems that arise out of the general assumptions about symbolism, made before a system gets under weigh. Likewise, he is interested in the paradoxical conclusions that are sometimes reached in the construction of a symbolic system.

One such paradox arose in connection with the definition of number in Principia Mathematica. The notion of 'class of all classes' was the cause of it. For evidently the class of all classes is itself a class, and therefore belongs to the class of all classes; it thus contains itself as one of its members. There are, of course, many other classes that do not have this property. The class of all voters does not itself enjoy the benefits of universal suffrage. The paradox now arises when we consider the class of all classes which are not members of themselves.

The question is whether this class is a member of itself or not. If we suppose that it is a member of itself, then it is not an instance of a class that does include itself. But in order to be a member of itself, it must be of the kind that is being considered in the first place, that is, not a member of itself. If, on the contrary, we assume that the class under discussion is not a member of itself, then it is not an instance of a class that does not include itself. But in order to be no member of itself, it must be one of the classes in the class about which the original question was asked, and so it is a member of itself. In either case we reach a contradiction.

The difficulty can be removed if we note that one must not treat classes on quite the same footing as classes of classes, just as normally one would not speak of men on the same level as of nations. It then becomes evident that we should not talk about classes that are their own members so glibly as we did in setting up the paradox. The difficulties concerning the paradoxes have been tackled in various ways, and no general agreement has yet been reached on how they should be disposed of. But in the meantime, this problem has made philosophers aware once again of the great need to scrutinize the way in which sentences are constructed, and words used.

PRINCIPIA MATHEMATICA

BY

ALFRED NORTH WHITEHEAD, Sc.D., F.R.S.
Fellow and late Lecturer of Trinity College, Cambridge

AND

BERTRAND RUSSELL, M.A., F.R.S.
Lecturer and late Fellow of Trinity College, Cambridge

VOLUME I

Cambridge
at the University Press
1910

The authors of Principia Mathematica

Contemporary

In dealing with the philosophy of the last seventy or eighty years, we are faced with some special difficulties. For we are still so near to these developments that it is difficult to view them with proper distance and detachment. The thinkers of the remoter past have had to stand the test of critical assessment by later generations. Along with the passage of time there goes a gradual sifting, which helps to lighten the task of selection. It is very rare indeed that a minor thinker should in the long run achieve a measure of fame that his work does not warrant; though it does happen that important men are unjustly forgotten.

With recent thinkers, questions of choice become more difficult, and the chances of achieving a balanced outlook more precarious. Where for the past it is possible to see phases of development in their entirety, the present is too close upon us to allow us to disentangle the various strands of the story with the same confidence. Indeed, it cannot be otherwise. It is comparatively easy to be wise after the event and come to understand the growth of the philosophic tradition. But it would be an Hegelian illusion to imagine that the significance of contemporary changes can be deduced in all their specific detail. At best, one may hope to see some general trends that can be linked with earlier events.

As life grows in complexity, so do the means for ruling it: part of an 'electronic brain'

The later nineteenth century is marked by a number of new developments that have affected the intellectual climate of our own time. There is first of all the breakdown of old ways of life that were grounded in the pre-industrial era. The tremendous growth of technical power has made life a very much more intricate business than once it used to be. Whether this is good or bad is not here at issue. We merely note the fact that the demands on our time are vastly more varied, and our requirements for ordinary living a great deal more complex, than ever before.

All this is reflected in the intellectual sphere as well. Where at one time it had been possible for a single person to master several disciplines, it was now becoming increasingly more difficult for anyone to acquire a thorough grasp of even one single field. The breaking up of intellectual pursuits into compartments of ever more narrow scope has in our own time brought about a veritable confusion of tongues. This unhealthy state of affairs is the outcome of certain changes that have imposed themselves with the growth of contemporary technological society. In the not so distant past there prevailed, not only within a given country, but to a large measure throughout Western Europe, a common background which was shared by all those who had reached a certain level of education. This was not, of course, a universal or egalitarian polish. Education was usually a matter of privilege, an exclusiveness which has since been largely eliminated; the only admissible criterion now is competence, which is a privilege of a different sort. This common basis for understanding has since disappeared. The demands and pressures of specialisation direct young people into narrow channels before there is time to develop broader interests and understanding. As a

result of all this, it is often extremely difficult for those who devote themselves to different branches of enquiry to communicate with each other.

But the nineteenth century has brought forth another even more literal confusion of tongues. For it has seen the decay and ultimate death of what had from time immemorial served as the common medium of expression amongst the learned of all nations. Latin had been the language of scholars, thinkers and scientists, from the time of Cicero to the renaissance. Gauss, in the early nineteenth century, wrote his famous work on curved surfaces in Latin, but this was already somewhat of a curiosity. Today the enquirer in any field has to be able to cope with two or three languages other than his own, if he wishes to have access to the work that goes on in his own speciality. This has become a problem of some magnitude. So far no solution of this difficulty has been found, though it seems some modern tongue will eventually have to fulfil the function that Latin once did.

Another new feature of the intellectual life of the nineteenth century is the break between artistic and scientific pursuits. This was a retrograde step when set over against the temper of mind displayed by the humanists of renaissance times. Where these earlier thinkers pursued science and art in the light of the one general principle of harmony and proportions, the nineteenth century, under the impact of romanticism, produced a violent reaction against the inroads that scientific progress seemed to make on man. The scientific way of life with its laboratories and experiments seemed to stifle the spirit of freedom and adventure which the artist demanded. The view that the experimental approach would not reveal the secrets of nature was oddly enough expressed already by Goethe, no doubt in one of his romantic moods. At all events, the contrast between the laboratory and the artist's studio well describes the break we have mentioned.

The astringency of science: Madame Curie in her laboratory

At the same time, there developed a certain divergence between science and philosophy. During the seventeenth and early eighteenth centuries, those who made significant contributions to philosophy were very often men who were more than amateurs in scientific matters. Largely as a result of the German Idealist philosophy, this scope of philosophic outlook disappeared in the course of the nineteenth century, at any rate in England and Germany. The French, as we have already suggested, were at the time somewhat immune to German Idealism, simply because their tongue does not take kindly to this sort of speculation. As a result, the rift between science and philosophy did not affect France in the same measure. This break has on the whole continued ever since. Scientists and philosophers do not, of course, ignore one another completely. But it would seem a fair comment that each often fails to understand what the other is doing. The excursions of contemporary scientists into philosophy are often no more felicitous than were the idealist philosopher's sallies in the reverse direction.

In the political field, the nineteenth century in Europe is an era of sharpening national differences. The previous century had not the same fierce attitude to such matters. It was possible, then, while France and England were at war, for English noblemen to spend the winter months on the shores of the Mediterranean as was their custom. The business of war, for all its ugliness, was on the whole a somewhat relaxed affair. Not so with the great national wars of the last hundred years. Like much else in contemporary affairs, war has become a great deal more efficient. What has hitherto tended to save the world from utter ruin is the perennial incompetence of its rulers. But let the direction of public business fall into the hands of some latter day Archimedes, whose engines of war are atomic rather than ballistic, and we should swiftly find ourselves disintegrated.

However, the late nineteenth century did not quite foresee these changes. On the contrary, there prevailed at that time a kind of scientific optimism which made men believe that the Kingdom of heaven was about to break out on earth. The vast strides accomplished by science and technology made it seem not unplausible that the solution of all problems was close at hand. Newtonian physics was the instrument that was going to accomplish this task. But here, the discoveries of the following generation dealt a rude shock to those who had thought that it only remained to apply to special cases the well-known principles of physical theory. In our own time the discoveries concerning atomic structure have shattered the complacent outlook that had developed by the turn of the century.

The romantic exuberance in art: Sarah Bernhardt in her salon

Nevertheless, some of this scientific optimism survives in the present. The scope for scientifically and technologically transforming the world appear indeed to be without limit. At the same time, there is a growing suspicion, even amongst the experts themselves, that a brave new world is perhaps not quite so undiluted a blessing as some of its over-eager advocates seem to imagine. That to a large extent the differences between men can be ironed out is an unhappy commonplace we have had ample occasion to observe in our own lifetime. This may well make human society a more efficient and stable machine. But it would surely spell the end of all intellectual endeavour, in science as much as anywhere else. At bottom, this kind of dream is a Hegelian illusion. It supposes that there are ultimates that can be reached, and that enquiry is a process which comes to an end. This is, however, an unsound view; it seems clear, on the contrary, that enquiry is limitless. Perhaps this circumstance will in the end preserve us from the kind of goal that architects of Utopian phantasies dream up from time to time.

The enormous scope of scientific control raises new social problems of an ethical character. In themselves, the discoveries and inventions of the scientist are ethically neutral. It is the power which they confer on us that can be turned to good or bad account. As a problem, this is indeed not really new. What makes the repercussions of science more dangerous today is the fearful efficacy of the means of destruction now available. Another difference seems to lie in the indiscriminate character of modern scientific sources of power and control when used for destruction. We have indeed come a long way from the time of the Greeks. One of the most heinous crimes that a Greek could commit in times of war was to cut down olive trees.

But after sounding all these warnings, we ought perhaps to remember that it is a very precarious business to see one's own time in proper perspective. Besides, there has never yet been, in the entire history of our civilization, an occasion on which men of vision and enterprise have not in the end come forth to set things right when all seemed to be lost. Still, it might well be said that we are facing a situation unlike anything that ever happened. In the last hundred years the West has undergone a material change unprecedented in history.

The reaction of science against philosophy is in the last analysis an outcome of the positivism of Comte. We saw in this connection that Comte was intent on ruling out the setting up of hypotheses. Natural processes were to be described but not explained. This kind of programme is in some ways linked with the general state of scientific optimism of the times. Only when it is felt that the scientific enterprise has reached some measure of completeness, and the end is in sight, could such an attitude to theory emerge. It is worth noting that on this head there is a passage in Newton which is usually quoted out of context and thus distorted. Speaking of the way in which lightrays travel, he says, in a guarded manner, that he frames no hypotheses. An explanation is not attempted, but it is not suggested that this could not be done. Nevertheless, we may recognize that a powerful theory, like Newton's, when once set going, will find sufficient employment for a time without the need for such hypotheses. In so far as scientists thought that Newtonian physics was on the point of settling all outstanding problems, it was natural enough that they should insist on description at the expense of explanation. The Idealist philosophers had tended, in the Hegelian manner, to run together all branches of enquiry into one vast and comprehensive system. Against this the scientists felt that their researches should not be submerged in a monistic philosophy. As to the positivist demand to remain within the bounds of experience and the description of it, this was consciously linked with an appeal to Kant and his followers. To look for the reasons of phenomena and to purport to furnish explanations amounts to transgressing into the noumenal, where the categories of explanation do not apply. It therefore must be a chimerical undertaking.

De Chirico's 'Great Metaphysician', symbol of the search for meaning. (Mus. Mod. Art, New York)

This kind of approach to scientific theory is characteristic of a whole group of scientists who were interested in the philosophical implications of the activities of the enquirer. When the name of Kant is invoked here, it is well to remember that the outlook which informs these thinkers is not Kantian in the orthodox sense. For, as we saw, Kant's theory of knowledge makes the framework of the categories of explanation a pre-requisite for experience. In this present context, explanation is declared to be unscientific because it is supposed to go beyond experience. It cannot be said that these scientific positivists had understood Kant too well.

The best known representative of this group is E. Mach (1838-1916), whose 'Science of Mechanics' provides a positivist account of mechanics. In so doing it studiously avoids using the scholastic terminology which had to some extent found its way into Newtonian physics. A term like force is a case in point. A force is not something that one can see. All we can say is that bodies move in certain ways. Mach therefore eliminates force and defines it in terms of the purely kinematic concept of acceleration. Mach does not, of course, purport to produce a mechanics that will be more powerful as a science. The positivist exercise is really an application of Occam's razor to what seemed to be a clearly superfluous growth of idle scientific concepts. We cannot here examine in detail how far this pruning operation might have been justified. But it is of some importance to insist on one point concerning scientific method in general. To rule hypotheses out of court is to misunderstand the function of explanation in science. A hypothesis explains in so far as it saves the appearances and predicts the future. If not itself the object of enquiry, it may continue to explain, so long at least as it does not do violence to the facts. But it explains only because it remains itself unexplained. When it in turn requires saving, it no longer explains, but must be accounted for in terms of some other hypothesis which now remains unexplained. This is not in the least mysterious. You cannot in one and the same breath explain everything at once. But the positivists are wrong in holding that you cannot explain anything at all. For suppose you really decided to abandon all hypotheses. How are we then to go about doing science? All that seems to be left is Baconian classification; and this, as we have seen, does not lead us very far. Thus, the very fact that science does go on gives the lie to the positivism of men like Mach. The most outspoken criticism of the positivist doctrine is to be found in the work of Meyerson (1859-1933), where we find an epistemology which is genuinely Kantian in principle, though not in detail.

In their attempts at finding scientific substitutes for what they called disparagingly 'metaphysics', the scientific philosophers very often fell into metaphysical difficulties of their own. This is in a way not surprising. For although they might with some justice reject the metaphysical speculations of philosophers, they were prone to forget that scientific enquiry itself proceeds on the basis of certain presuppositions. To this extent, at least, Kant seems to have been right. Thus, to take an example, the general notion of causality is a prerequisite for scientific work. It is not the outcome of research, but rather a presupposition, even if only tacit, without which research could not get under weigh. When viewed in this light, the philosophic novelties that have of late appeared in the writings of scientists are not quite so inspiring as they might seem at first.

$$\nabla^2\psi + \frac{8\pi^2 m}{h^2}(E - V)\psi = 0$$

An equation of theoretical science, usually interpreted as mere manipulation of signs

As to the significance of scientific statements and procedures, these have tended to be set aside in favour of a kind of mathematical ritual. The findings of science had somewhat upset the rigid and closed Newtonian view of the world. But instead of trying to enlarge this view, scientists have on the whole been content to handle their problems with the help of mathematical theories that produce adequate results when suitably interpreted. The intermediate stages of calculation and transformation are left alone and function merely as a set of rules. This attitude which, though not universal, is widespread, is curiously reminiscent of the numerical mysticism of the Pythagoreans and of their followers in late renaissance times.

In philosophy itself, these general trends have produced a movement away from science. This is true not only of the resurgence of Idealist strains on the continent, but also of the largely linguistic philosophy of Great Britain. As to this latter, it is true, in a sense, that it is not the business of philosophy to make discoveries, but to assess the merit of different ways of talking about what is admitted on all hands. At any rate, this is one of the things philosophy always has done. Nevertheless, different philosophic views may help or hinder, in various degrees, the progress of scientific enquiry.

F. H. Bradley (1846-1924)

His book, Appearance and Reality, was first published in 1893

APPEARANCE AND REALITY

A Metaphysical Essay

BY

F. H. BRADLEY, LL.D. GLASGOW

Fellow of Merton College, Oxford

SECOND EDITION (REVISED), WITH AN APPENDIX

London

SWAN SONNENSCHEIN & CO., LIM.

NEW YORK: THE MACMILLAN COMPANY

1897

As to philosophy proper, to which we must now return, the English scene was dominated, during the later nineteenth century, by the Idealism that had drifted across from the continent. In Britain, rain comes from Ireland, and Idealism from Germany. The dominant figure in the field was not, however, quite in the Hegelian tradition. F. H. Bradley (1846–1924), who studied and wrote at Oxford, worked out a critical rejection of materialism and aimed at reaching an Absolute reminiscent of Spinoza's god or nature, rather than of Hegel's absolute idea. As to the dialectic method which he adopts in his discussions, this is not a principle of organic growth, as it purports to be in Hegel, but rather a discursive weapon in the tradition of Plato and his Eleatic precursors. Indeed, Bradley is at pains to oppose the somewhat intellectual monism of Hegel, in which there is a tendency to equate knowing and being; a view which goes back ultimately to Socrates and the Pythagoreans. Bradley tries to go below rational thought and its categories to the level of bare feeling or experience. It is at this stage that we can speak of reality. As to thought, this is always a kind of falsification of what really is. It gives rise to mere appearances, because it distorts the real by imposing on it an alien framework of classifications and connections. Bradley thus holds that in the process of thinking we must inevitably entangle ourselves in contradictions. This doctrine is set out in a book entitled 'Appearance and Reality'.

The main burden of Bradley's attack on thought is that it is necessarily relational; and relations, as he tries to show, involve us in contradictions. To establish this odd conclusion Bradley uses a form of third man argument as was used by the Platonic Parmenides against Socrates' theory of participation. As qualities and relations are on the one hand distinct and on the other hand inseparable, we should be able to distinguish, in any given quality, that part which is strictly qualitative from that which gives purchase to the relational links. But we cannot so distinguish between different parts of a quality, and even if we could, we should now be faced with the problem of connecting the two parts together again. This involves a new relation, and the third man argument has got under weigh.

The sphere of thought, and with it science, thus suffers from contradiction, and therefore belongs to appearance rather than reality. In a curiously round about way Bradley here reaches the same conclusion as Hume, though on rather different grounds. But, like Hume, he rejects the notion of the self because it involves relations. As to the God of established religion, He too must be dismissed as appearance, for precisely the same reason.

Having thus disposed of appearance, Bradley finds reality in the Absolute, which seems to be some kind of Eleatic One that is experienced from within, at a level more direct and immediate than that of rational thought. In this Absolute all differences are united and all conflicts resolved. But this does not mean that appearances are abolished. In everyday life we think, and do science, which involves us in appearance. Likewise, the evil that men commit is firmly entrenched, as appearance, in the ordinary world. But at the level of the Absolute these imperfections seem to disappear.

Another form of Idealism which is in some ways derivative from Hegelianism is found in the philosophy of Benedetto Croce (1866–1952), though here the direct influence of Vico is perhaps even more important. Croce was not an academic philosopher, and enjoyed economic independence throughout his long life. Because of his international standing he survived the Fascist era without being too much molested; since the war he had held several positions in the Italian government.

He wrote voluminously on history and literature, and in 1905 founded 'La Critica', a literary journal of which he retained the editorship. Characteristic of his approach to philosophy is his emphasis on aesthetics, because of the concrete experience the mind is involved in when it contemplates a work of art.

With Hegel, whose monism simply does not allow room for the epistemological difficulties of British Empiricism, or even of Kant's theory, Croce shares the view that reality is spiritual. But though Hegel had insisted, in his emphasis on the dialectic, that mental processes involve the active conquest of obstacles, Croce seems here to go straight back to the 'verum factum' equation of Vico. At any rate, he is aware of some of the chief weaknesses of Hegelianism. Of these the application of dialectic to nature is one; the numerical mystery-mongering of tripartite divisions is another. But, above all, Hegel is at fault in his conception of an idealist system. We have already given some critical comment on this; here we may add that the doctrine of dialectic development and the attainment of ultimate goals are somehow incompatible. Croce retains the notion of development, though he does not accept a Hegelian account of it. Instead of dialectic progression, he adopts a modified form of Vico's theory of phases. Vico had thought that these developments are cyclical, so that in the end everything will return to the same starting point. This view, as we have seen, goes back to Empedocles. However, Croce thinks of these changes as progressive, so that, in returning to its initial stage, the mind has acquired some new insight in the process.

For all his rejection of Hegel, it must be confessed that Croce retains a fair measure of dialectic in his writings. Thus, in the book whose title-page is shown here, he speaks in terms that are almost reminiscent of Hegel's logic. 'The intimate link between error and truth arises because a mere and utter error is inconceivable; and because it is inconceivable it does not exist. Error speaks with two voices: one of these asserts the false, but the other denies it; and this is a clash of yes and no, which is called contradiction'. This excerpt also serves to underline the point that for Croce the mind is adequate to reality. There is nothing in the world that we cannot in principle discover. Whatever is inconceivable cannot exist, and therefore what exists is also conceivable. It is worth pointing out that Bradley held a view which is converse to this. To him what was conceivable must therefore exist, which he expressed in the formula 'what may be and must be, is.' Finally, the Hegelian influence is responsible for making Croce present Vico as a nineteenth century rationalist, when in fact he was a seventeenth century Platonist.

Benedetto Croce (1866–1952)

This essay (1913) was an inaugural lecture for the Rice Institute, University of Houston, Texas

PICCOLA BIBLIOTECA FILOSOFICA

BENEDETTO CROCE

BREVIARIO

DI

ESTETICA

QUATTRO LEZIONI

QUARTA EDIZIONE
CON AGGIUNTA DI DUE SAGGI
(RISTAMPA)

BARI
GIUS. LATERZA & FIGLI
TIPOGRAFI EDITORI LIBRAI
1933

In France, the most influential philosopher of the late nineteenth and early twentieth centuries took a different turn in his reaction against science. Henri Bergson (1859–1941) stands in the irrationalist tradition which goes back to Rousseau and the romantic movement. Like the pragmatists, Bergson emphasizes action above all. In this, he mirrors a certain impatience with the careful and dispassionate exercise of reason in philosophy and scientific enquiry. One of the principal features of rational thought is its striving for precision. The Cartesian precepts in the Discourse are quite a good description of it. Above all, in trying to capture the fleeting movement of experience within the framework of language, we seem to arrest the flux of reality and put in its place a pale and static verbal picture of it. We have here the old problem of Heraclitus and Parmenides. What Bergson is trying to do is to uphold the reality of flux in experience as against the travesty of rigid forms that pertain to reason and its picture of the world.

Henri Bergson (1859-1941)

Thus far the problem of Bergson is somewhat reminiscent of Bradley. But the solution of it is here quite different. Bradley's metaphysics is in the end closely linked with his logical theories, and more particularly with a coherence theory of truth. For Bergson, logic itself is the influence which must be overcome. In this sense Bradley may be described as rationalist and Bergson as irrationalist.

The philosophy of Bergson, in contrast to the idealist and materialist monisms of the nineteenth century, returns to a dualist view of the world. The two divisions of the universe are however not quite those of earlier dualist theories. One of them is matter, as with Descartes; the other is some sort of vital principle which is different from the mental portion of the rationalist's world. These two great forces, the vital on one side, and the material on the other, are involved in a permanent struggle in which the active impulse of life tries to overcome the obstacles put in its way by inert matter. In this process the life-force is to some extent moulded by the material conditions in which it operates, but nevertheless it retains its basic feature of freedom in action. Bergson rejects the traditional theories of evolution because of their rationalist leanings, which do not allow the emergence of anything fundamentally new. The later seems somehow already contained in the earlier, or predetermined by it, and this seems to undermine the freedom of action that Bergson attributes to the life-force. For him, evolution produces genuine novelty, it is creative in the literal sense. This doctrine is set forth in his best-known work, which bears the title of 'Creative Evolution'. The sort of evolutionary process that Bergson postulates is taken directly from the analogy of artistic creation. Just as the artist is moved to action by some kind of creative urge, so is the life-force working in nature. Evolutionary changes occur through persistent creative urges that aim at certain new characteristics hitherto not existing.

As to man, the evolutionary process has landed us with an animal in which intellect has supervened over and above instinct. This Bergson counts as somewhat of a misfortune, as indeed Rousseau had done before him. Man's intellect has tended to stifle his instincts and has thus robbed him of his freedom. For the intellect imposes its own conceptual constraints on the world and thus gives a distorted picture of it. We have indeed come a long way from the rationalist doctrine that sees in the intellect a force for liberation.

The highest form of instinct is intuition, which is some kind of mental activity directly in tune with the world. Where intellect distorts, intuition grasps experience as it is. The trouble with intellect, according to Bergson, is that it is adequate only to the discontinuity of the material world. This view is evidently linked with the notion of language as a framework of discontinuous concepts. As for life, this is essentially continuous, the intellect cannot understand it. Here, it seems, we must fall back on intuition. The distinction between intellect and intuition is connected, for Bergson, with a parallel distinction between space and time. The intellect, which breaks up or analyses the world operates in a timeless, dreamlike fashion. To use our previous contrast between the theoretical and the practical, in the etymological sense of these words, the intellect is theoretical. It looks at the world in a geometrical way, for it there is space but not time. But life is a practical business which flows in time, and this is where intuition intervenes. The spatial dissections effected by the intellect have some point, of course, but they are a hindrance to a proper understanding of life. The time of physical theory is not a genuine time, but rather a kind of spatial metaphor; the real time of intuition Bergson calls duration. What this might be is however not easy to explain. Bergson seems to think of it as a kind of bare experience which overwhelms us when we refrain from rational thought and merely let ourselves drift on the crest of time. It may be suggested that this notion is somewhere akin to the existential modes of cognition mentioned by Kierkegaard and taken up, in modified form, by later existentialists.

BIBLIOTHÈQUE
DE PHILOSOPHIE CONTEMPORAINE

L'ÉVOLUTION
CRÉATRICE

PAR

HENRI BERGSON

PARIS
FÉLIX ALCAN, ÉDITEUR

1907

Title page of Creative Evolution, Bergson's best known work

Bergson's theory of time is linked with his account of memory. In memory the conscious mind contrives some kind of communion between the past and the present. The past is acting no longer while the present is active now. This way of talking, of course, assumes precisely that mathematical time which elsewhere he is at pains to discard in favour of duration. The past and present must be separate for the statement about activity to make sense. Besides, there is a simple confusion which arises from the double meaning that attaches to the word memory. By memory we understand sometimes the mental activity of remembering here and now, and sometimes the past event, which is being thus remembered. By confusing the mental activity with its object, Bergson is led to speak of past and present as mingling.

It is in line with the anti-rationalist bent of Bergson's thinking that, on the whole, he is not given to providing reasons, either good or bad, for the views he invites us to accept. Instead, he relies on a certain poetic quality in his illustrations. This is all very colourful and pleasing but does not necessarily convince the reader. Indeed, this is a difficulty with any set of maxims which intends to curtail the scope of reason. For to speak of grounds for acceptance is already to move within the sphere of the rational.

I. P. Pavlov (1849-1936), Russian physiologist, worked on the conditioned reflex

Pavlov in his laboratory

The Bergsonian theory may perhaps best be regarded as suggesting some psychological rather than logical features of experience. In this sense it is in line with certain trends in psychological theory. Similar considerations apply to existentialism. The great new development in the field of psychology was the theory of psycho-analysis. But before embarking on a brief discussion of it, we must mention another trend in psychology which is in many ways opposed to this, to wit an approach which is generally called behaviourism.

The behaviourist school of psychology is an offshoot from positivism. It denies the seemingly occult entities of the old introspective kind of psychology and declares in favour of overt behaviour. Only what people are observed to be doing counts. At best we may use, in our conceptual framework for describing behaviour, dispositions to act in certain ways under given circumstances. These are openly observable matters that can be tested much in the way that experiments are conducted by the physical scientist. A simple extension of this approach is to seek purely physico-chemical and physiological explanations for pyschological events. This kind of theory thus tends to be materialist and positivist in the sense explained. One of the most widely publicised aspects in this line of development is the work of the Russian physiologist Pavlov on conditioned reflexes. Everyone has heard of Pavlov and his salivating dogs. Very roughly the experiment consists in providing food for the animal at the same time as showing it some signal, for instance a shape on a screen. After a while the shape alone came to be sufficient to produce the physiological effects that one would have expected to go with the provision of food. Saliva started to flow at the mere showing of the signal. This kind of reaction was called a conditioned reflex.

What these researches are supposed to show is that the concrete, observable situation reveals certain linked events, with connections that can be to some extent altered through enforced habits. On this point the explanation uses associationist psychology in a fairly traditional, Humean manner. But in addition the implication seems to be that there is no need to postulate such occult entities as thought; all that can be said is covered by the observable linked events.

This is perhaps an extreme formulation of the case, and no doubt some qualifications are required. However, for our present purpose it is enough to indicate the trend. In philosophy, a somewhat similar development is found in certain forms of linguistics which do away with meaning in the traditional sense and substitute actual use of language, or the disposition to use it in certain ways on the appropriate occasion. Like Pavlov's dogs, we are supposed to salivate rather than think.

Quite the opposite approach is found in the psychological doctrines that are associated with the name of Sigmund Freud (1856–1939). Starting from a fairly biological point of view, Freud eventually moved to a psychology that embraces hidden entities without stint. Of central importance to his theory is the notion of the subconscious mind, which by its very nature is not directly observable. Leaving aside, for the moment, the question whether this theory is sound, it must be repeated here that it is at any rate quite a proper scientific hypothesis. Those who reject it out of hand from a positivist bias fail to understand the function of hypothesis in scientific method. But to return to Freud, the theory of the subconscious mind and its ways of working provide the means for several important developments in psychological theory. The first of these is Freud's general theory of dreams, published in 1900 under the title of 'The Interpretation of Dreams'; the second, connected with the former, is his theory of forgetting, a layman's account of which appeared, in 1904, in the 'Psychopathology of Everyday Life'.

What distinguishes dreaming from being awake and conscious is that the former allows a kind of freedom and phantasy, which in our waking life would not stand up to the hard facts that confront us. But this freedom of the dreamer is after all more apparent than real. This must be the outcome of any general theory of dreams. In Freud's work, the general hypothesis is that in dreams we attain the fulfilment of wishes and desires which in ordinary life are repressed for a variety of reasons. The mechanism of repression and the detailed structure of the individual's psychological apparatus we cannot go into here. It is sufficient to point out that the dreamer shuffles and reconstructs, with some latitude, a variety of elements grounded in immediate experience, and the repressed wishes not only of the day, but those that reach back sometimes even to early childhood. The task of interpretation is to unravel the real meaning of the dream. This involves the recognition of certain symbols that intervene in the process of repression, in order to hide some uncomfortable truth, or avoid calling a spade a spade when this might not be countenanced. In the course of these interpretations Freud built up a whole list of symbols, though in all fairness it must be said that he himself was more guarded in their use than were his followers. On the therapeutic side, and it must be remembered that Freud was a medical man, an uncovering or psycho-analysis of these processes was held to be necessary for the adjustment of neurotic disorders occasioned by repression. Analysis was indeed not sufficient to effect a cure, but without it no attempt was even possible. The therapeutic conception of knowledge is, of course, not new. As we have seen, it was held already by Socrates. Contemporary linguistic analysts hold a very similar view about philosophic puzzles, which they assimilate to linguistic neuroses, to be cured by analysis.

As to forgetting, Freud connects this with a similar mechanism of repression. We forget because in some sense we are afraid to remember. In order to cure our forgetfulness we must come to understand what it is that makes us shrink from remembering.

The Freudian theory has in any case the merit of making a serious attempt at giving a general scientific account of dreams. In some of its details it is no doubt not altogether convincing. The Freudian dictionary of symbols, for instance, does not seem altogether acceptable. What has, of course, brought psycho-analysis greater notice than it might otherwise have had was the frank recognition of sexual behaviour and its repression. At the same time, this circumstance has made it the target of much unenlightened abuse.

Sigmund Freud (1856-1939), founder of psycho-analysis. His Psychopathology of Everyday Life (1904) saw three editions by 1910

Zur

Psychopathologie des Alltagslebens

(Über Vergessen, Versprechen, Vergreifen, Aberglaube und Irrtum)

Von

Prof. Dr. Sigm. Freud

in Wien

Dritte, vermehrte Auflage

Nun ist die Luft von solchem Spuk so voll,
Daß niemand weiß, wie er ihn meiden soll.
Faust, II. Teil, V. Akt.

BERLIN 1910
VERLAG VON S. KARGER
KARLSTRASSE 15

Since the turn of the century, the dominant force in American philosophy has been a modified form of pragmatism. The chief representative of this movement was John Dewey (1859–1952). Of New England ancestry, he was steeped in the old liberal tradition of that region. His interests were always widespread and went beyond academic philosophy. Perhaps his main influence has been in the field of education, a subject on which he had much to say from the time when, in 1894, he became professor of philosophy at the university of Chicago. If in our own time the distinction between education in the traditional sense, and vocational training as increasingly demanded by a technological society, has become somewhat blurred, this is in part due to the influence of Dewey's work.

There are, in Dewey's philosophy, three central notions that link it with certain earlier developments. The pragmatic element we have already mentioned. Dewey shares with Peirce the view that inquiry is all-important. There is next an emphasis on action, which is Bergsonian rather than pragmatist. It is true, as we saw, that the pragmatists also were convinced of the importance of action. But here we must recall that James misunderstood Peirce, and that Peirce's activity is much rather the sort of thing that Vico had in mind when he formulated the 'verum factum' equation. Thirdly, there is in Dewey's theory a strong measure of Hegelian thinking. This comes out in particular in his insistence on organic or unified wholes as the ultimate goal of inquiry. The logical steps which occur in the process are thus viewed as instruments towards the whole. This instrumental conception of logic has much in common with the Hegelian dialectic, if we consider this as an instrument that leads to the complete system. Following the pragmatist school, Dewey does not wish to be hamstrung by the traditional conceptions of truth and falsehood as they have come down to us from the mathematical philosophy of Pythagoras and Plato. Instead, Dewev speaks of warranted assertability, a notion which is derivative from Peirce; though we should add the rider that the later Peirce allowed the existence of one answer to any question, however remote the attaining of it.

John Dewey (1859-1952)

On this general question of doing away with truth in the absolute sense, we can apply the criticism that was mentioned already in connection with Protagoras. Suppose someone asserts that I am a nuisance. If, in a pragmatist mood, I were to ask him whether he had warrant for this assertion, what is the fellow to reply? It may in fact be useful to him to hold such views about me, in which case he might feel tempted to answer my question in the affirmative. But whether he say yes or no, he at once goes beyond his own pragmatist principles. For this is no longer a question of warrant. He does not think of second order expediences or warrants at all; this, indeed, leads straight into an infinite regress. On the contrary, in answering yes or no, he implicitly recognizes an absolute sense of truth. This is not altered by the eventual circumstance of his being mistaken as to the facts of the matter. He may in good faith give a reply that turns out to be false. Nevertheless, he must implicitly accept an absolute standard in order to give any answer at all. This kind of criticism applies not only to pragmatic theories of truth, but to any theory that seeks to define truth in terms of other criteria.

It is not too difficult to see whence springs this sort of attempt at subsuming logic under action. At bottom, it is the Bergsonian complaint that on traditional objective views of logic nothing genuinely new can arise in the world. It is the demand for novelty and social expansion that inspires this sort of theorizing. In this there is, in the end, a confusion between the variety of human activity and the invariable framework in which it is given expression in language and logic. A failure to recognize these standards is apt to make men overstep the measures and forget the limitations of their powers.

A. N. Whitehead (1861-1947)

The other main figure we must mention here is my former colleague A. N. Whitehead (1861–1947). We have already met him as a mathematical logician. After Principia Mathematica his interests gradually changed in the direction of philosophic problems arising from contemporary science, and ultimately he turned to metaphysics. In 1924, he virtually began a new career, being appointed professor of philosophy at Harvard. The writings that belong to these later years are often very obscure and difficult to read. Though, of course, to say that a book is difficult is not in itself a criticism, I must confess that the metaphysical speculations of Whitehead are somewhat strange to me. I will try, however, to state them briefly.

Whitehead holds that in order to grasp the world we must not follow the tradition of Galileo and Descartes, which divides the real into primary and secondary qualities. On this path we merely reach a picture distorted by rationalist categories. The world much rather consists of an infinite collection of full-blooded events, each of which seems to be somewhat reminiscent of a Leibnizian monad. However, unlike monads, events are momentary and die away to give rise to new events. These events somehow happen to objects. Sets of events might be thought of as a Heraclitean flux, and objects as Parmenidean Spheres. Separately they are, of course, abstractions; in actual processes both are inseparably connected.

As for genuine contact with the real, this seems to require a knowing from within, a conflation of the knower and his object into a single entity. We are reminded of Spinoza here, and Whitehead does, indeed, maintain that every proposition should ultimately be viewed in its relation to the universal system. This is clearly a form of systematic Idealism, though it is not quite of the character of the Idealist strains in Dewey's philosophy. Where Dewey's conception of wholes goes back to Hegel, the Idealism of Whitehead has more in common with the organic notions of the later Schelling.

This, very briefly, seems to be the theme of Whitehead's metaphysics. What standing it will come to have in the history of philosophy I do not profess to know. What is, however, of immediate interest is the way in which a metaphysical doctrine here arises directly from an interest in certain general problems of science. Indeed, we have seen the same thing in the case of the seventeenth century rationalists and the nineteenth century idealists. Insofar as scientific theory attempts to embrace the whole world, it pursues an aim which is similar to that of metaphysics. Where science differs is in its greater responsibility to hard, recalcitrant facts.

If the nineteenth century may be said to have changed the world more thoroughly than anything up till then, the same holds for the last fifty years, in which the transformation has been, if anything, even more intense. The first world war marks the end of an era.

The leading idea that had inspired men for several generations was the notion of progress. It seemed that the world was moving towards a better and more civilized condition, with Western Europe as the benevolent master, and the rest of the world in political and technical dependence. In some ways this view of the world was not unjustified. The West was certainly dominant both politically and in its grasp of material power provided by industry. All this was backed by tremendous self-confidence, and the feeling that God was on the side of progress. The growth of industrial society brought with it a steep rise in population. Within a century numbers in England increased five-fold, and yet the gloomy prophesies of Malthus had not come true. On the contrary, as industrial society began to overcome its initial problems, the general way of life of the community became gradually more comfortable.

As a result of these changes there prevailed a feeling of optimism and confidence in the future which, on the whole, has since been somewhat shaken. This general optimistic tone is shared by all the major intellectual trends of the century. Utilitarianism, pragmatism and materialism are all imbued with it. The most spectacular example is perhaps the case of Marxist doctrine. This has succeeded in preserving its belief in the inevitability of progress even into the present. It is the only political theory which has maintained its ingenuous faith in spite of the disturbances that have upset the world since then. In its inflexible dogmatism and its utopian outlook Marxism is a relic of the nineteenth century.

In Victorian times, life seemed solid, set and sound. The world was well-organized and stable

In such an atmosphere of progress, it seemed to men that the world was set on firm foundations. This bias coloured the thinking not only of those whose material condition there and then allowed them to take such an optimistic view. The underprivileged, likewise, felt that their lot could and would be improved, a hope which was indeed not disappointed in the event. Meanwhile, the provision of universal education served to show the way in which men could better themselves. For in this new society those who had not the advantage of position could rise above their station through knowledge and skill.

This competitive element is something new in the social field. Competition between traders is, of course, as old as trade itself. But the notion that a man could better himself through his own efforts was of more recent origin. In medieval times it was universally accepted that everyone had been put into his appointed place by God, and that it was sinful to tamper with an order divinely ordained. These older views had been called into question by the thinkers of the renaissance; the nineteenth century dismissed them altogether.

The conditions we are here describing belong, of course, to those regions only where industrialism was gaining a foothold. This includes England and parts of Western Europe. It is well to remember that these areas amount to a minute fraction of the inhabited globe. The influence these countries have had on world history as a result of their greater development has been quite out of proportion to their numbers. But this, too, is nothing new in human affairs. In sheer size, the Persian Empire of old was vast compared with Greece, its influence was ultimately negligible.

To those who lived in this period inspired with the thought of progress, it seemed possible to plan ahead with confidence. Conditions were settled enough to make it reasonable for men to view their prospective careers as a whole. At the same time, these plans were entirely a personal matter. It was through one's own sustained efforts that one achieved standing and security. As to the underprivileged, the attitude was one of charity and voluntary assistance by high-minded and responsible private citizens. The first steps towards the provision of social welfare were taken, oddly enough, by Bismarck, who introduced a form of health insurance for workers, in order to take the wind from the sails of his socialist opponents.

Funeral procession, in 'Entr'acte', René Clair's film (1924): the old values ridiculed, stability gone

Another outstanding feature of this period was its generally liberal outlook in politics. It was taken for granted that government was a marginal activity, whose function it was to adjudicate between clashing interests. Interference in the running of industry or trade was not even thought of. That nowadays governments themselves run a variety of enterprises is the result of Marxist influence on our general approach to social questions. As to freedom of movement, this was completely unrestricted throughout most parts of Europe. Then, as now, Russia was somewhat of an exception. You could travel anywhere in Western Europe without papers of any kind, except in the Tsar's Empire, where a passport was required. At the same time, people did not travel as much as they do now. Partly this was due to the greater cost involved which restricted movement to those who were relatively well-to-do. The controls that have since been introduced show how far international confidence has decayed.

In the political sphere, Western Europe from 1870 onwards enjoyed nearly fifty years of peace. This happy state of affairs was indeed not world-wide. There were colonial conflicts in Africa, and in the Far East, Russia suffered defeat at the hands of Japan, which had made rapid strides in its attempt at absorbing the technical civilization of the West. Still, to someone living in our parts, the world seemed a reasonably peaceful place. This was the situation only fifty years ago. When one looks back on it, one is apt to feel that people in those times lived as though in a world of dreams.

This entire framework of values and preconceptions was destroyed by the World War of 1914–1918. In spite of the greater national consciousness that had developed in the course of the nineteenth century, those differences had so far been contained. Now they broke loose upon the world a blood-bath the like of which had not until that time been experienced. Along with this catastrophe went the decay of confidence in progress and the growth of a climate of suspicion from which the world has never quite recovered.

FEBRUARY, 1920. *League of Nations—Official Journal.*

The Covenant of the League of Nations.

THE HIGH CONTRACTING PARTIES,

In order to promote international co-operation and to achieve international peace and security

by the acceptance of obligations not to resort to war,

by the prescription of open, just and honourable relations between nations,

by the firm establishment of the understandings of international law as the actual rule of conduct among Governments, and

by the maintenance of justice and a scrupulous respect for all treaty obligations in the dealings of organised peoples with one another,

Agree to this Covenant of the League of Nations.

ARTICLE I.

The original Members of the League of Nations shall be those of the Signatories which

The League of Nation's articles, outcome of the first World War

On the purely technical side the first World War showed how far the refinement of weapons had outpaced the tactical conceptions of military men. The result was a tremendous and inconclusive slaughter which greatly weakened Western Europe. The weak and unstable condition of France since 1918 is to a large extent the legacy of this blood-letting. At the same time the United States now began to play an increasingly central role in world affairs. On the other side, Russia went through the Bolshevik revolution and built up a new industrialised society vastly more powerful than the Tsarist Empire ever had been. Nationalist feelings that had been smouldering beneath the surface since the Congress of Vienna now found expression in the form of new national states, each of which was suspicious of its neighbours. Freedom of movement became hedged about with restrictions which are only now beginning to disappear again.

Nevertheless, it had become clear that further internecine warfare amongst European nations was going henceforth to threaten the very survival of Western Civilization. This was the main driving force behind the setting-up of the League of Nations in 1919. One of the chief protagonists of this attempt at laying the foundation for peaceful co-operation amongst nations was President Wilson of the United States. The fact that his proposals were not in the end supported by his own country did much to weaken the position of the League from its very beginning. In the meantime, the defeat of the central powers called forth, by way of reaction, a fiercer and more uncompromising nationalist revival than had yet arisen. The National Socialist dictatorship of Germany led, within twenty years of the foundation of the League of Nations, to the second World War, which in scope and destruction surpassed any previous war in history. The greater technical power of armaments and the stronger ideological motives at stake turned the business of warfare between armies into total war, which directly affected civilians as much as soldiers. Atomic warfare saw its first spectacular demonstration in Japan. This ultimate achievement in destructive power has now placed within man's reach the possibility of self-extermination. Whether we shall be wise enough to resist this temptation remains to be seen. It is to be hoped that the United Nations, which after the Second World War took the place of the old League, will succeed in restraining men from blasting each other out of existence.

Throughout history, the two main forces that have given special impetus to technical development are trade and war. Recent events have done this in a spectacular manner. The growth of electronic and communication engineering has produced what is now called by some the second industrial revolution. This is transforming the world under our very eyes in a manner more radical even than the first industrial revolution, which was based on the steam engine.

Likewise, the means of transport have undergone a change undreamt of in the nineteenth century. Modes of travel had changed relatively little from Roman times until the advent of railways. Since then man has turned the legend of Icarus into reality. Only some eighty years ago it seemed fantastic that one might circle the globe in eighty days. Now it is possible to do it in as many hours.

These far-reaching developments have in some ways gone ahead faster than man has been able to adjust himself to his new surroundings. To begin with, the great international conflicts have done something towards undermining the sense of security which had prevailed in the previous century. It was no longer possible to take a long range view of things quite in the same way. At the same time, the activities of states have heavily encroached upon the freedom of action that once belonged to the individual. For this there are a variety of reasons. In the first place, the growing complexity of the economic life of industrial nations has rendered them very sensitive to all kinds of disturbances. Compared with medieval times, our own society is much less stable. It is therefore necessary to exercise some measure of control over forces that can upset the body politic. Secondly, there arises the problem of providing some balancing influence to counteract the inevitable fluctuations that do occur. This involves state action in economic matters. Thirdly, the loss of security independently achieved is now to some extent compensated by services provided by the state. These changes have very little to do with the political system of a country. They depend primarily on the technology of our civilization. It is indeed remarkable how much alike these matters look in countries that are politically very different from each other.

The crushing weight of organization in modern living has called forth new strains of irrationalist thinking in philosophy. In some sense these outbursts are a reaction against the power philosophies that have inspired contemporary autocratic regimes. It is also a revolt against what is felt to be the threat of science to human freedom.

The main philosophic brand of irrationalism is to be found in the revived existentialist doctrines that have of late played such a dominant role in the philosophy of France and Germany. About this we shall presently make some brief comments; the important thing to note here is that this trend covers a vast range of different doctrines that are often at odds with each other.

Alongside the existentialist doctrines there has been, on the continent a return to traditional metaphysics. In Great Britain, philosophy has of late moved mainly in the linguistic groove. Never has the gap between continental and British philosophy been so great as it is today. Indeed, it is no longer even allowed by either side that the other is really doing philosophy.

This in the barest outline is the setting of the contemporary scene. In venturing to draw a general sketch one runs not only the risk of distortion, but also of lack of perspective. For this there is no remedy. Nevertheless, we may note one general conclusion. What has hitherto enabled Western civilization to dominate the world was its technology together with the scientific and philosophic tradition which gave rise to it. At the moment these forces still seem to be in command, though there is nothing in the nature of things why they must remain so. As the technical skills that were developed in the West spread to other parts of the world, so our position of vantage declines.

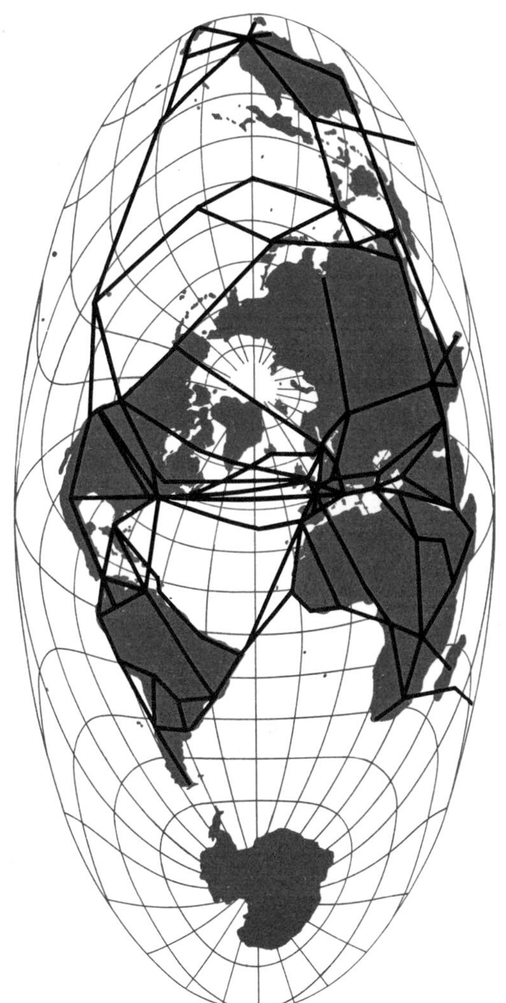

With the growth of air links, distances have shrunk

The existentialist philosophy of the continent is in some ways a rather puzzling business. Indeed, it is at times difficult to see in it anything that is recognizable as philosophy in the traditional sense. However, the general point of departure which is common to the entire movement seems to be this: rationalism as a philosophy is held to be unable to provide a viable account of the meaning of human existence. In using a system of concepts, the rationalist gives general descriptions that fail to catch the specific tang of individual human experience. To overcome this apparent failure, existentialists fall back on the sort of thing that Kierkegaard had called existential modes of thinking. Rationalism, in tackling the world from the outside, falls short of doing justice to the immediacy of living experience; this must be grasped existentially from within.

Karl Jaspers

To this apparent puzzle one may give different kinds of treatment. One might to begin with be tempted to suggest that human life has no meaning or significance in the sense required for these speculations. The purpose of life is to live it in as interesting a manner as possible; ulterior purposes are chimerical. Besides, there is a serious weakness in the very conception of existential modes of thinking. If you reflect on the existence of anything, you must be thinking of something of a given kind. Existence by itself alone is a vicious abstraction. Not even Hegel is unaware of this.

But these are sledge-hammer arguments; valid no doubt, yet apt to prevent us from seeing clearly what these thinkers are hinting at. We must therefore take a somewhat ampler view of existentialism, and attempt to indicate briefly what it is trying to show.

For all its rejection of Idealist metaphysics, the existential philosophy of Karl Jaspers, in its recognition of three kinds of being, retains a certain element of dialectic in the Hegelian sense. Jaspers (1883–) came to philosophy through an earlier interest in psychology, and more especially problems of psycho-pathology. Thus, man stands at the centre of his philosophic studies. In this sense we may describe his existentialism as humanist, a phrase that has been used by Sartre about his own brand of philosophy. But in contrast to the objective humanism of the renaissance, existentialism provides at best a subjective humanism. It is therefore somewhat misleading for existentialist philosophers to use Sartre's dictum.

In Jaspers' theory of being, we are confronted with three different notions. At the lowest level, we have the objective world which is simply there. Its being is thus a being-there, grasped from the outside, objectively. It covers the field of science in all its aspects. But it is not adquate to the proper recognition by the self of its own existence. Indeed, the objective existence that holds in the scientific field is a hindrance to a feeling for this higher kind of being, which Jaspers calls being-I, or simply existence. This mode of being is no longer responsible to the rational categories that rule the field of objective being. The being-I, or personal existence, is said always to point beyond itself. It would not do Jaspers an injustice to describe this in Aristotelian terms by saying that, for him, personal existence contains within itself an indeterminate fund of potentialities. In striving

Karl Jaspers

beyond itself, the I attunes itself to a third sort of being, which may be called transcendent, a being-in-itself that includes both former varieties. Although Jaspers does not pursue the kind of aim that inspired the Idealists, it is nevertheless very obvious that his three kinds of being constitute a pretty example of dialectic progression. To this extent they must somehow be within the scope of the rational. This, as we have seen before, is an inherent difficulty of any theory which attempts to curtail reason in principle. It is, of course, quite proper to point out simple home-truths like the fact that men are moved by passions as much or even more than by reason; this is not in principle a restriction of reason. But when it comes to a theory of reason that tries to invalidate reason itself, there arises an uncomfortable contradiction. For it is necessary to enlist reason in order to give an account of anything whatever. A denial of the competence of reason can thus not be given a theoretical cloak; it remains ineffable and constrains us to silence. To some extent this is indeed vaguely recognized by existentialists, who therefore at times advocate silence, even if they do not themselves practise it. As to Jaspers, he is aware of the difficulty and tries to make amends by allowing that reason is after all important.

Martin Heidegger

On the basis of this division of being, Jaspers maintains that science, being of necessity interpretative in character, must fail to gain a genuine grasp of reality. For, in allowing a distinction between the interpretation and its object, we implicitly admit that we have failed. The assumption seems to be that all statements are a distortion of facts, merely because a statement is not identical with the situation that is its object. Thus, because statements are about something else, they are held to be inadequate. It is to be noted that a statement is here regarded as inadequate of its very nature, and not, as with Idealism, because it stands in isolation from a range of other statements that would give it its full meaning.

Philosophy, for Jaspers, pertains to the transcendent kind of being, or being-in-itself. Or rather, philosophy is the striving of the individual in its endeavour to transcend. As to the moral life of the individual, this operates on the plane of personal existence. It is at this level that men understand each other, and experience the feeling of freedom. Since freedom lies outside the rational sphere, we can not give a rational account of it. We must content ourselves to recognize its manifestations in certain moods. Our feeling that we are free is said to go with a certain mood of apprehension, or dread, as Jaspers calls it, borrowing a phrase from Kierkegaard. In general we may say that whereas the level of being-there is governed by reason, the field of being-I is ruled by moods.

While the existentialism of Jaspers, at the transcendent level, allows room for religion, as did Kierkegaard's, a very different tone prevails in the more metaphysically coloured works of Heidegger (1889–). Highly eccentric in its terminology, his philosophy is extremely obscure. One cannot help suspecting that language is here running riot. An interesting point in his speculations is the insistence that nothingness is something positive. As with much else in existentialism, this is a psychological observation made to pass for logic.

In France, the existentialist movement has had more intimate connections with literature. Its best-known exponent, Jean Paul Sartre (1905–) has written not only a weighty philosophic treatise, but also novels. In these much of his existentialist thinking is presented through characters faced with the kind of call for action which is so important a facet of existentialism. The literary medium of the novel provides the perfect vehicle for reflections on the human predicament.

In Sartre, the existentialist view of human freedom is taken to the limit. Man continuously chooses his destiny. There are no links with tradition or with preceding events in the life of the individual. It is as though every new decision requires some kind of total commitment. Those who are frightened by this unpleasant truth will try to seek protection from rationalising the world. In this the man of science is at one with the religious believer. Both are trying to escape from reality. But for Sartre they are both sadly mistaken. The world is not as science sees it; and as for God, it would seem that He has been dead since the time of Nietzsche. The person who is prepared to face the world as it is reminds one indeed of Nietzsche's hero. It is from this source that Sartre derives his atheism.

Jean Paul Sartre

What is at bottom opposed by Sartre is the rationalist conception of necessity, as found in Leibniz and Spinoza, and inherited by the Idealist philosophers. It will be recalled that for these thinkers everything that is can in principle be seen as necessary, provided we take a sufficiently ample view. It is then inevitable that a doctrine of freedom takes the form we find in Spinoza or Hegel. Freedom consists in a being attuned to the workings of necessity. Once such a view of freedom is rejected, as it is by Sartre, the rest seems to follow almost of itself. The rationalist view of necessity dominates, as we have previously remarked, in the field of theoretical science. This must therefore be rejected as soon as we adopt the existentialist doctrine of freedom. Likewise, rationalist theology must be abandoned, though it would seem that Sartre is going too far in trying to tie this in with atheism. For if we are free in the sense in which Sartre thinks we are, then we can choose whatever we will. In this matter different existentialist thinkers have in fact chosen differently, as we have seen already.

In its criticism of the rationalist view of necessity, existentialism is drawing attention to an important point. However, it does not make a philosophic criticism so much as an emotional protest on psychological grounds. It is from a mood of feeling oppressed that existentialism stages its rebellion against rationalism. This leads into a somewhat strange and personal attitude towards the world of fact which constitutes an obstacle to freedom. The rationalist sees his freedom in a knowledge of how nature works; the existentialist finds it in an indulgence of his moods.

The basic logical point behind all this goes back to Schelling's criticism of Hegel. Existence cannot be deduced from general logical principles. This is a criticism that any orthodox empiricist would cheerfully endorse. But this much having been said, nothing more needs to be added. Indeed, it seems that one would subvert this admirable criticism by proceeding to deduce, on the basis of it, an existentialist psychology. For this is precisely what Sartre's theory comes to. There is much interesting and valuable observation in the description of a variety of psychological states. But that men behave and feel in this manner is not a logical consequence of the fact that existence is not logically necessary. To go the other way would be to admit and reject Schelling's point in one and the same breath. While, therefore, one may well recognize the psychological observations as accurate, it will not do to turn this material into an ontology. This is precisely the object of Sartre's treatise entitled 'Being and Nothingness'. For poetic vagueness and linguistic extravagance this is in the best of German traditions. Its attempt at turning a particular outlook on life into an ontological theory seems somewhat eccentric to the traditional philosopher, whether he belong to the rationalist or the empiricist camp. It is as though one were to turn Dostoevsky's novels into philosophic text-books.

Gabriel Marcel

It may be remarked that existentialists would probably reject our criticisms as beside the point. For, they would say, we are using rationalist criteria. Instead of addressing ourselves to existential issues we are moving within the field of rationalist logic. This may indeed be so. But the objection can be turned against itself. This is merely another way of saying that any criteria whatsoever operate within the field of reason. So, too, does language. It is therefore dangerous to make use of it in advocating existentialist doctrines. Alternatively, one may, of course, content oneself with a kind of poetic effusion from which everyone may profit as best he may.

The existentialist philosophy of Gabriel Marcel (1889–), unlike that of Sartre, is religiously inclined. In this it somewhat resembles the theories of Jaspers. Like all existentialist thinkers, Marcel is particularly interested in the individual and his concrete experience of peculiarly human situations. As to philosophy in general, what Marcel emphasizes is the need to go beyond the ordinary kind of reflection which dissects and analyses. In order to see reality in the fullest sense we must put the slices of our rationalist dissection together again. This synthetic operation is achieved through what Marcel calls reflection to the second power. This is meant to convey the notion of a more intense and higher form of reflection. Where reflection to the first power is directed outwards, this higher reflection to the second power looks inwards on itself.

One of the problems which Marcel is concerned with is the body-mind relation. This arises from his interest in the human predicament as it strikes the individual in some given real setting. The criticism he levels at the dualism of the Cartesians is reminiscent of Berkeley's criticism against those who confuse seeing with geometrical optics. We might say that the division of mind from body presupposes a metaphor that regards the mind as somehow hovering over the person and seeing itself and the body as two distinct things. This, roughly, seems to be Marcel's point, and it is sound enough. However, he connects the resolution of the problem to the exercise of synthetic reflection, whereas we should feel inclined to hold that here a little linguistic analysis will show what has gone wrong.

The positivism which grew about the turn of the century was represented by men like Mach, whose work on mechanics we have already mentioned. During the twenty years that followed, there gradually developed a somewhat wider interest in symbolic logic. These two tendencies combined led to the formation of a new movement which centred round Schlick. Like Mach, he was a professor at the University of Vienna. The group of which he was the leader was called the Vienna Circle, and their philosophy came to be known as Logical Positivism.

As the name implies, this doctrine was in the first instance positivist. It holds that the sum total of our knowledge is provided by science, and that metaphysics in the old style is strictly empty verbiage. There is nothing we can know beyond experience. In this we find some affinity with Kantian ideas, if we omit noumena. Along with their insistence on empirical observation goes a criterion of meaning which is somewhat linked with the routine pragmatism of the laboratory scientist. This is the famous principle of verifiability, according to which the meaning of a proposition is its method of verification. It derives from Mach, who used this kind of procedure in defining the terms used in mechanics.

The logical positivist movement which started in Vienna did not survive where it was born. Schlick was killed in 1936 by one of his students, and the other members found it necessary to settle elsewhere owing to the impending strictures of the Nazi regime. All of them eventually found their way to America or England. Carnap is still at Chicago, and Waissmann at Oxford. In line with the general unifying tendency of the language of science, the movement began to publish, just before the war, the first monographs of what was to become an International Encyclopedia of Unified Science. The series is published by the Chicago University Press; its first editor, O. Neurath, died in England in 1945. Logical positivism thus came to be transplanted from its native soil to the English speaking countries, where it linked up again with the old tradition of British Empiricism, to which it is in some measure indebted. In England, the logical positivist doctrine first gained widespread notice through A. J. Ayer's 'Language, Truth and Logic' (1936).

Within the positivist movement, there reigned a shared contempt for metaphysics, and reverence for science. But for the rest, there were considerable differences on matters of logic and scientific method. In particular, the verifiability principle gave rise to a number of different interpretations. The history of the movement really hinges on the discussion that developed round questions concerning the status and significance of the principle.

One preliminary criticism against the verifiability theory of meaning is that it suffers from the same kind of difficulty as the pragmatic theory of truth. For suppose that we have found some method of verifying a proposition. If we give a descriptive account of the procedure we may now ask what is the meaning of this account. This leads at once into an infinite regress of meanings to be verified, unless at some stage we admit that the meaning of a proposition

International Encyclopedia of Unified Science

Editor-in-chief Otto Neurath

Associate Editors Rudolf Carnap Charles W. Morris

Foundations of the Unity of Science

(Volumes I-II of the Encyclopedia)

Committee of Organization

Rudolf Carnap	Charles W. Morris
Philipp Frank	Otto Neurath
Joergen Joergensen	Louis Rougier

Advisory Committee

Niels Bohr	R. von Mises
Egon Brunswik	G. Mannoury
J. Clay	Ernest Nagel
John Dewey	Arne Ness
Federigo Enriques	Hans Reichenbach
Herbert Feigl	Abel Rey
Clark L. Hull	Bertrand Russell
Waldemar Kaempffert	L. Susan Stebbing
Victor F. Lenzen	Alfred Tarski
Jan Lukasiewicz	Edward C. Tolman
William M. Malisoff	Joseph H. Woodger

Copyright 1939 by the University of Chicago
All Rights Reserved. Published May 1939
Fourth Impression 1947

The advisory committee of the Encyclopedia of Unified Science

simply stares us in the face. But if that were admitted, the original principle is destroyed, we might then as well allow that we can discern meanings directly at once.

A further difficulty in the positivist position is the rejection of all philosophic speculation as gibberish. For the verifiability theory is itself a philosophic doctrine. Schlick tried to avoid this impasse by arguing that the principle of verifiability is really ingrained in our behaviour, and to state it in so many words merely reminds us of how we do in fact proceed. But if this be so, then the principle is sound after all, and thus states a philosophic position. For it is agreed on all hands that it is not a statement of empirical science.

What Schlick attempts to do is to avoid the infinite regress of successive verifications. He holds that ultimately meanings are derived from self-illuminating experiences which in turn confer meaning on sentences. A similar aim was pursued by Carnap, who tried to work out a formal logical system reducing the epistemological problem to primitive ideas linked by the one basic relation of recognizing similarity.

This method of attack is based on a tacit assumption of some correspondence theory of truth. The weakness of such a theory as an account of the problem of knowledge is that it requires us to stand outside the arena in which experiences and sentences are to be compared. Neurath saw this difficulty and insisted that a sentence can be compared only with another sentence. What gives support to a sentence is, according to him, a 'protocol statement', which he regards as on the same level as ordinary empirical statements; that is to say, they are not necessary. Carnap adopted a similar view, but held that protocol statements were indubitable starting points, which somewhat smacks of Cartesianism. In either case, this way of tackling the problem lands us with a coherence theory of truth in the traditional rationalist fashion.

Carnap ultimately turned his attention to a very different approach to the central problem of the logical positivist philosophy. If one could invent a formalized language which is so constructed that unverifiable statement cannot be formulated within it, then the adoption of such a language would meet all positivist requirements. The principle of verifiability is, as it were, built into the syntax of the system. However, this way of dealing with the problem is inadequate too. For one thing, questions of meaning cannot be reduced to syntactic constructions, which concern the ways of putting words together. Besides, the construction of such a system tacitly assumes that all discoveries have by now been made. It is in some ways an equivalent to Hegel's systematizing, which was based on the similar view that the world had moved into its final stage.

One figure of some importance to the logical positivists, though not a member of the Vienna Circle, was Wittgenstein. His early logical theories had considerable influence on their thinking. It was, however, Wittgensteins' later, linguistic developments that gave logical positivism a new twist once it gained a foothold in England.

A sample of O. Neurath's use of pictorial symbols to overcome problems of communication

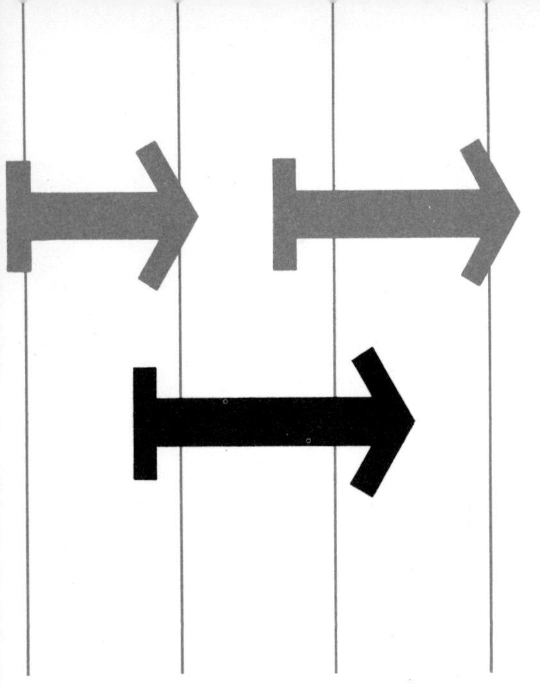

Of everything beginning in time we may ask what came before it

The positivist movement has given rise to a number of different branches. Of these one of the most important is the school of linguistic analysis which has dominated British philosophy for the last few decades. It shares with orthodox logical positivism the principle that all philosophical perplexities are the outcome of slovenly use of language. Every properly formulated question, so they would hold, has a clear and precise answer. It is the task of analysis to show that 'philosophical' questions arise from careless misuse of language. Once the ambiguities of such questions have been exhibited in broad daylight, the problems are shown to be meaningless and simply dissolve. Philosophy, when properly employed, is thus to be regarded as some kind of linguistic therapy.

A simple example will illustrate the method, though I do not accept the particular argument on this point. It often happens that someone asks himself the question of how it all began. What has started the world off, from what beginning did it take its course? Instead of providing an answer, let us first scrutinize the wording of the question. The central word figuring in it is the word 'beginning'. How is this word used in ordinary discourse? To settle this subsidiary query we must look at the kind of situation in which we ordinarily use the word. We might think perhaps of a symphony concert and speak of it as beginning at eight o'clock. Before the beginning we might have gone out to dinner in town, and after the concert we shall go home. The important thing to note is that it makes sense to ask what came before the beginning and what came after it. A beginning is a point in time marking a phase of something taking place in time. If now we return to the 'philosophical' question it is at once clear that there we are using the word 'beginning' in a different way altogether. For it is not intended that we should ever ask what came before the beginning of everything. Indeed, putting it this way we can see what is wrong with the question. To ask for a beginning with nothing preceding it is like asking for a round square. Once we have seen this we shall stop asking the question, because we see that it is senseless.

The philosophy of analysis in England has been greatly influenced by Wittgenstein (1889–1951), who at one time was in touch with the Vienna Circle. Like its members, he left before the gathering storm of Hitler's Germany and came to live in Cambridge, where he was appointed professor in 1939 when G. E. Moore retired. His only book to appear during his lifetime is the Tractatus Logico-Philosophicus, which was published in 1921. In this work he developed the view that all the truths of logic are tautological. A tautology in his technical sense is a proposition of which the contradictory is self-contradictory. The word tautological in this sense corresponds roughly to the more usual term analytic. In later years his interests led him away from logic to linguistic analysis. So far as records of his views exist they are to be found in lecture notes and in the posthumous collection of his papers, of which two volumes are so far to hand. Because of his peculiar and somewhat esotoric style he is not easy to describe in a summary fashion. Perhaps a fair statement of the basic tenet of his later philosophic theory is that the meaning of a word is its use.

A page from Wittgenstein's Tractatus Logico-Philosophicus

LOGISCH-PHILOSOPHISCHE ABHANDLUNG

würdige Tatsache, dass jeder Satz eine dieser Eigenschaften besitzt. Das scheint nun nichts weniger als selbstverständlich zu sein, ebensowenig selbstverständlich, wie etwa der Satz, „alle Rosen sind entweder gelb oder rot" klänge, auch wenn er wahr wäre. Ja, jener Satz bekommt nun ganz den Charakter eines naturwissenschaftlichen Satzes und dies ist das sichere Anzeichen dafür, dass er falsch aufgefasst wurde.

6.112 Die richtige Erklärung der logischen Sätze muss ihnen eine einzigartige Stellung unter allen Sätzen geben.

6.113 Es ist das besondere Merkmal der logischen Sätze, dass man am Symbol allein erkennen kann, dass sie wahr sind, und diese Tatsache schliesst die ganze Philosophie der Logik in sich. Und so ist es auch eine der wichtigsten Tatsachen, dass sich die Wahrheit oder Falschheit der nichtlogischen Sätze n i c h t am Satz allein erkennen lässt.

6.12 Dass die Sätze der Logik Tautologien sind, das z e i g t die formalen — logischen — Eigenschaften der Sprache, der Welt.

Dass ihre Bestandteile s o verknüpft eine Tautologie ergeben, das charakterisiert die Logik ihrer Bestandteile.

Damit Sätze, auf bestimmte Art und Weise verknüpft, eine Tautologie ergeben, dazu müssen sie bestimmte Eigenschaften der Struktur haben. Dass sie s o verbunden eine Tautologie ergeben, zeigt also, dass sie diese Eigenschaften der Struktur besitzen.

6.1201 Dass z. B. die Sätze „p" und „$\sim p$" in der Verbindung „$\sim(p \, . \sim p)$" eine Tautologie ergeben, zeigt, dass sie einander widersprechen. Dass die Sätze „$p \supset q$", „p" und „q" in der Form „$(p \supset q) \, . \, (p) : \supset : (q)$" miteinander verbunden eine Tautologie ergeben, zeigt, dass q aus p und $p \supset q$

156

In the course of presenting his account, Wittgenstein introduced the simile of 'language games'. According to this view, the actual use of some part of language is like a game, let us say like chess. It has certain rules that must be observed by those who play the game, and there are certain restrictions on the moves that are allowed. Wittgenstein completely repudiates his earlier logical work of the Tractatus. At that time it had seemed to him possible to analyze all statements into simple ultimate constituents that cannot be broken down any further. This theory is accordingly sometimes called logical atomism, and has much in common with earlier rationalist doctrines of simple ultimates. It is at the basis of all attempts at working out a perfect language, which will state everything with utmost precision. The later Wittgenstein denies that such a language can be constructed. We can never eliminate confusion completely.

Thus, by learning to play a variety of language games, we acquire the meaning of words through and in their use. Another way in which this is sometimes put speaks of our learning the 'grammar' or 'logic' of a word, a technical phrase which has gained widespread currency in linguistic analysis. The raising of metaphysical problems would then be the result of a defective grasp of the 'grammar' of words. For once the rules are properly understood, there survives no temptation to ask such questions. Linguistic therapy has cured us from the desire.

The influence of Wittgenstein on linguistic philosophy has been considerable. Nevertheless, linguistic analysis has in some measure gone its own several ways. In particular, there has evolved a new interest in linguistic distinctions irrespective of what beneficial cures this might effect. A new kind of scholasticism has sprung up, and like its medieval forerunner, is running itself into a somewhat narrow groove. What most of the various strands of linguistic analysis share is a belief that ordinary language is adequate, and puzzles arise from philosophic solecism. This view ignores the fact that ordinary language is shot through with the fading hues of past philosophic theories.

The example given earlier shows how the common use therapy is to be understood. This kind of analysis is certainly a useful weapon in clearing away much abstruse and tangled metaphysical cobweb. As a philosophical doctrine it has however some weaknesses. I should have thought, indeed, that philosophers had been doing this sort of thing on the quiet all along. That this is not willingly acknowledged nowadays is due to a certain intellectual parochialism which has been somewhat the fashion recently. A more serious matter is the enthronement of ordinary language as an arbiter in all disputes. It does not seem at all clear to me that ordinary language could not itself be seriously confused. At the very least it must be a risky business to treat it like the form of the Good without asking what language is, how it arises, functions and grows. The tacit assumption is that language as ordinarily used is possessed of some superior genius or hidden intelligence. A further assumption, linked indirectly with this, allows that one may ignore all un-linguistic knowledge, a dispensation liberally indulged by its adherents.

Ludwig Wittgenstein (1889-1951)

Epilogue

We have come to the end of our story. The reader who has followed thus far may ask himself what profit he has drawn from it. To him we must address a word of warning. On each of the main topics that we have discussed whole libraries have been written. Some small fraction of this mass of material will have been considered in the writing of the present volume. The perusal of one book, however vast its scope, has never yet transformed the reader into an expert. Indeed, no amount of mere reading will of itself improve one's understanding of anything. What is required in addition to the acquiring of information is some measure of intense reflection upon the several matters thus gathered in. This, too, is one excuse for histories of philosophy, when on each single issue that comes up for treatment so much more detailed works have been provided by specialists. To the layman, and indeed to the scholar too, it is of some importance at times to sit back and take a synoptic view. For this he needs a survey which is not too bulky nor too detailed, and above all one that has gone through a single brain. Our account is not encyclopaedic in the literal sense. There has, of necessity, been some selection, both of men and ideas. At best one can hope to provide an outline of the general trends. Likewise, the historical background material is severely schematic and condensed. This book does not set out to teach the reader history; rather, it tries to remind him of it from time to time, so that the setting in which philosophic views have grown should not be forgotten. At the same time it underlines the continuity in the cultural traditions of the West from early Greece to our own day.

It may be asked us why in a history such as this we leave no room for what is usually called the wisdom of the East. To this one may give several answers. In the first place, the two worlds have grown in isolation from each other, so that a self-contained account of Western thought is permissible. Besides, this is already a sufficiently formidable task; and we have chosen to restrict our scope to that subject. But there is another, more compelling reason why one might do this. For in some vital respects the philosophic tradition of the West differs from the speculations of the Eastern mind. There is no civilization but the Greek in which a philosophic movement goes hand in hand with a scientific tradition. It is this that gives the Greek enterprise its peculiar scope; it is this dual tradition that has shaped the civilization of the West.

It is of some moment to be clear on this peculiar relationship. The pursuit of scientific enquiry in some given field is not the same thing as philosophy. But one of the sources of philosophic reflection lies in science. When we consider what it is, in general, to be scientific, we are dealing with a philosophic question. The study of the canons of scientific method is a philosophic study. One of the perennial problems that has occupied the attention of philosophers is the attempt of giving an account of what the world is like, in its general features. But let us be careful here to draw a distinction. It is not a proper aim for philosophic study to give a description of facts in the way of science. A failure to respect this limitation caused the systematic idealists to go astray at times. What philosophy can provide is a way of looking at the results of empirical enquiry, a frame-work, as it were, to gather the findings of science into some kind of order. Insofar as idealism has tried to do no more than that, it is quite within its proper bounds. At the same time we may point out that in setting out to do science we are already involved in some kind of philosophic view of the world. For what we call the ordinary common sense attitude is in fact a tissue of general tacit assumptions about the nature of things. To have drawn attention to this circumstance is perhaps the principal merit of the critical philosophy. It is in any case not superfluous to remind ourselves that scientific theories aim at stating something that is true of the world, whatever profitable actions they might enable us to take. This point is at times forgotten by those who see in theories no more than abstract formal systems, just as they forget that numbers are used for counting.

The philosopher, as seen through contemporary eyes

The world that is the object of enquiry is not of our making. We do indeed contrive our own mistakes and illusions, and often find it difficult to discover that we are in error. But it is not the pleasure or comfort that some belief affords us that makes it true. A man might think that he had unlimited financial resources because this view caused him some satisfaction. There are, indeed, people who do adopt this outlook, but bank managers and law courts are on the whole not inclined to share their views. The findings of enquiry are sometimes erroneous, but this does not make them subjective. It might with some justice be remarked that error at least requires a perpetrator. Nature herself cannot err, because she makes no statements. It is men who may fall into error, when they formulate propositions. Perhaps one motive for pragmatic theories is derived from this fact. For if error is subjective in the sense of being tied to someone committing it, and furthermore there is no guarantee against error, it might be felt that we are always enclosed within our own subjective opinions. But this is altogether wrong. It is one things to say that errors may always creep in, but quite another to assert that we are never right. If I say of something that it is so when in fact it is, nothing subjective enters such a judgment. Equally in the case of error, if I am wrong, then that I am wrong is a fact about the world. It is important to emphasize the objective character of disinterested enquiry, and the independent nature of the truths that it pursues. Those who insist that truth is something malleable and subjective fail to observe that on this view enquiry is impossible. Besides, they err in thinking that an enquirer cannot follow his curiosity quite independently of gain or usefulness in his discoveries. No one denies that much research is not of this kind, but some of it is. The history of science cannot be accounted for in terms of pragmatic conceptions. A respect for objective truth is apt to operate as a brake on the illusions of unlimited power that spring from the subjectivist bias.

This brings us to the other mainspring of philosophic speculation. So far we have mentioned only science and the general principles of its operation, which are an object of philosophic study. But man as a social animal is not only interested in finding out about the world: one of his tasks is to act within it. The scientific side is concerned with ὁ δὲ ἀνεξέταστος βίος οὐ βιωτὸς ἀνθρώπῳ

'The unexamined life is not worth living for man' (*Apology, 38a*)

means, here we are dealing with ends. It is mainly because of his social nature that man is faced with ethical problems. Science can tell him how certain ends might best be reached. What it cannot tell him is that he should pursue one end rather than some other.

As to the ethical problem, we have seen a number of different approaches to it. In Plato, the ethical and the scientific are ultimately run together. The good is identified with knowledge. It would be comforting if this were so. But unfortunately Plato's view is altogether too optimistic. Those who know most may sometimes turn this knowledge to evil account. In any case, however much one knows, it does not in itself resolve the problem of what is to be done.

This, then, is the general problem of reason and the will. If one rejects the view that with sufficient scope the two will coincide, one has to allow, as has been done by Occam, that they are independent. This does not, of course, imply that they are totally unrelated. Reason can and does act as a control and guide to the will and the passions. But, in all strictness, it is the will that chooses ends.

One consequence of this fact is that we cannot give scientific justifications for the goals that we might pursue, or for the ethical principles that we adopt. We can begin to argue only if we admit, from the outset, some ethical premiss. Thus, one might take it for granted that one's actions should be such as to preserve the society in which one lives; or, perhaps, it might be held that one's actions should promote some transformation of the social system. Whatever the ethical premiss, on such a basis it is possible to produce arguments to show why this or that course of action is to be followed. The vital thing to note is that without a premiss containing an 'ought', we cannot derive a conclusion telling us what should be done.

Now, clearly, ethical demands may differ from one person to the next, and it is indeed a commonplace that people often disagree on such matters. The question then arises whether it is possible to find an ethical principle that has some measure of universal validity. This requires, at any rate, that the demand should not depend, for its acceptability, on the person who makes it. We conclude from this that if there are ethical principles of universal scope they must apply to human society in general. This is not the same thing as saying that all men are equal in all respects. Indeed, it would be foolish to assert that they are, because the fact is that they are not. Men differ in scope and in abilities, and in many other ways. But insofar as ethical judgments are made, it will not do to limit them to a particular group. If, for example, it is held that one should act with honesty, then this does not depend on the size, shape or colour of those with whom one happens to be dealing. In this sense, then, the ethical problem gives rise to the conception of the brotherhood of man. It is a view first stated explicitly in the ethical doctrine of stoicism, and later found its way into Christianity.

Most of the principles which make for civilized living are of this ethical character. No scientific reason can be given why it is bad to inflict wanton cruelty on one's fellows. To me it seems that it is bad, and I imagine that this view is fairly widely held. As to why cruelty is a bad thing, I am not sure that I can supply satisfactory reasons. These are difficult questions and take time to settle. Perhaps in due course a solution may be found. But meanwhile it might be well to suggest to those who hold the opposite view that they should ask themselves whether their own opinions on these matters are independent of the fact of their holding them. It might then appear that what looks like a general ethical principle is no more than a piece of special pleading.

I have said earlier that while a genuine ethical principle is no respecter of persons, this does not mean that all men are equal. One particular in which there are notorious differences is as regards knowledge. I do not mean just information, but articulate knowledge. We have seen that in the Socratic view, knowledge tends to be identified with the good, and we have criticized this theory as too rationalistic. There is, however, an important point here that must not be overlooked. It is recognized quite freely by Socrates that the sum total of what a man knows is vanishingly small. What seems in the end more important is that one should pursue knowledge. It is disinterested enquiry that is the good. This is an ethical principle that stems from Pythagoras. The pursuit of a truth which is acknowledged as independent of the seeker, this has been, from the time of Thales, the ethical driving-force behind the scientific movement. Admittedly, this does leave untouched the ethical problem arising from possible uses and abuses of invention. But while this problem must be faced, it does not help our understanding of these matters if we mix up together these quite distinct and separate issues.

The enquirer is thus confronted by a twofold task. On the one hand, it is his business to pursue, to the best of his powers, the independent objects of his study. He must do this regardless of whether his findings will soothe or upset. Just as ethical principles are no respecters of persons, so the results of enquiry are not bound to respect our feelings. On the other hand, there is the problem of turning discovery to good account, in the ethical sense.

There remains the question of how we are to take this ethical principle that the pursuit of truth is a good thing. For evidently we are not all of us endowed with the ability to engage in scientific enquiry. Nor is it possible on all occasions to suspend judgment. Men must act as well as think. But there is one thing that every man can do, and that is to allow others the freedom to suspend judgment on matters that he himself may not wish to question. This shows, incidentally, how the pursuit of disinterested enquiry is linked with freedom, which is counted as another good. Tolerance is a pre-requisite in a society in which enquiry is to flourish. Freedom of speech and thought are the great promoters of a free society in which it is possible for the enquirer to let the truth lead him whither it will. To this extent, every one can contribute to the good here at stake. This does not mean that we shall all have the same opinions on everything, but it ensures that no avenue is closed by artificial strictures. For man, the unexamined life is, indeed, not worth living.

The author of this book

Index

Illustrations

Acknowledgements

Académie Royale de Belgique 192. Allen and Unwin 290. Courtesy American Philosophical Society 276. Archives K. 197, 287. Archives Photographiques 128, 148. Archiv für Kunst und Geschichte, Berlin 248, 250, 270. Arts et Métiers Graphiques 140, 144. Basel Picture Gallery 178, 179. Biblioteca Capitolare, Verona 125. Bibliotheque Nationale 12, 65, 123, 133. Bild Post 302. Bridal Georges, Lausanne 182. British Museum 33, 37, 42, 52, 53, 55, 95, 104, 123, 124, 126, 127, 181, 184, 223, 232, 243, 263. Brückmann 23, 57, 59, 81. By gracious permission of Her Majesty the Queen 184. Courtesy Cahiers d'Art 96, 126. Cambridge University Library 137. Cambridge University Press 283. Courtesy Clarendon Press 225. Courtesy the Governing Body, Christchurch, Oxford 215. Editions Tel, Paris 14, 46, 87, 92, 98. Ehem Städtische Museen zu Berlin 251. Fritz Eshen 303. Courtesy Faber and Faber 221. Frommans Verlag, Stuttgart 245. Giraudon 13, 32. Gräfe und Unzer Verlag, München 238. De Gruyter Verlag 17. Courtesy the Hanover Gallery, London 311. Courtesy Harvard University Press 277. Heliotopia Artistica Española, Madrid 129. Herder Verlag, Freiburg 124, 132, 134, 135. Courtesy I.B.M. United Kingdom Ltd. 284. Courtesy S. Karger A. G., Basle 295. Courtesy Alfred Knopf 278. Courtesy Laterza, Bari 291. Librairie Hachette, Arts du Monde, Paris 95, 96. Courtesy Librairie Orientaliste Paul Geuthner 133. Librairie Renouard Henri Laurens Editeur, Paris 42. Libreria dello Stato, Roma 131. Mansell Collection 6, 23, 27, 45, 50, 51, 54, 58, 102, 106, 112, 113, 114, 115, 116, 120, 125, 129, 135, 136, 139, 146, 152, 156, 158, 162, 164, 165, 167, 168, 176, 177, 179, 180, 182, 186, 188, 189, 193, 194, 198, 199, 228, 230, 232, 234, 235, 236, 244, 257, 274, 286, 298. Marcel, J. M. 305. Courtesy Professor Roland Martin 111. Matson Photography Service 127. Courtesy Merton College, Oxford 290. Metropolitan Museum of Art, New York 109, 110. Courtesy Professor Ernest C. Mossner 224. Museum Extension Publications, Boston 35. Museum of Modern Art, New York 288. Museum of Science and Engineering, Newcastle upon Tyne 260. Courtesy National Archives, Washington 8. Trustees of the National Gallery of Scotland 226. National Portrait Gallery 190, 192, 220. New Statesman 313. Nietzche Archiv, Weimar 259. Courtesy Parker Gallery, London 223. Max Parrish 10, 11, 61. Phaidon Press 121. John Piper 7, 49, 103, 122, 143, 171, 231. Courtesy Presses Universitaires de France 293. Courtesy Propyläen-Verlag, Berlin 173, 210, 212, 213, 218. Radio Times Library 233, 241, 254, 268, 292. Courtesy the Executors of the late Sir William Rothenstein 283. Routledge and Kegan Paul 255, 308. Courtesy Bertrand Russell 282. Russell and Sons 288, 297. Courtesy Benno Schwabe and Co., Verlag, Basle 25. Science Museum 188, 212. Società Magna Grecia 29. Society for Cultural Relations with the U.S.S.R. 233, 294. Skira 108, 130, 131, 138, 139, 174. Svensktbalett Museum, Stockholm 299. Courtesy Thames and Hudson 145. United Press International Photography 296. University of Chicago Press 306. Vatican Museum 50, 54, 102, 108, 118, 148, 149, 157. Roger Viollet 34, 51.

On the Ball

"PROFESSOR AYER, the Hoad of philosophical discussion." (Sunday Times.)

Pancho Gonzales
Said, flexing his muscle,
"If Ayer is Hoad,
Then I'm Bertrand Russell."

From Peter Simple's column, Daily Telegraph, Feb. 11, 1959